THE
Good Home
COOKBOOK

THE
Good Home
COOKBOOK

MORE THAN 1,000 CLASSIC AMERICAN RECIPES

Edited by
Richard J. Perry

Stewart, Tabori & Chang
New York

Published in 2009 by Stewart, Tabori & Chang
An imprint of Harry N. Abrams, Inc.

Text copyright © 2009 by Richard J. Perry

Library of Congress Cataloging-in-Publication Data

The good home cookbook : more than 1,000 classic American recipes / edited by Richard J. Perry.
   p. cm.
 Includes bibliographical references and index.
 ISBN 978-1-58479-746-3 (alk. paper)
 1. Cookery, American. I. Perry, Richard J.,
 TX715.G6192 2009
 641.5973—dc22

          2008033388

Editor: Luisa Weiss
Design Team: Kevin A. Welsch, Lisa M. Douglass, Campion Primm
Jacket Design: Galen Smith
Original Illustrations: David Hahn
Production Manager: Tina Cameron

The text of this book was composed in Adobe Garamond, Mrs Eaves, and Trade Gothic Bold Extended.

Printed and bound in Hong Kong
10 9 8 7 6 5 4 3 2

HNA
harry n. abrams, inc.
a subsidiary of La Martinière Groupe

115 West 18th Street
New York, NY 10011
www.hnabooks.com

TABLE OF CONTENTS

Dedication

To our parents and grandparents, who taught us what we know today about cooking.

Credits

This book would not have been possible without an incredible development team behind it:

Special thanks to Andrea Chesman who researched a vast number of the recipes in this book.

Many thanks to Jennifer Weaver-Neist, Lindsay Brown, Carole Berglie, Rebecca Pepper, Laura Bartroff, Lindsay Burt, W. Gail Manchur, Tiffany Owens, Tasia Bernie, and a host of interns who did everything from proofreading to managing the recipe tester program.

Thanks also to graphic designers Kevin Welsch, Campion Primm, and Lisa Douglass; and to graphic novel artist David Hahn for the fun illustrations throughout this book.

I would also like to thank my agent, Janis Donnaud, for finding a "good home" for my book, and Luisa Weiss and everyone at Stewart, Tabori & Chang for their enthusiastic welcome.

And finally, a very warm thanks to my wife Lisa, who helped me pour through hundreds of recipe tester feedback forms and tested recipes side by side with me night after night, as our son Keaton and daughter Ava watched in awe.

For a complete list of recipe tester credits, please see pages 494–495.

PREFACE

The inspiration for this book stems from years of experimenting in the kitchen as a youth and then as a chef. My interests are diverse, like the jobs I've held, from line cook to executive chef. My passion for cooking is nothing less than addiction.

When I made the transition from chef to publisher, I left behind incredible memories of professional cooking, but not my love for the kitchen. More and more, I find myself cooking meals like the ones I grew up with—meals that remind me of good times past.

Whenever I think of good eating, it's my Granny Frieda's meals that come to mind—the vision of family suppers, accompanied by much laughter and happiness. Another great family cook was Nana Cathy, who loved to serve up Texas-sized feasts from her youth. One of my favorite memories is the day she taught me to make red-eye gravy using ham and coffee. Conversely, my mother was a simple meat-and-potatoes kind of cook. I remember helping Mom out in the kitchen—cooking and laughing together. That's where we forged our strongest bond. Just as it was for me as a child, I want my children to grow up with fond memories of us cooking together.

My childhood days may be gone, but the memories remain. I still cook supper from scratch nearly every night, have hearty weekend breakfasts with farm-fresh eggs, and cook elaborate Sunday meals. It's a labor of love, as it was for Granny, Nana, and Mom—much like developing this book was for me.

The idea for *The Good Home Cookbook* came on gradually. It started as a small collection of recipes based upon a retro cookbook series that I had developed. The idea of expanding the book into one big collection of classic recipes came to me when I couldn't find a single anthology-type American cookbook that hadn't changed with the times. Many of the traditional recipes in the new volumes I found had become either quick 'n'

easy, lowfat, low carb, or peppered with new international flavors. I wanted a cookbook that would stay true to its roots. I didn't want to lose sight of the great recipes that formed the backbone of today's popular creations.

As a collector of vintage kitchen gadgets, cookbooks, and food advertising, I've paid attention to our culinary past. I also collect contemporary cookbooks as a means to identify how recipes have evolved over time. My personal collection served as a valuable resource for editing this book.

What is a classic American recipe? My editors and I defined it simply as a recipe that has been handed down from generation to generation in various forms, from cookbooks to menus—recipes that have withstood the test of time. Then we created a list of enduring regional favorites. To qualify as a classic, the recipe had to be either a household name or a popular item on menus, like Caesar salad. Once a recipe was selected, we researched and compared recipes to ensure that it could represent them all as the "standard."

We then launched a "recipe testers wanted" campaign that targeted newspapers nationwide. The response was staggering. More than 1,500 applied. My home soon became a test kitchen, and in the evenings, my family and I would test and retest recipes to verify tester comments as needed. The end results are the recipes found within these pages.

Ultimately, *The Good Home Cookbook* is a heartfelt tribute to our parents and grandparents—for their dedication to family and for all that they passed on to us: their love, their best recipes, and their simple, old-fashioned belief that life is short, so live well…and eat well.

From our family to yours,

Richard J. Perry

INTRODUCTION

There was a time in the not-too-distant past when families sat down together every Sunday evening to reconnect by sharing stories and each other's company over a hearty, made-from-scratch meal. On warm summer afternoons, friends and neighbors gathered together with loaves of bread and bowls of salad and fruit to share. Fresh-squeezed lemonade, grilled ribs and burgers, and homemade potato salad were the mainstays of every great backyard barbecue or celebration. Here, lasting friendships and family memories were made.

Now that we're adults, the aroma and taste of these classic family dishes can easily (and instantly) transport us back to those fond childhood memories. These wholesome recipes, handed down from generation to generation, are kept alive because they connect us to good times spent with the people we've known and loved throughout our lives. They are both tributes and family heirlooms.

The Good Home Cookbook is a collection of more than a thousand classic, timeless recipes that commemorates and preserves our distinctively American cuisine to prevent recipes from being lost, forgotten, or overshadowed by microwave ovens, convenience foods, and our faster pace of life.

AN AMERICAN TRADITION IS BORN

Amelia Simmons made history in 1796 when she published the first edition of *American Cookery*, widely regarded as the first cookbook written by an American for Americans. Although a slim volume at just 47 pages with recipes, or "receipts" (often no more than one or two lines long—mere suggestions, rather than fully crafted recipes), the book quickly became a bestseller. *American Cookery* called for indigenous ingredients, such as cornmeal or cranberry sauce to accompany roast turkey, as well as a recipe for "Pompkin Pie" and tips on how to use corncobs to smoke bacon.

The cookbook was also notable because the author called herself "an American orphan"—no mother was handing down family recipes to her. Modern cookbooks continue to replace the teachings of our mothers in the kitchen. As two-worker households have become the norm, a new generation has been forced to turn to cookbooks as teachers instead.

Fannie Merritt Farmer published her *Boston Cooking-School Cook Book* almost a century later, in 1896, which went on to sell more than three million copies. Her book had a profound effect on American cuisine. For one thing, she defined American cookery as "English thoroughness and French art," giving an official nod to the classic French cuisine that forms the foundation of Western cooking. Farmer offered recipes for everyday dishes and provided complete menus for family dinners that consisted of soup, meat or fish, potatoes or sweet potatoes, two vegetables, dessert, cheese, and coffee. While the cheese course has gone by the wayside, Farmer's definition of a proper meal has been amazingly enduring. Farmer also introduced a system of standardized measurements, which made it possible to duplicate her recipes.

Over time, American cooking has also made some notable transitions, from open-hearth cooking to wood-fired ovens, to electric and gas ovens. Similarly, the invention of baking powder and commercially produced yeast saved cooks hours of beating and kneading. By the early 1900s, labor-saving kitchen devices offered more leisure time for cooks, allowing for a greater enjoyment of food as entertainment. Toasters, waffle irons, stand mixers, and coal-burning ovens made a huge difference in the kitchen, as did the electric refrigerator, introduced in 1914. By 1937 it could be found in more than two million American homes.

Little by little, convenience foods began to replace cooking from scratch. In 1925 the average American homemaker prepared all her food at home, but by the 1930s, food manufacturers introduced products that simplified meal preparation. Bisquick claimed to "[Make] Anybody a Perfect Biscuit Maker" in 1931, and in 1934 Campbell's introduced chicken noodle and cream of mushroom soups, which went on to become staples on stovetops everywhere. In 1937 Kraft rolled out the Kraft Dinner, a 19-cent boxed meal with claims of "A Meal for Four in Nine Minutes." Recipe pamphlets accompanied the latest kitchen devices to demonstrate a plethora of innovative and tasty ways to use their products. Food manufacturers also got in on the act and showed new (and often wacky) ways their foods could be used, inventing the Spam Shake, Sauerkraut Jell-O Mold, and the Tomato Soup Cake. By 1965, more than 75 percent of food prepared in the average kitchen had undergone some sort of processing.

However, it was the end of World War II that brought the most remarkable and rapid transformation of American cookery. Returning GIs brought back a taste for the exotic flavors of the South Pacific and rationed canned goods, which now made their way into the home. Likewise, international food festivals began to gain popularity in cities across the country. America's culinary traditions were evolving yet again.

THE HOME COOKING SPIRIT LIVES ON

Change has always been one of America's defining characteristics—and that includes its history of and attitudes toward food. American cuisine has progressed significantly since the colonial-day staples of beans, corn, and squash, and throughout its itinerant and colorful course, it has inspired some exceedingly diverse and delicious fare.

But while most other countries of the world boast a cuisine they are readily associated with—like Italian pasta or German bratwurst—American food heritage is as diverse as its people. The fact that American cuisine is so multifaceted and multinational is the rich result of our country's blended ethnic heritage. Many agree that this great American melting pot is what also makes our nation so distinctive and inviting.

Ultimately, American home cooking is a creative mix of regional styles developed from the cultural influences of European settlers combined with native peoples and their close ties to the land and its seasonal produce. It was their creativity and innovation with these ingredients that came to define what American cuisine truly is. These early home cooks experimented with, substituted, and modified recipes over the years, developing new dishes with many regional variations to create the American standards that we all know and love today.

But before they became American standards, these best-loved recipes were first handed down through families like treasured heirlooms, or otherwise gained momentum on the menus of roadside or city cafés. America's expanding economy and transportation advancements also contributed to many of these foods' rapid and widespread popularity. Suddenly, regional dishes and patterns could not be so clearly defined. For example, when oysters began to be shipped to landlocked states from the Atlantic coast, we instantly became a nation of oyster lovers; and fried chicken, once considered the pride and joy of the South, quickly became standard picnic fare nationwide.

Today, American cuisine still continues to change, evolve, and embrace the influence of new immigrants, traditions, and technology. It is that collective, can-do spirit that ultimately defines American home cooking—a craft that knows no real boundaries, borrows and adapts, and refuses to be limited.

Just as recipes have been handed down and modified through generations, it is our hope that *The Good Home Cookbook* will serve as the foundation for others to create their own family classics. Cooking is an art, a necessity, and a process that brings families, friends, and communities together. Serving a meal made from scratch and with heartfelt pride is a time-honored tradition that is passed on with this book. Indeed, the recipes here will serve as a lasting reminder to current—and future—generations of how we lived and ate together as families, not only in America's earlier days, but in today's world too, as we continue to share and create traditions that will keep us connected to our culinary heritage, past and future.

HOW TO USE THIS BOOK

Since you may not have a mother at your elbow passing down cooking knowledge, this section of the book is devoted to explaining a few things about how to follow a recipe and how to select the best ingredients for these recipes.

BEFORE YOU START COOKING

It's always a good idea to read the entire recipe before you begin. If any of the language confuses you, check the definitions of the cooking terms (page 482). Then gather your ingredients together (they are listed in the order in which they will be used), and collect the utensils and equipment you will be using. Make sure you have the right size pans (size is especially important if you are baking).

Do as much advance preparation as you can. Chop, cut, grate, melt, and otherwise prepare your ingredients before you start. That way you won't find yourself lost in the middle of a recipe or needing to take the pan off the heat while you prepare the next ingredient. As the recipe will advise, preheat the oven and grease your baking pans as a first step when baking.

ONCE YOU START COOKING

Measure accurately. Liquids should be measured in glass measuring cups, which you can hold at eye level. Dry ingredients, such as flour, should be measured by the "spoon and sweep" method. Lightly spoon the ingredient into the measuring cup or measuring spoon. Level it off by sweeping a flat-bladed knife across the surface. Never pack the ingredient down; never shake or tap the cup. Brown sugar is the exception to these rules. It should be packed into the cup with the back of a spoon, and then leveled off.

It's always a good idea to clean up as you go. Wash empty bowls and measuring utensils and let them dry in a drying rack to keep the sink clear.

Throw away packaging and wipe up spills. Cleanup after the meal will be less daunting and the cooking process will be much more pleasant.

INGREDIENTS

This is a cookbook that focuses on good food made from scratch. There is very little in the way of convenience foods, like condensed cream of mushroom soup. Most of the ingredients are generally available in any supermarket. A few ingredients are regional specialties, such as pure maple syrup or sorghum. You can find mail-order sources of these ingredients on the Internet if your local grocery store doesn't carry them.

Butter: Unless otherwise noted, recipes in this book are made using salted butter. Usually it is best to use unsalted butter in baked goods. Unsalted butter tastes fresher, is generally superior to salted butter, and is less likely to allow sticking when used to grease pans. Your recipes should turn out just fine with salted butter, however, so it is your choice. Do not substitute whipped butter or margarine in any recipe calling for butter.

Cream: This is made from the fat portion of milk. Light cream, also called table cream or coffee cream, contains only 18 percent butterfat. In some parts of the country, light cream is difficult to find. In that case, substitute half-and-half, which is a mixture of milk and cream and contains about 12 percent butterfat. Whipping cream and heavy cream can be used interchangeably. When making whipped cream, try to find cream that is not ultrapasteurized; it will whip better.

Milk: The recipes have been tested and developed using whole milk, unless otherwise stated. One percent, two percent, and skim milk can be used, though with the resulting dish tasting a little less rich and creamy.

Oil: When a recipe calls for oil, the choice of what type of oil to use is yours. These days, because of health concerns, many people use canola oil when a neutral-tasting oil is required (baking and frying), and olive oil in salad dressings and sautés. When olive oil is called for in a recipe, use either pure or extra virgin olive oil. Extra virgin olive oil has the best flavor, especially for salad dressings. Peanut oil is sometimes preferred for deep-frying because of its high smoking point.

Shortening: When a recipe calls for shortening, it is referring to refined hydrogenated vegetable oil, such as Crisco, or lard. Vegetable shortening is neutral in flavor; lard does impart some flavor. Butter can be used instead.

Salt and pepper: While some recipes give specific amounts of salt and pepper to add, others instruct to "season with salt and pepper." Some people prefer to use sea salt to season foods; others are happy with regular table salt. Likewise, some people prefer freshly ground black pepper, while others are happy with regular ground pepper. The choice is yours. Salted water is also called for in some recipes. This is made by combining 1 tablespoon of salt per gallon of water.

Sizes of vegetables and fruits: If a recipe calls for 1 onion or 1 apple, unless otherwise stated, the onion and apple should be medium sized. A medium onion should give you about 1 cup of chopped pieces.

Cooking is not an exact science and if a little more or a little less onion is used, the outcome of the recipe will be fine. Likewise, 1 apple sliced equals about 1 cup, but don't worry if you have a little more or less—dessert will be delicious either way. The same holds true for every celery rib, carrot, potato, or peach that a recipe calls for. A little more or a little less won't hurt anything.

EGG SAFETY

When eating eggs and other raw foods from animals, there is a small possibility of Salmonella food poisoning. The risk is greater for pregnant women, the elderly and very young, and people with impaired immune systems. These individuals should avoid raw and undercooked animal foods.

Treat eggs and other raw animal foods accordingly. Use only properly refrigerated, clean, sound-shelled, fresh, grade AA or A eggs and avoid mixing yolks and whites with the shell. Refrigerate broken-out eggs, prepared egg dishes, and other foods if you won't be consuming them within an hour.

If you are concerned about Salmonella contamination when cooking with eggs, you can always use reconstituted powdered egg whites, such as Just Whites, or pasteurized eggs, such as Davidson's.

CHAPTER ONE

Breakfast

The sun peeks over the trees. Smoke drifts out of the chimney as Ma stokes the huge Monarch wood stove, and soon the delightful aromas of honest, rib-stickin' biscuits and bacon waft throughout the house. With a chorus of yawns, the children throw aside their cozy quilts and sniff the fragrant air filled with promises of griddle cakes, ham 'n' eggs, biscuits 'n' gravy, and bowls of oatmeal with thick cream. Hard work and long days on the farm call for hearty fuel for the body.

Fast forward to 1950. The house is located in suburbia; the stove is shiny and new; the coffee is brewing in the chrome electric percolator; and freshly squeezed orange juice is served in little juice glasses. Breakfast might be a bowl of cold cereal or pancakes served by a cheerful stay-at-home mom.

Home-cooked breakfast on weekdays may be a thing of the past in today's busy world, but the weekends are for indulgence! Bring back the delight of plopping down a platter of fluffy pancakes. Set a delectable omelet or breakfast casserole on the table to comments like, "I remember my Mom making that!" or "Is this Grandma's recipe?" Or consider one of Great Aunt's flowered plates heaped high with mouthwatering waffles. Grab a waffle, slap on the butter, pour on the pure maple syrup, and coast back to the era of comfort food. Consider starting a tradition, or breathe life back into a fondly remembered Sunday ritual of a breakfast that holds warm-hearted memories and creates new ones.

Grandma grew up helping out in the kitchen, learning how to cook alongside her mother. Your mother probably learned how to cook the same way. Today some of that cooking know-how has been lost, or mislaid, along the way. Though Grandma instinctively knew when to flip a flapjack, how to poach an egg, and how to fold an omelet, some of us could use a little instruction to do the same. Here's a collection of recipes from simple scrambled eggs to luxurious eggs Benedict, from hearty whole-grain pancakes to comforting buttery grits that are guaranteed to get you up and cooking confidently in the kitchen.

Soft-boiled Eggs

If you can boil water, you can boil an egg. The trick is to watch the timing carefully. You can also cook multiple eggs at the same time as long as there is room for water to circulate around each egg in the pan.

MAKES 2

2 large eggs

1. Fill a small saucepan three-quarters full with water and bring to a boil over medium-high heat.

2. Gently lower the eggs into the boiling water. Reduce the heat enough to maintain a very gentle boil and boil the eggs for 3 to 4 minutes depending on desired doneness. At 3 minutes, the yolks will be runny and the whites not fully set; at 4 minutes, the whites will be set and the yolks will be beginning to harden.

3. Using a small strainer or slotted spoon, scoop the eggs out of the water and briefly run under cold water until cool enough to handle. Crack the tops of the eggs open and eat directly out of the shell or spoon out onto toast.

TIP: To make hard-boiled eggs, put the eggs in a small saucepan of cold water. Cover the saucepan, bring the water to a boil, and turn off the heat. Leave the eggs in the water for 10 minutes. Drain and immediately run the eggs under cold water until they are cold.

Poached Eggs

Some restaurant cooks poach eggs in advance, trim off the ragged edges, and reheat the eggs in barely simmering water for about 30 seconds. Your poached eggs won't look as perfect, but it'll taste just as good. Also, the fresher the egg, the better it will hold its shape. Don't try to poach more than four eggs at a time.

MAKES 2

1 teaspoon salt
1 tablespoon white vinegar
2 large eggs

1. Fill a small saucepan with about 3 inches of water, add the salt and vinegar, and bring the water to a boil. Reduce the heat so the water is just simmering (it barely bubbles).

2. Break 1 egg into a shallow dish and slide it into the water. Repeat with the second egg. Cover the pan and cook for 3 to 5 minutes, until the white is set and the yolk has filmed over.

3. Remove the eggs with a slotted spoon and serve hot.

Fried Eggs

Don't rush these! Low heat and slow cooking will make delicate fried eggs, while high heat turns the whites to rubber.

MAKES 2

1 tablespoon butter
2 large eggs
Salt and pepper

1. Heat a medium skillet over medium heat. Melt the butter in the skillet, swirling the pan to coat it evenly.

2. Crack the eggs into the pan. Season with salt and pepper, cover, and keep cooking until the whites are firm, 2 to 3 minutes. (If the eggs are very fresh, the whites won't spread out much and they will be slow to cook. If you want the yolks to stay runny, make a cut in the whites to encourage the uncooked white to spread out faster in the pan.)

3. When the whites are firm, remove the eggs from the pan with a spatula and serve.

Scrambled Eggs

Low and slow is the secret to perfectly scrambled eggs: low heat and slow cooking. Adding water to the eggs makes them lighter; adding milk or cream makes them creamier.

SERVES 2

4 large eggs
Salt and pepper
1 to 2 tablespoons water, milk, or heavy cream (optional)
1 tablespoon butter

1. Break the eggs into a medium mixing bowl, add a little salt and pepper, and beat with a fork until just blended. Beat in the water, if using.

2. Heat a medium skillet over medium heat. Melt the butter in the skillet, swirling the pan to coat evenly. Pour in the eggs, reduce the heat to medium-low, and cook, stirring frequently with a wooden spoon, until the eggs are just set, 2 to 4 minutes. Don't overcook. Serve hot.

TIP: To make the scrambled eggs more interesting, mix in 1 tablespoon chopped fresh herbs (especially chives); 1 diced tomato; ½ cup chopped smoked salmon, salami, or ham; or ½ cup diced roasted pepper or chopped scallions.

Hearty Vegetable Scramble

Though this dish is a great way to start the day, it also makes a fine supper. Serve with plenty of whole-wheat toast or biscuits and your favorite salsa.

SERVES 4

2 tablespoons oil
1 tablespoon butter
½ pound hot or sweet Italian-style sausage, removed from its casings
½ medium onion, finely chopped
¼ cup finely chopped green bell pepper
1 medium waxy potato, such as thin-skinned red or white, cooked, peeled, and cubed
8 large eggs
½ cup chopped cooked spinach, squeezed to remove excess liquid
½ cup seeded and chopped tomato or drained canned tomato
½ teaspoon salt
Pinch of black pepper
Dash of hot pepper sauce, such as Tabasco
1 tablespoon chopped fresh parsley
¼ cup grated Parmesan cheese

1. Heat the oil and butter in a large skillet over medium heat. Add the sausage meat, onion, bell pepper, and potato. Sauté the sausage, breaking it up with a wooden spoon, until well browned, about 8 minutes.

2. Whisk the eggs in a medium bowl until well blended. Stir in the spinach, tomato, salt, pepper, and hot pepper sauce.

3. Pour the egg mixture into the skillet with the sausage. Gently stir with a wooden spoon, scraping the eggs off the bottom of the skillet, until they are set, about 4 minutes.

4. Sprinkle the parsley and cheese over the eggs and serve hot.

Egg-in-a-Nest

Here is a dish that kids will love to help out with.
Use different–shaped cookie cutters for variety.
It's as fun to make as it is to eat.

SERVES 4

4 thick slices white bread (homemade is great)
8 slices bacon
4 large eggs
Salt and pepper

1. Use a round biscuit cutter or cookie cutter to cut a hole out of the center of each slice of bread. Set aside the cut-out rounds.

2. Fry the bacon slices in a large skillet over medium heat, turning frequently, until they are crisp, 10 to 15 minutes. Drain them on paper towels and keep them warm. Pour off all but a thin layer of the bacon fat from the pan (reserving the remaining bacon fat).

3. Return the skillet to medium heat and add as many bread slices as will comfortably fit. Break an egg into each hole and cook until the egg whites are set, about 1 minute. Use a spatula to carefully flip over the slices. Cook an additional minute for "over easy," 2 to 3 minutes more for firm yolks. The bread should be lightly toasted on both sides. Season with salt and pepper and set aside.

4. Add 2 tablespoons of the reserved bacon fat, increase the heat to medium-high, and fry the cut-out rounds on each side until they are lightly toasted, about 30 seconds per side.

5. Prepare 1 "nest" (egg-bread slice) for each person, balancing a round over each hole to conceal the egg. Serve with 2 slices of bacon alongside each nest.

Eggs Benedict

Poached eggs, taken to the height of luxury, become eggs
Benedict, a dish first made at the legendary Delmonico's
Restaurant in New York City in the 1890s.

SERVES 4

4 English muffins
1 tablespoon butter, plus more to spread
8 slices Canadian bacon
Hollandaise sauce (recipe follows)
½ teaspoon salt
1 teaspoon white vinegar
8 large eggs

1. Preheat the oven to 250°F.

2. Lightly toast the English muffins, spread them with butter, and set them on a baking sheet. Place the baking sheet in the oven.

3. Melt 1 tablespoon of butter in a large skillet over medium heat. Add the Canadian bacon and cook, turning frequently, until heated through, 3 to 5 minutes. Place a slice of bacon on each muffin half in the oven.

4. Make the Hollandaise sauce as directed and keep it warm.

5. Fill a small saucepan with about 3 inches of water, add the salt and vinegar, and bring to a boil. Reduce the heat so the water is just simmering (it barely bubbles). Break 1 egg into a shallow dish and slide it into the water. Repeat with 3 more eggs. Cover the pan and cook for 3 to 5 minutes, until the whites are set and the yolks have filmed over. Remove the eggs with a slotted spoon and drain briefly on a paper towel while you poach the remaining 4 eggs. Trim the ragged edges from the eggs as needed.

6. To assemble the dish, place 2 English muffin halves (with the Canadian bacon) on each plate. Top each with a poached egg. Spoon the Hollandaise sauce over each egg and serve immediately.

Huevos Rancheros

Here are Mexican-style ranch eggs. There are more versions of this dish than there are ranches in Mexico, but this one is fairly simple. You might want to add a serving of refried beans or a garnish of avocado slices or guacamole. You can also run the finished dish under the broiler to brown the cheese.

SERVES 4

3 tablespoons oil
Pinch of chili powder
1 small onion, finely chopped
1 medium green bell pepper, seeded and finely chopped
1 teaspoon minced garlic
1 (15-ounce) can diced tomatoes
1 (4-ounce) can chopped roasted chile peppers, drained
Salt and pepper
4 (6-inch) corn tortillas
4 large eggs
1 cup shredded Monterey Jack cheese (about 4 ounces)

1. Heat 1 tablespoon of oil in a medium saucepan over medium-high heat. Add the chili powder, onion, bell pepper, and garlic and sauté until the onion is softened, about 3 minutes. Add the tomatoes and chile peppers, season with salt and pepper, and bring to a boil. Reduce the heat to low and let simmer while you prepare the rest of the dish.

2. Heat the remaining 2 tablespoons oil in a large skillet over medium heat. One at a time, fry the tortillas until they are lightly browned, about 30 seconds per side. Set them aside on individual plates.

3. Break the eggs into the skillet and cook them until the whites just begin to set. Reduce the heat and continue cooking until the whites are just barely firm.

4. Top each tortilla with an egg. Spoon the tomato sauce over the eggs (the heat of the sauce will continue to cook the eggs), sprinkle with the cheese, and serve immediately.

Hollandaise Sauce

This rich, buttery sauce can be traced back to eighteenth-century France, though its name refers to Holland, which is known for its butter and eggs. (Note: This recipe contains raw eggs. For more information, see page 11.)

MAKES ABOUT 1 CUP

½ cup (1 stick) butter
3 large egg yolks
½ teaspoon salt
Pinch of cayenne pepper
1 tablespoon lemon juice, or more to taste

1. Melt the butter in a small saucepan over low heat. Keep warm.

2. Combine the egg yolks, salt, cayenne pepper, and lemon juice in a blender and process briefly until blended. With the motor running, very slowly pour in the warm butter. The sauce will thicken. Taste, and add more lemon juice if needed.

3. Keep the sauce warm by placing it in a thermos, in the top of a double boiler over barely simmering water, or in a pitcher that is placed in a bowl of hot water (like a water bath).

Huevos a Caballo

Fried eggs and toast are fine for workday mornings, but when the weekend rolls around, there's plenty of time to both cook and work off a big breakfast—like this one.

SERVES 4

2 tablespoons oil
2 medium red or yellow bell peppers, seeded and finely chopped
12 ounces thinly sliced beef steak (top round, sirloin tip, eye of the round, or boneless eye of chuck)
Salt and pepper
2 tablespoons butter
8 large eggs
4 (6-inch) corn tortillas
2 medium avocados, peeled, pitted, and finely chopped
1 cup salsa of choice (page 56)

1. Heat the oil in a large skillet over medium-high heat. Add the bell peppers and sauté until softened, about 4 minutes. Remove with a slotted spoon and keep warm. Add half the beef, season with salt and pepper, and cook until lightly browned, about 1 minute. Remove from the pan and repeat with the remaining meat. Set aside.

2. Melt 1 tablespoon of butter in a small skillet over medium heat. Break the eggs into the skillet and cook until the whites begin to set. Reduce the heat to low and continue cooking until the whites are firm.

3. Meanwhile, in another small skillet, melt the remaining tablespoon of butter over medium-high heat. Fry each of the tortillas until lightly browned, about 30 seconds per side. Drain on paper towels.

4. Lay a tortilla on each plate. Cover with strips of steak and bell peppers. Place 2 cooked eggs on top of each serving, then top the eggs with a sprinkle of avocado and a spoonful of salsa. Serve at once, offering the remaining salsa at the table.

Basic Omelet

Here's the method for making a classic omelet. Use a filling and topping of your choice, or choose from one of the variations that follow.

SERVES 1 TO 2

3 large eggs
3 tablespoons milk
¼ teaspoon salt
Pinch of black pepper
1 to 2 tablespoons butter
Filling, such as shredded cheese, chopped vegetables, or cubed cooked ham (optional)
Salsa of choice (page 56), to serve (optional)

1. Use a fork to beat together the eggs, milk, salt, and pepper in a medium bowl until blended but not foamy.

2. Melt the butter over medium-high heat in a medium nonstick skillet. Swirl the butter around in the pan until it stops foaming. Pour in the eggs and reduce the heat to medium. As the mixture sets, lift the edges of the egg with a spatula and tilt the skillet so uncooked egg flows underneath. Do not stir. Continue cooking until the omelet is moist but not runny, about 3 minutes.

3. If making a filled omelet, top it with your choice of filling. Use a large spatula to loosen the edge of the omelet and fold it in half. Slide it onto a plate, top with a few spoonfuls of salsa, if using, and serve.

Broccoli-Cheese Omelet

Make a Basic Omelet. Sprinkle on ¼ cup finely chopped cooked broccoli and ¼ cup shredded cheese, then fold the omelet in half, and serve.

Spinach-Feta Omelet

Squeeze ½ cup chopped cooked spinach to remove excess moisture. Make a Basic Omelet. Sprinkle on the spinach and ¼ cup crumbled feta cheese, fold the omelet in half, and serve.

Spinach-Mushroom Omelet

Squeeze ½ cup chopped cooked spinach to remove excess moisture. Melt 1 tablespoon butter in a medium nonstick skillet over medium-high heat. Add ½ cup sliced mushrooms and sauté until the mushroom juice evaporates, about 5 minutes. Remove from the pan and keep warm. Make a Basic Omelet in the same skillet. Sprinkle on the spinach and mushrooms, fold the omelet in half, and serve.

New York Diner Omelet

Make a Basic Omelet. Sprinkle on 2 tablespoons cubed cooked ham; 1 slice crisp bacon, crumbled; 2 tablespoons shredded cheese; 2 tablespoons finely chopped green bell pepper; 2 tablespoons chopped mushrooms; and 1 tablespoon finely chopped onion. Fold the omelet in half and serve.

Tomato-Herb Omelet

Seed and finely chop half a small tomato and mince half a garlic clove. Melt 2 teaspoons butter in a medium nonstick skillet over medium heat. Add the tomato, garlic, and 1 teaspoon finely chopped fresh parsley. Sauté until the tomato has given up its juice, about 5 minutes. Remove from the skillet and keep warm. Make a Basic Omelet in the same skillet. Add the filling, fold the omelet in half, and serve.

Mushroom-Ham Omelet

Melt 2 teaspoons butter in a medium nonstick skillet over medium-high heat. Add ¼ cup thinly sliced mushrooms and sauté until the mushroom juice evaporates, about 5 minutes. Add ¼ cup chopped cooked ham and sauté for another 2 minutes. Remove from the skillet and keep warm. Make a Basic Omelet in the same skillet. Add the filling, fold the omelet in half, and serve.

Shrimp-Mushroom-Cheese Omelet

Melt 2 teaspoons butter in a medium nonstick skillet over medium-high heat. Add ¼ cup thinly sliced mushrooms and sauté until the mushroom juice evaporates, about 5 minutes. Stir in ¼ cup chopped cooked shrimp, remove the mixture from the skillet, and keep warm. Make a Basic Omelet in the same skillet. Add the filling, sprinkle with 2 tablespoons shredded cheese, fold the omelet in half, and serve.

Spanish Omelet

Melt 2 teaspoons butter in a medium nonstick skillet over medium-high heat. Add ¼ cup finely chopped tomato and 1 tablespoon finely chopped onion. Sauté about 5 minutes. Remove the mixture from the skillet and keep warm. Make a Basic Omelet in the same skillet. Add the filling, fold the omelet in half, and serve.

Western Omelet

Melt 2 teaspoons butter in a medium nonstick skillet over medium-high heat. Add 2 tablespoons minced onion and 2 tablespoons minced green bell pepper. Sauté until the vegetables are softened, about 3 minutes. Add ¼ cup chopped cooked ham and sauté for another 2 minutes. Remove the mixture from the skillet and keep warm. Make a Basic Omelet in the same skillet. Add the filling, fold the omelet in half, and serve.

Crab-Cheddar Omelet

Make a Basic Omelet. Sprinkle on ¼ cup chopped lump crabmeat and ¼ cup shredded Cheddar cheese, fold the omelet in half, and serve.

Santa Barbara Omelet

In this omelet, the egg whites are beaten, then folded into the yolks to create a puffy, light texture. The omelet is then finished in the oven, creating a dish that is a cross between an omelet and a soufflé.

SERVES 4 TO 5

3 tablespoons butter or oil
¼ cup finely chopped sweet onion, such as Maui, Walla Walla, or Vidalia
3 tablespoons finely chopped green bell pepper
1 large tomato, seeded and finely chopped
¼ cup finely chopped celery
½ cup thinly sliced mushrooms
6 large eggs, separated
¼ teaspoon salt
¼ teaspoon cayenne pepper
⅛ teaspoon black pepper
5 tablespoons hot water
½ cup shredded sharp Cheddar cheese

1. Melt 1½ tablespoons of butter in a large oven-proof skillet over medium heat. Add the onion and bell pepper and sauté until tender, about 3 minutes. Add the tomato, celery, and mushrooms. Turn the heat to low and cook, stirring occasionally, until the celery is tender, about 5 minutes. Remove the mixture from the pan and keep warm.

2. Preheat the oven to 350°F.

3. With an electric mixer or whisk, beat the egg yolks in a medium bowl until thick and lemon colored; add the salt, cayenne pepper, black pepper, and hot water.

4. In a separate bowl, beat the egg whites until almost stiff. With a rubber spatula, fold one-third of the whites into the egg yolks until well blended, then fold in the remaining egg whites until lightly blended.

5. Melt the remaining 1½ tablespoons butter in the same skillet over low heat. Pour in the egg mixture. As the egg mixture sets, lift the edges with a spatula and tilt the skillet so the uncooked egg flows underneath. Cook until very lightly browned on the bottom but still very moist on top, about 3 minutes.

6. Place the skillet in the oven and bake for about 10 minutes, until the center of the omelet lightly springs back when touched in the center.

7. Sprinkle the cheese on top, and cut the omelet into wedges. Spoon the tomato mixture over the wedges and serve.

Baked Ham and Eggs

When you are making eggs for several people and don't want to be a short-order cook, just multiply this recipe to serve your crowd.

SERVES 2

2 tablespoons diced cooked ham
2 large eggs
Salt and pepper
2 teaspoons sour cream
2 teaspoons dry bread crumbs
1 teaspoon butter, melted

1. Preheat the oven to 350°F.

2. Grease 2 custard cups or ramekins with butter. Divide the ham evenly between the cups. Break an egg into each and season with salt and pepper. Drop 1 teaspoon of sour cream onto each egg. Top each with 1 teaspoon of crumbs. Drizzle ½ teaspoon of melted butter on top.

3. Place the custard cups in a baking dish and fill the pan with enough hot water to come halfway up the sides of the cups.

4. Bake for 13 to 14 minutes, until the yolks are set and the whites are just barely firm. Check for doneness by inserting the tip of a knife into the whites; it should come out with a little white sticking to it. (Unless you are serving immediately, it is better to undercook these eggs because they will continue baking in the cups.)

5. If desired, preheat the broiler and then slip the custard cups under the broiler for 1 to 2 minutes, until the tops are lightly browned. Serve hot.

Corned Beef Hash and Eggs

You'll never go back to the canned stuff once you taste this version. The hash is best made the night before, so it's ready to fry in the morning.

SERVES 4

¼ cup (½ stick) butter
1 small onion, finely chopped
1 pound corned beef, fat trimmed, finely chopped
3 medium baking potatoes, boiled, peeled, and finely diced
½ teaspoon Worcestershire sauce
10 large eggs
2 tablespoons oil
Pinch of black pepper

1. Melt the butter in a small skillet over medium heat. Add the onion and sauté until softened, about 3 minutes. Transfer to a large bowl.

2. Add the corned beef, potatoes, and Worcestershire sauce. Beat 2 eggs with a fork and add them to the corned beef mixture; mix well with a spoon. Form the mixture into 8 patties and refrigerate, preferably overnight.

3. Heat the oil in a large skillet over medium heat and cook the patties until the bottoms are browned, 10 to 15 minutes. Turn them over and season with pepper.

4. Make a depression in the top of each patty and crack an egg into it. Reduce the heat to low and cover the pan. Cook for about 3 minutes, until the eggs are set. Serve hot, egg side up.

TIP: The patties are not intended to stay together perfectly. The eggs will help to set them.

Eggs Florentine

Sometime in the sixteenth century, cooks in Florence, Italy, are said to have introduced the French to spinach. Since then, any dish with spinach often receives the name "Florentine." This is one of those classic dishes.

SERVES 4

3 (10-ounce) packages fresh spinach, washed and trimmed
2 tablespoons oil
½ small onion, finely chopped
1 teaspoon minced garlic
8 large eggs
Salt and pepper
½ cup grated Parmesan cheese
½ cup dry bread crumbs

1. Preheat the oven to 350°F. Grease a 9 x 13-inch baking dish.

2. Place the spinach in a large pot with 1 inch of water over high heat. Cover and steam until the spinach is wilted, 2 to 3 minutes. Drain well. Squeeze the spinach to remove any excess water.

3. Heat the oil in a large skillet over medium-high heat. Add the onion and garlic and sauté until softened, about 2 minutes. Use a wooden spoon to stir in the spinach and cook just until heated through, about 3 minutes. Use a slotted spoon to transfer the spinach to the baking dish.

4. Spread out the spinach in an even layer. Using the back of a spoon, make 8 indentations in the spinach. Crack an egg into each indentation. Season with salt and pepper. Sprinkle the cheese and crumbs evenly over the baking dish.

5. Bake for 15 to 20 minutes, until the egg whites are white and firm. Serve hot.

Hangtown Fry

A miner walked into a restaurant in Hangtown, California, in 1849, carrying a sack of gold over his shoulder. "Give me your most expensive grub," he ordered. The cook said he could cook some oysters and eggs—two very expensive ingredients in those days. The miner told the cook to add some bacon, and this famous dish was born, or so legend has it. You won't find Hangtown in an atlas, by the way; the name has been changed to Placerville.

SERVES 4

12 small oysters, shucked
¼ cup all-purpose flour
¼ teaspoon salt, plus more to taste
⅛ teaspoon black pepper, plus more to taste
1 large egg, well beaten
½ cup fine cracker crumbs or dry bread crumbs
¼ cup (½ stick) butter
8 large eggs
8 slices bacon, cooked until crisp

1. Preheat the broiler.

2. Drain the oysters.

3. In a small bowl, combine the flour with the ¼ teaspoon salt and ⅛ teaspoon black pepper. Dip each oyster in the flour mixture, then in the beaten egg, then in the cracker crumbs. Set aside.

4. Melt the butter in a heavy ovenproof skillet over medium heat. Add the oysters and fry until lightly browned on both sides, about 1 minute per side.

5. Beat the eggs with a fork, season lightly with salt and pepper, and pour over the cooked oysters in the skillet. Cook until the eggs are set on the bottom, about 3 minutes. Place the skillet under the broiler for 2 to 3 minutes, until lightly browned on top. Serve hot, with the bacon on the side.

Herb Frittata

Omelets have you running scared? Let's call the frittata an easy-to-make baked omelet. Frittatas can be served hot, straight out of the oven, or at room temperature, making them ideal for buffets and grab-and-go breakfasts. Several variations follow.

SERVES 4

6 large eggs
½ cup chopped fresh parsley
¼ cup chopped mixed fresh herbs (basil, oregano, mint, tarragon, and/or thyme)
1 teaspoon minced garlic
½ cup shredded cheese, such as Cheddar or Monterey Jack
Salt and pepper
2 tablespoons butter or oil

1. In a small bowl, use a fork to beat together the eggs with the parsley, mixed herbs, garlic, and cheese. Season with salt and pepper.

2. Melt the butter in a large ovenproof skillet over medium heat. Pour in the egg mixture and reduce the heat to medium-low. Cook, without stirring, until the eggs are set on the bottom, about 5 minutes.

3. While the eggs are cooking, preheat the oven to 350°F.

4. Transfer the skillet to the oven and bake for 10 to 12 minutes, just until the eggs are completely set. Slice and serve the frittata hot or at room temperature.

Herb and Goat Cheese Frittata

Replace the shredded cheese in the Herb Frittata with ¼ cup (4 ounces) crumbled chèvre (goat cheese), and complete the recipe as directed.

Spinach Frittata

Replace the herbs in the Herb Frittata with 1 cup chopped cooked spinach, and complete the recipe as directed.

Broccoli Frittata

Replace the herbs in the Herb Frittata with 1 cup chopped cooked broccoli, and complete the recipe as directed.

Breakfast Frittata

Combining potatoes and vegetables with the eggs, this frittata has everything you need to start the day well.

SERVES 6

1 medium waxy potato, such as thin-skinned red or white, peeled and thinly sliced
2 tablespoons oil
1 small onion, finely chopped
1 medium green or red bell pepper, seeded and finely chopped
½ cup finely chopped cooked ham or ¼ cup crumbled crisp bacon (optional)
6 large eggs
½ cup shredded cheese, such as Cheddar or Monterey Jack
Salt and pepper

1. Cover the potato with salted water in a small saucepan. Bring the water to a boil, cover, and cook until the potato is tender, about 10 minutes. Drain well.

2. Heat the oil in a large ovenproof skillet over medium-high heat. Add the onion and bell pepper and sauté until softened, 3 to 4 minutes. Stir in the potato and ham, if using.

3. Use a fork to beat the eggs and cheese together in a medium bowl. Season with salt and pepper.

4. Pour the eggs into the skillet and reduce the heat to medium-low. Cook, without stirring, until the eggs are set on the bottom, about 5 minutes.

5. While the eggs are cooking, preheat the oven to 350°F.

6. Transfer the skillet to the oven and bake for 10 to 12 minutes, just until the eggs are completely set.

7. Remove the frittata from the oven, cut into wedges, and serve hot or at room temperature.

Bacon and Cheese Breakfast Strata

Stratas are layered casseroles of bread, eggs, cheese, and sometimes meats and vegetables. Usually they must sit overnight in the refrigerator to allow the bread to absorb the milk-and-egg mixture, so be sure to plan ahead. Still, they are simple to make and wonderful to eat. Accompany this strata with a cup of coffee and you will be raring to go. And next time, try the variation that follows.

SERVES 6 TO 8

6 large eggs
3 cups milk
½ teaspoon salt
¼ teaspoon black pepper
6 tablespoons (¾ stick) butter, softened
15 slices white sandwich bread
1 pound sliced bacon, cooked and crumbled
1½ cups shredded sharp Cheddar cheese (about 6 ounces)
¼ cup chopped scallions

1. Grease a 9 x 13-inch baking dish.

2. Whisk the eggs, milk, salt, and pepper in a large bowl until well blended.

3. Spread some butter on one side of each slice of bread. Arrange the slices buttered side up in overlapping rows in the prepared baking dish. Crumble the bacon over the bread in an even layer. Sprinkle the cheese and scallions over the bacon. Pour the egg mixture over all.

4. Cover the baking dish with aluminum foil or plastic wrap and refrigerate overnight.

5. The next morning, preheat the oven to 350°F.

6. Uncover and bake the strata for 50 minutes, until the top is puffed up and the center is cooked through when tested with a toothpick. Serve hot.

TIP: For a more attractive presentation, cut the crust off the bread slices before using them.

Ham and Eggs Strata

Replace the bacon in the Bacon and Cheese Breakfast Strata (page 23) with 2 cups chopped cooked ham and complete the recipe as directed.

Quiche Lorraine

The most famous of all quiches, quiche Lorraine was originally made without cheese. This recipe, popularized in the 1960s, contains cheese and is the version best known today.

SERVES 6

Crust:
1¼ cups all-purpose flour
¼ teaspoon salt
⅓ cup shortening
5 to 7 tablespoons water

Filling:
8 slices bacon, cooked and crumbled
2 cups shredded Swiss cheese (about 8 ounces)
¼ cup finely chopped scallions
3 large eggs, lightly beaten
1½ cups half-and-half
⅛ teaspoon salt
¼ teaspoon black pepper
Pinch of cayenne pepper

1. To make the crust, combine the flour and salt in a medium bowl. Cut in the shortening with a fork or pastry cutter until the dough pieces are the size of peas. Sprinkle half of the water over the dough and mix until the water is absorbed. Sprinkle on the remaining water and continue to gently stir until the dough is moistened. Form the dough into a ball, wrap tightly in plastic wrap, and refrigerate for at least 3 hours.

2. When chilled, unwrap the dough and place on a lightly floured surface. Roll out into a 12-inch circle and gently lay in a 9-inch pie pan. Cut off any excess dough with kitchen scissors or a knife and crimp the edge.

3. Preheat the oven to 425°F.

4. To make the filling, sprinkle the bacon, cheese, and scallions in the pastry shell.

5. Combine the eggs, half-and-half, salt, black pepper, and cayenne pepper in a medium bowl. Beat with a fork until well blended and pour the mixture into the crust.

6. Bake for 15 minutes. Reduce the oven temperature to 300°F and bake for another 30 minutes, or until a knife inserted near the center comes out clean. Let the quiche stand for 10 minutes before cutting. Serve warm or at room temperature.

Broccoli Quiche

A quiche made with vegetables can be served for breakfast, lunch, or dinner. This one is made with broccoli; variations with spinach and asparagus follow.

SERVES 4 TO 6

1 (9-inch) pie crust, unbaked (see quiche
    Lorraine crust on this page)
1 cup shredded Swiss cheese (about 4 ounces)
1 cup chopped cooked broccoli
½ small onion, finely chopped
3 large eggs
Milk or heavy cream
Salt and pepper

1. Preheat the oven to 425°F.

2. Roll out the dough and place in a 9-inch pie pan. Prick it all over with a fork. Bake for 8 to 10 minutes, until lightly colored. Remove it from the oven and let cool. Reduce the oven temperature to 375°F.

3. Sprinkle ½ cup of cheese in the crust. Make a layer of the broccoli and onion on top of the cheese.

4. Beat the eggs in a glass measuring cup using a fork. Add enough milk to make 1½ cups and mix well. Season the mixture with salt and pepper. Pour it over the broccoli. Sprinkle the remaining ½ cup cheese over the top.

5. Bake for 30 to 35 minutes, until the quiche is puffed and browned on top. Let stand for at least 10 minutes, then slice and serve warm or at room temperature.

Spinach Quiche

Replace the broccoli in the Broccoli Quiche with 1½ cups chopped cooked spinach, carefully squeezed to remove excess liquid. Complete the recipe as directed.

Asparagus Quiche

Replace the broccoli in the Broccoli Quiche with 1 cup chopped cooked asparagus, in 1½-inch pieces. Complete the recipe as directed.

Fluffy Flapjacks

Here's a classic pancake recipe made a little lighter because the egg whites are beaten separately. Flapjacks is another name for pancakes.

SERVES 4 TO 6

2 cups all-purpose flour
2 tablespoons sugar
2 teaspoons baking powder
½ teaspoon salt
2 cups milk
4 large eggs, separated
2 tablespoons butter, melted
Toppings of choice, such as pure maple syrup, fresh fruit, and butter

1. Preheat the oven to 200°F. Preheat a griddle or large skillet over medium-high heat.

2. Combine the flour, sugar, baking powder, and salt in a large bowl. Add the milk, egg yolks, and melted butter, and beat with a whisk until well blended.

3. In a separate large bowl, beat the egg whites with a mixer until they are stiff. Fold the whites into the batter.

4. Grease the griddle, then ladle about ⅓ cup of batter onto the griddle for each pancake. Cook for 2 to 4 minutes, until the tops are bubbly. Flip the pancakes with a spatula and cook for another 2 to 4 minutes. Don't let the griddle smoke; adjust the heat as needed. Remove the pancakes from the griddle as they are finished and serve hot, or place them on a heatproof plate to keep warm in the oven. Continue making pancakes until all the batter is used, greasing the griddle as needed. Serve the pancakes with toppings as desired.

Whole-Wheat Pancakes

Whole-wheat flour and wheat germ enrich these hearty cakes. Serve them with butter and a selection of your favorite toppings.

SERVES 4 TO 6

1 cup whole-wheat pastry flour
¾ cup all-purpose flour
¼ cup wheat germ
1½ teaspoons baking powder
1 teaspoon baking soda
¼ teaspoon salt
2 cups milk
2 large eggs, lightly beaten
3 tablespoons butter, melted
Toppings of choice, such as pure maple syrup, fresh fruit, and butter

1. Preheat the oven to 200°F. Preheat a griddle or large skillet over medium-high heat.

2. Combine the whole wheat flour, all-purpose flour, wheat germ, baking powder, baking soda, and salt in a large bowl.

3. In a separate large bowl, whisk the milk, eggs, and melted butter until well blended. Stir into the flour mixture just until moistened.

4. Grease the griddle, and ladle about ⅓ cup of batter onto the griddle for each pancake. Cook for 2 to 4 minutes, until the tops are bubbly. Flip the pancakes with a spatula and cook for another 2 to 4 minutes. Don't let the griddle smoke; adjust the heat as needed. Remove the finished pancakes and serve hot, or place them on a heatproof plate to keep warm in the oven. Continue making pancakes until all the batter is used, greasing the pan as necessary. Serve the pancakes with toppings as desired.

Buttermilk Pancakes

Griddle cakes, flapjacks, hotcakes—we certainly have plenty of names for pancakes. Buttermilk makes particularly tender pancakes, but you can substitute milk, if desired.

SERVES 4 TO 6

2 cups all-purpose flour
1 tablespoon sugar
2 teaspoons baking powder
1 teaspoon baking soda
1 teaspoon salt
2½ cups buttermilk
2 large eggs, well beaten
¼ cup butter, melted
Toppings of choice, such as pure maple syrup
    and butter

1. Preheat the oven to 200°F. Preheat a griddle or large skillet over medium-high heat.

2. Stir together the flour, sugar, baking powder, baking soda, and salt in a medium bowl.

3. In a large bowl, beat the buttermilk, eggs, and melted butter until well blended. Stir in the flour mixture just until moistened.

4. Grease the griddle, and ladle about ⅓ cup of batter onto the griddle for each pancake. Cook for 2 to 4 minutes, until the tops are bubbly and the bottoms are browned. Flip the pancakes with a spatula and cook for another 2 to 4 minutes. Don't let the skillet smoke; adjust the heat as needed. Remove the finished pancakes from the skillet and serve hot, or place them on a heatproof plate and keep warm in the oven. Continue making pancakes until all the batter is used, greasing the griddle as necessary. Serve with toppings as desired.

Blueberry Pancakes

Gently fold 1 cup fresh blueberries (or frozen, defrosted, and drained) into the Buttermilk Pancakes batter and complete the recipe as directed.

Corn Pancakes

Fold fresh (or frozen, defrosted, and drained) corn kernels into the Buttermilk Pancakes batter and complete the recipe as directed.

Apple-Cornmeal Pancakes

Made with a touch of cinnamon and hearty, flavorful ingredients like fresh apples and cornmeal, these pancakes are perfect for a frosty fall weekend.

SERVES 6 TO 8

1¼ cups all-purpose flour
1¼ cups yellow cornmeal
¼ cup sugar
1½ tablespoons baking powder
½ teaspoon salt
½ teaspoon ground cinnamon
2 large eggs, beaten
1¾ cups milk
¼ cup plus 2 tablespoons oil
2 medium tart apples, such as Granny Smith
    or Rome Beauty, peeled, cored, and finely
    chopped
Toppings of choice, such as pure maple syrup,
    butter, and confectioners' sugar

1. Preheat the oven to 200°F. Preheat a griddle or large skillet over medium-high heat.

2. Combine the flour, cornmeal, sugar, baking powder, salt, and cinnamon in a large bowl.

3. In a separate large bowl, whisk the eggs, milk, and oil until well blended. Stir into the flour mixture just until moistened. Fold in the apples.

4. Grease the griddle, and ladle about ⅓ cup of batter onto the griddle for each pancake. Cook for 2 to 4 minutes, until the tops are bubbly and the bottoms are browned. Flip the pancakes with a spatula and cook for another 2 to 4 minutes. Don't let the griddle smoke; adjust the heat as needed. Remove the finished pancakes from the skillet and serve hot, or place them on a heatproof plate and keep warm in the oven. Continue making pancakes until all the batter is used, greasing the griddle as necessary. Serve with toppings as desired.

Buckwheat Pancakes

Nothing beats the earthy flavor of buckwheat pancakes. Serve them with your favorite syrup—pure maple or a fruity syrup such as blackberry, apricot, or blueberry. You might also want to try some thick preserves or honey. They're all delicious.

SERVES 4

1 large egg
1¼ cups buttermilk
½ cup buckwheat flour
½ cup all-purpose flour
2 tablespoons sugar
½ teaspoon baking powder
½ teaspoon baking soda
½ teaspoon salt
2 tablespoons butter, melted
Toppings of choice, such as pure maple or fruit syrup and butter

1. Preheat a griddle or large skillet over medium-high heat.

2. Whisk together the egg and 1 cup of buttermilk in a small bowl until well blended.

3. Combine the flours, sugar, baking powder, baking soda, and salt in a large bowl. Make a well in the mixture and pour in the buttermilk mixture. Stir long enough only to moisten thoroughly. Gently stir in the melted butter. Add as much of the remaining ¼ cup buttermilk as needed to achieve the consistency of heavy cream.

4. Grease the griddle, and ladle about ⅓ cup of batter onto the griddle for each pancake. Cook for 2 to 4 minutes, until the tops are bubbly and the bottoms are browned. Flip the pancakes with a spatula and cook for another 2 to 4 minutes. Don't let the griddle smoke; adjust the heat as needed. Continue making pancakes until all the batter is used, greasing the griddle as necessary. Serve immediately with your toppings of choice; buckwheat pancakes lose something when kept warm in the oven.

Sourdough Hotcakes

If you happen to have sourdough starter bubbling away in your refrigerator, you have a good head start toward this old-fashioned breakfast treat.

SERVES 4

1 large egg, separated
½ cup evaporated milk
1 tablespoon oil
1 tablespoon sugar
1 teaspoon baking soda
1 teaspoon salt
2 cups sourdough starter (page 338)
Toppings of choice, such as pure maple syrup, fresh fruit, and butter

1. Preheat a griddle or large skillet over medium-high heat.

2. In a small bowl, beat the egg white with a mixer until stiff but not dry.

3. In a large bowl, whisk together the egg yolk, milk, oil, sugar, baking soda, and salt until well blended. As quickly as possible, blend in the starter with a spoon. Try not to break the bubbles in the starter; they function as leavening. Gently fold in the egg white.

4. Grease the griddle, and ladle about ⅓ cup of batter onto the griddle for each pancake. Cook for 2 to 4 minutes, then flip with a spatula and cook for another 2 to 4 minutes. Don't let the griddle smoke; adjust the heat as needed. Continue making pancakes until all the batter is used, greasing the griddle as needed. Serve immediately with your toppings of choice; sourdough hotcakes lose something when kept warm in the oven.

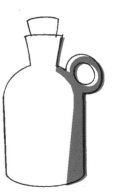

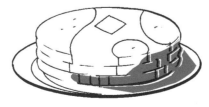

Aebleskivers

Aebleskivers are puffed Danish pancakes that are a cross between a pancake and a doughnut. Ideally they are made in an aebleskiver pan, which is a cast-iron pan with seven rounded, 2¼-inch indentations. You can make these pancakes on a regular griddle, however.

SERVES 6

2 cups all-purpose flour
2 tablespoons sugar
1 teaspoon baking powder
1 teaspoon baking soda
½ teaspoon salt
2 cups buttermilk
3 large eggs, separated
3 tablespoons butter, melted
Toppings of choice, such as pure maple syrup, fresh fruit, and butter

1. Preheat the oven to 200°F. Preheat an aebleskiver pan or large skillet over medium-high heat.

2. Sift the flour, sugar, baking powder, baking soda, and salt into a medium bowl.

3. In a small bowl, whisk together the buttermilk, egg yolks, and butter. Add the buttermilk mixture to the flour mixture and stir just until blended.

4. In a large bowl, beat the egg whites with a mixer until stiff. Fold them into the batter.

5. Heat the aebleskiver pan over medium heat. Generously grease the pan and spoon 1 heaping tablespoon into each indentation. Don't let the pan smoke; adjust the heat as needed. Cook for 3 minutes. Using a toothpick, turn each one over at the crusty edge. Reduce heat to medium-low and cook for 4 more minutes. Remove the finished pancakes and serve hot, or place them on a heatproof plate and keep warm in the oven. Repeat until all the batter is used, greasing the pan as needed. Serve the pancakes with toppings as desired.

German Pancake

A German pancake puffs up in the oven and makes a lovely presentation. The pancake is also known as a "Dutch baby." Bread flour is recommended for the pancake because its higher gluten content helps the batter rise. All-purpose flour can be substituted, but the results won't be as dramatic. Instead of the apple mixture, try a simple dusting of confectioners' sugar and serve with lemon wedges.

SERVES 4

7 tablespoons butter, softened
2 large apples, peeled, cored, and sliced
2 tablespoons granulated sugar
½ teaspoon ground cinnamon
6 large eggs, at room temperature
1 cup milk, at room temperature
1 cup bread flour
¼ teaspoon vanilla extract
Confectioners' sugar, to serve

1. Preheat the oven to 450°F. Place a large oven-proof skillet in the oven to preheat.

2. Melt 1 tablespoon of butter in a medium skillet over medium heat. Add the apples and sauté until softened, about 5 minutes. Stir in the granulated sugar and ¼ teaspoon of cinnamon and heat until the sugar is melted. Remove the skillet from the heat and set aside.

3. In a large bowl, beat the eggs with an electric mixer until light and frothy. Add the milk, flour, vanilla extract, and remaining ¼ teaspoon cinnamon. Beat for 5 minutes more. The batter will be thin but smooth and creamy.

4. Remove the hot skillet from the oven. Add the remaining 6 tablespoons butter, tilting the pan to melt the butter and coat the skillet. Pour the batter into the hot skillet all at once, and immediately place the skillet in the oven.

5. Bake for 15 to 20 minutes, until the pancake is puffed and golden brown on top.

6. Remove the pancake from the oven, bringing it to the table in its pan or sliding it onto a serving plate. Once out of the oven, the pancake will begin to deflate. Dust it with confectioners' sugar, cut it into wedges, and transfer the wedges to individual plates. Top the wedges with the apple mixture and serve immediately.

Golden Waffles

If you can find an old, well-seasoned waffle iron at a yard sale or flea market, go for it. Old irons turn out the crispiest, tastiest waffles. And for a bit of variety, try pouring in the batter and sprinkling it with cooked sausage, bits of bacon, or ham. Plunk down the lid and inhale the wonderful aroma. Serve your luscious waffles with sliced fresh fruits, jams, maple or fruit syrup, or honey. A variation made with blueberries follows.

SERVES 4

2 cups all-purpose flour
1 tablespoon baking powder
2½ teaspoons sugar
1 teaspoon salt
2 large eggs, separated
1½ cups milk
6 tablespoons (¾ stick) butter, melted
Toppings of choice, such as pure maple syrup, fresh fruit, and butter

1. Brush a waffle iron lightly with vegetable oil and preheat.

2. Sift together the flour, baking powder, sugar, and salt in a medium bowl.

3. In a large bowl, beat the egg yolks, milk, and melted butter with a fork.

4. Make a well in the center of the flour and add the milk mixture. Mix with a spoon just until moistened.

5. In a medium bowl, beat the egg whites with a mixer until stiff. Gently fold the egg whites into the batter with a rubber spatula.

6. Pour about ½ cup batter (or according to the manufacturer's recommendations) onto the hot iron and spread it with the back of a spoon to within ¼ inch of the grid's edge. Close the lid and bake for about 4 minutes, until golden brown with crisp edges. Remove the waffle with a fork and put on a plate. Serve hot with toppings as desired, and continue making waffles until all the batter is used.

Blueberry Waffles

After folding in the egg whites when making Golden Waffles, fold in 1 cup fresh blueberries. Complete the recipe as directed.

Crêpes

Crêpes are surprisingly easy to make, and extras can be stored in the refrigerator between sheets of waxed paper and filled later. Store for up to 1 day.

SERVES 4 TO 6

3 tablespoons butter
2 cups milk
2 large eggs
1 cup all-purpose flour
½ teaspoon baking powder
2 tablespoons granulated sugar
Pinch of salt
¼ cup jelly or jam
¼ cup confectioners' sugar

1. Melt 2 tablespoons of butter.

2. Combine the milk, eggs, flour, baking powder, granulated sugar, salt, and melted butter in a blender and process until the batter is smooth. Cover and chill for 30 minutes in the refrigerator.

3. Melt a little of the remaining 1 tablespoon butter in a crêpe pan or medium cast-iron skillet over medium heat. Pour in only enough batter to cover the bottom of the pan (2 to 3 tablespoons), tipping the pan to spread the batter to make a very thin pancake. Lightly brown on both sides and turn out onto a plate.

4. When all the crêpes are made (about 16 crêpes), spread each with jelly or jam and roll them up. Sprinkle a little confectioners' sugar over the tops and serve.

Cheese Blintzes

Blintzes are Jewish pancakes, very similar to French crêpes and Russian blini. They are typically served during the harvest holiday, Shavuoth, and may be filled with cheese or fruit. These blintzes are filled with a mixture of farmer cheese and cottage cheese. If you can't find farmer cheese, use well-drained cottage cheese or ricotta cheese instead.

SERVES 4 TO 6

Blintzes:
3 large eggs
¼ cup water
¼ cup milk
½ cup all-purpose flour
1½ teaspoons sugar
½ teaspoon baking powder
3 tablespoons butter
Sour cream, to serve
Jam of choice, to serve

Filling:
1½ cups farmer cheese
1 (16-ounce) container cottage cheese (about 2 cups)
¼ cup sugar
1½ teaspoons ground cinnamon
1 tablespoon all-purpose flour

1. To make the blintzes, combine the eggs, water, milk, flour, sugar, and baking powder in a blender and blend until the batter is smooth. Let stand for 30 minutes.

2. Melt 1 tablespoon of butter in an 8-inch non-stick crêpe pan or skillet over medium-high heat. Pour in only enough batter to cover the bottom of the pan, tipping the pan to spread the batter to make a very thin pancake. Cook until the top is set; do not turn over. Transfer to a plate, cooked side down. Continue making the blintzes until all the batter is used, stacking them between sheets of waxed paper.

3. To make the filling, combine the farmer cheese, cottage cheese, sugar, cinnamon, and flour in a food processor and process until the mixture is smooth.

4. Place 3 tablespoons of filling in the middle of each blintz. Fold the opposite edges to the middle and tuck in the sides to form a packet.

5. Melt the remaining 2 tablespoons butter in the skillet over medium heat. Cook the blintzes seam side down, 3 or 4 at a time, for 2 to 3 minutes, until golden brown.

6. Serve the blintzes hot, passing the sour cream and jam at the table.

French Toast

They don't call this dish "French toast" in France. There is "pain perdu," or "lost bread," which is what Cajun and Creole cooks in Louisiana also might call it. French toast is also known as German toast, Spanish toast, or nun's toast. Serve it with maple syrup or homemade preserves. Honey is also a good choice.

SERVES 4

4 large eggs
¼ cup half-and-half or milk
½ teaspoon ground cinnamon
½ teaspoon ground nutmeg
½ teaspoon vanilla extract
8 thick slices white or raisin bread
Confectioners' sugar, to serve
Pure maple or fruit syrup, to serve (optional)

1. Preheat the oven to 200°F. Preheat a griddle or large skillet over medium heat.

2. Whisk the eggs in a shallow bowl until foamy. Whisk in the half-and-half, cinnamon, nutmeg, and vanilla extract until well blended.

3. Grease the griddle or skillet.

4. Dip the bread slices in the batter for a few seconds on each side and place on the griddle. Cook, flipping once with a spatula, until golden brown on each side, about 4 minutes total. Don't let the griddle smoke; adjust the heat as needed. As the slices cook, place on an ovenproof plate to keep warm in the oven.

5. Sprinkle the French toast lightly with the confectioners' sugar and serve with syrup at the table, if desired.

Baked French Toast with Apples

If you're in the mood for French toast but don't have time to get out the skillet, this is a simple alternative. Featuring the same warm flavors of the original, this recipe combines apples and custard to create a delicious one-dish meal.

SERVES 4 TO 6

6 thick slices white or French bread
2 large eggs
1½ cups milk
2 teaspoons vanilla extract
3 large tart apples, such as Granny Smith or Rome Beauty, peeled, cored, and thinly sliced
½ cup sugar
1 teaspoon ground cinnamon
1½ tablespoons butter
Pure maple syrup, to serve

1. Preheat the oven to 400°F. Grease a 9 x 13-inch baking dish.

2. Arrange the bread in the bottom of the dish.

3. Whisk the eggs, milk, and vanilla extract in a medium bowl until smooth. Pour over the bread slices, then arrange the apple slices on top of the bread. Combine the sugar and cinnamon and sprinkle over the apple slices. Dot with the butter.

4. Bake for 35 minutes, until the apples are soft and the custard is set. Serve hot with maple syrup.

Creamy Oatmeal

When it comes to comfort foods, nothing beats a bowl of sweetened oatmeal, especially if it is topped with heavy cream or half-and-half. And the sweetener makes all the difference—Yankees clamor for maple syrup, but brown sugar, honey, and even sorghum all have their advocates.

SERVES 4

½ teaspoon salt
4 cups cold water
1⅓ cups rolled oats
Heavy cream, half-and-half, or milk, to serve
Sweetener of choice, such as brown sugar, honey, or pure maple syrup, to serve

1. Combine the salt and water in a medium saucepan and bring to a boil over high heat.

2. Stir in the oats with a spoon, reduce the heat to very low, and simmer, stirring occasionally, until the oatmeal is the desired consistency, about 5 minutes.

3. Cover the saucepan and let stand for 5 minutes more. Serve the oatmeal hot, offering cream and a sweetener at the table.

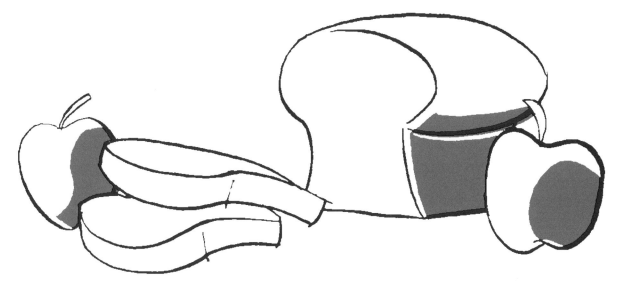

Burgoo

While Southerners enjoy a thick stew of meats and/or game and vegetables known as burgoo, New Englanders sometimes call their morning porridge by the same name. The word once described an oatmeal porridge that was part of English sailors' diet in the mid-1700s.

SERVES 4

1 teaspoon salt
3½ cups water
1 cup steel-cut oats (Scottish or Irish oatmeal)
3 tablespoons butter
¼ cup sugar or brown sugar
¼ cup raisins, dates, or chopped fresh fruit
Heavy cream, half-and-half, or milk, to serve

1. Combine the salt and water in a medium saucepan over medium heat and bring to a boil.

2. Stir in the oats and turn the heat to low. Simmer for 40 to 45 minutes, stirring frequently, until the oats are tender.

3. Remove the saucepan from the heat and stir in the butter, sugar, and fruit. Serve hot, offering the cream at the table.

Hot Wheat Cereal

Wheat flakes are rolled kernels of wheat, just as rolled oats are rolled kernels of oat grain. Both make delicious hot cereals. You can find wheat flakes, or rolled wheat, at health food and natural food stores.

SERVES 4

3 cups water
1½ cups rolled wheat or wheat flakes
½ teaspoon salt
Sweetener of choice, such as brown sugar, honey, or pure maple syrup, to serve
Heavy cream, half-and-half, or milk, to serve

1. Bring the water to a boil in a medium saucepan over high heat.

2. Stir in the wheat and reduce the heat to medium-low. Cover and gently cook, stirring occasionally, until the water is absorbed and the cereal has a smooth consistency, about 10 minutes.

3. Remove the saucepan from the heat and let stand, covered, for 5 minutes. Serve the cereal hot, sprinkled with your favorite sweetener. Offer the cream at the table.

Grits

When corn kernels are dried, they are sometimes treated with an alkali (such as lye) to remove the hulls, producing hominy. Cracked into a coarse meal, hominy becomes hominy grits, or simply grits. Grits are served with butter and pepper throughout the South. They may appear at any meal, but they are most popular at breakfast. Instant grits and quick-cooking grits cut down cooking time, but they are poor imitations of the real thing.

SERVES 4 TO 6

4 cups water
1 teaspoon salt
1 cup yellow or white grits
Black pepper
Butter

1. Combine the salt and water in a medium saucepan over medium heat and bring to a boil.

2. Slowly stir in the grits, cover the saucepan, and reduce the heat to medium-low. Cook for 30 to 40 minutes, stirring often, until the grits are creamy and the water is absorbed.

3. Season the grits with pepper and stir in as much butter as desired. Serve hot.

Creamy Cheese Grits

Cheese in the grits adds substance, texture, and flavor. It makes a wonderful variation on plain grits, especially at brunch.

SERVES 4

3 cups water
3 cups milk
1 teaspoon salt
½ teaspoon white pepper
2 tablespoons butter
¾ cup white grits
2 cups finely shredded white Cheddar cheese
  (about 8 ounces)

1. Combine the water, milk, salt, pepper, and 1 tablespoon of butter in a large saucepan over medium heat. Bring the liquid to a gentle boil.

2. Slowly stir in the grits. Simmer for 1 to 1¼ hours, stirring occasionally. If the grits get too thick, add hot water to thin them.

3. Remove the pan from the heat and stir in the remaining 1 tablespoon butter and the cheese. Serve hot.

Cornmeal Mush

There's no difference between good, old-fashioned American cornmeal mush and Italian polenta—except that Americans are likely to enjoy their mush for breakfast, whereas Italians eat polenta as part of dinner.

SERVES 4

4 cups water
1 cup coarsely ground yellow cornmeal
1 teaspoon salt
Sweetener of choice, such as brown sugar,
  honey, or pure maple syrup, to serve

1. Bring 2 cups of water to a boil in a medium saucepan. Whisk in the cornmeal and salt, and stir vigorously until the mush is smooth.

2. Slowly add the remaining 2 cups water, stirring constantly to avoid lumps. Cover and cook over very low heat for 25 to 30 minutes, until the mixture is thick. Serve hot, offering a sweetener at the table.

TIP: Pour any leftover mush into a greased loaf pan and refrigerate overnight. The next morning, cut the loaf into ½-inch slices and fry them in butter until lightly browned on both sides. Serve the slices with pure maple syrup.

Granola

Fresh granola is so superior to the boxed variety that there is no comparison. Serve it with milk if you must, but cream is heavenly. Besides being a great breakfast dish, granola is terrific when sprinkled on ice cream.

MAKES 8 CUPS

¾ cup (1½ sticks) butter (preferably unsalted)
½ cup honey
½ teaspoon salt
1½ teaspoons vanilla extract
4½ cups rolled oats
1 cup raw wheat germ
1 cup sweetened coconut flakes
1 cup almonds, whole or halved

1. Preheat the oven to 300°F.

2. Melt the butter with the honey and salt in a small saucepan over medium heat. Stir occasionally until the mixture is warm and well mixed. Remove the saucepan from the heat and stir in the vanilla extract.

3. Mix the oats, wheat germ, coconut, and almonds in a large bowl. Pour the warm butter over the oats and stir until moistened. Scoop the granola into two 9 x 13-inch baking pans.

4. Bake for 35 to 40 minutes, until the granola is nicely browned. Stir every 8 to 10 minutes or so to make sure it browns evenly.

5. Cool the pans on wire racks, stirring occasionally so no big lumps form. The granola will keep for about a week in a closed container.

Homesteader Scrapple

This combination of cornmeal porridge and pork is a Pennsylvania Dutch creation—and perhaps an acquired taste. It was originally a way to use up leftover meat.

SERVES 6 TO 8

8 cups water
2 cups yellow cornmeal
1 tablespoon salt
1½ to 2 cups chopped cooked pork or ham
3 tablespoons shortening or oil
Topping of choice, such as apple butter, applesauce, honey, or pure maple syrup, to serve

1. Bring 6 cups of water to a boil in a large saucepan.

2. Use a spoon to vigorously stir together the cornmeal, salt, and remaining 2 cups water in a medium bowl. Slowly stir the cornmeal mixture into the boiling water and use the back of the spoon to break up any lumps that may form. Stir slowly and constantly for at least 10 minutes, until the mixture has thickened. Stir in the pork.

3. Grease two 9 x 5-inch loaf pans and divide the cornmeal mixture between the pans. Refrigerate overnight.

4. In the morning, cut the scrapple loaves into ½-inch-thick slices.

5. Heat the shortening in a heavy skillet over medium-high heat and fry the slices until they are golden brown on both sides and the edges are crisp, about 8 minutes total. Serve the scrapple hot with your choice of topping.

Biscuits and Gravy

This is a true farmland standby. It is often found in those tiny hole-in-the-wall cafés where the locals come by at sunrise. They share the latest corn prices, discuss the newest tractor on the market, drink strong coffee with real cream, and fill up for the long day's work.

SERVES 4

Biscuits:
2 cups all-purpose flour
4 teaspoons baking powder
½ teaspoon salt
½ teaspoon cream of tartar
2 teaspoons sugar
½ cup shortening
⅔ cup milk

Sausage gravy:
½ pound ground breakfast sausage of choice (page 37)
¼ cup all-purpose flour
3 cups milk
Salt and pepper

1. Preheat the oven to 425°F.

2. To make the biscuits, sift together the flour, baking powder, salt, and cream of tartar in a medium bowl. Stir in the sugar with a spoon. Using a pastry cutter or your fingers, blend in the shortening until the mixture is crumbly. Mix in the milk with a fork until the dough is soft but not sticky.

3. Place the dough on a floured board and knead it for a minute or so. Roll it out to a thickness of 1¼ inches and cut it into biscuits with a 2-inch round cutter or the rim of a small water glass. Arrange the biscuits 2 inches apart on a baking sheet.

4. Bake the biscuits for 18 to 20 minutes, until lightly browned on top. Take the baking sheet out of the oven and set the biscuits aside.

5. To make the sausage gravy, cook the sausage in a large skillet over medium-high heat until browned, about 8 minutes.

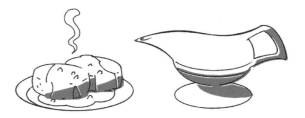

6. Sprinkle the flour over the meat and stir with a spoon until blended. Stir in the milk. Bring the mixture to a boil, stirring until thickened. Reduce the heat and simmer for 5 minutes. Season to taste with salt and pepper.

7. Cut the biscuits in half horizontally and place them cut side up on plates. Spoon the sausage gravy over the biscuits and serve immediately.

Breakfast Sausage

With the help of a food processor, it is not difficult to make your own sausage.

MAKES 2 POUNDS

1½ pounds boneless pork butt, cut into
    1-inch cubes
½ pound pork fatback, trimmed of rind,
    cut into 1-inch cubes
2 teaspoons salt
1½ teaspoons dried sage
1 teaspoon black pepper
½ teaspoon dried marjoram
Pinch of ground cloves
Pinch of cayenne pepper

1. In a food processor, mince about one-third of the meat with one-third of the fatback until finely chopped. Do not process to a purée; mince in pulses to retain some texture. Transfer the meat to a bowl. Repeat two more times, working with one-third of the meat and one-third of the fatback at a time.

2. Mix in the salt, sage, black pepper, marjoram, cloves, and cayenne pepper. Pinch off a small piece of the meat mixture and cook in a small skillet over medium heat until it is browned. Taste and adjust the seasoning accordingly.

3. Form the remaining meat mixture into 12 sausage patties. (The sausage patties can be frozen at this point, if you wish.)

4. To cook the sausage patties, preheat a large skillet over medium heat. Add the patties in a single layer. Cook until they are browned on the bottom, 5 to 8 minutes. Turn over and brown, 4 to 8 minutes. Serve hot.

Ham with Red-Eye Gravy

A Southern classic, red-eye gravy is made from pan drippings flavored with coffee. Be sure to choose a country ham (brine cured and smoked—a method used to preserve the meat before the invention of refrigeration) with plenty of fat on it. Country ham has a high salt content, so taste the gravy before adding more seasonings. The key to good red-eye gravy is to use an iron skillet so the brown parts stick to the pan. Serve it with biscuits or grits—or both.

SERVES 4 TO 6

2 pounds country ham
1 teaspoon sugar
1 cup brewed coffee
Salt and pepper

1. Preheat the oven to 200°F.

2. Cut the fat from the ham, then cut the ham into equal serving slices no thicker than 1 inch; set aside. Place the fat in a large skillet over medium-high heat and cook until it is well browned, about 10 minutes. Remove the larger pieces, leaving the drippings behind. Add the ham pieces, turning frequently with a spatula, and cook until browned on both sides, 8 to 10 minutes total. Remove from the pan and keep warm in a covered dish in the oven.

3. Spoon out about half the fat and discard. Add the sugar to the skillet and continue to cook over medium-high heat, stirring frequently, allowing it to caramelize, 2 to 3 minutes.

4. Pour the coffee into the skillet and bring to a boil, stirring with a wooden spoon to scrape up all the browned bits. The gravy will turn slightly red. Simmer for 10 minutes to reduce slightly and season to taste with salt and pepper.

5. Place the ham slices on plates and serve, passing the gravy at the table. If a smoother gravy is desired, strain before serving.

New Hampshire Fried Apples

Apples are a terrific accompaniment to pancakes, waffles, and sausage. In the old days, before orange juice was found on every breakfast table, apples were commonly served for breakfast. This recipe is more than a hundred years old. Choose a good cooking apple, such as Granny Smith or Rome Beauty.

SERVES 4

2 tablespoons butter
3 tablespoons sugar
2 tablespoons light molasses
1 tablespoon water
6 medium apples, peeled, cored, and cut into eighths
Pinch of ground cinnamon (optional)
Pinch of ground nutmeg (optional)

1. Melt the butter in a medium skillet over medium heat. Add the sugar, molasses, and water. Stir well with a wooden spoon to melt the sugar. Add the apples, cinnamon, and nutmeg, if using, and cover the skillet. Cook until the apples are tender but not mushy, about 10 minutes.

2. Remove the cover and continue cooking until the liquid is mostly gone and the apples are lightly browned, about 5 minutes more. Serve warm.

Home Fries

These potatoes are a crunchy alternative to hash browns. Using a waxy potato helps to keep their shape.

SERVES 4

4 medium waxy potatoes, such as thin-skinned red or white
3 tablespoons butter
1 medium onion, finely chopped
1 teaspoon salt
¼ teaspoon black pepper

1. Cover the potatoes with water in a medium saucepan. Bring the water to a boil, and boil until the potatoes are tender, 15 to 20 minutes. Drain and run the potatoes under cool water until cool enough to handle.

2. Peel and dice the potatoes.

3. Heat the butter in a large, heavy skillet over medium heat. Add the potatoes, onion, salt, and pepper. Cook until lightly browned and crisp, turning occasionally, 15 to 20 minutes. Serve hot.

Hash Browns

Hash browns are generally finer in texture than home fries, and they are cooked long enough to form a crust on both sides. The insides are tender and moist.

SERVES 4

3 medium baking potatoes, peeled and shredded
Salt and pepper
3 tablespoons oil

1. Using a large spoon or your hands, toss the potatoes in a medium bowl with salt and pepper to taste.

2. Heat the oil in a large, heavy skillet over medium-high heat. Add the potatoes by handfuls of ⅓ to ½ cup. Flatten with a spatula and cook until golden, 5 to 7 minutes.

3. Flip the hash browns over, reduce the heat to medium, and cook until browned on the bottom, another 5 to 7 minutes. Serve hot.

COOKING BREAKFAST BACON, SAUSAGE, AND HAM

Bacon

The smoky, sweet smell of bacon cooking in the morning is one of the best things about breakfast. Here's how you can cook it right every time.

▶ Allow 2 to 3 slices per serving.

▶ Some people like their bacon soft and chewy; others prefer it crisp, almost burned. Watch the pieces carefully as you cook them and remove them when they are done to your liking.

▶ Bacon cooked on the stovetop will spatter and requires constant monitoring to avoid burning. Roasting the bacon in the oven takes longer, but it doesn't require as much attention. Roasting is an especially good method if you want to cook a large quantity.

▶ To cook bacon on top of the stove, place it in a large, heavy skillet over medium-high heat. When the bacon begins to sizzle, turn frequently so the slices cook evenly. Reduce the heat as needed to keep the bacon from burning. The total cooking time will be 8 to 20 minutes.

▶ To cook bacon in the oven, preheat the oven to 450°F. Arrange the bacon in a single layer in a large roasting pan. Roast, turning the slices occasionally and pouring off excess fat every 5 minutes or so, until the bacon is crisp, about 30 minutes. Drain the slices well and serve hot.

Sausage

▶ You can make your own sausage (page 35) or buy it ready-made; it is sold in bulk, as patties, or in links.

▶ To cook links, place them in a large, heavy skillet. Add ½ cup boiling water. Cover the skillet and simmer for 8 to 10 minutes, until the sausages are almost done and no pink shows. Pour off the liquid, return the skillet to low heat, and cook until the sausages are evenly browned, turning frequently. Drain well and serve hot.

▶ To cook patties, preheat a large skillet over medium heat. Add the patties in a single layer and cook for 5 to 8 minutes. Turn them over with a spatula and brown for 4 to 8 minutes more, until browned on both sides. Drain the patties well and serve them hot.

▶ To cook bulk sausage, lightly grease a heavy skillet with vegetable oil and heat over medium-high heat. Add the sausage meat and cook, stirring frequently, until well browned, about 8 minutes. Drain well and serve.

Ham

▶ Cooking a ham steak for breakfast is simply a matter of heating the precooked ham and giving it a nice browned finish.

▶ Slice the ham ¼ to ½ inch thick.

▶ Melt 1 teaspoon of butter in a large skillet over medium-high heat. Add the ham steak and cook until browned on both sides, 6 to 10 minutes total. Serve hot.

CHAPTER TWO

Lunch

America is a nation of sandwich eaters. It is no accident that an entire fast-food industry sprang up around America's favorite sandwich, the hamburger. But even before the Golden Arches, there were diners and dining cars, stretching from one end of America to the other, serving lunch between two slices of bread or on a bun.

The sandwich, of course, is British in origin. In legend it is said to have been invented by John Montagu, the fourth Earl of Sandwich, who insisted on convenient foods that could be eaten without utensils, so as not to disturb his card games. It spread to Scandinavia, where cooks specialized in open-faced sandwiches, and to Italy, where sandwiches—or panini—were typically grilled on a press that squashes the bread flat. But nowhere was it found in more variations—on fresh bread or toast, open faced or triple stacked, regular sized or supersized into a hero—than in America.

Sandwiches were arguably the most important items on the menus of diners. Convenient and inexpensive, diners began as simple sandwich carts parked across from mills and factories to supply weary blue-collar workers with sandwiches, pie, and coffee. By the turn of the century, pre-fab dining cars replaced horse-drawn lunch wagons, and the American diner was born.

Diners helped popularize sandwiches as a favorite lunch item, and the country gradually shifted to having their main meal of the day in the evening. Regional specialty sandwiches ruled the menus, from cheese steak in Philadelphia, to muffulettas in New Orleans, to Reuben sandwiches in New York City. Heroes, grinders, submarines, bombers, and hoagies all appealed to sandwich lovers with big appetites. Skippy peanut butter was invented in 1932, and it wasn't long before American children were carrying PB&J every day in their lunchboxes.

Meanwhile, the hamburger—unadorned or dressed with onion, pickles, ketchup, and mustard—was found everywhere, from roadside shacks to expensive restaurants. Today the average American eats about three hamburgers per week—about 38 billion burgers annually.

Lunch, however, hasn't been limited to just sandwiches. Mexican favorites such as tacos and burritos were enjoyed long before the "wrap" was invented. So whether your favorite condiment is ketchup or salsa, you're sure to find a lunchtime treat that pleases in this chapter.

Egg Salad Sandwiches

Many speculate that Columbus brought the first chickens to the New World in 1493. We do know that by colonial times, chickens—and their eggs—were quite common. The origin of egg salad, however, is lost in time. If you like, replace the pickle relish with finely chopped onion.

SERVES 4

4 large eggs
¼ cup sweet pickle relish, well drained
3 tablespoons mayonnaise
¼ cup finely chopped celery
1 teaspoon prepared yellow mustard
½ teaspoon salt
Pinch of black pepper
4 teaspoons butter, softened
8 slices white or whole-wheat sandwich bread
1 medium tomato, sliced

1. Place the eggs in a small saucepan and cover with cold water. Cover the saucepan and bring the water to a boil. Remove the pan from the heat and let the eggs sit in hot water for 10 minutes. Pour off the hot water and run the eggs under cold water until completely cooled.

2. Peel and dice the eggs.

3. Combine the eggs, pickle relish, mayonnaise, celery, mustard, salt, and pepper in a medium bowl. Mix well.

4. Butter each slice of bread. Spread the egg mixture on the buttered side of 4 slices. Top each with a slice of tomato, then the remaining bread. Cut the sandwiches in half and serve.

Tuna Salad Sandwiches

Tuna salad preferences are often based on what Mom made. Here's a version that includes sweet pickles. If you like, substitute chopped dill pickles for the sweet pickle relish.

SERVES 4

1 (6-ounce) can albacore tuna (packed in water or oil), drained
¼ cup mayonnaise
¼ cup sweet pickle relish, well drained
3 tablespoons finely chopped celery
3 tablespoons finely chopped sweet onion, such as Maui, Walla Walla, or Vidalia
½ teaspoon salt
Pinch of black pepper
4 teaspoons butter, softened
8 slices sandwich bread of choice
4 lettuce leaves of choice

1. Use a fork to flake the tuna in a medium bowl. Add the mayonnaise, relish, celery, onion, salt, and pepper, and mix well.

2. Butter each slice of bread. Spread the tuna mixture on the buttered side of 4 slices. Top each with a piece of lettuce, then the remaining bread. Cut the sandwiches in half and serve.

Chicken Salad Sandwiches

Afternoon teas often include chicken salad on white bread with the crusts removed. For other occasions, pile the chicken salad on rye or whole-wheat bread and serve with chips and pickles. Sliced almonds and red onions can be added for extra flavor and crunch.

SERVES 4

1½ cups chopped cooked chicken
1 medium celery rib, finely chopped
¼ cup mayonnaise
1 teaspoon lemon juice
Salt and pepper
4 teaspoons butter, softened
8 slices white sandwich bread
1 medium tomato, sliced
4 lettuce leaves of choice

1. Combine the chicken, celery, mayonnaise, and lemon juice in a medium bowl. Season to taste with salt and pepper.

2. Butter each slice of bread. Spread the chicken mixture on the buttered side of 4 slices. Top each with a slice of tomato, a lettuce leaf, and the remaining bread. Cut the sandwiches in half and serve.

TIP: Substitute leftover turkey for the chicken.

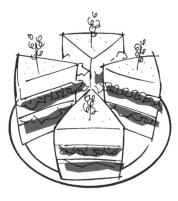

Club Sandwiches

This triple-decker sandwich is a variation on the BLT, with the addition of a layer of sliced chicken breast (sometimes sliced turkey). Many agree that it was invented in 1894 at the Saratoga Club in upstate New York and was made popular in restaurants and clubhouses throughout the country. Since the layers can easily come apart, hold the sections together with toothpicks until you're ready to eat.

SERVES 4

12 slices white sandwich bread
¼ cup mayonnaise
8 lettuce leaves of choice
2 large tomatoes, thinly sliced
½ pound thinly sliced cooked turkey breast or chicken breast
16 thick slices bacon, cooked crisp

1. Toast the bread. Spread mayonnaise on one side of all the slices.

2. Lay 4 slices of bread on a work surface, mayonnaise side up. Top each slice with a lettuce leaf, tomato slice, and one-fourth of the turkey slices. Top with another slice of bread, mayonnaise side up. Top with another lettuce leaf, a tomato slice, and 4 slices bacon. Top with the final slices of bread, mayonnaise side down. Press the sandwiches together and cut each diagonally in half, then cut the halves in half again so you have 4 triangular pieces. Secure each triangle with a toothpick to hold the layers together, and serve.

BLT Sandwiches

The bacon, lettuce, and tomato (BLT) sandwich is one of the most popular, for good reason. The sandwich is a study in contrast: the crispy toast and bacon, the soft tomato and creamy mayonnaise, the salt of the bacon. It is all there.

SERVES 4

8 slices white sandwich bread
¼ cup mayonnaise
4 lettuce leaves of choice
2 medium tomatoes, sliced
12 thick slices bacon, cooked crisp
4 teaspoons butter (optional)

Toast the bread. Spread mayonnaise on one side of 4 bread slices. Top the mayonnaise side of each slice with a lettuce leaf, 2 slices of tomato, and 3 slices of bacon. If desired, butter the remaining 4 slices of bread and top the sandwiches, butter side down. Alternatively, you can spread these pieces of bread with more mayonnaise. Cut each sandwich in half and serve.

Lobster Rolls

The lobster roll may come as a surprise to folks who didn't grow up in New England. But it's simply lobster salad that's been stuffed into a top-sliced hot dog roll. Lobster rolls are sold at clam shacks and lobster pounds all along the coast.

SERVES 4

2 (1½-pound) live lobsters
½ cup mayonnaise, plus more as needed
¼ cup minced celery (optional)
Salt and pepper
4 hot dog rolls, split on the top, lightly toasted
Melted butter
4 lettuce leaves of choice

1. Bring a very large pot of salted water to a boil. Add the lobsters and cook until they turn bright red, 10 to 15 minutes. Drain the cooking water and run the lobsters under cold water to cool them.

2. When cool enough to handle, remove the lobster meat from the shells (page 147). Finely chop the meat and refrigerate until the meat is chilled.

3. Combine the lobster meat with the mayonnaise and celery, if using, in a medium bowl. Season with salt and pepper, and stir gently to mix.

4. Brush the insides of the rolls with melted butter. Stuff the rolls with a lettuce leaf, then the lobster filling, and serve.

Muffuletta

The New Orleans muffuletta is a hero sandwich created at the Central Grocery in 1906. Popular variations of the classic abound. A round loaf of Italian bread is filled with ham, salami, cheese, and a mixture called olive salad.

SERVES 4

Olive salad:
½ cup chopped pimento-stuffed green olives
½ cup chopped pitted brine-cured black olives, such as kalamata
¼ cup minced pimentos
¼ cup minced pepperoncini (Italian pickled peppers)
⅓ cup minced celery
¼ cup olive oil
¼ cup red-wine vinegar
1 tablespoon chopped fresh parsley
1 teaspoon minced garlic
1 teaspoon dried oregano
¼ teaspoon black pepper

Sandwiches:
1 (10-inch) round loaf Italian bread, sliced horizontally
¼ pound thinly sliced Cappicola ham or other cooked ham
¼ pound thinly sliced Genoa salami
¼ pound thinly sliced provolone cheese

1. To make the olive salad, combine the olives, pimentos, pepperoncini, celery, olive oil, vinegar, parsley, garlic, oregano, and black pepper in a medium bowl. Toss with a fork to mix well, then cover the bowl and refrigerate for at least 8 hours, or overnight.

2. To make the sandwiches, remove most of the soft inner part of the bread and discard it (or use to make bread crumbs for another dish).

3. Drain the olive salad, reserving the marinade. Brush the marinade on the inside of the bread, top and bottom.

4. On the bottom half of the bread, layer the ham, salami, and cheese. Top with the olive salad and cover with the top half of the bread. Wrap the loaf tightly in plastic wrap and weight it down with a heavy plate. Set the loaf aside at room temperature for 30 minutes, or refrigerate for up to 6 hours.

5. To serve, remove the plastic wrap and cut the loaf into wedges.

Great Sandwich Combos

Some of the best classic sandwiches are straightforward and simple. The following seven sandwiches combine the basic elements of meat, cheese, fresh vegetables, and condiments to produce a variety of tasty results.

EACH SERVES 1

Roast Beef Sandwich 1

Spread mayonnaise on 1 side of 2 slices rye sandwich bread. Spread prepared horseradish over the mayonnaise. Top 1 bread slice with thinly sliced roast beef, a lettuce leaf, a tomato slice, and then the second bread slice. Cut the sandwich in half and serve.

Roast Beef Sandwich 2

Spread Russian dressing or Thousand Island dressing on a slice of rye, wheat, or white sandwich bread. Top with thinly sliced roast beef, a lettuce leaf, and a second bread slice. Cut the sandwich in half and serve.

Turkey Sandwich

Spread mayonnaise on a slice of white or wheat sandwich bread. Spread cranberry sauce or mango chutney over the mayonnaise. Top with thinly sliced cooked turkey breast, a lettuce leaf, and a second bread slice. Cut the sandwich in half and serve.

Roast Pork Sandwich

Spread barbecue sauce on a slice of white sandwich bread or half of a Kaiser roll. Top with sliced roast pork, coleslaw, and a second bread slice or half of roll. Cut the sandwich in half and serve.

Ham Sandwich

Spread mayonnaise on a slice of rye sandwich bread and follow with mustard. Top with alternating layers of sliced cooked ham and sliced Swiss cheese. Top with a lettuce leaf and a second bread slice. Cut the sandwich in half and serve.

Tomato Sandwich

Generously spread mayonnaise on a slice of white or wheat sandwich bread. Top with tomato slices. (When tomatoes are in season, make the tomato slices thick.) Sprinkle the tomato generously with salt and pepper, and top with a second bread slice. Cut the sandwich in half and serve.

Spicy Peanut Butter–Bacon Sandwich

Spread peanut butter and hot pepper jelly on a slice of white or wheat sandwich bread. Top with crisp bacon and a second bread slice. Cut the sandwich in half and serve.

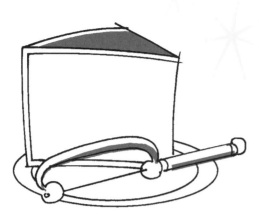

Grilled Cheese Sandwiches

In the 1950s, a Campbell's soup jingle included the refrain "Soup and sandwich, soup and sandwich, go together like a horse and carriage." The combination everyone thinks of is grilled cheese and tomato soup—something every mom served at one time or another—with or without the Parmesan cheese (included here).

SERVES 4

¼ cup (½ stick) butter, softened
3 tablespoons grated Parmesan cheese
8 thick slices sourdough bread
8 slices American cheese
8 slices Swiss cheese

1. Preheat a griddle or large, heavy skillet over medium heat.

2. Combine the butter and Parmesan cheese in a small bowl. Spread on one side of each bread slice.

3. Place 4 slices, buttered side down, on the griddle. Top with 2 slices of each cheese, then 1 bread slice, buttered side up.

4. When the cheeses start to melt, after 3 to 4 minutes, check the sandwiches for a light golden-brown color and gently flip over with a spatula. Grill until the undersides are lightly browned, about 3 minutes. Cut each sandwich in half and serve.

Welsh Rabbit

Both Welsh rabbit and Welsh rarebit are correct names for this dish of melted cheese and beer served on toast or crackers. The Welsh part comes as an insult to the Welsh, who were presumably too poor to eat meat. Welsh "rarebit" is an attempt either to avoid offending the Welsh or to dignify the original (and slightly silly) name.

SERVES 4

8 slices bread of choice
3 tablespoons butter, softened
1 tablespoon all-purpose flour
½ cup porter or ale
¼ cup milk
1 teaspoon dry mustard
⅛ teaspoon black pepper
1½ cups extra-sharp Cheddar cheese, coarsely
    shredded (about 6 ounces)
1 large egg yolk

1. Preheat the broiler.

2. Spread one side of each bread slice with butter, using 2 tablespoons of butter. Arrange the slices, buttered side up, on a baking sheet. Broil 4 to 6 inches from the heat until golden brown, 1 to 4 minutes.

3. Melt the remaining 1 tablespoon butter in a small saucepan over low heat. Stir in the flour to form a smooth paste; cook for 1 minute. Slowly add the beer and milk, stirring constantly until the mixture is smooth. Whisk in the mustard, pepper, and cheese. Cook until the cheese is melted and smooth, about 2 minutes.

4. Remove the sauce from the heat and immediately whisk in the yolk.

5. To serve, arrange the bread on plates, toasted side up, and spoon the cheese sauce over the top.

American Pizzas

Very few children made it through the 1950s and 1960s without eating "American" pizza, or pizza made with an English muffin. It was often heated in a toaster oven, an appliance that most households acquired in those years.

SERVES 4

4 English muffins, split
1 (8-ounce) can tomato sauce
Onion salt
Garlic salt
Dried oregano
½ cup shredded mozzarella cheese
½ cup grated Parmesan cheese

1. Preheat the broiler or toaster oven.

2. Toast the English muffins in a toaster until golden brown. Arrange them, cut side up, on a baking sheet or oven pan.

3. Spoon some tomato sauce on each muffin half, dividing the sauce equally among them. Sprinkle each with onion salt, garlic salt, and oregano. Sprinkle 1 tablespoon of each cheese on top of the tomato sauce.

4. Broil until the cheeses have melted and the muffins have reached the desired crispness, about 4 minutes. Serve hot.

Grilled Ham and Cheese Sandwiches

*What's better than a grilled cheese?
Why, a grilled ham and cheese, of course!*

SERVES 4

¼ cup mayonnaise
3 tablespoons prepared mustard (preferably honey mustard)
¼ teaspoon prepared horseradish (optional)
4 (¼-inch-thick) slices cooked ham
3 tablespoons butter, softened
8 thick slices sourdough bread
4 thick slices sharp Cheddar cheese

1. Preheat a griddle or large, heavy skillet over medium heat.

2. Combine the mayonnaise, mustard, and horseradish, if using, in a small bowl and mix well. Spread the mixture on each slice of ham.

3. Spread butter on 1 side of each bread slice.

4. Place 4 slices of bread, buttered side down, on the griddle. Top with a slice each of ham and cheese and cover with the remaining 4 slices of bread, buttered side up.

5. When the cheese starts to melt, after 3 to 4 minutes, check the bread for a light golden-brown color and gently flip the sandwiches over with a spatula. Grill the underside until lightly browned, about 3 minutes. Cut each sandwich in half and serve.

Monte Cristo Sandwiches

The Monte Cristo is a cross between French toast and a grilled chicken and cheese sandwich. It is closely related to the "croque monsieur," an egg-dipped, grilled ham and cheese sandwich.

SERVES 4

3 large eggs, well beaten
1 cup milk
Pinch of salt
8 slices white sandwich bread
4 slices cooked chicken breast
4 thick slices Monterey Jack cheese
4 thick slices Cheddar cheese
3 tablespoons butter
1 tablespoon oil

1. Combine the eggs, milk, and salt in a shallow bowl and mix well with a whisk.

2. Top 4 slices of bread with the chicken and cheese slices. Cover with the remaining slices of bread.

3. Melt the butter with the oil in a large, heavy skillet over medium heat.

4. Dip both sides of the sandwiches in the egg mixture and carefully add to the skillet. Cook until browned on the bottom, 3 to 4 minutes. Turn over with a spatula and cook until browned on the other side, 3 to 4 minutes. Cut each sandwich in half and serve.

Tuna Melts

You don't have to choose between a tuna sandwich and a grilled cheese; the tuna melt has the best of both.

SERVES 4

1 (6-ounce) can albacore tuna (packed in water or oil), drained
6 tablespoons mayonnaise
3 tablespoons finely chopped sweet onion, such as Maui, Walla Walla, or Vidalia
3 tablespoons finely chopped celery
1 tablespoon finely chopped pitted black olives
2 teaspoons lemon juice
¼ teaspoon salt
Pinch of black pepper
4 teaspoons butter, softened
8 thick slices sourdough bread
2 teaspoons grated Parmesan cheese
4 slices Cheddar cheese

1. Flake the tuna in a small bowl with a fork and combine with the mayonnaise, onion, celery, and olives. Add the lemon juice, salt, and pepper, and mix well.

2. Spread butter on 1 side of each bread slice and sprinkle with Parmesan cheese.

3. Place 4 slices of bread, buttered side down, in a cold skillet. Top each with the tuna mixture and 1 slice of cheese. Place the remaining 4 slices of bread, buttered side up, on top of the cheese.

4. Grill the sandwiches over medium heat, turning once, until the bread is golden brown on both sides and the cheeses are melted, 7 to 8 minutes. Cut the sandwiches in half and serve hot.

Grilled Cuban Sandwiches

This popular sandwich was brought to Florida by Cuban immigrants who came to this country during the Spanish–American war in 1898. It is sometimes called simply a "Cuban."

SERVES 4

4 sandwich rolls
Butter, softened
8 slices roasted pork loin
8 slices baked or smoked ham
12 dill pickle chips
8 slices Swiss cheese
Dijon mustard

1. Slice the rolls lengthwise and spread butter lightly on each cut half.

2. Layer the pork, ham, pickle chips, and cheese on the bottom half of each roll. Spread the top half with mustard and top the sandwich with it. Press down firmly.

3. Preheat a griddle or cast-iron frying pan over medium heat.

4. Lightly butter one side of the sandwiches. Place them, buttered side down, on the griddle and cook for 1 minute. Lightly butter the top and turn over the sandwiches with a spatula and place a heavy weight on them. Continue cooking until the cheese is melted, 3 to 4 minutes. Flip and serve hot.

Hot Brown Sandwiches

Hot turkey sandwiches are frequently found on diner menus, but you have to go to Louisville, Kentucky, to enjoy the original hot brown. This famous open–faced sandwich of turkey and bacon under a blanket of cheese sauce was created in 1926 at the Brown Hotel, where big bands kept guests dancing late into the night. Chef Fred K. Schmidt created the sandwich for hungry dancers who were drawn to the restaurant for a midnight snack during the band break. Today the hot brown sandwich is still a Louisville favorite and the signature dish of the Camberley Brown Hotel.

SERVES 4

6 tablespoons (¾ stick) butter
6 tablespoons all-purpose flour
3 cups milk
1 cup grated Parmesan cheese
1 large egg
½ cup whipped cream
Salt and pepper
8 slices white sandwich bread, toasted, with crusts trimmed off

1 pound thinly sliced cooked turkey breast
1 (2-ounce) jar diced pimentos, drained
8 slices bacon, cooked crisp

1. Melt the butter in a large saucepan over medium heat. Stir in the flour to make a smooth paste and cook for 1 minute. Gradually stir in the milk until the sauce comes to a slight boil, stirring constantly. Remove the saucepan from the heat and stir in ½ cup of Parmesan cheese. Stir until the cheese is melted and well blended.

2. Beat the egg with a fork in a small bowl. Gradually add 1 cup of the hot sauce, stirring constantly. Stir the warmed egg back into the sauce, stirring constantly until well blended. Fold in the whipped cream, and season to taste with salt and pepper.

3. Preheat the broiler.

4. Place the toasted bread slices on a metal (or ovenproof) platter. Cover each piece with some turkey, dividing it evenly among them. Pour a generous amount of sauce over the turkey, and sprinkle each with the remaining ½ cup Parmesan cheese.

5. Place the dish under the broiler until the sauce is browned and bubbly, 1 to 2 minutes. Watch carefully.

6. Remove the sandwiches from the broiler, sprinkle with the pimentos, cross 2 slices of bacon over each one, and serve immediately.

Reuben Sandwiches

The Reuben was probably invented at Reuben's Restaurant in New York City in 1914. It is a brilliant combination of corned beef, Swiss cheese, sauerkraut, and Russian dressing on rye, which is then grilled. Buy sauerkraut that comes in the supermarket's refrigerated case and avoid canned sauerkraut if possible. And if you aren't a fan of sauerkraut, consider substituting coleslaw.

SERVES 4

¼ to ½ cup Russian dressing (page 90)
8 slices rye sandwich bread
1 pound thinly sliced corned beef
12 ounces sauerkraut, well drained
4 slices Swiss cheese
4 teaspoons butter, softened

1. Preheat a griddle or large, heavy skillet over medium heat.

2. Spread half the dressing on one side of 4 bread slices. Top the dressing with the corned beef, then the sauerkraut, then the cheese. Spread the remaining dressing on one side of each of the remaining bread slices and place them, dressing side down, on top of the cheese. Butter the top slices.

3. Carefully place the sandwiches, buttered side down, on the griddle and butter the top slice. Cook until browned on the bottom, 3 to 4 minutes. Using a spatula, turn over the sandwiches and cook until browned on the other side, 3 to 4 minutes more. Cut the sandwiches in half and serve hot.

Milwaukee Hot Corned Beef Sandwiches

This corned beef sandwich combines all of the ingredients and then the filling is baked. Toast the bread first if you prefer.

SERVES 4

½ pound corned beef, chopped
¼ cup minced onion
1 pound sauerkraut, drained
½ cup mayonnaise
1 teaspoon prepared horseradish
1½ cups shredded Swiss cheese (about 8 ounces)
8 slices rye sandwich bread (preferably marble rye)

1. Preheat the oven to 350°F.

2. Combine the corned beef, onion, sauerkraut, mayonnaise, horseradish, and Swiss cheese in a small casserole dish. Bake for 20 minutes, until the mixture is heated through.

3. Divide the mixture among 4 slices of bread. Top with the remaining bread slices. Press the sandwiches together gently, cut in half, and serve.

Philly Cheese Steaks

Invented in 1930 by Pat Olivieri, a Philadelphia hot-dog stand operator, this sandwich has thinly sliced beef steak topped with cheese and sautéed onions. Today it is popular to add sautéed bell peppers. Some devotees claim that Cheez Whiz makes the best cheese topping.

SERVES 4

4 Italian or French rolls (about 6 inches long),
    partially split lengthwise
3 tablespoons oil
2 medium onions, very thinly sliced
1 pound sirloin, very thinly sliced
Salt and pepper
4 slices American or provolone cheese

1. Preheat the oven to 250°F.

2. Wrap the rolls in aluminum foil and place in the oven to warm.

3. Heat 2 tablespoons of oil in a large skillet over medium-high heat. Add the onions and sauté until softened, 4 to 5 minutes. Remove from the skillet with a slotted spoon and keep warm in an ovenproof dish in the oven.

4. Heat the remaining 1 tablespoon oil in the skillet. Add the sirloin and sauté just until lightly browned, about 2 minutes. Season with salt and pepper.

5. Stuff the rolls with steak slices, then top with the onions and a slice of cheese. If the meat and onions are hot enough, the cheese should begin to melt. If not, wrap the sandwiches in aluminum foil again and warm in the oven for a few more minutes, just until the cheese begins to ooze. Serve hot.

TIP: Meat that is partially frozen is easier to slice than meat that is just chilled.

Fried Oyster Po' Boy Sandwiches

The po' boy is New Orleans's version of the hero. Although many different types of fillings may be used, fried oysters are the most popular and the most closely associated with New Orleans.

SERVES 4

Oil, for frying
2 cups yellow cornmeal
1 teaspoon salt
½ teaspoon black pepper
¼ teaspoon cayenne pepper
24 medium oysters shucked, drained
2 loaves soft-crusted French bread
½ cup tartar sauce (page 123)
2 medium tomatoes, thinly sliced
Shredded iceberg lettuce

1. In a large, heavy saucepan or deep fryer, heat 2 to 3 inches of oil to 375°F.

2. Mix the cornmeal, salt, black pepper, and cayenne pepper in a shallow bowl. Dip in the oysters and stir to coat with the cornmeal mixture, tapping off any excess.

3. Deep fry 6 oysters at a time until golden and just cooked through, about 1½ minutes. Transfer the oysters with a slotted spoon to paper towels to drain. Continue cooking batches of 6 until all the oysters are fried.

4. Halve the loaves horizontally, cutting them all the way through. Spread each with about 2 tablespoons of tartar sauce. Layer the oysters, tomatoes, and lettuce equally among the bottom pieces of bread. Top with the remaining bread slices, pressing down gently. Serve immediately.

Meatball Sub Sandwiches

Depending on where you live, you might call a sub a hero. They are also called bombers, grinders, or hoagies. Fill them with various meats and cheeses or with meatballs, tomato sauce, and cheese, as in this recipe.

SERVES 4

1 medium onion, quartered
2 garlic cloves
¼ cup chopped fresh parsley
½ pound ground pork
½ pound ground beef
1 cup fresh bread crumbs
1 large egg
1 teaspoon dried oregano
1 teaspoon salt
½ teaspoon black pepper
2 tablespoons oil
1 (15-ounce) jar seasoned Italian tomato sauce
4 Italian hero rolls (about 6 inches long), partially split lengthwise
1 cup grated Parmesan cheese
1 cup shredded mozzarella cheese (about 4 ounces)

1. Finely chop the onion, garlic, and parsley in a food processor. Add the pork, beef, bread crumbs, egg, oregano, salt, and pepper, and process until just mixed; do not overmix. Shape the mixture into 12 meatballs.

2. Heat the oil in a large skillet over medium-high heat. Add half the meatballs and brown all over, about 5 minutes. Remove from the skillet with a slotted spoon. Repeat with the remaining meatballs.

3. Drain any fat from the skillet. Return the meatballs to the skillet and add the sauce. Cover and simmer for 15 minutes.

4. Meanwhile, preheat the oven to 250°F.

5. Warm the rolls in the oven for 5 minutes.

6. Stuff 3 meatballs into each roll. Cover the meatballs with more sauce, and top with Parmesan cheese and mozzarella cheese.

7. Wrap the heroes tightly in aluminum foil and return to the oven for 5 to 10 minutes, until the cheese is melted. Serve hot.

Sausage and Pepper Rolls

This sandwich is only as good as the sausages you use—look for top-quality hot or sweet sausage made by a local butcher. Lining the buns first with mozzarella is an option for cheese lovers.

SERVES 4

4 Italian sausages, hot or sweet
3 tablespoons oil
2 medium green bell peppers, seeded and thinly sliced
2 medium red bell peppers, seeded and thinly sliced
1 medium sweet onion, such as Walla Walla, Maui, or Vidalia, thinly sliced
Salt and pepper
4 Italian hero rolls (about 6 inches long), split lengthwise

1. Pierce each sausage with a fork to release the fat as it cooks. Place the sausages in a cold skillet, turn the heat to medium, and cook until well browned and cooked through, about 15 minutes. Pour off the fat. Drain the sausages on paper towels. (Alternatively, grill the sausages over a gas or charcoal fire, 15 to 20 minutes.)

2. Heat the oil in the same skillet and add the bell peppers and onion. Sauté until tender but not browned, 6 to 7 minutes. Return the sausages to the skillet, season with salt and pepper, and cook for another 10 to 15 minutes, spooning off any excess fat.

3. Use tongs to place a sausage in each roll. Top with some bell peppers and onion and serve.

Patty Melts

What's the difference between a patty melt and a hamburger? A patty melt is always topped with cheese, often smothered with onions, and can be served on any sort of bread or roll, including rye bread, which is the choice here.

SERVES 4

1 pound ground beef
½ teaspoon salt
Pinch of black pepper
1 tablespoon oil
1 large sweet onion, such as Maui, Walla Walla, or Vidalia
1 tablespoon butter
8 slices rye sandwich bread, toasted
4 slices Monterey Jack cheese

1. Form the meat into 4 patties; sprinkle each with salt and pepper.

2. Preheat a large, heavy skillet over medium-high heat. Add the patties and brown on both sides, about 3 minutes per side for rare or 4 minutes for medium. Remove the patties and set aside.

3. Wipe out the skillet with a paper towel. Add the oil and heat over medium-high heat. Add the onion and sauté just until transparent, about 3 minutes. Remove and set aside.

4. Preheat the broiler.

5. Butter 1 side of 4 pieces of toast and place on a baking sheet, buttered side up. Top each with a patty, then with sautéed onion, and 1 slice of cheese.

6. Broil the sandwiches 5 inches from the heat for about 2 minutes, until the cheese is melted but not runny. Top each patty melt with 1 toasted bread slice and serve hot.

All-American Hamburgers

It is possible that the hamburger as we know it today—the ground meat patty on a bun—was invented in Hamburg, New York, in the summer of 1885 at the Erie County Fair. Regardless of its origin, this is a sandwich we've all grown up with and look forward to eating again and again. Several variations follow.

SERVES 4

1 pound ground beef
½ teaspoon salt
Pinch of black pepper
4 hamburger buns
4 thick slices sweet onion, such as Maui, Walla Walla, or Vidalia
4 lettuce leaves of choice
1 medium tomato, sliced
Ketchup, mustard, and pickle relish, to serve

1. Form the meat into 4 thick patties; sprinkle each with salt and pepper.

2. Preheat a large, heavy skillet over medium-high heat. Add the patties and brown on both sides, about 3 minutes per side for rare or 4 minutes for medium. (Alternatively, you can broil them, 3 minutes per side for rare or 4 minutes for medium.)

3. Meanwhile, preheat the broiler.

4. Toast the buns under the broiler, cut side up, for 1 minute, and remove from the oven.

5. Top each bun bottom with a patty, onion slice, lettuce leaf, and tomato slice. Top with the remaining bun halves. Serve immediately, with the ketchup, mustard, and pickle relish on the side.

Cheeseburgers

Follow steps 1 and 2 in making All-American Hamburgers. After browning the patties, top each with a slice of American, Cheddar, or Swiss cheese. Complete the recipe as directed.

Bacon Cheeseburgers

Follow steps 1 and 2 in making All-American Hamburgers. After browning the patties, top each with a slice of American, Cheddar, or Swiss cheese, then 1 slice of crisp bacon, cut in half. Complete the recipe as directed.

Sloppy Joes

Sloppy Joes are barely sandwiches—they are almost too messy to eat with your hands. If you grew up in the Midwest, you might know them as "loosemeat sandwiches."

SERVES 4

1 tablespoon oil
1 pound ground beef
1 medium onion, diced
1 medium red or green bell pepper, seeded and diced
1 teaspoon minced garlic
⅔ cup chili sauce or barbecue sauce (page 254)
1 tablespoon Worcestershire sauce
2 to 3 tablespoons brown sugar
Salt and pepper
Hot pepper sauce, such as Tabasco
4 hamburger buns

1. Heat the oil in a large skillet over medium-high heat. Add the beef, onion, bell pepper, and garlic and sauté until the meat is browned, about 10 minutes.

2. Add the chili sauce, Worcestershire sauce, and 2 tablespoons of brown sugar. Season to taste with salt, pepper, hot pepper sauce, and remaining 1 tablespoon brown sugar, if desired. Partially cover the skillet, reduce the heat, and let the meat mixture simmer for 15 minutes, until the flavors are blended and the sauce is slightly thickened.

3. Meanwhile, preheat the broiler.

4. Toast the buns, cut side up, under the broiler for about 1 minute.

5. To serve, arrange the bun bottoms on plates and spoon the filling on each; top with the remaining bun halves.

Chili Dogs

Hot dogs are a quintessential American sandwich. Top a hot dog with chili, shredded cheese, and onions, and you have a meal on a bun.

SERVES 6

1½ pounds ground beef
1 medium onion, finely chopped
2 garlic cloves, finely chopped
1½ cups peeled and diced tomatoes (fresh or canned)
¼ cup chopped green chile peppers (fresh or canned, drained)
1 tablespoon ground chili powder
1 teaspoon ground cumin
½ teaspoon salt
½ teaspoon black pepper
6 hot dogs
6 hot dog buns
1 cup shredded Cheddar cheese (about 4 ounces)
½ cup finely chopped sweet onion, such as Maui, Walla Walla, or Vidalia

1. Brown the beef in a large skillet over medium-high heat for about 8 minutes. Add the onion and garlic and continue cooking for 2 more minutes. Drain off any fat.

2. Stir in the tomatoes, chile peppers, chili powder, cumin, salt, and pepper. Simmer the mixture over low heat for 1 hour.

3. Cook the hot dogs in a skillet over medium-high heat, turning frequently, until browned, about 5 minutes.

4. Use tongs to place a hot dog in each bun and spoon some chili over each. Sprinkle with shredded cheese and sweet onion, and serve.

Corn Dogs

*The corn dog is a hot dog skewered on a stick,
covered with cornmeal batter, and deep fried. It has
been a popular fair food since the 1940s.
You will need six craft sticks for this recipe.*

SERVES 6

Oil, for frying
½ cup yellow cornmeal
½ cup all-purpose flour
1 tablespoon sugar
1 teaspoon baking powder
Pinch of salt
½ cup milk
1 large egg, lightly beaten
1 tablespoon butter, melted
6 hot dogs

1. In a large saucepan or deep fryer, heat 3 to 4 inches of oil to 375°F.

2. Stir together the cornmeal, flour, sugar, baking powder, and salt in a medium bowl. Add the milk, egg, and butter, and mix until the batter is smooth. Transfer to a pitcher or tall glass.

3. Skewer the hot dogs lengthwise almost all the way through. Dip each in the batter, coating evenly. (Be sure not to coat the sticks.)

4. Deep fry for about 2 minutes, until the batter coating is golden brown. Drain the corn dogs on paper towels, cool for 1 minute, and serve.

Bean Burritos

*The original "wrap" sandwich, a burrito is a filled flour
tortilla. If you like, serve the burrito with guacamole and/or
sour cream. Three variations follow.*

SERVES 4

4 large flour tortillas
2 cups canned or homemade refried beans
    (page 288)
2 cups shredded Monterey Jack or pepper Jack
    cheese (about 8 ounces)
½ cup salsa of choice (page 56)

Pickled peppers (optional)
Sliced pitted black olives (optional)
Shredded lettuce of choice (optional)

1. Preheat the oven to 300°F.

2. Wrap the tortillas in aluminum foil and warm them in the oven for about 10 minutes.

3. Warm the beans in a saucepan over low heat, stirring occasionally to avoid sticking.

4. Spread one-quarter of the beans on each tortilla. Sprinkle on one-quarter of the cheese, then add some salsa. Add a sprinkle of pickled peppers, black olives, and/or shredded lettuce, if using. Fold in the sides of the tortillas, then roll up. Serve immediately.

Chili Burritos

Replace the beans in Bean Burritos with your favorite chili (page 196) or beef taco filling (page 53). Complete the recipe as directed.

Chicken Burritos

Replace the beans in Bean Burritos with 2 cups shredded cooked chicken. Complete the recipe as directed.

Breakfast Burritos

Replace the beans in Bean Burritos with a batch of scrambled eggs (made with 4 eggs) mixed with 4 crisp, crumbled bacon slices. Complete the recipe as directed.

Chimichangas

*Chimichangas are deep-fried burritos, usually filled with
beef. There are several stories about the origin of this dish,
one being that chimichanga is the Mexican equivalent of
"whatchamacallit" or "thingamajig."*

SERVES 5 TO 10

3 pounds boneless beef shoulder or chuck
Salt and pepper
2 tablespoons oil, plus more for frying
1 small onion, chopped
1½ teaspoons minced garlic
1 cup beef broth (page 118)
10 large flour tortillas
Shredded Monterey Jack or Cheddar cheese,
    to serve
Sour cream, to serve
Diced fresh tomatoes, to serve
Salsa of choice (page 56), to serve

1. Rub the meat with salt and pepper.

2. Heat 2 tablespoons oil in a large Dutch oven over medium-high heat. Add the meat and brown on all sides, about 10 minutes. Add half the onion and the garlic, and sauté for 1 minute. Add the broth. Reduce the heat, cover the pot tightly, and simmer for about 1½ hours, until the meat is tender enough to be falling apart. Remove the meat from the broth and let cool.

3. Shred the beef and return it to the Dutch oven. Add the remaining onion and cook until the broth has evaporated.

4. Warm the tortillas in a skillet until soft enough to roll. Place ¾ cup of shredded beef in the center of each tortilla. Fold in the sides and roll up. Secure with toothpicks.

5. In a large saucepan or deep fryer, heat 4 to 5 inches of oil to 375°F.

6. Deep fry the chimichangas until golden brown, about 4 minutes. Drain on paper towels and serve hot. Offer the cheese, sour cream, tomatoes, and salsa as accompaniments.

Beef Tacos

Have a fiesta! Set up a taco bar by doubling this recipe, and let your guests make their own tacos. In addition to the fixings listed below, you can offer bowls of guacamole, sour cream, sliced black olives, and sliced pickled jalapeño chile peppers. Include Spanish rice and refried beans. The drink of choice is a margarita, of course. A soft taco variation follows.

SERVES 4

1 pound ground beef
1 tablespoon chili powder
1 teaspoon ground cumin
1 small onion, finely chopped
1 medium green bell pepper, seeded and finely
    chopped
1 teaspoon minced garlic
1 cup tomato sauce
Salt and pepper
Cayenne pepper or ground chile peppers, such
    as ancho or New Mexico
12 taco shells
2 cups shredded lettuce of choice
2 cups shredded Monterey Jack or pepper Jack
    cheese (about 8 ounces)
Salsa of choice (page 56), to serve

1. Brown the beef with the chili powder and cumin in a large skillet over medium-high heat, about 8 minutes. Add the onion, bell pepper, and garlic and continue cooking for 2 more minutes. Drain off any fat.

2. Stir in the tomato sauce. Season to taste with salt and pepper and cayenne pepper. Simmer over low heat for 30 minutes to blend the flavors.

3. Meanwhile, preheat the oven to 200°F.

4. Warm the taco shells on a baking sheet in the oven for about 10 minutes. Arrange the lettuce, cheese, and salsa in serving bowls.

5. Transfer the meat mixture to a serving bowl and place the warmed taco shells in a basket. Serve buffet style, allowing guests to fill the taco shells as desired with meat, lettuce, cheese, and salsa.

Soft Beef Tacos

Replace the taco shells in Beef Tacos with soft corn tortillas, wrapped in aluminum foil and warmed in the oven.

CHAPTER THREE

Appetizers

Everyone loves a party. After a hectic day, a party takes us outside our workaday world and brings us together with old friends and new. Parties give us the opportunity to play matchmaker with friends—or make new connections ourselves. They give us the opportunity to pull out the pearls or the bow ties, the Fiestaware or the crystal. We talk, we drink, we dance, we eat.

There is no such thing as "authentic" American appetizers, only creative adaptations based on period recipes. The smorgasbord, a buffet meal of Swedish origins, became very fashionable in the United States after it first appeared in American print in 1893. By the 1940s it was believed that a party was successful only when the hostess supplied ample platters of appetizers and the host kept the cocktails flowing.

The nibbles and noshes that start a party are very important for setting the tone and making your guests comfortable. You can simply put out a bowl of potato chips with some onion dip, or tortilla chips and salsa, but why stop there? Add a few dips and spreads for crackers, or raw vegetables and some spiced nuts or olives, and you are well on your way to making your gathering a special occasion.

Some of the foods you may want to offer require little or no preparation. A wooden board with an assortment of cheeses makes a quick party fix. A tray of rolled deli meats is always inviting. Crudités, or attractively cut raw vegetables, carefully arranged around a bowl of ranch salad dressing, are a party standard.

For a retro look (to go with those pearls), set a head of purple cabbage, stem side down, on a festive plate. Use the cabbage as a holder for mini-kebabs, which you make using colorful cocktail toothpicks. Some possible kebab combinations are ham and cheese or ham and pineapple cubes, shrimp and mandarin orange segments, little smoked sausages, squares of multicolored bell peppers and cherry tomatoes, or stuffed olives with cheese cubes.

Even if you aren't the "hostess with the mostest" or the original party lover, you are probably a snack lover—who isn't? The recipes in this chapter make terrific snacks for those times when you want to kick back and relax with a book, a movie, a jigsaw puzzle with the kids, or an evening of cards. Let the good times roll!

Pico de Gallo

This salsa is also known as salsa cruda ("cruda" means "raw" in Spanish) because of its simple combination of fresh tomatoes and chile peppers. This is best made with vine-ripened tomatoes at season's peak. Serve alone as a dip with tortilla chips or as a topping on eggs or Mexican dishes.

MAKES 2 CUPS

2 large tomatoes, seeded and finely chopped
¼ cup finely chopped onion
¼ cup finely chopped chile peppers, such as jalapeño
¼ cup seeded and finely chopped green or red bell pepper
2 tablespoons finely chopped fresh cilantro
1 to 2 tablespoons lime or lemon juice
Salt and pepper

1. Mix the tomatoes, onion, chile peppers, bell pepper, cilantro, and 1 tablespoon lime juice in a medium bowl. Season to taste with salt and pepper.

2. Let the salsa sit for 15 to 30 minutes. Taste and adjust the seasoning, adding additional lime juice, salt, and pepper as needed.

Qué Bueno Salsa

This recipe makes a large amount so there's extra for canning the salsa and your enjoyment well past summer.

MAKES 4 PINTS

8 to 10 large tomatoes, peeled, seeded, and quartered
4 to 5 medium yellow or red bell peppers, seeded and quartered
2 large sweet onions, such as Maui, Walla Walla, or Vidalia, quartered
2 (4-ounce) cans diced mild green chile peppers, drained
½ cup cider vinegar
1 (6-ounce) can tomato paste
2 large garlic cloves
2 tablespoons chopped fresh cilantro
1 tablespoon salt
2 teaspoons chili powder
½ teaspoon dried oregano

1. Coarsely chop the tomatoes, bell peppers, and onions in a food processor.

2. Transfer to a large, nonreactive saucepan and add the chile peppers, vinegar, tomato paste, garlic, cilantro, salt, chili powder, and oregano. Bring the mixture to a gentle boil, then reduce the heat and simmer for 30 minutes.

3. Fill 4 sterilized pint canning jars (or 3 if serving some immediately) with the hot salsa, leaving ½ inch of headspace. Wipe the rims clean and seal with the lids and screw caps. Process in a boiling water bath for 15 minutes, according to the directions from the jar manufacturer. If serving immediately, allow the salsa to cool to room temperature.

Guacamole

In an authentic guacamole, avocado is chopped into small cubes, the way fresh salsa ingredients are. Serve as a dip with tortilla chips. Finely chopped cilantro can be added just before serving for a garden-fresh taste.

MAKES ABOUT 2 CUPS

3 medium avocados, peeled, pitted, and diced
¼ cup salsa of choice, such as pico de gallo (this page) or qué bueno salsa (this page)
1 garlic clove, finely chopped
1 tablespoon olive oil
1 tablespoon lime or lemon juice
Salt and pepper

1. In a medium bowl, mix the avocados, salsa, garlic, oil, and lime juice. Season to taste with salt and pepper.

2. Cover the guacamole and chill for about 1 hour before serving.

TIP: Avocados are rarely ripe when you buy them, so buy them 2 or 3 days in advance and leave them in a paper bag at room temperature. A ripe avocado will give slightly when pressed at the stem end.

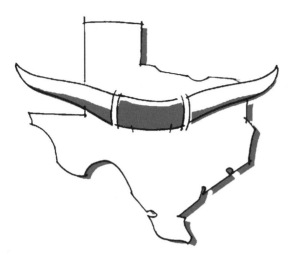

Texas Caviar

It's an old tradition to call a dish made with beans, or one that contains lots of seeds, "poor man's caviar." Serve this savory dip in a colorful bowl with tortilla chips alongside.

MAKES 4 CUPS

3 (15½-ounce) cans black-eyed peas, rinsed
  and drained
½ cup Italian dressing (page 89), or more
  to taste
1 tablespoon finely chopped canned jalapeño
  chile pepper
¼ cup seeded and finely chopped green bell
  pepper
¼ cup seeded and finely chopped yellow bell
  pepper
¼ cup seeded and finely chopped red bell
  pepper
½ cup finely chopped sweet onion, such
  as Maui, Walla Walla, or Vidalia
1 large garlic clove, finely chopped
Salt

1. Combine the peas, dressing, jalapeño, bell peppers, onion, and garlic in a medium bowl. Mix well. Season to taste with salt.

2. Refrigerate the dip for at least 2 hours, or up to 2 days to allow the flavors to blend.

3. Taste for salt and add more as needed. If the mixture is a bit dry, add a little more dressing. Serve at room temperature.

Pimento Cheese

Pimento cheese, or "PC" as it is sometimes called, is the "paste" that holds Southern food traditions together. Rarely served outside of the South, it is typically made with cheese, pimentos, mayonnaise, salt, pepper, and maybe a pinch of sugar. It is served as a spread for crackers and a filling for sandwiches; in South Carolina you may see it as a topping for hamburgers and hot dogs.

MAKES ABOUT 1 CUP

1 cup shredded sharp Cheddar cheese (about
  4 ounces)
¼ cup diced pimentos
¼ cup mayonnaise
2 tablespoons lemon juice
¼ teaspoon salt
Dash of hot pepper sauce, such as Tabasco
  (optional)
Pinch of sugar (optional)

1. Combine the cheese, pimentos, mayonnaise, lemon juice, and salt in a food processor. Process until smooth.

2. Taste and add hot pepper sauce and sugar, if desired.

3. Chill well before serving.

Green Onion Dip

A zesty dip made from dried onion soup mix was de rigueur at 1950s-era parties. But in other homes, where everything was made from scratch (except perhaps the potato chips), green onion dip offered an alternative.

MAKES 2 CUPS

1 (16-ounce) container sour cream (about
  2 cups)
½ cup chopped scallions
1 teaspoon minced garlic
½ to 1 teaspoon cayenne pepper or crushed
  red pepper
Salt and pepper

1. In a medium bowl, mix the sour cream, scallions, and garlic. Add the cayenne pepper, then salt and pepper to taste.

2. Refrigerate overnight. Serve chilled.

Bacon Horseradish Dip

The year 1966 was an important one in entertaining history, as it was the year General Foods introduced Bac-Os, bits of soy protein isolate artificially flavored to taste like bacon. But here's a dip still made with the real thing.

MAKES ABOUT 2½ CUPS

1 (16-ounce) container sour cream (about 2 cups)
½ cup finely chopped crisp bacon
1 tablespoon Worcestershire sauce
2 tablespoons prepared horseradish
½ teaspoon hot pepper sauce, such as Tabasco
Pinch of garlic powder

1. In a medium bowl, stir together all the ingredients until well blended. Cover.

2. Refrigerate for several hours or until chilled. Serve with chips and/or crackers.

Herbed Cheese Spread

Fresh herbs can dress up cream cheese to make a spread that comes close to the famous Boursin cheese from France. Dried herbs can be substituted at one-third the fresh amount, but the flavor will not be as intense.

MAKES ABOUT 1½ CUPS

2 scallions, trimmed and chopped
2 tablespoons chopped fresh basil
1 tablespoon chopped fresh parsley
1 tablespoon chopped fresh dill
1 garlic clove
1 (8-ounce) package cream cheese, softened
1 tablespoon lemon juice
½ teaspoon Worcestershire sauce

1. Combine the scallions, basil, parsley, dill, and garlic in a food processor and process until finely chopped. Add the cream cheese, lemon juice, and Worcestershire sauce and process until well blended.

2. Use a spatula to transfer the mixture to a medium bowl and let stand for 30 minutes to allow the flavors to blend, or refrigerate for several hours. Serve chilled.

Beer Cheese Dip

When the party is casual, serve this savory dip with chips, crackers, or fresh vegetable sticks.

MAKES ABOUT 3 CUPS

2½ cups shredded extra-sharp Cheddar cheese (about 10 ounces)
½ cup beer
¼ cup mayonnaise
1½ teaspoons Worcestershire sauce
1 teaspoon caraway seeds
Salt and pepper

1. Process the cheese, beer, mayonnaise, and Worcestershire sauce in a blender or food processor until smooth. Transfer the mixture to a medium bowl and stir in the caraway seeds. Season to taste with salt and pepper.

2. Cover and refrigerate. Serve cold.

Party Cheese Ball

Set a cheese ball on a plate and surround it with an assortment of crackers. It will look like you spent some time preparing this, but it is really quite easy.

MAKES 1

2 scallions, trimmed and chopped
1 garlic clove
6 (3-ounce) packages cream cheese, softened
2 cups shredded sharp Cheddar cheese (about 8 ounces)
2 teaspoons Worcestershire sauce
1 teaspoon prepared horseradish
1¼ cups finely chopped pecans or walnuts

1. Combine the scallions and garlic in a food processor and process until finely chopped. Add the cream cheese, Cheddar cheese, Worcestershire sauce, and horseradish and process until smooth.

2. Transfer the mixture to a large piece of plastic wrap and shape into a ball. Wrap the ball and place in a deep bowl to help keep its shape. Refrigerate until firm, at least 1 hour.

3. Unwrap the ball. Place the nuts on a plate and roll the cold cheese ball over the nuts, pressing them into the surface to adhere. Rewrap and store in the refrigerator for up to 3 days.

4. Remove the cheese ball, unwrap, and let sit for about 1 hour to soften a bit before serving.

Hot Crab Dip

If possible, serve this hot dip in a chafing dish, a fondue pot, or a crockery bowl set on a hot plate. Accompany with slices of baguette, small chunks of sourdough bread, or your favorite crackers. For a variation, add ¼ cup marinated artichoke halves chopped into bite-size pieces and a pinch of cayenne pepper.

MAKES ABOUT 2½ CUPS

12 ounces lump crabmeat
1 (3-ounce) package cream cheese, softened
¼ cup sour cream
¼ cup mayonnaise
½ teaspoon prepared horseradish (optional)
1 tablespoon lemon juice
1 tablespoon minced pimento or roasted red bell pepper
2 tablespoons minced sweet onion, such as Maui, Walla Walla, or Vidalia

1. Preheat the oven to 400°F.

2. Drain the crabmeat; pick through and discard any cartilage or shell, then set aside.

3. In a large bowl, combine the cream cheese, sour cream, mayonnaise, horseradish, and lemon juice. Stir well, then add the pimento, onion, and crabmeat; stir until well mixed.

4. Transfer the mixture to a shallow baking pan and bake for 15 minutes, or until bubbly. Serve at once.

Hot Artichoke Dip

Artichoke dip is a great, last-minute appetizer that is simple to make. Serve with various crackers or sliced bread, such as French bread, which can be used to scoop up the dip without breaking.

MAKES ABOUT 3½ CUPS

2 (3-ounce) packages cream cheese, softened
½ cup mayonnaise
½ cup sour cream
¾ cup grated Parmesan cheese
¼ cup diced pimento
1 teaspoon minced garlic
1 (14-ounce) can artichoke hearts, drained and chopped

1. Preheat the oven to 375°F.

2. In a large bowl, blend the cream cheese, mayonnaise, sour cream, Parmesan cheese, pimento, and garlic. Fold in the artichoke hearts. Pack the mixture into a small ovenproof crock or casserole dish.

3. Bake for 15 to 20 minutes, until hot and lightly browned on top. Serve immediately.

Smoked Salmon Spread

Garnished with a dab of red caviar, this pink spread becomes an elegant holiday offering. And even without the caviar, it is terrific on bagels for Sunday brunch.

MAKES ABOUT 2½ CUPS

2 (8-ounce) packages cream cheese, softened
2 tablespoons lemon juice
8 ounces smoked salmon, flaked
¼ cup finely chopped fresh chives
Salt and pepper

1. Whip the cream cheese with the lemon juice in a food processor until light. Fold in the salmon and chives, and season to taste with salt and pepper.

2. Transfer to a serving bowl or crock and refrigerate. Serve chilled or at room temperature.

Chopped Chicken Livers

Before there were food processors, chicken livers were minced with a knife, ground with a hand-cranked meat grinder, or spun in a blender. Now the food processor is the essential tool for making this spread. Enjoy chopped chicken liver on crackers (or matzos), or call it "chicken liver pâté" and serve with slices of baguette and cornichons (small pickles).

SERVES 8

4 tablespoons oil
2 large onions, halved and thinly sliced
1 pound chicken livers, trimmed of fat and
    halved
Salt and pepper
2 large eggs, hard-boiled, peeled, and
    quartered
¼ cup coarse chopped fresh parsley
1 to 2 tablespoons brandy or dry sherry
    (optional)

1. Heat 2 tablespoons of oil in a large skillet over medium heat. Add the onions and sauté until golden brown, about 10 to 12 minutes. Remove the onions from the skillet.

2. Heat the remaining 2 tablespoons oil in the skillet over medium-high heat. Add the livers and season with salt and pepper. Sauté until the livers are cooked through, about 3 minutes. Do not overcook.

3. Combine the onions, livers, eggs, and parsley in a food processor and pulse until very finely chopped and well mixed. Taste and adjust the seasoning, adding the brandy if desired. Chill for 1 to 2 hours before serving.

Spiced Nuts

Nothing is more irresistible than salty, spiced nuts. Adding 1 teaspoon onion powder, garlic powder, cinnamon, nutmeg, or other spice (or a combination) will only add more character. You can double or triple this recipe easily.

MAKES 2 CUPS

2 cups mixed shelled nuts (almonds, Brazil
    nuts, cashews, peanuts, pecans, walnuts)
1½ tablespoons butter, melted
1 tablespoon chili powder
1 teaspoon salt

1. Preheat the oven to 350°F.

2. Spread out the nuts in a single layer in a baking dish. Roast for about 10 minutes, stirring occasionally, until very lightly browned.

3. Combine the butter, chili powder, and salt in a small bowl. Pour over the nuts and toss to coat well. Spread out in a single layer, reduce the temperature to 300°F, and continue roasting for 20 minutes more, until browned.

4. Let cool until the nuts are crisp. Serve warm or at room temperature.

Toasted Pumpkin Seeds

Pumpkins were an important part of the early settlers' diets, and pumpkin seeds were eaten as snacks. Pumpkin seeds are also a snack throughout Central America, where they are known as "pepitas."

MAKES 2 CUPS

2 cups fresh pumpkin seeds
¼ cup Worcestershire sauce
2 tablespoons butter, melted
1 teaspoon salt

1. Preheat the oven to 250°F.

2. Use paper towels to wipe any fibers off the seeds. Do not wash the seeds.

3. Toss the pumpkin seeds with the Worcestershire sauce, butter, and salt on a baking sheet until evenly coated. Spread out the seeds to form a single layer.

4. Bake for 2 hours, stirring occasionally, until the seeds are crisp, dry, and golden.

5. Serve immediately or let cool and store in an airtight container.

Hot Buttered Popcorn

You might think that popcorn is always made in the microwave, but it used to be popped on top of the stove. The great thing about this method is that you get to add as little or as much butter as you choose. Two variations follow.

MAKES ABOUT 4 CUPS

2 tablespoons oil
½ cup popping corn
Melted butter
Salt

1. Place the oil and 3 popcorn kernels in a large, deep saucepan over high heat. Cover, and when you hear the first kernel pop, add the remaining popcorn, reduce the heat to medium, and replace the cover.

2. Cook, shaking the pot occasionally, until the popping sound nearly stops, about 5 minutes.

3. Pour the melted butter over the popcorn—¼ cup (½ stick) is an average amount—and salt to taste. Enjoy immediately.

Cheese Popcorn

Cook the popping corn as directed for Hot Buttered Popcorn. Pour ¼ cup melted butter over the popped corn and toss. Sprinkle ½ cup grated Parmesan cheese over the top and add salt to taste. Toss lightly to mix, and serve.

Nutty Popcorn

Cook the popping corn as directed for Hot Buttered Popcorn. Add 1 heaping tablespoon peanut butter (creamy or crunchy) to ¼ cup melted butter. Pour the mixture over the freshly popped popcorn. Toss lightly to mix, and serve.

Caramel Corn

In 1893, brothers Fred and Louis Rueckheim, German immigrants from Chicago, came up with the idea of covering popcorn with molasses. They called their confection "candied popcorn and peanuts." But the name "Cracker Jack" came into use in 1896 when a customer who tried the candied popcorn said, "That's really a cracker jack!" The term "cracker jack" was slang for "something very pleasing." The brothers loved the name and had it copyrighted. Their slogan was "The more you eat, the more you want," which was also copyrighted that year. This caramel corn will remind you of Cracker Jack, but the original formula is a trade secret.

MAKES ABOUT 12 CUPS

2 tablespoons oil
⅓ cup popcorn kernels
½ cup (1 stick) unsalted butter
1½ cups packed brown sugar
½ cup light corn syrup
¾ teaspoon salt
½ teaspoon baking soda
1 cup salted peanuts

1. Place the oil and 3 popcorn kernels in a large, deep saucepan over high heat. Cover, and when you hear the first kernel pop, add the remaining popcorn, reduce the heat to medium, and replace the cover.

2. Cook, shaking the pan occasionally, until the popping sound nearly stops, about 5 minutes.

3. Line the bottom of a large, shallow baking pan with aluminum foil. Lightly oil the foil.

4. Melt the butter in a 6-quart heavy pot over medium heat. Add the brown sugar and corn syrup and bring to a boil. Boil, without stirring, until the syrup registers 300°F on a candy thermometer, 8 to 10 minutes. Remove from the heat.

5. Stir the salt and baking soda into the syrup. Quickly stir in the peanuts and popcorn to coat. Immediately spread the mixture in the baking pan as thinly and evenly as possible.

6. Cool completely, then break into bite-size pieces, and eat.

Nutty Party Mix

Party mixes are made up of whatever salty, crunchy foods you like. So tour the snack aisle of your local supermarket and come up with your own interesting variation.

MAKES ABOUT 5½ CUPS

¼ cup (½ stick) butter, melted
2 tablespoons soy sauce
2 teaspoons hot pepper sauce, such as Tabasco
1 teaspoon Worcestershire sauce
1 teaspoon garlic salt
1 cup oyster crackers or chow mein noodles
1 cup small pretzel sticks, broken into 1½- to 2-inch pieces
1 cup Rice Chex cereal
1 cup Wheat Chex cereal
½ cup roasted salted cashews
½ cup salted peanuts
½ cup almonds

1. Preheat the oven to 250°F.

2. Combine the butter, soy sauce, hot sauce, Worcestershire sauce, and garlic salt in a small bowl. Mix well.

3. Combine the oyster crackers, pretzel pieces, cereals, cashews, peanuts, and almonds in a large bowl. Add the butter mixture and toss gently to mix. Taste and add more hot pepper sauce, if desired.

4. Transfer the mixture to a large baking sheet or shallow roasting pan and spread into an even layer. Bake for 1 hour, stirring occasionally. Serve warm or at room temperature.

Roasted Chestnuts

Roasted chestnuts are a holiday tradition. At the grocery store, look for the meatiest chestnuts you can find. Select ones that are firm and whose skins are a rich, shiny brown. If they smell moldy, look blotchy, feel light, or have pinholes, do not buy them.

MAKES 1 POUND

1 pound chestnuts in the shell

1. Preheat the oven to 400°F.

2. Make a cut in the rounded side of each chestnut to keep them from exploding in the oven. Place the chestnuts in a single layer on a baking sheet.

3. Roast for about 20 minutes, until tender. To test, insert a fork through the cut in one of the shells.

4. Wrap the hot chestnuts in an old towel, squeeze them hard to crush the skins, and let them sit wrapped for 5 minutes. Open the towel, peel, and enjoy.

Cheese Straws

Now that puff pastry is readily available in the freezer case of most supermarkets, cheese straws are easy to make.

MAKES 24 STRAWS

2 sheets frozen puff pastry (16 to 17 ounces), thawed
1 large egg, lightly beaten
½ cup grated Parmesan cheese

1. Roll out the pastry on a lightly floured surface to make each 8½-inch square about ¼ inch thick. (For most commercial puff pastry sheets, this will simply involve unrolling or unfolding the sheet.) Brush the tops of both sheets with the beaten egg.

2. Sprinkle one of the pastry sheets with the cheese. Top with the second sheet of pastry, egg side down. Roll out the dough to form a thin rectangle, about 9 x 12 inches. Transfer the rectangle to a baking sheet and refrigerate for 30 minutes.

3. Generously grease a baking sheet.

4. Trim the pastry so the edges are even. Cut the pastry into ½ x 9-inch strips. Twist each strip by securing one end to the cutting board and twisting the other end about three times. Transfer the twisted strips to the prepared baking sheet, placing them about 1 inch apart.

5. Refrigerate until firm. (You can store the strips in the refrigerator for several hours.)

6. Preheat the oven to 425°F.

7. Bake the twists until light brown, about 12 minutes. Cool on wire racks and serve.

Caraway Sticks

A cracker rod is a handy tool for scooping up dips. This is a good cracker for Boursin cheese or Herbed Cheese Spread (page 58).

MAKES ABOUT 12 STICKS

Sticks:
2 cups all-purpose flour
1 teaspoon salt
⅔ cup butter
⅔ cup shortening
2 large egg yolks, lightly beaten
2 tablespoons water

Egg wash and topping:
1 large egg
2 teaspoons milk
Coarse or kosher salt
Caraway seeds

1. To make the sticks, mix the flour and salt in a medium bowl. Cut in the butter and shortening with a fork or two knives until the mixture resembles coarse meal. Mix in the egg yolks and water until blended. Gather the dough into a ball. Cover and refrigerate until firm, about 30 minutes.

2. Preheat the oven to 425°F.

3. Roll out the dough on a lightly floured surface and cut into ¾-inch-thick sticks about 4 inches long.

4. To make the egg wash, whisk the egg with the milk in a small bowl. Use a pastry brush to brush the wash on the sticks. Place the sticks on a baking sheet about ½ inch apart and sprinkle with the salt and caraway seeds.

5. Bake for 10 to 12 minutes, until lightly browned. Cool on wire racks, then serve.

Stuffed Cucumbers

Cucumbers make a cool and refreshing cup to hold this creamy filling. Look for unwaxed cucumbers—either pickling (Kirby) or the cellophane-wrapped long cucumbers variously called "English," "hothouse," or "gourmet" cucumbers.

MAKES 14 TO 18 PIECES

2 (3-ounce) packages cream cheese, softened
2 tablespoons sour cream
¼ cup finely minced pimento-stuffed green olives
1 tablespoon chopped fresh chives
Salt and pepper
2 English cucumbers or 4 Kirby cucumbers

1. Combine the cream cheese, sour cream, olives, and chives in a food processor and process until well blended. Season to taste with salt and pepper.

2. Cut the cucumbers into 1½-inch-thick slices. Hollow the slices halfway, making a well to hold the filling and leaving enough on the bottom to prevent the filling from seeping out.

3. Fill the cucumber cups with the cream cheese mixture. Chill for several hours before serving.

Deviled Eggs

Deviled eggs are such a standard on buffet tables that you can buy platters with indentations especially for them; they make serving these eggs all the easier. An alternative is to tuck lettuce or kale leaves around the stuffed eggs to hold them in place. If possible, use a pastry tube or bag with a star tip to fill the egg halves—it speeds up the process and gives a rippled surface that catches the dusting of paprika.

MAKES 16

8 large eggs, hard-boiled and peeled
¼ cup mayonnaise
2 tablespoons prepared yellow or Dijon mustard
1 teaspoon hot pepper sauce, such as Tabasco (optional)
Salt and pepper
Paprika

1. Carefully slice the eggs in half lengthwise and remove the yolks.

2. Mash the yolks in a small bowl. Mix in the mayonnaise, mustard, and hot pepper sauce until well blended. Season to taste with salt and pepper.

3. Spoon or pipe the filling into the hollows of the whites, mounding it slightly. Sprinkle lightly with paprika to garnish.

4. Refrigerate for 1 to 2 hours and serve cold.

Marinated Olives

This recipe requires imported brine-cured olives. Mixing several types of olives makes it even more interesting.

MAKES ABOUT 1½ CUPS

8 ounces brine-cured pitted green olives, drained
8 ounces brine-cured pitted black olives, drained
¼ cup olive oil
2 teaspoons red-wine vinegar
½ teaspoon minced garlic
1 sprig fresh rosemary or thyme
2 bay leaves
Pinch of crushed red pepper

1. Combine the olives, oil, vinegar, garlic, rose-mary, bay leaves, and crushed red pepper in a glass or earthenware container and stir with a spoon until well mixed. Cover and refrigerate for 1 to 2 days.

2. Bring to room temperature before serving.

Marinated Mushrooms

Here's a party dish that can be made ahead of time. And any leftover mushrooms can be added to salads, pasta sauces, or pizza.

MAKES ABOUT 3 CUPS

¾ cup olive oil
⅓ cup red-wine vinegar
1½ teaspoons salt
¾ teaspoon sugar
1 teaspoon minced garlic
2 bay leaves
1½ pounds button mushrooms, trimmed
2 tablespoons chopped fresh parsley
1 teaspoon dried basil

1. Combine the oil, vinegar, salt, sugar, garlic, and bay leaves in a medium saucepan over high heat and bring to a boil.

2. Add the mushrooms, parsley, and basil; reduce the heat and simmer until the mushrooms are tender, 3 to 5 minutes.

3. Pour the mushrooms and their marinade into a glass or earthenware container and refrigerate overnight, or up to 3 days.

4. Bring to room temperature before serving.

Lobster Puffs

This lobster salad is served in tiny cream puffs made from choux pastry—an elegant, fast-rising dough that's incredibly easy to make. The pastry can also be used to make sweet cream puffs and éclairs.

MAKES 24

Choux pastry:
1 cup water
½ cup (1 stick) butter, cut into small pieces
⅛ teaspoon salt
1 cup all-purpose flour
4 large eggs

Lobster salad:
1 cup cooked lobster meat
½ cup sour cream
¼ cup minced red bell pepper
2 scallions, minced
1 tablespoon minced fresh parsley
1 teaspoon fresh lemon juice
Salt and pepper

1. Preheat the oven to 400°F.

2. To make the pastry, combine the water, butter, and salt in a small saucepan and bring to a full boil over medium heat. Add the flour all at once and stir vigorously until the mixture pulls away from the sides of the pan. Continue to cook for 1 minute, stirring constantly.

3. Transfer the dough to a bowl and let cool for 5 minutes, stirring occasionally.

4. Beat in the eggs, one at a time, making sure the dough is smooth and shiny before adding the next egg.

5. Transfer the dough to a pastry bag fitted with a plain tip. Pipe out 24 puffs about 1 inch in diameter on a baking sheet, spacing them about 1 inch apart.

6. Bake the puffs in the lower third of the oven for 15 minutes. Reduce the oven temperature to 350°F and bake until golden brown, 10 to 15 minutes more. Turn off the oven, but leave the puffs in the oven for 10 minutes to dry.

7. Slice off the top third of the pastries and set aside. Remove the undercooked dough to make room for the filling.

8. To make the salad, combine the lobster, sour cream, bell pepper, scallions, parsley, and lemon juice in a medium bowl and toss to mix well. Season to taste with salt and pepper.

9. Fill each puff with 1 teaspoon of salad and place the tops back on. Serve immediately.

Shrimp Cocktail

Shrimp can be purchased precooked, and you can even buy bottles of cooked shrimp in cocktail sauce—but fresh seafood and homemade sauce take so little time to prepare and taste so much better.

SERVES 8

3 quarts water
1 tablespoon salt
2 pounds large shrimp
Cocktail sauce (recipe follows)
Lettuce of choice, to serve

1. In a large saucepan, bring the water and salt to a boil over high heat. Reduce the temperature to medium-low, add the shrimp, and cook just until the shrimp are pink and firm, 3 to 4 minutes. Drain, rinse with cold water, and drain again. Peel and devein the shrimp, then place in the refrigerator.

2. To serve, line a platter with lettuce, place a bowl of cocktail sauce in the middle, and arrange the shrimp on the lettuce. The shrimp can also be hooked over the edge of the bowl.

Cocktail Sauce

Shrimp cocktail would not be complete without this tangy sauce. The jarred variety is convenient, but making the sauce is as easy as, if not easier than, making a trip to the grocery store. And the fresh taste will be well worth the minimal effort.

MAKES ABOUT 1⅓ CUPS

1 cup ketchup
¼ cup prepared horseradish
1 teaspoon Worcestershire sauce, or to taste
2 teaspoons chili powder, or to taste
3 tablespoons lemon juice, or to taste
Salt and pepper

1. In a small bowl, combine the ketchup, horseradish, Worcestershire sauce, chili powder, and lemon juice. Season to taste with salt and pepper.

2. Cover and chill for at least 15 minutes or up to 8 hours. Before serving, taste and adjust the seasonings as desired.

Stuffed Mushrooms

This rich, bite-sized appetizer is a favorite at parties. Mushrooms 1 to 1 ½ inches in diameter are ideal.

SERVES 6 TO 8

1 pound button mushrooms
2 tablespoons oil
¼ cup finely chopped onion
½ teaspoon minced garlic
¼ cup fresh bread crumbs
½ cup grated Parmesan cheese
½ cup chopped fresh parsley
Salt and pepper
¼ cup (½ stick) butter, melted

1. Preheat the oven to 400°F. Lightly grease a baking sheet.

2. Trim the bottoms of the mushrooms and snap off the stems, leaving the caps whole. Finely chop the stems.

3. Heat the oil in a medium skillet over medium-high heat. Add the mushroom stems and the onion and sauté until softened, about 5 minutes. Add the garlic and cook for another 2 minutes. Remove from the heat and stir in the bread crumbs, Parmesan cheese, and parsley. Season to taste with salt and pepper.

4. Brush each mushroom cap with some melted butter. Pour the remaining butter into the crumb mixture and mix well. Stuff each mushroom with a spoonful of crumbs and place, stuffing side up, on the baking sheet.

5. Bake for 15 minutes, until the tops are lightly browned. Serve hot or warm.

Stuffed Grape Leaves

Stuffed grape leaves, or "dolmades," are served throughout Greece and the Middle East as part of a large and varied appetizer plate. The stuffing is usually flavored rice or a rice and meat combination. Brined grape leaves are found in jars where Middle Eastern or Greek foods are sold.

SERVES ABOUT 12

1 (16-ounce) jar grape leaves, drained and rinsed
6 tablespoons oil
⅓ cup pine nuts
1 cup long-grain white rice
½ cup finely chopped onion
3 tablespoons dried currants
1 tablespoon sugar
1½ teaspoons ground cinnamon
4 cups hot water
¼ cup lemon juice
2 tablespoons finely chopped fresh dill or mint leaves
2 tablespoons finely chopped fresh parsley
Salt and pepper
Lemon wedges, to serve

1. Bring about 2 quarts of water to a boil in a medium saucepan. Carefully unroll the grape leaves, add to the boiling water, and remove the saucepan from the heat. Let stand for 2 to 3 minutes to soften the leaves and rid them of excess salt.

2. Remove the leaves from the water with a slotted spoon and drain on paper towels. Cut away any protruding stems or hard veins with scissors or a sharp knife. Set aside.

3. Heat 2 tablespoons of oil in a medium saucepan over medium heat. Add the pine nuts and sauté for about 2 minutes, until golden brown. Stir in the rice, onion, currants, sugar, cinnamon, and 2 cups of hot water. Cover and simmer for 15 to 20 minutes, until the water has been absorbed. Remove from the heat and stir in 2 tablespoons of lemon juice, the dill, and the parsley. Season to taste with salt and pepper. Let the stuffing cool for 30 to 40 minutes.

4. Carefully spread out a grape leaf on a flat plate with the veins facing upward (shiny side down). If the leaf is torn or has a hole in it, use a damaged leaf as a patch, placing it over the hole. Put 1 to 2 tablespoons of stuffing near the stem end of the leaf (the amount of stuffing will depend on the size of the leaf). Mold the stuffing into a small sausage shape. Fold the stem end of the leaf over the filling, then fold both sides toward the middle, and roll up into a cigar shape (it should be snug but not overly tight because the rice will swell once it is fully cooked). The rolls should

be cylindrically shaped, about 2 inches long and ½ inch thick. Continue stuffing and filling the leaves until all the filling is used.

5. Line the bottom of a large Dutch oven with half of the remaining grape leaves. Arrange the stuffed grape rolls on top of the leaves, seam side down, packing them close together. Make up to 3 layers. Don't pack the rolls too tightly or they won't cook well, but don't leave too much space between them or they may unravel.

6. Preheat the oven to 350°F.

7. Pour the remaining 2 cups hot water, the remaining ¼ cup olive oil, and the remaining 2 tablespoons lemon juice over the rolls. Weigh down the rolls with an ovenproof plate and cover the Dutch oven.

8. Bring the liquid in the Dutch oven to a boil over medium heat. Transfer to the oven and bake for 45 to 60 minutes, until the grape rolls are tender and the water has been absorbed.

9. Serve chilled or at room temperature, garnished with lemon wedges.

Cheese Quesadillas

When the party is Mexican-themed, serve these little snacks to whet everyone's appetite. Quesadillas also make a fine snack any time of the day!

SERVES ABOUT 6

1½ cups shredded Monterey Jack or pepper Jack cheese (about 6 ounces)
1 cup shredded Cheddar cheese (about 4 ounces)
½ cup chopped roasted green chile peppers
⅓ cup finely chopped scallions or onion
6 large flour tortillas
Salsa of choice (page 56), to serve

1. Preheat the oven to 375°F.

2. In a medium bowl, mix the cheeses, chile peppers, and scallions.

3. Lightly oil a griddle and heat over medium heat. Add the tortillas, one at a time, and fry lightly until faintly colored on each side.

4. Arrange 3 tortillas on a large baking sheet. Top each with one-third of the cheese mixture. Cover with the remaining tortillas and press together lightly.

5. Bake for 10 minutes, or until the cheese begins to run. Cut into wedges and serve immediately, passing the salsa at the table.

Crunchy Clam Puffs

This creamy clam spread on toast is a classic hot canapé, and one that's overdue to be revived. Canapés are slices of toast or crackers spread with any variety of meats, cheeses, vegetables, or fish, usually served on trays before the first course.

SERVES 10 TO 15

1 (3-ounce) package cream cheese, softened
1 tablespoon heavy cream
½ cup canned minced clams, well drained
1 teaspoon minced onion
½ teaspoon Worcestershire sauce
¼ teaspoon salt
Pinch of dry mustard
Pinch of black pepper
24 baguette slices
Paprika
1 tablespoon finely chopped fresh chives

1. Preheat the broiler.

2. Combine the cream cheese, cream, clams, onion, Worcestershire sauce, salt, mustard, and black pepper in a food processor. Pulse just to combine; do not overprocess.

3. Arrange the bread rounds on a baking sheet. Broil just until browned on one side, about 30 seconds.

4. Turn the bread over and spread a little clam filling on each. Broil until lightly browned, about 1 minute.

5. Sprinkle with paprika and chives, and serve hot.

Clams Casino

Clams Casino was invented in the early part of the twentieth century at the Casino at Narragansett Pier in Rhode Island. The combination of sweet, salty clams and crisp bacon is irresistible. Cherrystone, mahogany, and Manila clams are 2 to 3 inches across—just the right size for this dish.

MAKES 24

24 small hard-shell clams
¼ cup (½ stick) butter, softened
2 tablespoons minced onion
2 tablespoons minced green bell pepper
2 tablespoons minced fresh parsley
1 tablespoon lemon juice

1. Shuck the clams by prying each open with a knife. Cut the clam from the shell. Slit the skin of the clam's siphon (neck) and pull off and discard the tough skin. Scrub the bottom shells and discard the tops.

2. Place a clam in each bottom shell and place the shells on a baking sheet.

3. Combine the butter, onion, bell pepper, parsley, lemon juice, and Worcestershire sauce in a small bowl and mix well.

4. Preheat the broiler.

5. Spoon about 1 teaspoon of butter mixture into each clam. Sprinkle the crumbled bacon on top.

6. Broil for 3 minutes, until the butter is bubbling. Serve hot.

Oysters Rockefeller

In 1899 Chef Jules Alciatore, of Antoine's restaurant in New Orleans, decided to create a new appetizer using local products. Oysters were readily available, and it was a novelty to cook them at that time because they were mostly enjoyed raw. His creation combined oysters with a green sauce that may or may not have contained spinach; the result was so rich it was named after one of the wealthiest men in America, John D. Rockefeller.

MAKES 24

24 oysters
1½ cups cooked or frozen and thawed spinach
¼ cup fresh bread crumbs
¼ cup finely chopped scallions
2 slices bacon, cooked crisp and crumbled
1 teaspoon chopped fresh tarragon
¼ cup (½ stick) butter, softened
Salt and pepper
Hot pepper sauce, such as Tabasco
Coarse or kosher salt

1. Preheat the oven to 450°F.

2. Shuck the oysters. Scrub the bottom shells and discard the top shells. Place 1 oyster in each bottom shell.

3. Combine the spinach, bread crumbs, scallions, bacon, and tarragon in a food processor and process until very finely chopped. Add the butter and process until well mixed. Season to taste with salt, pepper, and hot pepper sauce.

4. Spoon a heaping teaspoon of spinach mixture over each oyster.

5. Make a layer of coarse salt on a rimmed baking sheet. Nestle the oyster shells in the salt so they are held firmly in place.

6. Bake for 6 minutes. Run under the broiler for 1 to 2 minutes, until the tops are browned. Serve hot.

Sweet-and-Sour Meatballs

Sweet-and-sour flavors are found all over the world. The Chinese are famous for their sweet-and-sour pork and fish dishes. The Germans weigh in with sweet-and-sour cabbage. These meatballs have a Hawaiian flair. Serve in a chafing dish or on a hot plate and provide small plates and toothpicks.

SERVES 12 TO 15

1 pound ground beef
1 pound ground pork
2 large eggs, lightly beaten
⅓ cup minced onion
1 teaspoon salt
¼ teaspoon ground nutmeg
Pinch of black pepper
1½ cups pineapple juice
3 tablespoons cornstarch
3 tablespoons oil
2 medium green bell peppers, seeded and cut into 1-inch squares
1 teaspoon minced garlic
¼ cup rice vinegar
2 tablespoons soy sauce
¼ cup firmly packed brown sugar
2 cups pineapple chunks

1. Mix the beef, pork, eggs, onion, salt, nutmeg, and black pepper in a large bowl. Form into 1-inch balls.

2. Combine ½ cup of pineapple juice with the cornstarch and set aside.

3. Heat 2 tablespoons of oil in a large, heavy skillet over medium heat. Working in batches, brown the meatballs in a single layer on all sides, about 5 minutes per batch. Remove the meatballs from the skillet and set aside.

4. Heat the remaining 1 tablespoon oil in the skillet and add the bell peppers and garlic. Sauté until the bell peppers are just limp, about 2 minutes.

5. Add the remaining 1 cup pineapple juice, the vinegar, soy sauce, and brown sugar. Scrape up all the browned bits on the bottom of the pan and bring to a boil. Stir in the cornstarch mixture, return the sauce to a boil, and cook until thick and translucent.

6. Return the meatballs to the pan along with the pineapple chunks. Simmer for 5 minutes. Serve hot.

Greek Meatballs

Although meatballs in sauce (from Italy or Sweden) are familiar, meatballs without sauce are less common—unless you happen to come from the Mediterranean or the Middle East. The Greeks serve "keftedes." Kefta are common throughout the Middle East. And in India these meatballs are called "kofta." The meatballs may be fried as they are here, or shaped into sausages and grilled.

SERVES ABOUT 4

1 pound ground pork
1 large red onion, minced or grated
1 large tomato, grated
2 tablespoons dried mint
2 tablespoons chopped fresh parsley
Salt and pepper
¼ cup milk
¼ to ½ cup dry bread crumbs
½ to ¾ cup all-purpose flour
Oil, for frying

1. Combine the pork and onion in a medium bowl. Add the tomato, mint, and parsley. Season with salt and pepper and blend well. Pour in the milk and continue mixing until the liquid is absorbed. Add the bread crumbs a few tablespoons at a time until the mixture will hold a shape if pressed together.

2. Cover and refrigerate for 1 to 6 hours.

3. In a shallow bowl, season the flour with salt and pepper. Form the meat mixture into balls about 1½ inches in diameter. Roll the meatballs in the flour and place on a clean plate. Continue until all the meatballs are formed.

4. Heat about ½ inch of oil in a large skillet over medium heat. Add meatballs in a single layer and fry until browned, turning carefully to brown all sides, about 8 minutes. Remove the meatballs with a slotted spoon and keep warm. Repeat until all the meatballs are browned. Serve hot or at room temperature.

Kal-Bi Short Ribs

Although this is a signature Korean dish, it is also a long-time Hawaiian favorite. The thin-cut ribs and the marinade's sweet concentrated flavors make this dish perfect for quick cooking under the broiler or on the grill.

SERVES 6 TO 8

⅓ cup finely chopped scallions
¼ cup soy sauce
¼ cup minced white onion
3 tablespoons sesame oil
3 tablespoons toasted sesame seeds
1 tablespoon minced fresh ginger
1 tablespoon minced garlic
2 teaspoons brown sugar
Pinch of black pepper
4 pounds flanken cut beef short ribs

1. Mix the scallions, soy sauce, onion, sesame oil, sesame seeds, ginger, garlic, brown sugar, and pepper in a shallow, nonreactive bowl or zippered plastic bag. Add the short ribs and toss to coat. Marinate for 2 to 3 hours.

2. Preheat the broiler or prepare the grill.

3. Grill or broil the ribs for 5 to 6 minutes per side. If bite-size pieces are desired, cut the ribs between the bones before serving. Serve hot.

Pigs in a Blanket

This 1950s party favorite remains popular today. One particular version of pigs in a blanket wraps breakfast sausages in pancakes; this version uses hot dogs wrapped in biscuit dough. Serve this fun snack with saucers of mustard and ketchup for dipping.

MAKES 32

8 hot dogs
3 cups all-purpose flour
1 tablespoon baking powder
1 teaspoon salt
1 cup milk or buttermilk

1. Preheat the oven to 400°F. Lightly oil 2 large baking sheets.

2. Cut the hot dogs in half vertically and horizontally and set aside.

3. In a large bowl, stir together the flour, baking powder, and salt. Add the milk and mix lightly with a fork to form a soft dough.

4. Transfer the dough to a lightly floured surface and knead lightly about 10 times or until springy. Roll out the dough to a large, thin rectangle. Cut the dough into 32 rectangles, about 4 inches from tip to tip. Wrap a rectangle of dough around each hot dog. Pinch the dough closed around the middle of the hot dog, then arrange on the baking sheets.

5. Bake for about 15 minutes, until the dough is lightly browned and the hot dogs are slightly plump. Cool for 5 minutes before serving.

Homemade Beef Jerky

Native Americans taught early settlers how to make beef jerky by cutting meat into long strips, which were then cured, seasoned, and smoked. Cowboys carried beef jerky in their saddle bags when out on the range for long periods of time, as this was their only source of protein. This jerky can be stored in a sealed container in the refrigerator for 4 to 6 weeks or in the freezer, preferably for no more than 6 months.

MAKES ABOUT 1 POUND

3 pounds flank steak (partially frozen for easy slicing)
⅔ cup soy sauce
⅔ cup Worcestershire sauce
1 teaspoon black pepper
1 teaspoon garlic powder
1 teaspoon onion powder
1 teaspoon salt
2 teaspoons liquid smoke flavoring
2 teaspoons hot pepper sauce, such as Tabasco

1. Slice the meat, with the grain, about ¼ inch thick and set aside.

2. Mix the soy sauce, Worcestershire sauce, pepper, garlic powder, onion powder, salt, liquid smoke, and hot pepper sauce in a large (gallon-size) resealable plastic bag or bowl. Add the meat. Refrigerate overnight.

3. Place a sheet of aluminum foil on the bottom of the oven (for easier cleanup), and preheat the oven to 150°F.

4. Drain the meat in a strainer and pat dry with paper towels.

5. Place the meat strips directly on the oven racks. Leave the oven door open to allow the moisture to escape while you roast and dry the strips for 8 to 10 hours. The meat should feel firm and dry, not spongy, when done. (It is overdried if it snaps in two easily. Check frequently toward the end to prevent this.) Remove from the oven and store as desired.

Prosciutto with Melon

Prosciutto is ham that has been seasoned, salt cured, and air dried, resulting in a delicately flavored, salty meat with a firm, dense texture. It is best served on its own, with a slice of bread, or paired with melon, figs, or pears. Prosciutto with melon is a classic first course.

SERVES 6

1 large cantaloupe or Crenshaw melon, cut into 6 wedges with rinds removed
18 paper-thin slices prosciutto

Place 1 melon wedge on each of 6 plates. Arrange 3 prosciutto slices alongside the melon or drape them over the melon and serve.

Bounteous Trays of Simple Foods

You don't have to spend hours in the kitchen preparing dainty hors d'oeuvres for a party. Arrange a selection of prepared foods, using your imagination to create a beautiful display. Here are some ideas to get you started.

EACH SERVES A CROWD

Sliced Cold Cuts and Cheese

Wood carving boards, lacquerware, and glass platters are good choices for setting out cold cuts and cheese. Arrange the sliced or rolled meats and cheeses in a pattern—straight rows, spirals, wagon wheels, or sunbursts. Set bowls of mayonnaise and mustard in the center, and have a bread basket nearby.

Antipasto Tray

Arrange marinated mushrooms, marinated artichoke hearts, and sliced roasted bell peppers on a tray. Add sliced provolone cheese and Genoa salami. Breadsticks or slices of Italian bread go well with these Mediterranean dishes.

Fruit and Cheese

Fresh fruit and an assortment of cheeses are always welcome. Think about variety: Offer a soft cheese such as Brie, a hard cheese such as Cheddar or Gruyère, a blue-veined cheese such as Stilton, and a goat cheese such as Montrachet. Snip bunches of grapes into small clusters for easier eating. Brush apple and pear slices with lemon juice to keep them from discoloring. Figs, sliced kiwifruits, sliced starfruit, pineapple wedges, and berries add color and variety to your presentation.

Crudités

An array of crisp vegetables is irresistible, especially for those on a diet. Mound some sweet red bell pepper strips, bright orange carrot sticks, celery sticks, radishes, cucumber slices, cherry tomatoes, and snow peas on a large platter. Place a dish of dipping sauce alongside, choosing a thick, creamy dressing such as ranch dressing, which clings better to raw vegetables than an oil-based dressing.

CHAPTER FOUR

Salads

Americans love their salads so much that they serve them first—before the main course, unlike Europeans, who often serve their green salad after the main course. And our salads are endlessly varied, with all sorts of ingredients tossed together or artistically composed. They are as rich in flavor as they are in history.

Mention the word "salad," and the first vision in our mind is a tossed green salad—a tempting combination of leafy greens, perhaps with a few slices of cucumber, tomato, and carrots. The dressing may be sweet-and-sour or creamy, or a simple combination of oil and vinegar, and it may be garnished with red onion rings, croutons, or sprouts.

Before the days of refrigerated boxcars and trucks, green salads came out of the backyard garden or not at all. Lettuce seeds traveled to America on Columbus' ships, and early colonists ate lettuce to cool the stomach and relieve heartburn. With the exception of California and Florida, few places in America are suited to year-round growing, so green salads were once a special, summer-only treat. Salad oils were also rare, so salad dressings were usually warm and made with bacon grease, or cool and made from cream or buttermilk.

Cabbage offered another option for greens. It could be stored in the root cellar through a long winter, making coleslaw very popular. Even today coleslaw is an essential accompaniment to barbecue and fried fish, and it holds its own with fried chicken as well. It can even be enjoyed when stuffed into a sandwich like lettuce.

Fruit salads were common with the Shakers and were often served as luncheon dishes. They became especially prevalent in the Midwest in the form of "molded" or "congealed salad," made with gelatin, and later with Jell-O. The Waldorf salad, made with apples and celery, was invented in New York City in the 1890s and experienced wild popularity, showing up on menus across the country.

Fortunately, potatoes have always been available year round, and so potato salads are well loved, with plenty of regional differences. It's hard to imagine a picnic that doesn't feature some variation of the classic.

And then there are all those other kinds of salads, made with avocados, carrots, beets, beans, tomatoes, pastas, chicken, fish, seafood: The list of possibilities is endless. This chapter offers a sampling of some of the good old-fashioned favorites.

Mixed Green Salad

You can use whatever greens you have on hand. The combination listed below mixes sweet, mild lettuces with stronger-tasting greens. Shaved carrot curls or very thin carrot slices are also a nice addition, and crispy croutons are always welcome.

SERVES 4 TO 8

½ medium head Boston, Bibb, or iceberg lettuce
½ medium head curly endive or frisée
2 cups spinach or romaine lettuce
1 small cucumber, thinly sliced
¼ cup sliced radishes
½ to ¾ cup salad dressing of choice (pages 89–91)

1. Tear the lettuce, endive, and spinach into bite-size pieces and combine in a large salad bowl. Add the cucumber and radishes and toss gently with 2 forks or your hands.

2. Just before serving, add the dressing and toss gently with the forks to coat the greens.

Caesar Salad

On July 4, 1924, a group of airmen from San Diego arrived hungry at a restaurant in Tijuana, Mexico, owned by Caesar Cardini. There wasn't much food to feed them, but somehow Caesar's brother Alex managed to whip up a salad of eggs, romaine lettuce, Parmesan cheese, garlic, olive oil, lemon juice, and pepper. Thus, the aviator salad was born, later renamed the Caesar salad. The salad became quite popular, especially with movie folks, and was voted "the greatest recipe to originate from the Americas in 50 years" by the International Society of Epicures in Paris. The original recipe did not include anchovies, but due to many years of popularity we have included them here. (Note: This recipe contains raw eggs. For more information, see page 11.)

SERVES 6

3 to 4 anchovy fillets
¼ cup olive oil
Juice of 1 medium lemon
1 garlic clove, halved
½ teaspoon salt
6 dashes Worcestershire sauce
Pinch of black pepper

1 large head romaine lettuce
1 cup store-bought croutons or homemade (page 75)
¼ cup grated Parmesan cheese
1 large egg, coddled (see tip)

1. In a large salad bowl, mince the anchovies using the back of a fork. Add the oil, lemon juice, garlic, salt, Worcestershire sauce, and pepper. Cover the bowl and let stand for about 1 hour. Discard the garlic.

2. Mix the dressing again. Tear the lettuce into bite-size pieces and add to the dressing. Add the croutons and cheese and toss well.

3. Lightly beat the egg, if using, and pour into the salad. Toss again. Serve immediately.

TIP: To coddle the egg, lower it into simmering water with a slotted spoon. Cook for 1 minute. Remove the egg and set aside until needed.

Greek Salad

During the first half of the twentieth century, Greek immigrants started or took over diners all along the East Coast of the United States. Their recipe for Greek salad became an instant classic.

SERVES 4 TO 6

¼ cup olive oil
3 tablespoons lemon juice
2 tablespoons white-wine vinegar
1 tablespoon minced fresh oregano
½ medium red onion, thinly sliced
½ cup kalamata olives
¾ cup feta cheese, crumbled (about 4 ounces)
1 large head iceberg lettuce or 2 medium heads romaine lettuce
1 medium cucumber, sliced
2 large tomatoes, chopped

1. Combine the oil, lemon juice, vinegar, and oregano in a large salad bowl and mix well. Add the onion, olives, and feta cheese. Cover the bowl and let stand for 1 hour.

2. Tear the lettuce into bite-size pieces and add to the dressing. Add the cucumber and tomatoes and use 2 forks to toss gently. Serve immediately.

Salade Niçoise

French foods became the fashion at stylish restaurants in the 1960s, and Julia Child further popularized French cooking with her cookbooks and TV show. This salad is as big on looks as it is on taste. Hailing from Nice, France, it artfully arranges fresh greens and vegetables with cooked string beans and potatoes, egg slices, anchovies, tuna, and niçoise olives flavored by a light, lemon–garlic oil dressing.

SERVES 6

Dressing:
1 cup olive oil
1 cup chopped fresh basil
¼ cup lemon juice
1 teaspoon minced garlic
Salt and pepper

Salad:
1 large head Boston lettuce
1 pound green beans, trimmed
1 pound yellow wax beans, trimmed
2 pounds extra-small new potatoes, scrubbed
1 medium red bell pepper, seeded and
    julienned
20 anchovy fillets (packed in oil), drained
4 medium tomatoes, cut into wedges
4 large eggs, hard-boiled, peeled, and cut into
    wedges
2 (6-ounce) cans albacore tuna (packed in
    water or oil), drained
1 cup niçoise olives
Sprigs of fresh parsley and chervil, to serve

1. To make the dressing, whisk together the oil, basil, lemon juice, and garlic in a small bowl to blend. Season to taste with salt and pepper.

2. To make the salad, line a large serving platter with lettuce.

3. Blanch the green and yellow wax beans in a large pot of boiling salted water until just tender, about 3 minutes. Plunge into cold water to stop the cooking. Drain well.

4. Bring a medium pot of salted water to a boil, and add the potatoes. Cook just until they are tender all the way through, about 15 minutes. Drain. Transfer the potatoes, still warm, to a large bowl and add about one-third of the dressing. Toss well.

5. In a separate large bowl, toss the beans and the bell pepper with about one-third of the remaining dressing and arrange them in the center of the platter. Top them with the anchovy fillets, arranging them attractively on top. Arrange the potatoes around the beans. Place the tomato and egg wedges around the edge of the platter. Break the tuna apart into large pieces, and arrange the pieces attractively atop the potatoes and tomatoes. Sprinkle with the olives. Drizzle with the remaining dressing, and garnish with several sprigs of parsley and chervil. Serve immediately.

Crispy Croutons

What to do with that loaf of bread getting stale in the bread box? Croutons are a tasty solution.

MAKES ABOUT 2 CUPS

3 tablespoons olive oil or butter
½ teaspoon minced garlic
½ teaspoon salt (optional)
3 cups bread cubes

1. Heat the oil in a large, heavy skillet over medium heat.

2. Stir in the garlic and salt, if using. Add the bread cubes and toss gently to coat. Cook, stirring and turning the croutons until they are light brown and crispy, about 10 minutes.

3. Drain the croutons on paper towels. Use immediately, or cool and store in an airtight container for up to a week.

Bermuda Salad Bowl

In the days before Vidalia, Walla Walla, and Maui onions had wide distribution, people enjoyed Bermuda onions when they had the urge for a sweet onion. This vintage salad has many variations but always includes a sweet onion.

SERVES 4 TO 6

Dressing:
⅓ cup ketchup
¼ cup white-wine vinegar
½ teaspoon sugar
⅔ cup olive oil

Salad:
1 medium head iceberg lettuce, torn into bite-
    size pieces
1 medium head cauliflower, broken into florets
1 medium Bermuda or other sweet onion,
    sliced
½ cup sliced pimento-stuffed green olives
½ cup crumbled Roquefort cheese

1. To make the dressing, combine the ketchup, vinegar, and sugar in a blender and process until well mixed. While the motor is running, add the oil in a slow, steady stream. Set aside.

2. To make the salad, combine the lettuce, cauliflower, onion, olives, and cheese in a large salad bowl. Toss with 2 forks to blend well. Add the dressing and toss again. Serve immediately.

Vegetables à la Grecque

The French were fond of assigning names to recipes based on the cooking styles of other countries, despite the fact that you were much more likely to encounter such dishes in France than you were in the supposed country of origin. À la Grecque is a Greek technique of cooking vegetables in a wine and olive oil broth. If you don't have the vegetables suggested for this recipe, use whatever you have on hand.

SERVES 6

1 medium head cauliflower, cut into florets
2 cups white boiling onions, peeled
1 fennel bulb, trimmed and thinly sliced
2 medium carrots, thinly sliced

1 cup dry white wine
Juice of 1 medium lemon
¼ cup olive oil
2 teaspoons coriander seeds
1 teaspoon dried thyme
1 tablespoon salt

1. Combine the cauliflower, onions, fennel, and carrots in a wide, nonreactive saucepan or Dutch oven. Add the wine, lemon juice, oil, coriander seeds, thyme, and salt. Bring the liquid to a simmer over medium heat. Cover, reduce the heat, and simmer for 10 to 15 minutes, until the vegetables are cooked but not mushy.

2. Transfer the vegetables and their cooking liquid to a bowl and cool to room temperature. Then refrigerate for at least 1 hour, or up to 3 days.

3. Allow the vegetables to lose a little bit of the chill from the refrigerator before serving.

Asparagus Salad with Lemon-Mustard Dressing

There are all sorts of recipes that combine asparagus and eggs. Besides the fact that asparagus goes well with eggs, the season for cutting asparagus corresponds with a lengthening of the daylight hours and an increase in egg laying by free-range hens.

SERVES 4 TO 6

1 to 1½ pounds asparagus, trimmed
2 tablespoons lemon juice
1 teaspoon Dijon mustard
¼ cup olive oil
Salt and pepper
2 large eggs, hard-boiled and peeled
Paprika, to serve

1. Bring a large saucepan of salted water to a boil. Add the asparagus and cook until the spears are tender but not mushy, about 4 minutes. Drain, plunge into cold water to stop the cooking, and drain again. Pat dry with paper towels.

2. Combine the lemon juice and mustard in a small bowl. Whisk in the oil until the dressing is smooth. Season to taste with salt and pepper.

3. Arrange the asparagus on a platter or individual salad plates. Drizzle the dressing over the top.

4. Grate the eggs on the coarse side of a box grater and sprinkle over the asparagus.

5. Lightly dust with paprika and serve immediately.

Three Bean Salad

This all-American classic is made far too often from canned green and wax beans, and with a dressing that is too sweet. But made with fresh beans and a balanced vinaigrette, it is a delicious salad.

SERVES 4 TO 6

1½ cups green beans, cut into 2-inch pieces
1½ cups yellow wax beans, cut into 2-inch pieces
1 (15-ounce) can kidney beans, rinsed and drained
½ red onion, thinly sliced
¼ cup red-wine vinegar
¼ cup sugar
1 teaspoon salt
¼ teaspoon black pepper
½ cup olive oil

1. Bring a medium pot of salted water to a boil. Add the green and yellow beans and blanch until barely tender, about 3 minutes. Drain, plunge into a bowl of cold water to stop the cooking, and drain again.

2. Combine the blanched beans in a large salad bowl with the kidney beans and onion. Toss gently to mix. Set aside.

3. Stir together the vinegar, sugar, salt, and pepper until the sugar is dissolved. Whisk in the oil until smooth.

4. Pour the dressing over the beans and toss gently to coat. Serve immediately or chill in the refrigerator for up to 2 hours.

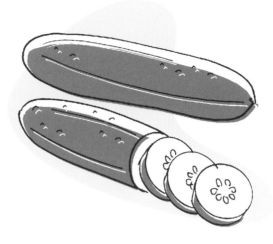

Beet and Cucumber Salad

This is a beautiful salad featuring alternating slices of white cucumbers and purple beets. If the cucumbers are not waxed, then peeling is unnecessary. Use a peeler to remove strips of peel in a decorative fashion.

SERVES 4

4 medium beets, trimmed
1 bunch watercress, trimmed
1 large cucumber, sliced ¼ inch thick
2 tablespoons chopped fresh mint
¼ cup white-wine vinegar
1 teaspoon salt
¼ teaspoon black pepper
½ cup olive oil

1. Place the beets in a medium saucepan and cover with water. Bring to a boil, reduce the heat, and simmer, partially covered, until tender when pierced with a fork, about 30 minutes, depending on the size. Drain and cool.

2. When the beets are cool enough to handle, peel and slice ¼ inch thick.

3. Make a bed of watercress on a platter. Alternate overlapping slices of beets and cucumbers on top. Sprinkle with the mint and set aside.

4. Stir together the vinegar, salt, and pepper in a small bowl. Whisk in the oil until smooth.

5. Pour the dressing over the vegetables and serve immediately.

Creamy Coleslaw

The Dutch brought coleslaw, or "koolsla," to our shores in the 1700s. It has been a popular salad ever since. This is the coleslaw of choice for serving at a barbecue or on a sandwich.

SERVES 8

Dressing:
¾ cup mayonnaise
3 tablespoons sugar
2 tablespoons cider vinegar
1 teaspoon dry mustard
½ teaspoon salt
¼ teaspoon black pepper
Pinch of celery salt

Salad:
1 medium head cabbage, cored and shredded
    (a combination of red and green makes the
    dish more colorful)
½ cup shredded carrot
½ cup finely chopped sweet onion, such as
    Maui, Walla Walla, or Vidalia
¼ cup finely chopped celery

1. To make the dressing, combine the mayonnaise, sugar, vinegar, mustard, salt, pepper, and celery salt in a small bowl and mix well.

2. To make the salad, use 2 forks or your hands to toss together the cabbage, carrot, onion, and celery in a large salad bowl.

3. Pour the dressing over the vegetables and toss with the forks. Refrigerate for a few hours, or overnight, before serving.

Pineapple Coleslaw

Adding pineapple to coleslaw gives it a tropical touch—perfect for a Polynesian party or adding a little sunshine to a wintry day.

SERVES 10

1 medium head green cabbage, cored and
    shredded
3 tablespoons cider vinegar
1 tablespoon sugar
3 medium celery ribs, thinly sliced
1 medium carrot, shredded
¼ cup finely chopped red or green bell pepper
2 tablespoons finely chopped sweet onion,
    such as Maui, Walla Walla, or Vidalia
1 (8-ounce) can pineapple tidbits, drained
    (juice reserved)
¼ cup mayonnaise
Salt and pepper

1. Combine the cabbage with the vinegar and sugar in a large bowl and toss with 2 forks. Let stand for about 1 hour. Drain well.

2. Combine the celery, carrot, bell pepper, onion, and pineapple in a large salad bowl. Mix in the cabbage.

3. In a small bowl, combine the mayonnaise with enough pineapple juice to make a dressing the consistency of cream. Pour over the cabbage mixture and toss to coat. Season to taste with salt and pepper.

4. Refrigerate for 1 to 2 hours to allow the flavors to blend. Gently toss before serving.

Grated Carrot and Raisin Salad

The naturally sweet carrot is a child-friendly vegetable. Moms first made this sweet salad in an effort to get the kids to eat their vegetables.

SERVES 6 TO 8

6 cups grated carrots (about 2 pounds)
1 cup raisins
1 cup slivered almonds (optional)
1 cup mayonnaise or ½ cup mayonnaise and
    ½ cup plain yogurt
2 tablespoons cider vinegar
2 tablespoons sugar
1½ teaspoons salt
Black pepper

1. Combine the carrots, raisins, and almonds, if using, in a salad bowl.

2. Mix together the mayonnaise, vinegar, sugar, and salt in a small bowl. Pour over the carrot mixture and toss with 2 forks. Season to taste with pepper.

3. Refrigerate for at least 30 minutes, or up to 2 hours, to allow the flavors to blend before serving.

Cucumbers with Sour Cream Dressing

Tables throughout the South are set with this delightfully refreshing salad of cucumbers, sour cream, and dill.

SERVES 4 TO 6

5 medium cucumbers, peeled and very thinly sliced
2 teaspoons salt
1 cup sour cream
3 tablespoons cider or red-wine vinegar
3 tablespoons chopped fresh dill
1 teaspoon sugar
Black pepper

1. Combine the cucumbers and salt in a strainer and toss with 2 forks. Set aside to drain for 30 to 60 minutes. Transfer the cucumbers to a medium bowl.

2. Mix the sour cream, vinegar, dill, and sugar in a small bowl. Season to taste with pepper.

3. Add the dressing to the cucumbers and toss gently with the forks.

4. Serve immediately or chill in the refrigerator for up to 4 hours before serving.

Marinated Cucumbers

It is a custom among the Pennsylvania Dutch to set out seven sweets and seven sours at every dinner. This cucumber salad is a traditional sour dish.

SERVES 6

½ cup cider vinegar
2 teaspoons sugar
1 teaspoon salt
6 cups cucumbers, peeled and very thinly sliced
1 medium red onion, thinly sliced

1. Combine the vinegar, sugar, and salt in a small saucepan and heat just enough to completely dissolve the sugar. Cool to room temperature.

2. Combine the cucumbers and onion with the vinegar mixture and toss gently using 2 forks. The cucumbers will seem dry, but the salt will draw out moisture from the cucumbers to create more liquid.

3. Cover and refrigerate for at least 30 minutes before serving. The cucumbers can be stored for up to a week in the refrigerator.

Creamy Pea Salad

There is no farm chore more pleasant than sitting on the back porch shucking peas. This is a classic salad that was whipped together with those peas. You can use frozen peas if you don't have the garden or the back porch.

SERVES 4 TO 6

3 cups fresh or frozen peas
2 tablespoons finely chopped red onion
2 tablespoons finely chopped fresh mint
½ cup sour cream
1 tablespoon red-wine vinegar
Salt and pepper

1. Blanch the peas in boiling water until just barely tender (1 minute for frozen peas, 3 to 5 minutes for fresh). Drain, then immediately plunge the peas into cold water to stop the cooking. Drain well.

2. Transfer the peas to a medium bowl. Add the onion and mint and toss gently with 2 forks.

3. Mix the sour cream and vinegar in a small bowl. Season to taste with salt and pepper.

4. Add the dressing to the peas and toss gently with the forks. Serve immediately or chill for up to 2 hours in the refrigerator before serving.

Wilted Spinach Salad

After a long, hard winter, our ancestors craved greens. Their first "sallets" of the season were likely made with wild greens, such as dandelions. And the dressing was often made of rendered bacon fat because salad oils were not available in northern climates.

SERVES 6

1 pound tender young spinach, washed and
    trimmed
6 slices bacon
4 scallions, trimmed and finely chopped
½ teaspoon minced garlic
¼ cup cider or red-wine vinegar
½ teaspoon salt
¼ teaspoon black pepper

1. Pat the spinach leaves dry with paper towels, place in a large salad bowl, and refrigerate.

2. Cook the bacon in a large, heavy skillet over medium heat until all of the fat is rendered and the bacon is crisp, 10 to 15 minutes, turning frequently. Place the bacon on paper towels to drain, and reserve the fat in the skillet. Cut the bacon into small pieces.

3. Add the scallions and garlic to the skillet and gently cook over low heat for 2 minutes. Stir in the vinegar, salt, and pepper and bring to a boil.

4. Pour the hot dressing over the spinach, sprinkle bacon bits over the top, and serve.

Sliced Tomato Salad

In the good old days, a tomato was plump, sun-warmed, and flavorful, and a plate of sliced tomatoes was set on the dinner table for as long as the tomato season lasted. Sometimes the tomatoes were dressed with no more than a sprinkling of salt and pepper. Sometimes it got a little fancier, as this recipe tastefully demonstrates.

SERVES 4 TO 6

4 medium tomatoes, sliced
1 medium red onion, sliced
3 tablespoons chopped fresh basil
2 tablespoons red-wine vinegar
3 tablespoons olive oil
Salt and pepper

1. Arrange the tomato and onion slices so they are overlapping on a platter.

2. Sprinkle with the basil. Drizzle with the vinegar, then the oil. Season to taste with salt and pepper. Serve at once.

Macaroni Salad

Before there was pasta salad, there was macaroni salad—always made with elbow macaroni, always dressed with mayonnaise. The crunch varied—often there was celery, sometimes bell peppers or carrots, and sweet pickles. It was a favorite for everyone.

SERVES 6

8 ounces elbow macaroni
¾ cup mayonnaise
½ teaspoon salt
3 tablespoons sweet pickle relish
3 tablespoons finely chopped sweet onion,
    such as Maui, Walla Walla, or Vidalia
½ cup thinly sliced celery
¼ cup finely chopped green bell pepper
1 cup frozen baby peas, thawed
4 large eggs, hard-boiled, peeled, and chopped
Salt and pepper

1. Cook the macaroni according to the package directions. Drain well, rinse, and cool.

2. Mix the mayonnaise, salt, relish, and onion in a small bowl. Set aside.

3. Combine the macaroni, celery, bell pepper, and peas in a large bowl. Add the mayonnaise mixture and toss to coat.

4. Gently toss in the eggs. Season to taste with salt and pepper.

5. Chill well, about 2 hours. Taste and adjust the seasoning before serving.

Potato Salad

Can you even have a picnic without potato salad?
A mayonnaise dressing makes this all–American
favorite the perfect accompaniment to hot
dogs, hamburgers, and deli sandwiches.

SERVES 8 TO 10

3 pounds waxy potatoes, such as thin-skinned
    red or white
3 large celery ribs, finely chopped
1 cup mayonnaise
1½ tablespoons prepared yellow mustard
½ cup finely chopped sweet onion, such as
    Maui, Walla Walla, or Vidalia
½ cup sweet pickle relish or finely chopped
    sweet pickles
¼ cup sweet pickle juice or white vinegar
1½ teaspoons salt
½ teaspoon black pepper, or more to taste
½ teaspoon garlic powder
6 large eggs, hard-boiled and peeled
½ teaspoon paprika

1. Put the potatoes in a large pot and cover with
water. Cook until tender, 15 to 25 minutes,
depending on the size. Drain and cool. Peel the
potatoes and cut into cubes.

2. Combine the celery, mayonnaise, mustard,
onion, relish, pickle juice, salt, pepper, and garlic
powder in a large bowl and mix well. Gently fold
in the potatoes. Chop 4 eggs and mix into the
salad. Taste and add salt and pepper as needed.

3. Cover and chill for at least 1 hour. Slice the
last 2 hard-boiled eggs and arrange them on top
of the salad. Sprinkle the paprika over the top,
and serve.

TIP: The best potatoes for potato salads are waxy, low-
starch potatoes, not the kind used for baking. Red Bliss
and Yellow Finn are both excellent choices. If you don't
feel like peeling, choose new potatoes with thin skins.

Warm German Potato Salad

At the turn of the last century, German immigrants
brought their unique warm potato salad to the attention of
their American neighbors. The rest of the country readily
adopted this salad. It is terrific served with any grilled meat.

SERVES 8 TO 10

3 pounds waxy potatoes, such as thin-skinned
    red or white
1 pound sliced bacon
1 medium onion, chopped
2 tablespoons all-purpose flour
2 tablespoons sugar
1½ teaspoons salt
1 teaspoon celery seeds
¼ teaspoon black pepper
½ cup water
½ cup cider vinegar

1. Put the potatoes in a large pot and cover with
water. Cook until tender, 15 to 25 minutes,
depending on size. Drain and cool enough to
allow easy handling. Peel and thinly slice.

2. Cook the bacon in a large, heavy skillet over
medium heat, turning frequently, until almost
crisp, 10 to 15 minutes. Put the bacon on paper
towels to drain, and chop into small pieces.

3. Add the onion and sauté until transparent,
about 4 minutes. Stir in the flour, sugar, salt,
celery seeds, and pepper. Cook over medium heat
for 2 minutes.

4. Remove the skillet from the heat and stir in
the water and vinegar, scraping the bits off of the
bottom of the pan. Increase to medium-high heat
and bring to a simmer, stirring constantly for
about 2 minutes. Transfer to a large ceramic or
other non–heat conducting bowl.

5. Add the potatoes and bacon and stir gently,
taking care not to break up the potatoes. Let stand
until you are ready to serve.

French Potato Salad

German potato salad is served warm and is flavored with bacon. A French-style potato salad has an oil and vinegar dressing. The dressing is added to warm potatoes so the potatoes absorb the maximum amount of flavor.

SERVES 8 TO 10

3 pounds waxy potatoes, such as thin-skinned
　　red or white
6 tablespoons red-wine vinegar
½ medium red onion, minced
3 tablespoons chopped fresh parsley
1 tablespoon Dijon mustard
1 tablespoon chopped fresh tarragon or
　　1 teaspoon dried
1 teaspoon minced garlic
1 teaspoon salt, or more to taste
¼ teaspoon black pepper, or more to taste
½ cup olive oil

1. Put the potatoes in a large pot and cover with water. Cook until tender, 15 to 25 minutes, depending on size. Drain and cool enough to allow easy handling. Peel and thinly slice.

2. Whisk together the vinegar, onion, parsley, mustard, tarragon, garlic, salt, and pepper in a small bowl. Whisk in the oil in a slow, steady stream until the dressing is smooth.

3. Pour over the potatoes and toss gently with a spoon. Taste and adjust the salt and pepper as needed. Serve warm, at room temperature, or chilled.

Rice Salad

Thrifty cooks of the past thought up many crafty ways to use up leftovers. This salad takes advantage of leftover rice. If you happen to have leftover chicken or shrimp, toss that in, and turn this salad into a main dish.

SERVES 4

2 cups cooked long-grain white rice
2 tablespoons lemon juice
¼ cup olive oil
1 small sweet onion, such as Maui, Walla
　　Walla, or Vidalia, finely chopped
2 medium tomatoes, chopped
¼ cup finely chopped green or red bell pepper

3 tablespoons chopped fresh parsley
2 tablespoons capers
Salt and pepper

1. Combine the rice, lemon juice, oil, onion, tomatoes, bell pepper, parsley, and capers in a large bowl. Mix thoroughly and season to taste with salt and pepper.

2. Chill in the refrigerator for at least 30 minutes, or up to 4 hours. Taste and adjust the seasonings as needed before serving.

Summertime Fruit Salad

Nothing perks up a flagging appetite in the summer like a fresh fruit salad. Feel free to vary the fruit, depending on what you have on hand. If you like, garnish with flaked almonds.

SERVES 4 TO 6

Salad:
2½ cups melon balls or cubes (watermelon,
　　honeydew, cantaloupe, etc.)
1 cup strawberries, hulled and cut in half
½ cup blueberries
1 cup peeled and sliced peaches or nectarines
1 teaspoon lemon juice

Dressing:
½ cup honey
½ cup sweet sherry or port wine
½ cup water
1 teaspoon crushed fresh mint leaves
Pinch of ground cardamom

1. To make the salad, use a spoon to gently toss together the fruits with the lemon juice in a large bowl. Chill.

2. To make the dressing, combine the honey, sherry, and water in a small saucepan and warm over low heat, stirring constantly just until the honey blends with the other liquids. Remove from the heat, stir in the mint and cardamom, and cool to room temperature.

3. Pour the dressing over the fruit and chill for at least 1 hour, or up to 4 hours, before serving.

Autumn Fruit Salad

Salad or dessert? It doesn't really matter when you serve this dish; everyone will love it. If you like, add a pinch of cinnamon or nutmeg to the dressing.

SERVES 4 TO 6

Salad:
2 large apples, peeled, cored, and sliced
2 large pears, peeled, cored, and sliced
2 large bananas, peeled and sliced
1 cup seedless green grapes
1 cup seedless red grapes
1 teaspoon lemon juice

Dressing:
1 cup sour cream
2 tablespoons lemon or lime juice
2 tablespoons sugar or honey
Pinch of salt

1. To make the salad, combine the fruit in a large bowl with the lemon juice and toss gently with a spoon. Set aside in the refrigerator.

2. To make the dressing, stir together the sour cream, lemon juice, sugar, and salt in a small bowl.

3. Divide the fruit among 4 to 6 bowls, top each with a generous spoonful of dressing, and serve.

TIP: For more color, don't peel the apples and pears.

Winter Fruit Salad

In the summer, we almost take fruit for granted because it is so readily available. In the winter, fruit is even more welcome, especially when someone else takes the time to prepare it. To make this salad truly special, it is served in hollowed-out pineapple shells.

SERVES 4 TO 6

1 large pineapple
2 medium oranges, peeled and divided into
    sections
2 medium bananas, peeled and sliced
1 medium grapefruit, peeled and divided into
    sections

1. Remove the top from the pineapple and slice in half. Hollow out the fruit and cut into bite-size wedges, discarding the portions of core.

2. In a large bowl, combine the pineapple, oranges, bananas, and grapefruit. Toss gently with a spoon to combine.

3. Spoon the fruit into the pineapple shells and serve.

TIP: Choose a pineapple that is slightly soft to the touch. The stem end should smell sweet and the leaves should be crisp and green with no brown tips. Avoid fruit with soft or dark areas on the skin. Golden pineapples are dependably sweet. Keeping slightly underripe pineapple at room temperature for a few days won't make the fruit any sweeter, but it will make it less acidic.

Grapefruit and Avocado Salad

This classic salad appears in many vintage cookbooks, though the avocado is more likely to be called an alligator pear. The acidic grapefruit is tamed by the creamy nature of the avocado.

SERVES 4

Boston or butter lettuce, to serve
2 medium grapefruits, peeled and divided into
    sections
2 large avocados, peeled, pitted, and sliced
½ medium red onion, thinly sliced
Olive oil, to serve

1. Line four salad plates with the lettuce.

2. Arrange alternating slices of grapefruit and avocado on each plate. Scatter the onion over the fruits.

3. Drizzle with olive oil and serve.

Waldorf Salad

New York City at the turn of the twentieth century was a dazzlingly sophisticated place, with hotel restaurants offering the pinnacle of haute cuisine. Waldorf salad was invented at the Waldorf-Astoria Hotel and soon appeared on menus throughout the country—wherever high society gathered. The original recipe did not contain walnuts or grapes. These embellishments were added sometime later and remain staples to this day.

SERVES 4 TO 6

Juice of ½ medium lemon
1 medium apple, diced
1 large celery rib, diced
½ cup chopped walnuts
½ cup red seedless grapes, halved
½ to ¾ cup mayonnaise
Salt and pepper

1. Combine the lemon juice with the apple in a large bowl. Add the celery, walnuts, and grapes, and stir in enough mayonnaise to coat and bind the salad.

2. Season to taste with salt and pepper. Serve cold or at room temperature.

Chef's Salad

Who is the anonymous chef who invented this salad? The answer is apparently lost, but it is likely that the salad is meant to use up leftovers, just as the equally popular Cobb salad does. You can choose to use whatever salad dressing you like best: Russian, Catalina, and Thousand Island are particularly good choices. This is a composed salad, so take time with the arrangement of the ingredients.

SERVES 4 TO 6

10 cups torn salad greens, such as an assortment of romaine lettuce, Boston lettuce, and tender young spinach
¾ cup salad dressing of choice (pages 89–91)
4 ounces cooked turkey breast, cut into long, thin strips
4 ounces cooked ham, cut into long, thin strips
4 ounces Swiss cheese, cut into long, thin strips

2 medium tomatoes, seeded and cut into wedges
2 large eggs, hard-boiled, peeled, and cut into wedges
12 pitted black olives

1. In a large salad bowl, combine the greens with the dressing and toss lightly with 2 forks.

2. Arrange the turkey, ham, and cheese in a decorative fashion on top of the greens, like spokes on a wheel. Around the edges, arrange the tomatoes, eggs, and olives. Serve immediately.

Cobb Salad

According to legend, this recipe was created by Bob Cobb, the owner of the Brown Derby Restaurant in Los Angeles, to use up some leftovers that had gathered in the refrigerator.

SERVES 4 TO 6

Dressing:
2 tablespoons red-wine vinegar
½ teaspoon finely minced garlic
1 teaspoon salt
½ teaspoon black pepper
½ teaspoon Worcestershire sauce
½ teaspoon lemon juice
⅛ teaspoon sugar
½ cup olive oil

Salad:
6 cups torn lettuce (preferably Bibb, romaine, iceberg, or a combination)
1 bunch watercress, trimmed
2 cups torn curly endive or frisée
2 medium tomatoes, chopped
6 slices bacon, cooked crisp and crumbled
3 cups diced cooked chicken
3 large eggs, hard-boiled, peeled, and diced
1 large avocado, peeled, pitted, and diced
½ cup crumbled Roquefort cheese
2 tablespoons chopped fresh chives

1. To make the dressing, combine the vinegar, garlic, salt, pepper, Worcestershire sauce, lemon juice, and sugar in a small bowl. Whisk in the oil in a slow, steady stream until the dressing is smooth. Set aside.

2. To make the salad, line a large platter with the lettuce. On top of the lettuce, arrange the watercress and curly endive. Arrange the tomatoes, bacon, chicken, eggs, and avocado in a decorative manner on top. Sprinkle with the Roquefort cheese and chives.

3. Drizzle half the dressing over the salad. Serve at once, passing the remaining dressing at the table.

Crab Louis Salad

Crab salads are particularly popular in the Pacific Northwest region of the United States, where the Dungeness crab commands tremendous culinary respect. This simple preparation highlights the crab's unique flavor.

SERVES 4

Dressing:
1 cup mayonnaise
3 tablespoons chili sauce
2 tablespoons chopped scallion
1 tablespoon Worcestershire sauce
1 tablespoon red-wine vinegar
2 teaspoons lemon juice
Pinch of cayenne pepper
Salt and pepper

Salad:
Lettuce, such as romaine or iceberg, to serve
1 pound lump crabmeat
3 large eggs, hard-boiled, peeled, and chopped

1. To make the dressing, combine the mayonnaise, chili sauce, scallion, Worcestershire sauce, vinegar, lemon juice, and cayenne pepper in a small bowl. Mix well. Season to taste with salt and pepper. Chill in the refrigerator for 30 minutes to allow the flavors to blend.

2. To make the salad, line a platter or individual salad plates with lettuce. Heap the crab in the center of the plate(s). Sprinkle the egg over the crab and serve at once, passing the dressing at the table.

TIP: Fresh dungeness crab is seasonal and is far superior to canned. It is well worth the wait for fresh crab in this dish.

Crab Rémoulade

Rémoulade is a classic French sauce similar to tartar sauce. It was adapted by Louisiana cooks, who gave it an extra kick by adding cayenne pepper. Rémoulade sauce can also be served with other seafood, especially shrimp.

SERVES 4

Sauce:
¾ cup mayonnaise
¼ cup ketchup
2 tablespoons capers
2 tablespoons finely chopped shallots
1 tablespoon lemon juice
1 tablespoon anchovy paste
1 tablespoon chopped fresh parsley
2 teaspoons paprika
1 teaspoon chopped fresh thyme
¼ teaspoon cayenne pepper, or to taste
Salt and pepper
Hot pepper sauce, such as Tabasco

Salad:
1 pound lump crabmeat
Lettuce, such as romaine or iceberg, to serve

1. To make the sauce, combine the mayonnaise, ketchup, capers, shallots, lemon juice, anchovy paste, parsley, paprika, thyme, and cayenne pepper in a medium bowl. Mix well. Season to taste with salt, pepper, and hot pepper sauce.

2. To make the salad, fold the crabmeat into the sauce and chill in the refrigerator for 30 minutes to allow the flavors to blend.

3. Line a platter or individual salad plates with lettuce. Heap the crab mixture in the center of the plate(s) and serve.

Lobster Salad

If you are working with freshly cooked lobster, and if you are lucky enough to have a female lobster, then you may find the body cavity filled with red roe (eggs), known as coral. Use the coral to flavor the mayonnaise and give it an attractive pink color. You can also make this salad substituting shrimp or crabmeat for the lobster.

SERVES 4

3 tablespoons red-wine vinegar
½ teaspoon Dijon mustard
Pinch of sugar
¾ cup olive oil
Salt and pepper
3 cups cooked lobster meat
1 shallot, finely chopped
2 medium celery ribs, diced
1 medium red bell pepper, diced
½ cup mayonnaise
2 tablespoons lobster coral (optional)
Lettuce, such as romaine or iceberg, to serve

1. In a medium bowl, combine the vinegar, mustard, and sugar. Whisk in the oil in a slow, steady stream until the dressing is smooth. Season to taste with salt and pepper. Add the lobster meat and toss gently to mix. Cover and marinate in the refrigerator for 1 hour.

2. Drain the lobster. Mix in the shallot, celery, bell pepper, mayonnaise, and coral, if using. Taste and adjust the seasoning as needed.

3. Line a platter with the lettuce, spoon the lobster mixture on top, and serve.

Shrimp and Rice Salad

For a while it seemed that pasta salads would edge all the rice salads off the table. But rice salad is a lovely summer tradition in the South.

SERVES 4 TO 6

1 pound shrimp, peeled and deveined
1½ cups cooked long-grain white rice
1 cup frozen peas
1 medium celery rib, diced
3 scallions, thinly sliced
2 tablespoons finely chopped red bell pepper
½ to ¾ cup mayonnaise
2 tablespoons lemon juice
½ teaspoon celery seed
Salt and pepper
Lettuce, such as romaine or iceberg, to serve
2 medium tomatoes, cut into wedges, to serve

1. Bring about 6 cups of salted water to a boil. Add the shrimp and boil just until pink and firm, about 3 minutes. Drain well. Cover and refrigerate.

2. Just before serving, combine the shrimp, rice, peas, celery, scallions, and bell pepper. Add ½ cup mayonnaise, lemon juice, and celery seed and gently mix. Season to taste with salt and pepper. Add the remaining ¼ cup mayonnaise if the mixture seems dry.

3. Line a platter with lettuce leaves and mound the shrimp salad on top. Decorate with the tomato wedges and serve.

Orange, Shrimp, and Spinach Salad

Spinach salad with oranges and shrimp was a popular variation of the spinach and tomato salad in the 1950s and 1960s. If you like, substitute canned mandarin oranges for fresh oranges.

SERVES 4

Dressing:
⅓ cup Dijon mustard
¼ cup honey
¼ cup orange juice
1 tablespoon red-wine vinegar

Salad:
6 cups torn spinach
1 small red onion, thinly sliced
1 medium cucumber, peeled and thinly sliced
2 large oranges, peeled, sectioned, and
  chopped

1 pound small shrimp, peeled, deveined, and
   cooked
Salt and pepper
1/3 cup toasted almond flakes

1. To make the dressing, combine the mustard, honey, orange juice, and vinegar in a small jar. Cover and shake to blend; refrigerate.

2. To make the salad, create a bed of the spinach leaves on a large serving platter or on individual salad plates. Layer the onion slices, cucumber slices, orange pieces, and shrimp on top of the spinach. Season with salt and pepper, and sprinkle with the almond flakes.

3. Drizzle the honey-mustard dressing over the salad and serve immediately.

Tuna Macaroni Salad

Familiar macaroni salad becomes a main-dish salad with the addition of canned tuna. Served on a bed of lettuce, this is a wonderful, quick summer supper when the heat makes you crave simple foods.

SERVES 6

8 ounces elbow macaroni
1 (7-ounce) can albacore tuna (packed in water
   or oil), drained
2 large celery ribs, thinly sliced
1 small red or green bell pepper, diced
1 medium carrot, grated
1/4 cup finely chopped sweet onion, such as
   Maui, Walla Walla, or Vidalia
1/4 cup chopped fresh parsley
1 cup mayonnaise
2 tablespoons lemon juice
Salt and pepper
Lettuce such as romaine or iceberg, to serve

1. Cook the macaroni according to the directions on the package. Drain well, rinse, and cool.

2. Flake the tuna in a large bowl. Add the macaroni, celery, bell pepper, carrot, onion, and parsley, and mix gently. Add the mayonnaise and lemon juice and toss to coat. Season to taste with salt and pepper.

3. Line a bowl or platter with the lettuce, and heap the tuna salad on top. Serve immediately.

Crunchy Chicken Salad

Chow mein noodles have no counterpart in China, yet we love them as a crunchy topping to contrast the creamy, fresh flavors of homemade chicken salad.

SERVES 4 TO 6

Chicken:
3 to 4 boneless, skinless chicken breasts
1/2 cup chicken broth (page 119)

Dressing:
1/4 cup rice vinegar
2 tablespoons sugar
1/2 teaspoon salt
1/4 teaspoon black pepper
1/4 cup sesame oil

Salad:
1/2 medium head lettuce, such as iceberg,
   shredded
3 scallions, finely chopped
3 tablespoons sesame seeds
1/4 cup toasted slivered almonds
1 cup Chinese chow mein noodles

1. To make the chicken, combine the chicken and broth in a medium saucepan over medium heat. Simmer the chicken, covered, until cooked through, about 12 minutes. Let the chicken cool in the broth. Drain off the broth and reserve for another use.

2. Cut the chicken into bite-size pieces and chill in the refrigerator.

3. While the chicken cools, make the dressing. Combine the vinegar, sugar, salt, and pepper in a small bowl. Stir to dissolve the sugar. Whisk in the oil until the dressing is smooth.

4. To make the salad, combine the lettuce, scallions, sesame seeds, and almonds in a large bowl. Add the chicken and toss with 2 forks. Add the dressing and toss again. Add the noodles, toss gently, and serve immediately.

Stuffed Tomato Salad

Any salad mixture can be used to stuff tomatoes—think tuna salad, egg salad, etc. In this recipe, it is curried chicken salad.

SERVES 4

8 medium tomatoes, cored
2 cups finely chopped cooked chicken
2 large celery ribs, finely chopped
1 medium apple, cored and finely chopped
½ medium red bell pepper, finely chopped
¾ cup mayonnaise
1 tablespoon lemon juice
½ teaspoon curry powder
Salt and pepper
Lettuce, such as romaine or iceberg, to serve

1. Cut the tops off the tomatoes. Cut a thin slice off the bottom so they sit level. Scoop out the pulp from inside each tomato and finely chop.

2. Combine the chicken, celery, apple, bell pepper, and chopped pulp in a medium bowl. Add the mayonnaise, lemon juice, and curry powder. Mix well. Season to taste with salt and pepper.

3. Line four salad plates with lettuce.

4. Transfer the tomatoes to the plates. Carefully stuff each tomato with ⅛ of the chicken salad, and serve immediately.

Turkey Salad

Of course, turkey and chicken can be used interchangeably in salads. This salad is perfect for Thanksgiving leftovers—it has a distinctive autumnal touch. As an acceptable option, add ½ cup seedless grape halves.

SERVES 4

⅔ cup mayonnaise
2 tablespoons cider vinegar
1 teaspoon salt
4 to 5 cups cooked turkey, diced
2 large celery ribs, sliced
1 large red apple (do not peel), cored and diced
⅔ cup walnuts
2 teaspoons grated onion
Lettuce, such as romaine or iceberg, to serve

1. Combine the mayonnaise, vinegar, and salt in a large bowl. Add the turkey, celery, apple, walnuts, and onion. Mix gently. Cover and refrigerate for 30 minutes to allow the flavors to blend.

2. Make a bed of lettuce on a platter or individual plates. Mound the salad on top of the lettuce and serve.

Taco Salad

Taco salads are a Western favorite that spread to the East along with tacos, burritos, and other Tex-Mex favorites. In restaurants it is usually served in a bowl made from a deep-fried flour tortilla. At home, tortilla chips add the necessary crunch.

SERVES 4

1 pound ground beef
1 teaspoon chili powder
½ teaspoon garlic powder
1 teaspoon salt
1 large head lettuce, such as iceberg, shredded
1 cup mixed torn tender greens (butter lettuce, baby romaine lettuce, etc.; optional)
½ medium red onion, thinly sliced
2 large tomatoes, chopped
2 cups shredded Cheddar cheese (about 8 ounces)
1¼ cups Catalina dressing (page 90)
1 large avocado, peeled, pitted, and sliced
2 cups tortilla chips

1. Brown the beef in a large, heavy skillet over medium-high heat, about 8 minutes, using a wooden spoon to break up the clumps. Pour off the fat and drain the meat on paper towels. Sprinkle with the chili powder, garlic powder, and salt. Set aside to cool.

2. In a large bowl, toss together the lettuce, greens, onion, tomatoes, and cheese. Chill for at least 30 minutes.

3. Pour the dressing over the lettuce mixture and toss to coat. Transfer to a large platter. Mound the meat filling over the greens. Garnish with avocado slices and tortilla chips, and serve.

Basic Vinaigrette

This is a basic salad dressing that is known by many names. Some might simply call it oil and vinegar dressing because oil and vinegar are the main ingredients. Others might call it Italian Dressing—which is a variation that follows.

MAKES ABOUT 1 CUP

2 tablespoons red-wine vinegar
½ teaspoon minced garlic or shallot
1 teaspoon Dijon mustard
6 tablespoons olive oil
Salt and pepper

Whisk together the vinegar, garlic, and mustard in a small bowl. Slowly whisk in the oil until the dressing is smooth. Season to taste with salt and pepper. Refrigerate in an airtight container for up to 2 weeks. Let the dressing come to room temperature before serving.

Italian Dressing

This variation on Basic Vinaigrette becomes Italian dressing with the addition of fennel and oregano.

MAKES ABOUT 1 CUP

2 tablespoons red-wine vinegar
1 teaspoon minced garlic
1 teaspoon Dijon mustard
1 teaspoon fennel seeds, lightly crushed
1 teaspoon dried oregano
6 tablespoons olive oil
Salt and pepper

Whisk together the vinegar, garlic, mustard, fennel seeds, and oregano in a small bowl. Slowly whisk in the oil until the dressing is smooth. Season to taste with salt and pepper. Refrigerate in an airtight container for up to 2 weeks. Let the dressing come to room temperature before serving.

Ranch Dressing

The original ranch dressing is credited to the Hidden Valley Guest Ranch in Santa Barbara in the 1950s, but buttermilk and cream dressings go back to the days when oil was a scarce commodity rarely used in salads.

MAKES ABOUT 1 CUP

½ teaspoon minced garlic
1 tablespoon chopped fresh parsley
1 tablespoon chopped fresh chives
½ cup buttermilk
½ cup mayonnaise
2 tablespoons white-wine vinegar
Salt and pepper

Combine the garlic, parsley, and chives in a blender and process until finely chopped. Add the buttermilk, mayonnaise, and vinegar and process until well blended. Season to taste with salt and pepper. Refrigerate in an airtight container for up to 2 weeks.

Green Goddess Dressing

This creamy dressing predates ranch dressing and was very popular in its time. It was invented at the Palace Hotel in San Francisco in the 1920s in honor of a hit play of the same name.

MAKES ABOUT 2 CUPS

1 cup mayonnaise
½ cup sour cream
2 scallions, finely chopped
¼ cup finely chopped fresh parsley
1 tablespoon lemon juice
1 tablespoon red-wine vinegar
1 teaspoon anchovy paste
Salt and pepper

Stir together the mayonnaise, sour cream, scallions, parsley, lemon juice, vinegar, and anchovy paste in a small bowl. Season to taste with salt and pepper. Refrigerate in an airtight container for up to 2 weeks.

Catalina Dressing

For the perfect summer salad, try chopped iceberg lettuce, chopped avocado, grated carrot, and sliced cucumber. Toss with this sweet-sour dressing and sit back for the compliments. Catalina dressing is terrific on most green salads.

MAKES ABOUT 2 CUPS

½ cup sugar
½ cup ketchup
1 small onion, grated
¼ cup cider vinegar
½ teaspoon salt
Pinch of black pepper
1 cup olive oil

1. Whisk together the sugar, ketchup, onion, vinegar, salt, and pepper in a small bowl. Slowly whisk in the oil until the dressing is smooth.

2. Let stand for at least 30 minutes to allow the flavors to blend. Serve immediately or chilled. Refrigerate in an airtight container for up to 2 weeks.

Russian Dressing

Russian dressing is an American favorite not seen in Russia. How it got its name is a mystery, though some versions of the original recipe contained caviar, a signature Russian product. It is a wonderful dressing for a wedge of chilled iceberg lettuce, and it is the perfect spread for a roast beef or turkey sandwich.

MAKES ABOUT 1¼ CUPS

1 cup mayonnaise
¼ cup chili sauce or ketchup
1 tablespoon prepared horseradish
1 teaspoon Worcestershire sauce
1 teaspoon grated onion
Salt and pepper

1. Mix the mayonnaise, chili sauce, horseradish, Worcestershire sauce, and onion in a small bowl. Season to taste with salt and pepper.

2. Let stand for at least 30 minutes to allow the flavors to blend. Serve immediately or chilled. Refrigerate in an airtight container for up to 2 weeks.

Thousand Island Dressing

Similar to Russian dressing, thousand island dressing adds chopped pickles or pickle relish. It received its name because the chopped pickles resemble thousands of little islands in a sea of dressing.

MAKES ABOUT 1½ CUPS

1 cup mayonnaise
¼ cup chili sauce
3 tablespoons minced gherkins or pickle relish
3 tablespoons finely chopped green bell pepper
1 tablespoon finely chopped red bell pepper
2 tablespoons finely chopped sweet onion, such as Maui, Walla Walla, or Vidalia
Salt and pepper

1. In a small bowl, stir together the mayonnaise and chili sauce. Stir in the gherkins, bell peppers, and onion. Season to taste with salt and pepper.

2. Let stand for at least 30 minutes to allow the flavors to blend. Serve immediately or chilled. Refrigerate in an airtight container for up to 2 weeks.

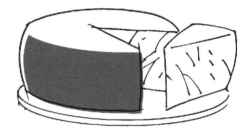

Blue Cheese Dressing

Roquefort cheese has just the right blend of creaminess and pungency to make it perfect for this salad dressing, but any blue cheese will work. Try Gorgonzola as an alternative.

MAKES ABOUT 2½ CUPS

¾ cup crumbled Roquefort or other blue cheese
⅓ cup half-and-half or evaporated milk
1 cup mayonnaise
½ cup buttermilk
½ teaspoon minced garlic
Salt and pepper

1. Melt ½ cup of cheese with the half-and-half in the top of a double boiler over barely simmering water. Stir until smooth. Let cool.

2. Stir in the mayonnaise, buttermilk, and garlic. Gently fold in the remaining ¼ cup cheese. Season to taste with salt and pepper.

3. Let stand for at least 30 minutes to allow the flavors to blend. Serve immediately or chilled. Refrigerate in an airtight container for up to 2 weeks.

Creamy Parmesan Dressing

Here's a creamy dressing without the pungency of blue cheese dressing, but it is equally good on green salads.

MAKES ABOUT 1 CUP

½ cup grated Parmesan cheese
¾ cup mayonnaise
6 tablespoons olive oil
¼ cup white-wine vinegar
1 teaspoon minced garlic
Salt and pepper

1. Process the Parmesan cheese in a food processor until it is a very fine powder. Add the mayonnaise, oil, vinegar, and garlic and process until well mixed. Season to taste with salt and pepper.

2. Let stand for at least 30 minutes to allow the flavors to blend. Serve immediately or chilled. Refrigerate in an airtight container for up to 2 weeks.

Homemade Mayonnaise

Homemade mayonnaise is far richer tasting than the convenient bottled kind. But because it uses raw eggs, it spoils very quickly. (For more information about egg safety, see page 11.)

MAKES ABOUT 1¼ CUPS

1 large egg
½ teaspoon dry mustard
2 tablespoons lemon juice
1 cup olive oil
Salt

1. Combine the egg, mustard, and lemon juice in a blender or food processor. With the motor running, very slowly add the oil in a thin, steady stream. Season to taste with salt.

2. Refrigerate in an airtight container for up to 2 days.

TIP: If your homemade mayonnaise is too thick, thin it with a little warm water.

Boiled Salad Dressing

Before there was Miracle Whip, there was boiled salad dressing, also known as cooked salad dressing.

MAKES ABOUT 2 CUPS

2 tablespoons all-purpose flour
2 tablespoons sugar
1¼ teaspoons salt
½ teaspoon dry mustard
Pinch of cayenne pepper
2 large eggs
1 cup water
⅓ cup lemon juice or cider vinegar
3 tablespoons olive oil

1. Combine the flour, sugar, salt, mustard, and cayenne pepper in a small saucepan.

2. In a medium bowl, use a fork to beat together the eggs, water, and lemon juice. Whisk into the saucepan until smooth.

3. Cook over low heat, stirring constantly, until the mixture thickens. Remove from the heat and stir in the oil.

4. Chill for at least 2 hours. Refrigerate in an airtight container for up to 2 days.

Sunshine Salad

Carrots plus pineapple in a gelatin salad equals a sunshine salad. It is a beautiful salad to display and a refreshing side dish.

SERVES 8

1 (20-ounce) can crushed pineapple
1 (6-ounce) package orange or lemon gelatin
4 cups grated carrots
½ cup finely chopped pecans
Watercress, to serve

1. Drain the crushed pineapple, reserving the juice in a 2-cup glass measuring cup. Add water to the juice to make 2 cups. Set aside the pineapple.

2. Combine the juice mixture and gelatin in a small saucepan over low heat. Stir until the gelatin is completely dissolved. Stir in 2 cups cold water.

3. Chill until partially set, about 1½ hours. The mixture should mound slightly when dropped from a spoon and have the consistency of unbeaten egg white.

4. Fold in the pineapple, carrots, and pecans.

5. Rinse an 8-cup ring mold with cold water. Pour in the gelatin mixture and chill until set, about 3 hours.

6. Line a platter with the watercress, unmold the salad on top, and serve.

Ginger Ale and Fruit Salad Mold

Gelatin salads have been popular in the Midwest ever since they were introduced in the late nineteenth century. They have almost disappeared from tables on the East and West Coasts. Sparkling, bubbly ginger ale provides the liquid for this refreshing gelatin mold.

SERVES 6 TO 8

2 cups ginger ale
1 (3-ounce) package lemon gelatin
2 cups diced apples, pears, or peeled orange sections
¼ cup chopped pecans

1 tablespoon chopped candied (crystallized) ginger
Lettuce, such as romaine or iceberg, to serve
Mayonnaise, to serve

1. Combine 1 cup of ginger ale with the gelatin in a small saucepan. Heat over low heat, stirring constantly until the gelatin is completely dissolved. Set aside to cool.

2. Add the remaining 1 cup ginger ale.

3. Chill until partially set, about 1 hour. The mixture should mound slightly when dropped from a spoon and have the consistency of unbeaten egg white.

4. Fold in the apples, pecans, and ginger.

5. Rinse a decorative 4-cup mold with cold water. Pour the gelatin mixture into the mold and refrigerate until set, about 3 hours.

6. To serve, line a platter with the lettuce. Unmold the salad onto the platter. Place a bowl of mayonnaise in the center if you are using a ring mold, or dollop onto the molded salad as desired.

Pineapple and Lime Gelatin Salad

Pineapple and lime gelatin is a classic combination. If you like, add a cup of miniature marshmallows to the gelatin mixture to turn this into a "millionaire" salad.

SERVES 10

1 (6-ounce) package lime gelatin
2 cups boiling water
1 cup sour cream
1 (20-ounce) can crushed pineapple, drained
1 cup mandarin orange sections
Lettuce, such as romaine or iceberg, to serve

1. Dissolve the gelatin in the boiling water in a medium bowl.

2. Chill until partially set, about 1 hour. The mixture should mound slightly when dropped from a spoon and have the consistency of unbeaten egg white.

3. Stir in the sour cream, pineapple, and orange sections.

4. Rinse a 6-cup ring mold with cold water. Pour in the gelatin mixture and chill until set, about 3 hours.

5. To serve, line a platter with the lettuce, and unmold the salad onto the platter.

Cranberry-Nut Gelatin Salad

Cranberries may show up in many guises on the Thanksgiving table—in the muffins, in the juice on the children's table, as an accompaniment to the turkey, and in this wonderful salad.

SERVES 6

1 (6-ounce) package orange gelatin
3 cups boiling water
¾ cup whole cranberry sauce
¼ cup finely chopped celery
¼ cup chopped walnuts
1 tablespoon lemon juice
½ teaspoon salt
Lettuce, such as romaine or iceberg, to serve

1. Dissolve the gelatin in the boiling water in a medium bowl. Stir in the cranberry sauce.

2. Chill until partially set, about 1½ hours. The mixture should mound slightly when dropped from a spoon and have the consistency of unbeaten egg white.

3. Fold in the celery, walnuts, lemon juice, and salt.

4. Rinse a 6-cup ring mold with cold water. Pour in the gelatin mixture and chill until set, about 3 hours.

5. To serve, line a platter with the lettuce, and unmold the salad onto the platter.

THE ART OF GELATIN SALADS

▚▚▚▚▚▚▚▚▚▚▚

There are many kitchens decorated with beautiful copper gelatin molds, but there is no one to make molded salads. Don't let gelatin salads intimidate you!

▶ If you are making your own recipe, 1 (¼-ounce) envelope of unflavored gelatin will gel 2 cups of liquid (broth or fruit or vegetable juice).

▶ Gelatin added to cold liquid should be soaked for 3 to 5 minutes before dissolving to soften it first.

▶ Dissolve gelatin in hot liquid, stirring until it is completely dissolved, but don't let the mixture come to a boil.

▶ Rinse out the mold with cold water before using or spray with nonstick spray to make the gelatin easier to unmold.

▶ To speed the setting of a gelatin mixture, place the mold in a bowl of ice water, stirring constantly until the mixture is partially set.

▶ Don't add solids to a gelatin until it is partially set and has the consistency of unbeaten egg white, or the solids will sink to the bottom of the mold.

▶ To remove gelatin from a mold, insert a knife between the mold and the gelatin to release the vacuum. Then dip the mold in hot water up to its edge for about 5 seconds. Place a plate over the top of the mold and, holding both the plate and the mold tightly, invert the mold and give it a firm shake. The gelatin should drop onto the plate. If it doesn't, repeat the dip and try again.

CHAPTER FIVE

Soups

Soup—the very word brings visions of steaming bowls of delicious vegetables and fragrant broth served with warm, crusty bread on a cold winter evening. It is perhaps the best known and most soothing of all comfort foods, and Mom's chicken soup always seemed to cure the worst cold or stomach ache.

The very first fast food was soup. As early as 600 B.C., Greek street vendors sold pea, bean, and lentil soups from carts on the street. In medieval times, broth made from boiled meat was served over a piece of bread in a bowl. That bread was known as "sop," and from "sop" came the words "soup" and "supper."

Early American colonists made fish soups and chowders because fish was so readily available. Colonial travelers carried a form of dried soup known as "pocket soup," which was easily reconstituted with a little hot water. Commercially canned and dehydrated soups became available in the nineteenth century. These supplied the military, covered wagon trains, cowboy chuck wagons, and the home pantry.

In 1869, a fruit merchant named Joseph Campbell and an icebox manufacturer named Abraham Anderson formed a business that became one of the most recognized in the world and would serve as a symbol of Americana: Campbell Soup Company. In 1897, a major company milestone was reached when out of its laboratory came the invention of condensed soup. By eliminating most of the water, Campbell's lowered the costs for packaging, shipping, and storage of canned soups.

Some of the most popular varieties of Campbell's soups have been enjoyed by generations of soup lovers: Tomato was introduced in 1897, and cream of mushroom and chicken noodle first appeared in 1934. Combined, Americans consume approximately 2.5 billion bowls of these three soups alone each year.

But the desire for homemade soup has never faded. Simmering soup, whether on the back burner of a wood-fired stove or on the front burner of an electric one, fills a home with aromas that promise warmth, comfort, and security.

Our American soup menu has been widely influenced by people of all the various ethnic cultures that have made their homes here. We enjoy Russian borscht, Italian minestrone, and Spanish gazpacho, as well as French onion, Portuguese kale, and Mexican tortilla soups—all recipes that are featured in this chapter.

There's soup simmering on the stove, so grab a spoon.

Borscht

Borscht is a beet soup brought to this country by immigrants from Eastern Europe. Ukrainians consider it their national soup, but borscht is widespread in the region, and has been made with so many variations since its medieval development that it is hard to be precise about what constitutes authentic borscht. This is the version most like that served in Jewish delis in New York City. It is so closely associated with Jewish emigrants to America that resorts in the nearby Catskills, which featured Jewish comedians as entertainers, became known as the "borscht belt."

SERVES 4

8 cups beef broth (page 118)
2 cups peeled and diced beets
1½ cups chopped green cabbage
2 medium carrots, diced
1 medium onion, diced
1 bay leaf
2 tablespoons red-wine vinegar
Salt and pepper
Sour cream, to serve
Chopped fresh dill, to serve

1. Combine the broth, beets, cabbage, carrots, onion, and bay leaf in a large soup pot or saucepan. Bring to a boil, reduce the heat, and simmer, partially covered, for 30 minutes, until the beets and carrots are tender.

2. Remove the bay leaf. Add the vinegar, salt, and pepper to taste. Serve hot, or chill and serve cold, topping each serving with a dollop of sour cream and a pinch of fresh dill.

TIP: For a vegetarian version, substitute vegetable broth (page 118) for the beef broth.

Cheddar-Broccoli Soup

Although Thomas Jefferson did plant broccoli in his garden in Monticello, broccoli was not a common vegetable in the United States until Italian immigrant farmers grew it in the 1920s. Broccoli pairs well with cheese in all sorts of dishes.

SERVES 4 TO 6

1 large head broccoli, trimmed and chopped
¼ cup (½ stick) butter
1 medium onion, diced
¼ cup all-purpose flour
3 cups chicken broth (page 119)
3 cups milk
1 pound Cheddar cheese, shredded (about 4 cups)
Salt and pepper

1. Blanch the broccoli in boiling water for 3 minutes, until bright green and tender but not mushy. Drain, plunge into cold water to stop the cooking, and drain again. Set aside.

2. Melt the butter in a large soup pot or saucepan over medium-high heat. Add the onion and sauté until translucent, about 3 minutes. Stir in the flour until well blended. Gradually add the broth and bring to a boil, stirring constantly. Pour in the milk and heat just to a boil, stirring constantly.

3. Remove from the heat and stir in the cheese until melted. Stir in the broccoli. Return to very low heat and heat just until the broccoli is warmed, 1 to 2 minutes.

4. Taste and add salt and pepper as needed. Serve hot.

Cheddar Cheese Soup

Cheddar was the most popular American-made cheese in the nineteenth century. Throughout New England, every mom-and-pop grocery kept a wheel of Cheddar from which they cut wedges for their customers.

SERVES 4 TO 6

½ cup (1 stick) butter
½ medium onion, finely chopped
6 tablespoons all-purpose flour
4 cups chicken broth (page 119)
4 cups milk
⅛ teaspoon paprika
3 cups Cheddar cheese, shredded (about 12 ounces)
Salt and pepper
Finely chopped fresh parsley, to serve (optional)

1. Melt the butter in a large saucepan over medium-low heat. Add the onion and sauté until softened, about 5 minutes.

2. Sprinkle in the flour and blend well. Stir in the chicken broth and milk. Bring to a boil, stirring constantly. Reduce heat to medium and cook for 10 minutes.

3. Stir in the paprika and cheese. Reduce the heat to low and cook until the cheese is melted.

4. Season to taste with salt and pepper. Serve hot, garnished with parsley, if using.

Cream of Cauliflower Soup

Cauliflower, like broccoli, comes from the cabbage family and has been used for thousands of years. However, cauliflower has been an important crop in America only since the 1920s.

SERVES 4 TO 6

2 cups chicken broth (page 119) or vegetable broth (page 118)
1 large head cauliflower, trimmed and chopped
1 cup dry white wine
1 medium onion, diced
3 tablespoons butter
1 teaspoon minced garlic
⅛ teaspoon ground nutmeg (optional)
¼ cup all-purpose flour
3 cups milk or half-and-half
Salt and pepper
Chopped fresh parsley, dill, or chives, to serve (optional)

1. Combine the broth, cauliflower, wine, and onion in a large soup pot or saucepan over high heat. Bring to a boil, reduce the heat to medium-low, then cover and cook for 10 to 15 minutes, until the cauliflower is tender. Remove a few pieces for garnishing and set aside.

2. Purée the cauliflower mixture in a food processor or blender until smooth. Set aside.

3. In the same pot, melt the butter over medium heat. Add the garlic and nutmeg, if using, and sauté for about 1 minute. Stir in the flour and cook for another minute.

4. Add the milk and cook until thick and bubbly, stirring constantly.

5. Stir in the cauliflower mixture. Simmer briefly to reheat, and season to taste with salt and pepper.

6. Serve hot, garnishing each bowl with parsley and reserved cauliflower florets, if using.

Cream of Broccoli Soup

Broccoli is a powerhouse of nutrition. Although this classic, creamy soup is best made when fresh, you can use thawed frozen broccoli and skip the first step of cooking it. Just set aside a few florets to use as a garnish before serving.

SERVES 4 TO 6

1 large head broccoli, trimmed and chopped
2 cups chicken broth (page 119)
1 cup heavy cream
3 tablespoons butter
Salt and pepper

1. Cook the broccoli in a large pot of boiling salted water until tender but still bright green, about 5 minutes. Drain the broccoli. Remove a few florets for garnishing and set aside.

2. Combine the broth, cream, and butter in a large, heavy saucepan and bring to a boil.

3. Working in batches, purée the broccoli and broth mixture in a blender until smooth. Return the soup to the same pan. Season to taste with salt and pepper.

4. Bring the soup to a simmer and serve, garnishing each serving with the reserved florets.

Cream of Celery Soup

Celery used to be a much more popular vegetable than it is today. Mostly it is used now as a snack or in salads. In a soup, celery takes on a clean and fresh taste. It is nicely pronounced in this recipe.

SERVES 4

3 cups chicken broth (page 119) or vegetable broth (page 118)
6 large celery ribs, chopped
½ medium onion, finely chopped
3 tablespoons butter
¼ cup all-purpose flour
2 cups milk or half-and-half
Salt and pepper
Chopped fresh parsley, dill, or chives, to serve (optional)

1. Combine the broth, celery, and onion in a large soup pot or saucepan over high heat. Bring to a boil, reduce the heat to medium-low, then cover and cook for 15 to 20 minutes, until the celery is tender.

2. Purée the celery mixture in a food processor or blender until smooth. Set aside.

3. In the same pot, melt the butter over medium heat. Stir in the flour and cook for 2 minutes. Add the milk and cook until thick and bubbly, stirring constantly.

4. Stir in the celery mixture. Simmer briefly to reheat, and season to taste with salt and pepper.

5. Serve hot, garnishing each bowl with a sprinkling of parsley, if using.

Corn Chowder

Corn was grown by native Americans long before Christopher Columbus set sail in 1492. It did not become widely adopted by settlers until the nineteenth century, when it became one of the most popular vegetables for home gardens. Cooks make the most of the corn season by using it in many dishes, including this soup. Fresh corn tastes best, but frozen corn may be used.

SERVES 4

½ cup rinsed and finely chopped salt pork
1 medium onion, chopped
3 medium waxy potatoes, such as thin-skinned red or white, peeled and diced
2 cups water
2 cups fresh or frozen corn
1½ cups milk
1½ cups half-and-half
Salt and pepper

1. Fry the pork in a large soup pot or saucepan over medium-high heat until rendered and lightly browned, about 4 minutes. Add the onion and continue cooking until transparent, about 4 minutes.

2. Add the potatoes and water and bring to a boil. Reduce the heat and simmer for 25 to 30 minutes, until the potatoes are tender. Stir in the corn, milk, and half-and-half. Season to taste with salt and pepper. Simmer until the soup is heated through, about 15 minutes.

3. Taste and adjust the seasonings as needed. Serve hot.

TIP: To remove whole kernels from a cob, hold an ear of corn vertically, resting the tip end down. Using a sharp knife, carefully slice the kernels off in long rows, turning the cob after each row is removed.

Chilled Cucumber Soup

This delicious soup travels well and makes a lovely first course. The combination of cucumber, cream, and dill give this soup its simple and charming character.

SERVES 4 TO 6

1 tablespoon oil
1 medium onion, thinly sliced
2 large cucumbers, peeled, seeded, and diced
2 cups chicken broth (page 119)
½ cup dry vermouth
1 teaspoon cornstarch
3 tablespoons water
1 cup heavy cream
1 tablespoon chopped fresh dill
Salt and pepper

1. Heat the oil in a large soup pot or saucepan over medium-high heat. Add the onion and sauté until soft, about 3 minutes. Reduce the heat and add the cucumbers, broth, and vermouth.

2. Mix together the cornstarch and water in a small dish or jar until dissolved. Stir into the soup and simmer gently for 15 minutes. Cool briefly.

3. Purée the soup in a blender or food processor in small batches until smooth. Stir in the cream and dill. Season to taste with salt and pepper.

4. Chill thoroughly before serving.

Portuguese Kale Soup

Portuguese immigrants brought caldo verde ("green soup") to America in the nineteenth century. It is still served in homes and in restaurants from Cape Cod to Providence, Rhode Island, where a large Portuguese population resides today. This version of the soup is its simplest form, but it can also be made with tomatoes and beef broth—only the linguiça sausage and kale is universal. If you can't find linguiça, substitute chorizo or kielbasa.

SERVES 4 TO 6

½ pound linguiça sausage
8 cups chicken broth (page 119)
3 to 4 medium baking potatoes (about
    1 pound), peeled and diced
8 cups chopped kale, trimmed and lightly
    packed
Salt and pepper

1. Combine the sausage and broth in a large soup pot or saucepan. Bring to a boil, reduce the heat, and simmer while you prepare the potatoes.

2. Cover the potatoes with salted water in a medium saucepan. Bring to a boil, cover, and cook until tender, about 8 minutes. Drain and briefly mash with a potato masher for an uneven, lumpy texture.

3. Add the potatoes to the sausage. Add the kale and simmer for 15 minutes, until the kale is tender. Season to taste with salt and pepper. Serve hot.

Cream of Mushroom Soup

In the not-so-distant past, white button mushrooms were the only variety available. Today this soup can be made with a wide range of fresh wild mushrooms for diverse flavor.

SERVES 4

¼ cup (½ stick) butter
1 pound mushrooms, trimmed and finely
    chopped
¼ cup finely chopped onion
2 tablespoons all-purpose flour
2 cups chicken broth (page 119)
2 tablespoons dry sherry or Madeira wine
½ teaspoon dried thyme
1 cup heavy cream
Salt and pepper

1. Melt the butter in a large soup pot or saucepan over medium heat. Add the mushrooms and onion and sauté until the mushrooms give up their juice, 5 to 10 minutes, depending on the type of mushroom used.

2. Sprinkle the mushrooms with the flour and stir until the flour forms a paste. Slowly stir in the broth. Add the sherry and thyme and bring to a boil, stirring. Reduce the heat and simmer for 20 minutes.

3. Stir in the cream and season to taste with salt and pepper. Cook just until the cream is heated through. Serve hot.

TIP: Clean mushrooms by wiping them with a toothbrush and damp paper towels. Trim the bottom ¼ inch off the stem ends of button or crimini mushrooms.

Barley-Mushroom Soup

Barley makes a hearty, healthful, whole-grain base for a soup. The soup will thicken on standing, so if you are making this ahead of time, be prepared to thin it with a little broth or water before reheating to serve.

SERVES 6 TO 8

2 tablespoons oil
1 pound mushrooms, trimmed and finely chopped
2 medium celery ribs, finely chopped
2 medium carrots, finely chopped
1 medium onion, finely chopped
8 cups vegetable broth, chicken broth, or beef broth (pages 118–119)
⅔ cup pearl barley
2 tablespoons dry sherry or Madeira wine
¼ cup chopped fresh parsley
Salt and pepper

1. Heat the oil in a large soup pot or saucepan over medium heat. Add the mushrooms, celery, carrots, and onion and sauté until the onion and mushrooms are well browned and the liquid has mostly evaporated, about 15 minutes.

2. Add the broth and barley. Bring to a boil, reduce the heat, and simmer, partially covered, until the barley is tender, 40 to 60 minutes.

3. Stir in the sherry and parsley. Season to taste with salt and pepper and serve hot.

French Onion Soup

Onion soups were enjoyed by ancient Greeks and Romans; they can also be found in the earliest American cookbooks. French onion soup (with the characteristic bread and cheese topping) is highly reminiscent of medieval soups. It enjoyed a resurgence of popularity in the 1960s, when famed chef Julia Child introduced French home cooking to a wide American TV audience.

SERVES 6

3 tablespoons butter
2 tablespoons oil
5 medium onions, thinly sliced
½ cup dry sherry or cognac
8 cups beef broth (page 118)
½ teaspoon dried thyme

Salt and pepper
12 slices baguette, cut ¼ inch thick
2¼ cups shredded Gruyère or Swiss cheese (about 9 ounces)

1. Melt the butter with the oil in a large soup pot or saucepan over medium heat. Add the onions and sauté, stirring frequently, until they begin to brown, about 15 minutes. Reduce the heat to medium-low and continue to sauté, still stirring frequently, until the onions are a rich brown, about 30 minutes. Do not allow the onions to burn.

2. Add the sherry, increase the heat to high, and cook until most of the liquid evaporates, 4 to 5 minutes.

3. Stir in the broth, bring to a boil, and reduce the heat. Add the thyme, season to taste with salt and pepper, and simmer, partially covered, for 30 minutes.

4. Meanwhile, preheat the oven to 350°F.

5. Arrange the bread slices in a single layer on a baking sheet and toast in the oven until dry and lightly colored, 10 to 15 minutes. Remove the bread from the oven and increase the oven temperature to 450°F.

6. Place 6 ovenproof soup bowls or crocks on a baking sheet. Ladle the hot soup into the bowls. Top each bowl with 2 slices of bread and top each slice with about 3 tablespoons shredded cheese.

7. Place the baking sheet with the bowls in the oven and bake for 4 to 6 minutes, until the cheese is melted and bubbling. Serve hot.

Fresh Pea Soup

Once picked, peas convert their sugar to starch as rapidly as corn does, maintaining their sweet flavor for no more than two days. To enjoy this soup the way farmers and their families do, use garden-fresh peas when possible. For a creamier version, stir a tablespoon or two of heavy cream into each bowl.

SERVES 4 TO 6

¼ cup (½ stick) butter
1 medium onion, finely chopped
7 cups fresh or frozen sweet peas
3 cups chicken broth (page 119)
1 tablespoon chopped fresh tarragon (optional)
Salt
White pepper

1. Melt the butter in a large soup pot or saucepan over low heat. Add the onion and sauté until translucent, about 5 minutes.

2. Add the peas, broth, and tarragon, if using. Simmer fresh peas for 20 minutes, or frozen peas for 5 minutes, until the peas are completely tender. Allow to cool slightly.

3. Purée the soup in a blender or food processor until smooth. Pour the soup through a fine-mesh strainer to remove any pea skins. Return to the pot and reheat over low heat.

4. Season to taste with salt and pepper and serve hot.

TIP: If you are buying fresh peas, figure that 1 pound of peas in the pod equals 1 cup of shelled peas.

Vichyssoise

Despite the French name, this chilled potato-leek soup was created in New York City. The chef, however, was French, and he named it after the city in which he grew up—Vichy.

SERVES 4

3 tablespoons butter
6 leeks, white parts only, trimmed and sliced
5 cups chicken broth (page 119), plus more as needed
3 medium baking potatoes, peeled and thinly sliced
1 cup heavy cream
Salt and pepper
Chopped fresh chives, to serve

1. Melt the butter over low heat in a large soup pot or saucepan. Add the leeks and sauté until tender but not browned, about 15 minutes.

2. Add the 5 cups broth and the potatoes. Cover and bring to a boil over medium-high heat. Reduce the heat and simmer until the potatoes are soft, 20 to 30 minutes. Cool slightly.

3. Purée the soup in a food processor or blender until smooth. Return the soup to the pot and stir in the cream. Chill thoroughly.

4. Before serving, thin, if necessary, with additional broth. Season to taste with salt and pepper. Garnish each bowl with a sprinkling of chives.

TIP: Leeks tend to harbor dirt between their leaves, so it is important to clean them thoroughly. Trim off the root ends, then trim the stalks to about 5 inches above the roots. Slit the leeks from top to bottom without cutting all the way through. Rinse under cold running water, flipping through the leaf layers to remove all the hidden grit and soil.

Cream of Tomato Soup

Cream of tomato soups are tricky because the acidity of the tomatoes can curdle the milk. The baking soda here helps neutralize some of that acid. Canned tomato soup doesn't hold a candle to this homemade version.

SERVES 4 TO 6

2½ cups diced canned tomatoes
¼ cup finely chopped onion
½ teaspoon salt
½ teaspoon baking soda
Pinch of celery salt
2 tablespoons butter
2 tablespoons all-purpose flour
2 cups half-and-half
Sour cream, to serve (optional)
Croutons (page 75), to serve (optional)
Crumbled crisp bacon, to serve (optional)

1. Combine the tomatoes, onion, salt, baking soda, and celery salt in a large soup pot or saucepan. Simmer gently for 10 minutes.

2. Press the tomato mixture through a fine-mesh strainer. Return the mixture to the pan and reheat over low heat.

3. Melt the butter in a small saucepan over medium heat. Stir in the flour until you have a smooth paste. Slowly add the half-and-half, stirring constantly until smooth, about 1 minute.

4. Blend the half-and-half mixture into the soup. Stir until the soup is thickened. Be careful it doesn't scorch. Pour into bowls, top with sour cream, croutons, and bacon, if using, and serve hot.

Gazpacho

Although this chilled tomato soup is of Spanish origin, gazpacho has been served in America for at least two centuries. It first appeared as a layered salad in "The Virginia Housewife," a cookbook by Mrs. Mary Randolph, published in 1824. Today, it is more popularly known as a soup, served chilled. But in Spain, there are numerous versions of gazpacho, including many without tomatoes and many that are served hot.

SERVES 4 TO 6

1 small onion, quartered
½ cup fresh parsley leaves
2 garlic cloves
2½ pounds tomatoes, peeled, seeded, and coarsely chopped
1 cup tomato juice
¼ cup red-wine vinegar
3 tablespoons oil
1 medium cucumber, peeled, seeded, and finely chopped
Salt and pepper

1. Combine the onion, parsley, and garlic in a food processor and finely chop, using a rubber spatula to scrape down the sides of the food processor bowl between pulses. Add the tomatoes and process until finely chopped.

2. Transfer the mixture to a large bowl. Stir in the tomato juice, vinegar, oil, and cucumber. Season to taste with salt and pepper.

3. Refrigerate for at least 2 hours. Taste and adjust the seasoning as needed before serving. Serve cold.

TIP: To peel tomatoes, use a slotted spoon to lower each tomato into a pot of boiling water for 15 to 20 seconds, or until the skin splits, then plunge into ice water to cool quickly. Peel with a paring knife. To seed tomatoes, cut each in half horizontally and squeeze out the seeds.

Tomato Vegetable Soup

Who needs canned soup when you can make a homemade soup that is tasty and good for you in less than an hour? Serve with grilled cheese sandwiches (page 44), or make a meal of it paired with salad and fresh bread.

SERVES 4 TO 6

2 tablespoons oil
1 medium onion, finely chopped
2 medium celery ribs, sliced
2 medium carrots, diced
1 (28-ounce) can diced tomatoes
4 cups chicken broth (page 119) or vegetable broth (page 118)
1 teaspoon dried oregano
Salt and pepper
1 cup sliced (1½-inch lengths) fresh or frozen green beans
1 cup fresh or frozen corn

1. Heat the oil in a large soup pot or saucepan over medium-high heat. Add the onion, celery, and carrots and sauté until the onion is softened, about 3 minutes.

2. Stir in the tomatoes, broth, and oregano and season to taste with salt and pepper. Bring to a boil, reduce the heat, and simmer, covered, for 30 minutes.

3. Stir in the green beans and corn. Simmer for another 30 minutes, until the flavors have blended and the vegetables are heated through.

4. Taste and adjust the seasonings as needed before serving. Serve hot.

Minestrone Soup

Cooks all over Italy and America make minestrone soup, and each version differs from the next. Usually it is a tomato-vegetable soup with beans and pasta—a hearty, healthy soup served fresh or as leftovers the next day.

SERVES 6 TO 8

2 tablespoons oil
1 medium onion, finely chopped
1 teaspoon minced garlic
6 cups chicken broth (page 119) or vegetable broth (page 118), plus more as needed
1 (28-ounce) can diced tomatoes
1 medium carrot, diced
1 medium celery rib, diced
2 teaspoons dried oregano
1 teaspoon dried thyme
1 bay leaf
Salt and pepper
1 cup small soup pasta, such as rings, ditalini, alphabets, or bow ties
1 cup chopped fresh or frozen green beans
1 (15-ounce) can cannellini beans, rinsed and drained

1. Heat the oil in a large soup pot or saucepan over medium heat. Add the onion and garlic and sauté for 2 minutes. Add the 6 cups of broth, tomatoes, carrot, celery, oregano, thyme, and bay leaf. Season to taste with salt and pepper. Bring to a boil, reduce the heat, and simmer for about 20 minutes.

2. Return the soup to boiling. Add the pasta and boil gently until the pasta is partially cooked, about 5 minutes. Add the green beans and cannellini. Simmer for 10 minutes more, or until the green beans are tender.

3. Remove the bay leaf. Taste and adjust the seasoning as needed. The soup will thicken on standing; thin with additional broth or water if needed. Serve hot.

Split Pea Soup

Split peas are dried sweet peas. The peas split when they are fully dried, hence the name. Like lentils, split peas do not require presoaking. This recipe uses split peas, salty ham, a touch of sweetness from carrots, and onions for a classic flavor combination.

SERVES 4 TO 6

8 cups water
2 cups dried split peas, rinsed and debris removed
1 meaty ham bone or 2 smoked ham hocks
1 leek, white part only, trimmed and chopped
1 medium onion, chopped
½ teaspoon salt, or more to taste
Black pepper
2 medium carrots, finely chopped (optional)

1. Combine the water, split peas, and ham bone in a large soup pot or saucepan. Bring to a boil. Skim off any foam that rises to the top.

2. Add the leek, onion, and salt and pepper to taste. Reduce the heat and barely simmer, partially covered, for 3 hours, stirring occasionally.

3. Remove the ham bone, and cut the meat from the bone. Finely chop the meat and return to the soup. Discard the bone.

4. Add the carrots, if using, and continue to simmer until the carrots are tender, about 15 minutes.

5. Taste and adjust the seasoning as needed; serve hot.

Black Bean Soup

Black beans are popular in Central America and in the Caribbean. This particular version, flavored with a ham hock, chicken broth, sherry, and cayenne pepper, is a favorite in Cuban-American communities in Florida.

SERVES 4 TO 6

1 pound dried black beans, debris removed, soaked overnight, and drained
1 smoked ham hock
2 medium onions, chopped
1½ teaspoons minced garlic
7 cups chicken broth (page 119)
2 cups water
¼ cup dry sherry
1 tablespoon red-wine vinegar
¼ teaspoon cayenne pepper
Salt and pepper
Chopped scallion, to serve
1 medium lime, thinly sliced, to serve (optional)

1. Combine the beans, ham hock, onions, garlic, broth, and water in a large soup pot or saucepan. Bring to a boil, partially cover, and simmer, stirring occasionally, until the beans are completely tender, about 2 hours.

2. Remove the ham hock. Strip the meat from the bone and chop; discard the bone.

3. Remove about half the beans with some broth and purée in a blender.

4. Return the puréed beans and meat from the ham hock to the soup. Stir in the sherry, vinegar, and cayenne pepper. Season to taste with salt and pepper.

5. Serve hot, garnished with chopped scallion and lime slices, if using.

Pasta e Fagioli

This pasta and bean soup is also known as "pasta fazool." It is a hearty dish, adding bacon, tomatoes, and cheese to the pasta and beans to make it a fine meal accompaniment as well as a suitable main course.

SERVES 4

2 tablespoons oil
1 medium onion, finely diced
2 slices bacon, finely diced, or ¼ cup rinsed
    and diced salt pork
½ teaspoon minced garlic
4 cups chicken broth (page 119)
1 (15-ounce) can diced tomatoes
1 (15-ounce) can cannellini beans, rinsed and
    drained
1 cup freshly grated Romano cheese
1 tablespoon chopped fresh parsley
½ teaspoon dried oregano
¼ teaspoon crushed red pepper
Salt and pepper
½ cup ditalini pasta

1. Heat the oil in a large saucepan or soup pot over medium heat. Add the bacon and cook for 5 minutes. Add the onion and sauté until the onion is translucent, about 5 minutes. Add the garlic and cook for 2 more minutes.

2. Add the chicken broth and tomatoes and bring the mixture to a boil. Reduce the heat and add the beans, cheese, parsley, oregano, and crushed red pepper. Simmer for 3 to 4 minutes. Season to taste with salt and pepper.

3. Bring a medium pot of salted water to a boil. Add the pasta and cook until just done. Drain and add the pasta to the soup. Serve hot.

Roman Holiday Soup

Minestrone soup comes in many forms. Here the beans are dried, not canned, so the soup must simmer on the back burner for a couple of hours. While the soup simmers, it fills your home with wonderful aromas. Serve with a loaf of homemade or bakery bread and you have a meal suitable for a holiday or a lazy Sunday.

SERVES 6 TO 8

2½ pounds beef soup bones (with some meat)
4 quarts water
1 cup dried red kidney beans, debris removed,
    soaked overnight, and drained
2 teaspoons salt, plus more to taste
¼ teaspoon black pepper, plus more to taste
2 tablespoons oil
2 medium onions, finely chopped
2 medium carrots, finely chopped
2 medium celery ribs, finely chopped
¼ small head green cabbage, cored and
    shredded
1 (10-ounce) package frozen peas
1 medium zucchini, finely chopped
1 cup puréed fresh or canned tomatoes
½ cup uncooked elbow macaroni
¼ cup uncooked long-grain white rice
¼ cup chopped fresh parsley
½ teaspoon crushed dried sage
½ teaspoon minced garlic
Freshly grated Parmesan cheese, to serve

1. Preheat the oven to 425°F.

2. Spread the bones on a baking sheet and roast in the oven until browned, about 30 minutes, turning every 10 minutes to get even browning.

3. Combine the soup bones, water, kidney beans, salt, and black pepper in a large soup pot or saucepan. Bring to a boil, then use a spoon to skim off any foam that rises to the top. Reduce the heat, and simmer until the meat is falling off the bones and the beans are tender, 2½ to 3 hours.

4. Remove the soup bones with a slotted spoon and cut any meat from the bones. Finely chop the meat and return to the soup. Discard the bones.

5. Heat the oil in a large skillet over medium-high heat. Add the onions, carrots, and celery, and sauté until the onions are transparent, about 3 minutes. Add to the soup pot.

6. In the same large skillet, add the cabbage, peas, zucchini, tomatoes, macaroni, rice, parsley, sage, and garlic. Simmer for about 30 minutes or until the macaroni, rice, and vegetables are tender.

7. Taste and adjust the seasonings as needed. Serve hot, passing the Parmesan cheese at the table.

Lentil Soup

Lentils have been around for at least eight thousand years—long enough for farmers in India to have cultivated more than fifty different varieties, although American markets rarely carry more than the familiar green, red, yellow, and brown varieties. Of all the dried beans, only lentils and split peas don't require presoaking, which makes them practically a convenience food. This dish uses vegetables, the smoky flavor of bacon, and a touch of lemon juice to enhance the lentil base.

SERVES 6

4 slices bacon, chopped
2 medium onions, sliced
2 medium carrots, sliced
2 medium celery ribs, sliced
1 pound (2¼ cups) lentils, rinsed and debris removed
8 cups hot water
1 teaspoon dried thyme
2 bay leaves
1 teaspoon salt, plus more to taste
½ teaspoon black pepper, plus more to taste
1 (15-ounce) can diced tomatoes
2 tablespoons lemon juice or red-wine vinegar, or to taste

1. Cook the bacon over medium-high heat in a large soup pot or saucepan until lightly browned, about 4 minutes. Add the onions, carrots, and celery and sauté until tender, about 5 minutes.

2. Drain off any excess fat. Add the lentils, water, thyme, bay leaves, salt, and pepper. Cover and simmer over low heat for about 1 hour, until the lentils are completely tender.

3. Stir in the tomatoes and simmer for 15 minutes.

4. Remove the bay leaves. Taste and add the lemon juice and more salt and pepper as needed. Serve hot.

Lentil-Sausage Soup

This robust soup makes for good wintertime eating and excellent leftovers. It also makes a great vegetarian soup; just leave out the sausage and use vegetable broth.

SERVES 4 TO 6

2 tablespoons oil
1 large onion, finely diced
2 medium celery ribs, finely diced
1 teaspoon minced garlic
6 cups chicken broth (page 119)
⅔ cup green or brown lentils, rinsed and debris removed
2 bay leaves
1½ teaspoons dried thyme
1 (15-ounce) can diced tomatoes
12 ounces smoked sausage, such as kielbasa, finely diced
Salt and pepper

1. Heat the oil in a large soup pot or saucepan over medium heat. Add the onion, celery, and garlic and sauté until soft, about 5 minutes.

2. Add the broth, lentils, bay leaves, and thyme. Bring to a boil, cover, and simmer for 45 minutes, until the lentils are tender.

3. Add the tomatoes and sausage, and season to taste with salt and pepper. Simmer for 20 minutes, until the flavors have blended.

4. Remove the bay leaves. Serve hot.

Senate Navy Bean Soup

Although several senators are credited for its popularity, Joseph G. Cannon, U.S. Speaker of the House, 1903–1911, is the one most referenced. Various politicians have openly stated their affection for this soup as it appears on the menus of all eleven Capitol dining rooms.

SERVES 6 TO 8

2 cups dried white navy beans or black-eyed peas, debris removed, soaked overnight, and drained
1 meaty ham bone or 2 smoked ham hocks
12 cups water
1 teaspoon dried thyme
1 bay leaf
1 medium onion, finely chopped
2 medium celery ribs, finely chopped
1½ teaspoons finely minced garlic
1 cup mashed potatoes (optional)
¼ cup chopped fresh parsley
Salt and pepper
Minced fresh chives, to serve (optional)

1. Combine the beans, ham bone, water, thyme, and bay leaf in a large soup pot or saucepan over high heat. Bring to a boil, skim off any foam that rises to the surface, then reduce the heat, cover, and simmer for 2 hours, until the beans are tender.

2. Stir in the onion, celery, garlic, potatoes, if using, and parsley. Season to taste with salt and pepper, and simmer for 30 minutes, until the vegetables are tender.

3. Remove the ham bone and bay leaf from the pot. Remove the meat from the bone and cut into small pieces. Return the meat to the pot and discard the bone. Taste and adjust the seasoning as needed.

4. Garnish each bowl with a sprinkling of chives, if using, and serve hot.

Bouillabaisse

If you were a fisherman in the South of France, this seafood stew would be the typical "catch of the day" special. It is distinguished from cioppino, the famous seafood soup of San Francisco, by the presence of saffron and fennel in the broth. Try to make it with a variety of fish and seafood, and be sure to serve it with crusty French bread.

SERVES 4 TO 6

3 tablespoons oil
1 medium onion, diced
1 medium fennel bulb, trimmed and diced
    4 cups fish broth (page 118) or chicken broth (page 119)
1 (15-ounce) can diced tomatoes
1½ teaspoons minced garlic
¼ teaspoon saffron threads
Salt and pepper
Pinch of crushed red pepper (optional)
24 small hard-shell clams or mussels
1½ pounds firm white fish fillets, cut into large chunks
¾ pound shrimp, peeled and deveined
¾ pound sea scallops
1 tablespoon Pernod or other anise-flavored liqueur

1. Heat the oil in a large soup pot or saucepan over medium-high heat. Add the onion and fennel and sauté until the onion is translucent, about 3 minutes.

2. Add the broth, tomatoes, garlic, and saffron. Bring to a boil, reduce the heat, and simmer for 10 minutes. Season to taste with salt and pepper, and crushed red pepper, if using.

3. Add the clams to the broth and continue to cook, covered, for 5 minutes. Add the fish, cover, and cook for another 5 minutes, until the clams begin to open.

4. Add the shrimp, scallops, and Pernod to the broth and cook for 3 to 5 minutes, until all the seafood is cooked through.

5. Taste and adjust the seasoning as needed. Serve hot.

Cioppino

Italian immigrants brought their fish stews to America. Many speculate that cioppino (pronounced cho-PEEN-o) first became famous in San Francisco. The seafood may vary depending on the catch of the day, but it usually includes crab.

SERVES 4 TO 6

2 tablespoons oil
2 leeks, white parts only, trimmed and thinly sliced
1 medium onion, diced
1 medium green bell pepper, seeded and diced
1 (28-ounce) can diced tomatoes
1 (8-ounce) can tomato sauce
1½ teaspoons minced garlic
½ teaspoon dried thyme
1 bay leaf
2 cups dry white wine
Salt and pepper
12 small hard-shell clams, shucked (liquor reserved)
1 pound firm white fish fillets, cut into 2-inch chunks
1 pound shrimp, peeled and deveined
1 pint shucked oysters with liquor
2 pounds lump crabmeat

1. Heat the oil in a large soup pot or saucepan over medium-high heat. Add the leeks, onion, and bell pepper and sauté until softened, about 5 minutes.

2. Add the tomatoes, tomato sauce, garlic, thyme, and bay leaf. Cover, reduce the heat, and simmer for 2 hours.

3. Add the wine. Season to taste with salt and pepper and simmer for 10 minutes.

4. Layer the clams, fish, and shrimp in a separate large pot. Pour the tomato mixture over. Cover and simmer for 5 to 7 minutes, until the seafood is almost cooked through. Add the oysters and crabmeat and cook for 3 more minutes.

5. Remove the bay leaf. Taste and adjust the seasoning as needed. Serve hot.

Shrimp and Crab Gumbo

The catch of the day in the bayous of Louisiana is often turned into a soup that is thickened with a browned paste of flour and fat called "roux." The roux and filé powder (ground sassafras) gives gumbo its unique flavor.

SERVES 6 TO 8

¼ cup plus 1 tablespoon oil
¼ cup all-purpose flour
1 medium onion, diced
1 medium green bell pepper, seeded and diced
2 medium celery ribs, thinly sliced
1 teaspoon minced garlic
6 cups fish broth or chicken broth (page 119)
1 pound fresh or frozen okra, trimmed (about 4 cups)
½ pound andouille or other spicy smoked sausage, sliced
2 bay leaves
½ teaspoon dried thyme
½ teaspoon cayenne pepper
Salt and pepper
1½ pounds shrimp, peeled and deveined
1 pound lump crabmeat
Filé powder
4 to 6 cups cooked white rice, to serve

1. Combine ¼ cup oil and the flour in a large frying pan, stirring with a wooden spoon until you have a smooth paste. Cook over medium heat, stirring frequently, until the roux is a rich chocolate brown, 20 to 30 minutes. Set aside.

2. Heat the remaining 1 tablespoon oil in a large soup pot or saucepan over medium-high heat. Add the onion, bell pepper, celery, and garlic and sauté until the onion is translucent, about 5 minutes.

3. Add the broth and carefully stir in the roux. Add the okra, sausage, bay leaves, thyme, and cayenne pepper. Season to taste with salt and pepper. Bring to a boil, reduce the heat, and simmer for about 30 minutes.

4. Add the shrimp, crabmeat, and filé powder. Taste and adjust the seasonings as needed. Simmer for another 5 minutes.

5. Remove the bay leaves. Ladle the gumbo over rice in large soup bowls and serve.

New England Fish Chowder

When the first settlers arrived in what we know today as New England, seafood was abundant along the Atlantic shore. Although clam chowder became the most famous of New England soups, all kinds of seafood found its way into the chowder pots.

SERVES 4 TO 6

¼ pound salt pork, rinsed and chopped
1 medium onion, diced
2 medium celery ribs, diced
4 medium waxy potatoes, such as thin-skinned red or white, peeled and diced
4 cups fish broth (page 118) or bottled clam juice
1½ pounds firm white fish fillets, cut into 1-inch chunks
1 cup half-and half
Salt and pepper

1. Cook the salt pork in a large soup pot or saucepan over medium heat until it has rendered its fat, about 4 minutes. Increase the heat to medium-high and continue to cook until it begins to brown, about 3 to 4 minutes. Add the onion and celery and continue to cook until the onion is soft, about 4 minutes.

2. Add the potatoes and broth. Bring to a boil, reduce the heat, and simmer until the potatoes are tender, about 20 minutes.

3. Stir in the fish and simmer, covered, until the fish is just cooked, about 3 minutes. Add the half-and-half. Taste and add salt and pepper as needed. Heat just long enough to bring the liquid back to a simmer. Serve hot.

Salmon-Corn Chowder

Salmon are saltwater fish that spawn in fresh water. Their pink flesh stands out among other fish. This distinctive chowder includes the smoky taste of bacon, a bit of white wine, a slight touch of cayenne pepper, and hearty diced potatoes.

SERVES 6 TO 8

¼ pound thick-sliced bacon, chopped
2 medium onions, diced
¾ cup dry white wine
1 cup bottled clam juice
1 cup milk
½ teaspoon dried thyme
⅛ teaspoon cayenne pepper
4 medium waxy potatoes, such as thin-skinned red or white, peeled and diced
Kernels from 4 sweet corn ears (3 to 4 cups)
1 cup heavy cream
1¼ pounds salmon fillet, skinned and cut into 1-inch pieces
Salt and pepper
¼ cup minced fresh chives, to serve

1. Fry the bacon over medium heat in a large soup pot or saucepan until nearly crisp and lightly browned, about 10 minutes. Remove the bacon and set aside on paper towels to drain.

2. Add the onions to the pan and sauté, stirring occasionally, until golden, 5 to 7 minutes.

3. Pour in the wine and boil over high heat until reduced by half, about 3 minutes. Add the clam juice, milk, thyme, and cayenne pepper and bring to a boil. Add the potatoes, reduce the heat to medium, and cook for 8 minutes, until the potatoes are tender but still medium-firm.

4. Add the corn and cream and cook for 3 to 5 minutes longer, until the corn is almost tender but still slightly crunchy.

5. Season the salmon with salt and pepper. Add to the soup along with the bacon and simmer until the fish is just opaque, 5 to 7 minutes.

6. Taste and adjust the seasoning as needed. Serve hot, sprinkling some chives on each serving.

New England Clam Chowder

There are chowder houses all along the coast of New England—family restaurants whose reputations rest on the quality of the milk-based clam soup they serve. The only proper accompaniment to this clam chowder is pilot crackers—unsalted crackers that are a direct descendant of hardtack, which sailors ate in place of bread on long voyages. If you can't find pilot crackers, unsalted saltines will do.

SERVES 4 TO 6

½ cup dry white wine
5 pounds hard-shell clams, such as Manila or
    littleneck
¼ cup rinsed and finely chopped salt pork
    (rind removed)
1 small onion, chopped
2½ cups milk
1 cup heavy cream
3 medium waxy potatoes, such as thin-skinned
    red or white, peeled and diced
2 tablespoons butter
Salt and pepper

1. Heat the wine in a large saucepot over medium-high heat. Add the clams, cover, and cook until the clams have opened, 5 to 10 minutes depending on the size of the clams. Remove the clams from the pot, discarding any that are unopened, and remove the clams from the shells. Coarsely chop the clams and set aside. Strain the clam liquor through cheesecloth or a clean kitchen towel to remove sand, and set aside.

2. Fry the salt pork in a large soup pot or saucepan over medium heat until crisp, about 10 minutes. Add the onion and sauté until golden, about 10 minutes.

3. Add the clam liquor, milk, cream, and potatoes. Simmer until the potatoes are tender, about 20 minutes.

4. Stir in the butter and clams. Cook for 2 to 3 more minutes. Season to taste with salt and pepper, and serve hot.

TIP: If fresh clams are not available when making clam chowder, skip step 1 and substitute the liquid from 4 (7-ounce) cans chopped clams (setting the clams aside).

Manhattan Clam Chowder

No one really knows how this red chowder got its name, but its tomato base and other savory flavors offer a tangy variation to the cream-based New England clam chowder. Serve with pilot crackers or toasted garlic bread.

SERVES 4 TO 6

½ cup water or red wine
5 pounds hard-shell clams, such as Manila or
    littleneck
3 slices bacon, chopped
1 medium onion, diced
1 medium celery rib, diced
1 medium carrot, diced
3 cups tomato juice
2 medium waxy potatoes, such as thin-skinned
    red or white, peeled and diced
1 (28-ounce) can diced tomatoes, undrained
1 bay leaf
1 teaspoon salt, plus more to taste
1 teaspoon chopped fresh thyme
¼ teaspoon black pepper, plus more to taste
2 tablespoons chopped fresh parsley

1. Heat the water or red wine in a large saucepot over medium-high heat. Add the clams, cover, and cook until the clams have opened, 5 to 10 minutes, depending upon the size of the clams. Remove the clams from the pot, discarding any that are not open, and remove the clams from the shells and set aside. Strain the clam liquor through cheesecloth or a clean kitchen towel to remove the sand, and set aside.

2. Fry the bacon over medium-high heat in a large soup pot or saucepan until lightly browned, about 5 minutes. Add the onion, celery, and carrot and sauté until tender, about 5 minutes.

3. Add the tomato juice, potatoes, clam liquor, tomatoes, bay leaf, salt, thyme, and black pepper. Bring to a boil, reduce the heat, and simmer, covered, for 20 minutes, until the potatoes are tender.

4. Add the clams and cook for 2 to 3 more minutes. Remove the bay leaf and add the parsley. Taste and adjust the seasoning as needed. Serve hot.

Shrimp Bisque

What makes a soup a bisque? A bisque is traditionally a thick cream soup made of shellfish or puréed fish that is usually thickened with rice rather than flour. Its rich taste and texture makes it an elegant first course or a stand-alone dinner. Small shrimp with shells on will work fine in this recipe.

SERVES 4 TO 6

3 tablespoons butter
¼ cup finely diced onion
¼ cup finely diced celery
¼ cup finely diced carrot
1 (15-ounce) can diced tomatoes, drained
2 tablespoons oil
1 pound shrimp
5 cups shrimp broth (see tip), fish broth
   (page 118), or chicken broth (page 119)
½ cup vermouth or dry white wine
½ cup uncooked rice
1 cup heavy cream
Salt and pepper

1. Melt 1 tablespoon of butter in a large soup pot or saucepan over medium heat. Add the onion, celery, and carrot and sauté until the vegetables are soft but not browned, about 5 minutes. Add the tomatoes and sauté for another 5 minutes. Scrape out into a bowl and reserve.

2. Return the pan to medium heat and heat the oil. Add the shrimp and cook until the shells are red and crisp, 4 to 5 minutes. Remove from the pan and let cool.

3. While the shrimp are cooling, heat the broth and vermouth in a large saucepan over medium-high heat. Add the sautéed vegetables and the rice. Bring to a boil, reduce the heat, partially cover, and simmer for 20 minutes.

4. Meanwhile, peel the cooled shrimp.

5. Purée the soup in a blender and strain back into the pot through a fine-mesh strainer.

6. Purée half the shrimp in the blender, slowly adding enough hot broth to completely purée them. Add to the pot.

7. Whisk in the remaining 2 tablespoons butter and the cream. Season to taste with salt and pepper. Cover, reduce heat to low, and cook for 10 minutes to allow the flavors to blend.

8. Divide the remaining whole shrimp among the soup bowls, ladle in the hot soup, and serve.

TIP: To make shrimp broth, in a medium saucepan, heat 1 tablespoon oil over medium heat. Add 1 pound shrimp shells and cook for 3 to 4 minutes, until the shells have all turned pink. Add 6 cups water and simmer on low with the lid on for 20 minutes, then strain. It takes a lot of shrimp to make 1 pound of shells. You can accumulate them in the freezer over time.

Lobster Bisque

There was a time in American history when lobsters were so common they were considered food for the poor. In Maine, at the end of the nineteenth century, one dozen lobsters sold for twenty-five cents. This classic French soup, if made back then, would not have been the sheer extravagance it is today.

SERVES 4 TO 6

5 cups water
3 cups fish broth (page 118) or chicken broth
   (page 119)
2 live lobsters, 1 to 1½ pounds each
4 tablespoons (½ stick) butter
¼ cup finely diced onion
¼ cup finely diced celery
¼ cup finely diced carrot
1 (15-ounce) can diced tomatoes, drained
1 tablespoon cognac or brandy
1 cup heavy cream
Salt and pepper

1. Combine the water and broth in a very large pot and bring to a boil. Place the lobsters tail first into the pot, cover, and cook for 12 minutes, until the lobsters are bright red. Remove the lobsters from the broth and set aside to cool.

2. Remove the meat from the shells and chop, reserving the shells. Set the meat aside. Return the shells to the broth and simmer for 45 minutes.

3. Pour the broth through a fine-mesh strainer into a large bowl. Measure the broth and add enough water to make 6 cups. Discard the solids, and set aside.

4. Melt 1 tablespoon of butter in a large soup pot or saucepan over medium heat. Add the onion, celery, and carrot and sauté until the vegetables are soft but not browned, about 5 minutes. Add the tomatoes and sauté for another 5 minutes. Add the broth and bring to a boil. Reduce the heat, partially cover, and simmer for 45 minutes.

5. Purée the soup in a blender and pour back through the strainer into the pot.

6. Purée half the lobster meat in the blender, slowly adding enough hot soup to completely purée the meat. Add to the pot.

7. Whisk in the remaining 3 tablespoons butter, the cognac, and cream. Season to taste with salt and pepper. Reduce heat to low and cook for 10 minutes to allow the flavors to blend.

8. Divide the remaining lobster pieces among 4 to 6 soup bowls, ladle in the hot soup, and serve.

Chicken Noodle Soup

No soup is as comforting as chicken noodle soup. Highly variable, the soup can be found in many forms, in many different cultures.

SERVES 6

8 cups chicken broth (page 119)
2 cups chopped or shredded cooked chicken
2 medium carrots, diced
2 medium celery ribs, diced
3 ounces uncooked egg noodles (about 2 cups)
Salt and pepper

1. Bring the broth to a boil in a large soup pot. Add the chicken, carrots, celery, and egg noodles. Stir well and let simmer until the noodles and vegetables are tender, 10 to 15 minutes.

2. Add salt and pepper to taste. Serve hot.

Chicken Soup with Rice

Replace the noodles in Chicken Noodle Soup with 1 cup long-grain rice and complete the recipe as directed.

Pennsylvania Dutch Chicken-Corn Soup

In Lancaster County, Pennsylvania, chicken-corn soup has been a favorite for generations. The noodles are often homemade, but store-bought noodles are perfectly acceptable. Plan on serving this hearty soup as a main dish.

SERVES 6

8 cups chicken broth (page 119)
¼ teaspoon saffron threads
Salt and pepper
3 ounces uncooked egg noodles (about 2 cups)
2 cups chopped or shredded cooked chicken
4 cups fresh or frozen corn
¼ cup minced fresh parsley
2 large eggs, lightly beaten

1. Bring the broth and saffron to a boil in a large soup pot or saucepan. Season to taste with salt and pepper. Add the egg noodles, stir well, and simmer for 5 minutes.

2. Stir in the chicken and corn, return the broth to a boil, and simmer for 3 minutes.

3. Add parsley. Slowly stir in the eggs in a swirling manner.

4. Test a noodle. It should be firm but not chewy. Taste and adjust the seasonings as needed. Serve hot.

Chicken Soup with Matzo Balls

During the Jewish holiday of Passover, leavened foods are not eaten. However, matzo, a thin, brittle bread made with only water and flour, can be eaten plain or ground into meal that can be used in baking and cooking. This soup, with dumplings made of matzo meal, is so popular that it is eaten year-round. These matzo balls are small, but sometimes a large, single ball (a little smaller than a tennis ball) is served with the bowl of chicken soup.

SERVES 4 TO 6

¼ cup oil
¼ cup water
3 large eggs
1 teaspoon salt
1 cup matzo meal
8 cups chicken broth (page 119)
2 cups shredded cooked chicken
2 medium carrots, diced
2 medium celery ribs, diced
2 sprigs fresh dill, chopped, plus more to serve

1. Whisk together the oil, water, eggs, and salt in a medium bowl. Stir in the matzo meal, cover, and refrigerate for at least 15 minutes.

2. Meanwhile, bring a large pot of salted water to a boil. Reduce the heat to medium-low to keep the water gently boiling.

3. Form the chilled matzo-meal batter into 1-inch balls and carefully ease into the water using a slotted spoon. Cover the pot and simmer for 15 minutes. The balls will puff up a little and rise to the top when done (firm and cooked through in the center). Remove them from the pot with the slotted spoon and set aside.

4. Meanwhile, bring the broth to a boil in a separate large soup pot or saucepan. Add the chicken, carrots, celery, and dill; reduce the heat and simmer, covered, until the vegetables are tender, about 15 minutes.

5. To serve, place 1 or 2 matzo balls in each bowl, ladle the soup over, and sprinkle with dill.

Avgolemono

This is comfort food, Greek style. This classic soup of chicken and rice is distinctively flavored with lemon and thickened with egg.

SERVES 6

6 cups chicken broth (page 119)
1 boneless, skinless chicken breast
Zest of 1 lemon, finely grated
⅔ cup uncooked long-grain rice
¼ cup lemon juice
3 large egg yolks
1 tablespoon chopped fresh mint or
    1 teaspoon dried
1 teaspoon dried oregano
1 tablespoon chopped fresh parsley
1 teaspoon black pepper
Salt

1. Bring the broth to a boil in a large saucepan. Reduce the heat and add the chicken breast with half the lemon zest. Cover and simmer for 15 minutes. Remove the chicken, let cool, then thinly slice.

2. Return the broth to a boil and add the rice. Reduce the heat to a simmer and cook for 20 minutes, until the rice is tender. Return the chicken to the soup and simmer.

3. Whisk the remaining zest, lemon juice, and egg yolks in a small bowl. Gradually add about 1 cup of hot soup to the lemon juice mixture. Very slowly stir this mixture into the simmering soup, continuing to stir until the soup thickens.

4. Stir in the mint, oregano, parsley, and pepper. Season to taste with salt and serve immediately.

Cock-a-Leekie Soup

Scottish immigrants brought their national dish, cock-a-leekie soup, to these shores. Some add Scotch whiskey in the end, but we'll leave that to your discretion. The prunes make this dish practically exotic.

SERVES 6

3 tablespoons butter
3 leeks, white parts only, trimmed and thinly sliced
6 to 8 cups chicken broth (page 119)
1 small waxy potato, such as thin-skinned red or white, peeled and diced
½ cup pearl barley
1 medium carrot, finely chopped
1 large celery rib, finely chopped
2 cups diced cooked chicken
2 cups half-and-half or milk
Salt and pepper
½ cup pitted prunes, cut into slivers, to serve

1. Melt the butter in a large soup pot or saucepan over medium heat. Add the leeks and sauté until softened but not browned, about 5 minutes.

2. Add the broth, potato, barley, carrot, and celery. Bring to a boil, reduce the heat, cover, and simmer for 30 minutes, until the potato and barley are tender.

3. Stir in the chicken and cream and simmer until heated through, about 10 minutes. Season to taste with salt and pepper.

4. Garnish each bowl with prune pieces and serve hot.

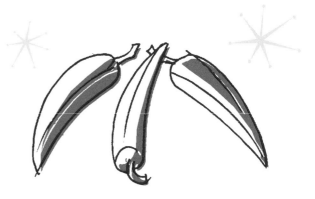

Chicken Gumbo

Gumbo is the soup most closely associated with Cajun cooking. It contains the "holy trinity" of onions, celery, and bell peppers, as well as the distinctive brown roux, which gives the soup its silky texture. Tasso is a smoked pickled pork sausage that gives this dish a unique smoky flavor. Smoked ham or andouille sausage will also work.

SERVES 6 TO 8

¼ cup oil
¼ cup all-purpose flour
¼ pound bacon
1 medium onion, diced
1 medium green bell pepper, seeded and diced
2 medium celery ribs, thinly sliced
2 jalapeño chile peppers, seeded and diced
1 teaspoon minced garlic
6 cups chicken broth (page 119)
1 pound fresh or frozen okra, trimmed and sliced
½ pound tasso or smoked ham, diced
1½ cups diced tomatoes, fresh or canned
¼ cup chopped fresh parsley
2 bay leaves
2 cups diced cooked chicken
2 tablespoons filé powder
Salt and pepper
½ teaspoon cayenne pepper
4 to 6 cups cooked white rice, to serve
Louisiana-style hot sauce, to serve

1. Combine the oil and flour in a large frying pan, stirring with a wooden spoon, until you have a smooth paste. Cook over medium heat, stirring frequently until the roux is a rich chocolate brown, 20 to 30 minutes. Set aside.

2. Fry the bacon in a large soup pot or saucepan over medium heat until crisp, 10 to 15 minutes. Remove the bacon and reserve for another use.

3. Add the onion, green pepper, celery, jalapeños, and garlic to the bacon fat and sauté over medium heat until the onion is limp, about 4 minutes.

4. Add the chicken broth and carefully stir in the roux. Add the okra, tasso, tomatoes, parsley, and bay leaves. Bring to a boil, stirring frequently; reduce the heat and simmer for about 30 minutes.

5. Add the chicken and filé powder. Season to taste with salt, pepper, and cayenne pepper. Simmer for another 15 minutes.

6. Remove the bay leaves. To serve, ladle the gumbo over rice in large soup bowls. Pass the hot sauce at the table.

Mulligatawny Soup

Mulligatawny comes from the southern Indian (Tamil) word for "pepper water" or "pepper broth." The spicy soup became popular with the British stationed in India during colonial times. When the British troops returned home, they brought with them the taste for this rich curried soup, which ultimately made its way across the Atlantic to America.

SERVES 6

2 tablespoons butter
2 medium celery ribs, diced
1 medium carrot, diced
1 medium onion, diced
1 green chile pepper, such as jalapeño, seeded and diced
1 tablespoon curry powder
4 cups chicken broth (page 119)
¼ cup red lentils, rinsed and debris removed
Salt and pepper
½ cup coconut milk or heavy cream
¾ cup cooked long-grain white rice (preferably basmati)
½ to 1 cup shredded cooked chicken
1 medium tart green apple, finely chopped
¼ cup chopped fresh parsley, to serve

1. Melt the butter in a large soup pot or saucepan over medium heat. Add the celery, carrot, onion, and chile pepper and sauté until the onion is translucent, about 3 minutes. Stir in the curry powder and cook for a minute.

2. Pour in the broth, add the lentils, and bring to a boil. Reduce the heat and simmer, partially covered, until the lentils are tender, 30 to 45 minutes.

3. Season the soup to taste with salt and pepper. Purée in a blender and return to the pot.

4. Bring the soup to a simmer over medium heat. Stir in the coconut milk, rice, chicken, and apple. Cook long enough to heat through. Taste and adjust the seasonings as needed. Serve hot, garnishing each bowl with the parsley.

Mexican Tortilla Soup

Never letting anything go to waste, many cooks in Mexico use leftover tortillas in this tomato-based chicken soup. It's a meal-in-a-bowl, with rich contrasts in flavors and textures.

SERVES 6

6 corn tortillas, cut into strips
1 tablespoon oil
Salt
8 cups chicken broth (page 119)
1 cup tomato purée
1 green chile pepper, such as jalapeño, seeded and cut into strips
1 canned chipotle chile pepper in adobo sauce, minced
2 cups chopped cooked chicken
Black pepper
1 medium lime, cut into wedges, to serve
1 large avocado, peeled, pitted, and diced, to serve
2 cups shredded Monterey Jack cheese (about 8 ounces), to serve
Sour cream, to serve

1. Preheat the oven to 425°F.

2. Toss the tortillas with the oil in a medium bowl and spread out in a single layer on a baking sheet. Bake until crisp, about 10 minutes. Season with salt and transfer to paper towels to absorb excess oil.

3. Heat the broth, tomato purée, and chile pepper in a large soup pot or saucepan over medium-high heat until boiling. Reduce the heat and simmer for 20 minutes to allow the flavors to blend. Add the chicken and continue to simmer until heated through, about 5 minutes. Season to taste with salt and pepper.

4. To serve, ladle the soup into bowls and top with the tortilla strips. Pass the lime wedges, avocado, shredded cheese, and sour cream at the table.

Leftover Turkey Soup

The Thanksgiving turkey always provides plenty of leftovers. After a few days of sandwiches and maybe a pot pie or casserole, the turkey carcass remains. Don't let it go to waste: Make soup.

SERVES 6

Carcass from 1 roasted turkey
Leftover gravy (optional)
2 medium onions, cut into large chunks
4 medium celery ribs, cut into large chunks
1 bunch parsley
1 bay leaf
Salt
1 sprig fresh thyme or ½ teaspoon dried
3 tablespoons uncooked rice
1 medium carrot, thinly sliced
1 cup diced cooked turkey

1. Break the carcass into 4 or 5 pieces. Cover with water in a large soup pot. Add the leftover gravy (if using), onions, celery, parsley, bay leaf, some salt, and thyme. Bring to a boil. Reduce the heat and simmer for 2 to 3 hours.

2. Remove the turkey pieces and pour the liquid through a fine-mesh strainer into a large bowl, pressing on the solids to extract as much flavor as possible.

3. Return the strained soup to the pot. Skim off the fat and season with salt as needed. Bring to a boil. Add the rice and carrot and simmer for 15 to 20 minutes, until the rice is tender.

4. Add the turkey and simmer long enough to heat through, about 10 minutes. Serve hot.

Beef Barley Soup

This rib-sticking soup has old-fashioned flavor. Serve it as a main course, accompanied by toasted bread and a green salad.

SERVES 6 TO 8

2 tablespoons oil
2½ cups diced beef stew meat
6 cups beef broth (page 118)
1 medium onion, diced
1 bay leaf
2 teaspoons salt, plus more to taste
¼ teaspoon black pepper, plus more to taste
½ cup pearl barley
3 medium celery ribs, diced
2 medium carrots, diced
1 leek, white part only, trimmed and sliced
½ teaspoon dried thyme

1. Heat the oil in a large soup pot or saucepan over medium-high heat. Add the meat and brown on all sides, about 12 minutes.

2. Add the broth, onion, bay leaf, salt, and pepper. Bring to a boil, reduce the heat, and simmer, covered, for 1½ hours.

3. Stir in the barley, celery, carrots, leek, and thyme. Simmer for 30 minutes, until the meat is completely tender.

4. Discard the bay leaf. Taste and adjust the seasonings as needed. Serve hot.

Meatball-Tomato Soup

Meatballs are always popular, whether served with spaghetti, packed into a sub sandwich, or in this tasty, tomato-based broth.

SERVES 4 TO 6

3 cups beef broth (page 118)
1 (15-ounce) can diced tomatoes
1 pound ground beef or ground turkey
1 large egg, lightly beaten
½ cup fresh bread crumbs
1 teaspoon dried oregano
½ teaspoon salt, plus more to taste
¼ teaspoon black pepper, plus more to taste
2 tablespoons oil
1 medium onion, finely chopped
2 medium carrots, diced
2 medium celery ribs, diced
⅓ cup uncooked rice
1 teaspoon dried oregano
1 teaspoon dried thyme
1 bay leaf

1. Combine the broth and tomatoes in a large soup pot or saucepan and simmer over low heat for 10 minutes

2. Meanwhile, combine the beef, egg, bread crumbs, oregano, salt, and pepper in a large bowl. Using your hands, combine the mixture until thoroughly blended, then shape 18 to 24 meatballs, about 1 inch in diameter.

3. Heat the oil in a large skillet over medium-high heat. Add a single layer of meatballs and brown on all sides, about 8 minutes. Transfer the meatballs

to the pot containing the broth mixture. Add another layer of meatballs to the skillet and continue browning until all the meatballs are cooked.

4. Sauté the onion in the oil remaining in the skillet until soft and translucent, about 3 minutes. Transfer to the soup.

5. Add the carrots, celery, rice, oregano, thyme, and bay leaf to the soup. Season to taste with salt and pepper. Bring to a boil, reduce the heat, and simmer until the rice and vegetables are tender, about 20 minutes.

6. Remove the bay leaf. Taste and adjust the seasonings as needed. Serve hot.

Hamburger Soup

If American goulash (hamburger, macaroni, and tomatoes) is a favorite dish of school kids, this soup has to be a close second.

SERVES 4 TO 6

1 tablespoon oil
1 pound ground beef or ground turkey
1 medium onion, finely chopped
3 cups beef broth (page 118)
1 (28-ounce) can diced tomatoes
3 tablespoons chili powder
2 teaspoons Worcestershire sauce
Salt and pepper
1 cup uncooked elbow macaroni
1 cup frozen corn
1 cup frozen green beans or peas
Grated Parmesan cheese (optional), to serve

1. Heat the oil in a large soup pot or saucepan over medium-high heat. Add the meat and brown, about 8 minutes, stirring to break up any clumps. Add the onion and sauté until soft and translucent, about 3 minutes. Drain off any fat.

2. Add the broth, tomatoes, chili powder, and Worcestershire sauce. Season to taste with salt and pepper. Bring to a boil. Stir in the macaroni, reduce the heat, and simmer until the macaroni is tender, 15 to 20 minutes.

3. Stir in the corn and green beans or peas. Simmer until tender and heated through, about 10 minutes. Serve hot, passing the cheese, if using, at the table.

Beef Broth

There is no question that making beef broth takes time. If you prefer, you can substitute canned beef broth in any recipe calling for beef broth.

MAKES ABOUT 10 CUPS

5 pounds beef bones
2 medium carrots, quartered
2 medium onions, quartered
2 medium celery ribs, quartered
16 cups cold water, plus more as needed

1. Preheat the oven to 425°F. Lightly grease a large roasting pan.

2. Put the bones in the prepared pan and roast for 15 minutes. Add the vegetables and continue roasting for 45 minutes, until the bones are well browned.

3. Transfer the bones and vegetables to a large soup pot.

4. Add 2 cups of cold water to the roasting pan and stir, scraping up any browned bits. Add to the soup pot along with the remaining 14 cups water, to cover the bones.

5. Bring to a boil over high heat, skim off any foam that rises to the surface, reduce the heat, and simmer for 8 hours, skimming off additional foam as needed. The bones should stay covered; add water as needed.

6. Strain into another large pot and discard the solids. Chill, covered, in the refrigerator for up to 3 days, or freeze for 4 to 5 months. Remove the layer of fat that hardens on the surface of the broth before using.

Vegetable Broth

This broth can fill in for chicken broth when cooking for vegetarians.

MAKES 3½ TO 4 QUARTS

2 medium carrots, quartered
2 leeks, trimmed and chopped
1 large onion, quartered
¼ small head green cabbage, cored and chopped

4 garlic cloves
1 bunch fresh parsley
4 sprigs fresh thyme
1 cup dried porcini mushrooms
4 quarts water
1 cup dry white wine
1 tablespoon black peppercorns
Salt (optional)

1. Combine the carrots, leeks, onion, cabbage, garlic, parsley, thyme, and mushrooms in a large soup pot or saucepan. Add the water. Cover, bring to a boil, reduce the heat, and simmer for 30 minutes.

2. Add the wine and peppercorns and continue to simmer, covered, for 10 minutes. Strain into a clean pot and discard all the solids.

3. Season to taste with salt, if using. Use immediately or cool, cover, and refrigerate. The broth will keep for about 5 days in the refrigerator or 4 to 5 months in the freezer.

Fish Broth

To make fish broth, you will need fish heads and bones from your local fish monger. If this proves difficult, substitute bottled clam juice for fish broth in your next recipe.

MAKES ABOUT 6 CUPS

2 pounds fish heads and bones, well rinsed and drained
1 medium onion, quartered
1 medium carrot, quartered
1 medium celery rib, quartered
1 bunch fresh parsley
6 cups water
1 cup dry white wine

1. Combine all the ingredients in a large soup pot or saucepan. Bring to a boil. Reduce the heat and simmer for 40 minutes, skimming off any foam that rises to the surface.

2. Strain into a clean pot. Cool, cover, and refrigerate until you are ready to use it. Fish broth will keep for 2 days in the refrigerator or 3 to 4 months in the freezer.

Chicken Broth

When a recipe calls for chicken broth and/or cooked chicken, this is the place to start.

MAKES 2 TO 3 QUARTS, PLUS ABOUT 8 CUPS COOKED CHICKEN

3 to 4 pounds chicken parts
1 large onion, quartered
4 medium celery ribs, chopped
4 garlic cloves
1 bunch fresh parsley
4 quarts water
Salt (optional)

1. Combine the chicken, onion, celery, garlic, and parsley in a large soup pot or saucepan. Add the water. Cover and bring just to a boil. Immediately reduce the heat and simmer gently for 2 hours with the lid partially on. Season to taste with salt, if using.

2. Strain into a clean pot and discard the vegetables. Remove the meat from the bones.

3. Refrigerate or freeze the meat. Chill the broth for several hours. Skim off and discard the fat that rises to the surface and hardens. Use the broth immediately or cool, cover, and refrigerate. The broth and meat will keep for about 3 days in the refrigerator or 4 to 5 months in the freezer.

Turkey Broth

You can make a perfectly acceptable soup broth with a leftover roasted turkey carcass. Turkey broth can be used in any soup calling for chicken broth.

MAKES ABOUT 10 CUPS

Carcass from 1 roasted turkey
1 medium carrot, cut into large chunks
2 medium onions, cut into large chunks
4 medium celery ribs, cut into large chunks
1 bunch fresh parsley
1 bay leaf
Salt (optional)

1. Break the carcass into 4 or 5 pieces. Cover with cold water in a large soup pot. Add the carrot, onions, celery, parsley, and bay leaf. Bring to a boil. Reduce the heat and simmer for 1½ hours.

2. Remove the turkey pieces and strain the liquid, pressing on the solids to extract as much flavor as possible. Season with salt, if using.

3. Remove any meat from the bones and finely chop; discard the bones. Chill the broth and meat, in separate covered containers, in the refrigerator for up to 3 days, or freeze for 4 to 5 months. Remove the layer of fat that hardens on the surface of the broth before using.

Defatting Soup

▰▱▰▱▰▱▰▱▰▱

Nobody needs extra fat calories in his or her soup. Removing excess fat is easy. Most of these tips work for stews as well.

▶ If you have the time, make the soup a day ahead. Chill the soup in the refrigerator overnight. The fat will rise to the surface and harden. You will then be able to easily lift the fat off and discard it. As an added bonus, the flavors will improve overnight.

▶ If you have just a couple of hours, you can chill the soup and the fat will harden so you can lift it off.

▶ With the back of a large metal spoon, gently swirl in a circular motion from the center outward, scooping up the fat along the edges.

▶ Wrap a few ice cubes in paper towels and skim them over the top of the soup.

▶ Substitute smoked turkey for ham or sausage in soups to reduce the amount of fat. Replace bacon or salt pork with olive oil. You will lose flavor, but you can replace it with a little chopped smoked turkey.

CHAPTER SIX

Fish and Shellfish

When settlers first came to these shores, they were blessed with an abundance of seafood. Cod was so plentiful off the shores of the northern colonies that they named a great tract of land "Cape Cod." Lobsters, some six feet in length and weighing twenty-five to thirty pounds, filled the harbors. There were rivers teeming with trout and salmon, and lakes filled with perch, bass, and carp.

No doubt this abundance made a difference to the colonists, who persevered under harsh conditions. The heavily forested land required clearing before crops could be planted or animals grazed. Oysters harvested from the Elizabeth River enabled the first colonists in Virginia to survive a winter of scarcity, when the normal ration for each person was one pint of ground corn per week. Fish of all kinds were so plentiful that when the settlers planted corn, they used fish as a fertilizer—a method learned from friendly natives. According to early American historical records, mill workers and prisoners protested their daily diet of salmon or lobster. This ready supply, and the more casual life of the new Americans, created traditions that are with us today—clam fritters, seafood Newburg, the Maryland crab boil, and the Cajun crawfish boil. The alfresco seafood feast is a living part of our American culinary tradition.

New Englanders, with their penchant for simple foods, created dishes we still enjoy today—simple combinations like oyster stew or chowders made with fish, shellfish, and cream. Meanwhile, Creole and Cajun cooks performed their magic with spice, peppers, and tomatoes to create mouth-tingling dishes like shrimp Creole and crawfish étouffée.

As settlers moved west, they discovered vast networks of rivers, streams, lakes, and bayous that produced plenty of fresh fish and shellfish. Then they found the Pacific coast, with its Olympia oyster beds, Dungeness crabs, and razor clams. When it comes to fish and shellfish, American resources abound from sea to shining sea.

Many of the recipes in this chapter specify a particular type of fish or shellfish, but in some, whatever fish looks and smells best at the market may be substituted.

Fried Fish Fillets with Hushpuppies

Using cornmeal, as in this recipe, is the Southern way to fry fish. Make sure you season the cornmeal generously with black pepper. Hushpuppies are the traditional accompaniment. In the old days, a cook would add the milk that the fish soaked in to the leftover cornmeal and add an egg to make it all hold together. Balls of this batter were then dropped in hot fat to fry and fed to the dogs to keep them quiet.

SERVES 4

Oil, for frying
1½ pounds firm white fish fillets cut into
    4- to 6-ounce pieces
1 cup milk or buttermilk
1 cup yellow cornmeal
¾ cup dry bread crumbs
Salt and pepper
Pinch of cayenne pepper
Hushpuppies (recipe follows), to serve

1. Heat at least 2 inches of oil in a large, deep skillet to 375°F.

2. While the oil heats, soak the fish fillets in the milk.

3. Mix the cornmeal and bread crumbs in a shallow bowl. Season with salt, lots of pepper, and the cayenne pepper. Dredge the fish in the cornmeal, patting to make the breading stick.

4. Fry until golden on both sides, about 6 to 8 minutes total. Remove with a slotted spoon and drain well on paper towels. Serve hot with hushpuppies on the side.

Hushpuppies

If you don't mind the extra work, these traditional cornmeal dabs go perfectly with fried fish. Instead of using fresh cornmeal and fresh buttermilk, you can use the leftover crumb mixture and the leftover cornmeal from the fish for this recipe.

SERVES 4

2½ cups yellow cornmeal
2 teaspoons finely chopped onion
1 teaspoon salt
1 teaspoon baking soda
1½ cups buttermilk
2 cups oil, for frying

1. In a large bowl, combine the cornmeal, onion, salt, and baking soda. Stir in the buttermilk and mix until stiff (cornmeal will swell).

2. Heat the oil in a large, deep saucepan to 375°F. Carefully drop a small bit of cornmeal mix into the hot fat; when the dough bubbles and sizzles the oil is ready. Make spoon-size balls of the batter and carefully drop into the oil. Don't crowd the pan. Cook until golden brown on both sides, about 2 minutes total. Remove with a slotted spoon and drain on paper towels. Serve hot.

Batter-Fried Fish Fillets with Tartar Sauce

This is the fish to serve with chips—that is, french fries. The British call fries "chips," and they call their potato chips "crisps." If you are making french fries, you'll see that the potatoes are twice fried. Fry them once, then fry the fish. While the fish are draining, fry the potatoes a second time, and serve the fish and chips together. The British eat fish and chips with salt and malt vinegar, while Americans prefer tartar sauce and ketchup.

SERVES 4

1 cup all-purpose flour
1 teaspoon baking powder
1 teaspoon salt
½ teaspoon black pepper
1 cup milk
1 large egg
Oil, for frying

1½ pounds firm white fish fillets, cut into
    4- to 6-ounce pieces
Tartar sauce (recipe follows), to serve

1. Stir together the flour, baking powder, salt, and pepper in a shallow bowl. Beat in the milk and egg until smooth.

2. Heat at least 2 inches of oil in a large, deep skillet to 375°F.

3. Dip the fish in the batter, one piece at a time. Let the excess batter drip off, then slide the fish pieces into the oil and fry for 2 to 3 minutes per ¼ inch of thickness. Remove with a slotted spoon and drain on paper towels. Continue until all the pieces are cooked. Serve hot, passing the tartar sauce at the table.

Tartar Sauce

This sauce is the classic complement to fried fish and shellfish. Add cayenne pepper for a spicy version, or add chopped fresh basil for a richer, herbed flavor.

MAKES ABOUT 1 CUP

¾ cup mayonnaise
¼ cup snipped fresh dill or sweet pickle
2 tablespoons finely chopped onion
1 tablespoon chopped fresh parsley
2 teaspoons drained capers
½ teaspoon white vinegar

1. Combine the mayonnaise, dill, onion, parsley, capers, and vinegar in a small bowl and mix well.

2. Refrigerate for 1 hour or more to allow the flavors to blend (overnight is best).

Fish Cakes

Before there were frozen fish sticks, there were delicious homemade fish cakes. These light, crispy cakes are loved by adults and kids alike.

SERVES 4

1½ pounds baking potatoes, peeled and cut
    into large chunks
1 pound firm white fish fillets
1 medium onion, finely chopped
3 tablespoons chopped fresh parsley
2 teaspoons seafood seasoning mix, such as
    Old Bay or Zatarain's
½ teaspoon hot pepper sauce, such as Tabasco
Salt and pepper
Oil, for frying
Tartar sauce (this page), to serve

1. Cover the potatoes with salted water in a medium saucepan. Cover the saucepan and bring to a boil. Boil until the potatoes are very soft, 15 to 20 minutes. Drain well. Run the potatoes through a ricer or mash with a potato masher.

2. Fill a second medium saucepan with salted water and bring to a boil. Add the fish, reduce the heat to maintain a simmer, and poach the fish until it flakes easily with a fork, 5 to 10 minutes. Drain well. Finely chop the fish.

3. Combine the fish and potatoes in a large bowl. Add the onion, parsley, seafood seasoning, and hot pepper sauce. Mix well. Season to taste with salt and pepper.

4. Use your hands to shape the mixture into 8 cakes, each about ½ inch thick.

5. Heat ¼ inch of oil in a large skillet over medium heat. Add a single layer of fish cakes and cook until browned on both sides, 7 to 10 minutes total. Drain on paper towels while you cook the remaining cakes. Serve hot, passing the tartar sauce at the table.

Salt Cod Cakes

Substitute 1 pound salt cod for the fresh fish in the Fish Cakes. Freshen the salt cod first, by soaking it in three changes of water over a period of 18 hours in the refrigerator. Poach the salt cod for 10 minutes in unsalted water and complete the recipe as directed.

Oven-Fried Fish Fillets

When you don't want to go through the fuss of deep frying, oven frying is the perfect, less–fattening alternative. This recipe coats the fish in milk and bread crumbs before frying.

SERVES 4

3 tablespoons butter, melted
1½ pounds firm white fish fillets, cut into
    4- to 6-ounce pieces
1½ cups milk or buttermilk
1½ cups fresh bread crumbs
Salt and pepper
Lemon wedges, to serve
Tartar sauce (page 123), cocktail sauce
    (page 65), or salsa (page 56), to serve

1. Preheat the oven to 500°F. Generously brush a baking sheet with half of the butter.

2. While the oven preheats, soak the fish in the milk.

3. Put the bread crumbs in a large bowl and season with salt and pepper. Dredge the fish in the bread crumbs, patting to make the crumbs stick. Arrange in a single layer on the baking sheet. Drizzle with the remaining butter.

4. Bake for 6 to 10 minutes on the top rack of the oven, until the fish is tender and opaque through-out. Serve hot, with the lemon wedges, passing the tartar sauce at the table.

Broiled Fish Fillets with Garlic Herb Sauce

This is an easy, basic recipe for cooking fresh, white fish fillets, such as flounder or sole—the kind of fish you might pick up at the supermarket to make a quick supper. This dish is delicious served with rice and a green salad.

SERVES 4

⅓ cup olive oil
¼ cup lemon juice
½ teaspoon minced garlic
¼ cup minced fresh chervil, parsley, basil, or
    dill
Salt and pepper
1½ pounds firm white fish fillets

1. Preheat the broiler. Grease a baking sheet.

2. Whisk together the oil, lemon juice, garlic, and chervil in a small bowl. Season to taste with salt and pepper.

3. Arrange the fillets on the prepared baking sheet. Drizzle with some of the flavored oil. If the fillets are less than ¼ inch thick, broil for 2 to 4 minutes, until the fish is firm and barely cooked through. If the fillets are thicker, broil for 8 to 10 minutes per inch of thickness. Serve hot, passing the additional flavored oil at the table.

TIP: For a more complete list of white
fish fillets, see page 144.

Sautéed Fish Fillets with White Wine Sauce

Another quick way to prepare fish is to sauté it in a skillet and finish with a light white-wine sauce.

SERVES 4

Sauce:
1 tablespoon oil
1 tablespoon finely chopped shallots
½ cup dry white wine
1 tablespoon lemon juice
4 tablespoons (½ stick) butter
1 tablespoon drained capers
1 tablespoon chopped fresh parsley
Salt and pepper

Fish:
2 pounds white fish fillets
Salt and pepper
½ cup all-purpose flour
¼ cup oil
Lemon wedges, to serve

1. To prepare the sauce, heat the oil in a small saucepan over medium heat. Add the shallots and sauté until softened, about 2 minutes. Add the wine and lemon juice, bring to a boil, and continue to boil until the sauce is reduced to ¾ cup, 3 to 5 minutes. Remove the pan from the heat and whisk in the butter, 1 tablespoon at a time. Add the capers and parsley. Season to taste with salt and pepper. Cover and keep warm.

2. To make the fish, season the fillets with salt and pepper. Dip the fillets in the flour in a shallow bowl until lightly coated.

3. Heat 2 tablespoons of oil in a large skillet over high heat. Add half the fillets in a single layer, reduce the heat to medium-high, and cook until the bottoms are lightly browned, 2 to 3 minutes for fillets ¼ inch thick. Increase the time to 3 to 4 minutes for fillets that are 1 inch thick.

4. Flip the fillets with a spatula and cook on the second side until the fillet is firm, 30 to 60 seconds for thin fillets, 2 to 3 minutes for thick fillets. Transfer to a serving platter and tent with aluminum foil. Repeat with the remaining oil and fillets and transfer to the serving platter when done. Serve the fish hot, accompanied by lemon wedges and passing the sauce at the table.

TIP: Fish is done when the flesh is opaque and the juices are milky white. If you poke it with a fork, the fish should loosen in large flakes.

Lemon-Baked Fish Fillets

Lemon is a natural partner for fish. Besides making a perfect flavor marriage, it can be used to remove fish odors from hands and cutting boards.

SERVES 4

1½ pounds firm white fish fillets
½ teaspoon minced shallot
¼ cup minced fresh parsley
¼ cup lemon juice
1 teaspoon sugar
1 teaspoon salt
¼ cup oil
½ medium lemon, very thinly sliced

1. Preheat the oven to 450°F. Grease a large baking dish.

2. Arrange the fish in the baking dish in a single layer.

3. Stir together the shallot, parsley, lemon juice, sugar, and salt in a small bowl. Whisk in the oil until well blended. Pour over the fish. Top with lemon slices.

4. Bake until the fish is just cooked through, 5 to 8 minutes, allowing about 10 minutes per inch of thickness. Serve hot.

TIP: If your fillets are of uneven thickness, fold under the thin portions so the fillets are of uniform thickness. This will promote even cooking. Be sure to thaw frozen fish prior to baking.

Tuna Noodle Casserole

What would we do if a certain soup company, with the familiar red and white cans, stopped production? We would make tuna noodle casserole from scratch and wonder why we didn't do it sooner!

SERVES 4

6 tablespoons (¾ stick) butter
½ cup finely chopped mushrooms
½ medium red bell pepper, seeded and finely chopped
½ medium onion, finely chopped
2 tablespoons all-purpose flour
2½ cups milk
2 (6-ounce) cans albacore tuna (packed in water or oil), drained
Salt and pepper
3 cups cooked egg noodles
1 cup frozen peas or frozen mixed carrots and peas
½ cup dry bread crumbs

1. Preheat the oven to 350°F. Grease a 2-quart casserole dish.

2. Melt 4 tablespoons of butter over medium heat in a large saucepan. Add the mushrooms, bell pepper, and onion and sauté until the mushrooms give up their juice, about 4 minutes. Stir in the flour until it forms a paste. Stir in the milk, increase the heat, and bring to a boil. Remove from the heat and stir in the tuna, breaking up any clumps. Season to taste with salt and pepper.

3. Add the egg noodles and peas to the sauce and mix well. Taste and adjust the seasoning as needed.

4. Transfer the mixture to the casserole dish and sprinkle the top with the bread crumbs. Melt the remaining 2 tablespoons butter and drizzle over the casserole.

5. Bake for 25 to 35 minutes, until the topping is browned. Serve hot.

Baked Fish Provençal Style

In this dish, aromatic vegetables bake with the fish in a tomato sauce. The garlic and vegetables are signatures of Provence, the region of France that inspires this recipe. Serve with rice.

SERVES 4

2 tablespoons oil
1 medium onion, finely chopped
1 fennel bulb, trimmed and finely chopped, or ½ teaspoon fennel seed, crushed
½ teaspoon minced garlic
1 (15-ounce) can diced tomatoes, drained
¼ cup chopped brine-cured black olives, such as kalamata
¼ cup chopped fresh basil or parsley, plus more to serve
1 tablespoon grated lemon zest
Salt and pepper
1½ pounds firm white fish fillets

1. Heat the oil in a large skillet over medium-high heat. Add the onion and fennel and sauté until softened, about 3 minutes. Stir in the garlic, tomatoes, olives, basil, and lemon zest. Season to taste with salt and pepper. Bring to a boil, reduce the heat, and simmer until thickened, about 20 minutes.

2. Meanwhile, preheat the oven to 425°F. Lightly grease a medium baking dish.

3. Place the fish fillets in the baking dish and cover evenly with the tomato mixture.

4. Bake for 8 to 12 minutes, until the fish is opaque in the center and begins to flake when touched with a fork. Serve hot, garnished with basil.

Baked Fish with Cream and Mushrooms

When our grandmothers and great-grandmothers prepared fish baked in a cream sauce with mushrooms, they made a delicate sauce like this one. Sole is the perfect fish for this dish due to its firm but tender texture.

SERVES 4

1½ pounds sole or other firm white fish fillets
3 tablespoons lemon juice
½ cup all-purpose flour
1½ teaspoons salt
¼ teaspoon black pepper
¼ cup chopped fresh parsley
2 tablespoons chopped fresh chives
1 teaspoon chopped fresh tarragon
1½ cups heavy cream
5 tablespoons butter
3 cups sliced mushrooms

1. Preheat the oven to 350°F. Grease a large, shallow baking dish.

2. Sprinkle the fish with the lemon juice.

3. Mix the flour, salt, and black pepper in a shallow bowl. Dredge the fish in the flour mixture, shaking off the excess. Arrange in a single, or slightly overlapping, layer in the baking dish. Sprinkle with the parsley, chives, and tarragon. Slowly pour the cream on and around the fish.

4. Bake for 15 minutes.

5. While the fish bakes, melt the butter in a large skillet over medium heat. Add the mushrooms and sauté until they give up their juice, about 8 minutes.

6. When the fish flakes with a fork, remove from the oven and pour the mushrooms over the fish. Serve hot, spooning the cream from the baking dish over each serving.

Seafood-Stuffed Fillets

Stuffing fish with crabmeat doubles the flavor and makes an elegant dish. If you prefer, substitute chopped shrimp or lobster for the crab.

SERVES 4

1 tablespoon oil
2 tablespoons finely chopped onion
1 teaspoon minced garlic
½ cup lump crabmeat
¼ cup fresh bread crumbs
1 tablespoon minced fresh parsley
Salt and pepper
1½ pounds thin white fish fillets
2 tablespoons butter, melted
2 tablespoons dry vermouth
2 tablespoons heavy cream

1. Preheat the oven to 375°F. Grease a medium, shallow baking dish.

2. Heat the oil in a medium skillet over medium heat. Add the onion and garlic and sauté for 4 minutes, until the onion is softened. Stir in the crabmeat, bread crumbs, and parsley. Season to taste with salt and pepper.

3. Spread the crab mixture along the length of each fillet, dividing evenly. Roll up the fillets and secure each with a toothpick. Place in a single layer in the baking dish.

4. Mix the butter, vermouth, and cream in a small bowl and pour evenly over the fish. Bake, basting the fish occasionally with the pan liquids until the fish begins to flake when touched with a fork and the stuffing is heated through, 20 to 25 minutes.

5. Remove the toothpicks and serve hot, spooning some of the pan juices over each serving.

Broiled Fish Steaks with Tomato Glaze

A fish steak is a cross-section of a round fish with a bone in the center. Fish steaks tend to be hearty in flavor and suitable for both broiling and grilling.

SERVES 4

4 fish steaks, at least 1 inch thick, such as swordfish, tuna, salmon, or halibut
2 tablespoons oil
Salt and pepper
1 cup fresh or canned diced tomatoes (drained if canned)
½ teaspoon minced garlic
Lemon wedges, to serve

1. Preheat the broiler. Brush a baking sheet with oil.

2. Lay the fish on the baking sheet in a single layer. Brush with 1 tablespoon of oil and season with salt and pepper.

3. Combine the tomatoes and garlic in a small bowl. Stir in the remaining 1 tablespoon oil. Season with salt and pepper.

4. Broil the fish for 4 minutes. Turn over with a spatula, top with the tomato mixture, and continue to broil for another 4 to 5 minutes. Check doneness by inserting a knife between layers of the flesh. The meat should be just translucent.

5. Spoon the pan juices back over the fish and serve with lemon wedges.

TIP: You can grill the fish instead of broiling it. The cooking time will be approximately the same.

Poached Fish Steaks with Hollandaise Sauce

Hollandaise sauce is the perfect accompaniment to fish steaks poached in white wine and served warm. If you want to serve the fish at room temperature or slightly chilled, offer mayonnaise, tartar sauce, or lemon wedges instead.

SERVES 4

2 cups dry white wine
2 cups water
1 teaspoon salt
¼ teaspoon black peppercorns
1 bay leaf
4 fish steaks, ¾ to 1 inch thick, such as swordfish, tuna, salmon, or halibut
¾ to 1 cup warm Hollandaise sauce (page 17)

1. Combine the wine, water, salt, peppercorns, and bay leaf in a large skillet or Dutch oven and bring to a boil. Reduce the heat and simmer for 5 minutes.

2. Gently slide the fish steaks into the simmering liquid and adjust the heat to maintain the simmer. Cook for about 10 minutes, until the fish is mostly opaque but still slightly translucent in the center.

3. Remove the steaks from the water with a slotted spoon and serve hot, with the Hollandaise sauce spooned on top or passed at the table.

Salmon Pea Wiggle

It is a mystery why the tuna noodle casserole lives on while the salmon pea wiggle has faded from view. Children and adults alike will love this creamy dish.

SERVES 6

3 cups milk
3 tablespoons all-purpose flour
2 (14¾-ounce) cans pink salmon, drained and flaked
2 cups frozen peas, thawed
Salt and pepper
Crackers, toast points, or cooked egg noodles, to serve

1. Heat the milk in a large saucepan over medium heat until almost boiling, stirring constantly. Gradually whisk in the flour and continue cooking and stirring until slightly thickened, about 5 minutes.

2. Stir in the salmon and peas, and season to taste with salt and pepper. Continue cooking and stirring until thick and heated through, about 10 minutes. Serve over crackers, toast points, or egg noodles.

Broiled Salmon Steaks with Herbs

This simple recipe highlights the rich flavor of salmon. The herbs add contrast while the lemon balances the acidity. Here's a convenient way to prepare salmon on a hot summer night.

SERVES 4

6 tablespoons butter (¾ stick), melted
4 salmon steaks, ¾ to 1 inch thick
Salt and pepper
1 tablespoon chopped fresh dill, basil, chervil, parsley, or tarragon
Juice of 1 medium lemon
Lemon wedges, to serve

1. Preheat the broiler.

2. Place the fish on a baking sheet. Brush 2 tablespoons of butter over the salmon. Season with salt and pepper.

3. Broil the salmon for 5 minutes. Turn over with a spatula and broil for 2 more minutes.

4. Combine the remaining 4 tablespoons butter with the dill and lemon juice. Pour the sauce over the fish and continue to broil until the fish is mostly done, or still faintly translucent in the center. Serve hot, with lemon wedges.

TIP: Restaurant chefs are leading the way in serving salmon and tuna steaks cooked rare, or translucent in the center. If you prefer, increase the time and cook until the fish is opaque throughout.

Salmon with Egg Sauce

Salmon with egg sauce is served on the Fourth of July in northern New England, a custom that may have originated with Abigail Adams, wife of President John Adams. This salmon dish is usually served with the region's first crop of peas of the season.

SERVES ABOUT 8

5- to 7-pound whole salmon, cleaned and dressed
1 medium lemon, thinly sliced
3 tablespoons butter
3 tablespoons all-purpose flour
2 cups milk
2 tablespoons chopped fresh parsley
2 hard-boiled eggs, peeled and coarsely chopped
Salt and pepper

1. Preheat the oven to 450°F.

2. Rinse the fish and pat dry with paper towels. Lay the fish on a large piece of heavy-duty aluminum foil. Put half the lemon slices inside the fish's cavity; place the remainder on top. Fold the foil to encase the fish, securing the ends so no liquid escapes during baking. Place the package in a large roasting pan.

3. Bake for about 45 minutes, until the fish flakes easily.

4. While the fish bakes, prepare the sauce. Melt the butter in a medium saucepan over medium heat. Stir in the flour to form a smooth paste. Cook for about 2 minutes, then slowly stir in the milk and continue cooking, stirring constantly, until the sauce thickens, about 2 minutes more. Add the parsley, eggs, and salt and pepper to taste.

5. Divide the salmon into serving portions and spoon the sauce over each before serving.

Poached Salmon with Cucumber Sauce

Poaching is a way to lock in moisture without the addition of fat. If you want to serve the fish hot, consider serving it with Hollandaise sauce. When serving cold, offer a refreshing cucumber sauce.

SERVES 4

Fish:
2 cups dry white wine
2 cups water
2 teaspoons salt
1 medium onion, thinly sliced
1 medium carrot, thinly sliced
1 medium celery rib, thinly sliced
2 sprigs fresh dill
4 bay leaves
4 (6- to 8-ounce) salmon fillets, skin removed

Sauce:
1 medium cucumber, peeled and seeded
½ cup sour cream
2 tablespoons cider vinegar
1 tablespoon snipped fresh dill, plus sprigs to serve
Salt and pepper, to serve

1. To make the fish, in a large saucepan, combine the wine, water, salt, onion, carrot, celery, dill, and bay leaves. Bring to a boil, reduce the heat, and simmer for five minutes.

2. Place the fish gently in the simmering liquid, adding more water to cover the fish if needed. Adjust the heat to maintain a slight simmer for 8 to 10 minutes, until the fish begins to flake with a fork.

3. Remove the fish from the liquid with a slotted spatula and refrigerate until cold.

4. To make the sauce, grate the cucumber into a medium bowl. Add the sour cream, vinegar, and 1 tablespoon dill. Season to taste with salt and pepper. Let stand for at least 10 minutes to allow the flavors to meld, or refrigerate up to 4 hours.

5. Place the fillets on individual serving plates, spooning the sauce evenly over each fillet. Garnish each plate with a sprig of dill.

Sole Meunière

"Sole cooked in the style of the miller's wife" is how the title of this classic French recipe translates. Apparently, a miller's wife would be generous with the flour, dusting all that she cooks. In addition, the fish here is finished with a delicate pan sauce of browned butter. Use any thin white fish fillet in this recipe.

SERVES 2

1 cup all-purpose flour
Salt and pepper
12 ounces sole fillets
4 tablespoons (½ stick) butter
1 tablespoon chopped fresh parsley
1 teaspoon lemon juice
Lemon wedges, to serve

1. Season the flour with salt and pepper in a shallow bowl. Dip the fish in the flour, shake off any excess, and set aside on a plate.

2. Melt 3 tablespoons of butter in a large skillet over medium-high heat. Stir in the parsley. Add the fish, reduce the heat to medium, and cook for 2 to 3 minutes, until the fish is golden on the bottom. Turn the fillets over with a spatula and continue to cook for 1½ to 2 minutes, until the fish is golden and cooked through. Transfer to a serving plate.

3. Add the lemon juice and remaining 1 tablespoon butter to the pan juices. Increase the heat to medium-high and cook until the butter has melted and the foam subsides.

4. Pour the pan juices over the fish, garnish with the lemon wedges, and serve immediately.

Sole Florentine

Many dishes cooked with spinach acquired the name "Florentine," though spinach is popular in many other places besides Florence, Italy. Spinach is now available fresh year-round, so you might as well make this with the fresh vegetable. Two pounds may seem like a lot, but it cooks down to a very reasonable amount.

SERVES 4

2 pounds fresh spinach, washed and trimmed
5 tablespoons unsalted butter
1 shallot, finely chopped
2 tablespoons all-purpose flour
½ cup half-and-half
½ cup milk
⅛ teaspoon ground nutmeg
Salt and pepper
1 medium lemon, ½ juiced and ½ cut into
    4 wedges
1½ pounds sole fillets
¼ cup dry bread crumbs
¼ cup grated Parmesan cheese

1. Preheat the broiler. Grease a 9 x 13-inch baking dish.

2. Bring a large pot of salted water to a boil. Stir in the spinach and cook until wilted, 30 to 60 seconds. Drain well. Press out the excess moisture. Transfer to a cutting board and chop.

3. Heat 2 tablespoons of butter in a large skillet over medium-high heat. Add the shallot and sauté until softened, about 3 minutes. Add the flour and stir until you have a smooth paste. Slowly stir in the half-and-half and milk, bring to a boil, then remove from the heat. Stir in the spinach, nutmeg, and salt and pepper to taste. Transfer to the baking dish.

4. In a small saucepan, melt 2 tablespoons of butter, and add the lemon juice. Arrange the fillets in a single layer over the spinach, and brush the tops with the butter mixture. Sprinkle the bread crumbs and Parmesan cheese evenly over the fish. Dot with the remaining 1 tablespoon butter.

5. Broil for 5 to 6 minutes, until the fillets are opaque and the bread crumbs golden. Serve hot, with lemon wedges on the side of each plate.

Shrimp Florentine

Sole Florentine is easily adapted to shrimp. Replace the fish with 1¼ pounds shrimp, peeled and deveined. Prepare the spinach as directed. Arrange the shrimp over the spinach and continue with the recipe as directed.

FLORENCE

Trout Amandine

"Amandine" is a French term for a dish made with almonds. Many dishes are made with almonds, but trout and green beans is a classic combination.

SERVES 4

8 (4-ounce) lake or rainbow trout fillets
1 large egg
1 cup milk
1 cup all-purpose flour
Salt and pepper
2 tablespoons oil
4 tablespoons (½ stick) butter
¾ cup sliced almonds, blanched
Leaves from 1 bunch fresh parsley, finely
    chopped
Lemon wedges, to serve

1. Preheat the oven to 200°F. Set an ovenproof serving plate inside to heat. Rinse the fish fillets and pat dry with paper towels.

2. Use a fork to beat together the egg and milk in a shallow bowl. In a second shallow bowl, season the flour with salt and pepper. Coat the trout fillets in egg and milk, then in seasoned flour, and set aside on a plate.

3. Melt 1 tablespoon of oil with 1 tablespoon of butter in a large skillet over medium heat. Add a single layer of fillets and fry until golden on the bottom, 2 to 3 minutes. Turn with a spatula and cook until the second side is golden, 2 to 3 minutes more. Transfer the trout fillets to the warm platter in the oven to keep warm. Return the pan to the stove and repeat, using the remaining 1 tablespoon oil and 1 tablespoon of butter.

4. When all the trout is cooked and in the oven, add the remaining 2 tablespoons butter to the pan. When the butter melts, add the almonds and sauté until lightly golden, 1 to 2 minutes.

5. Remove the trout from the oven and pour the almonds and butter over the platter. Garnish with parsley and lemon wedges and serve hot.

TIP: The bones of freshwater fish, like trout, are thinner than those of saltwater fish and more likely to be eaten by mistake. If you think you have a small bone that has caught in your throat, eat a piece of bread to help it dislodge.

Bacon-Wrapped Trout

Like many recipes for fresh-caught trout, this one suggests the outdoors—a fishing camp by a wild river, where the cooking is simple and the fish is always fresh.

SERVES 4

4 whole trout, cleaned and dressed
Salt and pepper
8 slices bacon

1. Preheat the broiler with the rack 4 to 6 inches from the heat.

2. Rinse the fish and pat dry with paper towels. Season with salt and pepper, inside and out. Wrap 2 slices of bacon around each fish.

3. Broil in a nonstick baking pan for 3 to 4 minutes, until the bacon is crisp. Flip with a wide spatula and continue to broil until the bacon is crisp on the second side. Keep turning if needed to avoid burning the bacon. The total cooking time will be 12 to 15 minutes. Serve hot.

TIP: This recipe can be cooked on a grate over a campfire, if desired.

Basic Steamed Clams

The traditional clams to steam are soft-shell clams and razor clams, which are found in the Northwest. Soft-shell clams can be full of grit, so soaking them in salted water in advance is recommended. Eating these together is a fun, social event.

SERVES 4

5 pounds littleneck or soft-shell steamer clams
    (50 to 60 small clams)
1 tablespoon oil
2 tablespoons butter
2 teaspoons minced garlic
½ cup dry white wine
3 tablespoons chopped fresh parsley
French or sourdough bread, toasted, to serve

1. Soak the clams in a large pot of salted water for 2 hours. Rinse well.

2. In a large stockpot, heat the oil and butter over medium heat. Add the garlic and cook for 1 minute. Add the wine and increase the heat to high. Cook another 2 minutes. Add the parsley and clams, cover, and cook until the clams open, 5 to 7 minutes.

3. Divide the clams and broth into 4 bowls and serve with toasted French or sourdough bread to sop up the juices.

Clam Fritters

Clam fritters are a New England tradition. They are also known as "fannie daddies."

SERVES 4 TO 6

2 cups shucked clams (fresh or canned), finely chopped (liquor reserved)
1 cup cracker crumbs
¼ teaspoon cayenne pepper
2 large egg yolks (whites reserved), well beaten
½ teaspoon salt
¼ teaspoon black pepper
1 tablespoon minced fresh parsley
About ½ cup clam liquor
3 large egg whites
Oil, for frying
Tartar sauce (page 123), to serve

1. Mix together the clams, cracker crumbs, cayenne pepper, egg yolks, salt, pepper, and parsley. Add enough clam liquor to make a heavy batter (like a thick cake batter).

2. In a separate bowl, beat the egg whites until stiff. Fold the egg whites into the clam batter.

3. In a Dutch oven or tall, cast-iron skillet, heat 2 to 3 inches of oil to 365°F. Drop the batter by heaping tablespoons into the hot oil. Cook, turning once, until browned on both sides, 2 to 3 minutes total. Drain on paper towels and serve hot, passing the tartar sauce at the table.

Fried Clams

You'll find fried clams served at clam shacks throughout coastal New England, where everyone pretty much agrees on how the fried clam was invented. In 1916, in Essex, Massachusetts, Lawrence Woodman rolled the whole belly of a shucked soft-shell clam in some crumbs and fried it in the hot oil he used to fry a potato. And so a legend was born.

SERVES 4

2½ pints shucked soft-shell clams
Oil, for frying
1½ cups evaporated milk
1½ cups fine yellow cornmeal
¾ cup all-purpose flour
¼ teaspoon salt
Pinch of black pepper, or more to taste
Tartar sauce (page 123), to serve

1. Rinse the clams and dry thoroughly on paper towels.

2. In a tall skillet or saucepan, begin heating 2 to 3 inches of oil to 350°F. Preheat the oven to 200°F.

3. Pour the evaporated milk into a large bowl. Mix together the cornmeal, flour, salt, and pepper in a second large bowl.

4. Using your hands or a slotted spoon, dip several clams into the milk, then let the excess milk drain off. Dip the clams in the cornmeal mixture, shaking off the excess breading.

5. Slide the clams into the hot oil and fry until golden brown, 2 to 4 minutes. Drain on paper towels and place on an ovenproof plate in the oven to keep warm. Repeat with the remaining clams. Serve hot, passing the tartar sauce at the table.

Crab Boil

A crab boil is a backyard tradition wherever fresh crabs are readily available. To enjoy crabs this way, crack and eat them on a paper-covered picnic table. Lay out wooden crab mallets (for cracking the claws), serrated knives (for cutting open the bodies and helping with the picking), and rolls of paper towels. If you like, throw corn on the cob, shrimp in the shell, and clams into the steamer along with the crabs.

SERVES 4

Spice mix:
1 cup seafood seasoning mix, such as Old Bay or Zatarain's
½ cup coarse or kosher salt
2 tablespoons ground ginger
2 tablespoons ground black pepper
2 tablespoons garlic powder
1 tablespoon dry mustard
1 tablespoon yellow mustard seeds
1 tablespoon dried thyme
1 tablespoon onion powder
1 tablespoon cayenne pepper

Crabs:
3 cups water or beer, or a combination
24 live soft-shell crabs

1. To make the spice mix, combine all the ingredients in a jar and shake to mix. Use immediately or store in the jar for up to 6 months.

2. To cook the crabs, bring the water to a boil in a large pot with a steaming rack and a tight-fitting lid.

3. Place a layer of crabs, right side up, in the steamer, add a generous sprinkling of seasoning mix, and cover with another layer of crabs and more seasoning mix. Layer as many crabs as will fit and quickly cover the pan; steam for 15 to 20 minutes.

4. Remove and serve immediately. Continue steaming crabs until everyone has eaten more than his or her share.

Crawfish Boil

The crawfish boil is a Louisiana tradition. Into the pot with the crawfish go vegetables, potatoes, and sausage. Then it's all fished out of the liquid and set directly on paper-covered picnic tables. Serve with ice-cold beer.

SERVES 4

¼ cup coarse or kosher salt
2 medium lemons, cut in half
¼ cup seafood seasoning mix, such as Old Bay or Zatarain's
1 pound waxy potatoes, such as thin-skinned white or red, scrubbed
4 medium corn ears, shucked and cut in half
3 medium onions, quartered
¾ pound andouille sausage, cut into 2-inch lengths
5 pounds live crawfish, rinsed and cleaned

1. Fill a 5-gallon pot with about 3 gallons of water and bring to a boil.

2. Add the salt, lemons, and seasoning mix and boil for 5 minutes.

3. Add the potatoes and corn and cook for 10 minutes. Add the onions and sausage, and boil until the potatoes are cooked, about 10 more minutes. Turn off the heat, add the crawfish, and cook until the crawfish are red, 6 to 8 minutes. Drain immediately and serve.

TIP: To eat crawfish, hold the head in one hand and the tail in the other. Twist and pull the head from the tail. Suck out the juices in the head, if desired. Peel the shell off the tail and eat the meat inside.

Crab Cakes

Live crabs have always been prized in regions of the country where they are especially abundant—blue crabs in Maryland, stone crabs in Florida, Dungeness crabs in the Pacific Northwest, and king crabs in Alaska. But even where crabs aren't especially plentiful, crab cakes made with frozen or canned crabmeat are popular.

SERVES 4

1 large egg, beaten
1½ cups fresh white bread crumbs
3 tablespoons mayonnaise
2 tablespoons finely chopped scallion
1 tablespoon finely chopped fresh parsley
2 teaspoons Worcestershire sauce
1 teaspoon dry mustard
½ teaspoon salt
¼ teaspoon black pepper
1 pound lump crabmeat, or 4 (6-ounce) cans crabmeat, drained
3 tablespoons oil
Lemon wedges, to serve
Tartar sauce (page 123), to serve

1. Mix together the egg, bread crumbs, mayonnaise, scallion, parsley, Worcestershire sauce, mustard, salt, and pepper in a medium bowl. Fold in the crabmeat. Use your hands to form the mixture into 8 balls, then press into small patties.

2. Heat the oil in a large skillet over medium heat. Add the crab cakes and cook for 3 to 4 minutes on each side, until deep golden brown.

3. Transfer to paper towels to drain. Serve hot, passing lemon wedges and tartar sauce at the table.

Sautéed Soft-Shell Crabs

All crabs have hard shells except during the brief time when they molt and shed their outgrown shells, in late spring or early summer. It is at this point in their life cycle that the crabs can be eaten whole. Sautéed soft-shell crabs can be stuffed into baguettes, slathered with tartar sauce, and served as sandwiches for delicious, crunchy, casual dining.

SERVES 2 TO 4

4 soft-shell crabs, cleaned
1 cup all-purpose flour
1 large egg
1 cup dry bread crumbs
Salt and pepper
4 tablespoons (½ stick) butter
Tartar sauce (page 123), to serve
Lemon wedges, to serve

1. Rinse the crabs with water and pat dry with paper towels. Set aside.

2. Place the flour in a shallow bowl. Beat the egg in a second shallow bowl. Season the bread crumbs with salt and pepper in a third shallow bowl.

3. Melt the butter in a large skillet over medium-high heat. Dip the crabs first in the flour, then in the egg, then in the bread crumbs and place in the skillet. Cook until golden brown on both sides, about 3 to 4 minutes per side. Serve hot, accompanied by the tartar sauce and lemon wedges.

Deviled Crab

Crab and mustard flavors go well together. This is a classic spicy dish of which many versions exist.

SERVES 4

½ cup mayonnaise
2 tablespoons minced onion
2 tablespoons minced green bell pepper
1 tablespoon minced fresh parsley
2 teaspoons Worcestershire sauce
2 teaspoons lemon juice
1½ teaspoons dry mustard
¼ teaspoon cayenne pepper
Dash of hot pepper sauce, such as Tabasco
Salt and pepper
1 pound lump crabmeat, or 4 (6-ounce) cans
    crabmeat, drained
3 to 4 tablespoons butter
1 cup fresh fine bread crumbs
Lemon wedges, to serve

1. Preheat the oven to 425°F. Arrange 4 real crab or scallop shells, ceramic shells, or ramekins on a baking sheet.

2. Stir together the mayonnaise, onion, bell pepper, parsley, Worcestershire sauce, lemon juice, mustard, cayenne pepper, and hot pepper sauce. Season to taste with salt and pepper. Gently fold in the crabmeat.

3. Melt 3 tablespoons of butter in a small skillet and add the bread crumbs. Cook over low heat until just golden, adding a little more butter if it seems too dry. Scrape into a bowl and cool.

4. Divide the crab mixture among the shells or ramekins, mounding it a bit in the center so that it looks generous. Sprinkle the crumbs over the top.

5. Bake until bubbly and lightly browned, 10 to 15 minutes. Serve hot, with the lemon wedges.

Crawfish Étouffée

Crawfish are freshwater crustaceans that resemble miniature lobsters. What you call them depends on where you live; they are also known as crayfish, crawdads, and crawdaddies. Crawfish were once a major part of the diet of Native Americans in the South and are highly appreciated in Cajun country.

SERVES 6 TO 8

½ cup (1 stick) butter
1 cup chopped scallions
1 medium green bell pepper, seeded and diced
¼ cup chopped fresh parsley
2 pounds crawfish tails (sold vacuum-packed
    in seafood stores)
1 cup crawfish fat (sold frozen separately or
    with packaged tails), or 1 cup (2 sticks)
    butter
1 teaspoon cayenne pepper
Salt and pepper
2 teaspoons cornstarch dissolved in 1
    tablespoon water
Hot cooked white rice, to serve
Lemon slices, to serve

1. Melt the butter in a large skillet or Dutch oven over medium heat. Add the scallions and bell pepper and sauté until tender, about 10 minutes. Add the parsley, crawfish tails and fat, cayenne pepper, and salt and pepper to taste. Simmer for 15 to 20 minutes.

2. Bring the sauce to a boil, stir in the cornstarch mixture, and cook until thick and smooth, 1 to 2 minutes. Serve hot, over the rice, and garnish with the lemon slices.

Stuffed Broiled Lobsters

This is one of the most extravagant of dishes—perfect for a romantic evening for two.

SERVES 2

½ cup (1 stick) butter
1 medium onion, finely chopped
¼ pound raw small shrimp, peeled and
    deveined, or 1 cup lump crabmeat
¼ cup chopped fresh parsley
Salt and pepper

1 cup cracker crumbs
2 live lobsters, 2 to 3 pounds each
Lemon wedges, to serve

1. Melt half the butter in a medium skillet over medium heat. Add the onion and sauté until softened, about 3 minutes. Stir in the shrimp and continue to sauté until the shrimp are pink and firm, about 2 minutes. Stir in the parsley and salt and pepper to taste. Remove from the heat and let cool slightly.

2. Place the lobsters in a large pan in the freezer for 20 minutes to stun them. Remove them from the freezer and put one lobster on its back. Holding firmly with one hand, insert a sharp, heavy knife where the head meets the body, and quickly slice through the entire length of the body and tail. Spread the lobster open. With your fingers, remove and discard the food sac near the head. Remove and reserve the green tomalley (liver) and pink coral (eggs), if present. Remove and discard the gray tissue and the vein that runs down the middle of the tail. Crack the claws. Rinse the lobster under cold running water. Repeat with the second lobster.

3. Preheat the broiler.

4. Mix the tomalley and coral into the shrimp mixture. Gently fold in the cracker crumbs. Divide the mixture evenly between the two lobsters, spreading the stuffing into the body cavities. Melt the remaining butter and brush it on the tail, stuffing, and cracked claws.

5. Broil until the tail meat is white and firm and the stuffing is browned, 5 to 10 minutes. Serve hot, accompanied by the lemon wedges.

Lobster Thermidor

This is a classic baked dish of lobster, mushrooms, and sherry that is often served over rice. It is from the days when French cooking was the ultimate in American sophistication.

SERVES 4

½ cup (1 stick) butter
½ pound button mushrooms, sliced
2 shallots, finely chopped
½ cup all-purpose flour
2 cups milk
¼ cup heavy cream
2 large egg yolks, lightly beaten
2 tablespoons dry sherry
½ teaspoon dry mustard
4 cups cooked lobster meat
Salt and pepper
2 tablespoons chopped fresh parsley
⅓ cup grated Parmesan cheese

1. Preheat the oven to 400°F.

2. Melt 4 tablespoons of butter in a medium saucepan over medium heat. Add the mushrooms and shallots and sauté until the mushrooms give up their juice, about 6 minutes. Remove from the pan with a slotted spoon and keep warm.

3. Melt the remaining 4 tablespoons butter in the pan, with the bits of shallots. Stir in the flour until a smooth paste forms. Whisk in the milk, then the cream, and cook, stirring constantly, until the sauce thickens.

4. Spoon a little sauce into a small bowl. Mix in the egg yolks. Stir into the saucepan. Add the mushrooms, sherry, mustard, and lobster, and stir. Season to taste with salt and pepper, and stir in the parsley.

5. Transfer the mixture to a medium baking dish. Sprinkle the top with the cheese, and bake for 15 minutes. Serve hot.

Steamed Mussels in White Wine

Mussels are an incredibly abundant, inexpensive shellfish that have never achieved the popularity of other shellfish in America. Mussels steamed in white wine, or "moules marinière," is a classic French bistro dish that shows up occasionally on American menus. Serve with crusty French bread for sopping up the broth.

SERVES 4

2 cups dry white wine
¼ cup finely chopped onion
¼ cup finely chopped celery
1 teaspoon minced garlic
1 fresh thyme sprig or 1 teaspoon dried
1 bay leaf
6 pounds mussels, well scrubbed and beards removed
⅓ cup chopped fresh parsley

1. Bring the wine, onion, celery, garlic, thyme, and bay leaf to a boil in a large pot. Reduce the heat and simmer for 10 minutes.

2. Add the mussels, cover, and boil until the shells open, 5 to 7 minutes. Discard any mussels that do not open.

3. Spoon the mussels into soup bowls with the broth, sprinkle with the parsley, remove the bay leaf, and serve.

Oyster Stew

During the nineteenth century, "oyster cellars" were establishments where oysters were served in various ways. Oyster stew is one of the simplest—and is a Christmas tradition in many homes.

SERVES 4

¼ cup (½ stick) butter
¼ cup finely chopped onion
2 tablespoons finely chopped celery
1½ cups milk
½ cup heavy cream
1 pint shucked oysters with liquor
Salt and pepper
Chopped fresh parsley, to garnish

1. Melt the butter in a medium skillet over medium heat. Add the onion and celery and sauté until just softened, about 3 minutes.

2. Stir in the milk and cream, and heat thoroughly. Add the oysters with their liquor and heat until the edges of the oysters are curled and their flesh turns a silvery gray, about 5 minutes.

3. Season to taste with salt and pepper. Spoon into bowls and garnish with the parsley. Serve hot.

Oyster Fritters

Oysters were enormously popular in the United States during the nineteenth century. They were carried on horse-drawn wagons loaded with seawater-soaked hay and shipped from Baltimore all the way out west. Packed in saltwater tanks or buried in ice, they came up the Mississippi River on steamboats, and were also transported by rail. Some of those oysters were made into fritters.

SERVES 4

1 pint shucked oysters
1¾ cups all-purpose flour
1 tablespoon baking powder
1 teaspoon salt
Pinch of cayenne pepper (optional)
2 large eggs
1 cup milk
1 tablespoon butter, melted
Oil, for frying
Tartar sauce (page 123), to serve
Lemon wedges, to serve

1. Rinse and drain the oysters, then chop into bite-size pieces.

2. Mix together the flour, baking powder, salt, and cayenne pepper, if using, in a medium bowl.

3. In a large bowl, beat the eggs with a fork. Add the milk and butter, and blend well. Add the flour mixture and blend until smooth. Gently mix in the oysters, taking care not to crush the pieces.

4. In a Dutch oven or tall skillet, heat 2 to 3 inches of oil to 365°F. Drop spoonfuls of the oyster mixture into the oil and fry 1 to 2 minutes on each

side, until golden brown. Remove the fritters with a slotted spoon and drain on paper towels. Serve immediately, passing the tartar sauce and lemon wedges at the table.

Oyster Pie

Oysterville, Washington, is a tiny historic village on the Long Beach Peninsula. Almost every house has a sign stating "Built in 1856" or "Captain —'s house." The house is usually situated on a picket-fenced lot lined with old cedar trees. This recipe is rumored to have its origin in an Oysterville kitchen.

SERVES 4 TO 6

1 pint shucked oysters with liquor
Milk
¼ cup (½ stick) butter
½ cup diced green bell pepper (optional)
½ cup diced celery
1 teaspoon salt
¼ teaspoon black pepper
5 tablespoons all-purpose flour
1 (9-inch) pie crust, unbaked (page 374)

1. Preheat the oven to 350°F.

2. Drain the liquor from the oysters into a 2-cup glass measuring cup. Add enough milk to make 2 cups.

3. Melt the butter in a medium skillet over medium heat. Add the bell pepper, if using, and celery and sauté until tender, about 3 minutes. Stir in the salt, pepper, and flour. Cook for a few minutes until a paste forms, then slowly add the oyster liquid. Continue cooking until thickened and smooth, about 5 minutes. Stir in the oysters.

4. Spoon the oyster mixture into a 9-inch pie pan. Top with the crust, and cut a few slashes in the top to allow steam to escape.

5. Bake for 30 minutes, until the crust is light brown and the filling is bubbly. Let stand for a few minutes before cutting into wedges and serving.

Clam Pie

Substitute 1 pint shucked clams for the oysters in Oyster Pie and complete the recipe as directed.

Seafood Pie

Cooks in New England turn everything they can into pies, from apples to oysters. If lobster proves too expensive, substitute shrimp.

SERVES 6 TO 8

2½ cups chicken broth (page 119)
12 medium oysters, shucked
½ cup sea scallops
½ pound firm white fish fillets, cut into large chunks
¼ cup (½ stick) butter
½ cup minced onion
½ cup minced celery
¼ cup all-purpose flour
1 cup chopped cooked lobster meat
¼ cup dry sherry
Salt and pepper
2 (10-inch) pie crusts, unbaked (page 374)

1. Bring the chicken broth to a boil in a large saucepan. Add the oysters, scallops, and fish. Reduce the heat to a simmer and cook for 4 minutes, until the seafood is just done. Use a slotted spoon to transfer the seafood to a large bowl. Reserve the broth in a medium bowl and set aside.

2. Melt the butter in a medium saucepan over medium heat. Add the onion and celery and sauté until tender, about 3 minutes. Stir in the flour until a paste forms. Slowly pour in the broth and simmer, stirring, until thick, about 5 minutes.

3. Gently stir in the lobster and sherry. Season to taste with salt and pepper.

4. Line a deep 10-inch pie pan with one of the crusts. Spoon in the seafood filling and top with the remaining crust. Seal and cut slits in the top for steam to escape.

5. Bake for 30 to 35 minutes, until the crust is light brown. Let stand for a few minutes before cutting into wedges and serving.

Seafood Newburg

The first recipe for seafood Newburg is lost in time, but many agree that it was originally made with lobster for a Mr. Wenburg. Later, somehow "Wenburg" became "Newburg," seafood was added, and the name became "seafood Newburg." No matter the name, this is a rich and filling dish.

SERVES 4 TO 6

3 tablespoons dry sherry
2 large egg yolks, lightly beaten
¼ cup (½ stick) butter
1 shallot, finely chopped
2 tablespoons all-purpose flour
2 cups half-and-half
Pinch of cayenne pepper
½ pound shrimp, peeled and deveined
½ pound bay scallops
1 pound cooked chopped lobster meat or lump crabmeat
Salt
Hot cooked rice or toast, to serve

1. Use a fork to beat together the sherry and egg yolks in a small bowl, and set aside.

2. Melt the butter in a large saucepan over medium heat. Add the shallot and sauté until softened, about 3 minutes. Stir in the flour and cook for 3 minutes. Stir in the half-and-half, increase the heat to medium-high, and continue cooking, stirring constantly, until the sauce comes to a boil. Reduce the heat to a simmer.

3. Stir a few tablespoons of the cream sauce into the sherry mixture. Stir the remaining sherry mixture into the cream sauce and cook for 1 minute, until thickened. Add the cayenne pepper. Stir in the seafood and cook until heated through, about 5 minutes. Season to taste with salt, and serve hot, spooned over rice or toast.

Fried Shrimp

Batter frying is one of the more popular ways shrimp is prepared in the South. Some people like fried shrimp with cocktail sauce, some with tartar sauce, and some with a little of both. Serving with lemon wedges is optional.

SERVES 4

1½ teaspoons salt
24 large shrimp, peeled and deveined
Oil, for frying
½ cup half-and-half or milk
1 large egg
½ cup all-purpose flour
½ cup yellow cornmeal
1 teaspoon salt
¼ teaspoon black pepper
Cocktail sauce (page 65), to serve
Tartar sauce (page 123), to serve

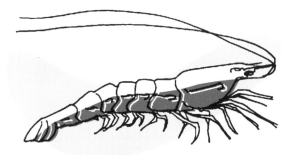

1. Season the shrimp with ½ teaspoon of salt and set aside.

2. In a large, heavy skillet or pot, begin heating 1 inch of oil to 350°F. Preheat the oven to 200°F.

3. Beat the half-and-half and egg together in a shallow bowl. In a second shallow bowl, stir together the flour, cornmeal, salt, and pepper.

4. One at a time, dip each shrimp into the milk mixture, then dip into the flour mixture until well coated.

5. Carefully slide a few shrimp into the oil and fry until golden brown, about 1 minute. Remove with a slotted spoon and place in the oven in a single layer on a baking sheet lined with paper towels. Continue frying the remaining shrimp. Serve hot, passing the cocktail sauce and tartar sauce at the table.

Shrimp Étouffée

The word "étoufée" means "smothered." In this case, the shrimp is smothered in flavor. It is a Cajun classic, using a dark roux—a blend of cooked oil and flower.

SERVES 4

¼ cup oil
¼ cup plus 2 tablespoons all-purpose flour
1 medium red or green bell pepper, seeded and finely chopped
1 large onion, finely chopped
2 medium celery ribs, finely chopped
2 scallions, finely chopped
2 cups shrimp broth (page 111) or chicken broth (page 119)
1½ teaspoons minced garlic
2 tablespoons chopped fresh parsley
Salt and pepper
Hot pepper sauce, such as Tabasco
1½ pounds shrimp, peeled and deveined
2 tablespoons butter
Hot cooked rice, to serve

1. Heat the oil in a large saucepan over medium heat. Stir in the flour until you have a smooth paste and continue to cook, stirring constantly, until the mixture darkens, about 10 minutes. Remove the roux from the heat.

2. Stir the bell pepper, onion, celery, and scallions into the roux. Return to low heat and sauté for 2 minutes.

3. Slowly whisk in the broth. Stir in the garlic and parsley and season to taste with salt and pepper and hot pepper sauce. Simmer for 15 minutes.

4. Stir in the shrimp and butter. Remove from the heat and let stand just until the shrimp are cooked through, about 5 minutes. Taste and adjust the seasonings, as needed. Serve hot, spooned over the rice.

Shrimp Creole

From New Orleans comes another classic shrimp dish, always served over rice. Creole dishes are usually spicy mixtures of tomatoes, green bell peppers, onion, and garlic.

SERVES 4

3 tablespoons butter
2 medium onions, finely chopped
3 medium celery ribs, finely chopped
1 medium green bell pepper, seeded and finely chopped
1½ cups diced and seeded tomatoes
1¼ cups shrimp broth (page 111) or chicken broth (page 119)
½ cup tomato sauce
3 tablespoons tomato paste
1 teaspoon minced garlic
2 bay leaves
¼ cup chopped fresh parsley
2 teaspoons white pepper
2 teaspoons dried thyme
¼ teaspoon cayenne pepper, plus more to taste
Salt
Black pepper
1 to 2 teaspoons brown sugar
1½ pounds shrimp, peeled and deveined
Hot cooked rice, to serve

1. Melt the butter in a large saucepan over medium heat. Add the onions, celery, and bell pepper and sauté until the vegetables are softened, about 5 minutes.

2. Add the tomatoes, broth, tomato sauce, tomato paste, garlic, bay leaves, parsley, white pepper, thyme, and cayenne pepper. Season to taste with salt and black pepper, and more cayenne pepper if needed. Stir in 1 teaspoon of brown sugar. Taste and add the second teaspoon if desired. Bring to a boil, then reduce the heat and simmer for 10 minutes.

3. Remove the bay leaves. Add the shrimp and simmer for 5 minutes, until the shrimp are pink and firm.

4. Spoon over the rice and serve hot.

Shrimp Scampi

Shrimp in garlic sauce is a favorite, whether served atop a bed of linguine or plain, with plenty of French bread to mop up the butter sauce.

SERVES 4

2 tablespoons butter
2 tablespoons oil
2 teaspoons minced garlic
3 tablespoons dry white wine
Salt and pepper
1½ pounds shrimp, peeled and deveined
¼ cup chopped fresh parsley

1. Preheat the broiler.

2. Melt the butter with the oil in a small saucepan over medium heat. Add the garlic and sauté until fragrant, about 30 seconds. Stir in the wine and season with salt and pepper.

3. Arrange the shrimp in a 9 x 13-inch baking dish and pour the butter mixture over it. Broil for 5 to 8 minutes, turning and basting once.

4. Sprinkle with the parsley and serve, spooning the pan juices over the shrimp.

Shrimp De Jonghe

In the days of speakeasies, bathtub gin, and gangsters, the De Jonghe Hotel and Restaurant was in its heyday in downtown Chicago. This simple casserole originated there.

SERVES 6

2 pounds shrimp, peeled and deveined
¾ cup (1½ sticks) butter
1½ teaspoons minced garlic
½ cup dry sherry
2 tablespoons chopped fresh parsley
1 teaspoon salt
½ teaspoon cayenne pepper
½ teaspoon paprika
1 cup dry bread crumbs

1. Preheat the oven to 350°F. Grease a 2-quart casserole dish.

2. Bring a medium pot of salted water to a boil. Add the shrimp and cook for 3 minutes, just until the shrimp turn pink. Drain, rinse in cold water to stop the cooking, and drain again.

3. Melt the butter in a large saucepan over medium heat. Add the garlic and sauté until fragrant, about 30 seconds. Stir in the shrimp, sherry, parsley, salt, cayenne pepper, and paprika. Add ¾ cup of bread crumbs and stir until moistened.

4. Transfer the mixture to the casserole dish. Sprinkle the remaining ¼ cup bread crumbs on top and bake for 25 minutes, until browned. Serve hot.

Greek Baked Shrimp

Greek immigrants in the early 1900s passed on their culinary traditions in diners and at Greek heritage festivals. Americans visiting these festivals experienced their first taste of exotic ingredients, like feta cheese.

SERVES 4

6 tablespoons oil
1 medium onion, finely chopped
1 teaspoon minced garlic
1½ cups seeded and diced tomatoes
⅓ cup dry white wine
½ cup chopped fresh parsley
Salt and pepper
2 pounds shrimp, peeled and deveined
2 tablespoons lemon juice
½ pound feta cheese, crumbled

1. Heat 3 tablespoons of oil in a medium saucepan over medium-high heat. Add the onion and garlic and sauté until the onion is softened, about 3 minutes. Add the tomatoes, wine, and parsley. Season to taste with salt and pepper. Bring to a boil, reduce the heat, and simmer until thickened, about 5 minutes. Remove from the heat.

2. Preheat the oven to 450°F. Grease a 9 x 13-inch baking dish.

3. Heat the remaining 3 tablespoons oil in a large skillet over medium heat. Add the shrimp and sauté until just beginning to turn pink. Pour the lemon juice over the shrimp and remove from the heat.

4. To assemble the dish, spoon half the tomato mixture into the baking dish. Spread the shrimp

evenly over the sauce, then top with the remaining sauce and the cheese.

5. Bake for 15 minutes, until bubbling. Serve hot.

Sautéed Scallops

Sea scallops are found from the Georges Bank off the East Coast all the way down the coast to Virginia. They are also harvested from Alaska to Oregon, although the Northwest scallops are in short supply.

SERVES 4

1 pound sea scallops
½ cup all-purpose flour
2 tablespoons oil
1 teaspoon minced garlic
Salt and pepper
Juice of 1 medium lemon

1. Rinse the scallops and pat dry with paper towels. Gently toss the scallops with the flour in a fine-mesh sieve and shake to remove all excess flour. The scallops should be lightly coated.

2. Heat the oil in a large skillet over medium-high heat. Add the scallops and sauté until just barely browned on all sides, about 1 to 2 minutes per side (less if the scallops are small). Add the garlic and continue to cook for about 30 seconds. Remove with a slotted spoon and keep warm on an ovenproof plate in a warm oven.

3. Add the lemon juice to the pan and cook until the liquid is slightly thickened, about 2 to 3 min-

utes. Return the scallops to the pan, season with salt and pepper, and toss to coat with the pan juices. Serve hot.

Scalloped Scallops

Seafood in a cream sauce is an easy and tasty dinner. Serve over rice, noodles, or toast points.

SERVES 4

1 cup water
1 pound sea scallops
3 tablespoons butter
3 tablespoons all-purpose flour
1 cup heavy cream
Salt and pepper
¾ cup fine dry bread crumbs

1. Preheat the oven to 400°F. Grease a 1½-quart casserole dish.

2. Bring the water to a simmer in a medium saucepan. Add the scallops and poach until just barely cooked, about 3 minutes. Drain, reserving ¾ cup of the cooking liquid.

3. Melt the butter in the same saucepan over medium heat. Stir in the flour until you have a smooth paste. Add the cream and scallop cooking liquid, bring to a boil, then turn off the heat. Season to taste with salt and pepper. Stir in the scallops.

4. Spoon the mixture into the prepared casserole and sprinkle the crumbs on top. Bake for 15 minutes, until browned and bubbly. Serve hot.

Coquilles St. Jacques

Scallops were named "Coquilles St. Jacques" ("Shells of St. James") in honor of St. James the Great, as was the dish. The scallop shell is the emblem of the Order of Saint James because James supposedly saved the life of a drowning knight who was covered in scallop shells when he emerged from the sea.

SERVES 6 TO 8

1½ cups water
½ cup dry sherry
1½ teaspoons salt
1½ teaspoons white pepper
2 pounds bay scallops
½ cup (1 stick) butter
½ pound mushrooms, sliced (about 3 cups)
½ medium onion, diced
½ cup all-purpose flour
1 cup half-and-half
¼ cup grated Parmesan cheese
¼ cup dry bread crumbs

1. Preheat the oven to 350°F. Grease the insides of 12 large scallop shells (available from gourmet cookware stores) or a large casserole dish.

2. Heat the water, sherry, salt, and pepper in a large saucepan until simmering. Add the scallops and poach until they are just cooked, about 3 minutes. Drain and set aside, reserving the cooking liquid.

3. Melt the butter in a medium saucepan over medium heat. Add the mushrooms and onion and sauté until the mushrooms give up their juice, about 8 minutes. Stir in the flour until you have a paste. Cook for 3 more minutes.

4. Stir in the half-and-half and liquid from the scallops. Cook, stirring, until thickened and smooth. Remove from the heat and add the scallops. Taste and adjust the seasoning as needed.

5. Spoon the mixture into the scallop shells or casserole dish. Mix the Parmesan cheese and bread crumbs in a small bowl and sprinkle over the top of each shell. Bake for 15 minutes, until browned and bubbly. Serve hot.

BUYING AND PREPARING SEAFOOD

▼▼▼▼▼▼▼▼▼▼

Basic Cooking Methods for White Fish Fillets

White fish include fillets of catfish, Chilean sea bass, cod, dogfish, flounder, fluke, grouper, haddock, hake, halibut, monkfish, ocean perch, orange roughy, pollock, red snapper, rockfish, sea bass, sole, striped bass, and tilapia. These may be sold as thin fillets, which are less than 1 inch thick. Thick white fish fillets are over 1 inch thick. In general, thick and thin fillets can be used interchangeably in recipes, though you must adjust the cooking times accordingly. Here are some general cooking tips.

▶ Suitable cooking methods for all fish fillets include broiling, poaching, sautéing, oven frying, and baking. Deep frying works well for firm, thick fillets such as catfish, red snapper, rockfish, and halibut. Fillets of these fish are less likely to fall apart in the deep fryer.

▶ By the time the outside of a thin fillet is opaque, the inside is done. Remove it from the pan soon after because the fish will continue to cook even when removed from the heat.

▶ When the thinnest part of a fillet flakes, the thicker part is done. By the time the thicker part flakes, it is overcooked.

▶ To broil thin white fillets, brush the fish with a little oil or melted butter and broil under a preheated broiler for 2 to 4 minutes without turning. To broil thick fillets, flip halfway through broiling and allow 4 to 6 minutes per ½-inch thickness.

▶ To sauté thin white fillets, coat the fish in flour before cooking. Add to very hot oil, but reduce the heat to medium-high as soon as the fish is added to the pan. Do not crowd the pan.

▶ To pan fry fillets or small panfish, heat ¼ inch butter or oil in a large skillet. Dip the fish in a mixture of 1 beaten egg and ¼ cup milk. Coat the fish in flour, cornmeal, or seasoned dry bread crumbs. Fry over medium-high heat, allowing 3 to 4 minutes on each side for ½-inch-thick fillets, 5 to 6 minutes on each side for 1-inch-thick fillets, and 5 to 8 minutes per side for panfish.

▶ To oven fry fillets, soak in milk or buttermilk. Then coat with bread crumbs and bake on a well-greased baking sheet at 500°F for about 10 minutes per inch of thickness.

▶ To poach fillets, bring 1½ cups water or a combination of water and wine to a boil. Reduce to a simmer, add the fish, and simmer, covered, for 4 to 6 minutes per ½-inch thickness.

▶ To bake fillets, place in a single layer in a baking dish, brush with butter, and bake, uncovered, in a 450°F oven for about 10 minutes per 1-inch thickness.

▶ When the fillets are of uneven thickness, fold under the thinnest part to form a folded fillet of even thickness. This will ensure more even cooking.

Fish Facts

Confused about cooking fish? Here are some tips.

▶ When buying fish, allow 4 to 6 ounces for each serving of steaks or fillets and 8 ounces of dressed fish (a dressed fish is whole but cleaned, scaled, and ready for cooking).

▶ Frozen fish should be thawed overnight in the refrigerator.

▶ To judge when a fish is done, poke the fish with a fork and twist gently. Properly cooked fish will be opaque and the flesh will pull away from the bones. The juices will be milky white. If the fish resists flaking, the flesh is translucent, and if the juices are clear, the fish is not done. If the fish looks dry, has no juices, and falls apart when prodded with the fork, it is overdone.

▶ In recent years, fish in restaurants has been served rare, or when the flesh is still slightly translucent in the center. If this is how you like your fish, remove it from the heat when it is still slightly underdone. The fish will still continue to cook for a few minutes.

Buying and Handling Clams

Clams are found all over the world. They fall into two basic categories: hard-shell (cherrystone, littleneck, quahog or chowder, mahogany, Manila) and soft-shell (steamers, razor clams, geoduck). Clams should be alive and in the shell when you buy them.

▶ When buying hard-shell clams, make sure the shells are tightly closed. If they are open, they should snap shut if lightly tapped. If they don't close, they are dead and should be discarded. To test a soft-shell clam, lightly touch the neck (siphon) that is sticking out; it will move if it is alive. Discard the clam if there's no movement.

▶ Store live clams in an open container covered with a moist cloth for up to 2 days in the refrigerator. Do not place in plastic bags.

▶ Store shucked clams in their liquor in the refrigerator for up to 3 days.

▶ To rid clams of sand, soak them in salted cold water for about 2 hours (use ¼ cup salt per gallon water).

▶ Before cooking, scrub the clamshells under cold running water.

▶ To open clams for serving on the half shell, place the live clam on a flat surface and insert a small knife into the hinged ligament. Using gloves and a kitchen towel around the clam, press, gently wiggle, and twist the knife until the shell pops open. Remove the shell, capturing as much of the liquor as possible.

▶ Cook clams briefly to avoid toughening.

Shucking Oysters

Raw oysters on the half shell are such a treat that everyone should know how to shuck them. Be sure to protect your hand from a slipping knife by wearing a glove or wrapping your hand in a towel.

To open, place the live oyster, cupped side down, on a flat surface and insert an oyster knife into the hinge. Using gloves and a kitchen towel around the oyster, press, wiggle, and twist the knife until the oyster pops open. Twist off the top shell, keeping as much of the liquor as possible. Detach the meat from the shell with the knife.

Buying and Cooking Shrimp

Americans buy more shrimp than any other seafood. Shrimp is widely available both fresh and frozen.

▶ When buying shrimp, allow about ½ pound per serving.

▶ Figure that 1 pound of raw shrimp in the shell (without the heads) will yield slightly more than ½ pound peeled shrimp.

▶ To peel shrimp, start at the large end and peel away the shell and legs.

▶ To devein shrimp (which really means pulling out the intestinal tract; some shrimp is sold deveined), use a sharp pointed knife to cut a shallow slit down the middle of the outside curve of the shrimp. Pull out the slightly darker tract, then rinse under cold water.

▶ Shrimp shells can be boiled for about 10 minutes to yield a flavorful broth. Shrimp boiled in the shell will be more flavorful than shrimp boiled after it has been peeled.

▶ Shrimp should be cooked briefly for the best texture—only until they turn pink, 3 to 5 minutes. Shrimp can be boiled, steamed, baked, grilled, broiled, sautéed, or fried.

Buying and Handling Soft-Shell Crabs

In fish markets where live crabs are sold, soft-shell crabs are available in late spring and early summer. They come in various sizes, such as hotels (weighing 2.5 ounces and measuring 4 to 4½ inches), primes (weighing 3 ounces and measuring 4½ to 5 inches), and jumbos (weighing 4½ ounces and measuring 5 to 5½ inches). Soft-shell crabs are usually stored at very cold temperatures to keep the shell from hardening and to prevent decomposition if the crabs die. Store cleaned crabs covered in plastic wrap in the coldest part of the refrigerator for up to 2 days.

How to Clean Soft-Shell Crabs

1. Hold the crab in one hand, and use a pair of kitchen shears to cut off the front of the crab, about ½ inch behind the eyes and mouth. Squeeze out the contents of the sac located directly behind the cut you just made.

2. Lift one pointed end of the crab's outer shell; remove and discard the gills. Repeat on the other side.

3. Turn the crab over and snip off the small flap known as the apron. Rinse the entire crab well and pat dry. Once cleaned, crabs should be cooked or stored immediately.

How to Remove Crabmeat from the Shell

It takes practice to get at all the crabmeat hiding in a crab. Here's how.

1. Pull off all of the crab's legs, and separate at the joints. Pull off the two large claws. Pound them lightly with your mallet; don't crush them, or the meat and shell will be crushed together. Just break the shell, then work with a knife, fork, pick, or your fingers to extract the meat. Continue with the remaining leg pieces.

2. Pick up the legless, clawless crab and stand it on its bottom edge, so that the white underbelly is facing you. The design on the underbelly that looks like a baseball catcher's chest protector should have an arrow-shaped flap on it that's pointing downward. With your fingers, grab that arrow, force it out of its groove, grab it with your fingers, and then, pulling upward, rip back and remove the whole "chest protector"—a triangular piece of soft shell.

3. Keep the crab standing on the same bottom edge. Planting one thumb at the top of the crab on the underbelly side, and another thumb on the top of the crab on the red top shell side, pry the crab open by moving your thumbs in opposite directions. The crab should pop open, and you'll have two pieces: the nearly empty top shell (which is red on the outside) and the white underbelly shell, filled with cartilage and crabmeat.

4. The nearly empty red shell may contain roe (eggs) and tomalley (the liver). Remove with a spoon and eat, if you like.

5. To remove the meat from the underbelly shell, break the body in half and pick it out.

Cooking Lobster

More lobsters are enjoyed steamed or boiled than prepared any other way. A freshly cooked lobster is so sweet and flavorful, it barely needs a dip in melted butter. The water in which the lobsters are steamed or boiled makes a great broth for use in soups.

▶ When buying, allow a 1½- to 2-pound lobster for each person.

▶ To kill a live lobster, either parboil for a few minutes or place it in a large pan in the freezer for 20 minutes to stun it. Remove and place the lobster on its back and hold firmly with one hand. Insert a sharp, heavy knife where the head meets the body and quickly slice through the entire length of the body and tail.

▶ To boil lobster, bring a very large pot of seawater to a boil, or use tap water plus a couple handfuls of salt. Plunge the lobster into the water, cover, and wait for the water to return to a boil. Cook 8 minutes for its first pound, plus 3 to 4 minutes for every additional pound.

▶ Boiled lobsters should be drained before serving. Poke a hole in the crosshatch directly behind the eyes and drain the water.

▶ To steam lobster, bring a few inches of seawater or salted tap water to a boil. Add the lobster and cook as above.

▶ Lobster can also be grilled (see Chapter 9).

▶ Lobsters are done when the meat is opaque and the shells are bright red.

Removing the Meat from a Lobster

To remove the meat from a lobster, you will need a nutcracker and pick (or long skewer) to pull out the meat.

1. First, twist the claws to remove them. Crack the claws with a nutcracker and pull out the meat.

2. Twist the lobster in half to separate the tail from the body. Cut through the soft side of the tail and crack it open. The meat is easily pulled out.

3. Pull off the legs, separate at the joints, and suck out the meat, if desired. Cut through the underside of the body, and pick out the small bits of meat in there. The red coral (eggs) on females and the green tomalley (the liver) are edible.

CHAPTER SEVEN

Poultry

Some historians believe the first chickens came to the New World with Christopher Columbus during his first voyages, and American cooks have been in love with them ever since. This is no surprise, since chicken is a popular ingredient in just about every culture in the world.

The native turkey was already held in great regard in the New World, and was domesticated in the Americas long before the Spaniards arrived. Although there is some doubt as to whether it was served at the first Thanksgiving in 1621, it most certainly appeared on tables at feasts soon thereafter. George Washington was the first president to declare Thanksgiving a holiday, in 1777, and the idea of a Thanksgiving turkey had doubled in popularity by the mid-1800s. It's no wonder the bird is still the most popular thing to eat on that holiday!

On American tables, wild ducks, geese, partridges, and other game birds made regular appearances wherever hunters lived. Pheasants were introduced from England by sportsmen in the late 1800s for hunting.

Meanwhile, chickens were roasted, poached, stewed, grilled, baked, and—especially—fried. Southern fried chicken is arguably the most beloved and distinctive of American chicken dishes, and is perhaps the most esteemed of all Southern meals. The details of this very simple dish vary from one state to another, with some cooks espousing lard and others insisting on oil. Some batter-dip the chicken, others call for crumbs. Some cook with the lid on, others with the lid off. Some insist on serving it hot with cream gravy, while others call for it served cold. Then there is the question of seasonings and spices. It seems as though the only aspect of Southern fried chicken on which there is agreement is the necessity to cook it in a cast-iron skillet.

Going to a supermarket to buy a package of parts—all breasts or all drumsticks, for example—is a fairly recent phenomenon. There's no shortage of recipes for any single part of the chicken, but recent diet trends have led Americans to prefer chicken breasts.

Here you will find a wide variety of recipes for perfect poultry every time—from a simple roasted chicken or savory duck to a festive Thanksgiving turkey.

Roast Chicken with Pan Gravy

Few dishes are as simple and as perfect as a beautifully roasted chicken. You don't need any special equipment to get the same results your grandmother did. Just use a rimmed baking sheet or very shallow roasting pan to encourage even browning.

SERVES 4 TO 6

1 (4- to 6-pound) roasting chicken
Salt and pepper
2 to 3 tablespoons butter, melted
Paprika
¼ cup dry white wine, sherry, Madeira wine, or water
2 tablespoons all-purpose flour
¾ cup chicken broth (page 119)

1. Preheat the oven to 400°F.

2. Remove the neck and giblets (heart, liver, and gizzard) from the cavity of the chicken and discard. Rinse the chicken and pat dry with paper towels. Season inside and out with salt and pepper. Arrange the chicken, breast side up, on a rimmed baking sheet. Brush the breasts and the legs with the butter and sprinkle with paprika.

3. Roast the chicken until the breast meat registers 170° to 175°F and the thigh runs with clear juices if poked with a fork. The roasting time will be about 60 minutes for the first 4 pounds, plus 8 minutes for every additional pound.

4. Remove the chicken from the pan and let stand on a large platter while you prepare the gravy.

5. To make the gravy, place the roasting pan over two burners, pour in the wine, and cook over medium-high heat, stirring and scraping with a wooden spoon to bring up all the browned bits from the bottom of the pan. Pour into a 4-cup glass measuring cup and let stand for a minute to allow the fat to rise to the top. Reserve 2 tablespoons of fat and discard the rest of the fat.

6. Heat the 2 tablespoons of fat in a small saucepan over medium heat. Stir in the flour and make a smooth paste and cook for 2 to 3 minutes. Stir in the remaining chicken juices from the glass measuring cup, any juices that have accumulated on the platter with the chicken, and the chicken broth. Bring to a boil, stirring, and cook until thickened. Season to taste with salt and pepper.

7. Cut the bird into serving pieces and serve hot, passing the gravy at the table.

TIP: Trussing the bird before roasting makes the presentation more attractive, but it is not essential. To truss a chicken, cut a length of string about 3 feet long. Place the center of the string under the rear end of the bird and loop it around the ends of the legs 2 to 3 times. Cross the string over the top of the breast. Loop the string under and around the wings. Tie a knot or bow on top of the bird to join the two ends.

Mushroom-Stuffed Roast Chicken

Stuffing a combination of mushrooms and herbs under the skin of a chicken creates a particularly aromatic bird.

SERVES 4 TO 6

1 (4- to 6-pound) roasting chicken
Salt and pepper
2 tablespoons butter
¼ cup minced shallots
1 tablespoon minced garlic
1 pound mushrooms, minced
2 tablespoons dry sherry
¼ cup dry bread crumbs
2 tablespoons chopped fresh parsley
½ teaspoon dried thyme
½ cup dry white wine
½ cup chicken broth (page 119)

1. Remove the neck and giblets (heart, liver, and gizzard) from the cavity of the chicken and discard. Rinse the chicken and pat dry with paper towels. Season inside and out with salt and pepper.

2. Melt the butter in a large skillet over medium heat. Add the shallots and garlic and cook until softened, about 2 minutes. Add the mushrooms and sherry and cook until the mushrooms give up their juice, about 8 minutes. Stir in the bread crumbs, parsley, and thyme. Season to taste with salt and pepper. Cool thoroughly.

3. Preheat the oven to 425°F. In a small bowl, combine the wine and broth; set aside.

4. Starting at the neck of the chicken, separate the skin from the flesh by gently working your fingers below the skin. Loosen the skin from the breast and legs, being careful not to tear it. Stuff the mushroom mixture under the skin to cover the leg and breast meat. Slip the tips of the wings under the back. Tie the legs together with string.

5. Place the chicken, breast side up, in a roasting pan and roast in the oven for 30 minutes.

6. Reduce the heat to 350°F and continue to roast for 30 minutes, basting the chicken with the wine and broth, until the breast meat registers 170° to 175°F and the thigh runs with clear juices when poked with a fork.

7. Remove the chicken from the oven and let stand in the pan for 15 to 20 minutes.

8. Cut the bird into serving pieces and place on a serving platter. Remove the fat from the pan juices and pour the juices into a gravy boat to pass at the table.

TIP: Instant-read thermometers take the guesswork out of judging when meat and poultry are cooked and are the most reliable way to tell if the meat is done. Alternatively, you can poke the bird with a fork at its thickest point in the thigh. The juices should run clear. Any sign of pink means the poultry is not done.

Southern Fried Chicken with Cream Gravy

This is the basic fried chicken recipe—as it has appeared in countless cookbooks written by countless cooks. Lard imparts rich flavor, but you can use shortening; however, the texture won't be as crisp as it would be otherwise.

SERVES 4 TO 6

3 to 4 pounds chicken parts
1½ cups buttermilk
2 cups all-purpose flour
2 teaspoons salt, plus more to taste
1 teaspoon black pepper, plus more to taste
3 or more cups of lard or shortening, for frying
2 cups milk

1. Cut the chicken legs to separate the thighs and drumsticks. Remove as much fat as possible. Put the chicken in a large bowl and cover with the buttermilk. Turn the pieces to coat. Refrigerate for at least 2 hours and up to 12 hours.

2. Spoon the flour into a sturdy brown paper bag or large resealable plastic bag. Add the 2 teaspoons salt and 1 teaspoon black pepper and shake to mix.

3. Remove a few chicken pieces from the buttermilk, add to the bag of flour, and shake to coat. Remove the pieces and set out to dry on wire racks. Repeat until all the chicken pieces are coated. Set the bag aside.

4. In a large, deep, heavy skillet, begin melting about 3 cups of lard to 350°F. The melted lard should be at least ½ inch deep.

5. Preheat the oven to 200°F. Place a baking sheet covered with wire racks in the oven.

6. Use tongs to gently lay a single layer of chicken in the skillet, skin side down, and fry for 10 to 12 minutes, until the bottom side is well browned. Turn and cook the second side for another 10 to 12 minutes. Keep the cooked chicken warm on the wire racks in the oven and continue to fry until all the chicken is cooked.

7. To make the gravy, pour off all but 2 tablespoons of the cooking fat in the skillet. Measure out 2 tablespoon of seasoned flour from the bag and sprinkle over the fat. Blend in with a wooden spoon until you have a smooth paste and cook for 2 minutes. Slowly pour in the milk, stirring until the gravy begins to thicken. Season to taste with salt and pepper. Serve the chicken hot, passing the cream gravy on the side.

Spicy Southern Fried Chicken

This recipe could give a certain colonel a run for his money. Lots of Southern cooks have experimented with spicing up their chicken recipes. Here's one version that is a terrific choice for taking on a picnic.

SERVES 4 TO 6

3 to 4 pounds chicken parts
1½ cups buttermilk
2 cups all-purpose flour
1 tablespoon salt
2 teaspoons dried basil
2 teaspoons dried oregano
2 teaspoons dried sage
2 teaspoons dried thyme
1 teaspoon black pepper
1 teaspoon cayenne pepper
1 teaspoon paprika
¼ teaspoon ground cumin
¼ teaspoon ground ginger
¼ teaspoon ground nutmeg
3 or more cups of lard or shortening, for frying

1. Cut the chicken legs to separate the thighs and drumsticks. Rinse the chicken and pat dry with paper towels. Remove as much fat as possible. Put the chicken in a large bowl and cover with the buttermilk. Turn to coat the pieces. Refrigerate for at least 2 hours and up to 12 hours.

2. Spoon the flour into a sturdy brown paper bag or large resealable plastic bag. Add the salt, basil, oregano, sage, thyme, black pepper, cayenne pepper, paprika, cumin, ginger, and nutmeg and shake to mix.

3. Remove a few chicken pieces from the buttermilk, add to the bag of flour, and shake to coat. Remove the pieces and set out to dry on wire racks. Repeat until all the chicken pieces are coated.

4. In a large, deep, heavy skillet, begin melting about 3 cups of lard to 350°F. The melted lard should be at least ½ inch deep.

5. Preheat the oven to 200°F. Place a baking sheet covered with wire racks in the oven.

6. Use tongs to lay a single layer of chicken in the skillet, skin side down, and fry for 12 to 15 minutes, until the bottom side is well browned. Turn and cook the second side for another 12 to 15 minutes. Keep the cooked chicken warm on the wire racks in the oven and continue to fry until all the chicken is cooked. Serve hot or cold.

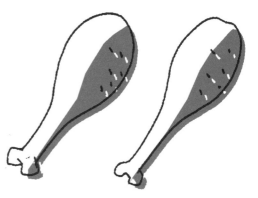

Oven-Fried Chicken

For those who haven't the courage or the time to make real Southern-style fried chicken, there is oven-fried chicken. If you run the chicken under the broiler for a minute before serving, the coating becomes remarkably crispy.

SERVES 4 TO 6

3 to 4 pounds chicken parts
1 large egg
2 tablespoons milk
2 cups dry bread crumbs
2 tablespoons butter, melted
1 teaspoon garlic powder
1 teaspoon onion powder
1 teaspoon salt
1 teaspoon dried oregano
½ teaspoon black pepper

1. Preheat the oven to 350°F. Grease a baking sheet.

2. Cut the chicken legs to separate the thighs and drumsticks. Rinse the chicken pieces and pat dry with paper towels. Remove as much fat as possible. Set aside.

3. Use a fork to beat the egg with the milk in a shallow bowl.

4. Combine the bread crumbs, butter, garlic powder, onion powder, salt, oregano, and pepper in a separate shallow bowl and mix.

5. Dip the chicken pieces in the egg, then roll in the bread crumbs, patting to make the crumbs adhere. Place on the baking sheet.

6. Bake for 45 to 60 minutes, until the crumbs are browned and chicken juices run clear when a piece is pierced with a fork.

7. Transfer the baking sheet to under the broiler and broil for 2 to 3 minutes to make the breading crisp. Serve hot or cold.

Oven-Fried Mustard Chicken

This is a real crowd pleaser. The mustard is subtle, which works well with the flavor of the chicken and the Parmesan cheese.

SERVES 4 TO 6

3 to 4 pounds chicken parts
1½ cups dry bread crumbs
½ cup grated Parmesan cheese
2 tablespoons butter, melted
1 teaspoon salt
1 teaspoon dried basil
½ teaspoon black pepper
⅓ cup Dijon mustard
1 teaspoon minced garlic

1. Preheat the oven to 350°F. Grease a baking sheet.

2. Cut the chicken legs to separate the thighs and drumsticks. Rinse the chicken and pat dry with paper towels. Remove as much fat as possible.

3. Mix the bread crumbs, cheese, butter, salt, basil, and pepper in a shallow bowl.

4. Combine the mustard and garlic in a small bowl. Brush the mustard mixture on the chicken. Dip the chicken pieces in the bread crumbs, patting to make the crumbs stick. Place on the baking sheet.

5. Bake for 45 to 60 minutes, until the crumbs are browned and the chicken juices run clear when a piece is pierced with a fork.

6. Transfer the baking sheet to the broiler and broil for 2 to 3 minutes to make the breading crisp. Serve hot or cold.

Broiled Herbed Chicken

A quick way to prepare chicken is to broil it with a coating of herbs and lemon. The resulting crisp, crackling skin is the best part.

SERVES 4 TO 6

3 to 4 pounds chicken parts
5 tablespoons butter, melted
1 tablespoon lemon juice
1 teaspoon minced garlic
1 tablespoon chopped fresh parsley
½ teaspoon salt
1 teaspoon onion powder
1 teaspoon dried thyme
1 teaspoon paprika
½ teaspoon black pepper

1. Preheat the broiler with the broiler pan in place, about 8 inches from the heat source.

2. Cut the chicken legs to separate the thighs and drumsticks. Rinse the chicken and pat dry with paper towels. Remove as much fat as possible.

3. Combine the butter, lemon juice, and garlic in a small bowl. In another small bowl, mix the parsley, salt, onion powder, thyme, paprika, and pepper.

4. Arrange the chicken, skin side down, on the hot broiler pan. Brush half the melted butter mixture onto the chicken pieces; sprinkle with half the herb mixture.

5. Broil for 20 minutes. Turn skin side up, brush with the remaining butter mixture, and sprinkle with the remaining herb mixture. Broil for another 20 minutes, until the chicken is tender and the juices run clear. Serve hot with the pan juices, if desired. The chicken is also good served cold.

Baked Barbecued Chicken

Nothing beats the taste of chicken barbecued on a grill, but sometimes the weather doesn't cooperate. This recipe provides a tasty rainy-day alternative, and homemade barbecue sauce will make it taste even better.

SERVES 4 TO 6

1½ cups barbecue sauce (page 254)
3 to 4 pounds chicken parts

1. Preheat the oven to 350°F.

2. Cut the chicken legs to separate the thighs and drumsticks. Brush the chicken with about two-thirds of the sauce, brushing both sides of each piece. Arrange the chicken in a shallow roasting pan or baking dish, skin side down. Bake for 20 minutes.

3. Turn the chicken, skin side up. Brush with the remaining sauce. Bake for another 20 to 30 minutes, until the chicken is tender and the juices run clear when pierced with a fork.

4. To crisp and color the skin, run the chicken under the broiler for about 5 minutes. Serve hot.

Chicken and Dumplings

Dumplings are very common throughout Europe and undoubtedly came to America with the earliest colonists. The dough is steamed rather than baked. Dumplings are an inexpensive way to extend a soup or stew.

SERVES 4 TO 6

Chicken:
3 to 4 pounds chicken parts
8 cups water
3 medium carrots, diced
3 medium celery ribs, diced
1 medium onion, diced
1 teaspoon dried thyme
1 teaspoon salt, plus more to taste
¼ teaspoon black pepper

Dumplings:
1 cup all-purpose flour
2 teaspoons baking powder
½ teaspoon salt

2 tablespoons butter, softened
1 large egg, beaten
½ cup milk

1. To make the chicken, cover the chicken with the water in a large pot. Bring to a boil, cover, and simmer for 1½ to 2 hours, until the chicken is completely cooked.

2. Strain and save the broth and let the chicken cool.

3. Remove the chicken meat from the bones. Discard the skin and bones, and cut the meat into bite-size pieces. Set aside. Skim the chicken fat off the surface of the broth and discard.

4. To make the dumplings, mix the flour, baking powder, and salt in a large bowl. Cut in the butter with a fork until well blended. Mix the egg and milk together in a small bowl. Add to the flour mixture and knead for a few seconds, until just mixed. If the dough is sticky, add more flour.

5. Heat the broth to a simmer in the large pot. Add the carrots, celery, onion, thyme, salt, and pepper and cook for 5 minutes. With a large spoon, pull the dumpling dough apart into rough-shaped balls the size of a walnut (do not press to form). Carefully drop the dumplings into the broth. Cover and reduce the heat so the broth is barely simmering. Cook for 7 to 8 minutes, until the dumplings are cooked through. Overcooking will turn the dumplings to mush.

6. Place the cooked chicken in a large bowl and ladle the hot broth, vegetables, and dumplings over the top. Serve immediately.

Smothered Southern Chicken

Many recipes start with fried chicken that is baked in a creamed (flour-thickened) gravy. These recipes were developed to tenderize tough old stewing hens that had lived past the age of productive egg laying. Mashed potatoes and biscuits are both traditional accompaniments.

SERVES 4 TO 6

3 to 4 pounds chicken parts
½ cup plus 3 tablespoons all-purpose flour
1 teaspoon salt, plus more to taste

¼ teaspoon black pepper, plus more to taste
¼ cup (½ stick) butter
¼ cup shortening
4 cups chicken broth (page 119)
1 bay leaf

1. Cut the chicken legs to separate the thighs and drumsticks. Rinse the chicken and pat dry with paper towels. Remove as much fat as possible.

2. Combine the ½ cup flour, 1 teaspoon salt, and ¼ teaspoon pepper in a paper or plastic bag. Add the chicken, a piece at a time, and shake to coat with the flour. Set aside the coated pieces on a large plate.

3. Melt the butter and shortening in a large skillet over medium-high heat. Use tongs to add a single layer of chicken pieces; do not crowd. Cook until browned all over, about 5 minutes per side. Transfer the chicken to a shallow roasting pan or baking dish. Repeat until all the pieces are browned.

4. Preheat the oven to 350°F.

5. Pour off all but 3 tablespoons of fat from the skillet. Stir in 3 tablespoons flour to make a paste. Continue to cook, stirring, until the paste is browned and thickened, about 5 minutes. Slowly add in the broth, stirring until smooth and thick. Season to taste with salt and pepper.

6. Pour the sauce over the chicken pieces, tuck a bay leaf into the pan, cover the pan tightly with aluminum foil, and bake for 1 hour.

7. Remove the bay leaf and serve hot.

Chicken Fricassee

The name "chicken fricassee" can be applied to any stewed chicken dish. Some recipes call for browning the chicken first, while some skip that step. Some call for mushrooms, others for an assortment of vegetables. A Cuban-style or Caribbean-style chicken fricassee may have raisins, brown sugar, and vinegar in the gravy. This basic version is widely made.

SERVES 4 TO 6

3 to 4 pounds chicken parts
½ cup plus 3 tablespoons all-purpose flour
1 teaspoon salt, plus more to taste
¼ teaspoon black pepper, plus more to taste

¼ cup (½ stick) butter
¼ cup shortening or oil
2 medium carrots, diced
2 medium celery ribs, diced
1 medium onion, diced
1 cup sliced mushrooms
1 teaspoon minced garlic
1 teaspoon fresh thyme
2½ cups chicken broth (page 119)
1 cup heavy cream
2 teaspoons lemon juice
1 bay leaf

1. Cut the chicken legs to separate the thighs and drumsticks. Rinse the chicken and pat dry with paper towels. Remove as much fat as possible.

2. Combine the ½ cup flour, 1 teaspoon salt, and ¼ teaspoon pepper in a paper or plastic bag. Add the chicken, a piece at a time, and shake to coat with the flour. Set aside the coated pieces on a large plate.

3. Melt the butter and shortening in a large skillet over medium-high heat. Use tongs to add a single layer of chicken pieces; do not crowd. Cook until browned all over, about 5 minutes per side. Transfer the chicken to a shallow roasting pan or baking dish. Repeat until all the pieces are browned.

4. Preheat the oven to 350°F.

5. Pour off all but 3 tablespoons of fat from the skillet and place over medium heat. Add the carrots, celery, onion, and mushrooms and sauté until the mushrooms give up their juice, about 8 minutes. Add the garlic and thyme and cook for 1 more minute.

6. Sprinkle in the 3 tablespoons flour and stir until the flour is completely moistened. Slowly add the broth, stirring until smooth and thick. Stir in the cream and lemon juice. Season to taste with salt and pepper.

7. Pour the sauce over the chicken pieces, tuck the bay leaf into the pan, cover the pan tightly with aluminum foil, and bake for 1 hour.

8. Remove the bay leaf and serve hot.

Chicken Étouffée

Cajun cooks take chicken fricassee or smothered chicken and spice it up, adding a considerable amount of flavor. First, the chicken is well seasoned. Then the roux is cooked until it is dark brown and rich in flavor. Aromatic vegetables and sausage or ham are added for flavor. And finally, the whole dish is spiced up with hot sauce. Serve over rice and provide plenty of ice-cold beer.

SERVES 4 TO 6

3 to 4 pounds chicken parts
Salt and pepper
Cayenne pepper
¼ cup oil
¼ cup (½ stick) butter
¾ cup all-purpose flour
1 medium onion, finely chopped
1 large celery rib, finely chopped
½ red or green bell pepper, finely chopped
1 teaspoon minced garlic
2 bay leaves
¼ cup chopped andouille sausage or smoked ham
1½ cups dark lager or amber beer
4 cups chicken broth (page 119)
¼ cup hot pepper sauce, such as Tabasco
1 tablespoon Worcestershire sauce
¼ cup chopped fresh parsley
¼ cup chopped scallions

1. Cut the chicken legs to separate the thighs and drumsticks. Rinse the chicken and pat dry with paper towels. Remove as much fat as possible. Sprinkle with salt, pepper, and cayenne pepper.

2. Heat the oil over medium-high heat in a large Dutch oven. Use tongs to add the chicken pieces in a single layer; do not crowd. Cook until browned all over, about 5 minutes per side. Transfer the cooked pieces to a platter and set aside. Repeat until all the chicken is browned.

3. To make the roux, add the butter to the drippings in the pan and melt over medium heat. Stir in the flour until you have a smooth paste. Continue to cook, stirring constantly, until chocolate brown, 12 to 15 minutes.

4. Immediately add the onion, celery, bell pepper, garlic, and bay leaves and cook until the vegetables are softened, 2 to 3 minutes. Use a wooden spoon to stir in the sausage and beer and continue stirring to loosen any brown bits from the bottom of the pan. Add the broth, hot pepper sauce, and Worcestershire sauce; stir and bring to a boil.

5. Return the chicken pieces to the pan, cover, and simmer for 1¼ hours, until the chicken is very tender.

6. Remove the bay leaves. Add the chopped parsley and scallions and stir well to combine. Taste and adjust the seasoning, if necessary. Serve hot.

Paprika Chicken

The soul of this dish is in the spice—paprika. The characteristic flavoring of Hungarian cooking, paprika should have a sweet and lively taste, never sharp or bitter. If your paprika is old, use it only for dusting the occasional deviled egg or potato salad. Buy a fresh supply for this recipe.

SERVES 4 TO 6

3 to 4 pounds chicken parts
2 teaspoons salt
⅛ teaspoon black pepper
¼ cup oil
2 large onions, chopped
3 tablespoons sweet or hot Hungarian paprika
1½ cups water
1 tablespoon all-purpose flour
1 cup sour cream

1. Cut the chicken legs to separate the thighs and drumsticks. Rinse the chicken and pat dry with paper towels. Remove as much fat as possible. Sprinkle with salt and pepper.

2. Heat the oil over medium-high heat in a large Dutch oven. Use tongs to add the chicken pieces in a single layer; do not crowd. Cook until browned all over, about 5 minutes per side. Transfer the cooked pieces to a platter and set aside. Repeat until all the chicken is browned.

3. Add the onions to the Dutch oven and cook until the onions are softened, about 3 minutes. Return the chicken to the Dutch oven. Add the paprika and water; cover and simmer slowly for 20 minutes.

4. Uncover and cook for 10 to 15 minutes, stirring occasionally, until the chicken is tender.

5. Transfer the chicken to a serving dish and keep warm.

6. In a separate medium bowl, stir the flour into the sour cream until well blended. Add the mixture to the Dutch oven and cook until the sauce thickens, 4 to 5 minutes. Pour over the chicken and serve.

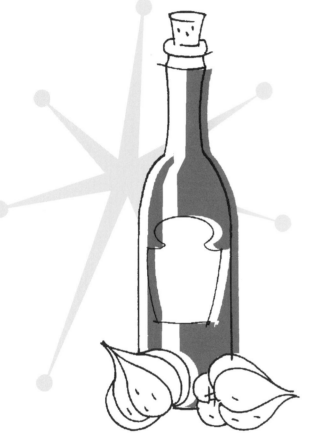

Coq au Vin

This dish is very similar to a fricassee, with the chicken stewed in wine with mushrooms, onions, and bacon. Serve with boiled potatoes or noodles.

SERVES 4

3 to 4 pounds chicken parts
4 slices bacon, chopped
2 tablespoons oil
¾ pound mushrooms, sliced
1 medium onion, chopped
2 medium carrots, chopped
1 teaspoon minced garlic
¼ cup all-purpose flour
2 cups red wine (such as Burgundy, Côtes du Rhône, or Pinot Noir)
About 2 cups chicken broth (page 119)
1 tablespoon tomato paste
16 to 20 white pearl onions, peeled
1 bay leaf
¼ teaspoon dried thyme
Salt and pepper

1. Cut the chicken legs to separate the thighs and drumsticks. Rinse the chicken and pat dry with paper towels. Trim off any excess fat.

2. Cook the bacon in the oil in a large Dutch oven over medium heat, about 5 minutes. Remove the bacon with a slotted spoon and set aside.

3. Increase the heat to medium-high. Use tongs to add the chicken pieces in a single layer; do not crowd. Cook until browned all over, about 5 minutes per side. Transfer the cooked pieces to a platter. Repeat until all the chicken is browned and set aside.

4. Add the mushrooms, chopped onion, carrots, and garlic to the Dutch oven and cook until the mushrooms give up their juice, about 8 minutes.

5. Stir in the flour, reduce the heat to low, and cook until the flour forms a paste and turns golden brown, about 5 minutes.

6. Stir in the wine, broth, and tomato paste until smooth. Return the chicken and bacon to the Dutch oven. Add the pearl onions, bay leaf, and thyme. Season to taste with salt and pepper. Cover and simmer for 25 to 35 minutes, until the chicken is completely tender. The sauce should be just thick enough to coat the chicken and vegetables lightly. If it is too thin, boil it down rapidly to concentrate it; if it is too thick, thin with spoonfuls of broth.

7. Remove the bay leaf and serve hot.

TIP: To make peeling pearl onions easier, place them in boiling water and let stand for 2 to 3 minutes. Cool in ice water, cut off the stem end, and slip the skins off.

Chicken Marengo

Chicken Marengo is said to have been invented by Napoleon's chef to celebrate the battle of Marengo in 1800. Make this flavorful dish in your Dutch oven on your next trip outdoors.

SERVES 4 TO 6

3 to 4 pounds chicken parts
Salt and pepper
⅓ cup oil
1 large onion, finely chopped
½ pound mushrooms, sliced
1 teaspoon minced garlic
1 (28-ounce) can Italian plum tomatoes, drained and diced
1 cup chicken broth (page 119)
½ cup dry white wine
1 tablespoon dried thyme
1 bay leaf

1. Cut the chicken legs to separate the thighs and drumsticks. Rinse the chicken and pat dry with paper towels. Remove as much fat as possible. Sprinkle with salt and pepper.

2. Heat the oil over medium-high heat in a large Dutch oven. Use tongs to add the chicken pieces in a single layer; do not crowd. Cook until browned all over, about 5 minutes per side. Transfer the cooked pieces to a platter and set aside. Repeat until all the chicken is browned.

3. Add the onion, mushrooms, and garlic to the Dutch oven and sauté until the mushrooms give up their juice, about 8 minutes.

4. Return the chicken to the Dutch oven. Add the tomatoes, broth, wine, thyme, and bay leaf. Cover and simmer until the chicken is tender, 25 to 35 minutes.

5. Remove the bay leaf and serve hot.

Country Captain Chicken

Country captain is a curried chicken dish that originated in the American South. Some credit the dish to a British army officer who brought the recipe back from his station in India. Others believe that the dish originated in Savannah, Georgia, which was a major shipping port for spices in the nineteenth century. Wherever its true origins, it is an unusual, delicious recipe.

SERVES 4 TO 6

3 to 4 pounds chicken parts
⅔ cup all-purpose flour
Salt and pepper
3 tablespoons oil
2 medium celery ribs, finely chopped
1 small onion, finely chopped
1 medium green bell pepper, seeded and finely chopped
1 teaspoon minced garlic
1½ cups diced fresh or canned tomatoes (drained if canned)
1 cup chicken broth (page 119)
½ cup dried currants or raisins
1 tablespoon curry powder
½ teaspoon ground ginger
½ teaspoon dried thyme
¼ teaspoon ground cinnamon
⅛ teaspoon ground cloves
⅛ teaspoon ground nutmeg
3 tablespoons lemon juice
1 tablespoon brown sugar
1 tablespoon chopped fresh parsley
½ cup slivered toasted almonds
Hot cooked white rice, to serve

1. Cut the chicken legs to separate the thighs and drumsticks. Rinse the chicken and pat dry with paper towels. Remove as much fat as possible. Dip the chicken in the flour and coat all sides. Season each piece with salt and pepper.

2. Heat the oil over medium-high heat in a large Dutch oven. Use tongs to add the chicken pieces in a single layer; do not crowd. Cook until browned all over, about 5 minutes per side. Transfer the cooked pieces to a platter and set aside. Repeat until all the chicken is browned.

3. Add the celery, onion, bell pepper, and garlic to the pan and sauté until the onion is softened, about 3 minutes. Add the tomatoes, broth, currants, curry powder, ginger, thyme, cinnamon, cloves, and nutmeg. Season to taste with salt and pepper. Bring to a boil, reduce the heat, cover, and simmer for about 10 minutes.

4. Return the chicken to the pan, cover, and cook, turning the pieces occasionally, until the chicken juices run clear when pricked with a fork, about 30 minutes.

5. Stir in the lemon juice and brown sugar. Taste and adjust the seasoning as needed and sprinkle with the parsley and toasted almonds. Serve hot, on a bed of rice.

Brunswick Stew

Brunswick stew, a relative of another stew known as Kentucky burgoo, is another Southern favorite. It was originally made with squirrel and was probably invented to serve those attending a political rally in Brunswick County, Virginia. The people of Brunswick, Georgia, also claim their stew is the original. It's just as likely that the stew, or at least a similar version, was created much earlier. The best Brunswick stew is a matter of great controversy in some parts, but most will agree that it should be slowly simmered until the meats are done and the vegetables are good and tender.

SERVES 6 TO 8

3 to 4 pounds chicken parts
⅓ cup all-purpose flour
1 teaspoon salt, plus more to taste
½ teaspoon black pepper, plus more to taste
1 teaspoon dried thyme
¼ teaspoon cayenne pepper

3 tablespoons oil
2 medium onions, chopped
6 ounces smoked ham, diced
4 cups chicken broth (page 119)
1 (28-ounce) can diced tomatoes, drained
1 medium green bell pepper, seeded and diced
1 bay leaf
2 cups shelled lima beans or 1 (10-ounce) package frozen lima beans, thawed
2 cups fresh or frozen corn

1. Cut the chicken legs to separate the thighs and drumsticks. Rinse the chicken and pat dry with paper towels. Remove as much fat as possible.

2. Mix the flour, 1 teaspoon salt, ½ teaspoon black pepper, thyme, and cayenne pepper in a shallow bowl. Dip the chicken pieces in the seasoned flour and set aside on a large plate. Reserve the excess seasoned flour.

3. Heat 2 tablespoons of oil in a large Dutch oven over medium-high heat. Use tongs to add a single layer of chicken pieces to the pan; do not crowd. Cook until browned all over, about 5 minutes per side. Transfer the chicken to a plate and keep warm.

4. Add the remaining 1 tablespoon oil and the onions to the Dutch oven. Sauté until softened, about 3 minutes. Add the ham and cook until lightly browned, about 3 minutes. Sprinkle the reserved seasoned flour over the ham and onions and cook, stirring, until the flour forms a paste.

5. Pour in 2 cups of broth and bring to a boil, using a wooden spoon to scrape up any brown bits from the bottom of the Dutch oven. Boil, stirring, until slightly thickened. Stir in the remaining 2 cups broth, tomatoes, bell pepper, and bay leaf. Return the chicken to the pan. Bring to a boil, reduce the heat to medium-low, and simmer, partially covered, for 30 minutes.

6. Add the lima beans and corn and simmer, uncovered, until the chicken and vegetables are tender, at least 30 minutes.

7. Skim any fat off the top of the stew. Remove and discard the bay leaf and season with additional salt and pepper as needed before serving. Serve hot.

Chicken Chili Verde

Starring chicken and tomatillos, this stew is different from the usual Tex-Mex ground beef dish. In New Mexico, chili verde is a traditional dish, prepared with meat—and no beans.

SERVES 6

1½ pounds boneless, skinless chicken thighs, cut into ½-inch pieces
Salt and pepper
3 tablespoons all-purpose flour
¼ cup oil
2 medium onions, chopped
1 tablespoon minced garlic
¾ cup seeded and chopped Anaheim or jalapeño chile peppers
1 medium green bell pepper, seeded and cut lengthwise into ¼-inch strips
2½ cups frozen corn, thawed
3 cups chicken broth (page 119)
6 tomatillos, husked and coarsely chopped
1 tablespoon chili powder
1½ teaspoons ground cumin
1½ teaspoons ground oregano
½ teaspoon paprika
1 cinnamon stick
½ cup chopped fresh cilantro
Tortilla chips, to serve

1. Sprinkle the chicken with salt and pepper. Toss with the flour in a medium bowl.

2. Heat 1 tablespoon of oil in a large skillet over medium-high heat. Add the chicken and sauté until golden brown, about 10 minutes. Transfer to a large saucepan.

3. Heat 1 tablespoon of oil in the same skillet over medium-high heat. Add the onions and garlic and sauté until the onions are softened, about 3 minutes. Transfer to the pan with the chicken.

4. Heat 1 tablespoon of oil in the same skillet over medium-high heat. Add the chile peppers and bell pepper. Sauté until tender, about 4 minutes. Transfer to the pan with the chicken.

5. Heat the remaining 1 tablespoon of oil in the same skillet. Sauté the corn until tender, about 2 minutes. Transfer to the pan with the chicken.

6. Add the broth, tomatillos, chili powder, cumin, oregano, paprika, and cinnamon stick to the pan with the chicken. Bring to a boil. Reduce the heat and simmer until the mixture thickens for about 1 hour, or to your liking.

7. Remove the cinnamon stick and stir in the cilantro. Serve hot, passing the tortilla chips at the table.

Chicken Cacciatore

The Italian recipe title translates as chicken "in the style of hunters." Presumably, this is how hunters traditionally prepare the game birds—or rabbits—they track down. It is an Italian-American favorite and should be served with a side dish of pasta and crusty Italian bread for sopping up the sauce.

SERVES 4 TO 6

3 to 4 pounds chicken parts
Salt and pepper
¼ cup oil
½ pound mushrooms, sliced
1 medium onion, diced
1 teaspoon minced garlic
1 (15-ounce) can tomato sauce
1 (6-ounce) can tomato paste
1 (28-ounce) can diced tomatoes
¾ cup dry red wine
1 teaspoon dried basil
1 teaspoon dried oregano
3 tablespoons all-purpose flour

1. Cut the chicken legs to separate the thighs and drumsticks. Rinse the chicken and pat dry with paper towels. Remove as much fat as possible. Salt and pepper lightly.

2. Heat the oil in a large Dutch oven over medium-high heat. Use tongs to add a single layer of chicken pieces to the pan; do not crowd. Cook until browned all over, about 5 minutes per side. Transfer the chicken to a plate and keep warm.

3. Add the mushrooms and onion to the Dutch oven and sauté until the onion is softened, about 3 minutes. Add the garlic and sauté for 1 more minute.

4. Return the chicken to the Dutch oven. In a separate bowl, mix the tomato sauce, tomato paste, tomatoes, wine, basil, and oregano. Add the flour and mix well. Season to taste with salt and pepper. Pour the mixture over the chicken. Cover and simmer for about 45 minutes, until the chicken is tender. Serve hot.

Chicken Pot Pie

It wasn't until 1951 that the first frozen pot pie was introduced by the C. A. Swanson Company. Like many pot pies of the day, these were made with a traditional two-crust pie pastry, as in this recipe. Many pot pies served today are single-crust, topped with biscuit dough or puff pastry.

SERVES 4 TO 6

Filling:
3 to 4 pounds chicken parts
7 to 8 cups water
1 medium onion, chopped
1 large carrot, chopped
1 medium celery rib, chopped
¼ cup chopped fresh parsley
1 teaspoon salt, plus more to taste
¼ teaspoon black pepper
2 tablespoons butter
5 tablespoons all-purpose flour
½ cup heavy cream or half-and-half
1 cup frozen peas and carrots, thawed
1 cup frozen green beans, thawed

Pastry:
2 cups all-purpose flour
½ teaspoon salt

4 teaspoons baking powder
5 tablespoons butter
¼ cup shortening
5 tablespoons milk

1. To make the filling, place the chicken in a large pot and cover with water. Add the onion, carrot, celery, parsley, and 1 teaspoon salt, if needed. Season to taste with additional salt and pepper. Simmer over low heat for 1½ hours, until the chicken is very tender. Let cool.

2. Remove the chicken from the bones and discard the bones and skin. Strain the broth, skim off the fat, and discard the solids. Refrigerate the fat for later. You will need 3 cups of broth; freeze the rest for another use.

3. In a shallow dish, pour 1½ cups of broth over the chicken meat and set aside.

4. Melt the butter with 2 tablespoons of reserved chicken fat in a medium saucepan over medium heat. Stir in the flour and heat until thick and smooth, about 2 minutes. Stir in the remaining 1½ cups broth and continue stirring until the sauce is smooth and thick. Stir in the cream and frozen vegetables and keep warm.

5. To make the pastry, sift together the flour, salt, and baking powder in a medium bowl. Cut in the butter and shortening (or use the reserved chicken fat) with 2 knives or rub in with your fingers. Add the milk a little at a time. Add just enough to hold the dough together. Divide the pastry in half and roll each half into a large circle big enough for a 10-inch pie pan.

6. Preheat the oven to 400°F.

7. Transfer one dough circle to the pie pan, allowing the dough to overhang the edges. With a slotted spoon, remove the chicken from its broth and place in the bottom of the pie. Pour the cream sauce over it and cover with the top pastry round. Poke a few steam holes with a knife, pinch together the top and bottom pastries, and crimp the edges.

8. Bake for 25 minutes, or until the top is golden brown.

9. Let stand for 10 minutes. Cut into wedges and serve hot.

Chicken Pies with Biscuit Crust

These pot pies have a crusty buttermilk-biscuit topping. They look particularly impressive when you make them in individual ramekins, though a single 9 x 13-inch baking dish works fine, too.

SERVES 6

Filling:
3 to 4 pounds chicken parts
7 to 8 cups water
1 medium onion, quartered
2 medium carrots, chopped
2 medium celery ribs, chopped
2 medium waxy potatoes, such as thin-skinned red or white, peeled and diced
6 tablespoons (¾ stick) butter
6 tablespoons all-purpose flour
3 tablespoons dry sherry
1 cup frozen peas or green beans, thawed
1 teaspoon dried thyme
Salt and pepper

Biscuit topping:
3 cups all-purpose flour
2 tablespoons baking powder
1½ teaspoons salt
⅔ cup butter, cut into pieces
1 cup buttermilk

1. To make the filling, place the chicken in a large pot and cover with the water. Add the onion, carrots, and celery. Bring to a boil, reduce the heat to maintain a slow simmer, and simmer for 1 hour, until the chicken is tender. Turn off the heat and allow the chicken to cool in the cooking liquid.

2. In a medium saucepan, cook the potatoes in boiling salted water until just tender, 5 to 8 minutes. Drain and set aside.

3. Remove the chicken from the broth. Remove the meat from the bones and discard the skin and bones. Chop the meat into bite-size pieces.

4. Strain the broth and discard the solids. Skim off any fat that rises to the top. Reserve 3 cups of broth for the pot pie and refrigerate or freeze the remainder for other recipes.

5. Melt the butter in a large saucepan over medium heat. Sprinkle in the flour and stir to form a smooth paste. Whisk in the reserved broth and sherry and stir until thickened and smooth. Stir in the chicken, potatoes, peas, and thyme. Taste and adjust the seasoning with salt and pepper. Bring to a boil. Keep hot while you prepare the topping.

6. Preheat the oven to 400°F. Set out six 12-ounce ramekins or ovenproof bowls, or a 9 x 13-inch baking dish.

7. To make the topping, combine the flour, baking powder, and salt in a food processor. Add the butter and process until the mixture resembles coarse crumbs. Pour in the buttermilk and process to make a soft dough. Knead a few times on a lightly floured board. Pat out the dough to a thickness of about 1 inch. Cut into 6 rounds the size of the ramekins or bowls; or, if using a baking dish, cut into 3-inch rounds.

8. Pour the hot chicken mixture into the baking pan(s) and place the biscuit rounds on top. Bake until the biscuits are golden and the chicken mixture is bubbling, 20 to 30 minutes. Let stand for a few minutes before serving.

Breaded Chicken Fingers with Peach Dipping Sauce

Kids love these! The dipping sauce is fruity and sweet, perfect for those with a sweet tooth; others may prefer homemade barbecue sauce. French fries are the perfect accompaniment, but also consider oven-fried sweet potato wedges or potato salad.

SERVES 4

Dipping sauce:
½ (8-ounce) can sliced peaches
Juice of 1 medium lemon (about ¼ cup)
3 tablespoons brown sugar
1 tablespoon butter, melted
1 tablespoon cider vinegar
Salt and pepper

Chicken Fingers:
4 boneless, skinless chicken breast halves
¼ cup all-purpose flour
1 cup dry bread crumbs
1 teaspoon onion powder
1 teaspoon dried thyme
1 teaspoon salt
½ teaspoon black pepper
1 large egg
1 tablespoon water
⅓ cup oil

1. To make the dipping sauce, purée the peaches and their juice in a blender until smooth. Add the lemon juice, brown sugar, butter, and vinegar. Pulse the blender until all is well mixed but not foamy. If the sauce is too thick, thin with a little water. Add salt and pepper to taste and set aside.

2. To make the chicken fingers, trim the fat from the breasts and remove the white tendons running through the tenderloins. Place each breast between sheets of wax paper and gently pound with a meat mallet until it is of even thickness. Slice into strips about 1 inch wide. Dust the chicken with the flour until well coated on all sides.

3. Stir together the bread crumbs, onion powder, thyme, salt, and pepper in a shallow bowl.

4. In another shallow bowl, use a fork to beat the egg with the water.

5. Heat the oil in a large skillet over medium-high heat until very hot but not smoking.

6. Dip the chicken pieces in the egg mixture, then roll in the seasoned bread crumbs until well coated, patting to make the crumbs adhere. Slip into the pan. Continue adding more pieces until the pan is full but not crowded. Fry until golden brown, 2 to 3 minutes per side. Use tongs to remove the cooked pieces and drain well on paper towels. Repeat until all the chicken is cooked. Serve hot, passing the dipping sauce on the side.

Cajun Popcorn Chicken

These are nuggets of deep-fried chicken, searingly spiced. The original Cajun popcorn was made with crawfish tails, but chicken is more easily found. It's the spices that make them so irresistible.

SERVES 4

1 cup all-purpose flour
1 cup finely ground yellow cornmeal
2 teaspoons garlic powder
2 teaspoons onion powder
2 teaspoons salt
1½ teaspoons dried thyme
1 teaspoon cayenne pepper
1 teaspoon black pepper
2 large eggs
2 tablespoons milk
1 pound boneless, skinless chicken breasts or
    thighs, cut into bite-size pieces
Oil, for frying

1. Stir together the flour, cornmeal, garlic powder, onion powder, salt, thyme, cayenne pepper, and black pepper in a shallow bowl.

2. In another shallow bowl, use a fork to beat the eggs with the milk. Add the chicken and turn until well coated.

3. Preheat the oven to 200°F. Place a couple of wire racks on a baking sheet and set in the oven.

4. Heat 2 inches of oil in a tall saucepan or large skillet until the oil reaches 375°F.

5. Use tongs to lift the chicken pieces, a few at a time, out of the egg mixture and dip in the seasoned flour until well coated. Slip into the pan. Continue adding more pieces until the pan is full but not crowded. Fry until golden brown, turning as needed, 2 to 3 minutes per side. Remove the cooked pieces, drain well on paper towels, and keep warm in the oven on the wire racks. Repeat until all the chicken is cooked. Serve hot.

Chicken Parmesan

Chicken Parmesan, veal Parmesan, eggplant Parmesan—these are all Italian-American classics. The main ingredient is breaded and fried, then layered in a casserole with tomato sauce and mozzarella and Parmesan cheese. Serve with pasta and marinara sauce on the side.

SERVES 4

4 boneless, skinless chicken breast halves
¼ cup all-purpose flour
¾ cup dry bread crumbs
½ cup grated Parmesan cheese
1 teaspoon garlic powder
1 teaspoon dried basil
1 teaspoon dried oregano
1 teaspoon salt
½ teaspoon black pepper
1 large egg
1 tablespoon water
⅓ cup oil
2 cups marinara sauce (page 260)
2 cups mozzarella cheese, shredded (about 8 ounces)

1. Trim the fat from the breasts and remove the white tendons running through the tenderloins. Place each breast between sheets of wax paper and gently pound with a meat mallet until less than ¼ inch thick. Dust the chicken with the flour until well coated on all sides.

2. Stir together the bread crumbs, Parmesan cheese, garlic powder, basil, oregano, salt, and pepper in a shallow bowl.

3. In another shallow bowl, use a fork to beat the egg with the water.

4. Heat the oil in a large skillet over medium-high heat until very hot but not smoking.

5. Dip the chicken in the egg mixture, then roll in the seasoned bread crumbs until well coated, patting to make the crumbs adhere. Use tongs to slip the chicken into the pan. Continue adding more pieces until the pan is full but not crowded. Fry until golden brown, 2 to 3 minutes per side. Remove the cooked pieces and drain well on paper towels. Repeat until all the chicken is cooked.

6. Preheat the oven to 375°F. Lightly oil a 9 x 13-inch baking dish.

7. Spread ½ cup of marinara sauce in the baking dish. Arrange the chicken pieces in the pan, overlapping as needed. Spoon the remaining 1½ cups sauce on top. Sprinkle the mozzarella over the sauce.

8. Bake for 15 to 20 minutes, until the cheese is melted and the chicken is hot. Serve hot.

Chicken Piccata

Americans eat a lot of chicken breasts and have adapted many Italian veal dishes by making them with chicken. In this recipe, the chicken is finished with a sauce of pan drippings, lemon juice, and chopped parsley. It is classic and delicious.

SERVES 4

4 boneless, skinless chicken breast halves
½ cup all-purpose flour
Salt and pepper
3 tablespoons olive oil
¾ cup chicken broth (page 119)
3 tablespoons lemon juice
2 tablespoons chopped fresh parsley
1 tablespoon capers, drained
3 tablespoons butter

1. Trim the fat from the breasts and remove the white tendons running through the tenderloins. Place each breast between sheets of wax paper and gently pound with a meat mallet until less than ¼ inch thick. Dust the chicken with the flour until well coated on all sides. Sprinkle with salt and pepper.

2. Heat the oil in a large skillet over medium-high heat until very hot but not smoking. Use tongs to add the chicken breasts in a single layer and sauté for 3 to 4 minutes on each side, until firm. Remove to a serving platter and cover with aluminum foil to keep warm.

3. Add the broth and lemon juice to the pan. Cook, stirring with a wooden spoon to loosen all of the browned bits stuck to the pan. Bring to a boil and cook until the mixture is reduced to about ⅓ cup, 3 to 4 minutes. Stir in the parsley and capers. Season to taste with salt and pepper.

Remove from the heat and whisk in the butter, 1 tablespoon at a time.

4. Pour the sauce over the chicken and serve immediately.

Chicken Marsala

This is another classic Italian veal dish adapted for chicken. Marsala wine is imported from Sicily and is Italy's most famous fortified wine. It has a rich, almost smoky flavor.

SERVES 4

4 boneless, skinless chicken breast halves
¼ cup all-purpose flour
Salt and pepper
2 tablespoons oil
2 cups sliced mushrooms
⅔ cup Marsala wine
2 tablespoons chopped fresh parsley
2 tablespoons butter

1. Trim the fat from the breasts and remove the white tendons running through the tenderloins. Place each breast between sheets of wax paper and gently pound with a meat mallet until less than ¼ inch thick. Dust the chicken with the flour until well coated on all sides. Sprinkle with salt and pepper.

2. Heat the oil in a large skillet over medium-high heat until very hot but not smoking. Use tongs to add the chicken breasts in a single layer and sauté for 3 to 4 minutes on each side, until firm. Remove to a serving platter and cover with aluminum foil to keep warm.

3. Add the mushrooms to the skillet and sauté until the mushrooms have given up their juice, about 8 minutes. Add the Marsala wine and cook, stirring with a wooden spoon to loosen all of the browned bits stuck to the pan. Bring to a boil and cook until the mixture is reduced to about ½ cup, 2 to 3 minutes. Stir in the parsley. Season to taste with salt and pepper. Remove from the heat and whisk in the butter, 1 tablespoon at a time.

4. Pour the sauce over the chicken and serve immediately.

Chicken Cordon Bleu

This stuffed chicken is a classic French dish that has been extremely popular over the years. The chicken, ham, and cheese create a spectacular combination, perfect for occasions when you want to impress a visitor.

SERVES 4

4 boneless, skinless chicken breast halves
1 teaspoon salt, plus more for seasoning
½ teaspoon black pepper, plus more for seasoning
4 thin slices ham or prosciutto, cut into 2 x ½-inch pieces
4 thin slices Gruyère or Swiss cheese, cut into 2 x ½-inch pieces
¼ cup all-purpose flour
1 large egg
1 cup dry bread crumbs
¼ cup minced fresh parsley
2 tablespoons oil

1. Trim the fat from the breasts and remove the white tendon running through the tenderloins. Place each breast between sheets of wax paper and gently pound with a meat mallet until less than ¼ inch thick. Sprinkle with salt and pepper.

2. Place a breast, skin side down, on a work surface. Cover half the piece with two pieces of ham. Top with 2 pieces of cheese. Fold the breast in half over the ham and cheese and secure the edges with a toothpick. Make a small vertical cut into the folded edge of the breast to keep it from opening during cooking. Repeat with the remaining 3 breasts.

3. Place the flour in a shallow bowl. Beat the egg with a fork in a second shallow bowl. Combine the bread crumbs, parsley, 1 teaspoon salt, and ½ teaspoon pepper in a third bowl. Working with one breast at a time, dip the breast into the flour, then into the egg, and roll in the bread crumbs, patting to make the crumbs adhere.

4. Set aside for 10 minutes to allow the breading to set.

5. Heat the oil in a large skillet over medium-high heat until very hot but not smoking. Use tongs to place the chicken in the skillet in a single layer and cook until browned, 3 to 4 minutes per side.

6. Drain on paper towels and serve immediately.

Chicken Kiev

This dish dates back to a time when boneless, skinless chicken breasts were not associated with austere diets. The butter and herb sauce makes it rich and decadent.

SERVES 4

4 boneless, skinless chicken breast halves
1 teaspoon salt, plus more for seasoning
½ teaspoon black pepper, plus more for seasoning
½ cup (1 stick) butter, softened
1 tablespoon lemon juice
2 tablespoons minced fresh parsley
1 tablespoon minced fresh chives or scallions
½ teaspoon minced garlic
¼ cup all-purpose flour
1 large egg
1½ cups dry bread crumbs
½ cup oil

1. Trim the fat from the breasts and remove the white tendon running through the tenderloins. Place each breast between sheets of wax paper and gently pound with a meat mallet until less than ¼ inch thick. Season with salt and pepper.

2. In a small bowl, combine the butter with the lemon juice, 1 tablespoon parsley, chives, garlic, a generous pinch of salt, and a pinch of pepper. Cream together using the back of a spoon until well mixed. Form the mixture into 4 equal logs about 2 inches long. Lay the butter logs on a sheet of waxed paper and freeze for 15 minutes, until hard.

3. Place the flour in a shallow bowl. Use a fork to beat the egg in a second shallow bowl. Combine the bread crumbs, the remaining 1 tablespoon parsley, 1 teaspoon salt, and ½ teaspoon pepper in a third bowl. Working with one breast at a time, place the breast, skin side down, on a work surface. Lay one piece of the butter across the wide part of the breast. Fold up the bottom, then roll the butter up inside the remainder of the breast, tucking in the sides to completely enclose the butter; secure with a toothpick. Dredge the breast in the flour, then dip into the egg, and roll in the bread crumbs, patting to make the crumbs adhere. Repeat with the remaining three breasts.

4. Refrigerate the breasts for at least 1 hour and up to 8 hours.

5. Preheat the oven to 350°F.

6. Heat the oil in a large skillet over medium-high heat. Use tongs to carefully place the chicken in the hot oil in a single layer and fry until the bottom sides are brown, 3 to 4 minutes. Turn and brown the second sides, 2 to 3 minutes. Transfer to a baking sheet and bake for 15 minutes. Serve immediately.

Chicken Chow Mein

Chinese workers came to this country to work the railroads, and many found themselves cooking in work camps and diners. This dish is probably an Americanized version of "ch'ao mien," or "fried noodles." After the 1970s, when Sichuan and other regional styles of Chinese cooking were introduced, chow mein was a favorite dish found in every Chinese restaurant in the United States.

SERVES 4

¼ cup peanut oil
1 pound boneless, skinless chicken breasts, cut into bite-size pieces
½ cup chopped mushrooms
2 medium celery ribs, chopped
½ cup chopped bok choy
1 medium onion, chopped
1 teaspoon minced garlic
1 cup chicken broth (page 119)
1 (15-ounce) can baby corn, drained
4 teaspoons cornstarch
⅓ cup cold water
1 cup mung bean sprouts
½ cup soy sauce, or to taste
Salt and pepper
Hot cooked rice, to serve
Chow mein noodles, to serve

1. Heat the oil over medium heat in a large saucepan. Add the chicken and cook, turning as needed, until white and firm, about 8 minutes. Remove the chicken from the pan and keep warm.

2. Add the mushrooms, celery, onion, and garlic to the saucepan and sauté until the mushrooms give up their juice, about 8 minutes. Return the chicken to the pan. Add the chicken broth and baby corn and bring to a boil.

3. Mix the cornstarch and water in a small bowl. Slowly stir half of the mixture into the vegetables; adding more as needed to reach desired thickness. Stir in the bean sprouts and continue cooking until heated through. Season to taste with soy sauce and salt and pepper.

4. Make a bed of the hot rice and spoon the chicken mixture over the top. Sprinkle the chicken with noodles and serve.

Chicken à la King

Many a politician's campaign luncheon used to feature chicken à la king, a dish of chicken in a rich, sherry-laced cream sauce. Serve over rice or noodles, or with toast points.

SERVES 4

3 tablespoons butter
1 cup finely chopped mushrooms
¼ cup minced green bell pepper
¼ cup minced onion
¼ cup all-purpose flour
1 teaspoon salt
½ teaspoon black pepper
⅛ teaspoon cayenne pepper
1½ cups milk
1 cup chicken broth (page 119)
3 cups chopped cooked chicken
1 tablespoon minced fresh parsley
1 tablespoon diced pimento
2 large egg yolks, lightly beaten
3 tablespoons sherry
Cooked rice or noodles or toast points,
    to serve

1. Melt the butter in a large saucepan over medium heat. Add the mushrooms, bell pepper, and onion and sauté until the mushrooms give up their juice, about 8 minutes.

2. Sprinkle in the flour, salt, black pepper, and cayenne pepper and stir to form a paste. Slowly add the milk and broth, stirring constantly. Cook until the sauce is thick and bubbly.

3. Stir in the chicken, parsley, and pimento. Simmer for 5 minutes.

4. Stir together the egg yolks and sherry in a small bowl. Stir in a few tablespoons of the chicken mixture to warm the eggs, then stir the egg mixture into the saucepan. Simmer for another 5 minutes. Pour over rice and serve immediately.

Chicken Divan

This casserole was created in the 1930s at the Divan Parisien restaurant in New York City. It helped make broccoli the popular vegetable it is today and is a tasty way to use leftover chicken.

SERVES 4

3 cups chopped broccoli
¼ cup (½ stick) butter
¼ cup all-purpose flour
1 cup chicken broth (page 119)
1 cup milk
¼ cup dry sherry
¾ cup shredded Gruyère cheese
Salt and pepper
3 boneless, skinless chicken breast
    halves, cooked and sliced

1. Bring a large pot of water to a boil. Add the broccoli and blanch for 3 minutes. Drain and immediately plunge the broccoli into cold water to stop the cooking. Drain well. Transfer to paper towels and pat dry.

2. Preheat the oven to 350°F.

3. Melt the butter in a medium saucepan over medium heat. Sprinkle in the flour and whisk until smooth. Stir in the broth, milk, and sherry and bring to a boil. Remove from the heat and stir in ½ cup of cheese. Season with salt and pepper.

4. Arrange the broccoli in a 9 x 13-inch baking dish. Pour half the sauce over it, then arrange the chicken on top. Cover with the remaining sauce. Sprinkle with the remaining ¼ cup cheese.

5. Bake for 30 to 35 minutes, until bubbling and hot. Serve immediately.

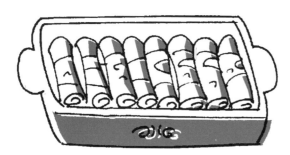

Chicken Enchiladas

A staple in Tex-Mex restaurants, an enchilada is a soft corn tortilla rolled around a filling of chicken, cheese, or meat. It is usually baked with a topping of cheese and served as a casserole. The casserole variation follows.

SERVES 4

2 tablespoons oil
1 medium onion, finely chopped
1 teaspoon minced garlic
1 (28-ounce) can diced tomatoes
1 (4-ounce) can chopped green chile peppers,
    drained
1 teaspoon dried oregano
1 teaspoon salt, or to taste
½ teaspoon sugar
1 to 1½ cups diced cooked chicken
8 to 10 corn tortillas
1 cup shredded Cheddar cheese (about
    4 ounces)
½ cup sour cream, to serve
Sliced pitted black olives, to serve

1. Preheat the oven to 400°F. Lightly grease a 9 x 13-inch baking dish.

2. Heat the oil in a large skillet over medium-high heat. Add the onion and garlic and sauté for 3 minutes, until softened. Stir in the tomatoes, chile peppers, oregano, salt, and sugar. Simmer for 15 minutes, stirring occasionally.

3. Combine ½ cup of sauce with the chicken in a small bowl and set aside.

4. Heat the remaining sauce until just boiling. Place a tortilla in the sauce to soften. Use tongs to remove it, letting the excess sauce drip back into the skillet. Place the tortilla on a plate and spread

2 tablespoons of the chicken mixture down the center. Roll it up and place it seam side down in the prepared baking dish. Repeat with the remaining tortillas. Pour the remaining sauce over the tortillas and sprinkle with the cheese.

5. Bake, uncovered, for 20 to 25 minutes, until bubbly and hot. Serve hot, topped with dollops of sour cream and a sprinkling of sliced olives.

Mexican Chicken Casserole

Instead of filling and rolling the tortillas in Chicken Enchiladas, layer the tortillas, chicken, sauce, and 2 cups grated cheese in a casserole dish. Bake at 400°F for 20 to 25 minutes and garnish as instructed.

Chicken Enchiladas with Creamy Green Chile Sauce

Enchiladas are often served with a creamy white sauce, robustly flavored with green chile peppers, instead of a red sauce. This dish makes good use of leftover chicken.

SERVES 4 TO 6

1 tablespoon butter
1 small onion, finely chopped
½ teaspoon minced garlic
¼ teaspoon ground cumin
2 tablespoons all-purpose flour
1½ cups chicken broth (page 119)
2 (4-ounce) cans chopped green chile peppers,
    drained
Salt and pepper
12 corn tortillas
Oil
2 cups coarsely shredded cooked chicken
2 cups shredded Monterey Jack cheese (about
    8 ounces)
1 cup whipping cream
⅓ cup sliced scallions
3 small tomatoes, seeded and chopped

1. Melt the butter in a medium saucepan over medium heat. Add the onion and sauté until softened, about 3 minutes. Add the garlic and cumin and sauté for 1 minute. Stir in the flour until well combined and cook for 1 minute. Slowly stir in the broth. Cook until the sauce thickens, about 3 minutes. Stir in the chile peppers, season to taste with salt and pepper, reduce the heat, and simmer for 15 minutes.

2. Preheat the oven to 350°F. Grease a 9 x 13-inch baking dish.

3. Place as many tortillas as will fit in a single layer on 2 baking sheets. Brush the tortillas lightly on both sides with oil. Bake for 3 minutes to warm and soften the tortillas before rolling. Stack on a plate and cover with aluminum foil to keep warm. Repeat until all the tortillas are warmed.

4. Combine the chicken with ½ cup of green chile sauce in a medium bowl.

5. Place 2 tablespoons of the chicken mixture and 2 tablespoons of cheese across the center of each tortilla. Roll up and place, seam side down, in the prepared baking dish. Pour the remaining sauce over the rolled enchiladas. Pour the cream evenly over the entire mixture and top with the remaining cheese. Sprinkle with the scallions.

6. Bake for 20 minutes. Sprinkle with the chopped tomatoes and serve.

King Ranch Chicken

This Tex-Mex take on chicken à la king used to be a favorite at ladies' luncheons in the Southwest. The dish may have been created at the King Ranch in Kingsville, Texas.

SERVES 6

Sauce:
6 tablespoons (¾ stick) butter
2 tablespoons chili powder
1 tablespoon ground cumin
6 tablespoons all-purpose flour
2 cups chicken broth (page 119)
1½ cups milk
Salt and pepper

Chicken tortillas:
2 tablespoons oil, plus more for frying
1 medium red bell pepper, seeded and diced
1 medium green bell pepper, seeded and diced
1 medium onion, diced
2 (4-ounce) cans chopped green chile peppers, drained
4 ounces mushrooms, sliced
4 cups chopped or shredded cooked chicken
1 (15-ounce) can diced tomatoes, drained
Salt and pepper
18 corn tortillas
2 cups shredded Monterey Jack cheese (about 8 ounces)
½ cup sliced pimento-stuffed green olives

1. Preheat the oven to 350°F. Grease a 9 x 13-inch baking dish.

2. To prepare the sauce, melt the butter in a medium saucepan over medium heat. Add the chili powder and cumin and sauté until fragrant, about 1 minute. Stir in the flour and make a smooth paste. Cook for 1 minute, stirring constantly. Add the broth, then the milk, stirring until the mixture is smooth and thick. Season to taste with salt and pepper. Keep warm.

3. To make the tortillas, heat the oil in a large skillet over medium-high heat. Add the bell peppers, onion, chile peppers, and mushrooms and sauté until the mushrooms give up their juice, about 8 minutes. Stir in the chicken and tomatoes. Season to taste with salt and pepper and remove from the heat.

4. Heat ½ inch of frying oil in a medium skillet over medium-high heat. Holding the tortillas with tongs, dip them one by one into the oil just long enough to soften, 10 to 15 seconds. Drain on paper towels.

5. Arrange 6 tortillas in the prepared baking dish. Cover with half the chicken mixture, one-third of the sauce, and one-third of the cheese. Scatter half the olives over the cheese. Repeat with another layer of 6 tortillas, chicken, sauce, cheese, and olives. Finish with the remaining tortillas, the remaining sauce, and the remaining cheese.

6. Bake for about 30 minutes, until browned and bubbly. Let sit for 5 minutes before serving.

Chicken Noodle Casserole

Leftover chicken makes a delicious next-day dinner when combined with noodles and a cheese sauce.

SERVES 4

½ pound egg noodles
½ cup (1 stick) butter
1 cup sliced mushrooms
3 scallions, finely chopped
⅓ cup all-purpose flour
2 cups chicken broth (page 119)
1 cup milk
1 cup grated Parmesan cheese
Salt and pepper
2 cups diced cooked chicken

1. Preheat the oven to 375°F. Grease a 2-quart baking dish.

2. Cook the noodles in a large pot of boiling salted water according to the package directions; drain.

3. Melt the butter in a large saucepan over medium heat. Add the mushrooms and scallions and sauté until the mushrooms give up their juice, about 8 minutes. Stir in the flour and make a paste. Gradually stir in the broth, milk, and ½ cup of Parmesan cheese, stirring constantly, until the sauce is thickened. Season to taste with salt and pepper.

4. Stir in the chicken and noodles and mix well.

5. Transfer the mixture to the baking dish and sprinkle the remaining ½ cup Parmesan cheese over the top.

6. Bake for 20 to 25 minutes, until heated through and golden. Serve hot.

Hot Chicken Salad

Hot chicken salads are simple casserole dishes made with traditional mayonnaise-based chicken salad that is baked, usually under a potato chip crust. Easy to make, it is a Midwestern favorite.

SERVES 4

3 cups chopped cooked chicken
4 large celery ribs, chopped
¾ cup cashews
1½ cups mayonnaise
1 medium onion, minced
1 tablespoon lemon juice
Salt and pepper
1 cup shredded Cheddar cheese (about
    4 ounces)
1 cup crushed potato chips

1. Preheat the oven to 400°F.

2. Mix the chicken, celery, and cashews in a medium bowl. Add the mayonnaise, onion, and lemon juice and mix well. Season to taste with salt and pepper.

3. Transfer the mixture to a 2-quart baking dish and top with the cheese and potato chips.

4. Bake for 20 minutes, until heated through and bubbly. Serve hot.

Chicken Livers and Bacon

Chicken livers can be tender and moist—the trick is to cook them in a very hot pan for a brief amount of time. Serve this dish with rice or mashed potatoes.

SERVES 4

1½ pounds chicken livers
Salt and pepper
8 slices bacon, cut into ½-inch pieces
1 medium onion, halved and sliced
¼ cup chopped fresh parsley

1. Rinse the livers, remove the connective strings, and separate the lobes. Pat dry with paper towels and season generously with salt and pepper. Set aside.

2. Cook the bacon in a large, deep skillet over medium-high heat until evenly brown, about 10 minutes. Remove the bacon and drain on paper towels.

3. Return the skillet to medium-high heat. Add about half the livers and quickly spread out into a single layer. Cook, undisturbed, for 1 minute, then turn and continue to cook until firm and

beginning to release their juices, 1 to 2 minutes more. Remove to a plate and keep warm. Repeat with the remaining livers.

4. Add the onion to the skillet and sauté until completely tender, about 8 minutes.

5. Drain the fat. Return the bacon and livers to the skillet and toss together until heated through.

6. Sprinkle with the parsley and serve hot.

Roasted Turkey Breast with Gravy

A roasted turkey breast fits the bill when you are cooking for just a few people on a holiday, and it can be just as satisfying as a whole turkey. The gravy and side dishes make all the difference.

SERVES 4 TO 6

Turkey:
1 (4- to 7-pound) turkey breast
Salt and pepper
Poultry seasoning
Paprika
2 tablespoons butter, melted

Gravy:
3 cups chicken broth (page 119)
3 tablespoons butter (optional)
¼ cup all-purpose flour

1. Preheat the oven to 350°F.

2. To make the turkey, rinse the turkey breast and pat dry with paper towels. Season on all sides with salt, pepper, poultry seasoning, and paprika. Place, skin side up, in a roasting pan. Brush the skin with the butter.

3. Roast for 15 to 20 minutes per pound, until the meat registers 160°F or releases clear juices when pricked with a fork.

4. Remove from the oven, transfer to a serving platter, and let stand while you prepare the gravy.

5. To make the gravy, place the roasting pan over 2 burners set on medium heat. Pour in the broth and bring to a boil, stirring with a wooden spoon, to release the browned bits on the bottom of the

pan. Pour into a 4-cup glass measuring cup and let stand for a few minutes to allow the fat to rise to the top.

6. If you can, skim off 2 tablespoons of fat and place in a medium saucepan; discard any additional fat. If there isn't enough fat, melt enough butter in the saucepan over medium heat to equal 3 tablespoons. Whisk in the flour to form a smooth paste. Whisk in the broth and pan drippings, bring to a boil, and cook for 5 minutes until thickened and smooth.

7. Carve the turkey breast and serve with the gravy.

Turkey Pie

This pot pie is topped with leftover mashed potatoes, but you may prefer the biscuit topping used for chicken pies with biscuit crust (page 162).

SERVES 6

8 tablespoons (1 stick) butter
6 tablespoons all-purpose flour
3 cups chicken broth or turkey broth
   (page 119)
4 cups chopped cooked turkey
2 cups frozen peas or green beans
2 medium carrots, diced
1 teaspoon dried thyme
Salt and pepper
3 to 4 cups mashed potatoes (page 302)

1. Preheat the oven to 400°F.

2. Melt 6 tablespoons of butter in a large saucepan over medium heat. Sprinkle in the flour and stir until a smooth paste forms. Whisk in the broth and stir until thickened and smooth. Stir in the turkey, peas, carrots, and thyme. Taste and adjust the seasoning with salt and pepper. Bring to a boil.

3. Transfer the turkey mixture to a 9 x 13-inch baking dish. Top with the mashed potatoes, making peaks and valleys with the back of a spoon. Cut the remaining 2 tablespoons butter into small pieces and scatter on top of the potatoes.

4. Bake until the potatoes are golden and the turkey mixture is bubbling, 20 to 30 minutes. Let stand for a few minutes before serving.

Roast Turkey with Giblet Gravy

Beautifully browned and seasoned, this is the roast turkey grandmothers serve. But every grandmother has her tricks. If you bake the stuffing separately, the bird will be juicier. You will also reduce the risk of undercooking the stuffing, which could lead to food poisoning.

SERVES 14

1 (10- to 25-pound) turkey
Salt
Poultry seasoning
Black pepper
Paprika
1 medium onion, quartered
2 medium celery ribs, quartered
6 tablespoons (¾ stick) butter, melted
Giblet gravy (recipe follows)

1. Preheat the oven to 325°F with the oven rack in its lowest position.

2. Remove the giblets (heart, liver, and gizzard) and neck from the turkey and reserve for making the gravy. Rinse the turkey with cold running water, drain well, and pat dry with paper towels.

3. Rub the turkey inside and out with salt. Sprinkle with poultry seasoning, pepper, and paprika. Stuff the body cavity with the onion and celery. Depending on the brand of turkey, tie the legs and tail together with kitchen string; or push the drumsticks under the band of skin; or use the stuffing clamp to secure the legs.

4. Place the turkey, breast side up, on the rack in a large roasting pan. Brush the turkey with half the butter and cover with aluminum foil. Roast for 10 to 12 minutes per pound, basting with the remaining butter every 30 minutes, until the deepest part of the breast registers 175° to 180°F.

5. While the turkey is roasting, prepare the giblets to use in the gravy (recipe follows).

6. To brown the turkey, remove the aluminum foil during the last hour of roasting and occasionally baste with pan drippings.

7. When the turkey is browned, place on a warm, large serving platter and keep warm. Prepare the gravy. Let the turkey stand for at least 20 minutes before carving. Serve with the gravy.

TIP: Allow 2 to 3 days for a frozen turkey to defrost in the refrigerator.

Giblet Gravy

Use the often discarded giblets (heart and gizzard) and neck from a whole, raw turkey to create this flavor-rich wine and herb gravy. Though the liver is usually included with the giblets, do not use it when making gravy. Serve the gravy with roasted turkey while it's still hot.

MAKES ABOUT 4 CUPS

Turkey gizzard, heart, and neck
2 tablespoons oil
½ medium onion, chopped
4 cups chicken broth (page 119)
½ cup dry white or red wine
1 large celery rib, chopped
¼ cup chopped fresh parsley
½ teaspoon dried thyme
⅓ cup all-purpose flour
Salt and pepper

1. Chop the neck into 2-inch pieces. Cut the heart in half and divide the gizzard into lobes.

2. Heat the oil in a medium saucepan over medium heat. Add the turkey parts and onion and cook until well browned, 10 to 20 minutes.

3. Add the broth, wine, celery, parsley, and thyme. Bring to a boil, reduce the heat, and simmer until the meat is tender, about 1 hour.

4. Strain the broth and add enough water to measure 4 cups. Set aside.

5. Finely chop the giblet and pull off the neck meat and set aside. Discard the vegetables and bones.

6. Pour the pan drippings through a strainer into a 4-cup glass measuring cup or medium bowl. Add 1 cup of giblet broth to the turkey roasting pan after the turkey is done and stir with a wooden spoon until the brown bits are loosened. Pour back into the drippings in the measuring cup. Let stand for a few minutes, until the fat rises to the surface.

7. Spoon 3 tablespoons of fat from the drippings into a large saucepan over medium heat; skim and discard any remaining fat. Stir the flour into the fat and cook until smooth and golden brown. Gradually stir in the broth mixture and cook, stirring, until the gravy boils and thickens slightly. Stir in the reserved giblets and neck meat, season to taste with salt and pepper, and heat through.

8. Pour the gravy into a gravy boat and serve with the roasted turkey.

Stuffed and Roasted Cornish Hens

The Cornish hens sold today are hybrids of Cornish and white rock chickens. It is preferable to serve one small hen to each diner, but it is getting progressively harder to find small ones, so you may have to serve half hens. You can choose to stuff with any stuffing you like. The wild rice stuffing here is very complementary.

SERVES 4

4 small (under 1½ pounds) Cornish hens
Salt and pepper
2 cups wild rice stuffing (page 178)
2 to 3 tablespoons butter, melted
1 medium onion, chopped
1 teaspoon dried thyme
1 cup chicken broth (page 119)

1. Preheat the oven to 400°F.

2. Remove the giblets (hearts, livers, and gizzards) and necks from the hens and discard. Rinse the hens and pat dry with paper towels. Season the birds inside and out with salt and pepper and stuff each with about ½ cup of stuffing. Tie the legs together at the ankles with kitchen string and arrange, breast side up, on a wire rack set in a roasting pan. Brush the skins with some of the butter and sprinkle the onion and thyme around them.

3. Roast for 40 to 45 minutes, basting occasionally with the remaining butter, until the meat is 170° to 175°F and the juices run clear when a fork is pricked in the thighs.

4. Transfer the birds to a serving platter and keep warm.

5. Place the roasting pan over 2 burners, add the broth, and bring to a boil, scraping up any browned bits from the bottom of the pan with a wooden spoon. Boil until the liquid is reduced slightly, about 2 minutes. Season to taste with salt and pepper and pour into a gravy boat.

6. Cut off the trussing strings, and serve one stuffed bird to each diner, passing the pan juices around the table.

Duck à l'Orange

This recipe was once the pinnacle of sophisticated French dining in this country. Remember, duck is all dark meat and is quite rich in taste.

SERVES 3 TO 4

1 (4- to 5-pound) duck
Salt and pepper
1 medium onion, sliced
1 teaspoon minced garlic
4 medium oranges
½ cup dry white wine
1 cup chicken broth (page 119)
1 tablespoon cornstarch
2 tablespoons water
1 tablespoon Cointreau, Grand Marnier, or
    triple sec

1. Preheat the oven to 375°F.

2. Rinse the duck and pat dry with paper towels. Remove as much fat as possible. With the point of a sharp knife, prick the entire surface of the skin, being careful not to cut into the flesh. Season the duck inside and out with salt and pepper. Stuff the cavity with the onion and garlic. Quarter one of the oranges and stuff into the duck. Truss the duck's legs together with kitchen string. Place the duck, breast side down, on a wire rack in a roasting pan.

3. Roast the duck for 15 minutes, prick the exposed skin again, then roast for another 15 minutes. Turn it breast side up. Prick again, then roast until the meat is done and all the juices run clear when the meat is pierced with a fork, about 45 minutes. The leg bone will wiggle a little in its socket, and the thigh will register about 180°F. Increase the oven temperature to 400°F for the last 10 minutes if the duck is not as brown as you'd like.

4. Transfer the duck to a serving platter. Discard the onion and orange in the cavity, and cover the duck with a loose tent of aluminum foil to keep warm.

5. Juice 2 oranges, then peel and chop the remaining orange.

6. Skim the fat from the roasting pan and discard. Place the roasting pan over 2 burners and heat over high heat. Add the wine and broth and cook, stirring and scraping the bottom of the pan with a wooden spoon, until the liquid is reduced

slightly, about 2 minutes. Add the orange juice and orange pieces, bring to a boil, and cook, for 3 to 4 minutes. Mix the cornstarch with water in a small cup. Stir in the cornstarch mixture and cook until thickened. Stir in the Cointreau and remove from the heat.

7. Carve the duck, spoon the sauce over it, and serve.

TIP: To carve a duck, cut off the legs and divide them at the thigh-drumstick joint. Cut off the wings and divide them in half. Cut each breast half from the bone, then divide each breast half. Serve each person a drumstick or thigh, half a wing, and a piece of breast meat.

Duck with Sauerkraut

Sauerkraut cuts the richness of duck meat. The apples and brown sugar in this recipe balance the acidity of the kraut. Together it is a wonderfully sweet and savory meal.

SERVES 4

1 (2- to 3-pound) duck
1 tablespoon coarse or kosher salt, plus more
    for seasoning
3 slices bacon, diced
1 medium onion, finely diced
4 cups sauerkraut with brine
1 medium tart apple, such as Granny Smith or
    Rome Beauty, cored and finely diced
6 tablespoons brown sugar
1 teaspoon caraway seeds
1 cup water
½ teaspoon black pepper

1. Preheat the oven to 400°F.

2. Rinse the duck and pat dry with paper towels. Remove as much fat as possible. Rub the duck inside and out with the 1 tablespoon salt and prick the skin. Place, breast side down, in a roasting pan and roast for 1 hour. Remove from the oven, discard the fat, and let cool. Reduce the oven temperature to 350°F.

3. Cook the bacon in a large Dutch oven or large, ovenproof saucepan over medium-high heat until crisp, about 10 to 15 minutes. Drain the grease.

4. Add the onion, sauerkraut, apple, 3 tablespoons of brown sugar, caraway seeds, and water. Taste and add salt, if needed. Make a hollow in the sauerkraut mixture and place the duck in the hollow so there is sauerkraut under and along the sides. Top the duck with the remaining 3 tablespoons brown sugar and the pepper. Cover and bake for 1 hour.

5. Carve the duck and strain the sauerkraut. Serve each person a piece of duck with some sauerkraut.

Roast Goose with Fruited Wild Rice Stuffing

Perfect on a fall day, this roasted goose highlights the best of the season's flavors with its apple-raisin wild rice stuffing. Note that a roasting goose renders a great deal of fat as it cooks. Use a baster to siphon fat out of the pan as it accumulates.

SERVES 6

5 tablespoons butter
½ medium onion, finely chopped
1 medium tart apple, such as Granny Smith or Rome Beauty, cored and finely diced
½ cup raisins
1½ cups cooked wild rice
½ teaspoon dried thyme
Salt and pepper
1 (12-pound) goose
3 medium carrots, chopped
3 medium celery ribs, chopped
1 bunch fresh sage
8 sprigs flat-leaf fresh parsley
1 bay leaf
1 teaspoon black peppercorns
10 cups water
½ cup dry white wine

1. Preheat the oven to 400°F.

2. Melt 4 tablespoons of butter in a large skillet over medium heat. Add the onion, apple, and raisins; cook until softened, about 3 minutes. Stir in the rice and thyme. Season to taste with salt and pepper; set aside.

3. Remove and reserve the giblets (heart, liver, and gizzard) and neck. Rinse the goose inside and out and pat dry with paper towels. Trim the excess fat from the opening of the cavity. Remove the first and second joints of the wings, and set them aside for use in making the broth. With the point of a sharp knife, prick the entire surface of the goose skin, being careful not to cut into the flesh. Fold the neck flap under the body of the goose, and pin the flap down with a toothpick. Generously sprinkle the cavity with salt and pepper, stuff loosely with the wild rice stuffing, and tie the legs together with kitchen string. Generously sprinkle the outside of the goose with salt and pepper, and place it, breast side up, on a wire rack set in a large roasting pan.

4. Roast the goose in the oven until it turns a golden brown, about 1 hour. With a baster, remove as much fat as possible from the roasting pan every 20 minutes. Reduce the oven temperature to 325°F and continue roasting until the goose is very well browned and the breast meat registers 180°F, about 1 hour.

5. Meanwhile, prepare broth for the gravy. Trim and discard any excess fat from the reserved wing tips and giblets. Place them in a saucepan along with the neck (if included). Add the carrots, celery, sage, parsley, bay leaf, peppercorns, and water. Bring to a boil over high heat, reduce the heat, and simmer for 1½ hours, skimming off any foam that forms on the surface. Strain the broth through a cheesecloth-lined strainer. Remove and discard the fat floating on the surface. Discard the solids and set the broth aside.

6. Remove the goose from the oven, and transfer to a large serving platter. Let the goose stand for 15 to 20 minutes.

7. Meanwhile, prepare the gravy. Pour off all the fat from the roasting pan, and place the pan over high heat. Pour in the wine and cook, stirring up any brown bits with a wooden spoon, until the liquid is reduced by three-quarters. Add 2 cups of goose broth and cook, stirring, until the liquid is again reduced by three-quarters. Season with salt and pepper to taste. Stir in the remaining 1 tablespoon butter and cook until slightly thickened. Pass the gravy through a cheesecloth-lined strainer into a gravy boat.

8. Carve the goose and serve with the stuffing and gravy on the side.

Roast Pheasant

Pheasants, like all game birds, are all dark meat. Wild birds may be quite lean; farm-raised birds will be less so. The legs take considerably longer to cook than the breast, so the pieces are separated and the breast is removed from the oven first. Traditional accompaniments include cranberry sauce, applesauce, and sweet-and-sour cabbage dishes.

SERVES 4 TO 6

2 or 3 (2- to 3-pound) pheasants, cut into
    serving pieces
½ medium lemon
Salt and pepper
5 tablespoons butter, melted
¾ cup dried cranberries or dried cherries
Juice of 3 medium oranges
1 teaspoon grated lemon zest
1 cup chicken broth (page 119)
⅓ cup dry white wine

1. Preheat the oven to 350°F.

2. Rinse the pheasant pieces and pat dry with paper towels. Rub with the lemon and season with salt and pepper. Place, skin side up, in a roasting pan. Brush with the butter.

3. In a bowl, mix the cranberries, orange juice, lemon zest, broth, and wine. Pour the broth mixture into the pan.

4. Roast for 45 minutes, basting with the pan mixture every 10 minutes. Check the breast pieces for doneness; the juices should run clear when the meat is pricked with a fork. Remove the breast pieces from the pan and keep warm on a plate loosely covered with aluminum foil. Continue to cook the legs until tender, about 20 more minutes. Serve with the pan juices.

Basic Bread Stuffing

Stuffing can easily be made from scratch, using day-old bread, with delicious results. Although typically used for turkey, this recipe works equally well with chicken.

SERVES 8 TO 10

1 pound sliced day-old white bread, French
    bread, or Italian bread, cut into ½-inch
    cubes (about 10 cups lightly packed)

½ cup (1 stick) butter
2 medium onions, finely chopped
2 medium celery ribs, finely chopped
½ cup minced fresh parsley
1 teaspoon dried sage
1 teaspoon dried thyme
1 teaspoon salt
½ teaspoon black pepper
1 cup chicken broth (page 119)

1. Preheat the oven to 400°F.

2. Spread the bread out on a large baking sheet. Toast until golden brown, 5 to 10 minutes, shaking the pan occasionally to avoid burning. Transfer to a large bowl. Reduce the oven temperature to 350°F.

3. Melt the butter in a large skillet over medium-high heat. Add the onions and celery and sauté, stirring, until tender, about 5 minutes.

4. Remove the skillet from the heat and stir in the parsley, sage, thyme, salt, and pepper.

5. Scrape the sautéed vegetables and butter into the bread cubes and toss until well combined. Mix in the broth until the stuffing is lightly moist but not packed together.

6. To use for stuffing, reheat just before spooning into the bird. As a side dish, spoon into a large, buttered, shallow baking dish. Bake in the 350°F oven until the top has formed a crust and the stuffing is heated through, 30 to 45 minutes. Serve hot.

TIP: The stuffing in a bird should register 160°F in the center before it is safe to eat. If the bird is done but the stuffing is not hot enough, spoon the stuffing into a buttered baking dish and finish baking in a hot oven while the bird rests before carving.

Sausage-Apple Stuffing

Sausage, apples, pecans, and cranberries add lots of flavor and texture to this stuffing. It is perfect for a Thanksgiving turkey, especially since the pecan is a native American nut.

SERVES 8 TO 10

1 pound sliced day-old white bread, French
     bread, or Italian bread, cut into ½-inch
     cubes (about 10 cups lightly packed)
8 tablespoons (1 stick) butter
2½ cups boiling water
1 pound pork sausage, removed from the
     casings
1 large onion, finely chopped
1½ teaspoons minced garlic
3 medium celery ribs, finely chopped
1 teaspoon dried thyme
1 teaspoon dried sage
1 cup chopped pecans
3 medium tart apples, such as Granny Smith
     or Rome Beauty, cored and finely diced
1 cup dried cranberries

1. Preheat the oven to 400°F. Grease a large, shallow baking dish.

2. Spread the bread out on a large baking sheet. Toast until golden brown, 5 to 10 minutes, shaking the pan occasionally to avoid burning. Transfer to a large bowl. Reduce the oven temperature to 350°F.

3. In a large skillet over medium heat, melt 4 tablespoons of butter. Add the melted butter to the bread along with the boiling water. Toss to combine.

4. Return the skillet to medium-high heat. Melt 1 tablespoon of butter and add the sausage. Sauté until well browned, breaking up the meat with a spoon, about 8 to 10 minutes. Transfer the meat to paper towels to drain.

5. Melt the remaining 3 tablespoons butter in the skillet over medium-high heat. Add the onion, garlic, celery, thyme, and sage and sauté until the onion is softened, about 3 minutes. Add the pecans and sauté for 1 minute. Add the apples and cranberries and sauté for 1 minute more.

6. Combine the sausage and sautéed ingredients with the bread mixture and toss to mix.

7. To use as a stuffing, reheat just before spooning it into the bird. As a side dish, spoon into the prepared baking dish. Bake for 30 to 45 minutes, until the top has formed a crust and the stuffing is heated through. Serve hot.

Cornbread-Sausage Dressing

Some people say stuffing is baked inside a bird, while dressing is baked in a baking dish alongside the bird. Actually, the two terms can be used interchangeably. Stuffing is the original term, but Victorians found the term to be vulgar and changed it to dressing.

SERVES 8 TO 10

8 tablespoons (1 stick) butter
1 pound pork sausage, removed from the
     casings
1 medium onion, finely chopped
1 large celery rib, finely chopped
½ red or green bell pepper, finely chopped
5 cups dry white bread cubes
5 cups crumbled cornbread
¼ teaspoon black pepper
1 teaspoon poultry seasoning
½ cup milk
1 cup chicken broth (page 119)

1. Preheat the oven to 350°F. Grease a large, shallow baking dish.

2. Melt 1 tablespoon of butter in a large skillet over medium-high heat. Add the sausage and sauté until well browned, breaking the meat up with a spoon, about 8 to 10 minutes. Transfer the meat to paper towels to drain.

3. Return the skillet to medium heat and add the remaining 7 tablespoons butter. When the butter is melted, add the onion, celery, and bell pepper and sauté just until softened, about 3 minutes. Scrape with a wooden spoon into a large bowl.

4. Add the sausage, bread cubes, cornbread crumbs, pepper, and poultry seasoning to the bowl and toss to mix. Mix in the milk and broth.

5. To use as a stuffing, reheat just before spooning it into the bird. As a side dish, spoon into the prepared baking dish. Bake for 30 to 45 minutes, until the top has formed a crust and the stuffing is heated through. Serve hot.

Herbed Oyster Stuffing

During the nineteenth century, oyster men kept the middle region of the country supplied with oysters, which they sold from horse-drawn wagons. At holiday times, these entrepreneurs also sold oranges. In those days, oysters were almost commonplace and oranges were a once-a-year treat; both made the holidays special.

SERVES 8 TO 10

1 pound sliced day-old white bread, French bread, or Italian bread, cut into ½-inch cubes (about 10 cups lightly packed)
½ pound sliced bacon, cut into ½-inch pieces
2 medium onions, finely chopped
3 medium celery ribs, finely chopped
1 tablespoon minced garlic
1 tablespoon dried thyme
2 teaspoons dried sage
½ teaspoon salt, plus more for seasoning
¼ teaspoon black pepper, plus more for seasoning
⅔ cup finely chopped fresh parsley
½ cup (1 stick) unsalted butter, melted
18 medium oysters, shucked, drained, and chopped (about ¾ cup)
2½ cups chicken broth (page 119)

1. Preheat the oven to 400°F. Grease a large, shallow baking dish.

2. Spread the bread out on a large baking sheet. Toast until golden brown, 5 to 10 minutes, shaking the pan occasionally to avoid burning. Transfer to a large bowl. Reduce the oven temperature to 325°F.

3. Meanwhile, cook the bacon in a large heavy skillet over medium heat, stirring and turning often, until crisp, about 10 to 15 minutes. Use a slotted spoon to transfer the bacon to paper towels to drain, reserving the grease in the skillet.

4. Add the onions, celery, garlic, thyme, sage, salt, and pepper to the skillet and sauté over medium heat, stirring occasionally, until the vegetables are softened, 5 to 8 minutes.

5. Use a wooden spoon to scrape the sautéed vegetables into the bowl with the bread cubes. Stir in the bacon, parsley, butter, and oysters. Drizzle with the broth, season with additional salt and pepper to taste, and toss well.

6. Spoon the stuffing into the prepared baking dish and cover. Bake for 30 minutes, then uncover and bake until browned, about 30 minutes more. Serve hot.

Wild Rice Stuffing

Because wild rice is native to America, it is a popular ingredient for stuffing on Thanksgiving, when we celebrate the bounty of this country. This particular stuffing is very good with game birds as well as turkey.

SERVES 12

¼ cup (½ stick) butter
2 cups thinly sliced mushrooms
1 medium onion, finely chopped
1 medium celery rib, minced
1 teaspoon minced garlic
6 ounces bulk pork sausage
¼ cup chopped pecans
1 tablespoon chopped fresh parsley
¼ teaspoon dried sage
2 teaspoons salt
2 teaspoons black pepper
1 medium apple, cored, peeled, and finely chopped
3 to 4 cups cooked wild rice (page 278)

1. Melt the butter in a large skillet over medium-high heat. Add the mushrooms, onion, celery, and garlic and sauté until the mushrooms give up their juice, about 8 minutes. Use a slotted spoon to transfer to a food processor.

2. Cook the sausage in the skillet over medium-high heat until well browned, about 10 minutes. Transfer to the food processor.

3. Add the pecans, parsley, sage, salt, and pepper to the food processor. Pulse until roughly chopped and mixed but not puréed. Transfer to a large bowl.

4. Add the apple and rice to the bowl and mix well.

5. Use the mixture to stuff a turkey, goose, or 2 pheasants. If serving as a side dish, spoon into a greased baking dish and bake at 350°F for 1 hour. Serve hot.

Potato, Sausage, and Apple Stuffing

Thanksgiving stuffings for German-Americans often included potatoes, sausages, and apples. This historical recipe makes an interesting change from the stuffings made strictly from bread.

SERVES 10

¾ cup (1½ sticks) butter
1 turkey liver, finely chopped
1 pound bulk pork sausage
2 medium white waxy potatoes, peeled and diced
3 medium celery ribs, diced
1 medium onion, diced
1 medium apple, cored and diced
9 cups soft bread cubes (preferably a mixture of white, whole wheat, and rye)
1 teaspoon dried thyme
½ teaspoon ground sage
½ to ¾ cup chicken broth (page 119)
Salt and pepper

1. Preheat the oven to 350°F. If you are planning to roast the turkey unstuffed, grease a large baking dish.

2. Melt the butter in a large skillet over medium-high heat. Add the liver, sausage, potatoes, celery, onion, and apple and sauté until the sausage is crumbled and evenly cooked, about 15 minutes.

3. Transfer the mixture to a large bowl. Add the bread cubes, thyme, and sage and toss to mix. Add as much of the broth as needed to moisten the mixture. Season to taste with salt and pepper.

4. If you are planning to stuff the mixture into a turkey, the mixture is ready for stuffing. If serving as a side dish, transfer to the prepared baking dish, cover, and heat for about 45 minutes, until heated through. For a crunchy top, uncover the baking dish for the last 15 minutes of baking. Serve hot.

Herbed Chestnut Stuffing

Did the early colonists make chestnut stuffing? They could have. At that time, eastern North America was covered with tall American chestnut trees, and chestnuts were an important food source for Native Americans. A blight introduced from the Far East in 1904 virtually wiped out native chestnut trees.

SERVES 8 TO 10

1 pound chestnuts
6 cups cubed day-old white bread
½ cup (1 stick) butter
2 medium onions, chopped
4 medium celery ribs, chopped
1 tablespoon dried sage
2 teaspoons dried thyme
1½ teaspoons dried crumbled rosemary
½ cup finely chopped fresh parsley
Salt and pepper

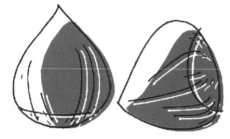

1. Preheat the oven to 400°F.

2. Make a cut in the rounded side of each chestnut to keep them from exploding in the oven. Place the chestnuts in a single layer on a baking sheet. Roast for about 20 minutes, until tender. Wrap the hot chestnuts in an old towel, squeeze hard to crush the skins, and let sit, wrapped, for 5 minutes before peeling. Coarsely chop them and set aside.

3. Reduce the oven temperature to 325°F. If you plan to roast the turkey unstuffed, grease a large baking dish.

4. Spread the bread in a single layer on 2 baking sheets and toast in the oven, stirring occasionally, for 10 to 15 minutes, until golden. Transfer to a large bowl.

5. Melt the butter over medium heat in a large skillet. Add the onions, celery, sage, thyme, and rosemary and sauté until the vegetables are soft-ened, about 8 minutes. Add the chestnuts and cook the mixture, stirring, for 1 minute.

6. Add the vegetable mixture to the bread cubes along with the parsley, tossing the mixture well. Season to taste with salt and pepper.

7. If you are planning to stuff the mixture into a turkey, the mixture is ready for stuffing. If serving as a side dish, transfer to the prepared baking dish, cover, and heat for about 45 minutes, until heated through. For a crunchy top, uncover the baking dish for the last 15 minutes of baking. Serve hot.

BUYING, CUTTING, AND CARVING POULTRY

Buying Poultry

▶ When buying poultry, allow ¾ to 1 pound of chicken or turkey (including bones) for each serving. With duck or goose, allow 1 to 1½ pounds per serving.

How to Cut Raw Chicken

▶ Be scrupulous about sanitation in the kitchen, keeping the poultry refrigerated and thoroughly washing any cutting boards and utensils that have had contact with raw meat.

▶ Cutting a whole chicken into pieces is a good idea. Whole chickens cost less per pound than packaged chicken pieces. Also, precut meat is often poorly trimmed, so you get less meat per pound. Cutting up a chicken is not hard, but a sharp knife or poultry shears and a cutting board are essential.

1. First, remove the legs. Place the chicken, breast side up, on the cutting board. Pull one leg away from the body and cut through the skin between the body and both sides of the thigh. Bend the whole leg firmly away from the body until the ball

of the thigh bone pops from the hip socket. Cut between the ball and the socket to separate the leg. Repeat with the other leg.

2. Place the leg, skin side down, on the cutting board. Cut down firmly through the joint between the drumstick and the thigh. Repeat with the second leg.

3. Next, remove the wings. Turn the chicken on its back. Cut down inside the wing just over the joint. Pull the wing away from the body and cut down through the skin and the joint. Repeat with the other wing.

4. Now, cut the carcass in half. Cut through the cavity of the bird from the tail end and slice through the thin area around the shoulder joint. Cut parallel to the backbone and slice the bones of the rib cage. Repeat on the opposite side of the backbone.

5. Pull apart the breast and the back. Cut down through the shoulder bones to detach the breast from the back. Cut the back into two pieces by cutting across the backbone where the ribs end.

6. Leave the breast whole if your recipe requires it. If you need halves, use strong, steady pressure to cut downward along the length of the breastbone and separate the breast into two pieces.

How to Carve a Chicken

▶ The goal of carving a chicken is to separate the chicken into pieces, rather than creating slices like you do when you carve a turkey.

1. Cut straight down on either side of the breastbone. Turn the bird over and continue to cut on either side of the backbone until you have cut the bird in half.

2. Separate the leg and breast sections by cutting through the skin that holds them together and continuing through the joint, holding the knife almost parallel to the cutting board.

3. Separate the wing from the breast.

4. Separate the leg and thigh by cutting through the joint.

5. Arrange the meat on a serving platter and serve.

How to Carve a Turkey

▶ A whole roasted turkey is an impressive sight, but the bird must be carved before it can be served. You will need a sharp 10-inch knife (no serrated blades), a carving fork for arranging the meat, and a serving platter. Before carving the turkey, let it stand at room temperature for 20 to 30 minutes to allow the juices to saturate the meat.

1. Remove the drumsticks first. Place the knife against the thigh, and cut down to expose the leg's second joint. Apply pressure at the joint with the knife point; twist the knife, and cut through to sever the drumstick. Repeat with the other drumstick.

2. Slice the thigh meat from the bone.

3. Place the knife horizontally at the bottom curve of the bird's breast, and slice in toward the rib cage to create a "guide cut." Then make a slice from the top down alongside the rib cage. Cut vertically through the breast meat to create medallion (small, circular) slices, being careful to preserve some of the skin on each slice. Repeat on the other side of the breast.

4. Place the knife at the first wing joint; insert the knifepoint, and twist it to sever the wing. Repeat with the other wing.

5. Arrange the meat on the serving platter and serve.

CHAPTER EIGHT

Meat

Meat has always played an integral role in the American diet, with pork being the most commonly consumed, and beef the most highly prized. Our rich farmland and endless tracts of grazing lands have made it possible to raise vast quantities of meat—some eaten fresh, some smoked, and some cured. In our grandmother's day the entire meal was planned around the meat, with a complementary starch and vegetable.

The first domesticated pigs arrived in the New World in 1539, brought to Tampa, Florida, by explorer Hernando de Soto. It is from these thirteen pigs that all North American domesticated pigs descend. The early settlers found pigs easy to raise because the pigs foraged on their own and lived off of scraps. Lard, or rendered pork fat, was also especially important as a cooking fat.

The demand for beef rose dramatically after the Civil War and led to the era of the great cattle drives and expansion of the West. This period in history was brief, ended by the introduction of barbed wire in the 1870s and the settlement of new farms.

By the 1920s, beef had overtaken pork as the most popular meat in America. In those times, a good meal came to be defined as a thick steak accompanied by a baked potato. With the exception of ground beef, most prime cuts of beef were—and still remain—expensive.

Roasts and steaks—beef, pork, veal, or lamb—continue to be the highest-ticket items on our grocery lists, so it is important that these meats be thoughtfully prepared. One thing has changed, however: The meat we buy today is significantly leaner than the cuts our grandmothers served. Therefore, meat dishes prepared with recipes from bygone eras typically do not produce the same results. All the classic ingredients are preserved in this chapter's meat recipes, but *The Good Home Cookbook*'s versions include updated and easy-to-follow cooking and preparation methods for optimal results in today's kitchens.

Standing Rib Roast with Horseradish Sauce

The ultimate holiday and company food, a standing rib roast is perfect for all occasions. This is the same cut as a prime rib, although if the meat is not USDA prime grade, it is not a prime rib. Be sure the chine (backbone) is removed to make carving easier. This roast is served with a cold horseradish sauce, but the gravy recipe with boneless rib roast provides a flavorful alternative.

SERVES 8

1 (9- to 10-pound) standing rib roast (4 ribs)
Salt and pepper
Horseradish sauce (recipe follows), to serve

1. Preheat the oven to 450°F.

2. Place the roast, fat side up, on the rack in a shallow roasting pan. Generously sprinkle the meat with salt and pepper.

3. Roast for 10 minutes.

4. Reduce the oven temperature to 325°F and roast for 15 to 30 minutes per pound, 2¼ to 3 hours. For rare, the internal temperature should be about 120°F, medium-rare will be about 130°F, and medium will be about 135°F. (The temperature will continue to rise 5 degrees while the meat rests.)

5. Remove the roast from the oven and let stand, covered loosely with aluminum foil, for 15 to 30 minutes before carving.

6. Carve the roast and serve, passing the horseradish sauce at the table.

Horseradish Sauce

This creamy sauce adds snap and character to steaks and poultry. Exchange the cream for mayonnaise and use on sandwiches.

MAKES 1 CUP

½ cup heavy cream
3 tablespoons lemon juice
2 tablespoons prepared horseradish
Salt and pepper

1. Use an electric mixer to beat the cream until stiff in a medium bowl. Beat in the lemon juice and horseradish. Season to taste with salt and pepper.

2. Chill before serving.

Boneless Rib Roast with Gravy

This is traditionally served at the holiday table, but it makes a wonderful meal any time of the year and the leftovers make great sandwiches. Leave the string in place when you roast and remove it just before carving.

SERVES 8 TO 10

1 (4½- to 5-pound) boneless rib roast
Salt and pepper
2 tablespoons all-purpose flour
2 cups beef broth (page 118) or water
2 tablespoons butter

1. Preheat the oven to 450°F.

2. Place the roast, fat side up, on the rack in a shallow roasting pan. Generously rub the meat with salt and pepper.

3. Roast for 20 minutes. Reduce the heat to 325°F and roast for 20 minutes per pound, 1¼ to 2½ hours. For rare, the internal temperature should be about 120°F, medium-rare will be about 130°F, and medium will be about 135°F. (The temperature will continue to rise 5 degrees while the meat rests.)

4. Remove the roast from the oven and let stand, covered loosely with aluminum foil, while making the gravy. Strain the pan drippings into a medium saucepan. Skim two-thirds of the fat off the top and discard.

5. Whisk the flour into the drippings until smooth. Cook on medium heat until thickened. Stir in the butter. Season with salt and pepper to taste.

6. Carve the roast and serve the gravy with the sliced meat.

Herbed Tenderloin with Mushroom Wine Sauce

The tenderloin is a long muscle that runs on either side of the backbone and contains the filet mignon, châteaubriand, and tournedos. It is a highly tender and rich cut of meat. Add the warm red wine sauce with mushrooms and experience the ultimate steak pleasure.

SERVES 8

Red wine sauce:
2¼ cups beef broth (page 118)
2½ tablespoons all-purpose flour
1 teaspoon minced garlic
1 teaspoon Worcestershire sauce
1 tablespoon tomato paste
1 tablespoon butter
1 cup sliced mushrooms
¼ cup dry red wine
Salt and pepper

Tenderloin:
1 whole beef tenderloin (about 5 pounds)
1 garlic clove, halved
2 tablespoons butter, softened
½ teaspoon dried oregano

¼ teaspoon dried basil
¼ teaspoon dried rosemary
¼ teaspoon dried thyme
½ teaspoon black pepper

1. To make the sauce, heat 2 cups of broth to boiling in a large saucepan. Mix the flour into the remaining ¼ cup broth in a small bowl. Whisk the flour mixture into the hot broth and add the garlic, Worcestershire sauce, and tomato paste. Simmer, uncovered, for 45 minutes.

2. Melt the butter in a medium skillet over medium heat. Add the mushrooms and sauté until lightly browned, about 5 minutes.

3. Add the sautéed mushrooms and red wine to the sauce and simmer for 10 minutes. Season to taste with salt and pepper and keep warm.

4. Preheat the oven to 425°F.

5. To make the roast, trim the meat by removing the thin, tough bluish membrane underneath the fat. Tuck the thin tail end under the roast and tie at 1½-inch intervals with kitchen string. Rub the roast all over with the cut side of the garlic and discard. Rub the butter over the meat.

6. In a small bowl, combine the oregano, basil, rosemary, thyme, and pepper. Rub the herbs over the roast, pressing evenly into the meat.

7. Place the roast on a rack in a shallow roasting pan. Roast, uncovered, for 25 to 45 minutes. For rare, the internal temperature should be about 120°F, medium-rare will be about 130°F, and medium will be about 135°F. (Do not cook beyond medium.) Let stand for 10 to 15 minutes. (The temperature will continue to rise about 5 degrees as it sits.)

8. Carve into ½-inch slices and serve with the red wine sauce.

Broiled Marinated Steaks

T-bone, porterhouse, New York, rib-eye, top sirloin, and tenderloin steaks are all good choices for broiling (or grilling). This marinade is simple and adds a lot of flavor to broiled steak.

SERVES 4

1½ cups soy sauce
1 teaspoon minced garlic
1 tablespoon dry mustard
1 tablespoon black pepper
4 (6- to 12-ounce) beef steaks

1. Mix the soy sauce, garlic, mustard, and pepper in a shallow baking dish. Add the steaks, turn to coat both sides well, cover, and refrigerate for 3 to 5 hours, turning every hour or so.

2. Preheat the broiler and broiler pan.

3. Discard the marinade and place the steaks on the broiler pan and position the pan 4 to 5 inches from the heat. Broil, turning once, to the desired doneness (check the center of one steak), according to the chart on page 223. Serve hot.

London Broil

Despite what you might find at the local meat market, London broil is not a cut of beef but rather a method of cooking. It was one of the first recipes to become popular in early restaurants. Originally it was made only with flank steak, but over the years the name has been applied to almost any cut of beef that is very lean and not very tender. The original method of preparing London broil was to pan fry a flank steak to medium-rare, slice across the grain, and serve. This method is perfect for a flank steak because it becomes very tough if cooked too long. Today London broil might also be grilled or broiled.

SERVES 4

5 garlic cloves
1 teaspoon salt
¼ cup dry red wine
2 tablespoons balsamic vinegar
1 tablespoon soy sauce

1 teaspoon honey
1 (1½-pound) beef flank steak or top round (about 1¼ inches thick)
1½ tablespoons oil

1. Mince the garlic to a paste with the salt. Combine in a blender with the wine, vinegar, soy sauce, and honey and pulse until blended.

2. Place the meat in a heavy-duty resealable plastic bag or shallow baking dish and pour the marinade over the meat. Marinate in the refrigerator, turning occasionally, for at least 4 hours and up to 24 hours.

3. Heat the oil in a large, heavy skillet over high heat. Lift the steak out of the marinade and pat dry with paper towels. Sear the steak on one side, 4 to 6 minutes. Turn and sear on the second side, 3 to 5 minutes.

4. Transfer the steak to a cutting board and let stand for 5 minutes. Holding a knife at a 45-degree angle, cut the steak across the grain into thin slices. Serve hot.

Sautéed Steak Strips with Mushrooms

This elegant dinner takes almost no time to prepare. Serve with rice or potatoes and a green salad. Choose a lean cut such as beef sirloin tip or top round for this recipe.

SERVES 4

1 (1½-pound) beef sirloin tip, or top round, well-trimmed
Salt and pepper
3 tablespoons oil
1 pound button mushrooms, quartered (or choose a mix of wild mushrooms)
1 medium carrot, diced
½ medium onion, diced
3 tablespoons dry red wine
¼ cup beef broth (page 118)
2 tablespoons cold butter, cut into pieces

1. Cut the beef into thin, 2 x ¼-inch strips. Season with salt and pepper.

2. Heat 2 tablespoons of oil in a large, heavy skillet over medium-high heat. Add the meat and

sear for approximately 1 minute on each side or until just browned. Remove from the skillet with a slotted spoon and keep warm.

3. Add the remaining 1 tablespoon oil to the skillet and heat. Add the mushrooms, carrot, and onion and sauté until the mushrooms give up their juice, about 8 minutes.

4. Return the beef to the skillet and stir in the wine and broth. Continue to sauté until the meat is just done, 1 to 2 minutes for rare. Stir in the butter until melted. Season to taste with salt and pepper. Serve immediately.

Chicken-Fried Steak with Cream Gravy

Chicken-fried steak is beef, usually round steak, that has been breaded and fried like Southern fried chicken. It is often made with cube steak, but it tastes best when made with round steak.

SERVES 4 TO 5

1 (1½- to 2-pound) beef round steak, cut into
    4 or 5 portions
1½ cups all-purpose flour
2 teaspoons black pepper, plus more to taste
2 teaspoons salt, plus more to taste
¼ teaspoon cayenne pepper
1 large egg
1¼ cups milk
Oil or shortening, for frying
½ to ¾ cup water

1. Place the meat between sheets of plastic wrap or wax paper. Pound with a meat mallet until less than ½ inch thick.

2. Stir together the flour, black pepper, salt, and cayenne pepper in a shallow bowl. Beat together the egg and ¼ cup of milk in a second shallow bowl.

3. Dip the steaks in the seasoned flour, shaking off any excess. Then dip each cutlet in the egg mixture, and back into the seasoned flour. Set the coated cutlets aside on a piece of wax paper and reserve the flour.

4. Pour ½ inch of oil into a large skillet and heat over medium-high heat. Carefully slide the steaks into the hot oil and fry until golden brown, 2 to 3 minutes per side.

5. Pour off all but 1 to 2 tablespoons of oil and reserve. Reduce the heat to low and cook the steaks for 4 or 5 minutes more.

6. Drain the hot cutlets on paper towels and keep warm while preparing the gravy.

7. Return ½ cup of reserved oil to the skillet and heat over medium heat. Sprinkle in 3 tablespoons of leftover seasoned flour. Stir until the flour is lightly browned. Gradually whisk in the remaining 1 cup milk and ½ cup of water, stirring constantly. Continue cooking and stirring for a few minutes until the gravy reaches the desired thickness. Add the remaining ¼ cup water, if needed. Taste and add salt and pepper, if needed.

8. Place a steak on each plate and serve, passing the gravy on the side.

Beef Stroganoff

Beef stroganoff is the prize-winning combination of beef, mushrooms, and sour cream created for an 1890s cooking competition in St. Petersburg, Russia. The chef who devised the recipe worked for the Russian diplomat Count Pavel Alexandrovich Stroganov. Presumably, the recipe traveled to America along with the great wave of Russian immigrants at the beginning of the twentieth century.

SERVES 4 TO 6

1 (1½-pound) beef sirloin tip, or top round,
 well trimmed
Salt and pepper
2 tablespoons butter
1 tablespoon plus 1 teaspoon all-purpose flour
1 cup beef broth (page 118)
3 tablespoons oil
1 pound button mushrooms, quartered
¼ cup sour cream
Hot cooked egg noodles, to serve
Chopped fresh parsley, to serve

1. Cut the beef into thin 2-inch strips, about ¼ inch thick. Season with salt and pepper.

2. Melt the butter in a medium saucepan over medium heat. Stir in the flour until you have a smooth paste. Slowly whisk in the broth and simmer until smooth and thick. Reduce the heat to low.

3. Heat 2 tablespoons of oil in a large, heavy skillet over medium-high heat. Add the mushrooms and sauté until they give up their juice, about 8 minutes. Use a slotted spoon to transfer the mushrooms to the sauce. Stir in the sour cream and season to taste with salt and pepper. Keep warm; do not allow the sauce to boil.

4. Add the remaining 1 tablespoon oil to the skillet and heat. Add the meat and sauté for about 2 minutes. The meat should be browned on the outside and still rare on the inside.

5. Arrange the egg noodles on a serving platter and lay the meat on top. Spoon the sauce over the meat and garnish with the parsley. Serve immediately.

Pan-Seared Steak

Open the windows or turn the exhaust fan on high when you try this. If you are serving more than two people, you will need two skillets. Steak sauce goes well with this simple cooking method.

SERVES 2

2 (6- to 12-ounce) beef steaks, such as New
 York or top sirloin
Oil
Salt and pepper

1. Brush both sides of the steaks with oil and season generously with salt and pepper.

2. Heat a large, heavy skillet over high heat. Add the steaks and sear on one side, about 5 minutes. Turn and sear on the second side for 3 to 4 minutes for rare, 5 to 8 minutes for medium. Serve hot.

Swiss Steak

Swiss steak is not an example of Swiss cuisine because it is an English recipe. The name most likely comes from relating the process of smoothing out cloth between rollers, called swissing, to the pounding and flattening of the meat. This dish is excellent served over rice or egg noodles.

SERVES 4

½ cup all-purpose flour
1 tablespoon dry mustard
1 (1½-pound) beef round steak, cut 1 inch
    thick
2 tablespoons oil
1 (15-ounce) can diced tomatoes
1 medium onion, sliced
2 medium celery ribs, sliced
2 medium carrots, sliced
2 tablespoons Worcestershire sauce
1 tablespoon brown sugar
Salt and pepper

1. Preheat the oven to 350°F.

2. Mix the flour with the mustard in a small bowl. Sprinkle the flour mixture over the steak and pound evenly with a meat mallet until the meat is ¼ inch thick. Cut the pounded steak into 4 serving-size pieces.

3. Heat the oil in a large skillet over medium-high heat. Add the meat and cook, turning once, until browned on both sides, 4 to 6 minutes. Transfer the meat to a shallow baking dish.

4. Add the tomatoes, onion, celery, carrots, Worcestershire sauce, and brown sugar to the dish, gently stirring to combine. Season to taste with salt and pepper. Cover the dish.

5. Bake until the meat is tender when pierced with a fork, about 1½ hours. Serve hot.

Beef Pot Pie with Biscuit Crust

Pot pies were a typical way to serve leftovers in days gone by, but only chicken pot pies seem to have made most modern menus. This hearty pot pie is sure to satisfy even the hungriest eater.

SERVES 6 TO 8

Filling:
¼ cup shortening
1 (1-pound) beef round steak, cut into ½-inch
    strips
1½ cups chopped onions
2 tablespoons all-purpose flour
1 cup canned diced tomatoes
1 cup water

1 (6-ounce) can tomato paste
1 tablespoon sugar
½ teaspoon Worcestershire sauce
Salt and pepper
1 cup sliced mushrooms
¾ cup sour cream

Biscuit topping:
1¼ cups all-purpose flour
2 teaspoons baking powder
½ teaspoon salt
¼ cup shortening
¾ cup sour cream

1. To make the filling, melt the shortening in a large skillet over medium-high heat. Add the beef and brown, about 1 minute per side. Add the onions and sauté until they are softened, about 3 minutes.

2. Sprinkle in the flour and stir until completely moistened. Stir in the tomatoes, water, tomato paste, sugar, and Worcestershire sauce. Season to taste with salt and pepper. Reduce the heat, cover, and simmer until the meat is tender, approximately 1 hour.

3. Preheat the oven to 425°F.

4. Stir the mushrooms and sour cream into the skillet and simmer for another 5 minutes. Do not let the mixture boil. Set aside.

5. To make the biscuit topping, sift together the flour, baking powder, and salt into a medium bowl. Cut in the shortening with a fork or pastry blender until the mixture resembles small peas. Mix in the sour cream until the dough comes together in a ball.

6. On a lightly floured surface, roll out the dough to a thickness of ¾ inch. Cut into 8 rounds with a biscuit cutter.

7. Transfer the beef mixture to a 2-quart baking dish. Top with the biscuits.

8. Bake for 20 to 25 minutes, until the biscuits are golden brown.

9. Let the pot pie stand for 5 minutes. Serve hot.

Yankee Pot Roast

When is a pot roast a Yankee pot roast? It is when vegetables are added midway through the cooking, turning an ordinary pot roast into a delicious, one-pot meal. Although the aroma is wonderful, seasoning the dish well with salt and pepper before serving will enhance the natural flavors.

SERVES 6

1 (3- to 4-pound) chuck roast or rump roast, tied if boneless
Salt and pepper
3 tablespoons oil, rendered beef fat, or lard
3 medium onions, sliced
2½ cups beef broth (page 118)
1 teaspoon dried thyme
1 bay leaf
6 large carrots, quartered and cut into 2-inch lengths
6 small waxy potatoes, such as thin-skinned red or white, peeled and quartered
4 medium turnips, peeled and quartered (optional)
3 medium parsnips, peeled and cut into 2-inch lengths
2 tablespoons all-purpose flour
2 tablespoons unsalted butter, softened

1. Season the meat with salt and pepper. Heat the oil in a large Dutch oven over medium-high heat. Add the beef and brown on all sides, 15 to 20 minutes. Remove the meat and set aside.

2. Add the onions and sauté until softened, about 5 minutes.

3. Return the beef to the Dutch oven. Add the broth, thyme, and bay leaf. Cover, reduce the heat to its lowest setting, and cook slowly, in liquid that is barely simmering, turning every 30 minutes. Flat roasts will require cooking for 1½ to 2½ hours; round roasts will take as long as 4 hours.

4. About 1 hour before the meat is done, add the carrots, potatoes, turnips, if using, and parsnips to the Dutch oven. Replace the cover and continue to cook until both the meat and vegetables are tender. Remove the bay leaf.

5. Transfer the meat and vegetables to a platter and cover with aluminum foil to keep warm. Skim off any fat from the surface of the pan juices and discard. Mix the flour and butter in a small bowl until smooth. Whisk into the pan juices, increase the temperature to medium-high and cook, stirring constantly until thickened, about 3 minutes. Taste and adjust the seasonings as needed. Pour into a gravy boat.

6. Slice the meat and serve alongside the vegetables, with the gravy on the side.

Braised Brisket

The brisket is the same cut of beef that is cured to make corned beef. This boneless cut is taken from the breast section under the first five ribs as a flat cut or point cut. The flat cut has minimal fat and is usually more expensive than the point cut, which is more flavorful. Both cuts require long, slow cooking. This recipe calls for cooking the meat a day before serving so all the fat can be removed from the gravy.

SERVES 6 TO 8

3 tablespoons oil
1 (4-pound) beef brisket
1 cup dry red wine
¼ cup ketchup
¼ cup Dijon mustard
3 tablespoons brown sugar
1 teaspoon salt, plus more to taste
½ teaspoon black pepper, plus more to taste
2 medium onions, quartered
1 garlic head, cloves peeled
3 medium carrots, coarsely chopped
2 bay leaves
2 to 4 cups beef broth (page 118)

1. Preheat the oven to 350°F.

2. Heat the oil over medium-high heat in a large Dutch oven or heavy roasting pan. Add the brisket and cook, turning once, until browned on both sides, 15 to 20 minutes. Remove the brisket and set aside.

3. Add the wine to the Dutch oven and bring to a boil, scraping the bottom of the pan with a wooden spoon to loosen all the browned bits. Continue

cooking the wine until reduced by about half. Remove the Dutch oven from the heat.

4. Mix the ketchup, mustard, brown sugar, salt, and pepper in a small bowl. Brush all over the brisket and return the meat to the Dutch oven. Scatter the onions, garlic, carrots, and bay leaves around the brisket and add enough broth so that the liquid comes halfway up the side of the meat.

5. Cover and roast for 2 to 3 hours, until the meat is completely tender, turning the brisket every half hour.

6. Transfer the brisket from the Dutch oven to a platter, cover, and refrigerate overnight. Strain the braising liquid and discard the bay leaves. Refrigerate the liquid and vegetables in separate containers.

7. The next day, remove the fat that has hardened on the top of the braising liquid and discard. Purée the vegetables and ½ cup of liquid in a food processor or blender.

8. Combine the puréed vegetables and remaining liquid in a large saucepan and heat over medium heat for 10 to 15 minutes. Taste and adjust the seasoning as needed.

9. Preheat the oven to 325°F.

10. Slice the brisket across the grain into thin slices and place in a clean roasting pan. Pour the vegetable gravy over the top. Cover and heat for about 30 to 45 minutes. Serve hot.

Beef Brisket with Dried Fruit

This is a traditional recipe of Jewish cooks who immigrated from Eastern Europe. The combination of dried fruit, sweet potatoes, and carrots makes a pleasant sweet-and-savory dish.

SERVES 8

3 tablespoons oil
3 medium onions, chopped
4 garlic cloves, chopped
1 teaspoon paprika
½ teaspoon ground allspice
¼ teaspoon crushed red pepper
3½ cups chicken broth (page 119)
1½ cups dry red wine
3 bay leaves
1 (4-pound) beef brisket
Salt and pepper
1 (6-ounce) package dried apricots
1½ cups pitted prunes
3 large sweet potatoes, peeled and cut into
     1½-inch pieces
6 large carrots, cut into 1½-inch pieces
Minced fresh parsley, to serve

1. Preheat the oven to 325°F.

2. Heat the oil in a large Dutch oven over medium-high heat. Add the onions and sauté until golden, stirring frequently, about 10 to 12 minutes. Add the garlic and cook another 2 minutes. Stir in the paprika, allspice, and crushed red pepper. Pour in the broth and wine. Add the bay leaves and bring to a boil, then reduce the heat and simmer for 10 minutes to blend the flavors.

3. Sprinkle the brisket with salt and pepper and add, fat side up, to the Dutch oven. Add the apricots and prunes and cover.

4. Bake for 1½ hours.

5. Add the sweet potatoes and carrots. Cover and bake until the brisket is very tender, another 2½ hours.

6. Remove the meat from the Dutch oven and place on a cutting board. Let stand for 20 minutes under a loose tent of aluminum foil. Meanwhile, use a slotted spoon to remove the fruits and vegetables and arrange on a platter. Cover and keep warm.

7. Remove the bay leaves from the pan juices and skim off the fat that rises to the surface. Keep warm.

8. Thinly slice the brisket against the grain. Arrange on the platter with the fruits and vegetables. Spoon the pan juices over the meat, garnish with parsley, and serve.

Sauerbraten

Sauerbraten translates as "sour roast," and it is made by marinating a pot roast for several days in a sweet-and-sour sauce of vinegar and/or beer and spices. Then the meat is braised in the marinade. Crumbled ginger snap cookie crumbs are frequently used to thicken the pan juices.

SERVES 6 TO 8

1 (4- to 5-pound) chuck roast or rump roast
Salt and pepper
1 cup cider vinegar or red-wine vinegar
1½ cups water
½ cup beer
¼ cup sugar
1 small onion, sliced
2 celery ribs, sliced
1 large carrot, sliced
12 whole black peppercorns
6 whole cloves
3 bay leaves
1 teaspoon mustard seeds
½ teaspoon dried thyme
All-purpose flour
2 tablespoons oil
¼ cup raisins (optional)
18 ginger snaps, crushed

1. Rub the beef with salt and pepper and place in a large bowl or crock. Add the vinegar, water, beer, sugar, onion, celery, carrot, peppercorns, cloves, bay leaves, mustard seeds, and thyme. Cover and marinate in the refrigerator for 2 to 4 days, turning the meat a few times a day.

2. When you are ready to cook, remove the meat from the marinade and pat dry with paper towels. Dust the meat with flour.

3. Heat the oil in a large Dutch oven over medium-high heat. Add the meat and brown on all sides, 15 to 20 minutes.

4. Add the marinade, including the vegetables and spices, cover, and simmer slowly for 3 hours, until the meat is tender.

5. Remove the meat from the Dutch oven and keep warm. Strain the cooking liquid and discard the solids. Let stand for a few minutes and skim off the fat that rises to the surface.

6. Return the liquid to the Dutch oven and add the raisins, if using, and ginger snaps. Cook over medium heat, stirring until thickened.

7. Slice the meat and place on a platter to serve, passing the raisin-ginger snap gravy on the side.

Oven-Barbecued Brisket

How do you make authentic barbecued beef brisket without a barbecue? Try this recipe. The meat will be tender, succulent, and full of delicious barbecue flavor.

SERVES 8 TO 10

1 cup barbecue sauce, bottled or homemade (page 254)
½ cup water
¼ cup Worcestershire sauce
2 tablespoons liquid smoke, such as Wright's Concentrated Hickory Seasoning™
1 tablespoon garlic powder
2 teaspoons celery salt
2 teaspoons black pepper
1 teaspoon salt
1 (5- to 6-pound) beef brisket, well trimmed
1 medium onion, chopped

1. Preheat the oven to 275°F.

2. Combine the barbecue sauce, water, Worcestershire sauce, liquid smoke, garlic powder, celery salt, pepper, and salt in a medium bowl and stir until well blended.

3. Place the brisket in a large roasting pan. Pour the sauce over and turn to coat the meat. Scatter the onion over the top.

4. Seal the roasting pan tightly with heavy-duty aluminum foil and bake for 5 to 7 hours (about 1¼ hours per pound).

5. Remove the meat from the oven, transfer to a serving platter, and allow to stand for 1 hour before slicing.

6. To serve, slice across the grain. Spoon the pan sauce into a bowl and pass at the table.

New England Boiled Dinner

Boiled dinners are found in many cuisines. The French have their "pot-au-feu," the Spanish their "cocido," and the Irish their corned beef and cabbage. Add root vegetables to corned beef and cabbage and you have a traditional New England dinner.

SERVES 8 TO 12

1 (6-pound) corned beef brisket
2 medium onions, chopped
4 whole cloves
6 whole black peppercorns
2 bay leaves
1 garlic clove
10 to 12 medium beets, trimmed
12 boiling onions, peeled
6 medium waxy potatoes, such as thin-skinned red or white, peeled and chopped
6 medium carrots, peeled and chopped
3 medium turnips, peeled and chopped
3 medium parsnips, peeled and chopped
1 large head green cabbage, cored and cut into wedges

1. Place the corned beef in a large pot and cover with water. Simmer for 1 hour, skimming off any foam that forms on the surface of the water.

2. Pour off the water; cover with fresh water. Add the chopped onions, cloves, peppercorns, bay leaves, and garlic. Cover and simmer for 3 to 4 hours or until the meat is tender.

3. Meanwhile, boil the beets in a large saucepan with enough water to cover, until tender (about 1 hour). Drain, cool, peel, and cut into quarters.

4. Transfer the meat from the liquid to a serving platter and keep warm.

5. Bring the meat's cooking liquid to a boil. Add the boiling onions, potatoes, carrots, turnips, and parsnips. Cover and simmer for 20 minutes. Add the cabbage and continue to simmer for 15 minutes more, until all the vegetables are tender.

6. Slice the brisket across the grain and serve with the beets and other vegetables.

TIP: Leftovers can be used to make red flannel hash, so called because the beets stain the dish pink. Just include beets with the corned beef in your favorite hash recipe.

Corned Beef and Cabbage

Eating corned beef and cabbage on St. Patrick's Day is a purely American tradition. Corned beef and cabbage is so delicious it deserves to be enjoyed more than once a year. Serve with boiled potatoes.

SERVES 8 TO 12

1 (6-pound) corned beef brisket
2 medium onions, chopped
4 whole cloves
6 whole black peppercorns
2 bay leaves
1 garlic clove
1 medium carrot, cut into large chunks
1 medium celery rib, cut into large chunks
1 large head green cabbage, cored
Horseradish sauce (page 184)

1. Place the corned beef in a large pot and cover with water. Simmer for 1 hour, skimming off any foam that forms on the surface of the water.

2. Pour off the water and cover with fresh water. Add the onions, cloves, peppercorns, bay leaves, garlic, carrot, and celery. Cover and simmer for 3 to 4 hours or until the meat is tender.

3. Cut the cabbage into 6 wedges and place on top of the meat. Cover and simmer until tender, about 15 minutes. Remove the cabbage with a slotted spoon and keep warm.

4. Remove the meat from the cooking liquid and let stand on a serving platter for 15 minutes. Cut into thin slices across the grain. Serve with the cabbage and pass the horseradish sauce at the table.

TIP: Use leftover corned beef and boiled potatoes to make corned beef hash.

Beef Stew

Tender chunks of beef, rich brown gravy, sweet chunks of vegetables—a steaming bowl of beef stew is one of the simple pleasures in life. Serve with good sourdough or French bread and enjoy with a bottle of red wine.

SERVES 6 TO 8

½ cup all-purpose flour
1 teaspoon dried thyme
1 teaspoon dried rosemary
Salt and pepper
1 (2-pound) boneless beef chuck or bottom round, cut into 1-inch pieces
¼ cup oil
1 medium onion, diced
3½ cups beef broth (page 118)
½ cup dry red wine
1 teaspoon minced garlic
2 bay leaves
½ teaspoon paprika
Pinch of ground allspice
6 to 8 new potatoes, halved or quartered
6 medium carrots, cut into large chunks
3 small turnips, peeled and quartered
1 pound boiling onions, peeled
1 cup frozen peas or cut green beans
2 tablespoons cold water

1. Combine the flour, thyme, and rosemary in a medium bowl. Season with salt and pepper. Add the meat and toss to coat.

2. Heat the oil in a large Dutch oven over medium-high heat. Remove about one-third of the meat from the flour with a slotted spoon, shaking off excess flour. Add the meat to the oil in a single layer. Brown on all sides, about 10 minutes. Remove with the slotted spoon and keep warm. Repeat until all the meat is browned; reserve the remaining flour.

3. Sauté the onion in the oil remaining in the Dutch oven until softened, about 3 minutes. Stir in the broth and wine, using a wooden spoon to scrape up any bits stuck to the bottom of the pan. Return the meat to the Dutch oven. Add the garlic, bay leaves, paprika, and allspice. Season to taste with salt and pepper. Bring to a boil, reduce the heat, and simmer, covered, for about 1½ hours, until the meat is nearly tender.

4. Add the potatoes, carrots, turnips, and boiling onions and return to a boil. Reduce the heat and simmer, covered, for 20 minutes.

5. Add the frozen peas and continue to cook until all the vegetables are tender, about 15 minutes.

6. Discard the bay leaves. Transfer the meat and vegetables to a serving dish and keep warm.

7. Stir 1 tablespoon of reserved flour into the 2 tablespoons cold water in a small bowl until smooth. Stir into the cooking liquid in the Dutch oven. Cook over medium heat and stir until thickened and bubbly. Continue to cook and stir for 3 minutes more.

8. Pour the gravy over the meat and vegetables and serve hot.

TIP: If you don't have a Dutch oven large enough to accommodate a hearty stew, you can bake it in a roasting pan in the oven at 300°F.

Beef Stifado

This Greek version of beef stew is a wonderfully complex dish, flavored with feta cheese and walnuts.

SERVES 4

2 tablespoons all-purpose flour
Salt and pepper
1 (1½-pound) boneless beef chuck, or bottom round, cut into 1½-inch cubes
¼ cup oil
12 ounces boiling onions, peeled
1 pound tomatoes, chopped
1½ teaspoons minced garlic
1 bay leaf
1 teaspoon ground cumin
1 teaspoon dried oregano
1 teaspoon dried rosemary
1 teaspoon dried thyme
2 cups dry red wine
1½ cups feta cheese, crumbled (about 8 ounces)
½ cup chopped walnuts
Salt and pepper

1. Preheat the oven to 350°F.

2. Season the flour with salt and pepper in a large bowl. Add the beef and toss to coat.

3. Heat the oil in a large Dutch oven over medium-high heat. Add a single layer of beef to the Dutch oven and cook until browned, stirring occasionally, about 10 minutes. Transfer the browned beef to a medium bowl.

4. Add the onions to the Dutch oven and sauté until browned, about 5 minutes. Add the tomatoes, garlic, bay leaf, cumin, oregano, rosemary, and thyme. Stir in the wine and bring to a boil. Return the meat to the Dutch oven and cover.

5. Bake until the beef is tender, about 2 hours.

6. Remove the bay leaf. Stir in the feta cheese and walnuts. Return to the oven and continue baking until the cheese is heated through, about 10 minutes. Season with salt and pepper and serve.

Beef Burgundy

"Boeuf à la bourguignon" is French for a beef stew made in the style of Burgundy, meaning the beef is marinated in a red Burgundy wine and usually cooked with onions and mushrooms. The longer the marinating time, the richer the wine flavor. Beef burgundy should be served with boiled new potatoes, mashed potatoes, rice, or noodles. A green salad and crusty French bread complete the meal.

SERVES 8

2 cups dry red wine
3 tablespoons oil
1¼ teaspoons salt
1 teaspoon black pepper
½ teaspoon dried thyme
1 bay leaf
3 medium onions
2 medium carrots
4 to 5 garlic cloves
1 medium celery rib
1 (3-pound) boneless beef chuck or bottom
    round, cut into 2-inch cubes
7 tablespoons butter
¼ cup all-purpose flour
½ cup beef broth (page 118)
1 tablespoon tomato paste

2 cups boiling onions, peeled
¼ teaspoon sugar
2 cups sliced mushrooms
5 medium tomatoes, diced

1. Mix the wine, 2 tablespoons of oil, 1 teaspoon of salt, the pepper, thyme, and bay leaf in a large bowl. Slice 1 onion, 1 carrot, 1 garlic clove, and the celery. Add to the wine mixture. Marinate the beef in this mixture in the refrigerator for at least 2 hours and up to 24 hours, turning occasionally.

2. Preheat the oven to 350°F.

3. Remove the meat from the marinade and pat dry with paper towels. Strain the marinade and reserve.

4. Heat 2 tablespoons of butter with the remaining 1 tablespoon oil in a heavy skillet over medium-high heat. Add a single layer of meat and brown the meat on all sides, about 10 minutes. Use a slotted spoon to transfer the meat to a 2-quart baking dish.

5. Add ¼ cup of reserved marinade to the skillet and cook, stirring with a wooden spoon to scrape up any browned bits, for 3 minutes. Add to the baking dish.

6. Finely chop the remaining 2 onions, 1 carrot, and 3 garlic cloves.

7. Melt 4 tablespoons of butter in the skillet over medium-high heat. Add the chopped onions, carrot, and garlic and sauté until golden, about 5 minutes. Blend in the flour and cook, stirring, for 1 minute. Add the remaining marinade, broth, and tomato paste and stir until the mixture comes to a boil. Pour over the meat and cover the baking dish.

8. Bake for 2½ hours.

9. Meanwhile, melt the remaining 1 tablespoon butter in the skillet over medium-high heat and add the boiling onions. Sprinkle with the remaining ¼ teaspoon salt and the sugar. Sauté until golden, 5 to 10 minutes. Add the mushrooms and sauté for 2 minutes more.

10. Add the sautéed onions, mushrooms, and tomatoes to the beef. Continue to bake for 10 more minutes. Serve hot.

Hungarian Goulash

Paprika, used mainly as a garnish in America, is an important flavoring in Hungarian cuisine. It is made by grinding dried sweet red peppers, and the flavor can range from sweet to hot. Supermarket paprika is quite mild, but spice markets and specialty food stores may also carry hot paprika, in which case you adjust the flavor to your liking.

SERVES 6 TO 8

¼ cup all-purpose flour
4 tablespoons paprika
1 teaspoon salt, plus more to taste
½ teaspoon black pepper, plus more to taste
3 pounds boneless beef chuck or bottom
    round, cut into 1-inch pieces
¼ cup oil
1½ medium onions, chopped
1 (15-ounce) can diced tomatoes
1½ cups beef broth (page 118)
1 bay leaf
1½ teaspoons caraway seeds
2 tablespoons water
1 cup sour cream (optional)
Hot cooked egg noodles, to serve

1. Mix together the flour, 1 tablespoon of paprika, salt, and pepper in a large bowl. Reserve 2 tablespoons of the flour mixture. Add the meat to the remaining flour mixture and toss to coat well.

2. Heat the oil in a large Dutch oven over medium-high heat. Remove about one-third of the meat from the flour with a slotted spoon, shaking off excess flour. Add the meat to the oil in a single layer. Brown on all sides, about 10 minutes, and transfer to an ovenproof plate using the slotted spoon. Keep warm. Repeat until all the meat is browned.

3. Add the onions and remaining 3 tablespoons paprika to the Dutch oven and sauté until the onions are softened, about 3 minutes.

4. Return the browned meat to the Dutch oven. Add the tomatoes, broth, bay leaf, and caraway seeds. Season to taste with salt and pepper.

5. Cover and simmer for 2 hours, stirring occasionally.

6. Remove the bay leaf and discard. Collect the meat from the cooking juices with the slotted spoon and transfer to an ovenproof plate. Keep warm.

7. Skim the fat from the top of the cooking liquid. In a small bowl, dissolve the reserved 2 tablespoons flour mixture in the water and stir into the cooking liquid. Bring to a boil and cook until the liquid thickens, about 3 minutes.

8. Remove from the heat and stir in the sour cream, if using. Return the meat to the sauce.

9. To serve, make a bed of the noodles and spoon the goulash on top.

Chili con Carne

This is an unapologetic chili—made with chunks of beef instead of ground beef. And the beef is browned in beef fat (suet), not vegetable oil. Unlike other chilis, this dish's red coloring comes from the hot red chile peppers, not tomatoes. At one time, this chili would have simmered over a campfire and been spooned out to dust-covered cowboys after a long day herding cattle. Serve the chili with rice and beans on the side.

SERVES 6 TO 8

3½ cups boiling water
5 dried red chile peppers, such as serrano or
    New Mexico
½ pound beef suet or lard
3 pounds boneless beef chuck or bottom
    round, cut into ½-inch cubes
3 bay leaves
1 tablespoon ground cumin
1 tablespoon minced garlic
1 tablespoon dried oregano
3 tablespoons paprika
1 tablespoon sugar
1 tablespoon salt

3 tablespoons masa harina or yellow cornmeal,
dissolved in ¼ cup water
1 teaspoon cayenne pepper (optional)

1. Pour the boiling water over the chile peppers in a medium bowl. Let soak for 30 to 45 minutes. Strain the liquid through a fine-mesh strainer and reserve. Chop the chile peppers and set aside.

2. Melt the suet over medium heat in a large saucepan, stirring often. Remove the suet bits and reserve ¼ cup.

3. Return the rendered fat to the saucepan. Add the beef and cook until the meat is lightly browned, about 10 minutes.

4. Add 2½ cups of reserved chile pepper liquid and bring it to a boil. Stir in the bay leaves and reduce the heat to low. Simmer for 1 hour.

5. Stir in the soaked chile peppers, remaining chile pepper water, the cumin, garlic, oregano, paprika, sugar, and salt. Simmer for 30 minutes.

6. Slowly stir in the masa harina mixture to thicken the stew.

7. Taste the chili and adjust the seasonings as needed. Add the cayenne pepper to taste, if using. Serve hot.

TIP: Exercise caution when handling chile peppers. Oils from the seeds and membranes can severely irritate your skin and eyes, so avoid touching your face with your hands while cutting them. Wash your hands, the cutting board, and the utensils with soap and water as soon as you have finished handling the chile peppers.

Ropa Vieja

Ropa vieja, which means "old clothes," is a Cuban classic—beef that is cooked to the point where it falls apart in shreds, resembling rags. Ropa vieja tastes better the day after it is made, once the flavors have had an opportunity to mingle. Serve over rice.

SERVES 6

2 pounds boneless beef chuck or bottom round
2 medium onions, thinly sliced
2 teaspoons minced garlic
Salt and pepper
¼ cup oil
1 large green bell pepper, seeded and finely chopped
2 green chile peppers, such as jalapeños, seeded and finely chopped
3 large tomatoes, finely chopped
2 tablespoons tomato paste
2 tablespoons dry sherry
2 bay leaves
2 teaspoons ground cumin

⅓ cup diced pimento, to serve

1. Cover the meat with water in a large saucepan. Add 1 sliced onion and half the garlic and season with salt and pepper. Bring to a boil. Cover, reduce the heat, and simmer gently until the meat is completely tender and falling apart, about 1½ hours.

2. Use a slotted spoon to place the meat on a plate. Reserve the broth in which the meat was cooked. Refrigerate until cool to the touch.

3. Shred the meat with 2 forks, and set aside.

4. Heat the oil in a large skillet over medium heat. Add the remaining onion and garlic, bell pepper, and chile peppers and sauté until tender, about 10 minutes.

5. Add the tomatoes, tomato paste, sherry, bay leaves, cumin, and 1½ cups of reserved meat broth. Bring to a boil. Reduce the heat and simmer for about 25 minutes, stirring occasionally.

6. Remove the bay leaves. Add the shredded meat and continue to cook until the meat is heated through, about 5 minutes. Serve hot over rice, garnished with the pimento, passing the hot sauce at the table.

Short Ribs

...ions of rib, about 2 to 3 inches
...f fat, meat, and bone. Long,
...izes this flavorful cut.

...ef short ribs

... oil

2 medium onions, diced
2 medium carrots, diced
1 medium garlic head, cloves separated and
    smashed
3 tablespoons all-purpose flour
4 cups dry red wine
1 tablespoon tomato paste
4 cups chicken broth (page 119)
¼ cup chopped fresh parsley
1 teaspoon dried thyme
1 teaspoon dried rosemary
2 bay leaves

1. Preheat the oven to 300°F.

2. Generously season the short ribs on both sides
with salt and pepper.

3. Heat the oil in a large skillet over medium-high
heat. Add a single layer of short ribs and cook
until browned on all sides, about 10 minutes.
Use tongs to transfer the ribs to a Dutch oven or
large roasting pan. Repeat until all the meat is
browned.

4. Pour off all but about 2 tablespoons of fat from
the skillet and reduce the heat to medium. Add
the onions and carrots and sauté until soft, about
5 minutes. Add the garlic and cook, stirring, for
1 more minute.

5. Stir in the flour until well combined, about
1 minute more. Add the wine to the skillet and
bring to a simmer, using a wooden spoon to scrape
up any browned bits remaining at the bottom
of the skillet. Add the contents of the skillet to the
Dutch oven.

6. In a large bowl mix the tomato paste with the
broth and add the parsley, thyme, rosemary and bay
leaves and pour over the short ribs. Cover tightly.

7. Bake until the meat is fork-tender, 2½ to 3 hours.

8. Using the tongs or a slotted spoon, transfer the
ribs to a large plate, removing excess vegetables
and herbs that may have clung to them. Discard
any loose bones that have fallen away from the
meat. Cover and keep warm. Strain the braising
liquid through a fine-mesh strainer into a large
glass measuring cup, pressing out the liquid from
the solids. Allow the fat to rise to the top, then
spoon off.

9. Pour the liquid into a clean saucepan and bring
to a boil over medium-high heat. Briskly simmer
until the sauce is reduced to the consistency of
heavy cream, 5 to 10 minutes. Add the ribs to the
saucepan. Reduce the heat to medium-low, cover,
and cook until the meat is heated through, about
10 minutes. Serve immediately.

Quintessential Meat Loaf

Meat loaf is an ancient combination of ground meat,
sometimes a starch such as bread or rice, vegetables, spices, and
a thickener for binding it all. Meat loaf is the epitome of home
cooking, capturing all the comforts of hearty flavor in a filling,
one-dish meat entrée. Serve with other home classics like
mashed potatoes and fresh steamed vegetables.

SERVES 8

¼ cup (½ stick) butter
1¼ cups finely chopped onions
1 cup finely chopped green bell pepper
2 garlic cloves, finely chopped
2 large eggs
½ cup beef broth (page 118)
1 tablespoon Worcestershire sauce
1 teaspoon hot pepper sauce, such as Tabasco
1 tablespoon soy sauce
1 pound ground round or other lean ground
    beef
½ pound ground pork
½ pound ground turkey
1 cup finely crushed saltine crackers
½ cup ketchup
5 thick slices bacon, cut in half

1. Preheat the oven to 350°F. Lightly grease a loaf
pan.

2. Melt the butter in a large skillet over medium-
high heat. Add the onions, bell pepper, and garlic

198   *The Good Home Cookbook*

and sauté until the onions are softened, about 3 minutes. Remove from the heat and cool slightly.

3. Whisk together the eggs, broth, Worcestershire sauce, hot pepper sauce, and soy sauce until well blended in a large bowl. Add the sautéed onion mixture, beef, pork, turkey, and cracker crumbs. Mix until well blended; your hands work best.

4. Shape into the loaf pan. Spread the ketchup over the top of the loaf and arrange the bacon on top of the ketchup.

5. Bake about 1½ hours or until the juices run clear and the center of the loaf reads 160°F.

6. Pour off the excess fat and let stand for 15 minutes before serving.

TIP: If you have a bulb baster, you can use it to remove the excess grease from the pan instead of pouring it out.

Salisbury Steak

A Salisbury steak is just a glorified hamburger. It was named in the nineteenth century after English physician Dr. J. H. Salisbury, who prescribed eating beef as a remedy for any number of ailments.

SERVES 4

1 pound ground beef
⅓ cup dry bread crumbs
½ small onion, finely chopped
1 large egg, lightly beaten
1 teaspoon Worcestershire sauce
1 teaspoon salt
¼ teaspoon black pepper
1 tablespoon butter
1 tablespoon oil
1 large onion, thinly sliced
1 cup sliced mushrooms
2 cups beef broth (page 118)
3 tablespoons cornstarch
3 tablespoons cold water

1. Mix the beef, bread crumbs, onion, egg, Worcestershire sauce, salt, and pepper with your hands in a medium bowl. Shape into 4 patties, each about ¾ to 1 inch thick.

2. Melt the butter with the oil in a large skillet over medium-high heat. Add the patties and fry for 4 to 5 minutes on each side. Use a spatula to transfer the patties from the skillet to an oven-proof plate; keep warm.

3. Add the sliced onion and mushrooms to the skillet and sauté until the mushrooms give up their juice, about 8 minutes. Stir in the broth, using a wooden spoon to scrape up any browned bits from the bottom of the skillet. Heat to boiling, then reduce the heat, cover, and simmer for 10 minutes.

4. Dissolve the cornstarch in the water in a small bowl. Stir into the mushroom mixture and bring to a boil. Cook, stirring, until thickened.

5. Pour the mushroom gravy over the patties and serve.

Cabbage Rolls

Cabbage rolls are a specialty among immigrants from eastern and central Europe. The most typical fillings use a mixture of ground beef and rice, and the cabbages are often baked in a sweet-and-sour tomato sauce. The crinkled leaves of savoy cabbage are more tender and easier to work with than regular green cabbage leaves.

SERVES 6 TO 8

Cabbage rolls:
1 large head savoy cabbage or other green
    cabbage
1 pound ground beef
¾ cup cooked rice
1 small onion, finely chopped
1 large egg
2 teaspoons salt
1 teaspoon black pepper

Sauce:
2 tablespoons oil
1 medium onion, diced
1 (8-ounce) can tomato sauce
1 (15-ounce) can diced tomatoes
3 tablespoons brown sugar
2 tablespoons cider vinegar
½ cup water

1. To make the cabbage rolls, bring a large pot of salted water to a boil. Remove the core from the cabbage and gently drop, cut side down, into the water. Boil for 5 to 10 minutes. Remove the soft-ened outer leaves and return the head to the water. Continue boiling and removing softened leaves until you have 12 large leaves. Trim away the back spine of each leaf so the leaf will be easier to roll.

2. Combine the ground beef, rice, onion, egg, salt, and pepper in a large bowl. Mix well with a spoon or your hands and divide into 12 portions.

3. Place a portion of the filling in the center of each cabbage leaf. Fold in the sides, then loosely roll the leaf around the filling; fasten with a toothpick. Place in a baking dish and repeat until all the leaves are rolled.

4. Chop enough of the remaining cabbage to make 1 cup and set aside.

5. Preheat the oven to 350°F.

6. To make the sauce, heat the oil in a medium saucepan over medium-high heat. Add the onion and chopped cabbage and sauté until golden, about 10 minutes. Stir in the tomato sauce, tomatoes, brown sugar, vinegar, and water and pour over the cabbage rolls.

7. Cover and bake for 40 to 45 minutes.

8. Remove and discard the toothpicks. Serve hot.

Swedish Meatballs

Swedish meatballs are indeed a Swedish dish, brought to America's northern Midwest by Scandinavian immigrants. It is traditionally served at Christmas in Swedish homes as one of many dishes and is also served at smorgasbords. This dish makes excellent leftovers.

SERVES 4 TO 6

⅔ cup milk
2 cups fresh bread crumbs
1 tablespoon butter
1 small onion, finely chopped
1½ pounds ground beef
3 large eggs, lightly beaten
2 teaspoons salt, plus more to taste
½ teaspoon black pepper, plus more to taste
1 teaspoon ground nutmeg
1 teaspoon paprika
¼ cup oil
3 tablespoons all-purpose flour

2 cups beef broth (page 118)
1 cup sour cream
Hot buttered egg noodles, to serve

1. Pour the milk over the bread crumbs in a medium bowl and set aside.

2. Melt the butter in a small skillet over medium heat. Add the onion and sauté until softened, about 3 minutes.

3. Combine the softened bread crumbs, onion, and ground beef in a large bowl. Add the eggs, salt, pepper, nutmeg, and paprika. Mix thoroughly with a spoon or your hands until well blended. Shape into 2-inch balls.

4. Heat the oil in a large skillet over medium heat. Add the meatballs in a single layer and fry until browned, turning carefully with 2 spoons to brown all sides, about 10 to 12 minutes. Transfer the meatballs with a slotted spoon to an ovenproof plate and keep warm. Repeat until all the meatballs are browned.

5. Use a wooden spoon to stir the flour into the remaining drippings until well blended. Cook over low heat for 1 minute. Add the broth and cook, whisking constantly, until thickened. Reduce the heat to low and cook for 5 minutes. Stir in the sour cream, a little at a time, until thoroughly blended after each addition. Season to taste with salt and pepper.

6. Return the meatballs to the sauce. Reduce the heat to a low simmer, cover the pan, and cook for 5 minutes. Turn the meatballs over and simmer for another 5 minutes. Serve hot over the buttered noodles.

TIP: Be sure to cook the meatballs the full 10 to 12 minutes or they may fall apart. Turn frequently and don't rush the process.

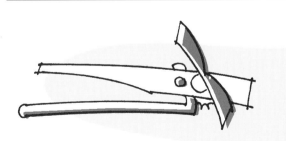

Tex-Mex Chili

As chili moved farther and farther from Mexico, it was adapted to American tastes. Ground beef was readily available and affordable, as was chili powder, a blend of ground dried chile peppers and other seasonings. This is the chili most Americans are raised on. It also makes a terrific filling for tacos and burritos.

SERVES 4

1 tablespoon oil
1 pound ground beef
1 medium onion, finely chopped
1½ to 2 tablespoons chili powder
2 teaspoons ground cumin
1 (15-ounce) can diced tomatoes
1 (15-ounce) can kidney beans, drained and
    rinsed
⅓ cup tomato paste
⅓ cup water
Salt and pepper
Sour cream, to serve
Shredded Cheddar cheese, to serve

1. Heat the oil in a large Dutch oven or saucepan over medium-high heat. Add the meat, onion, chili powder, and cumin and cook until the meat is well browned, about 8 minutes.

2. Stir in the tomatoes, kidney beans, tomato paste, and water. Season to taste with salt and pepper. Bring to a boil, reduce the heat, cover, and simmer for 20 minutes, stirring occasionally.

3. Ladle into warm soup bowls and serve, passing the sour cream and shredded cheese at the table.

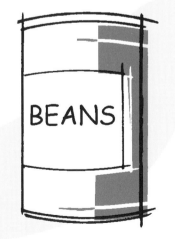

Tamale Pie

American cooks have been quite ingenious about simplifying dishes. A tamale pie combines the flavor of tamales, which are traditionally wrapped in corn husks, and layers them into a pie.

SERVES 6

2 tablespoons shortening
1 medium onion, diced
1 small green bell pepper, seeded and diced
1 pound ground beef
3 medium tomatoes, diced
1 tablespoon chili powder
1 tablespoon ground cumin
2 teaspoons salt
4 cups water
1 cup yellow cornmeal
4 cups shredded sharp Cheddar cheese (about 1 pound)

1. Preheat the oven to 350°F.

2. Melt the shortening in a large skillet over medium-high heat. Add the onion and bell pepper and sauté until softened, 4 to 5 minutes. Add the beef and continue cooking until the meat is well browned, 5 to 6 minutes. Stir in the tomatoes, chili powder, cumin, and 1 teaspoon of salt. Remove from the heat.

3. Bring the water to a boil in a large saucepan with the remaining 1 teaspoon salt. Slowly stir the cornmeal into the boiling water, stirring constantly. Continue cooking over low heat, stirring often, until thick, about 5 minutes. Remove from the heat.

4. Spread half the cornmeal mixture on the bottom of a 9 x 13-inch baking dish. Cover with the meat mixture and sprinkle with half the cheese. Cover with the remaining cornmeal mixture. Top with the remaining cheese.

5. Bake for 35 to 45 minutes. Let stand for 5 minutes before serving. Serve hot.

Southwestern Beef Casserole

There are as many names for this dish as there are recipes. It is often called Mexican lasagna, with corn tortillas playing the role that pasta performs in the Italian version.

SERVES 4

2 tablespoons oil
1 pound ground beef
1 medium onion, diced
1 medium green bell pepper, seeded and diced
1 (4-ounce) can diced green chile peppers, drained
1 tablespoon chili powder
1 (15-ounce) can diced tomatoes
Salt and pepper
1 (9-ounce) package corn tortillas, cut into wedges
2 cups shredded Monterey Jack or Cheddar cheese (about 8 ounces)
1 cup sliced black pitted olives
½ cup sour cream

1. Preheat the oven to 425°F.

2. Heat the oil in a large skillet over medium-high heat. Add the beef, onion, bell pepper, chile peppers, and chili powder and cook until the beef is well browned, about 10 minutes.

3. Stir in the tomatoes, season to taste with salt and pepper, and simmer for 5 minutes.

4. Spoon about ½ cup of tomato mixture into a 1½-quart baking dish. Arrange an overlapping layer of tortilla wedges on top (use one-third of the tortillas). Spoon 1 cup of tomato mixture on top. Sprinkle with ½ cup of cheese and ½ cup of olives. Layer with another third of tortillas and half the remaining tomato mixture. Top with ½ cup of cheese and the remaining olives. Arrange a final layer of tortillas on top. Spoon over the remaining tomato mixture. Top with the sour cream and the remaining 1 cup cheese.

5. Bake for about 25 minutes, until the cheese is melted and the filling is heated through. Let the casserole stand for 10 minutes before serving.

Creamed Chipped Beef

Some GIs came back from World War II with a fondness for a dish that they called SOS, which stands for "[expletive deleted] on a shingle." The recipe features chipped beef mixed in a warm cream gravy that is spooned over toast.

SERVES 4

Boiling water
½ cup dry chipped beef
½ cup oil
⅓ cup all-purpose flour
4 cups milk, heated
Salt and pepper
4 slices white sandwich bread, toasted
1 large egg, hard-boiled and chopped
   (optional)
Paprika, to serve

1. Pour boiling water over the chipped beef in a small bowl. Drain well. Break into small pieces.

2. Heat the oil in a medium skillet over medium heat. Slowly stir in the flour to form a paste. Remove from the heat and slowly stir in the milk until smooth.

3. Return to low heat and add the beef. Season to taste with salt and pepper.

4. To serve, spoon over toast on plates. Top with a little egg sprinkled over each, if desired, and lightly sprinkle with paprika.

TIP: To make the sauce richer, replace some of the milk with half-and-half.

Roasted Herbed Pork Loin and Potatoes

The advantage of using a boneless roast of pork is that it is so easy to carve. Also, roasting the pork with the potatoes adds flavor to the potatoes. Overall, this is a very easy-to-make and easy-to-serve dinner that is well suited to special occasions.

SERVES 8 TO 10

1 teaspoon minced garlic
2 teaspoons chopped dried rosemary
1½ teaspoons salt
1 teaspoon black pepper
1 (3- to 4-pound) boneless pork loin roast
4 to 6 medium waxy potatoes, such as thin-
   skinned red or white, peeled and quartered
2 tablespoons olive oil
1 teaspoon dried thyme

1. Preheat the oven to 325°F.

2. Mix the garlic, rosemary, 1 teaspoon of salt, and ½ teaspoon of pepper in a small bowl. Rub the pork loin with the mixture and place the pork on the rack in a shallow roasting pan. Roast for 50 minutes.

3. Meanwhile, cover the potatoes with water in a saucepan, bring to a boil, and cook for about 10 minutes until barely tender. Drain and let cool.

4. Toss the potatoes with the olive oil, thyme, remaining ½ teaspoon salt, and remaining ½ teaspoon pepper in a large bowl. Place the potatoes around the pork loin and roast for an additional 45 to 60 minutes or until the pork registers at least 155°F.

5. Cover the roast with aluminum foil and let stand for about 15 minutes before slicing. Serve on a large platter with the vegetables surrounding the meat.

Stuffed Roast Pork Loin

When the butcher removes the bones from a loin roast, he creates the perfect opportunity for making a stuffed roast. In this case, the stuffing is a conventional one of bread crumbs flavored with onions, celery, and thyme. If you like, add a finely chopped apple. Serve with applesauce.

SERVES 8

3 tablespoons butter
½ medium onion, finely chopped
1 large celery rib, finely chopped
1½ cups fresh bread crumbs
¼ cup chopped fresh parsley
1 teaspoon dried thyme
1 (3- to 5-pound) boneless pork loin roast, tied
Salt and pepper

1. Preheat the oven to 325°F.

2. Heat the butter over medium heat in a medium skillet. Add the onion and celery and cook until softened, 3 to 4 minutes. Transfer to a medium bowl.

3. Add the bread crumbs, parsley, thyme, and onion mixture to the bowl and mix well. Untie the pork roast and separate into halves. Sprinkle with salt and pepper on all sides. Spread the stuffing on the top side of the bottom half. Top the stuffing with the other half of roast. Secure well with skewers or toothpicks or retie and place in a shallow roasting pan.

4. Roast for 1½ to 2 hours, until the internal temperature registers 155°F.

5. Let stand for 10 minutes before slicing and serving.

TIP: You can make fresh bread crumbs by grating stale bread on the coarse side of a box grater.

Apple-Stuffed Pork Crown Roast

A crown roast is a magnificent cut of meat. It is made by tying standing ribs of pork into a circle. The roast's hollow center section can be filled with stuffing. Some people like to decorate the rib tips with paper frills before serving. You won't find this cut in the meat case of most supermarkets; you'll have to ask a butcher to prepare one for you. Double the stuffing recipe if you like and cook alongside the roast in a separate pan.

SERVES 16

1 (8-pound) pork crown roast
2 teaspoons salt
2 teaspoons black pepper
½ cup sugar
2 cups fresh or frozen cranberries
½ cup (1 stick) butter
1 medium onion, diced
4 medium celery ribs, sliced
3 cups dry bread cubes
2 cups chopped tart apples, such as Granny
   Smith or Rome Beauty (about 2 medium)
½ cup apple cider
1 large egg, slightly beaten
1 teaspoon poultry seasoning

1. Preheat the oven to 325°F.

2. Rub the roast with 1 teaspoon each of salt and pepper. Place the roast, ribs down, onto a rack in a shallow roasting pan.

3. Roast for 2 hours.

4. Meanwhile, mix the sugar and cranberries in a medium bowl and let stand for 1 hour.

5. Melt the butter in a large saucepan over medium heat. Add the onion and celery and sauté until softened, about 3 minutes. Stir in the cranberry mixture, remaining 1 teaspoon salt and 1 teaspoon pepper, the bread cubes, apples, cider, egg, and poultry seasoning. Cook, stirring, for 2 minutes. Remove from the heat.

6. Using tongs, remove the roast from the pan. Drain the drippings and discard or reserve for another use.

7. Return the roast, ribs up, to the rack in the roasting pan. Fill the center with the cranberry mixture. Continue to roast for 60 to 90 minutes

more, until the stuffing registers 155°F. If the stuffing is getting too brown, cover it lightly with aluminum foil.

8. Remove the roast from the oven and let it rest for 15 minutes. Cut into individual chops and serve each with a spoonful of stuffing.

Roasted Fresh Ham

Another crowd-pleaser is a whole pork leg, also known as a fresh ham. Most commonly, ham is cured, like country ham or prosciutto. Fresh ham is a nice change.

SERVES 8 TO 10

1 (6- to 8-pound) bone-in half ham with skin, preferably shank end
1 cup lightly packed fresh sage leaves or ¼ cup dried
½ cup fresh parsley leaves
8 garlic cloves, peeled
1½ teaspoons salt
1 tablespoon black pepper
¼ cup oil
2 cups dry white wine
2 cups chicken broth (page 119)
3 tablespoons cornstarch
3 tablespoons water

1. Preheat the oven to 500°F, with the oven rack in its lowest position.

2. Carefully slice through the skin and fat of the ham with a serrated knife, making a 1-inch diamond pattern. Be careful not to cut into the meat. Place the ham, cut side down, on the rack in a shallow roasting pan.

3. Combine the sage, parsley, garlic, salt, pepper, and oil in a food processor and process until the mixture forms a smooth paste. Rub the paste onto all sides of the ham.

4. Roast the ham for 20 minutes. Reduce the oven temperature to 350°F and continue to roast, basting the ham with the wine every 45 minutes, until the ham's center registers 155°F, about 2½ hours longer.

5. Remove the ham from the pan and cover loosely with aluminum foil. Let stand for 30 to 60 minutes.

6. Meanwhile, pour out the fat from the pan and discard. Add the broth to the pan and bring to a simmer, using a wooden spoon to scrape up any browned bits from the bottom of the pan. Continue to simmer until slightly thickened. Taste and adjust the seasonings as needed. In a small bowl, dissolve the cornstarch in the water and whisk into the pan juices to thicken.

7. Carve the ham and serve with the gravy on the side.

Roasted Pork Tenderloin with Rosemary

Pork tenderloin is a very popular cut of meat because it is so low in fat and can be cooked quickly. This dish combines garlic, olive oil, and rosemary for a simple yet flavor-rich roasting treatment. The tenderloin should be roasted in a very hot oven to prevent it from drying out.

SERVES 4 TO 6

2 (1-pound) pork tenderloins
2 garlic cloves, halved
1 tablespoon olive oil
1 tablespoon dried rosemary, crumbled
Salt and pepper

1. Preheat the oven to 500°F. Line a baking dish with aluminum foil, spray with cooking spray, and place in the oven.

2. Trim the fat from the pork tenderloins and butterfly the meat, cutting nearly in half lengthwise. Open the tenderloins and lay flat. Rub the meat all over with the cut sides of the garlic halves. Brush with olive oil, then sprinkle rosemary, salt, and pepper on both sides. Use tongs to place the pork on the hot baking dish.

3. Roast for 15 to 20 minutes, until the meat registers 150° to 155°F.

4. Let stand for 5 minutes, then slice and serve.

Bacon-Wrapped Pork Tenderloin

Is today's pork too lean? Here's a method of cooking tenderloin that compensates for the tendency of pork to dry out as it cooks, while adding a rich, smoky flavor.

SERVES 4 TO 6

2 teaspoons minced garlic
¼ cup chopped fresh parsley
2 teaspoons salt
2 teaspoons black pepper
2 teaspoons dried basil
1 teaspoon dried oregano
2 (1-pound) pork tenderloins
6 slices bacon
2 tablespoons oil

1. Preheat the oven to 400°F.

2. Combine the garlic, parsley, salt, pepper, basil, and oregano in a small bowl. Rub the seasoning all over the tenderloins. Wrap each tenderloin with 3 slices of bacon and secure with toothpicks. Brush with oil and place in a shallow roasting pan.

3. Roast for about 1 hour, until the bacon is crisp and the meat registers 150° to 155°F.

4. Cover with a tent of aluminum foil and let stand for 10 minutes before slicing. Serve immediately.

Pork Medallions with Madeira

Topped with a wine and vinegar sauce, this dish is suitable for a special occasion but quick enough to make in the middle of a busy work week. Serve with mashed potatoes or rice pilaf.

SERVES 4

2 (1-pound) pork tenderloins
2 teaspoons dried rosemary
½ teaspoon salt
¼ teaspoon black pepper
2 tablespoons oil
1 small onion, finely chopped
1 teaspoon minced garlic
¼ cup Madeira wine

¼ cup water
1 tablespoon red-wine vinegar
2 tablespoons butter
2 tablespoons chopped fresh parsley

1. Cut each tenderloin into 1-inch-thick medallions. Sprinkle with the rosemary, salt, and pepper.

2. Heat the oil in a large skillet over medium-high heat. Add a single layer of pork slices and sauté for about 2 minutes per side, until browned well on the outside and slightly pink on the inside. Transfer the cooked meat to a serving platter and keep warm. Repeat with the remaining slices until all are cooked.

3. Drain the fat from the skillet, add the chopped onion and garlic, and sauté until softened, about 3 minutes. Stir in the wine, water, and vinegar and bring to a boil. Reduce the heat and simmer until the liquid is reduced to about ⅓ to ½ cup. Whisk in the butter until melted.

4. Pour the sauce over the medallions, garnish with parsley, and serve immediately.

Braised Pork Roast with Sauerkraut

Pork shoulder, blade, and butt roasts require braising—long, slow, moist cooking—to become tender. They are flavorful, inexpensive cuts. Look for bone-in roasts, which will be more delicious than boneless ones.

SERVES 6

¼ cup oil
1 (4-pound) bone-in pork shoulder, butt, or blade roast, excess fat trimmed
Salt and pepper
1 cup water
6 cups sauerkraut, drained
3 medium carrots, sliced
4 bay leaves
1 tablespoon caraway seeds

1. Preheat the oven to 350°F.

2. Heat the oil in a Dutch oven over medium heat. Season the pork liberally with salt and pepper and add to the Dutch oven. Brown well on

all sides, about 10 minutes. Slowly add the water, sauerkraut, carrots, bay leaves, and caraway seeds. Cover the Dutch oven.

3. Roast for 1 hour, until the pork's internal temperature reaches 155°F and the meat is tender.

4. Remove the bay leaves. Slice and serve the meat on a large platter with the sauerkraut, carrots, and pan juices.

Breaded Pork Chops

For many years a well-seasoned cast-iron skillet was put to use almost every day. The skillet excelled for frying breaded meats—from chicken to catfish to pork chops. There is nothing fancy about this cooking, but the more that skillet is used, the better things taste. Here's a basic favorite featuring lightly herbed breading around juicy fried pork chops.

SERVES 4

8 center-cut pork chops, ½ inch thick
Salt and pepper
½ cup all-purpose flour
1 large egg
3 tablespoons milk
3 cups fresh bread crumbs
1 teaspoon dried thyme
¼ cup oil

1. Sprinkle the pork chops with salt and pepper.

2. Place the flour in a shallow bowl. Use a fork to beat the egg and milk together in another shallow bowl. Combine the bread crumbs and thyme in a third shallow bowl.

3. Dip each pork chop in the flour, shake off the excess, then dip into the egg mixture and roll in the bread crumbs. Pat to make the crumbs adhere.

4. Heat the oil in a heavy skillet over medium-high heat. Brown the chops on both sides for about 1 minute. Reduce the heat, cover the pan, and continue cooking for 4 minutes if the chops are boneless, 5 minutes if not. They should be browned on the outside and slightly pink inside. Serve hot.

Stuffed Pork Cutlets

Boneless pork chops cut thin are also known as cutlets. Rolled around a bread crumb stuffing and pan fried, they offer an elegant presentation.

SERVES 4 TO 6

8 thin boneless loin pork chops
¼ cup (½ stick) butter
1 small onion, finely chopped
1 small celery rib, finely chopped
1 small tart apple, such as Granny Smith or Rome Beauty, peeled, cored, and finely chopped
2 cups fresh bread crumbs
½ teaspoon poultry seasoning
Salt and pepper
¼ cup all-purpose flour
2 tablespoons shortening
⅓ cup chicken broth (page 119)

1. Lightly pound the pork chops with a smooth-sided meat mallet until very thin.

2. Melt the butter in a medium skillet over medium heat. Add the onion, celery, and apple and sauté until the onion is softened, about 4 minutes. Mix in the bread crumbs and poultry seasoning. Season to taste with salt and pepper.

3. Put a small mound of stuffing on each chop. Roll up and tie with kitchen string. Roll the pork rolls in flour; shake off the excess.

4. Heat the shortening in a large skillet over medium-high heat. Add the pork rolls and brown all over, about 1 minute per side. Add the broth, cover, and simmer for about 1 hour, until the meat is tender. Serve hot, spooning the pan juices over the pork rolls.

Milk-Braised Pork Chops

Braising pork in milk creates the most tender meat imaginable, which you might even mistake for veal. This is an adaptation of a classic Italian recipe, usually made with a pork loin roast.

SERVES 4

4 boneless loin pork chops, cut ¾ to 1 inch thick
2 tablespoons all-purpose flour
½ teaspoon salt
¼ to ½ teaspoon black pepper
1½ cups milk
2 teaspoons butter
2 teaspoons oil

1. Trim all the fat from the chops.

2. Combine the flour, salt, and pepper in a shallow bowl. Dip the chops in the mixture to coat thoroughly. Shake off any excess flour and set the chops aside on a plate.

3. To the flour remaining in the bowl, gradually stir in ½ cup of milk and set aside.

4. Melt the butter with the oil in a large skillet over medium-high heat. Add the chops and cook until browned, about 3 minutes per side. Pour off all but 2 teaspoons of drippings. Add the milk mixture to the skillet, cover, reduce the heat to low, and cook for 30 minutes, stirring occasionally.

5. Turn the chops over, then add the remaining 1 cup milk. Cover and cook for 30 minutes longer, stirring occasionally.

6. Uncover the skillet and cook the chops for 15 more minutes, until the liquid is reduced to about ¼ cup. Serve hot, spooning the pan juices over the pork.

Cider-Braised Pork Chops

Pork and apples are a classic German combination. In this recipe, pork chops are cooked in apple cider. Serve with applesauce on the side.

SERVES 4

4 bone-in pork chops, about 1 inch thick
Salt and pepper
2 tablespoons butter
1 tablespoon oil
2 leeks, trimmed and sliced
1 large celery rib, chopped
1 bay leaf
½ cup apple cider

1. Season the pork chops with salt and pepper.

2. Melt the butter with the oil in a large skillet over medium-high heat. Add the pork chops and cook until brown, about 3 minutes per side. Transfer the chops to a plate and set aside.

3. Add the leeks, celery, and bay leaf to the skillet. Sauté until the vegetables are softened, about 3 minutes. Add the cider and boil until the sauce is slightly reduced, about 6 minutes. Return the pork and any accumulated juices to the skillet. Simmer just until cooked through, about 5 minutes. Remove the bay leaf.

4. Season again with salt and pepper, if needed, and serve hot.

Baked Pork Chops and Apples

Applesauce is a traditional accompaniment to pork, but you can skip the applesauce and bake the pork with apples in a casserole. This is a terrific autumn dish.

SERVES 6

6 boneless pork chops, about ¾ inch thick
Salt and pepper
1 tablespoon oil
3 tablespoons all-purpose flour
2 cups hot water
1 tablespoon cider vinegar
½ cup raisins
3 medium tart apples, such as Granny Smith or Rome Beauty, peeled, cored, and sliced thick
3 tablespoons molasses

1. Preheat the oven to 350°F.

2. Season the pork chops with salt and pepper.

3. Heat the oil in a large, heavy skillet over medium-high heat. Add the pork chops and cook until browned, about 3 minutes per side. Transfer the chops to a large, shallow baking dish.

4. Stir the flour into the drippings in the skillet. Cook over medium heat, stirring, until browned. Slowly stir in the hot water and bring to a boil. Stir in the vinegar and raisins. Keep warm.

5. Arrange the apple slices over the pork chops. Pour the molasses over the apples.

6. Pour the sauce from the skillet over the apples and pork chops in the baking dish. Cover.

7. Bake for 1 hour and serve hot.

Sweet-and-Sour Pork

This is an Americanized version of a very popular Chinese restaurant dish of the same name. In the restaurant version, the pork is a tender cut that is batter dipped and quickly fried. This version doesn't have the frying step and it slow-cooks the pork to tenderness.

SERVES 4 TO 6

1 tablespoon oil
1½ pounds boneless lean country-style pork ribs, cubed
1 (20-ounce) can pineapple chunks
¾ cup water
¼ cup white vinegar
2 teaspoons soy sauce
¼ cup brown sugar
½ teaspoon salt
2 tablespoons cornstarch dissolved in 2 tablespoons water
1 large onion, diced
1 medium green bell pepper, seeded and diced
1 medium red bell pepper, seeded and diced
Hot cooked rice, to serve

1. Heat the oil in a large skillet over medium-high heat. Add the pork and sauté until lightly browned, about 10 minutes.

2. Drain the pineapple, reserving the juice in a small bowl. Add the water, vinegar, soy sauce, brown sugar, and salt to the juice. Pour over the pork in the skillet. Cover and simmer for 1 hour, or until the meat is tender.

3. Stir in the cornstarch mixture and cook, stirring constantly, until the mixture is thickened and bubbly.

4. Add the pineapple chunks, onion, and bell peppers. Cover and simmer for 10 minutes, or until the vegetables are tender.

5. Spoon the hot sweet-and-sour-pork over the rice and serve.

Posole

Posole is a traditional Mexican pork and hominy stew that has traveled north of the border wherever Mexicans have immigrated. It is often served at Christmastime. At the table, pass bowls of chopped lettuce, sliced radishes, chopped onions, and shredded cheese.

SERVES 12

2 tablespoons oil
1 (3-pound) boneless pork shoulder, cut into small cubes
Salt and pepper
1 medium onion, chopped
1 teaspoon minced garlic
1 dried red chile pepper, crushed, or 1 tablespoon cayenne pepper
6 cups water
6 cups canned hominy, drained
1 teaspoon dried oregano
2 tablespoons chopped fresh cilantro

1. Heat the oil in a large saucepan over medium-high heat. Add the pork, season with salt and pepper, and sauté until browned, about 10 minutes. Add the onion, garlic, and chile pepper and sauté until the onion is softened, about 3 minutes.

2. Stir in the water. Bring to a boil, cover, reduce the heat, and simmer until the meat is tender, about 1½ hours.

3. Add the hominy and oregano and simmer for another 30 minutes.

4. Stir in the cilantro and serve hot.

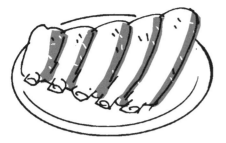

Oven-Roasted Spareribs

Have a hankering for ribs, but the weather outside isn't right for grilling? These tasty ribs are rubbed with spices, then slow-roasted to perfection in a low-heat oven. For even more flavor, put the rub on the ribs the night before, wrap them in a double layer of plastic wrap, and let them sit overnight in the refrigerator.

SERVES 4

2 tablespoons paprika
2 tablespoons firmly packed brown sugar
1 tablespoon chili powder
1 tablespoon ground cumin
1 tablespoon salt
1½ teaspoons dried oregano
1½ teaspoons black pepper
1½ teaspoons white pepper
½ teaspoon cayenne pepper
½ teaspoon ground allspice
2 full racks spareribs (about 6 pounds total), trimmed of excess fat
1½ cups barbecue sauce bottled or homemade (page 254), plus more to serve

1. Mix the paprika, brown sugar, chili powder, cumin, salt, oregano, black pepper, white pepper, cayenne pepper, and allspice in a small bowl.

2. Rub the spice mix on both sides of the ribs and let the ribs stand at room temperature for at least 1 hour.

3. Preheat the oven to 300°F.

4. Place the ribs, meatier side up, on a heavy rack set on a baking sheet with a rim. Cover with aluminum foil. Roast for 1 hour, remove the foil, and return to the oven.

5. Roast for another hour. Brush the meaty side of the ribs with the barbecue sauce.

6. Roast for another 1½ hours, until the bones have separated from the meat.

7. Unwrap the ribs, cut between the bones, and serve immediately, passing additional barbecue sauce at the table.

Baked Glazed Ham

Ham is a wonderful choice for serving to crowds. It doesn't require making gravy to accompany it—or stuffing, for that matter—and carving it is simpler than carving a turkey. Leftovers make terrific sandwiches and can be used in any number of soups and casseroles.

SERVES 12 TO 15

1 (12- to 14-pound) smoked ham
20 whole cloves
1½ cups firmly packed brown sugar
1 tablespoon Dijon mustard
½ cup orange marmalade
1½ cups apple juice
¼ to ½ cup bourbon or other whiskey

1. Preheat the oven to 300°F.

2. Trim as much fat off the ham as possible. Score the ham by cutting ½-inch-deep slashes (through the skin) to make diamond shapes. Make 20 tiny slits all over the ham and poke a whole clove in each slit. Place the ham on the rack in a roasting pan and set aside.

3. Mix the brown sugar and mustard in a small bowl. Stir in the marmalade to make a thick paste. Spread the glaze over the ham and be careful not to disturb the cloves.

4. In a small bowl, combine the apple juice with bourbon and pour into the roasting pan. Cover the pan with aluminum foil.

5. Roast for 2 hours, basting occasionally with pan juices.

6. Remove the aluminum foil and increase the oven temperature to 450°F. Roast for another 15 to 20 minutes, basting often, until the glaze is brown and thick.

7. Cool for a few minutes, remove the cloves, slice, and serve.

Baked Ham Steak with Brown Sugar Glaze

Ham steaks can provide all the good eating of a ham roast without the problems of dealing with endless leftovers. Try this tangy–sweet dish that's easy to make for a small, impromptu gathering or quick, after–work meal. A broiled variation follows.

SERVES 4

1 cup firmly packed brown sugar
¼ cup Dijon mustard
2 tablespoons cider vinegar
½ teaspoon ground cloves
1 (1½- to 2-pound) ham steak, 1 to 2 inches thick

1. Preheat the oven to 350°F.

2. Combine the brown sugar, mustard, vinegar, and cloves in a small bowl. Brush over the ham steak.

3. Bake, uncovered, for 15 to 20 minutes, until heated through and browned on top.

4. Spoon pan juices over each portion and serve hot.

Broiled Ham Steak with Brown Sugar Glaze

Brush one side of the steak with half the glaze in Baked Ham Steak with Brown Sugar Glaze. Broil, glazed side up, 2 inches from the heat for 5 to 7 minutes. Turn over, spread the remaining glaze on the steak, and broil for 5 to 7 minutes more, until well browned and heated through. Serve as directed.

Scalloped Potato and Ham Casserole

A casserole of ham, cheese, and potatoes provides a wonderful opportunity to use leftover ham while pleasing the family with a simple, one–dish meal.

SERVES 6 TO 8

½ cup (1 stick) butter
½ cup all-purpose flour
3 cups milk
3 cups shredded Cheddar cheese (about 12 ounces)
4 cups diced cooked ham
Salt and pepper
5 cups peeled and thinly sliced waxy potatoes, such as thin-skinned red or white
1 medium onion, diced
1 medium green bell pepper, seeded and diced

1. Preheat the oven to 350°F. Grease a large 9 x 13-inch baking dish.

2. Melt the butter in a medium saucepan over medium heat. Stir in the flour to make a paste and cook for 1 minute, stirring constantly. Stir in the milk and cook until thick, about 2 minutes. Stir in the cheese and cook until melted. Add the ham and season to taste with salt and pepper (you will not need much salt if the ham is cured).

3. Combine the potatoes, onion, and bell pepper in a large bowl. Pour in the sauce and mix well. Transfer to the baking dish and cover.

4. Bake for 90 minutes, until the potatoes are tender, removing the cover after the first 30 minutes. Cool for 15 minutes before serving.

Sausage and Sauerkraut Supper

German immigrants brought with them several culinary traditions. Sausage making, cabbage pickling, and beer brewing combine here in a delicious casserole. Serve with a hearty rye bread, and pass a good-quality German mustard at the table.

SERVES 6 TO 8

3 pounds sauerkraut
4 tablespoons (½ stick) butter or duck, chicken, or goose fat
¼ pound bacon, diced
3 medium onions, sliced
1 teaspoon dried thyme
1 garlic head, split in half
1 cup chicken broth (page 119)
2 cups dark or amber beer
2 bay leaves
1½ teaspoons whole black peppercorns
8 whole juniper berries, lightly crushed (if available)
1 tablespoon oil
1 pound garlic sausage, kielbasa, or knockwurst
1 pound bratwurst or veal sausage
1½ pounds small red new potatoes, well scrubbed

1. Preheat the oven to 325°F.

2. Drain the sauerkraut in a strainer, pressing to release most of the excess liquid.

3. Melt 3 tablespoons of butter in a large skillet over medium-low heat. Add the bacon and cook for 5 minutes; do not allow the bacon to brown. Add the onions and continue to cook until soft but not browned, 8 to 10 minutes.

4. Transfer the bacon-onion mixture to a 4-quart nonreactive baking dish or Dutch oven. Add the sauerkraut, thyme, and garlic and toss to combine. Add the broth and beer and stir to combine. Cut a 4 x 4-inch piece of cheesecloth. Place the bay leaves, peppercorns, and juniper berries on the cheesecloth, gather the 4 corners, and tie securely with a piece of string. Bury the cheesecloth packet in the sauerkraut. Cover the Dutch oven and bake for 1 hour, undisturbed.

5. While the sauerkraut is baking, heat the oil in a large skillet over medium-high heat and lightly brown the sausages on both sides, about 5 to 6 minutes. Set aside.

6. Place the potatoes on top of the sauerkraut in the Dutch oven. Cover and return to the oven. Bake about 20 minutes.

7. Remove the Dutch oven, place the browned sausages on top of the potatoes, cover, and return to the oven until the sausages are heated through and the potatoes are tender, about 30 more minutes.

8. Put the sausages, potatoes, and sauerkraut on each plate and serve hot.

Franks and Beans

This is an easy main dish to prepare, and it's easy on the budget, too. You start with canned beans and end up with homemade flavor.

SERVES 4 TO 6

2 (16-ounce) cans pork and beans in tomato sauce
1 pound hot dogs, sliced into 1-inch pieces
1 small onion, chopped
½ cup ketchup
¼ cup molasses
2 tablespoons brown sugar
1 tablespoon prepared yellow mustard
½ teaspoon Worcestershire sauce

1. Preheat the oven to 300°F.

2. Mix the beans, hot dogs, onion, ketchup, molasses, brown sugar, mustard, and Worcestershire sauce in a 2-quart baking dish.

3. Bake for 1½ hours and serve hot.

Roasted Leg of Lamb

In days past, lamb purchased at any time except spring had a very strong flavor because the animals were slaughtered when they were old, closer to mutton than to what we know as lamb today. Those days are gone, so don't be afraid to buy lamb any time of the year. And when you do, try this recipe, which highlights classic roasting herbs—rosemary and thyme—with heavy garlic and light wine overtones.

SERVES 8 TO 10

1 (6- to 9-pound) leg of lamb
20 peeled garlic cloves, larger ones sliced in
    half lengthwise
Fresh or dried rosemary
Fresh or dried thyme
Salt and pepper
3 tablespoons olive oil
1 cup dry red wine
½ cup water

1. Prepare the roast by removing most of the visible fat. Cut slits into the top portion with a small, sharp knife. Insert a garlic clove into each slit and push down with your finger until the garlic is no longer visible. Rub the rosemary, thyme, salt, and pepper all over the surface of the meat and follow with a rub of olive oil. Splash with 3 tablespoons of wine and rub again. Cover and let the lamb marinate for at least 3 hours (or overnight) in the refrigerator.

2. Remove the meat from the refrigerator about 1 hour before roasting.

3. Preheat the oven to 450°F and place the lamb in a shallow roasting pan.

4. Roast for 15 minutes, until the meat is browned. Reduce the oven temperature to 350°F and continue to roast 8 minutes per pound for rare (about 120°F), 10 minutes per pound for medium (about 135°F), or 18 minutes per pound for well-done (about 150°F). Occasionally baste with pan juices or additional wine. (The temperature will continue to rise 5 degrees while the meat rests.)

5. Remove the lamb from the oven, cover with a tent of aluminum foil, and let rest for 10 to 20 minutes before carving.

6. Meanwhile, pour the remaining wine and water into the pan. Bring to a boil, stirring constantly with a wooden spoon to bring up any browned bits from the bottom of the pan. Taste and adjust the seasoning as needed.

7. Slice the meat and serve immediately, passing the pan juices at the table.

TIP: Keep in mind that some portions of the leg will cook faster than others, so varying degrees of doneness can be achieved. Many people feel that today's lamb is best served rare and should never be cooked beyond medium.

Roasted Rack of Lamb with Garlic-Rosemary Sauce

Garlic and rosemary complement a rack of lamb as well as they do a leg of lamb. This version incorporates a thicker sauce that is spooned over the meat before serving. When you buy a rack of lamb, make sure the butcher has removed the chine (backbone) or has deeply scored it so you can cut through to serve individual chops.

SERVES 4 TO 6

8 garlic cloves, peeled
3 teaspoons fresh or dried rosemary
1 teaspoon salt, plus more to taste
½ teaspoon black pepper, plus more to taste
2 (8-rib) lamb racks, trimmed
½ cup dry red wine
1 cup water
2 tablespoons cornstarch dissolved in
    2 tablespoons water

1. Preheat the oven to 350°F.

2. Chop together 1 garlic clove and 1 teaspoon of rosemary. Mix with the 1 teaspoon salt and ½ teaspoon pepper in a small bowl. Rub the mixture all over the racks. Place the racks, bone side down, in a roasting pan. Scatter the remaining 7 garlic cloves and 2 teaspoons rosemary in the pan.

3. Roast for 20 minutes, until the thickest part of the meat registers 120°F for rare or 130°F for medium-rare. Remove the lamb from the pan and set aside on a plate. (The temperature will continue to rise 5 degrees while the meat rests.)

4. Place the roasting pan over high heat, add the wine, and cook, stirring with a wooden spoon to bring up any browned bits. Bring to a boil and boil until the wine is reduced by half.

5. Stir in the water and bring to a boil again. Strain the liquid into a small saucepan. Whisk in the cornstarch mixture over medium heat and cook until thickened. Taste and adjust the seasonings as needed. Keep warm.

6. Carve the lamb between the bones, arrange on a serving platter, spoon the warm sauce over, and serve.

Roasted Rack of Lamb with Mustard Crumbs

The rack is a portion of the rib section of a lamb, usually containing eight ribs. It is a very tender cut. In this recipe, bread crumbs and mustard provide a delicious crust that seals in the moist flavors and keeps the lamb tender.

SERVES 4 TO 6

1 cup dry bread crumbs
½ cup chopped fresh parsley
1 teaspoon coarse or kosher salt
4 tablespoons oil
2 (8-rib) lamb racks, trimmed
Salt and pepper
2 tablespoons honey
1 tablespoon Dijon mustard
1 teaspoon chopped fresh rosemary

1. Preheat the oven to 350°F.

2. In a food processor, combine the bread crumbs, parsley, and salt. Pulse briefly, add 2 tablespoons of oil, and process briefly. Place in a shallow bowl.

3. Heat the remaining 2 tablespoons oil in a large skillet over medium-high heat. Season the lamb loins liberally with salt and pepper. Carefully place the lamb in the oil with tongs and brown on all sides, 5 to 7 minutes. Remove the lamb from the pan and let it rest on a plate at room temperature.

4. Combine the honey, mustard, and rosemary in a small bowl and mix to form a paste. Spread this mixture liberally over the lamb loins, then dip the lamb in the seasoned bread crumbs, patting to make the crumbs adhere.

5. Roast for 15 to 17 minutes, until the thickest part of the meat registers 120°F for rare or 130°F for medium-rare. Remove the lamb from the pan and let rest for 5 minutes (the temperature will continue to rise 5 degrees)

6. Carve the lamb between the bones, arrange on a plate, and serve.

Irish Lamb Stew

In Ireland, Irish stew was made of mutton—older sheep that can no longer produce wool or milk for cheese, both of which drove the Irish farm economy. Mutton is rarely available in the United States, but fortunately the stew is delicious when made from lamb.

SERVES 5 TO 6

¾ pound thickly sliced bacon, chopped
3 pounds boneless lamb shoulder, cut into
    2-inch pieces
½ cup all-purpose flour
1 teaspoon salt, plus more to taste
1 teaspoon black pepper, plus more to taste
1½ teaspoons minced garlic
1 large onion, chopped
2 cups beef broth (page 118)
3 large carrots, diced
2 cups white pearl or boiling onions
2 medium waxy potatoes, such as thin-skinned
    red or white, peeled and cubed
1 teaspoon dried thyme
2 bay leaves
1 cup dry white wine

1. Cook the bacon in a large saucepan over medium-high heat until evenly brown, about 10 minutes. Remove the bacon with tongs and drain on paper towels. Set aside. Reserve the fat in the saucepan.

2. Combine the lamb and flour in a large bowl. Add the 1 teaspoon salt and ½ teaspoon pepper and toss to coat the meat evenly.

3. Heat the remaining bacon fat in the saucepan over medium-high heat. Add a single layer of lamb and brown on all sides, about 5 minutes. Remove from the saucepan and keep warm. Repeat until all the meat is browned.

4. Add the garlic and onion to the bacon fat and sauté until the onion is softened, about 3 minutes. Add the broth and cook, stirring with a wooden spoon, to release any browned bits from the bottom of the pan. Return the lamb to the pan and bring to a simmer. Reduce the heat to low, cover and continue to simmer for 1½ hours.

5. Add the bacon, carrots, pearl onions, potatoes, thyme, bay leaves, and wine to the saucepan. Cover and simmer for 1 to 1½ hours, to desired thickness and until the vegetables are tender.

6. Remove the bay leaves and serve hot.

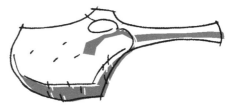

Shepherd's Pie

When the Sunday roast was lamb or mutton, Monday night's dinner took advantage of the leftovers in the form of shepherd's pie, a stew of meat topped with leftover mashed potatoes. This popular dish is so tasty that it readily adapts to using ground lamb and a topping of fresh mashed potatoes.

SERVES 4 TO 6

2 pounds baking potatoes, peeled and cubed
2 tablespoons sour cream
1 large egg yolk
½ cup milk
Salt and pepper
1 tablespoon oil
1½ pounds ground lamb
1 medium carrot, chopped
1 medium onion, chopped
2 tablespoons butter
2 tablespoons all-purpose flour
1 cup beef broth (page 118)
2 teaspoons Worcestershire sauce
½ cup frozen peas
½ cup fresh or frozen corn
1 teaspoon paprika
Chopped fresh parsley, to serve

1. Cover the potatoes with salted water in a large saucepan, bring to a boil, and boil until tender, about 12 minutes. Drain well.

2. Combine the potatoes, sour cream, egg yolk, and milk in a large bowl and mash until the mixture is almost smooth. Season to taste with salt and pepper and set aside.

3. Heat the oil in a large skillet over medium-high heat. Add the lamb and season with salt and pepper. Brown the meat for 3 or 4 minutes, breaking it up with a wooden spoon. Drain off any excess drippings.

4. Add the carrot and onion to the lamb. Sauté for 5 minutes, stirring frequently.

5. Meanwhile, melt the butter in a small saucepan. Stir in the flour to make a paste and cook for 2 minutes. Whisk in the broth and Worcestershire sauce and cook until thickened, about 1 minute. Add to the meat in the skillet and stir in the peas and corn.

6. Preheat the broiler.

7. Transfer the meat mixture to a shallow baking dish. Spoon the potatoes over the meat evenly and top with paprika.

8. Broil the casserole 6 to 8 inches from the heat until the potatoes are evenly browned. Top with chopped parsley and serve.

TIP: If you like, you can substitute ground beef for the lamb.

Moussaka

Moussaka is the shepherd's pie of Greece, often featured on the menu of Greek restaurants or served at Greek heritage festivals. The combination of fried eggplant, delicately spiced lamb, and rich cheese sauce is irresistible and well worth the rather lengthy preparation. It can be made earlier in the day for final cooking and browning in the oven.

SERVES 6

4 medium eggplants (about 4 pounds), peeled
    and cut into ¼-inch slices
Salt
8 tablespoons oil
1½ pounds ground lamb
1 medium onion, chopped
1 teaspoon minced garlic
1 (28-ounce) can tomato sauce
2 teaspoons dried oregano
1 teaspoon ground cinnamon
Black pepper
¼ cup (½ stick) butter
¼ cup all-purpose flour
2 cups milk
Pinch of ground nutmeg
1 cup grated Parmesan cheese

1. Arrange the eggplant on paper towels and sprinkle with salt on both sides. Cover with another layer of paper towels. Let drain while you prepare the lamb.

2. Heat 1 tablespoon of oil in a large skillet over medium-high heat. Add the lamb, onion, and garlic and sauté until the lamb loses its pink color, about 10 minutes. Drain off as much fat as possible.

3. Stir in the tomato sauce, oregano, and cinnamon. Season to taste with salt and pepper. Reduce the heat and let simmer while you prepare the eggplant.

4. Heat the remaining 7 tablespoons of oil in a large skillet over medium-high heat. Add the eggplant slices to fit in a single layer and fry until browned, 4 to 5 minutes per side. Drain on paper towels and repeat with the remaining eggplant slices.

5. Melt the butter over medium heat in a small saucepan. Stir in the flour to form a smooth paste; cook for 1 minute. Add the milk and cook, stirring frequently, until the sauce is smooth and thick. Add the nutmeg. Season to taste with salt and pepper and set aside.

6. Preheat the oven to 350°F.

7. To assemble, layer one-third of the eggplant in a 9 x 13-inch baking dish. Top with one-third of the meat sauce and sprinkle with one-third of the cheese. Repeat to make two more layers with the remaining eggplant, meat sauce, and cheese. Spoon the white sauce over the top.

8. Bake for 20 to 30 minutes, until the topping is browned. Serve hot.

Herbed Veal Rib Roast

Seasoned with garlic, thyme, and mustard roasted in the meat's surface, this dish highlights one of the most tender, most expensive veal cuts. Veal rib and loin roasts do best in hot ovens with brief cooking times. Have the butcher remove the chine (backbone) to make carving easy. Allow one rib per serving. A variation follows.

SERVES 6

1 (5- to 7-pound) bone-in veal rib roast
Salt and pepper
1 medium onion, chopped
10 garlic cloves, peeled
2 tablespoons dried thyme
1 cup whole-grain mustard
½ cup oil
½ cup dry wine white
½ cup chicken broth (page 119)

1. Generously season the roast with salt and pepper. Cut several slits in the meat.

2. Combine the onion, garlic, thyme, mustard, and oil in a food processor and process to form a paste. Rub the entire veal roast with the mustard mixture, pressing the mixture into the surface slits.

3. Place the roast on a rack in a roasting pan and cover tightly with plastic wrap. Refrigerate for 24 hours.

4. Remove the roast from the refrigerator and uncover. Bring the roast to room temperature.

5. Preheat the oven to 425°F.

6. Roast for 1¼ to 1½ hours, until the meat registers 135°F. Transfer the roast to a serving platter and let it rest for 20 to 25 minutes.

7. Meanwhile, place the roasting pan over high heat and add the wine and broth. Bring to a boil, scraping up the browned bits with a wooden spoon, and boil for 1 minute. Season to taste with salt and pepper.

8. Carve the roast by slicing the veal between the bones. Spoon the sauce over the meat and serve.

Herbed Boneless Veal Roast

Replace the bone-in roast in Herbed Veal Rib Roast with a one 3- to 4-pound boneless veal loin or rib roast. Have the butcher tie it into a neat, compact shape. Prepare the roast as directed. Roast for 45 to 60 minutes, until the meat registers 135°F. Complete the recipe as directed.

Braised Veal with Gravy

Tougher cuts from the shoulder or leg (top round) benefit from slow, moist cooking, which develops flavor and tenderizes the meat by gently breaking down tough fibers. Serve this dish with boiled or mashed potatoes and plenty of crusty French bread for mopping up the delicious gravy.

SERVES 6

1 (3-pound) boneless veal leg rump roast
¼ teaspoon salt
¼ teaspoon black pepper
2 tablespoons oil
¼ cup dry white wine
½ cup diced tomatoes
½ medium onion, diced
1 teaspoon minced garlic
1 tablespoon chopped fresh thyme or
    1 teaspoon dried
1 bay leaf
2 tablespoons all-purpose flour
½ cup chicken broth (page 119) and ½ cup
    beef broth (page 118)
1 tablespoon chopped fresh parsley

1. Preheat the oven to 250°F.

2. Rub the veal all over with the salt and pepper. Heat the oil in a large skillet over medium-high heat. Add the veal and brown on all sides, about 2 minutes per side. Remove the veal from the skillet and set aside on a plate.

3. Add the wine to the skillet and use a wooden spoon to scrape up any browned bits. Add the tomatoes, onion, garlic, thyme, and bay leaf.

4. Return the veal to the skillet. Cover and braise for 1¼ to 1¾ hours, until the internal temperature registers 145° to 150°F.

5. Transfer the veal to a serving platter, cover with a tent of aluminum foil, and let stand for 10 to 15 minutes while you prepare the gravy.

6. Remove the bay leaf from the skillet. Blend the flour with the broth in a small bowl and add to the pan juices. Bring to a boil. Reduce the heat to medium-high and cook until slightly thickened, about 3 minutes. Add the parsley and season to taste with salt.

7. Carve the veal and serve with the gravy.

Wiener Schnitzel

Breaded veal cutlet is an Austrian specialty. The meat is traditionally cooked in lard, but oil may be used instead. Lemon wedges are a traditional garnish, but sometimes hard-boiled eggs and capers or anchovies are used.

SERVES 4

1 pound veal scallopini slices (8 to 12), cut a
    little more than ¼ inch thick
½ cup all-purpose flour
2 large eggs
1 tablespoon milk
2 cups fresh bread crumbs
Salt and pepper
⅓ cup lard or oil
Lemon wedges, to serve

1. Preheat the oven to 200°F. Place an ovenproof platter in the oven.

2. Put 1 veal slice between 2 sheets of wax paper and gently pound with a meat mallet until it is less than ¼ inch thick. Repeat with the remaining slices and set aside on a plate.

3. Put the flour in a shallow bowl. Beat the eggs and milk in a second shallow bowl. Season the bread crumbs with salt and pepper in a third shallow bowl.

4. Heat the oil in a large skillet over medium-high heat.

5. Dip the veal in the flour, shaking off any excess, then dip the veal in the egg mixture. Roll in the bread crumbs until well coated, patting to make the crumbs adhere. Slip into the skillet. Continue adding more slices until the skillet is full but not crowded. Fry until golden brown, 2 to 3 minutes per side. Remove the cooked meat and drain well on paper towels. Place the cooked veal cutlets in the oven and continue cooking until all the veal is cooked.

6. Garnish the plates with lemon wedges and serve at once.

Veal Parmesan

If it weren't for veal Parmesan, many Americans would never taste veal, a tender and tasty, albeit expensive, form of meat. Veal Parmesan is a classic Italian dish of breaded veal cutlets baked with tomato sauce and cheese. Scallopini and cutlets are two different names for the same cut of veal—thin slices from the leg.

SERVES 4

1 pound veal scallopini slices (8 to 12), cut a
little more than ¼ inch thick
¼ cup all-purpose flour
1 cup dry bread crumbs
½ cup grated Parmesan cheese
1 teaspoon garlic powder
1 teaspoon dried basil
1 teaspoon dried oregano
1 teaspoon salt
½ teaspoon black pepper
1 large egg
1 tablespoon water
⅓ cup oil
1½ cups marinara sauce (page 260)
2 cups shredded mozzarella cheese (about
8 ounces)

1. Place 1 veal slice between 2 sheets of wax paper and gently pound with a meat mallet until it is less than ¼ inch thick. Repeat with the remaining slices. Dust the slices with the flour until well coated and set aside on a plate.

2. Stir together the bread crumbs, Parmesan cheese, garlic powder, basil, oregano, salt, and pepper in a shallow bowl.

3. In another shallow bowl, use a fork to beat the egg with the water.

4. Heat the oil in a large skillet over medium-high heat.

5. Dip the veal in the egg mixture, then roll in the seasoned bread crumbs until well coated, patting to make the crumbs adhere. Slip the cutlets into the skillet. Continue adding more slices until the skillet is full but not crowded. Fry until golden brown, 2 to 3 minutes per side. Remove the cooked meat and drain well on paper towels. Repeat until all the veal is cooked.

6. Preheat the oven to 375°F. Lightly grease a 9 x 13-inch baking dish.

7. Spread ½ cup of marinara sauce in the baking dish. Arrange the veal in the dish, overlapping as needed. Spoon the remaining 1 cup sauce on top. Sprinkle the mozzarella cheese over the sauce.

8. Bake for 15 to 20 minutes, until the cheese is melted and the veal is hot. Serve immediately.

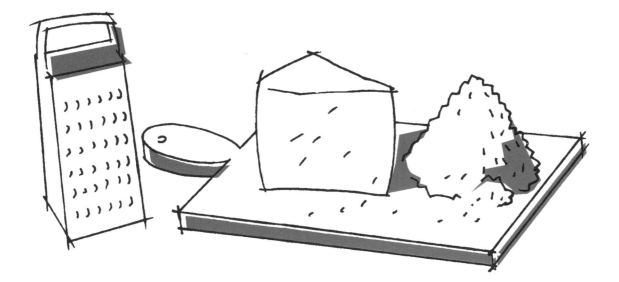

Veal Piccata

A classic Italian preparation, veal piccata is a breaded cutlet finished with a sauce of pan drippings, lemon juice, and chopped parsley.

SERVES 4

1 pound veal scallopini slices (8 to 12), cut a
  little more than ¼ inch thick
¼ cup all-purpose flour
Salt and pepper
3 tablespoons oil
¼ cup dry white wine
½ cup chicken broth (page 119)
3 tablespoons lemon juice
2 tablespoons chopped fresh parsley
1 tablespoon capers
3 tablespoons butter

1. Place 1 slice of veal between 2 sheets of wax paper and gently pound with a meat mallet until it is less than ¼ inch thick. Repeat with the remaining veal. Dust the slices with the flour until well coated. Sprinkle with salt and pepper.

2. Heat the oil in a large skillet over medium-high heat. Add a single layer of the veal and sauté for 3 to 4 minutes per side, until firm. Transfer to a serving platter and cover with aluminum foil to keep warm. Repeat with the remaining veal and set aside.

3. Pour off all but 1 tablespoon of fat from the pan. Add the wine, broth, and lemon juice. Cook, stirring with a wooden spoon to loosen all the browned bits stuck to the pan. Bring to a boil and boil until the mixture is reduced to about ⅓ cup, 3 to 4 minutes. Stir in the parsley and capers. Season to taste with salt and pepper. Remove from the heat and whisk in the butter, 1 tablespoon at a time.

4. Pour the sauce over the veal and serve immediately.

Veal Marsala

Marsala wine has a rich, almost smoky flavor, which gives this traditional Italian dish its distinctive taste.

SERVES 4

1 pound veal scallopini slices (8 to 12), cut a
  little more than ¼ inch thick
¼ cup all-purpose flour
Salt and pepper
3 tablespoons oil
2 cups sliced mushrooms
½ cup Marsala wine
½ cup chicken broth (page 119)
2 tablespoons chopped fresh parsley
2 tablespoons butter

1. Place 1 slice of veal between 2 sheets of wax paper and gently pound with a meat mallet until it is less than ¼ inch thick. Repeat with the remaining veal. Dust the veal with the flour until well coated. Sprinkle with salt and pepper.

2. Heat the oil in a large skillet over medium-high heat. Add a single layer of the veal and sauté for about 1½ minutes on each side, until firm. Transfer to a serving platter and cover with aluminum foil to keep warm. Repeat with the remaining veal and set aside.

3. Reduce the heat to medium, add the mushrooms to the skillet, and sauté until the mushrooms have given up their juice, about 8 minutes. Add the wine and broth and cook, stirring with a wooden spoon to loosen all the browned bits stuck to the pan. Bring to a boil and boil until the mixture is reduced to about ⅔ cup, 4 to 5 minutes. Stir in the parsley. Season to taste with salt and pepper. Remove from the heat and whisk in the butter, 1 tablespoon at a time.

4. Pour the sauce over the veal and serve immediately.

Osso Buco

"Osso buco" literally translates from the Italian as "bone with a hole." Osso buco is made with cross-sections of the veal shank. In the center of each slice is a hole containing the bone marrow, which traditionally is eaten with a special spoon. Risotto is the usual accompaniment.

SERVES 4 TO 6

½ cup all-purpose flour
8 slices veal shank, cut 1 to 1½ inches thick
Salt and pepper
¼ cup (½ stick) butter
2 tablespoons oil
2 medium carrots, finely chopped
2 medium celery ribs, finely chopped
1 medium onion, finely chopped
1 teaspoon minced garlic
½ cup dry white wine
1 (28-ounce) can diced tomatoes
½ cup chicken broth (page 119; optional)

1. Preheat the oven to 350°F.

2. Put the flour in a shallow bowl. Sprinkle the veal with salt and pepper and dip in the flour to coat all sides.

3. Melt the butter with the oil in a large skillet over medium-high heat. Add a single layer of veal shanks and brown on both sides, about 10 minutes total. Transfer to a roasting pan and repeat until the remaining veal is browned.

4. Add the carrots, celery, onion, and garlic to the skillet and sauté until the onion is softened, about 5 minutes. Transfer to the roasting pan with a slotted spoon and spoon over the veal.

5. Pour the wine and tomatoes over the veal. Cover the roasting pan tightly with aluminum foil.

6. Roast for about 1 hour. Uncover, then add the chicken broth if needed to keep the level of liquid halfway up the shanks. Roast for another hour, uncovered, until the veal is tender and offers no resistance when pierced with the tip of a knife. Serve immediately on a large platter, surrounded by the cooked vegetables.

Liver and Onions

Calf's liver is delicate in flavor and pale pink in color. "Baby beef" liver is not as delicately flavored and is much redder. If you can find it, and are willing to pay the higher price, choose calf's liver. Overcooking can ruin liver, so good timing with this recipe results in liver that is slightly pink inside.

SERVES 4

1 pound calf's liver
4 slices bacon, chopped
3 large onions, thinly sliced
½ cup all-purpose flour
Salt and pepper
2 tablespoons oil (optional)

1. Trim the liver to remove all the tough membranes. Cut into ½-inch slices and set aside.

2. Fry the bacon in a large skillet over medium-high heat until browned and crisp, about 10 to 15 minutes. Remove the bacon with a slotted spoon and drain on paper towels.

3. Add the onions to the skillet, reduce the heat to medium, and cook until lightly browned, 15 to 20 minutes. Remove from the skillet and set aside.

4. Lightly coat the liver with flour and sprinkle with salt and pepper.

5. Add the oil to the skillet, if needed, and heat over medium-high heat. Add the liver and fry until browned and cooked through, 2 to 3 minutes per side. Return the bacon and onions to the skillet to reheat.

6. Place the liver on individual serving dishes, topped with the onions and bacon. Serve immediately.

BUYING, STORING, AND PREPARING MEATS

Doneness	Beef and Lamb	Pork	Veal
Rare	125° to 135°F	N/A	N/A
Medium-rare	135° to 140°F	N/A	N/A
Medium	140° to 145°F	155° to 165°F	145° to 155°F
Medium-well	145° to 155°F	N/A	N/A
Well-done	155°F+	180° to 185°F	N/A

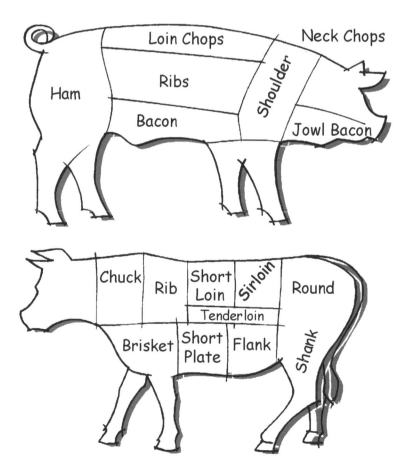

BEEF CUT	THICKNESS OR WEIGHT	APPROXIMATE BROILING TIME FOR MEDIUM-RARE TO MEDIUM	APPROXIMATE GRILLING TIME FOR MEDIUM-RARE TO MEDIUM
New York or Rib-eye steak	¾ inch 1 inch	8 to 10 minutes 8 to 10 minutes	6 to 8 minutes 11 to 14 minutes
Porterhouse	¾ inch	10 to 13 minutes	10 to 12 minutes
T-bone	1 inch	10 to 13 minutes 15 to 20 minutes	15 to 18 minutes
Tenderloin	1 inch 1½ inches	13 to 16 minutes 18 to 22 minutes	13 to 15 minutes 14 to 16 minutes
Top sirloin, boneless	¾ inch 1 inch	9 to 12 minutes 16 to 21 minutes	13 to 16 minutes 17 to 21 minutes
Flank	1½ to 2 pounds	13 to 18 minutes	17 to 21 minutes

▶ Trim excess fat to avoid flare-ups while broiling or grilling.

▶ Using tongs, turn the steaks halfway through the cooking time.

▶ Let steaks rest 5 minutes before serving.

▶ As a general rule, the less tender the cut of beef, the cheaper it is and the longer it takes to cook. Plan to stew or braise inexpensive cuts.

▶ When purchasing beef, look for brightly colored, deep-red meat.

▶ Allow about 6 ounces of boneless meat per person; allow 8 ounces for bone-in steaks.

▶ Store meat in the coldest part of the refrigerator. Store ground beef for up to 2 days and other cuts for up to 3 days.

▶ Ground beef can be frozen for up to 3 months. Roasts can be frozen for up to 6 months.

▶ When buying pork, look for meat that is pale pink with a small amount of marbling and not much fat. Darker pink indicates the pork came from an older animal.

▶ Store pork in the coldest part of the refrigerator for up to 2 days. Store ground pork and fresh pork sausage for up to 2 days.

▶ Pork can be frozen for up to 6 months.

▶ Cooking pork to 137°F kills all trichinosis-causing bacteria. For an extra measure of safety, most experts recommend cooking pork to an internal temperature of 150°F. Well-done pork tends to be dry and tough, though you will have to strike your own balance between method and safety.

CHAPTER NINE

Grilling

Memorial Day weekend marks the unofficial start of grilling season across America. The grill is ceremoniously wheeled out of the garage into its place of honor on the patio or deck, and the season of barbecue begins.

Although cooking over an open fire predates the beginnings of civilization, barbecue is a distinctly American phenomenon. In the pre–Civil War period, Southerners typically ate five pounds of pork for every one pound of beef. Pig slaughtering became a time of celebration, when entire communities gathered together to share in the feast. The traditional Southern barbecue grew out of these gatherings.

Meanwhile, as pioneers settled westward, barbecues quickly became a permanent feature of frontier life. In the nineteenth century, barbecues were a staple at political rallies, offering a popular and relatively inexpensive way for politicians to lobby for votes—complete with meat, lemonade, and, more often than not, whiskey.

At the turn of the twentieth century, barbecue restaurants began to appear throughout the South. Often these restaurants started as simple, weekend-only barbecue pits, where the "pit men" manned the grills. The subsequent introduction of the automobile gave these barbecue shacks a ready-made clientele.

By the 1950s, charcoal grills and briquettes were in full swing in the backyard. Hamburgers, hot dogs, and steaks were instant favorites because they required little grilling expertise. The home griller would cook the meat directly over the flame, which would rapidly sear the outer surface and create a delicious crust.

Some of the more adventurous cooks also developed techniques that enabled them to cook larger cuts of meat. For example, "slow cooking" utilized indirect heat in a closed grill—the meat cooked on one side, while the coals or propane burned brightly on the other. They also learned how to use wood chips to generate unique flavors of smoke and give the meat a variety of flavors. The chips were soaked for 30 minutes before being added to the fire in wood chip holders or packets of heavy-duty aluminum foil (pierced in several places).

To be sure, the advent of barbecue brought variety—and division—of cooking duties into the home. Mom was still queen of the kitchen, but Dad became the patio king!

Juicy Grilled Burgers

These juicy burgers won't dry out on the grill. The secret ingredient is the evaporated milk. Serve with all the traditional burger fixings—ketchup, mustard, sliced onions, and sliced pickles.

SERVES 4

1½ pounds ground beef
1 tablespoon finely chopped onion
⅔ cup evaporated milk
2 teaspoons Worcestershire sauce
1 teaspoon salt
¼ teaspoon black pepper
1 teaspoon minced garlic
4 hamburger buns (toasting optional)

1. Prepare a hot fire in a gas or charcoal grill.

2. Mix the beef, onion, milk, Worcestershire sauce, salt, pepper, and garlic in a medium bowl. Dampen your hands and shape the meat mixture into 4 equal patties.

3. Place the burgers on the grill and cover. Grill, turning once with a spatula, until the outside is well browned and the inside is still slightly pink, about 8 minutes for medium-rare. Remove the burgers from the grill, or move the burgers to a cooler spot on the grill and grill 2 minutes more for medium or 4 minutes more for well-done. Serve each patty sandwiched between a top and bottom bun.

TIP: Instead of serving soft white hamburger buns, give your burgers extra flavor by serving them on sourdough or hard rolls.

Grilled Blue Cheese Burgers

French bread is preferred for these burgers. Serve with red wine, not beer. These burgers have so much flavor, you probably won't want to offer the usual toppings of ketchup, tomatoes, or lettuce.

SERVES 4

2 tablespoons butter
½ cup sliced mushrooms
1½ pounds ground beef
1 large egg, well beaten
¼ cup dry red wine
8 thick slices French bread
¼ cup crumbled blue cheese

1. Prepare a hot fire in a gas or charcoal grill.

2. Melt the butter in a medium skillet over medium heat. Add the mushrooms and sauté until the mushrooms give up their juice, about 8 minutes.

3. Scrape the mushrooms into a medium bowl and add the ground beef, egg, and wine. Mix well. Dampen your hands and shape the meat mixture into 4 equal patties.

4. Place the burgers on the grill and cover. Grill, turning once with a spatula, until the outside is well browned and the inside is still slightly pink, about 8 minutes for medium-rare. Remove the burgers from the grill, or move the burgers to a cooler spot on the grill and grill 2 minutes more for medium or 4 minutes more for well-done.

5. Set each burger on a slice of French bread, sprinkle with blue cheese, and top with a second slice of bread. Serve immediately.

Stuffed Grilled Cheeseburgers

Smoked Cheddar gives extra flavor to these cheeseburgers. The ketchup, onion, and cheese are all inside the burgers, offering a twist on the standard way to dress a burger.

SERVES 5

2 pounds ground beef
½ cup ketchup
1 teaspoon salt
½ teaspoon black pepper
1 small onion, cut into 5 thin slices
5 thick slices smoked Cheddar cheese
5 hamburger buns

1. Prepare a hot fire in a gas or charcoal grill.

2. Divide the meat into 10 equal portions. Place the portions between sheets of wax paper or plastic wrap and flatten into patties ½ inch thick and 4 inches across. Spread ketchup on 5 patties. Season with the salt and pepper and top each with a slice of onion and cheese. Top with the remaining five patties and pinch around the edges to seal. Be careful to make a good seal so the filling doesn't leak out.

3. Place the burgers on the grill and cover. Grill, turning once with a spatula, until the outside is well browned and the inside is still slightly pink, about 8 minutes for medium-rare. Remove the burgers from the grill, or move them to a cooler spot on the grill and grill 2 minutes more for medium or 4 minutes more for well-done.

4. Serve on the buns.

TIP: Never press burgers with the spatula as they grill. Pressing squeezes out the juices and results in dry meat.

Grilled Kitchen-Sink Burgers

Everything except the kitchen sink goes into these burgers, including onions, carrots, and potatoes. Serve with the usual hamburger fixings.

SERVES 8

1 small sweet onion, such as Walla Walla, Maui, or Vidalia, quartered
1 medium carrot, coarsely chopped
1 medium baking potato, peeled and coarsely chopped
1 pound ground beef
1 cup dry bread crumbs
1 large egg
1 teaspoon finely chopped fresh parsley
1 teaspoon salt
¼ teaspoon black pepper
½ teaspoon paprika
8 hamburger buns or rolls

1. Prepare a hot fire in a gas or charcoal grill.

2. Combine the onion, carrot, and potato in a food processor and process until very finely chopped.

3. Combine the vegetables with the beef, bread crumbs, egg, parsley, salt, pepper, and paprika in a medium bowl and mix well. Dampen your hands and shape the meat mixture into 8 equal patties.

4. Place the burgers on the grill and cover. Grill, turning once with a spatula, until the outside is well browned and the inside is still slightly pink, about 8 minutes for medium-rare. Remove the burgers from the grill, or move them to a cooler spot on the grill and grill 2 minutes more for medium or 4 minutes more for well-done.

5. Serve on the buns.

TIP: Ground chuck is too fatty and ground sirloin is too lean, but 85% lean ground round is an excellent choice for grilled burgers.

Grilled Sausage Burgers

A combination of beef, sausage, green bell pepper, and onion makes these burgers irresistible. Serve these on bakery-fresh hard rolls and pass mustard on the side. Because the burgers are made from pork sausage, they should be cooked at least to medium.

SERVES 6

½ pound ground beef
½ pound pork sausage (also good with venison or elk sausage)
½ green bell pepper, finely chopped
¼ cup finely chopped onion
2 large eggs, lightly beaten
1 tablespoon finely chopped pimento-stuffed green olives
½ cup dry bread crumbs
¼ cup water
6 hamburger buns

1. Prepare a hot fire in a gas or charcoal grill.

2. Mix the beef, sausage, bell pepper, onion, eggs, olives, bread crumbs, and water in a medium bowl. Dampen your hands and shape the meat mixture into 6 equal patties.

3. Place the burgers on the grill and cover. Grill, turning once with a spatula, until the outside is well browned and the inside is still slightly pink, about 8 minutes. Move the burgers to a cooler spot on the grill and grill 2 minutes more for medium or 4 minutes more for well-done.

4. Toast the bun halves for about 1 minute. Set each burger on a bottom bun, top with a top bun, and serve immediately.

Grilled Reuben Burgers

Reuben sandwiches are typically made with corned beef, cheese, and sauerkraut, and are grilled indoors in a skillet. Here's a worthy variation that replaces the corned beef with a beef burger but keeps all the fixings.

SERVES 6

1½ pounds ground beef
½ teaspoon garlic powder
1 teaspoon salt
½ teaspoon black pepper
6 slices bacon
1 small onion, finely chopped
1 pound sauerkraut, well drained
12 thick slices rye bread
6 slices Swiss cheese

1. Prepare a hot fire in a gas or charcoal grill.

2. Mix the beef, garlic powder, salt, and pepper in a medium bowl. Dampen your hands and shape the meat mixture into 6 equal patties.

3. Cook the bacon in a large, heavy skillet over medium-high heat until crispy and browned, about 8 minutes. Drain away all but 1 tablespoon of fat. Pat the bacon with paper towels, crumble, and set aside.

4. Reheat the reserved bacon fat over medium heat and add the onion. Sauté until softened, about 3 minutes. Add the sauerkraut, mix well, and stir until heated through. Keep warm.

5. Place the burgers on the grill and cover. Grill, turning once with a spatula, until the outside is well browned and the inside is still slightly pink, about 8 minutes for medium-rare. Remove the burgers from the grill, or move them to a cooler spot on the grill and grill 2 minutes more for medium or 4 minutes more for well-done.

6. While the burgers are cooking, toast the rye bread on the grill, about 30 seconds on each side.

7. To serve, place a burger patty on a slice of toasted bread and top with the onion mixture, crumbled bacon, and a slice of cheese before adding the remaining slices of bread.

Grilled Marinated Steaks

Wine marinades enhance the natural flavors of meat while tenderizing it. The marinade in this recipe mingles red wine with the distinct flavors of garlic and bay leaves. T-bone, porterhouse, rib-eye, New York, sirloin, and tenderloin steaks are all good choices for grilling.

SERVES 4

1 to 1⅓ cups red wine marinade (page 251) or red wine pepper marinade (page 252)
4 (6- to 12-ounce) beef steaks, 1 to 1½ inches thick

1. Prepare the marinade in a shallow baking dish. Add the steaks, turn to coat, cover, and refrigerate for 3 to 5 hours, turning every hour.

2. Prepare a hot fire in a gas or charcoal grill with the grill rack 4 to 5 inches from the heat.

3. Remove the steaks from the marinade and pat dry with paper towels. Place on the grill, cover, and cook until well browned on the outside, about 8 minutes for medium-rare. Remove from the grill, or move the steaks to a cooler spot on the grill and continue grilling, covered, 3 minutes for medium, 5 minutes for well-done. Serve hot.

Grilled Dry Rub Rib-Eye Steak

This robust spice rub, which is typically used on barbecued ribs and brisket, complements the big, beefy flavor of the rib-eye.

SERVES 3 TO 4

1½ to 2 pounds beef rib-eye steaks, 1 inch thick
½ medium lemon
2 tablespoons Texas spice rub (page 251)

1. Prepare a hot fire in a gas or charcoal grill.

2. Squeeze the lemon on both sides of each steak. Rub the spice mix onto each side.

3. Place on the grill, cover, and cook until well browned on the outside, about 8 minutes for medium-rare. Remove from the grill, or move the steaks to a cooler spot on the grill and continue grilling, covered, 3 minutes for medium, 5 minutes for well-done. Serve hot.

Marinated Grilled Flank Steak

Flank steaks can be juicy and tender if properly cooked and sliced. Tamed by a marinade and grilled until rare, flank steaks are terrific. Be sure to let the meat rest before thinly slicing against the grain.

SERVES 4

1 (1½-pound) flank steak
1 to 2 cups red wine marinade (page 251), red wine pepper marinade (page 252), soy marinade (page 252), or Hawaiian soy marinade (page 253)

1. Place the steak in a large, heavy-duty resealable plastic bag or shallow baking dish and pour the marinade over the meat. Seal or cover, and refrigerate, turning occasionally, for at least 4 hours and up to 24 hours.

2. Prepare a hot fire in a gas or charcoal grill.

3. Mound the coals on just one side of the grill and place a drip pan on the other side. On a gas grill, turn off one gas burner and turn the other down to medium. Place a drip pan over the off burner.

4. Remove the steak from the marinade, letting excess marinade drip off. Sear the flank steak quickly on both sides over the hot burner or directly over the hot coals. Then move the steak over the drip pans, close the lid, and continue to grill for 15 minutes, turning once with a spatula. The flank steak will be cooked to rare; adjust the timing accordingly for medium.

5. Transfer the steak to a cutting board, cover loosely with aluminum foil, and let rest for 5 minutes.

6. Holding a knife at a 45-degree angle, cut the steak across the grain into thin slices and serve.

Grilled Steak Fajitas

The sautéed onion and bell peppers in fajitas are flavorful fixings, but what makes a fajita unique is the lime and cumin marinade, which gives the beef its special flavor.

SERVES 4

1 (1-pound) beef skirt steak or flank steak
¼ cup lime juice
5 tablespoons oil
2 teaspoons minced garlic
1 tablespoon chili powder
2 teaspoons ground cumin
1 teaspoon salt
Warm flour tortillas, to serve
1 large sweet onion, such as Maui, Walla Walla, or Vidalia, thinly sliced
1 medium green bell pepper, seeded and thinly sliced
1 medium red bell pepper, seeded and thinly sliced
1 medium yellow bell pepper, seeded and thinly sliced
Pico de gallo (page 56), to serve
Shredded Monterey Jack cheese, to serve
Sour cream, to serve
Guacamole (page 56), to serve

1. Place the steak in a large, heavy-duty resealable plastic bag or shallow baking dish. Combine the lime juice, 4 tablespoons of oil, garlic, chili powder, cumin, and salt in a small bowl. Set aside 3 tablespoons of marinade in the refrigerator. Pour the remaining marinade over the steak, seal or cover, and refrigerate for at least 2 hours, preferably overnight, turning occasionally.

2. Prepare a medium-hot fire in a gas or charcoal grill.

3. Remove the steak from the marinade, pat dry, and grill over medium-high heat for 4 to 5 minutes per side, until cooked through.

4. Cut the steak into thin strips; set aside and keep warm.

5. Preheat the oven to 225°F. Place the tortillas on an ovenproof plate, cover with aluminum foil, and keep warm in the oven until serving time.

6. Heat the remaining 1 tablespoon oil in a large skillet over medium-high heat. Add the onion and bell peppers and sauté until softened, about 5 minutes.

7. Remove from the heat and pour the reserved 3 tablespoons marinade over the vegetables. Add the steak and toss together.

8. Remove the tortillas from the oven and wrap in a clean cloth napkin. Serve the meat filling directly from the saucepan or in a prewarmed serving dish. Guests will assemble their own fajitas. Pass the pico de gallo, cheese, sour cream, and guacamole at the table.

Grilled Beef and Veggie Kebabs

Grilling hunks of meat on skewers is an ancient way of cooking. In the Middle East, where wood fuel was scarce, the meat was cut small and skewered to cook quickly. These kebabs have a definite Mediterranean flavor. Serve them on a bed of rice pilaf.

SERVES 6 TO 8

1 (2- to 2½-pound) boneless beef shoulder or top round, cut into 1-inch cubes
1 large sweet onion, such as Maui, Walla Walla, or Vidalia, cut into large chunks
2 large green bell peppers, seeded and cut into large chunks
¼ cup oil
⅓ cup lemon juice
2 teaspoons salt
1 teaspoon black pepper
2 garlic cloves, finely chopped
1 teaspoon dried rosemary leaves, crushed
16 cherry tomatoes
32 large pitted black olives
16 metal or bamboo skewers (soaked in water for 30 minutes)

1. Place the beef cubes, onion, and bell peppers in a large, heavy-duty resealable plastic bag or shallow baking dish. Whisk together the oil, lemon juice, salt, pepper, garlic, and rosemary in a small bowl. Pour over the meat and vegetables. Seal or cover and refrigerate for at least 4 hours and up to 8 hours, turning occasionally.

2. Prepare a hot fire in a gas or charcoal grill.

3. Drain off the marinade and thread the meat, onion, bell peppers, tomatoes, and olives onto the skewers, alternating until the skewers are full, leaving about ½ inch of open space on each end.

4. Grill over hot coals, turning often, until the meat is no longer pink, 8 to 12 minutes. Serve hot.

TIP: If you use metal skewers, choose flat-bladed ones because they make it easier to turn the kebabs. Bamboo skewers are more practical when cooking for a crowd, but they should be soaked in warm water for at least 30 minutes before using so they don't catch fire.

Herbed Grilled Steak Skewers

Cooking meat on skewers has the advantage of allowing you to customize each serving: a rare skewer comes off the grill quickly while a well-done skewer stays on a bit longer. If desired, you can also alternate the meat cubes on the skewers with large chunks of fresh vegetables like onions, bell peppers, and potatoes.

SERVES 6 TO 8

3 pounds beef top sirloin, cut into 1½-inch cubes
¾ cup dry red wine
¼ cup oil
1½ teaspoons minced garlic
2 teaspoons salt
¼ teaspoon black pepper
¼ teaspoon dried rosemary
¼ teaspoon dried thyme
Steak butter sauce (page 255)
6 to 8 metal or bamboo skewers (soaked in water for 30 minutes)

1. Place the beef cubes in a large, heavy-duty resealable plastic bag or shallow baking dish.

2. Whisk together the wine, oil, garlic, salt, pepper, rosemary, and thyme in a small bowl. Pour the marinade over the meat. Seal or cover and refrigerate for at least 4 hours, preferably overnight, turning occasionally.

3. Prepare a hot fire in a gas or charcoal grill.

4. Thread the meat onto the skewers until they are full, leaving about ½ inch of open space on each end.

5. Grill over hot coals, turning often and basting with the steak sauce, until the meat is no longer pink, 8 to 12 minutes. Serve hot.

Skewered Grilled Steak Teriyaki

Teriyaki is a sweet barbecue glaze, usually containing soy sauce. Use presoaked bamboo skewers and thread the meat strips so that each piece is pierced by the skewer in several places. Rice is the perfect accompaniment. Top sirloin makes a particularly good cut of beef for this recipe.

SERVES 6 TO 8

2 pounds top sirloin, cut into thin strips across the grain
¼ cup soy sauce
¼ cup dry sherry or rice wine
1 small onion, finely chopped
1 teaspoon minced garlic
1 tablespoon minced fresh ginger
6 to 8 metal or bamboo skewers (soaked in water for 30 minutes)

1. Place the meat in a large, heavy-duty resealable plastic bag or shallow baking dish.

2. Whisk together the soy sauce, sherry, onion, garlic, and ginger in a small bowl. Pour the marinade over the meat. Seal or cover and refrigerate for at least 4 hours, preferably overnight, turning occasionally.

3. Prepare a hot fire in a gas or charcoal grill.

4. Thread the meat strips onto the skewers until the skewers are full, leaving about ½ inch of open space on each end.

5. Grill briefly over hot coals, 3 to 4 minutes, turning often. Serve hot.

Grilled East-West Beef and Vegetable Kebabs

One theory is that the shish kebab was born when medieval Turkish soldiers would use their swords to grill small pieces of meat over fire. The method probably dates much earlier, given that the act of spit-roasting meat over fire has been around as long as fire has been used by humans. Chunks of beef partnered with vegetables is an American favorite, but lamb is still a big favorite in other countries.

SERVES 6 TO 8

2½ pounds beef round steak, cut into 1-inch cubes
¼ cup oil
½ cup soy sauce
⅓ cup lemon juice
2 tablespoons Worcestershire sauce
3 tablespoons finely chopped fresh parsley
1 to 2 garlic cloves, finely chopped
¼ teaspoon black pepper
12 small white boiling onions
1 large green bell pepper, seeded and cut into 1½-inch chunks
3 small zucchini, cut into 1½-inch chunks
16 cherry tomatoes
16 pineapple chunks (canned or fresh)
8 metal or bamboo skewers (soaked in water for 30 minutes)

1. Place the meat in a large, heavy-duty resealable plastic bag or shallow baking dish.

2. Whisk together the oil, soy sauce, lemon juice, Worcestershire sauce, parsley, garlic, and pepper in a small bowl. Reserve ¼ cup as a basting sauce. Pour the remaining marinade over the meat. Seal or cover and refrigerate for at least 4 hours, preferably overnight, turning occasionally.

3. Boil the onions in salted water for 3 minutes, until partially tender. Drain, immediately plunge into cold water to stop the cooking, drain well, and peel.

4. Prepare a hot fire in a gas or charcoal grill.

5. Thread the skewers with alternating pieces of meat, vegetables (including onions), and pineapple, using 4 cubes of meat on each skewer. Leave about ½ inch of open space on each end of the skewers.

6. Grill over hot coals, turning often, until the meat is no longer pink, 8 to 12 minutes, basting with the reserved marinade. Serve hot.

TIP: Never reuse marinade that has been in contact with raw meat.

Barbecued Beef Brisket

Texas barbecue must be cooked over an open fire on a spit or over a barbecue pit to be authentic. But a gas or charcoal grill can give you credible results. Using wood chips is best; add to the grill according to the manufacturer's directions.

SERVES 10 TO 12

1 (8- to 10-pound) beef brisket, untrimmed (it should have a thick layer of fat on one side)
Texas spice rub (page 251), Texas wet mop (page 253), or barbecue sauce of choice (page 254)
Wood chips (optional)
10 to 12 hamburger buns (optional)
Dill pickle slices, sliced onions, and/or pickled jalapeño chile peppers, to serve

1. Generously coat all sides of the brisket, particularly the fat layer, with the rub. Cover and let the meat come to room temperature, about 1 hour.

2. Prepare a medium fire in a gas or charcoal grill.

3. When the coals in the charcoal grill are covered with gray ash, push all the coals to one side of the grill and place a drip pan on the other side. Or turn off one side of the gas grill and place a drip pan over the off burner. If desired, add the wood chips according to the manufacturer's directions. Place the brisket on the grate over the drip pan. Cover the grill and cook, turning every hour or so and basting with the wet mop, until the brisket is tender and the internal temperature reaches 180°F, 8 to 10 hours. Keep a charcoal grill going by replenishing the coals and adding wood chips.

4. Remove the brisket from the grill and let rest for 20 minutes.

5. Trim off the fat layer and carve the brisket into thin slices across the grain.

6. Serve the slices on a plate with additional barbecue sauce, or stack slices between the bun halves and top with a little sauce. Pass the pickles, onions, and/or jalapeños at the table.

TIP: Disposable aluminum foil pans make excellent drip pans.

Barbecued Beef Short Ribs

Short ribs benefit tremendously from a tenderizing bath in a marinade, followed by long, slow, indirect grilling. Adding wood chips to the grill for extra smoke flavor is a tasty touch.

SERVES 4 TO 6

4 pounds beef short ribs
Red wine marinade (page 251), red wine pepper marinade (page 252), soy marinade (page 252), or Hawaiian soy marinade (page 253)
Wood chips (optional)

1. Place the ribs in a large, heavy-duty resealable plastic bag or shallow baking dish. Add the marinade, then seal or cover and refrigerate for 2 to 3 hours, turning occasionally.

2. Prepare a hot fire in a gas or charcoal grill.

3. Turn off one burner on a gas grill and place a drip pan over the off burner. Or push all the coals to one side of the grill and place a drip pan on the other side. Add the wood chips, if using. Remove the ribs from the marinade and position them on the grill over the drip pan. Cover the grill and cook, turning the ribs every 10 to 15 minutes, for 1¼ to 1½ hours, until tender. Serve hot.

Grilled Beef Back Ribs

Beef back ribs are grilled just as pork spareribs are—and in truth, this recipe would work for pork as well. The cider vinegar and dark flavors of the Texas rub make a marvelous combination. Wood chips added to the fire will give a smoky taste.

SERVES 10

10 pounds beef back ribs
1 cup cider vinegar
½ cup Texas spice rub (page 251)
Texas wet mop (page 253)
Wood chips (optional)

1. Rub the meat thoroughly with vinegar until it is moistened.

2. Rub the spice mixture into the meat, covering every surface well. Set aside.

3. Prepare a hot fire in a gas or charcoal grill.

4. When the coals in the charcoal grill are covered with gray ash, push all the coals to one side of the grill and place a drip pan on the other side. Or turn off one side of the gas grill and place a drip pan over the off burner. If desired, add wood chips according to the manufacturer's directions. Place the ribs, meat side up, on the grate over the drip pan. Cover the grill and cook, turning every half-hour or so and basting with the wet mop, until the ribs are tender, 2 to 2½ hours. Keep a charcoal grill going by replenishing the coals and adding wood chips. Serve hot.

Southern Barbecued Pork Spareribs

The fact that these ribs are made from pork, not beef, places the recipe's origins east of the Mississippi. The absence of tomato or ketchup in the marinade indicates that these spareribs are typical of those from the eastern part of North Carolina.

SERVES 4 TO 6

4 to 5 pounds pork spareribs
3 cups cider vinegar
2 cups firmly packed brown sugar
1 teaspoon salt
1 teaspoon black pepper
1 teaspoon paprika
½ teaspoon cayenne pepper
1½ to 2 teaspoons minced garlic
Wood chips (optional)

1. Place the ribs in a large, heavy-duty resealable plastic bag or glass baking dish. Combine the vinegar, brown sugar, salt, black pepper, paprika, cayenne pepper, and garlic in a large bowl. Pour over the ribs, cover, and refrigerate overnight, turning occasionally.

2. Prepare a hot fire in a gas or charcoal grill.

3. When the coals in the charcoal grill are covered with gray ash, push all the coals to one side of the grill and place a drip pan on the other side. Or turn off one side of the gas grill and place a drip pan over the off burner. If desired, add wood chips according to the manufacturer's directions. Transfer the ribs from the marinade to a plate and reserve the marinade.

4. Place the ribs, meat side up, on the grate over the drip pan. Cover the grill and cook for 30 minutes.

5. Meanwhile, pour the reserved marinade into a nonreactive saucepan and bring to a boil. Boil for 10 minutes.

6. After 30 minutes of grilling, turn the ribs and baste with the boiled marinade. Close the grill and continue cooking, turning every 30 minutes or so and basting with the marinade, until the ribs are tender, about 2 to 2½ hours. Keep a charcoal grill going by replenishing the coals and adding wood chips. Serve hot.

Grilled Pork Spareribs

Sweet and hot is a good way to describe these tender, juicy ribs. Have extra napkins on hand when serving.

SERVES 4 TO 6

2 cups hot water
1 cup ketchup
½ cup finely chopped onion
¼ cup Worcestershire sauce
¼ cup red-wine vinegar
¼ cup firmly packed brown sugar
1 medium lemon, thinly sliced
1 teaspoon chili powder
1 teaspoon celery salt
1 teaspoon salt
½ teaspoon ground ginger or 1 teaspoon grated fresh
¼ teaspoon black pepper
¼ teaspoon hot pepper sauce, such as Tabasco, or more to taste
Wood chips (optional)
4 to 5 pounds pork spareribs

1. Combine the water, ketchup, onion, Worcestershire sauce, vinegar, brown sugar, lemon, chili powder, celery salt, salt, ginger, pepper, and hot pepper sauce in a medium saucepan over medium heat. Simmer for 1 hour.

2. Prepare a hot fire in a gas or charcoal grill.

3. When the coals in the charcoal grill are covered with gray ash, push all the coals to one side of the grill and place a drip pan on the other side. Or turn off one side of the gas grill and place a drip pan over the off burner. If desired, add wood chips according to the manufacturer's directions. Place the ribs, meat side up, on the grate over the drip pan. Cover the grill and cook, turning every half-hour or so and basting with the sauce, until the ribs are tender, 2 to 2½ hours. Keep a charcoal grill going by replenishing the coals and adding wood chips. Serve hot.

Grilled Dry-Rub Pork Spareribs

These slow-grilled ribs take a while to cook, but they're well worth the wait. The tender, smoky-sweet flavor can only be achieved through patience, frequent visits to replenish the coals, and turning the ribs.

SERVES 4 TO 6

4 to 5 pounds pork spareribs
¼ cup liquid smoke, such as Wright's
    Concentrated Hickory Seasoning
1 small onion, chopped
½ teaspoon minced garlic
2 teaspoons chopped fresh parsley
1½ teaspoons salt
¼ teaspoon dried rosemary
¼ teaspoon ground ginger
¼ teaspoon black pepper
½ cup dry sherry
2 tablespoons brown sugar
2 tablespoons tomato paste

1. Brush the ribs well with liquid smoke and place in a shallow baking dish. In a small bowl, combine the onion, garlic, and parsley and sprinkle over the meat. Combine the salt, rosemary, ginger, and pepper in a separate small bowl and sprinkle over the meat. Cover with aluminum foil or plastic wrap and refrigerate overnight.

2. In a small bowl, combine the sherry, brown sugar, and tomato paste to make a basting sauce.

3. Prepare a hot fire in a gas or charcoal grill.

4. When the coals in the charcoal grill are covered with gray ash, push all the coals to one side of the grill and place a drip pan on the other side. Or turn off one side of the gas grill and place a drip pan over the off burner. Place the ribs, meat side up, on the grate over the drip pan. Cover the grill and cook, turning every half-hour or so and basting with the sauce, until the ribs are tender, 2 to 2½ hours. Keep a charcoal grill going by replenishing the coals. Serve hot.

Grilled Baby Back Ribs

Here's another recipe where liquid smoke replaces wood chips when grilling. This sauce is spicier than the sauce in the previous recipe. For even more spice, replace the paprika with cayenne pepper.

SERVES 4 TO 6

1½ tablespoons butter
1 medium onion, chopped
½ cup water
½ cup chili sauce
½ cup molasses
½ cup firmly packed brown sugar
¼ cup cider vinegar
2 tablespoons Worcestershire sauce
2 teaspoons liquid smoke, such as Wright's
    Concentrated Hickory Seasoning
2 teaspoons dry mustard
½ teaspoon black pepper
½ teaspoon paprika
3 to 4 pounds baby back ribs, trimmed of fat

1. Melt the butter in a medium saucepan over medium heat. Add the onion and sauté until softened, about 3 minutes. Stir in the water, chili sauce, molasses, brown sugar, vinegar, Worcestershire sauce, liquid smoke, mustard, pepper, and paprika. Bring to a boil over high heat. Reduce the heat and simmer for 30 to 35 minutes.

2. Prepare a hot fire in a gas or charcoal grill.

3. When the coals in the charcoal grill are covered with gray ash, push all the coals to one side of the grill and place a drip pan on the other side. Or turn off one side of the gas grill and place a drip pan over the off burner. Place the ribs, meat side up, on the grate over the drip pan. Cover the grill and cook, turning every half-hour or so and basting with the sauce, until the ribs are tender, about 2 hours. Keep a charcoal grill going by replenishing the coals. Serve hot.

TIP: Set aside some of the sauce for serving with the ribs, but do not dip your brush into this reserved sauce. This keeps the sauce free from contamination from uncooked meat.

Hawaiian Luau Pork Ribs

Turn your next backyard party into a luau with these ribs on the menu. Serve with an assortment of cold and hot pupus (appetizers), light the backyard with tiki torches, decorate the tables with flowers and imitation hula grass, adorn your guests with leis, sip Mai Tais, and throw on some Don Ho or Hawaiian slack-key guitar music.

SERVES 8 TO 10

½ cup soy sauce
½ cup sugar
½ cup firmly packed brown sugar
½ cup ketchup
2 tablespoons dry sherry
1 tablespoon minced fresh ginger
½ teaspoon minced garlic
1 teaspoon salt
8 to 10 pounds baby back ribs
Wood chips (optional)

1. Combine the soy sauce, sugars, ketchup, sherry, ginger, garlic, and salt in a small bowl. Place the meat in a baking dish. Rub the mixture into the meat. Pour half the remaining marinade over the top and reserve the rest. Cover and refrigerate for at least 3 hours, preferably overnight, turning occasionally.

2. Prepare a hot fire in a gas or charcoal grill.

3. When the coals in the charcoal grill are covered with gray ash, push all the coals to one side of the grill and place a drip pan on the other side. Or turn off one side of the gas grill and place a drip pan over the off burner. If desired, add wood chips according to the manufacturer's directions. Place the ribs, meat side up, on the grate over the drip pan. Cover the grill and cook, turning every half-hour or so basting with the reserved marinade, until the ribs are tender, about 2 hours. Keep a charcoal grill going by replenishing the coals and adding wood chips. Serve hot.

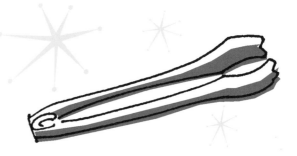

Pulled Pork Barbecue

Traditionally, pulled pork barbecue is served either straight, piled high on a plate with side dishes, or on hamburger buns with a side of coleslaw. When making sandwiches, pile on the meat and drizzle on a little barbecue sauce.

SERVES 6 TO 12

Pork:
2 (3-pound) boneless halves pork shoulder
    (also known as Boston butt), untrimmed
3 tablespoons black pepper
3 tablespoons brown sugar
2 tablespoons paprika
2 tablespoons salt
1 teaspoon cayenne pepper

Mop:
1 cup cider vinegar
½ cup water
1 tablespoon Worcestershire sauce
1 tablespoon black pepper
1 tablespoon salt
2 teaspoons oil

4 cups wood chips, soaked in water for about
    1 hour
Barbecue sauce of choice (page 254), to serve

1. To prepare the pork, place the meat, fat side up, on a clean work surface. Cut each piece in half lengthwise, to have four long strips. Place the strips on a baking sheet.

2. Combine the black pepper, brown sugar, paprika, salt, and cayenne pepper in a small bowl and mix well. Sprinkle the mixture all over the pork, rubbing it into the meat and covering it completely. Cover and chill for at least 2 hours or overnight.

3. To make the mop, combine all the ingredients in a medium bowl and set aside.

4. Prepare a hot fire in a gas or charcoal grill.

5. When the coals in the charcoal grill are covered with gray ash, push all the coals to one side of the grill and place an aluminum foil loaf pan on the other side. Or turn off one side of the gas grill and place an aluminum foil loaf pan over the off burner. Add wood chips according to the manufacturer's directions.

6. Fill the loaf pan halfway with water. Arrange the pork, fat side up, on the upper grill rack above the foil pan. Close the lid.

7. Check the temperature after 5 minutes. Use the vent to maintain a temperature of 225° to 250°F, opening the vent wider to increase heat and closing to decrease heat.

8. Keep a charcoal grill going by replenishing the coals and adding wood chips. Cook turning every half hour or so brushing the pork lightly with the mop. The pork is done when a meat thermometer inserted into the meat registers 165° to 170°F, about 3 hours total.

9. Transfer the pork to a baking sheet and let stand for 10 minutes. When the meat is cool enough to handle, use 2 forks or your fingers to pull apart the meat, shredding it into bite-size pieces and discarding any fat. Mix any meat juices from the baking sheet into the pork. Stir into the meat any crusty bits of meat from the edges of the meat—this is referred to as "outside." If desired, stir some barbecue sauce into the meat to moisten it, but don't overwhelm it with sauce. Serve with additional barbecue sauce at the table.

Grilled Pork Tenderloin with Mustard Glaze

The tenderloin is a fairly lean cut, so it benefits from being grilled away from direct heat. The mustard glaze helps to seal in flavor and juices.

SERVES 6 TO 8

½ cup Dijon mustard
3 tablespoons oil
1 teaspoon minced garlic
½ teaspoon dried rosemary
¼ teaspoon black pepper
2 (¾- to 1-pound) pork tenderloins

1. Combine the mustard, oil, garlic, rosemary, and pepper in a small bowl. Rub into the meat. Cover and refrigerate for 30 to 60 minutes.

2. Prepare a hot fire in a gas or charcoal grill.

3. When the coals in the charcoal grill are covered with gray ash, push all the coals to one side of the grill and place a drip pan on the other side. Or turn off one side of the gas grill and place a drip pan over the off burner. Place the meat on the grate over the drip pan. Cover the grill and cook, turning once or twice, for 25 to 35 minutes, or until the meat's internal temperature registers 150° to 155°F.

4. Let stand for 5 minutes, then slice and serve.

Caribbean Pork Roast

*Caribbean foods blend sweet and spicy flavors.
This dish is reminiscent of the spicy jerk pork sold at
roadside stands throughout the island of Jamaica.
Serve with grilled corn and rice.*

SERVES 6 TO 8

1 (3-pound) boneless pork shoulder roast
3 tablespoons soy sauce
2 tablespoons oil
2 tablespoons cider vinegar
2 tablespoons water
1 tablespoon minced onion
2 teaspoons sugar
2 teaspoons dried thyme
1 teaspoon ground allspice
1 teaspoon cayenne pepper
½ teaspoon ground cinnamon
¼ teaspoon ground nutmeg
Wood chips (optional)

1. With a sharp fork, poke 8 to 10 holes in the roast. Place the pork in a large, heavy-duty resealable plastic bag or glass baking dish. In a small bowl, mix the soy sauce, oil, vinegar, water, onion, sugar, thyme, allspice, cayenne pepper, cinnamon, and nutmeg. Pour over the roast, turning the meat so it is evenly coated. Seal or cover and refrigerate overnight, turning occasionally.

2. Prepare a hot fire in a gas or charcoal grill.

3. When the coals in the charcoal grill are covered with gray ash, push all the coals to one side of the grill and place a drip pan on the other side. Or turn off one side of the gas grill and place a drip pan over the off burner. If desired, add wood chips according to the manufacturer's directions. Place the meat on the grate over the drip pan. Cover the grill and cook, turning every half-hour or so, for 20 to 22 minutes per pound, until the meat is tender and its internal temperature registers 170°F, 1 to 1¼ hours. Keep a charcoal grill going by replenishing the coals and adding wood chips.

4. Remove the roast from the grill and let stand for 10 minutes on a serving platter. Slice and serve hot.

Beer Brats

*The beer brat is Wisconsin's soul food, served virtually
everywhere during grilling season, which runs May through
September in the North Country. At a Wisconsin "brat fry,"
the bratwurst are cooked on a grate over charcoal, usually
on a kettle grill, and served with "bratwash" (chilled beer).
In Sheboygan, brats are typically dressed with "the works"—
ketchup, mustard, chopped onion, and pickle. To be authentic,
serve on a proper brat bun, which is bigger and chewier than a
hot dog bun. A good-quality roll will also do the trick.*

SERVES 10

10 fresh bratwurst
3 (12-ounce) bottles or cans beer
1 large onion, chopped, plus more to serve
½ cup (1 stick) butter
10 brat buns or rolls
Ketchup, to serve
German brown mustard, to serve

1. Prepare a hot fire in a gas or charcoal grill.

2. Place the bratwurst on the grill 7 to 9 inches above the coals and grill, turning often, for 20 to 25 minutes, or until the brats feel firm when squeezed.

3. While the brats grill, mix the beer, onion, and butter in a large, shallow saucepan or ovenproof baking pan and bring to a simmer on the grill; do not allow it to boil.

4. Place the cooked bratwurst in the beer sauce, close the grill, and keep warm until ready to serve.

5. Place one bratwurst in each bun and serve, passing the ketchup, mustard, and additional onion at the table.

Patio Hot Dogs

When grilling for a crowd, never underestimate the popularity of a good old-fashioned hot dog. Kids may turn up their noses at lamb or shrimp, but for hot dogs, kids come in all ages. It is important to provide all the standard fixings.

SERVES 8

8 to 16 medium hot dogs (preferably natural casing)
8 to 16 hot dog buns (preferably bakery made)
Mustard relish or other sweet pickle relish with mustard, to serve
1 medium onion, chopped, to serve
Prepared yellow mustard, to serve
Ketchup, to serve

1. Prepare a hot fire in a gas or charcoal grill.

2. Grill the hot dogs directly over the hot fire, uncovered, for 3 to 5 minutes over high heat until deeply browned, rolling to cook all the surfaces. If you like, toast the buns on the edge of the grill for about 30 seconds; watch them carefully.

3. Arrange the dogs on the buns and supply the relish, onions, mustard, and ketchup as desired. Serve immediately.

Grilled Rack of Lamb

Lamb ribs or "chops" are much more delicate than pork or beef ribs. They benefit from quick grilling over hot coals in a grill that isn't covered. Americans often serve lamb with mint jelly, but here the mint appears in the marinade.

SERVES 4

2 (8-rib) racks of lamb
⅓ cup lemon juice
¼ cup dry white wine
¼ cup chopped fresh mint
3 tablespoons chopped shallots
2 tablespoons finely grated lemon zest
1 tablespoon chopped fresh rosemary or 1 teaspoon dried
1 teaspoon dried oregano
½ cup oil
Salt and pepper

1. Trim the fat from the racks, leaving a ⅛-inch layer. Place the rack in a large, heavy-duty resealable plastic bag or glass baking dish. Combine the lemon juice, wine, mint, shallots, lemon zest, rosemary, and oregano in a small bowl. Whisk in the oil until blended and season to taste with salt and pepper. Pour the marinade over the meat and marinate in the refrigerator for 2 to 8 hours, turning occasionally.

2. Prepare a hot fire in a gas or charcoal grill.

3. Transfer the meat from the marinade to a plate. Pour the marinade into a saucepan and bring to a boil. Boil for 10 minutes and set aside.

4. Place the racks, fat side down, on a grill over red-hot coals and sear on an open grill for 1 minute. Turn and sear the other side for 1 minute. Turn back onto the fat side and cook for approximately 12 minutes, basting occasionally with the boiled marinade. Turn again and cover the grill. Grill for about 12 minutes more, until the rack is medium-rare. Test for doneness by carving between the ribs and checking the color. Serve hot off the grill.

Mediterranean Lamb Shish Kebabs

Because meat tenderizes in a marinade, tougher meat from the lamb shoulder can be used, although meat from the leg is always an option. A large Greek salad is the perfect accompaniment.

SERVES 4 TO 6

2 pounds boneless leg of lamb, cut into 1¼-inch cubes

1 large sweet onion, such as Maui, Walla Walla, or Vidalia, cut into large chunks

2 large green bell peppers, seeded and cut into large chunks

¼ cup oil

⅓ cup lemon juice

2 teaspoons salt

1 teaspoon black pepper

1 teaspoon minced garlic

1 teaspoon dried rosemary leaves, crushed

16 cherry tomatoes

16 metal or bamboo skewers (soaked in water for 30 minutes)

1. Place the meat, onion, and bell pepper in a large, heavy-duty resealable plastic bag or shallow baking dish. Whisk together the oil, lemon juice, salt, pepper, garlic, and rosemary in a small bowl. Pour over the meat and vegetables. Refrigerate for at least 4 hours and up to 8 hours, turning occasionally.

2. Prepare a hot fire in a gas or charcoal grill.

3. Drain off the marinade and thread the meat, onion, bell peppers, and tomatoes onto the skewers. Alternate until the skewers are full, leaving about ½ inch of open space on each end.

4. Grill over hot coals, turning often, until the meat is light pink, 6 to 8 minutes. Serve hot.

Grilled Leg of Lamb

Grilling a boneless leg of lamb eliminates the carving quandary—it is difficult to cut around the bone. Also, opening up the tied roast guarantees that the garlicky herbal marinade penetrates every inch of meat. The use of wood chips is optional but recommended.

SERVES 8

1 (4- to 5-pound) boneless leg of lamb

¼ cup oil

¼ cup balsamic vinegar

1 tablespoon minced garlic

1 tablespoon minced fresh rosemary or 1 teaspoon dried

2 teaspoons salt

½ teaspoon black pepper

½ teaspoon sugar

Wood chips (optional)

1. Remove any netting or string from the lamb. Unroll the roast and place in a large, nonreactive roasting pan. Whisk together the oil, vinegar, garlic, rosemary, salt, pepper, and sugar in a small bowl. Pour over the lamb, cover, and refrigerate for 6 to 24 hours, turning occasionally.

2. Prepare a hot fire in a gas or charcoal grill.

3. Roll up the leg of lamb and tie with kitchen string.

4. When the coals in the charcoal grill are covered with gray ash, push all the coals to one side of the grill and place a drip pan on the other side. Or turn off one side of the gas grill and place a drip pan over the off burner. If desired, add wood chips according to the manufacturer's directions. Place the meat on the grate over the drip pan. Cover the grill and cook for 1¼ to 1½ hours, turning every half-hour or so, until the meat is tender and the internal temperature registers 120°F for rare or 135° for medium. Keep a charcoal grill going by replenishing the coals and adding wood chips.

5. Transfer the leg to a serving platter and let stand for 10 minutes. The meat will continue to cook another 5 degrees. Slice and serve hot.

Grill-Roasted Whole Chicken

A skilled griller can turn out a juicy whole chicken. The secret is indirect heat. This recipe calls for lemon in the cavity of the chicken to perfume the flesh.

1 (4- to 6-pound) roasting chicken
2 medium lemons
3 tablespoons oil
1 tablespoon minced garlic
1 teaspoon salt
¼ teaspoon black pepper
Wood chips (optional)

1. Prepare a hot fire in a gas or charcoal grill.

2. Wash the chicken thoroughly and pat dry with paper towels.

3. Juice the lemons, reserving the rinds. Mix the lemon juice, oil, garlic, salt, and pepper in a small bowl. Rub the chicken inside and out with the mixture. Stuff the chicken cavity with the lemon rinds.

4. When the coals in the charcoal grill are covered with gray ash, push all the coals to one side of the grill and place a drip pan on the other side. Or turn off one side of the gas grill and place a drip pan over the off burner. If desired, add wood chips according to the manufacturer's directions. Lightly oil the grill. Place the chicken, breast side up, on the grate over the drip pan. Cover the grill and cook for 1¼ to 1½ hours, until the interior temperature of the meat registers 170°F.

5. Transfer from the grill to a serving platter and let stand for 10 minutes. Carve and serve hot or cold.

Simple Grilled Chicken

There is nothing fancy about this recipe, but a perfectly grilled chicken is worthy of celebration. It should have crackling crisp skin and moist, tender flesh. Keep a close eye on it while grilling because the white meat may be done before the dark meat.

3 to 4 pounds chicken parts
¼ cup oil
¼ cup lemon juice
1 teaspoon minced garlic
1 tablespoon chopped fresh thyme
2 teaspoons salt
¼ teaspoon black pepper
Wood chips (optional)

1. Place the chicken in a large, heavy-duty resealable plastic bag or baking dish. Whisk together the oil, lemon juice, garlic, thyme, salt, and pepper in a small bowl. Pour half the mixture over the chicken, seal or cover, and refrigerate for 1 to 4 hours, turning occasionally. Reserve the remaining marinade to use as a basting sauce.

2. Prepare a hot fire in a gas or charcoal grill.

3. When the coals in the charcoal grill are covered with gray ash, push all the coals to one side of the grill and place a drip pan on the other side. Or turn off one side of the gas grill and place a drip pan over the off burner. If desired, add wood chips according to the manufacturer's directions. Lightly oil the grill. Place the chicken pieces, skin side down, on the grate over the drip pan. Cover the grill and cook for 25 minutes. Baste with the reserved marinade, turn the chicken over, skin side up, and baste again. Cover the grill and continue to cook for another 15 to 20 minutes, until the juices run clear and the chicken shows no pink against the bone.

4. Transfer the chicken to a serving platter and let stand for 10 minutes. Serve hot or cold.

Grilled Chicken with Barbecue Sauce

When someone mentions barbecued chicken, this is the recipe that comes to mind. Many people make the mistake of grilling chicken with the skin on directly over the coals, where the dripping grease inevitably causes flare-ups that char the outside of the chicken while leaving the meat raw near the bone. Grilling over indirect heat solves that problem.

SERVES 4 TO 6

Wood chips (optional)
3 to 4 pounds chicken parts
3 tablespoons butter
1 medium onion, chopped
1½ teaspoons minced garlic
1 (8-ounce) can tomato sauce
¼ cup chili sauce
2 tablespoons firmly packed brown sugar
2 tablespoons Worcestershire sauce
1 teaspoon chili powder
½ teaspoon salt
½ teaspoon black pepper

1. Prepare a hot fire in a gas or charcoal grill.

2. When the coals in the charcoal grill are covered with gray ash, push all the coals to one side of the grill and place a drip pan on the other side. Or turn off one side of the gas grill and place a drip pan over the off burner. If desired, add wood chips according to the manufacturer's directions. Lightly oil the grill. Place the chicken pieces, skin side down, on the grate over the drip pan. Cover the grill and cook for 25 minutes.

3. Meanwhile, melt the butter in a medium saucepan over medium heat. Add the onion and garlic and sauté until the onion is softened, about 3 minutes. Stir in the tomato sauce, chili sauce, brown sugar, Worcestershire sauce, chili powder, salt, and pepper. Simmer for about 5 minutes to blend the flavors.

4. Baste the chicken pieces with the barbecue sauce, turn over, skin side up, and baste again. Cover the grill and continue to cook for another 15 to 20 minutes, until the juices run clear and the chicken shows no pink against the bone.

5. Transfer the chicken from the grill to a serving platter and let stand for 10 minutes. Serve hot or cold.

TIP: Reserve some of the basting sauce in a bowl where it doesn't have contact with the basting brush. Serve with the chicken.

Beer-Basted Grilled Chicken

The beer is in the marinade, not in the can. It does a marvelous job of tenderizing the chicken, as well as deepening the color and enhancing the flavor.

SERVES 4 TO 6

3 to 4 pounds chicken parts
1 (12-ounce) bottle or can beer
3 tablespoons lemon juice
2 tablespoons brown sugar
1 tablespoon molasses
1 teaspoon grated orange zest
1 teaspoon salt
¼ teaspoon black pepper
Dash of hot pepper sauce, such as Tabasco
Wood chips (optional)

1. Place the chicken in a large, heavy-duty resealable plastic bag or baking dish. Whisk together the beer, lemon juice, brown sugar, molasses, orange zest, salt, pepper, and hot pepper sauce in a small bowl. Pour half the mixture over the chicken, seal or cover, and refrigerate for 1 to 4 hours, turning occasionally. Reserve the remaining marinade.

2. Prepare a hot fire in a gas or charcoal grill.

3. When the coals in the charcoal grill are covered with gray ash, push all the coals to one side of the grill and place a drip pan on the other side. Or turn off one side of the gas grill and place a drip pan over the off burner. If desired, add wood chips according to the manufacturer's directions. Lightly oil the grill. Place the chicken pieces, skin side down, on the grate over the drip pan. Cover the grill and cook for 25 minutes. Baste with the reserved marinade, turn the pieces over, skin side up, and baste again. Cover the grill and continue to cook for another 15 to 20 minutes, until the

juices run clear and the chicken shows no pink against the bone.

4. Remove from the grill and transfer to a serving platter; let stand for 10 minutes. Serve hot or cold.

Grill-Roasted Beer-Can Chicken

Grilling a chicken on a rotisserie guarantees moist results because the bird self-bastes as it turns. Not everyone owns a rotisserie, but a can of beer can act as a folksy backyard alternative. The chicken is positioned over a half-filled can of beer and the resulting recipe is called beer-can chicken or chicken on the throne.

SERVES 4 TO 6

1 (4- to 6-pound) roasting chicken
Salt and pepper
3 tablespoons Texas spice rub (page 251)
Wood chips (optional)
1 (12-ounce) can beer
2 tablespoons chopped onion
1½ teaspoons minced garlic

1. Prepare a hot fire in a gas or charcoal grill.

2. Wash the chicken thoroughly; pat dry with paper towels. Season the bird generously with salt and pepper inside and out. Massage the spice rub all over the chicken, inside and out. Lift up the skin over the breast and rub the spice mixture directly onto the meat beneath.

3. When the coals in the charcoal grill are covered with gray ash, push all the coals to one side of the grill and place a drip pan on the other side. Or turn off one side of the gas grill and place a drip pan over the off burner. If desired, add wood chips according to the manufacturer's directions.

4. Open the beer can and pour out (or drink) about ¼ cup. With a church-key can opener, punch 2 more large holes in the top of the can (for a total of 3 holes). Add the onion and garlic to the beer remaining in the can. Slide the chicken over the can so that the drumsticks reach down to the bottom of the can and the chicken is standing up on its legs. Place the chicken and beer can on the grate over the drip pan. Use the ends of the drumsticks to help steady the bird. Cover and grill for 1¼ to 1½ hours, rotating the bird and can 180 degrees after 35 to 40 minutes to ensure even cooking, until the thickest part of the thigh registers 170°F.

5. Carefully transfer the chicken and can to a platter or tray, making sure to keep the can upright. Let rest for 15 minutes.

6. Lift the chicken off the can and onto a platter or cutting board. Discard the remaining beer and can. Carve and serve.

Yucatan Chicken

This lime and cumin marinade is similar to the marinade used for fajitas. Indeed, if you wish to make chicken fajitas, replace the chicken pieces with boneless breasts and use this marinade. Serve with flour tortillas, guacamole, pico de gallo, sour cream, and shredded cheese.

SERVES 4 TO 6

3 to 4 pounds chicken parts
2 tablespoons oil
2 tablespoons lime juice
1 teaspoon minced garlic
1 teaspoon chili powder
1 teaspoon salt
½ teaspoon ground cumin
½ teaspoon grated lime zest
¼ teaspoon black pepper
Wood chips (optional)

1. Place the chicken in a large, heavy-duty resealable plastic bag or baking dish. Whisk together the oil, lime juice, garlic, chili powder, salt, cumin, lime zest, and pepper in a small bowl. Pour half the mixture over the chicken, seal or cover, and refrigerate for 1 to 4 hours, turning occasionally. Reserve the remaining marinade.

2. Prepare a hot fire in a gas or charcoal grill.

3. When the coals in the charcoal grill are covered with gray ash, push all the coals to one side of the grill and place a drip pan on the other side. Or turn off one side of the gas grill and place a drip pan over the off burner. If desired, add wood chips according to the manufacturer's directions. Lightly oil the grill. Place the chicken pieces, skin side down, on the grate over the drip pan. Cover the grill and cook for 25 minutes. Baste with the reserved marinade, turn over the pieces, skin side

up, and baste again. Cover the grill and continue to cook for another 15 to 25 minutes, until the juices run clear and the chicken shows no pink against the bone.

4. Transfer the chicken to a serving platter and let stand for 10 minutes. Serve hot or cold.

Skewered Grilled Chicken Teriyaki

A small hibachi grill isn't suitable for most chicken dishes because chicken grills best over indirect heat. Not so with these quick-cooking strips of delicious chicken; a tiny hibachi is perfect. The sugar in the glaze caramelizes the chicken, creating a crisp, savory crust.

SERVES 4

1¼ pounds chicken tenders
½ cup soy sauce
⅓ cup dry sherry
¼ cup oil
¼ cup firmly packed brown sugar
¼ cup rice vinegar
1 tablespoon minced fresh ginger
1 teaspoon minced garlic
Metal or bamboo skewers (soaked in water for 30 minutes)

1. Place the chicken in a large, heavy-duty resealable plastic bag or baking dish. Whisk together the soy sauce, sherry, oil, brown sugar, vinegar, ginger, and garlic in a small bowl. Pour the marinade over the chicken, seal or cover, and refrigerate for 1 to 2 hours, turning occasionally.

2. Prepare a medium fire in a gas or charcoal grill.

3. Thread the chicken strips onto the skewers, piercing the chicken with the skewers at least twice. Leave about ½ inch of open space on each end.

4. Lightly oil the grill. Cook the skewered chicken for 8 to 10 minutes, turning once. Check for doneness by cutting into one piece and checking to be sure it is opaque all the way through. Serve hot off the grill.

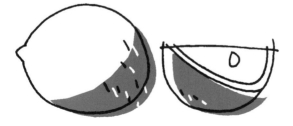

Grilled Halibut with Garlic-Basil Butter

Halibut is a great fish choice for grilling because it has moist, sweet, firm, mild, white flesh. To avoid having the fish stick to the grill, make sure that the grill is clean and hot before you put on the fish, and that the fish is well coated with oil. Another way to prevent sticking is to use a hinged wire grill basket sprayed with nonstick cooking spray.

SERVES 6

½ cup (1 stick) butter, softened
1 teaspoon minced garlic
Pinch of black pepper
½ cup finely chopped fresh basil
6 (6- to 8-ounce) halibut steaks, each about
    1 inch thick
3 tablespoons oil
Paprika
White pepper

1. Cream the butter with the garlic and black pepper in a small bowl. With a fork, work in the basil until the butter is thoroughly blended. Place on a sheet of wax paper or plastic wrap, form into a log shape, and refrigerate.

2. Prepare a medium-hot fire in a gas or charcoal grill.

3. Rinse the fish and pat dry with paper towels. Brush with the oil and sprinkle with the paprika and white pepper.

4. Lightly oil the grill. Cook the fish steaks 4 to 6 inches above the coals, turning once with a spatula, for a total of 8 to 10 minutes. Check doneness by inserting a knife between layers of the flesh. The meat should be just translucent. Serve hot with a slice of the garlic basil butter on top of each serving.

Grilled Salmon Steaks with Honey-Mustard Sauce

The sweet honey–mustard sauce is the perfect contrast to the white wine marinade. This recipe would also work with halibut, swordfish, or tuna. As with most fish, don't marinate for longer than 30 minutes or it will become soft.

SERVES 4

4 (6- to 8-ounce) salmon steaks, each about
    ¾ inch thick
White wine marinade (page 252)
1 tablespoon butter
2 tablespoons chopped shallots
⅓ cup Dijon mustard
2 tablespoons honey
1 teaspoon soy sauce

1. Place the fish in a large, heavy-duty resealable plastic bag or baking dish. Pour the marinade over the fish, seal or cover, and set aside for 30 minutes.

2. Prepare a medium fire in a gas or charcoal grill.

3. Meanwhile, melt the butter in a small saucepan over medium heat. Add the shallots and sauté until softened, about 3 minutes. Remove from the heat and stir in the mustard, honey, and soy sauce.

4. Lightly oil the grill. Cook the fish steaks 4 to 6 inches above the coals for 4 minutes. Turn the steaks with a spatula and spread each with one-quarter of the sauce. Cook until the fish is opaque when pierced in the center with the tip of a sharp knife, about 4 more minutes. Serve hot, passing the remaining sauce at the table.

Whole Grilled Fish

There's nothing more dramatic than presenting a grilled whole fish. This method applies to any fish, from a 2-pound snapper to a 6-pound salmon. Allow about 8 to 10 ounces of fish per person. To gauge the cooking time, lay the fish on a work surface and use a ruler to measure it at its thickest part. Give about 10 minutes of grill time for every inch of thickness.

SERVES 4 TO 10

1 (2- to 6-pound) whole fish, such as striped bass, sea bass, grouper, red snapper, or salmon, cleaned and dressed
2 to 6 tablespoons oil
1 to 3 tablespoons fresh lemon juice
½ teaspoon dried basil
½ teaspoon dried thyme
Salt and pepper
Wood chips (optional)
Lemon wedges, to serve

1. Rinse the fish inside and out and pat dry with paper towels. Cut 1- to 1½-inch-deep slashes into both sides of the fish. Rub the outside with oil and drizzle with the lemon juice. Sprinkle the basil, thyme, salt and pepper inside and out. Let stand at room temperature while the fire is being prepared.

2. Prepare a hot fire in a gas or charcoal grill.

3. When the coals in the charcoal grill are covered with gray ash, push all the coals to one side of the grill and place a drip pan on the other side. Or turn off one side of the gas grill and place a drip pan over the off burner. If desired, add wood chips according to the manufacturer's directions. Lightly oil the grill. Place the fish directly over the hot coals or the on burner. Grill, uncovered, for about 2 minutes, until the skin shows grill marks. Turn the fish over with a wide spatula and move to the side over the drip pan. Cover the grill and cook until the flesh looks opaque when pierced in the thickest part with the tip of a knife, 10 to 30 minutes, depending on the thickness of the fish.

4. Transfer to a serving dish (some skin may stick to the grill) and serve garnished with the lemon wedges.

Veracruz Grilled Snapper

Veracruz, along the Gulf Coast of Mexico, is famous for cooking fish and shellfish in a tomato sauce flavored with chile peppers, onion, garlic, oregano, and lime juice. This dish would appear as "Huachinango Veracruz" on menus there.

SERVES 6

3 pounds snapper fillets
Juice of 1 medium lime
Salt
2 tablespoons oil
1 large onion, chopped
1 teaspoon minced garlic
1 (15-ounce) can diced tomatoes
1 (8-ounce) can tomato sauce
1 (4-ounce) can diced roasted chile peppers, drained
½ cup sliced pimento-stuffed green olives
½ teaspoon dried oregano
½ teaspoon sugar, or more to taste
Black pepper
Wood chips (optional)
2 tablespoons capers

1. Wash the fillets and pat dry with paper towels. Drizzle the lime juice over the fish. Sprinkle lightly with salt.

2. Heat the oil in a medium saucepan over medium-high heat. Add the onion and garlic and sauté until the onion is softened, about 3 minutes. Add the tomatoes, tomato sauce, chile peppers, olives, oregano, and sugar. Season with salt and pepper; keep at a simmer while you prepare the fire.

3. Prepare a hot fire in a gas or charcoal grill.

4. When the coals in the charcoal grill are covered with gray ash, push all the coals to one side of the grill and place a drip pan on the other side. Or turn off one side of the gas grill and place a drip pan over the off burner. If desired, add wood chips according to the manufacturer's directions. Lightly oil the grill. Place the fish directly over the drip pan. Grill, covered, turning once with a wide spatula, until the flesh looks opaque when pierced in the thickest part with the tip of a knife, 6 to 10 minutes.

5. Transfer to a serving dish, spoon the sauce over the top, and garnish with capers. Serve hot.

Grilled Lobster

You'll only be able to fit two lobsters at a time on most grills, so this recipe is for a romantic dinner for two.

SERVES 2

2 (1½- to 2-pound) live lobsters
¼ cup (½ stick) butter
2 tablespoons lemon juice
Salt and pepper
Lemon wedges, to serve

1. Place the lobsters in a large pan in the freezer for 20 minutes to stun them.

2. Prepare a hot fire in a gas or charcoal grill.

3. Melt the butter in a small saucepan over medium heat. Remove from the heat and stir in the lemon juice. Keep warm.

4. Make sure the rubber bands around the lobster claws are secure. With the first lobster sitting so the tail curls toward the table, flatten it out and use one hand to grasp the tail where it joins the body. Using a heavy knife, cut the lobster at the crease behind the head. Press the point of the knife into the head until the point goes all the way through to the cutting board. Bring the blade down between the eyes to finish the cut of the head. Split the lobster in half lengthwise. Remove the dark matter in the head and discard the intestinal tube that runs through the length of the body. Reserve the green tomalley (liver) and red roe (eggs), if any, and stir into the melted butter. Crack the claws. Brush all the cut surfaces with the lemon butter and season with salt and pepper. Repeat with the second lobster.

5. Oil the grill rack. Place the lobsters, cut side down, on the grill and cover. Grill until the meat is opaque on the surface, about 4 minutes. Turn and brush with more butter. Cover and grill until the lobster shells are deep red and the lobster meat is opaque throughout, 10 to 15 minutes. Serve immediately with the lemon wedges.

Skewered Scallops with Bay Leaves

The bay leaves in this recipe impart an unusual but delicate perfume to the scallops. Julia Child introduced this now classic taste to America. Instead of skewering the bay leaves, make a bay leaf butter for basting and dipping. It is crucial that you do not overcook the delicate scallops.

SERVES 4

½ cup (1 stick) butter
4 bay leaves
Zest of ½ medium lemon, minced
1½ pounds sea scallops
Bamboo skewers, soaked in water for
    30 minutes
Salt and pepper
Lemon wedges, to serve

1. Prepare a medium fire in a gas or charcoal grill.

2. In a small saucepan, heat the butter until just melted. Add the bay leaves and lemon zest. Cook on low heat for 5 minutes. Turn off the heat, remove the bay leaves, and set the pan aside.

3. Rinse the scallops with cold water and pat dry with paper towels. Hold 2 bamboo skewers parallel to each other, no more than ½ inch apart, and thread 4 to 5 scallops onto the pair of skewers. Leave ½ inch of open space on either end of the skewers. Brush generously with the butter mixture and sprinkle with salt and pepper.

4. Lightly oil the grill. Place the skewers on the grill and cook for 3 to 5 minutes, turning once. Remove the skewers from the grill as soon as the scallops have turned opaque and white, no more than 3 to 4 additional minutes. Serve immediately with the lemon wedges, passing the remaining butter for dipping.

Grilled Shrimp Scampi

Use the largest shrimp you can afford here, because small shrimp cook quickly and are easily overcooked on the grill. Skewers are a good idea for this recipe, as you'll find turning the individual shrimp is a tedious process. Serve with pasta tossed with olive oil, grated Parmesan cheese, and fresh parsley.

SERVES 4

2 pounds large shrimp, peeled and deveined
White wine marinade (page 252), made with garlic
Bamboo skewers (soaked in water for 30 minutes)

1. Combine the shrimp with the marinade in a large, heavy-duty resealable plastic bag and refrigerate for about 1 hour.

2. Prepare a medium fire in a gas or charcoal grill.

3. Thread the shrimp onto 2 parallel bamboo skewers, piercing each shrimp through the top and bottom while threading so it keeps its natural C-shaped curve. Do not crowd the shrimp on the skewers, and leave about ½ inch of open space on both ends.

4. Lightly oil the grill. Place the shrimp on the grill, cover, and cook just until the shrimp are opaque, 3 to 4 minutes for large and extra-large shrimp, and 5 to 7 minutes for jumbo or larger shrimp, turning once. Serve immediately.

Grilled Shrimp Wrapped in Bacon

Similar to "angels on horseback" (at right), the angels here are shrimp. Marinating the shrimp first delivers extra flavor. Serve as a main dish or appetizer with an outdoor meal that includes grilled corn and sliced fresh tomatoes.

SERVES 4

½ cup oil
2 tablespoons white-wine vinegar
1½ teaspoons Dijon mustard
1 tablespoon chopped fresh dill
Salt and pepper

1 pound jumbo shrimp (13 to 15 per pound), peeled and deveined
5 slices bacon, cut lengthwise into thirds

1. Whisk together the oil, vinegar, mustard, and dill in a small bowl. Season to taste with salt and pepper. Pour over the shrimp in a larger, heavy-duty resealable plastic bag or glass baking dish. Seal or cover and refrigerate for about 1 hour.

2. Prepare a medium fire in a gas or charcoal grill.

3. Drain the shrimp. Wrap a piece of bacon around each one, securing each with a toothpick.

4. Lightly oil the grill. Place the shrimp on the grill and cook for 2 to 3 minutes per side, until the shrimp is cooked through, turning with tongs. Serve immediately.

Grilled Bacon-Wrapped Oysters

These are the famous "angels on horseback," a favorite hors d'oeuvre of the 1950s. Though oysters tend to overcook, the bacon here makes this a popular item nonetheless.

SERVES 4

12 to 16 fresh medium oysters, shucked
12 to 16 slices bacon
Salt and pepper
Lemon wedges, to serve
Melted butter, to serve
Hot pepper sauce, such as Tabasco, to serve

1. Prepare a hot fire in a gas or charcoal grill.

2. Wrap each oyster in a slice of bacon and secure with a toothpick. Arrange the wrapped oysters in a hinged wire rack.

3. Grill over hot coals until the bacon is cooked to your liking, about 5 minutes, turning at least once.

4. Remove the toothpicks and serve with lemon wedges, offering the butter and hot pepper sauce for dipping.

Grilled Corn

By grilling corn on the cob with the husks on, you provide enough steam to gently cook the corn and keep it moist. The charring of the husks adds even more flavor. Also, the husks will hold in the heat so you can set aside the corn while you grill the meat portion of your meal. Buy the freshest corn you can for this very simple recipe.

SERVES 6

6 large ears corn with husks
½ cup (1 stick) butter, melted, or oil
Salt and pepper

1. Pull off the dry outer husks until you get to the tender, light green inner ones; leave these on. Save a few of the removed husks and tear into ¼-inch strips; set aside. Pull back the inner husks gently and remove the silk. Baste the ears with the butter, sprinkle with salt and pepper, then close and tie with the reserved strips.

2. Prepare a hot fire in a gas or charcoal grill.

3. Place the corn on the grill and cover. Cook, turning occasionally, for 15 to 20 minutes, until the husks are streaked with brown.

4. Remove the husks just before serving.

Grilled Corn with Chile-Lime Butter

After a few meals of simple grilled corn, you may be ready for something new. This is the perfect corn to serve with chicken or beef fajitas. Fresh limes deliver much better flavor than bottled lime juice.

SERVES 8

½ cup (1 stick) butter
2 tablespoons lime juice
1 tablespoon chili powder

⅛ teaspoon cayenne pepper
Salt and pepper
8 large ears corn with husks

1. Melt the butter over medium heat in a small saucepan and stir in the lime juice, chili powder, and cayenne pepper. Season to taste with salt and pepper.

2. Pull off the dry outer husks until you get to the tender, light green inner ones; leave these on. Save a few of the removed husks and tear into ¼-inch strips; set aside. Pull back the inner husks gently and remove the silk. Baste the ears with the flavored butter, then close and tie with the reserved strips.

3. Prepare a hot fire in a gas or charcoal grill.

4. Place the corn on the grill and cover. Cook, turning occasionally, for 15 to 20 minutes, until the husks are streaked with brown.

5. Remove the husks just before serving.

Grilled Onion Slices

Grilled onions are the perfect accompaniment to any grilled meat, especially grilled steak. And they make a terrific topping for grilled hamburgers. By grilling the onion slices in aluminum foil packets, you solve the problem of how to keep the onion slices from falling into the fire.

SERVES 6

4 medium sweet onions, such as Walla Walla, Maui, or Vidalia, sliced ⅓ inch thick
4 teaspoons sugar
4 teaspoons beef bouillon granules

1. Prepare a hot fire in a gas or charcoal grill.

2. Tear off four 12-inch squares of aluminum foil. On each square, place one sliced onion, 1 teaspoon of sugar, and 1 teaspoon of bouillon granules. Fold in the sides to form a sealed packet.

3. Place on the grill, cover, and cook for 10 to 15 minutes, turning once. The aluminum foil should puff up.

4. Snip open the packets and serve.

Mixed Vegetable Kebabs

It makes sense to cook vegetable kebabs separately from meat kebabs because the vegetables often require more cooking time than the meat. If you have trouble keeping the vegetables from spinning on the skewers, try using two parallel skewers for each kebab.

SERVES 4

10 small white boiling onions
5 small zucchini or pattypan squash
2 large red bell peppers
2 teaspoons garlic powder
½ teaspoon salt
¼ teaspoon black pepper
Bamboo skewers (soaked in water for
    30 minutes)
¼ cup oil

1. Bring a small saucepan of salted water to a boil. Add the onions and boil for about 25 minutes, until nearly tender. Drain well, peel, and set aside.

2. Prepare a medium fire in a gas or charcoal grill.

3. Cut the zucchini into 1½-inch slices, or if you are using pattypan squash, cut into quarters. Seed and cut the bell peppers into large chunks. Set aside.

4. Mix the garlic powder, salt, and pepper in a small, shallow dish. Roll the vegetables in the mixture.

5. Thread the vegetables onto the skewers, alternating the squash, onion, and bell peppers. Leave ½ inch of open space on both ends.

6. Lightly oil the grill. Baste the vegetables with the oil and grill over medium heat, turning often and basting with oil, for 15 to 25 minutes, until tender. Serve hot.

Grilled New Potatoes

Potatoes are tricky on the grill because they can cook unevenly. Cooking in aluminum foil packets remedies this. The rosemary, garlic powder, and touch of cayenne pepper in this recipe flavor the potatoes as they cook.

SERVES 4

1 tablespoon oil
1 teaspoon dried rosemary
½ teaspoon garlic powder
½ teaspoon salt
¼ teaspoon black pepper
Pinch of cayenne pepper
1 pound new red or white potatoes, cut into
    wedges

1. Prepare a hot fire in a gas or charcoal grill.

2. Whisk together the oil, rosemary, garlic powder, salt, black pepper, and cayenne pepper in a medium bowl. Add the potatoes and toss to coat.

3. Tear off four 12-inch squares of aluminum foil. Place one-quarter of the potatoes on each square. Fold in the sides to form a sealed packet.

4. Place on the grill, cover, and cook for 20 to 30 minutes, turning every 5 minutes. The aluminum foil should puff up.

5. Snip open the packets and serve.

TIP: Heavy-duty aluminum foil is best for using on the grill. It is less likely to tear or fall apart than regular aluminum foil.

Grilled Baked Potatoes

Use the covered grill as an oven for baking potatoes. If you prefer crisp potato skins, remove the potatoes from the aluminum foil and grill directly over the heat for the final 5 to 10 minutes.

SERVES 4

4 large baking potatoes
Butter, to serve
Sour cream, to serve

1. Prepare a medium fire in a gas or charcoal grill.

2. Scrub the potatoes and pierce each in several places with the tip of a knife. Wrap each in a double layer of aluminum foil.

3. Mound all the coals on one side of the grill or turn one burner off. Position the potatoes over the grill where there are no coals or over the off burner. Cover the grill and cook until the potatoes are easily pierced with a knife, 45 to 60 minutes. Serve hot, passing the butter and sour cream at the table.

Grilled Garlic Bread

Nothing disappears quite as quickly as a rich, buttery garlic bread. You may even want to make more than one loaf if there are hungry kids at your table.

SERVES 4 TO 6

1 large loaf French or Italian bread
½ cup (1 stick) butter, softened
1 teaspoon minced garlic
½ teaspoon salt
1 teaspoon dried parsley

1. Prepare a hot fire in a gas or charcoal grill.

2. Slice the bread lengthwise. In a small bowl, mix the butter, garlic, salt, and parsley. Spread the butter on both sides of the bread and wrap in heavy-duty aluminum foil.

3. Mound all the coals on one side of the grill or turn one burner off. Position the bread over the grill where there are no coals or over the off burner. Cover the grill and cook until hot, about 10 minutes.

4. Unwrap and slice through diagonally. Serve hot.

Texas Spice Rub

In some parts of the country, mainly Texas and the South, meat is rubbed with this mix of spices before it is put on the grill. This particular combination of spices is good with beef, pork, and chicken. Simply rub the mixture into the meat the night before, then cover the meat in plastic wrap and leave in the refrigerator until you're ready to grill.

MAKES ABOUT ½ CUP

3 tablespoons brown sugar
2 tablespoons paprika
2 teaspoons onion powder
1½ teaspoons dried oregano
2 teaspoons dry mustard
2 teaspoons garlic powder
1 teaspoon crumbled bay leaf (about 1 leaf)
1 teaspoon salt, or to taste
1 teaspoon black pepper
½ teaspoon ground cumin
½ teaspoon ground coriander
½ teaspoon dried thyme

Mix all the spices in a small bowl or jar. Use immediately or store for up to 4 months in a sealed jar in a cool, dark place.

Red Wine Marinade

A marinade of red wine is perfect for beef and lamb. Choose a wine that you would be happy to drink with the finished grilled meat.

MAKES ABOUT 1¼ CUPS

¼ cup oil
¾ cup dry red wine
1 tablespoon wine vinegar
2 tablespoons minced garlic
1 tablespoon chopped fresh parsley
2 bay leaves
1 teaspoon salt
½ teaspoon black pepper

Mix all the ingredients in a small bowl. Use immediately.

Red Wine Pepper Marinade

In contrast to red wine marinade, this one has quite a bit of kick to it, using more garlic, some onion, and peppercorns.

MAKES ABOUT 1¼ CUPS

¼ cup oil
¾ cup dry red wine
⅓ cup tarragon vinegar or red-wine vinegar
2 teaspoons minced garlic
2 bay leaves
1 small onion, thinly sliced
1 tablespoon chopped fresh parsley
15 to 20 whole black peppercorns, crushed

Mix all the ingredients in a small bowl. Use immediately.

Wild Game Marinade

Hunters will love this for venison, moose, elk, or bear. It has enough tasty ingredients to cut any gamey flavor, while the vinegar and wine tenderize the meat. If you're going to cook a bear roast, be sure you remove absolutely all fat to avoid the rank flavor it otherwise imparts to the meat.

MAKES ABOUT 7 CUPS

5 cups dry white wine
¾ cup tarragon vinegar or red-wine vinegar
3 medium onions, finely chopped
1 cup finely chopped scallions
1 large carrot, finely chopped
1 large celery rib, finely chopped
2 garlic cloves, crushed
2 bay leaves
2 teaspoons salt
1 teaspoon black pepper

Combine all the ingredients in a large saucepan. Simmer for 5 minutes. Cool. Use immediately.

TIP: The game meat should be completely covered with the marinade. Refrigerate for 2 or 3 days. Discard the marinade and grill the meat. Remember, wild game usually has very little fat, so don't overcook it. You might want to consider basting with steak butter sauce (page 255).

White Wine Marinade

This white wine marinade should be used with poultry or fish. Its combination of lemon, pepper, and sweet onion is a classic. Replacing the onion with garlic provides another flavor option.

MAKES ABOUT 1¼ CUPS

½ cup oil
½ cup dry white wine
3 tablespoons lemon juice
½ teaspoon salt, or more to taste
½ teaspoon black pepper
3 tablespoons finely chopped sweet onion,
    such as Walla Walla, Maui, or Vidalia, or
    1½ teaspoons minced garlic

Mix all the ingredients in a small bowl. Use immediately.

Soy Marinade

Asian marinades are relatively new to the grilling scene, unless you live in Hawaii. This recipe works particularly well with chicken and fish, but it is hearty enough for beef, pork, or lamb.

MAKES ABOUT 3 CUPS

½ cup peanut oil
1½ cups water
⅔ cup soy sauce
¼ cup firmly packed brown sugar
1 tablespoon lemon juice
2 teaspoons Worcestershire sauce
¼ cup bourbon or brandy (optional)

Mix all the ingredients in a small bowl. Use immediately.

Hawaiian Soy Marinade

For your next backyard picnic, think about staging a Hawaiian luau. This marinade goes with all poultry and meats, particularly short ribs.

MAKES ABOUT 2½ CUPS

1 cup soy sauce
½ cup peanut oil
½ cup dry sherry
1 medium onion, finely chopped
1 to 1½ teaspoons minced garlic
2 teaspoons honey
1 teaspoon ground ginger
½ teaspoon black pepper

Mix all the ingredients in a small bowl. Use immediately.

Southern Barbecue Mop

This is the perfect sauce to brush on pork as it barbecues. The simple combination of vinegar, salt, and chili powder enhances the natural flavors of pork.

MAKES ABOUT 6 CUPS

3 cups cider vinegar
3 cups water
6 tablespoons salt
2 tablespoons chili powder

Mix all the ingredients in a medium bowl and mop on the grilling meat at least once an hour.

Texas Wet Mop

This baste is painted on brisket as it barbecues. The flavor is complex and adds greatly to the finished flavor.

MAKES ABOUT 2 CUPS

½ pound hickory-smoked bacon, diced
¼ cup chopped onion
¼ cup chopped celery
¼ cup chopped green bell pepper
2 tablespoons minced garlic
1 tablespoon Texas spice rub (page 251)
2 cups beef broth (page 118)
1½ tablespoons soy sauce
1½ tablespoons cider vinegar
1 tablespoon lemon juice
Salt and pepper
Cayenne pepper

1. Cook the bacon in a large saucepan over medium-high heat until crisp, about 10 minutes. Remove the bacon with a slotted spoon and set aside to drain on paper towels. Use the cooked bacon in another recipe. Pour off all but 2 tablespoons of bacon grease.

2. Add the onion, celery, bell pepper, garlic, and spice rub to the bacon grease in the saucepan and sauté until the onion is softened, about 5 minutes.

3. Stir in the broth, soy sauce, vinegar, and lemon juice. Bring to a boil, reduce the heat, and simmer, stirring occasionally, for 1 hour. Season to taste with salt and pepper, and cayenne pepper.

Garlic Lover's Baste

This baste should be used with quick-cooking fish so the garlic doesn't have a chance to char and become bitter. This baste can also be brushed onto steaks and burgers as a final flourish.

MAKES ABOUT ⅓ CUP

¼ cup oil
3 tablespoons lemon juice
2 teaspoons Worcestershire sauce
1½ teaspoons salt
2 teaspoons minced garlic

1. Combine the ingredients in a small jar. If time permits, cover and refrigerate overnight to let the flavors blend.

2. Brush over fish and shellfish before and during grilling.

Barbecue Sauce

Barbecue cook-offs have a special category of prizes for sauces, and prizewinners have a reputation for using secret ingredients. This is the classic American barbecue sauce: no secret ingredients, just honest, full, sweet, and spicy flavor.

MAKES ABOUT 2 CUPS

2 tablespoons butter
2 medium onions, finely chopped
½ cup ketchup
½ cup water
⅓ cup firmly packed brown sugar
⅓ cup Worcestershire sauce
¼ cup steak sauce
2 tablespoons cider vinegar
⅛ teaspoon hot pepper sauce, such as
　　Tabasco

1. Melt the butter in a medium saucepan over medium heat. Add the onions and sauté until softened, about 5 minutes.

2. Stir in the ketchup, water, brown sugar, Worcestershire sauce, steak sauce, vinegar, and hot pepper sauce. Bring to a boil, reduce the heat, and simmer, stirring occasionally, for 20 minutes.

3. Allow the sauce to cool to room temperature and serve. It can be stored in the refrigerator for 2 to 3 weeks.

Beer Barbecue Sauce

A little beer adds a surprising yeasty note to this otherwise typical barbecue sauce.

MAKES ABOUT 3 CUPS

2 tablespoons butter
½ medium onion, finely chopped
½ teaspoon minced garlic
1¼ cups ketchup
1 cup water
⅔ cup cider vinegar
¼ cup beer
¼ cup firmly packed brown sugar
1 tablespoon Worcestershire sauce
1 teaspoon salt
1 teaspoon chili powder
1 teaspoon hot pepper sauce, such as Tabasco

1. Melt the butter in a medium saucepan over medium heat. Add the onion and garlic and sauté until the onion is softened, about 5 minutes.

2. Stir in the ketchup, water, vinegar, beer, brown sugar, Worcestershire sauce, salt, chili powder, and hot pepper sauce. Bring to a boil, reduce the heat, and simmer, stirring occasionally, for 20 minutes.

3. Cool to room temperature and serve. The sauce can be stored in the refrigerator for 2 to 3 weeks.

TIP: If a smooth texture is preferred, strain the barbecue sauce prior to cooling.

Sweet-and-Spicy Barbecue Sauce

For those with a sweet tooth, this sauce is finger-licking good. Try it with grilled chicken, which goes well with sweet sauces. If you like your sauce extra spicy, just leave the jalapeño seeds in.

MAKES ABOUT 3½ CUPS

2 cups tomato sauce
½ cup cider vinegar
¼ cup firmly packed brown sugar
¼ cup molasses
¼ cup Worcestershire sauce
3 tablespoons tomato paste
1 tablespoon dry mustard
1 jalapeño chile pepper, seeded and minced
2 to 4 drops hot pepper sauce, such as Tabasco
½ cup crushed pineapple or apricot preserves
Salt and pepper

1. Combine the tomato sauce, vinegar, brown sugar, molasses, Worcestershire sauce, tomato paste, mustard, jalapeño, and hot pepper sauce in a medium saucepan over medium heat. Bring to a boil, reduce the heat, and simmer, stirring occasionally, for 20 minutes.

2. Remove from the heat and stir in the pineapple. Cool and season to taste with salt and pepper. Serve at room temperature. The sauce can be stored in the refrigerator for 2 to 3 weeks.

Bourbon Barbecue Sauce

Made from fermented corn, bourbon is the whiskey of choice in the South. It rounds out the flavor in this not-too-sweet barbecue sauce.

MAKES 2½ CUPS

2 cups ketchup
½ cup molasses
⅓ cup bourbon or other whiskey
¼ cup Dijon mustard
2 tablespoons Worcestershire sauce
1 to 3 teaspoons hot pepper sauce, such as Tabasco
2 teaspoons paprika
1 teaspoon garlic powder
1 teaspoon onion powder
Salt and pepper

1. Combine the ingredients in a medium sauce-pan over medium heat. Bring to a boil, stirring occasionally. Reduce the heat to medium-low and simmer, uncovered and stirring frequently, until the sauce thickens and flavors blend, about 20 minutes.

2. Cool and season to taste with salt and pepper. Serve at room temperature. The sauce can be stored in the refrigerator for 2 to 3 weeks.

Sweet Mustard Sauce

This mustard-and-vinegar-based barbecue sauce is perfect on any kind of pork, grilled or smoked. It makes a good change of pace from tomato-based sauces.

MAKES ABOUT 2 CUPS

1 cup prepared yellow mustard
½ cup molasses
¼ cup cider vinegar
¼ cup honey
1 tablespoon oil
¼ teaspoon dried oregano
¼ teaspoon dried thyme
¼ teaspoon black pepper
Pinch of cayenne pepper

1. Combine the ingredients in a medium sauce-pan over medium-high heat. Bring to a boil; reduce the heat and simmer, stirring frequently, for about 20 minutes.

2. Cool to room temperature and serve. The sauce can be stored in the refrigerator for 2 to 3 weeks.

Steak Butter Sauce

Butter on steak? Is that simply too decadent? As an alternative to barbecue sauce or a marinade, try this butter sauce on a tender cut of steak.

MAKES 1¼ CUPS

¾ cup (1½ sticks) butter
½ cup Worcestershire sauce
2 teaspoons chopped fresh rosemary

1. Melt the butter in a small saucepan. Stir in the Worcestershire sauce, then add the rosemary. Simmer for 15 minutes.

2. Brush on steaks before serving.

Classic Steak Sauce

Steak sauces are complex blends of spices in a sweet-sour base. This homemade version is delicious on grilled steaks and burgers.

MAKES ABOUT ¾ CUP

¼ cup oil
3 tablespoons finely chopped onion
½ teaspoon finely minced garlic
¼ cup cider vinegar
½ teaspoon salt
½ teaspoon dry mustard
¼ teaspoon ground nutmeg
¼ teaspoon ground mace
¼ teaspoon ground cloves

1. Heat the oil in a small saucepan over medium heat. Add the onion and cook for 3 to 4 minutes, until soft. Add the garlic and cook for 1 minute more. Add the vinegar, salt, mustard, nutmeg, mace, and cloves. Bring to a simmer and cook for 5 minutes.

2. Cool to room temperature and serve with steak.

THE ART OF GRILLING

Grilling Made Easy

Whether you grill with gas or charcoal, there are a few rules to follow that will guarantee success every time.

▶ Wait until the fire is ready for grilling. Fully preheat a gas grill until it reaches at least 550°F. Charcoal briquettes will be covered with gray ash when they are ready.

▶ Remove food from the refrigerator in time for it to lose its chill before putting it on the grill—about 30 minutes.

▶ Don't overmarinate foods. Leaving foods in a marinade too long will result in a mushy texture.

▶ Be sure the grill is scrubbed clean with a grill brush and lightly oiled before each use.

▶ Grill with the lid closed to increase the heat. Watch closely for flare-ups.

▶ To gauge the temperature of a fire, hold your hand just above the cooking rack. If the fire is hot, you will be able to hold your hand at that level for 1 or 2 seconds. For a medium fire, you should be able to hold your hand just above the cooking rack for 3 or 4 seconds.

▶ Be flexible about cooking times; some grills and some fires burn hotter than others.

Grilling Over Charcoal

Many people prefer the old kettle-style grill to the newer gas grills. They say the food tastes better when grilled over coals, and they are willing to deal with the inconvenience of fire starting.

▶ Never use lighter fluid to start a fire. Too much lighter fluid will flavor the food.

▶ Chimney starters take the work out of starting charcoal fires. They are tall canisters with a grate for holding the charcoal and a space below for holding kindling. Light the kindling and allow 20 to 30 minutes for the charcoal to fully ignite, then dump the coals out of the chimney and spread them out with a garden trowel.

▶ Five pounds of charcoal will generally yield the necessary number of coals for one cooking session.

▶ Hardwood charcoal burns hotter and faster than regular briquettes and imparts more wood-smoke flavor.

Grilling Over Indirect Heat

The patio grillers of days past had some clumsy grilling techniques. They built hot fires, placed the meat over the coals, and grilled, using a spray bottle of water nearby to quench flare-ups. Too often the result was meat—particularly chicken—that was charred on the outside and raw on the inside. Using indirect heat solves this problem. Grill over indirect heat whenever the food will take more than 25 minutes to cook through. This includes most chicken and roasts.

1. With a charcoal grill, build a hot fire with the normal amount of coals. In a gas grill, preheat with all the burners on high.

2. Heap the coals on one side of the grill and place a drip plan (disposable aluminum pans work best) next to the coals. In a gas grill, leave one side of the burners on high or medium (as the recipe directs), and turn off the other burners. Place a drip pan over the burner that has been turned off.

3. Place the food directly over the drip pan. Close the lid of the grill and grill as the recipe directs.

Grilled Fruit

Fruit cooks on grills surprisingly well, but it is essential that the grill be clean or the fruit will pick up flavors of previously grilled food. You can simply baste the fruit with melted butter or flavor the butter with 1 teaspoon ground cinnamon. Grill over a low to medium fire to avoid charring. If using bamboo skewers, presoak in warm water for 30 minutes before using to avoid burning.

▶ APPLES: Core, peel (if desired), and cut into halves. Grill for 10 to 12 minutes.

▶ APRICOTS: Cut into halves and discard the pits. Thread onto skewers, making sure the fruit lies flat. Grill for 4 to 6 minutes.

▶ BANANAS: Do not peel. Slit open 3 inches of peel, hold open enough to drizzle in 1 tablespoon honey mixed with ¼ teaspoon ground cinnamon. Let stand for about 30 minutes before placing on the grill and cooking for about 8 minutes.

▶ PAPAYAS: Peel, then cut crosswise into ¾-inch rings or cut lengthwise into quarters. Remove and discard the seeds. Grill for 5 to 8 minutes.

▶ PEACHES: Drain canned peach halves, or peel and halve if fresh. Drizzle each half with about 1 tablespoon honey or 1 tablespoon honey combined with ¼ teaspoon ground cinnamon, or brush with melted butter and sprinkle with 1 teaspoon brown sugar. Grill canned peaches for 4 minutes, fresh peaches for 6 to 8 minutes.

▶ PEARS: Peel, if desired. Cut small ones into halves lengthwise, large ones into ¾-inch wedges. Core. Thread onto skewers, making sure the fruit lies flat. Grill the wedges for 6 minutes, halves for 10 to 12 minutes.

▶ PINEAPPLE: Cut a fresh pineapple lengthwise into 8 sections. Peel and remove the core. Place in a shallow pan and drizzle with about 1 tablespoon honey per section. Let stand for about 30 minutes, then grill for 10 to 12 minutes.

CHAPTER TEN

Pasta and Rice

Like most people, Thomas Jefferson fell in love with pasta the first time he tried it. In fact, it was Mary Randolph, Jefferson's cousin, who published the first recipe for macaroni and cheese in her 1824 cookbook, *The Virginia Housewife*.

Along with the hamburger, macaroni and cheese is still considered one of America's best-loved foods. Its popularity surged when Kraft Foods introduced the Kraft Dinner in 1937; Kraft now sells more than one million boxes every day.

But our love affair with pasta doesn't end with macaroni; it encompasses noodles of all varieties. German immigrants (including the Pennsylvania Dutch) first brought egg noodles to America in the nineteenth century. The demand for these noodles grew as immigrants from Russia, Hungary, and the Ukraine merged their traditional noodle recipes into our melting-pot cuisine. Years later, when egg noodles were paired with Campbell soups, a whole new tradition of casserole dishes was born.

Italian immigrants in the nineteenth century brought pasta with them as well. Americans embraced this newfound Italian food with its exotic flavors—spaghetti with tomato sauce and meatballs quickly became part of the typical dinner menu. These traditional Italian recipes were Americanized in their mass production, made with overly sweetened, bottled spaghetti sauce and powdered Parmesan cheese. In recent years, however, Americans have become savvier about traditional ingredients and authentic cuisine.

Rice, on the other hand, has enjoyed a longer history in the United States. First grown in a garden in South Carolina in 1671, early rice plants thrived in the rich southeastern soil. It took time for South Carolinians to discover how to husk and prepare it for eating, but by the turn of the seventeenth century, it had become a major staple. Many of our beloved chicken-and-rice recipes, including chicken bog and chicken pilau, date from that same era. Rice later became particularly associated with the Creole and Cajun cooking of New Orleans, being a primary ingredient in such Big Easy favorites as dirty rice and jambalaya.

If the classic pasta and rice recipes in this chapter are not already favorites in your home, they soon will be!

Pesto Pasta

Pesto, whose name is derived from the Italian word for "pounded," is an uncooked sauce made from fresh basil, Parmesan cheese, olive oil, and pine nuts. Although you can buy bottled pesto sauce, it is easily prepared in a modern food processor—as opposed to using the traditional mortar and pestle. The fresh basil makes the homemade version infinitely better.

SERVES 4 TO 6

1½ cups tightly packed fresh basil leaves
2 garlic cloves
3 tablespoons pine nuts
¼ cup olive oil
3 tablespoons grated Parmesan cheese, plus
    more to serve
Salt and pepper
1 pound fettuccine, linguine, or spaghetti

1. Combine the basil, garlic, and pine nuts in a food processor fitted with a metal blade. Process until finely chopped.

2. Add the oil through the feed tube with the motor running and continue processing until you have a smooth paste. Briefly mix in the cheese and salt and pepper to taste.

3. Set aside for at least 20 minutes to allow the flavors to blend.

4. Meanwhile, begin heating a large pot of salted water for the pasta.

5. Cook the pasta in the boiling water until done, about 12 minutes. Reserve about ½ cup of the pasta cooking water and drain the rest.

6. Return the pasta to the pot. Add the pesto and as much of the reserved cooking water as needed to create a light sauce. Toss to coat. Sprinkle with Parmesan cheese and serve immediately.

Spaghetti with Olive Oil and Garlic

This simple Italian pasta recipe is very quick and easy to make. In Italian households, it is often whipped up as a late-night snack. If you don't have fresh mint, substitute another tablespoon of parsley.

SERVES 4 TO 6

½ cup olive oil
2 teaspoons minced garlic
½ teaspoon crushed red pepper
1 pound spaghetti
2 tablespoons chopped fresh parsley
1 tablespoon chopped fresh mint
Salt and pepper

1. Bring a large pot of salted water to a boil.

2. Meanwhile, heat the oil over medium-low heat. Add the garlic and crushed red pepper and simmer until the garlic is pale gold, about 3 minutes.

3. Cook the pasta in the boiling water until done, about 12 minutes, then drain and return to the pot. Add the oil mixture, parsley, and mint. Cook over low heat for 2 minutes, stirring constantly.

4. Season to taste with salt and pepper and serve immediately.

Pasta with Marinara Sauce

Marinara is a basic red sauce from which many recipes are derived. Since it's quick and easy to make, this dish can stand on its own as a meal or be served as a side dish with meat, seafood, or poultry courses.

SERVES 4 TO 6

¼ cup oil
1 small onion, chopped
1½ to 2 teaspoons minced garlic
2 (28-ounce) cans diced tomatoes
1 teaspoon salt, plus more to taste

1 teaspoon dried basil, plus more to taste
½ teaspoon dried thyme, plus more to taste
½ teaspoon dried oregano, plus more to taste
Black pepper
1 pound pasta of choice

1. Heat the oil in a large saucepan over medium heat. Add the onion and garlic and sauté for about 5 minutes, until softened.

2. Add the tomatoes with their juices to the pan. Add the salt, basil, thyme, oregano, and pepper. Cook, covered, for 10 minutes. Uncover, stir, and cook, uncovered, for another 20 to 25 minutes, until the flavors have blended. Taste and adjust the seasoning as needed.

3. Meanwhile, cook the pasta in a large pot of boiling salted water according to the package directions. Toss with the sauce and serve immediately.

Pasta Primavera

Primavera means "in the style of springtime" in Italian. Any dish can be made primavera style, but it is most often a dish of pasta and fresh vegetables. With all the different vegetables, this pasta dish is a colorful, flavorful feast.

SERVES 4 TO 6

10 asparagus spears, cut into 2-inch lengths
1 small head broccoli, cut into small florets
2 tablespoons butter
2 tablespoons oil
1 medium onion, thinly sliced
3 medium carrots, peeled and cut into thin strips
1 medium yellow bell pepper, seeded and cut into thin strips
1 medium red bell pepper, seeded and cut into thin strips
1 medium zucchini, cut into thin strips
1 cup heavy cream
1 tablespoon dried Italian seasoning
Salt and pepper
1 pound fettuccine
15 cherry tomatoes, halved
½ cup grated Parmesan cheese, plus more to serve

1. Bring a large pot of salted water to a boil. Add the asparagus and broccoli and cook for 1 minute. Remove from the water with a slotted spoon and set aside; save the cooking water in the pot.

2. Melt the butter with the oil in a large saucepan over medium heat. Add the onion, carrots, bell peppers, and zucchini and cook until softened, about 5 minutes. Add the asparagus and broccoli. Stir in the heavy cream and Italian seasoning, season to taste with salt and pepper, and simmer over low heat while the pasta cooks, about 12 minutes.

3. Meanwhile, return the vegetable cooking water to a boil, add the pasta, and cook until done, about 12 minutes. Drain well.

4. Add the pasta to the saucepan along with the cherry tomatoes and adjust the seasoning with salt and pepper. Toss well to mix. Sprinkle with the Parmesan cheese and serve immediately, passing more cheese at the table.

TIP: Dried Italian seasoning is an herb blend generally consisting of dried oregano, rosemary, savory, thyme, basil, marjoram, and sage.

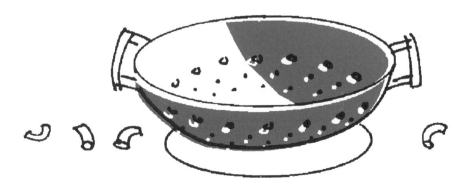

Fettuccine Alfredo

Fettuccine Alfredo was created by Roman restaurateur Alfredo Di Lelio in 1914 as a dish to tempt his wife to eat during her pregnancy. It originally did not contain heavy cream, but over time cream was added and became widely accepted. The nutmeg is a classic addition found in many cream sauces.

SERVES 4 TO 6

3 tablespoons butter
1 cup heavy cream
Pinch of ground nutmeg
1 pound fettuccine
¾ cup grated Parmesan cheese, plus more to serve
Salt and pepper
5 fresh basil leaves, cut into ribbons (optional)

1. Bring a large pot of salted water to a boil.

2. Meanwhile, melt 2 tablespoons of butter in a large saucepan over medium heat. Stir in the cream and nutmeg and keep warm over low heat.

3. Cook the pasta in the boiling water until done, about 12 minutes, and drain well.

4. Transfer the pasta to a warmed serving bowl. Toss with the remaining tablespoon butter and the cheese. Pour the sauce over the pasta and toss again. Taste and adjust the seasoning, adding salt and pepper as needed. Garnish with the basil and serve immediately, passing additional cheese at the table.

Spaghetti Carbonara

Made with smoked or cured bacon (pancetta), this dish is a nice blend of smoky flavor, wine, and cheese. It is best to eat directly after cooking. (Note: This recipe contains raw eggs. For more information, see page 11.)

SERVES 4 TO 6

3 tablespoons olive oil
½ pound pancetta or smoked bacon, diced
¼ cup dry white wine
4 large eggs
½ cup grated Romano cheese
½ cup grated Parmesan cheese, plus more to serve
Coarsely ground black pepper
2 tablespoons chopped fresh parsley
1 pound spaghetti

1. Bring a large pot of salted water to a boil.

2. Meanwhile, heat the oil in a large skillet over medium heat. Add the pancetta and cook until the pieces begin to crisp on the edges, about 5 minutes. Spoon out all but about 3 tablespoons of the oil. Stir in the wine and bring to a boil. Boil for 2 minutes, until reduced by at least half. Keep warm.

3. Break the eggs into a large serving bowl. Beat lightly with a fork, then add the cheeses, pepper, and parsley. Mix thoroughly.

4. Cook the pasta in the boiling water until just done, about 12 minutes. Drain briefly and immediately add to the bowl with the eggs. Toss rapidly to coat well. Add the pancetta and wine sauce. Toss again and serve immediately, passing more cheese at the table.

Baked Ziti

A boon for the busy family, this recipe couldn't be simpler, especially when made with store-bought tomato sauce. Make it ahead, make it at the last minute, make it often. Ziti are small, straight tubes of pasta. Feel free to substitute macaroni, penne, rotini, or any other shape you prefer.

SERVES 4 TO 6

1 pound ziti
1 (16-ounce) container ricotta cheese
3 cups shredded mozzarella cheese (about
    12 ounces)
3 cups marinara sauce (page 260)
½ cup grated Parmesan cheese

1. Preheat the oven to 350°F. Grease a 3-quart baking dish.

2. Cook the ziti in a large pot of salted boiling water until done, about 15 minutes. Drain and transfer to a large bowl.

3. Stir the ricotta cheese and 1½ cups of mozzarella cheese into the ziti.

4. Cover the bottom of the baking dish with 1½ cups of marinara sauce. Spoon the ziti mixture over the sauce. Cover with the remaining 1½ cups sauce. Sprinkle with the Parmesan cheese and the remaining 1½ cups mozzarella cheese.

5. Bake for 30 minutes, until hot and bubbling. Remove from the oven and let stand for 10 minutes before serving.

Ricotta-Spinach Manicotti

Manicotti are large tubes of pasta that are often stuffed with cheese, as they are here, and baked under a topping of tomato sauce. Like other baked pasta dishes, manicotti can be made ahead and refrigerated for a few days or frozen for a few months. A variation follows.

SERVES 6

4 cups fresh spinach, washed and trimmed
1 (14-count) box manicotti
2 (16-ounce) containers ricotta cheese
3 cups shredded mozzarella cheese (about
    12 ounces)
½ cup grated Parmesan cheese
1 teaspoon minced garlic
1 teaspoon dried Italian seasoning
Salt and pepper
2 to 3 cups marinara sauce, bottled or
    homemade (page 260)

1. Bring a large pot of salted water to a boil.

2. Add the spinach and cook until wilted, 1 to 2 minutes. Remove from the pot with a slotted spoon and drain well.

3. Return the water to a boil. Add the manicotti shells and cook according to the box directions; they should be barely tender. Drain and set aside on paper towels to dry.

4. Squeeze the spinach to remove any excess water. Chop fine and transfer to a large bowl. Mix in the ricotta cheese, 2 cups of mozzarella cheese, and ¼ cup of Parmesan cheese. Stir in the garlic, Italian seasoning, and salt and pepper to taste.

5. Preheat the oven to 350°F. Grease a 3-quart shallow baking dish.

6. Using a small spoon, carefully stuff the manicotti with the cheese mixture. Pour about half of the sauce in the bottom of the baking dish and spread evenly. Arrange the manicotti in the baking dish, then pour the remainder of the sauce on top. Sprinkle the remaining 1 cup mozzarella cheese and ¼ cup Parmesan cheese on top. Cover with aluminum foil.

7. Bake for about 40 minutes, until heated through. Let stand for 10 minutes before serving.

Stuffed Shells

Replace the manicotti with large, cooked pasta shells in Ricotta-Spinach Manicotti. Fill with the spinach-cheese mixture or omit the spinach and just use the cheeses. Complete the recipe as directed.

Baked Macaroni and Cheese

Warm noodles baked in Cheddar cheese and Velveeta conjures up nostalgic memories. There is, perhaps, no recipe that defines classic comfort food better than macaroni and cheese. It's a year-round favorite with kids, and adults are equally enthusiastic about this homemade variety.

SERVES 4 TO 6

1 pound elbow macaroni
¼ cup (½ stick) butter
3 tablespoons all-purpose flour
1 teaspoon dry mustard
5 cups milk
2 cups shredded sharp Cheddar cheese (about 8 ounces)
½ pound processed cheese, such as Velveeta, cut into cubes
Salt and pepper

1. Preheat the oven to 375°F. Grease a 9 x 13 baking dish.

2. Bring a large pot of salted water to a boil. Add the macaroni and cook until done, about 12 minutes. Drain well and transfer to the baking dish.

3. Melt the butter over medium heat in a medium saucepan. Stir in the flour and dry mustard to form a smooth paste. Slowly stir in the milk and bring to a boil, stirring often to prevent lumps. Reduce the heat to medium and stir in the cheeses until melted. Season to taste with salt and pepper.

4. Mix the sauce with the macaroni and bake for 30 to 35 minutes, until bubbly and lightly browned on top. Serve hot.

TIP: Velveeta gives this dish a creamy texture and unique flavor. However, you can replace it with more sharp Cheddar cheese (about 2 cups) if you prefer.

Spaghetti with White Clam Sauce

There are plenty of variations for this Italian classic, but one thing all the recipes have in common is a healthy dose of garlic. Serve this with plenty of crusty Italian bread. A simplified variation follows.

SERVES 4 TO 6

1½ cups water
½ cup dry white wine
4 pounds small hard-shell clams
¼ cup oil
2 teaspoons minced garlic
Pinch of crushed red pepper, or more to taste
4 tablespoons chopped fresh parsley
2 tablespoons chopped fresh thyme
1 pound spaghetti or linguine
Salt

1. Bring the water and wine to a boil in a large skillet. Add the clams, cover, reduce the heat, and simmer until the clams open, 5 to 7 minutes. Remove the clams with a slotted spoon and discard any unopened ones. Strain the liquid through a paper coffee filter and set aside. Shuck the clams or leave in the shells, set aside.

2. Heat the oil in a large saucepan over medium heat. Add the garlic and crushed red pepper, reduce the heat, and cook until the garlic is fragrant, 2 to 3 minutes. Add the reserved clam liquid, 2 tablespoons of parsley, and the thyme. Simmer over very low heat.

3. Meanwhile, cook the spaghetti in a large pot of boiling salted water until just done, about 12 minutes. Drain well.

4. Add the pasta and clams to the sauce and toss carefully. Toss with the remaining 2 tablespoons parsley and serve immediately.

TIP: If fresh clams are not available to make the clam sauce, omit step 1 and substitute 2 (8-ounce) bottles clam juice plus the liquid from 2 (7-ounce) cans chopped clams (setting the clams aside).

Spaghetti with Red Clam Sauce

Spaghetti with a tomato-based clam sauce is an Italian-American restaurant standard. The presentation is most dramatic when the dish is served with fresh clams still in the shell, but a variation using canned clams follows.

SERVES 4 TO 6

1½ cups water
½ cup dry white wine
4 pounds small hard-shell clams
2 tablespoons oil
1 medium onion, finely chopped
1 teaspoon minced garlic
Pinch of crushed red pepper, or more to taste
1 (28-ounce) can tomato sauce
4 tablespoons chopped fresh parsley
1 teaspoon dried oregano
½ teaspoon dried basil
Salt and pepper
1 pound spaghetti or linguine

1. Bring the water and wine to a boil in a large skillet. Add the clams, cover, reduce the heat, and simmer until the clams open, 5 to 7 minutes. Remove the clams with a slotted spoon and discard any unopened ones. Strain the liquid through a paper coffee filter and set aside. Shuck the clams or leave in the shells; set aside.

2. Heat the oil in a large saucepan over medium heat. Add the onion, garlic, and crushed red pepper and sauté until the onion is softened, about 3 minutes. Add the tomato sauce, reserved clam liquid, 2 tablespoons of parsley, oregano, and basil. Season to taste with salt and pepper. Simmer over very low heat, stirring occasionally.

3. Meanwhile, cook the spaghetti in a large pot of boiling salted water until just done, about 12 minutes. Drain well.

4. Add the pasta and clams to the sauce and toss carefully. Toss with the remaining 2 tablespoons parsley and serve immediately.

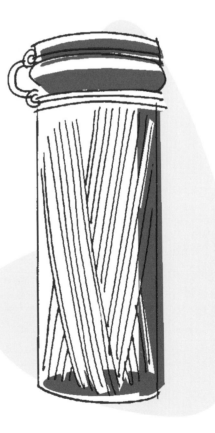

Turkey Tetrazzini

Leftover turkey dishes are part of the pleasure of the holiday season. This hearty casserole is a tasty way to use leftover chicken or turkey. It is named after opera star Luisa Tetrazzini, who was popular at the turn of the twentieth century.

SERVES 6

¼ cup (½ stick) butter
½ pound mushrooms, sliced
1 small onion, minced
¼ cup all-purpose flour
3 cups chicken broth (page 119)
½ cup milk
3 tablespoons dry sherry
4 cups shredded or chopped cooked turkey or chicken
2 cups frozen Frenched green beans, thawed
Salt and pepper
¾ pound thin spaghetti
½ cup toasted slivered almonds
¼ cup chopped fresh parsley
1 cup grated Parmesan cheese

1. Melt the butter in a large saucepan over medium heat. Add the mushrooms and onion and sauté until the mushrooms give up their juice, about 8 minutes. Stir in the flour to make a paste. Add the broth, milk, and sherry and stir until smooth and thick.

2. Add the turkey and green beans and season generously with salt and pepper. Set aside.

3. Preheat the oven to 350°F. Grease a 9 x 13-inch baking dish.

4. Cook the spaghetti in a large pot of boiling salted water until done, about 12 minutes. Drain well.

5. Mix the spaghetti into the creamed turkey mixture, then mix in the almonds and parsley. Transfer to the prepared baking dish and top with the Parmesan cheese.

6. Bake for 30 minutes, until the topping is golden and the filling is hot. Serve immediately.

TIP: If you can't find Frenched green beans, simply cut the beans down their length into long strips.

Two-Way Cincinnati Chili

Cincinnati chili is a uniquely American recipe. It's a crazy mixture of cultures—a little Greek, a little Italian, and a lot of creativity—made complete by an unusual blend of spices and ingredients. When served alone over spaghetti, it is known as two-way chili. Three-way chili has an additional topping of shredded Cheddar cheese, four-way chili adds chopped onions, and five-way chili adds kidney beans.

SERVES 4 TO 6

2 tablespoons oil
1 pound ground beef
1 large onion, chopped
½ teaspoon minced garlic
1 tablespoon chili powder
1 teaspoon ground allspice
1 teaspoon ground cinnamon
1 teaspoon ground cumin
½ teaspoon cayenne pepper
½ teaspoon salt
1½ tablespoons cocoa powder or ½ ounce grated baking chocolate
1 (15-ounce) can tomato sauce
1 tablespoon Worcestershire sauce
1 tablespoon cider vinegar
½ cup water
1 pound spaghetti
Oyster crackers, to serve

1. In a large skillet, heat the oil over medium-high heat. Add the ground beef, onion, and chili powder. Cook for 10 minutes. Add the garlic and cook for 3 more minutes.

2. Add the allspice, cinnamon, cumin, cayenne pepper, salt, cocoa powder, tomato sauce, Worcestershire sauce, vinegar, and water. Reduce the heat and simmer, uncovered, for 1½ hours. Remove from the heat.

3. Cook the spaghetti in a large pot of boiling salted water until done, about 12 minutes. Drain well.

4. Spoon the chili over the spaghetti and serve, passing the oyster crackers at the table.

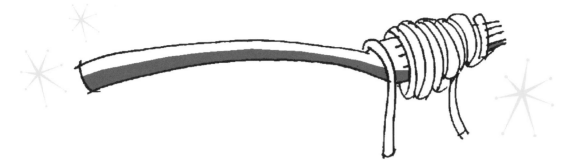

Spaghetti and Meatballs

The first Italian-inspired dish that Americans widely adopted was spaghetti and meatballs. It is a family favorite in households across the country.

SERVES 4 TO 6

Sauce:
2 tablespoons oil
1 medium onion, diced
1 teaspoon minced garlic
1 (28-ounce) can tomato sauce
1 (28-ounce) can diced tomatoes
½ cup dry red wine
½ cup chicken broth (page 119), tomato juice, or water
2 teaspoons dried oregano
1 teaspoon dried thyme
1 teaspoon dried rosemary
1 teaspoon sugar
Salt and pepper

Meatballs:
1 medium onion, chopped
¼ cup fresh parsley leaves
2 garlic cloves
2 slices white sandwich bread, finely diced
¾ pound ground beef
¾ pound ground pork, veal, turkey, or beef
2 large eggs
1 teaspoon dried oregano
1 teaspoon salt
¼ teaspoon black pepper
2 tablespoons oil

Pasta:
1 pound spaghetti
Freshly grated Parmesan cheese, to serve

1. To make the sauce, heat the oil in a large saucepan over medium-high heat. Add the onion and garlic and sauté until softened, about 3 minutes. Add the tomato sauce, diced tomatoes, wine, broth, oregano, thyme, rosemary, and sugar. Add salt and pepper to taste. Bring to a boil, reduce the heat, and simmer, partially covered, while you make the meatballs.

2. To make the meatballs, combine the onion, parsley, and garlic in a food processor and process until finely chopped. Add the bread and process to make fine crumbs. Add the beef, pork, eggs, oregano, salt, and pepper. Process until well mixed.

3. Heat the oil in a large skillet over medium-high heat. Form the meat mixture into meatballs the size of walnuts. Add a single layer to the skillet and fry, turning as needed, until browned all over, about 8 minutes. Remove the meatballs with a slotted spoon and add to the simmering sauce. Repeat until all the meatballs are browned.

4. Simmer the sauce and meatballs, partially covered, for about 1 hour.

5. To make the spaghetti, bring a large pot of salted water to a boil. Add the spaghetti and cook until done, about 12 minutes. Drain well.

6. Top the spaghetti with the sauce and meatballs and serve, passing the Parmesan cheese at the table.

TIP: Leftover meatballs make terrific hot meatball subs. Warm the meatballs and sauce in a saucepan over medium heat. Lightly toast sub rolls under the broiler. Spoon the meatballs into the rolls with a little sauce and top with sliced mozzarella cheese. Return to the broiler for 1 to 2 minutes to melt the cheese; serve hot.

Spaghetti with Meat Sauce

Bolognese sauce is the popular red meat sauce found on menus everywhere Italian dishes are served. Veal is sometimes added in addition to a splash of cream at the end. Many consider the optional sugar to be the secret ingredient. This recipe is also satisfying without these additions.

SERVES 4 TO 6

2 tablespoons oil
¾ pound ground beef
¾ pound ground pork or Italian sausage, removed from its casings
1 medium onion, diced
1 (28-ounce) can tomato sauce
1 (28-ounce) can diced tomatoes
½ cup dry red wine
1 teaspoon minced garlic
1 cup beef broth (page 118)
2 teaspoons dried oregano
1 teaspoon dried thyme
1 teaspoon fennel seeds, crushed
1 teaspoon sugar (optional)
Salt and pepper
1 pound spaghetti
Freshly grated Parmesan cheese, to serve

1. Heat the oil in a large saucepan over medium-high heat. Add the beef, pork, and onion and sauté, stirring to break up the pieces, until the meat is well browned, about 15 minutes. Add the tomato sauce, diced tomatoes, wine, garlic, broth, oregano, thyme, fennel seeds, and sugar. Season to taste with salt and pepper. Bring to a boil, reduce the heat, and simmer, partially covered, for 1 hour.

2. Cook the spaghetti in a large pot of boiling salted water until done, about 12 minutes. Drain well.

3. Top the spaghetti with the sauce and serve, passing the Parmesan cheese at the table.

Spaghetti with Sausage

Spaghetti with sausage adds a touch of spice and variety to the typical sauce. In restaurants, this is often served with link sausages, but cutting the sausage into bite-size pieces makes it easier to eat. Serve with lightly toasted Italian bread and a bright Italian red wine.

SERVES 4 TO 6

¼ cup oil
1 pound Italian sausages, cut into bite-size pieces
1½ teaspoons minced garlic
1 medium green bell pepper, seeded and cut into thin strips
1 (28-ounce) can diced tomatoes
2 bay leaves
Pinch of ground saffron
Salt and pepper
1 pound spaghetti
Freshly grated Parmesan cheese, to serve

1. Heat the oil in a heavy saucepan over medium-high heat. Add the sausage and cook until lightly browned, about 8 minutes. Remove with a slotted spoon and set aside.

2. Add the garlic and bell pepper to the saucepan and sauté until the pepper is softened, about 3 minutes.

3. Add the tomatoes, bay leaves, and saffron. Return the sausage to the saucepan, reduce the heat to medium, and cook covered for 20 minutes. Season to taste with salt and pepper.

4. Meanwhile, cook the spaghetti in a large pot of boiling salted water until done, about 12 minutes. Drain well.

5. Remove the bay leaves. Add the spaghetti to the sauce and toss gently to coat. Serve immediately, passing the Parmesan cheese at the table.

Stovetop Macaroni and Beef

Into the great melting pot of America went Italian home cooking and out came something streamlined and convenient for a busy cook. This dish requires only one pot and about 40 minutes to make from start to finish, though it doesn't take any shortcuts on taste.

SERVES 4 TO 6

2 tablespoons oil
1 pound ground beef
1 medium onion, chopped
1 medium green bell pepper, seeded and
    chopped
1 (15-ounce) can diced tomatoes
1 (15-ounce) can tomato sauce
1½ cups water
1 teaspoon minced garlic
1 tablespoon dried Italian seasoning
Salt and pepper
2 cups elbow macaroni
¼ cup grated Parmesan cheese
2 cups shredded mozzarella cheese (about
    8 ounces)

1. Heat the oil in a large skillet over medium-high heat. Add the beef and cook, stirring frequently to break up the pieces, until the meat is lightly browned, about 10 minutes. Drain off any excess fat. Add the onion and bell pepper and cook for 3 to 4 minutes longer, until the onion is soft.

2. Stir in the tomatoes, tomato sauce, water, garlic, and Italian seasoning. Season to taste with salt and pepper. Stir in the macaroni, cover the pan, and

simmer over medium-low heat for 15 to 20 minutes, stirring frequently, until the macaroni is tender.

3. Stir in the cheeses. Taste and adjust the seasonings as needed. Serve immediately.

American Goulash

Depending on where you grew up, you may know this dish as American goulash, American chop suey, or just hamburger casserole. It is a basic dish of ground beef, macaroni, and tomatoes that has been a staple in school cafeterias nationwide. Add corn if you like, or substitute marinara or spaghetti sauce for the tomato sauce.

SERVES 6

1 pound elbow macaroni
2 tablespoons oil
1 pound ground beef
1 medium onion, chopped
1 medium green bell pepper, seeded and
    chopped
1 (28-ounce) can tomato sauce
1 (28-ounce) can diced tomatoes
Salt and pepper
4 cups shredded mozzarella or Cheddar cheese,
    (about 1 pound)

1. Preheat the oven to 350°F. Grease a 9 x 13-inch baking dish.

2. Cook the macaroni in a large pot of boiling salted water until done, about 12 minutes. Drain well.

3. Heat the oil in a large skillet over medium-high heat. Add the beef, and cook, stirring frequently to break up the pieces, until the meat is lightly browned, about 10 minutes. Drain off any excess fat. Add the onion and bell pepper and cook for 3 to 4 minutes longer, until the onion is soft. Add the tomato sauce and diced tomatoes and mix well. Season to taste with salt and pepper. Stir in the macaroni until well mixed.

4. Transfer the mixture to the prepared baking dish and cover.

5. Bake for 25 minutes. Remove from the oven and top with the mozzarella cheese. Bake, uncovered, for 15 to 20 minutes more, until the cheese has melted and the mixture is hot. Serve immediately.

Ham and Noodle Casserole

*A holiday ham often results in days of leftovers.
Here's a popular casserole that makes good use of them,
adding peas, scallions, and noodles to an egg base.*

SERVES 4 TO 6

8 ounces wide egg noodles
2 to 3 cups diced baked or smoked ham
1 cup frozen peas
1 cup milk or half-and-half
2 large eggs, beaten
4 scallions, chopped
½ teaspoon salt, or to taste
½ teaspoon black pepper, or to taste
1½ cups shredded Cheddar or Swiss cheese
    (about 6 ounces)
2 tablespoons butter, melted

1. Preheat the oven to 350°F. Grease a 2-quart baking dish.

2. Cook the noodles in a large pot of boiling salted water until just done, about 10 minutes. Drain well.

3. Combine the noodles, ham, and peas in the baking dish.

4. Whisk together the milk and eggs in a small bowl. Mix in the scallions, salt, and pepper. Pour over the ham and noodles. Sprinkle with the cheese and drizzle with the melted butter.

5. Bake for 45 minutes and serve hot.

Lasagna

*In Italy there are many versions of lasagna, but this
is the one most widely seen in the United States. Because
it is time-consuming to make, it is a special-occasion dish.
Easily made in advance, lasagna can be stored, unbaked,
in the refrigerator for up to two days; or bake
and freeze it for up to two months.*

SERVES 8

1 tablespoon oil
1 pound ground beef
1 medium onion, diced
1½ teaspoons minced garlic
2 (15-ounce) cans diced tomatoes, drained
2 (15-ounce) cans tomato sauce
1 tablespoon dried Italian seasoning
1 teaspoon fennel seeds, crushed (optional)
Salt and pepper
1 pound lasagna noodles
1 large egg, beaten
1 (16-ounce) container ricotta cheese
½ cup grated Parmesan cheese
4 cups shredded mozzarella cheese, (about
    1 pound)

1. Heat the oil in a large saucepan over medium-high heat. Add the beef and onion and sauté until the meat is well browned, about 15 minutes, stirring frequently to break up the pieces. Add the garlic and cook for 1 more minute.

2. Stir in the tomatoes, tomato sauce, Italian seasoning, and fennel seeds, if using. Season to taste with salt and pepper. Bring to a simmer, reduce the heat, and simmer, covered, for at least 15 minutes, stirring occasionally.

3. Meanwhile, cook the noodles in a large pot of boiling salted water for 10 to 12 minutes, until tender but still firm. Drain the noodles and rinse with cold water. Drain well and set aside.

4. Combine the egg, ricotta cheese, and ¼ cup of Parmesan cheese in a medium bowl and set aside.

5. Preheat the oven to 375°F. Grease a 9 x 13-inch baking dish.

6. Spread about 1 cup of sauce over the bottom of the baking dish. Cover with a layer of pasta, overlapping the noodles by ½ inch. Spread with one-third of the ricotta cheese mixture. Scatter one-quarter of the mozzarella cheese on top. Spoon about 1½ cups of sauce over the cheese. Add another layer of noodles and continue layering until all the ingredients are used, ending with a layer of pasta, sauce, and mozzarella cheese. Sprinkle the remaining Parmesan cheese over the top.

7. Place the baking dish on a baking sheet and bake for 30 to 35 minutes, or until heated through. Let stand for 10 minutes before serving.

Buttered Noodles

Egg noodles were often used by the Pennsylvania Dutch when they settled in eastern Pennsylvania. These settlers were actually German, not Dutch. In fact, their name came from the word "Deutsch," which is German for "German." This is a very simple but popular way to serve egg noodles, enhanced by the fresh parsley.

SERVES 4 TO 6

1 (12-ounce) package egg noodles
¼ cup (½ stick) butter
Salt and pepper
Chopped fresh parsley

1. Cook the noodles in a large pot of boiling salted water until done, about 10 minutes. Drain and return to the pot.

2. Melt the butter in a small saucepan over medium-high heat and continue to cook until it turns brown, watching carefully to make sure it doesn't burn.

3. Pour the butter over the noodles. Add the salt, pepper, and parsley to taste and stir until well combined. Serve immediately.

Three-Cheese Noodle Bake

This creamy casserole can be served as a side dish with a simple main course, such as baked chicken or fish. The recipe can also be doubled to serve as a main dish.

SERVES 4 TO 6

8 ounces egg noodles
3 tablespoons butter
2 cups shredded Cheddar cheese (about 8 ounces)
1 cup cottage cheese
½ cup sour cream
3 tablespoons grated Parmesan cheese
1 large egg, lightly beaten
¼ cup milk
1 teaspoon Worcestershire sauce
¼ teaspoon salt
¼ teaspoon black pepper

1. Preheat the oven to 300°F. Grease a 2-quart baking dish.

2. Cook the noodles in a large pot of boiling salted water until done, about 10 minutes; drain. Transfer the noodles to a large bowl and stir in the butter until melted. Mix in 1½ cups of Cheddar cheese, the cottage cheese, sour cream, Parmesan cheese, egg, milk, Worcestershire sauce, salt, and pepper.

3. Transfer the noodles to the baking dish and sprinkle with the remaining ½ cup Cheddar cheese.

4. Bake for 1 hour or until set. Serve hot.

Noodles Romanoff

The Romanoff family ruled Russia until the revolution in 1917. A dish that contains sour cream is often thought of as Russian; this dish could have acquired its royal reference because it is rich enough for a Russian czar. You may know this delectably rich noodle dish under its other name, sour cream noodles.

SERVES 4 TO 6

1 (12-ounce) package wide egg noodles
2 tablespoons butter
1 (16-ounce) container sour cream (about 2 cups)
1 cup grated Parmesan cheese
½ cup chopped scallions
½ teaspoon minced garlic
2 teaspoons Worcestershire sauce
½ teaspoon salt
⅛ teaspoon black pepper

1. Preheat the oven to 350°F. Grease a 2-quart baking dish.

2. Cook the noodles in boiling salted water until done, about 10 minutes; drain. Transfer the noodles to a large bowl and stir in the butter until melted. Mix in the sour cream, ½ cup of cheese, the scallions, garlic, Worcestershire sauce, salt, and pepper.

3. Transfer the noodles to the prepared dish and sprinkle with the remaining ½ cup Parmesan cheese.

4. Bake for 30 minutes, just until heated through. Serve hot.

Noodles with Cabbage

The mixture of noodles and sour cream has many guises, including this dish, which immigrants from Poland and Hungary brought to these shores. Known variously as "haluska," "haluski," and "kapusta," it contains noodles, cabbage, onions, and sour cream. Though traditionally served as a side dish, it also makes a fine vegetarian main dish. To convert this to a main course for meat eaters, sauté one pound of sliced kielbasa with the cabbage and onion.

SERVES 6 TO 8

1 (16-ounce) package wide egg noodles
½ cup (1 stick) butter
1 medium head green cabbage, cored and
    coarsely shredded
2 medium onions, thinly sliced
2 teaspoons paprika
1 teaspoon salt
1 teaspoon celery salt
½ teaspoon black pepper
1 (16-ounce) container sour cream (about
    2 cups)

1. Cook the noodles in boiling salted water until done, about 10 minutes; drain.

2. Melt the butter in a large Dutch oven over medium-high heat. Add the cabbage and onions and sauté until the cabbage is wilted, about 5 minutes. Cover and simmer over medium heat for 10 minutes.

3. Stir in the paprika, salt, celery salt, pepper, and cooked noodles; cook until warmed through, about 5 minutes.

4. Remove from the heat and stir in the sour cream. Serve hot.

Noodle Kugel

Kugel translates as "pudding" in Yiddish, the everyday language of European Jews. The Jews of Eastern Europe brought their recipes for noodle kugel with them to America. Although this recipe is sweet enough to be served as dessert, it is traditionally a side dish. Note that it must be refrigerated overnight before it is baked; this allows the uncooked noodles to absorb enough moisture to soften before baking.

SERVES 8 TO 10

4 large eggs
¾ cup sugar
3 cups milk
1½ cups ricotta cheese
1 (12-ounce) package wide egg noodles
½ cup golden raisins
3 tablespoons sugar
1 teaspoon ground cinnamon

1. Grease a 9 x 13-inch baking dish.

2. Combine the eggs, sugar, milk, and ricotta cheese in a large bowl. Add the uncooked noodles and raisins and stir gently to mix.

3. Spoon the noodle mixture into the prepared baking dish, cover with plastic wrap, and refrigerate overnight. Check occasionally to make sure the noodles are immersed in the liquid.

4. Preheat the oven to 350°F.

5. Uncover the kugel. Mix the sugar and cinnamon in a small bowl and sprinkle over the top. Cover with aluminum foil.

6. Bake for 35 minutes. Uncover and bake for another 40 minutes, until firm in the center, puffed up, and browned a little on the top. Serve hot or at room temperature.

Spaetzle with Browned Butter

Tiny German dumplings, or "spaetzle," are very quick and easy to make and complement a variety of foods. Though theay are traditionally served with roasted veal or stews, you can serve them as you would noodles or other dumplings. There are several spaetzle makers available—one like a potato ricer with larger holes and another like a flat grater that fits on top of the pot. If you don't have a spaetzle maker, force the batter through the holes of a strainer with a rubber spatula.

SERVES 4

2½ cups sifted all-purpose flour
1 teaspoon baking powder
½ teaspoon salt, plus more to taste
¼ teaspoon ground nutmeg
2 large eggs, lightly beaten
1¼ cups milk
5 tablespoons butter
Black pepper

1. Stir together the flour, baking powder, salt, and nutmeg in a large bowl. Add the eggs and milk and stir until thoroughly combined. Let the dough rest for 15 minutes before cooking.

2. Bring a large pot of lightly salted water to a boil. Force the dough through a spaetzle maker and cook until done, about 4 minutes. Remove from the pot with a strainer or slotted spoon and drain well.

3. Melt the butter in a small saucepan or skillet over medium heat and continue cooking until the butter browns.

4. Place the spaetzle in a serving dish and pour the butter on top. Season to taste with salt and pepper, toss well to combine, and serve immediately.

Seafood Paella

Paella is one of the few dishes from Spain that is frequently cooked in American homes. There is no one recipe for paella, but it always includes saffron-flavored rice, often with a variety of meats like seafood and sausage.

SERVES 4

2 tablespoons oil
2 cups long-grain white rice
1 small onion, minced
1 medium red bell pepper, seeded and diced
½ teaspoon minced garlic
4 cups chicken broth (page 119)
½ teaspoon saffron threads, crushed
Salt and pepper
½ pound smoked sausage, thinly sliced
½ pound shrimp, peeled and deveined
¼ cup bay scallops or sea scallops cut into quarters
18 small hard-shell clams or mussels, well scrubbed and beards removed

1. Heat the oil over medium-high heat in a large, ovenproof skillet. Add the rice, onion, bell pepper, and garlic and sauté until the rice is toasted and dry, about 5 minutes.

2. Add the broth and saffron, reduce the heat to maintain a gentle simmer, cover, and cook until the liquid is absorbed, 15 to 18 minutes. Turn off and let the rice stand, covered for 5 to 10 minutes. Meanwhile, preheat the oven to 350°F.

3. When the rice is cooked, fluff with a fork. Season to taste with salt and pepper. Place the sausage, shrimp, scallops, and clams on top of the rice. Cover and bake for 15 to 20 minutes, until the shrimp are firm and the clams open (discard the closed ones).

4. Stir gently to mix all the ingredients. Serve immediately.

Arroz con Pollo

This dish is a classic combination made with many different flavorings found throughout Spain, Central America, and the Caribbean. Besides including chicken and rice, there are no steadfast rules for preparing this dish.

SERVES 4 TO 5

1 pound boneless, skinless chicken breasts, cut into bite-size pieces
Salt and pepper
2 tablespoons oil
1 medium onion, diced
1 medium green bell pepper, seeded and diced
2 cups long-grain white rice
1 teaspoon minced garlic
3 cups chicken broth (page 119)
¼ teaspoon saffron threads, crushed
4 medium tomatoes, seeded and diced, or 2 cups canned diced tomatoes, drained
1 cup frozen peas
¼ cup chopped fresh cilantro

1. Rub the chicken with salt and pepper. Heat the oil in a large skillet over medium-high heat. Add the chicken and sauté for 2 minutes. Add the onion, and bell pepper. Sauté until the vegetables are limp and the chicken is white and firm, 6 to 8 minutes. Add the rice and sauté for 3 to 5 minutes more, until toasted. Add the garlic and cook for 1 more minute.

2. Stir in the broth and saffron. Bring to a boil, cover, reduce the heat to maintain a gentle simmer, and cook until the liquid is absorbed, 15 to 18 minutes. Turn off the heat and let the rice stand, covered, for 10 to 15 minutes.

3. When the rice is cooked, fluff with a fork. Stir in the tomatoes, peas, and cilantro. Cover and cook over low heat for 3 minutes, until the peas are cooked through. Taste and season with salt and pepper as needed. Serve at once.

TIP: You can substitute ¼ teaspoon turmeric for the saffron. The flavor will be different, but it will give the rice its characteristic yellow color.

Chicken Pilau

While the South knows this chicken and rice dish as pilau, it can be found in various cultures by the names of pilaf or jambalaya. This recipe is quite similar to chicken bog, minus the smoked sausage.

SERVES 6 TO 8

3 to 4 pounds chicken parts
8 cups water
¼ pound bacon, diced
1 medium onion, finely chopped
3 large celery ribs, finely chopped
2 to 3 large tomatoes (about 1 pound), seeded and chopped
1 tablespoon fresh thyme leaves or 1 teaspoon dried
½ teaspoon crushed red pepper
2 cups long-grain white rice
Salt and pepper

1. Combine the chicken and water in a large saucepan and bring to a boil. Reduce the heat and simmer until the chicken is very tender, 1 to 1½ hours.

2. Remove the chicken from the broth and skim off the excess fat from the surface (if desired). Pull the meat from the bones and chop. Discard the skin and bones; reserve the chicken and the broth.

3. Cook the bacon over medium heat in a large skillet until crisp, 10 to 15 minutes. Remove the bacon with a slotted spoon and set aside. Drain off all but 2 tablespoons of bacon fat.

4. Add the onion and celery to the skillet and sauté until the onion is soft, about 4 minutes. Add the bacon, tomatoes, thyme, crushed red pepper, and rice.

5. Stir in 3 cups of reserved broth and the chicken. Season to taste with salt and pepper. Cover, bring to a simmer, reduce the heat, and cook slowly, without lifting the lid, for 30 minutes, until the rice is tender and all the broth is absorbed. Serve hot.

Cajun Dirty Rice

Various meats in this dish give the rice a dirty appearance, hence the name of this Cajun classic. It is served as a main course, a side dish, or a stuffing.

SERVES 6 TO 8

2 cups long-grain white rice
5 cups chicken broth (page 119)
¼ cup chicken livers
¼ cup chicken gizzard
2 tablespoons oil
1 medium onion, diced
1 medium green bell pepper, seeded and diced
2 teaspoons minced garlic
Salt and pepper
1 teaspoon dried thyme
1 bay leaf
¼ teaspoon cayenne pepper
¼ pound pork sausage meat
¼ pound ground pork

1. Combine the rice and 4 cups of broth in a large saucepan and bring to a boil. Cover and simmer for 15 to 18 minutes, until the liquid is absorbed. Set aside.

2. Meanwhile, cover the livers and gizzard with water in a small pot. Simmer for 30 minutes. Drain, let it cool enough to handle, then dice and add to the rice.

3. Heat the oil in a large skillet over medium-high heat. Add the onion, bell pepper, and garlic, and sauté until softened, about 5 minutes. Season to taste with salt and pepper, then add the thyme, bay leaf, and cayenne pepper. Add to the rice.

4. Return the skillet to medium-high heat. Add the sausage and pork and sauté until well browned, about 10 minutes. Add to the rice.

5. Mix in the remaining 1 cup broth and let simmer on the lowest heat for 30 minutes, stirring continuously, until the flavors meld. Remove the bay leaf and serve hot.

Chicken Bog

Chicken bog apparently gets its name because the chicken is "bogged" in rice. It's a traditional Southern dish served on the Fourth of July and at barbecues and picnics. The dish may have originated years ago at tobacco barns or warehouses, where it was served at barn suppers. There are many versions of the dish, but all have in common the rice, chicken, smoked sausage, and plenty of black pepper. If serving as leftovers, add water or additional chicken broth as needed.

SERVES 6 TO 8

3 to 4 pounds chicken parts
4 cups water
1 tablespoon salt
1 medium onion, finely chopped
1 pound smoked sausage, cut into ½-inch pieces
2 cups long-grain white rice
1 tablespoon chopped fresh thyme
½ teaspoon black pepper, or more to taste
¼ teaspoon crushed red pepper

1. Combine the chicken and water in a large saucepan and bring to a boil. Reduce the heat and simmer, covered, until the chicken is tender, 1 to 1½ hours.

2. Remove the chicken from the broth and skim off the excess fat from the broth's surface (if desired). Remove the meat from the bones and chop. Discard the skin and bones. Return the chicken to the broth.

3. Stir in the salt, onion, sausage, rice, thyme, black pepper, and crushed red pepper. Bring to a boil, reduce the heat, cover, and gently simmer for 30 minutes. Taste and add more salt and pepper as needed. Serve hot.

Jambalaya

There are many ways to make jambalaya—any meat goes in, including duck and alligator. A Creole-style red jambalaya has tomatoes or tomato sauce, while a Cajun-style brown jambalaya uses meat broth to color the rice. This recipe is for a red jambalaya with ham, chicken, and shrimp.

SERVES 6

2 slices bacon
1 medium onion, diced
1 medium green bell pepper, seeded and diced
2 medium celery ribs, diced
1½ teaspoons minced garlic
2 cups long-grain white rice
2 tablespoons tomato paste
4 cups chicken broth (page 119)
1 (15-ounce) can diced tomatoes
2 dashes hot pepper sauce, such as Tabasco,
　　plus more to taste
1 teaspoon dried thyme
1 bay leaf
½ pound smoked ham, diced
2 cups shredded cooked chicken or turkey
2 cups cooked shrimp, peeled and deveined
¼ cup chopped fresh parsley
Salt and pepper

1. Cook the bacon in a large skillet over medium heat until crisp, 10 to 15 minutes. Transfer to paper towels to drain.

2. Return the skillet to medium-high heat. Add the onion, bell pepper, celery, and garlic and sauté until the vegetables are softened, about 5 minutes.

3. Add the rice and tomato paste to the skillet and sauté until the tomato paste turns a mahogany color, about 4 minutes. Stir in the broth, tomatoes, hot pepper sauce, thyme, and bay leaf. Cover and bring to a boil. Reduce the heat to maintain a gentle boil and cook until the liquid is absorbed, about 15 minutes.

4. Uncover and add the ham, chicken, shrimp, and parsley. Replace the cover and let stand for 15 minutes.

5. Fluff the rice with a fork. Crumble the bacon and mix in. Season to taste with salt and pepper and more hot sauce, if desired. Remove the bay leaf and serve hot.

Louisiana Red Beans and Rice

Red beans and rice is a delicious and popular Louisiana dish, traditionally served on Mondays, using the ham bone left from Sunday's ham dinner. Since Mondays were busy wash days, cooks needed an easy dish that could simmer on the back of the stove while they did their chores.

SERVES 6

1 pound red beans, soaked overnight, debris
　　removed, and drained
6 cups water
1 pound andouille or other smoked sausage,
　　cut into ¼-inch slices
3 medium celery ribs, chopped
1 large onion, chopped
1 medium green bell pepper, seeded and
　　chopped
3 bay leaves
½ teaspoon minced garlic
2 teaspoons dried thyme
1 teaspoon dried sage
1 teaspoon red-wine vinegar
¼ teaspoon hot pepper sauce, such as Tabasco
3 tablespoons chopped fresh parsley
Hot cooked rice, to serve

1. Combine the beans and water in a large saucepan. Bring to a boil, reduce the heat, and simmer, partially covered and stirring occasionally, for about 1½ hours, until the beans are tender.

2. Add the sausage, celery, onion, bell pepper, bay leaves, garlic, thyme, sage, vinegar, and hot pepper sauce. Simmer for about 1 hour, stirring occasionally. Add water if the mixture becomes dry.

3. Remove the bay leaves, sprinkle with parsley, and serve hot over the rice.

Spanish Rice with Beef

This one-dish meal combines beef and rice with Tex-Mex seasonings. If desired, add crushed red pepper to spice it up. It also makes wonderful leftovers.

SERVES 6

1 pound ground beef
½ medium onion, finely chopped
½ medium green bell pepper, seeded and
   finely chopped
1 tablespoon chili powder
1 teaspoon ground cumin
2 cups long-grain white rice
1 (15-ounce) can diced tomatoes
Salt and pepper

1. Brown the beef with the onion, bell pepper, chili powder, and cumin in a large skillet over medium-high heat, breaking it up with a spoon, about 10 minutes.

2. Stir in the rice and sauté, stirring constantly, until the rice is lightly toasted, about 5 minutes.

3. Drain the tomatoes, pouring the juice into a 4-cup glass measuring cup. Add enough boiling water to the juice to make 4 cups. Add to the skillet with the tomatoes, and season to taste with salt and pepper. Stir well.

4. Cover, bring to a boil, reduce the heat, and simmer until the liquid is absorbed, 15 to 18 minutes. Turn off the heat and let the rice stand, covered, for 10 to 15 minutes.

5. Fluff the rice with a fork and serve immediately.

Basic Cooked White Rice

The goal when cooking white rice is to make tender, fluffy rice, with each kernel separate and firm, not mushy. Never stir rice while it's cooking; this is what turns rice gummy.

SERVES 4 (ABOUT 3 CUPS)

2 cups water
1 tablespoon butter (optional)
1 cup long-grain white rice
½ teaspoon salt (optional)

1. Bring the water to a boil in a medium saucepan with the butter, if using. Stir in the rice and salt, if using.

2. Cook over medium-low heat until most of the water is absorbed, 15 to 18 minutes.

3. Turn off the heat and let the rice stand, covered, for 10 to 15 minutes. Fluff the rice with a fork and serve.

Basic Cooked Brown Rice

Brown rice is chewier than white rice and has more nutrients because it is less polished. It also takes longer to cook. The proportion of water to brown rice varies depending on the type of rice. For long-grain brown rice, use 1 cup rice to 2¼ to 2½ cups water. For short-grain brown rice, use 1 cup rice to 2 to 2¼ cups water.

SERVES 4 (ABOUT 3 CUPS)

2 to 2½ cups water
1 tablespoon butter (optional)
1 cup brown rice
½ teaspoon salt (optional)

1. Bring the water to a boil in a medium saucepan with the butter, if using. Stir in the rice and salt, if using.

2. Cover and cook over very low heat until all the water is absorbed, 35 to 45 minutes.

3. Turn off the heat and let the rice stand, covered, for 10 to 15 minutes. Fluff the rice with a fork and serve.

Basic Cooked Wild Rice

Wild rice is not really rice at all; it is a cereal grain native to North America. It grows wild in the Great Lakes region and is also grown as a field crop. Native Americans have harvested wild rice for centuries, and it was a valuable commodity to early explorers, both as a food supply and for trading.

SERVES 4 (ABOUT 3 CUPS)

1 cup wild rice
4 cups water
½ teaspoon salt (optional)
Butter (optional)

1. Rinse the rice thoroughly in a strainer. Combine with the water in a large, heavy saucepan, adding the salt, if using. Bring to a boil. Reduce the heat, cover loosely, and simmer for 45 to 60 minutes, until the rice has puffed. Remove from the heat.

2. Fluff the rice with a fork, cover tightly, and let stand for 5 to 10 minutes.

3. Drain off any excess water. Stir in the butter, if using, and serve.

Lemon Parsley Rice

The easiest way to dress up rice is to add a flavoring ingredient. In this recipe, a little lemon and parsley give the rice flavor and color. Don't even think about using bottled lemon juice or dried parsley; only fresh will do here. This is the perfect accompaniment to fish and shellfish.

SERVES 4 (ABOUT 3 CUPS)

2 cups water
1 cup long-grain white rice
½ teaspoon salt
2 tablespoons finely chopped fresh parsley
2 tablespoons butter, or more to taste
1 teaspoon grated lemon zest

1. Bring the water to a boil in a medium saucepan. Stir in the rice and salt.

2. Cook over medium heat until most of the water is absorbed, 15 to 18 minutes.

3. Turn off the heat. Add the parsley, butter, and lemon zest and let the rice stand, covered, for 10 to 15 minutes more. Fluff the rice with a fork and serve.

Rice Pilaf

Pilaf is rice that has been stirred in hot butter or oil, then cooked in broth—a method of cooking that has spread throughout the world and is particularly popular in the Middle East and India. When pilafs traveled to the American South, they were called pilau, purlow, or perlew.

SERVES 6 TO 8 (ABOUT 6 CUPS)

2 tablespoons butter
1 tablespoon oil
½ medium onion, chopped
2 cups long-grain white rice
4 cups chicken broth (page 119)
1 teaspoon salt
Pinch of black pepper
2 tablespoons chopped fresh parsley

1. Melt the butter in the oil in a medium saucepan over medium heat. Add the onion and rice and sauté until the rice is golden brown, about 5 minutes.

2. Stir in the broth and bring to a boil. Add the salt and pepper, reduce the heat, and gently simmer for 15 to 18 minutes, until the liquid is mostly absorbed.

3. Turn off the heat and let the rice stand, covered, for 10 to 15 minutes.

4. Fluff the rice with a fork, mix in the parsley, and serve.

Saffron Rice

Saffron is the world's most expensive spice. It is the stigmas from the fall-flowering crocus flower. There are only three stigmas (referred to as saffron threads when harvested) per flower, and these are hand harvested. It takes thousands of threads to make one ounce of saffron, but even a little saffron added to rice lends a warm yellow color and a distinct flavor that especially complements chicken.

SERVES 6 TO 8 (ABOUT 6 CUPS)

2 tablespoons butter
1 tablespoon oil
½ medium onion, chopped
2 cups long-grain rice
4 cups chicken broth (page 119)
¼ teaspoon saffron threads, crushed
½ cup raisins
2 tablespoons toasted pine nuts
Salt and pepper

1. Melt the butter in the oil in a medium sauce-pan over medium-high heat. Add the onion and rice and sauté until the rice is golden brown, about 5 minutes.

2. Stir in the broth and saffron and bring to a boil. Reduce the heat, and simmer for 15 to 18 minutes, until most of the liquid is absorbed.

3. Turn off the heat and let the rice stand, covered, for 10 to 15 minutes.

4. Fluff the rice with a fork, mix in the raisins and pine nuts, season to taste with salt and pepper, and serve.

Spanish Rice

Spanish rice, red rice, Mexican rice—there are many names for rice cooked with tomatoes and bell peppers. This is a great side dish with Mexican foods and with chicken, beef, and pork.

SERVES 4 TO 6 (ABOUT 4 CUPS)

2 tablespoons oil
1 cup long-grain white rice
1 medium onion, finely chopped
1 medium green bell pepper, seeded and finely chopped
1 teaspoon minced garlic
1 teaspoon chili powder
2½ cups water
1 (8-ounce) can tomato sauce
1½ teaspoons salt

1. Heat the oil in a large skillet over medium heat. Add the rice, onion, bell pepper, garlic, and chili powder and sauté for about 5 minutes, stirring frequently.

2. Stir in the water, tomato sauce, and salt. Bring to a boil, reduce the heat, and simmer for 15 to 20 minutes, until the liquid is mostly absorbed.

3. Turn off the heat and let the rice stand, covered, for 10 to 15 minutes.

4. Fluff the rice with a fork and serve.

Green Rice

"Arroz verde," or green rice, is not as well known as Spanish rice, but it is an equally good choice to accompany Mexican food. Fresh cilantro and parsley lend the rice the green color and distinct herbal flavor.

SERVES 4 (ABOUT 3 CUPS)

2 tablespoons oil
½ medium onion, finely chopped
1 jalapeño chile pepper, seeded and minced
1 teaspoon minced garlic
1 teaspoon ground cumin
½ teaspoon salt
¼ cup chopped fresh cilantro, plus more to serve
¼ cup chopped fresh parsley
2 cups chicken broth (page 119)
1 cup long-grain white rice

1. Heat 1 tablespoon of oil in a large, heavy skillet over medium-high heat. Add the onion and jalapeño and sauté until softened, about 3 minutes. Add the garlic, cumin, salt, cilantro, and parsley and cook, stirring, for 30 seconds.

2. Remove from the heat and transfer to a blender with ½ cup of broth. Blend until smooth and set aside.

3. Heat the remaining 1 tablespoon oil in the skillet over medium heat. Add the rice and cook, stirring, until translucent, 1 to 2 minutes. Add the herb purée and cook, stirring, to evaporate most of the liquid, 2 to 3 minutes. Add the remaining 1½ cups broth, stir, cover, and reduce the heat to medium-low. Simmer, without stirring, until the rice is tender and the liquid is absorbed, about 20 minutes.

4. Remove from the heat and let sit, covered, for 10 to 15 minutes.

5. Fluff with a fork and serve, garnished with additional cilantro.

Southern Red Rice

This recipe is quite similar to Spanish rice. Both are flavored with tomatoes, bell peppers, and onion, but Spanish rice has chili powder, typical of Tex–Mex cooking. Southern red rice has bacon, which is characteristic of many Southern dishes.

SERVES 6 TO 8 (ABOUT 6 CUPS)

4 to 6 slices bacon
1 medium onion, finely chopped
1 medium green bell pepper, seeded and finely chopped
2 medium celery ribs, finely chopped
2 cups long-grain white rice
1 (28-ounce) can diced tomatoes
1½ cups water
2 teaspoons salt, or to taste
¼ teaspoon black pepper
3 to 4 drops hot pepper sauce, such as Tabasco, or to taste

1. Preheat the oven to 350°F. Grease a 2-quart baking dish.

2. Fry the bacon until crisp in a large skillet over medium heat, about 10 to 15 minutes. Use a slotted spoon to transfer it from the pan to paper towels to drain. Crumble and set aside.

3. Add the onion, bell pepper, and celery to the bacon fat in the skillet and sauté until softened, about 5 minutes. Stir in the rice, tomatoes, water, salt, pepper, hot pepper sauce, and crumbled bacon.

4. Pour into the prepared baking dish. Cover tightly with aluminum foil and bake for about 1 hour, until the rice is tender. Serve hot.

San Francisco Rice

Rice-A-Roni was introduced in 1958, and thanks to a very effective advertising campaign, it became a favorite packaged side dish. The dish is actually an old Armenian pilaf recipe consisting of rice, vermicelli pasta, and chicken broth. There's nothing to relate it to San Francisco, other than the fact that Vince DeDomenico lived in San Francisco when he decided to produce his version for sale in grocery stores. He placed the rice and pasta in a box, added a dry seasoning mix in place of the liquid chicken broth, and called it Rice-A-Roni.

SERVES 4 (ABOUT 3 CUPS)

2 tablespoons butter
½ cup vermicelli (broken into small pieces) or ½ cup orzo
½ cup long-grain white rice
1 teaspoon minced garlic
2 cups chicken broth (page 119)
½ teaspoon seasoned salt
1 tablespoon chopped fresh parsley

1. Melt the butter in a large saucepan over medium heat. Add the vermicelli and sauté until browned, about 5 minutes. Mix in the rice and garlic and sauté until the garlic is fragrant, about 1 minute. Add the broth and salt, cover, and simmer for 15 to 18 minutes, until the liquid is absorbed.

2. Fluff with a fork and stir in the parsley. Cover and let stand for 10 to 15 minutes. Serve hot.

Curried Rice with Peas

If you are serving a simple roast or cutlet and want an exotic side dish, curried rice is a good choice. If you like, substitute frozen green beans or carrots.

SERVES 6 TO 8 (ABOUT 6 CUPS)

¼ cup (½ stick) butter
2 cups long-grain white rice
¼ cup finely chopped onion
1 teaspoon minced garlic
2 tablespoons curry powder
4 cups chicken broth (page 119) or water
1½ cups frozen peas
¼ cup chopped pimentos or roasted red bell pepper
Salt and pepper

1. Melt the butter in a large skillet over medium heat. Add the rice, onion, garlic, and curry powder and sauté for about 5 minutes, stirring frequently.

2. Stir in the broth. Bring to a boil, reduce the heat, and simmer for 15 to 18 minutes, until the liquid is absorbed.

3. Turn off the heat, add the peas and pimentos, and let the rice stand, covered, for 10 to 15 minutes.

4. Fluff the rice with a fork. Season to taste with salt and pepper and serve.

Fried Rice

You can enjoy fried rice as a side dish or main dish. As a main dish for four people, double the recipe and add diced or slivered cooked pork or chicken and some cooked vegetables, such as chopped broccoli or carrots.

SERVES 4 (ABOUT 3 CUPS)

2 tablespoons oil
2 cups cooked white rice
¼ cup finely chopped onion
¼ cup soy sauce, or more to taste
2 large eggs
¼ cup chopped scallions
¼ cup frozen peas

1. Heat the oil in a large skillet over medium-high heat. Add the rice and onion and sauté for about 10 minutes, until the onion is cooked and the rice is heated through and evenly browned. Add the soy sauce and cook for 3 more minutes.

2. Move the rice aside and crack the eggs into the skillet. Stir constantly to break up the eggs as they cook.

3. Add the scallions and peas and continue to cook, stirring frequently, until the peas are heated through. Serve hot.

Risotto with Mushrooms

Making a risotto requires constant attention, so make sure you have 30 to 40 minutes to devote. The amount of broth you add will vary depending upon your stove's temperature. Use a variety of mushrooms, if desired.

SERVES 4 TO 6 (ABOUT 5 CUPS)

1 tablespoon oil
1 tablespoon butter
½ medium onion, diced
2 cups mushrooms, chopped
½ teaspoon salt
Pinch of black pepper
1 cup Arborio rice
5 cups chicken broth (page 119), plus more as needed
½ medium lemon, juiced
½ cup grated Parmesan cheese

1. In a medium saucepan, heat the broth over medium-high heat; keep hot.

2. In a large saucepan, heat the oil and butter over medium-high heat. Add the onion, mushrooms, salt, and pepper, and cook for 4 to 5 minutes. Add the rice and cook for 2 minutes longer, stirring constantly.

3. Add 1 cup of hot broth and the lemon juice. Stir continuously until the liquid is absorbed. Gradually add the remaining 2 cups hot broth in 3 equal portions, allowing the rice to absorb the broth before each addition. Add more hot broth as needed to reach a firm but not crunchy texture.

4. Turn off the heat. Stir in the Parmesan cheese and serve immediately.

Hoppin' John

There is more than one theory as to how this Southern dish, traditionally served on New Year's Day, got its name. Some say that children would hop around the table once, as a New Year's ritual, before eating the dish. Others claim the name is a derivation of a French term for "pigeon peas." In any event, eating Hoppin' John on the first day of the new year is supposed to ensure good luck through the rest of it.

SERVES 6 TO 8 (ABOUT 6 CUPS)

1 cup dried black-eyed peas, rinsed and debris removed
6 cups water
2 small smoked ham hocks
1 medium onion, finely chopped
1 teaspoon crushed red pepper
1 teaspoon salt
1 teaspoon black pepper
½ teaspoon dried thyme
1 cup long-grain white rice
Hot pepper sauce, such as Tabasco, or hot pepper vinegar, to serve

1. Combine the black-eyed peas with the water in a large saucepan. Add the ham hocks, onion, crushed red pepper, salt, black pepper, and thyme. Bring to a boil over high heat, reduce the heat, and simmer gently until the peas are soft but not mushy, about 1½ hours.

2. Remove the ham hock and set aside to cool.

3. Drain the cooking liquid from the peas into a 4-cup measuring cup. You will need 2 cups of liquid to cook the rice. Discard any extra liquid or, if necessary, add hot water to equal 2 cups.

4. Pour the liquid back into the pea mixture. Cut the meat from the ham hock and add it to the pot. Stir in the rice, cover, and cook over low heat for about 20 minutes.

5. Without lifting the lid, set the mixture aside to steam for 10 to 15 minutes.

6. Fluff the mixture with a fork and serve immediately with hot pepper sauce.

PREPARING PASTA AND RICE

Guide to Rice

In addition to the familiar white and brown rice, there are now black, purple, and red rice. You can also divide rice into short grain, medium grain, and long grain.

▶ **Brown rice:** With its nutty taste and chewy texture, this unpolished rice tastes best when paired with strong seasonings and sauces. It is available in supermarkets and natural food stores.

▶ **Long-grain white rice:** The majority of the rice consumed in America is long grain. This rice's neutral taste and firm texture make it a perfect side dish with almost anything. When cooked, the grains remain separate and fluffy. Jasmine is a type of long-grain rice with a mild popcorn aroma. Basmati also has a popcorn aroma. When cooked, its long grains separate well. Long-grain rice is excellent paired with seafood dishes. It is available in most supermarkets, Asian and Indian groceries, natural food stores, and gourmet stores.

▶ **Short-grain white rice:** This is the rice to use when you prefer a stickier texture and a softer grain after cooking. It pairs well with many Asian dishes and is used in dishes such as paella and risotto. One popular type of short-grain rice is Arborio. Grown in both America and Italy, it is sometimes labeled "risotto rice." When cooked, Arborio rice produces a slightly chewy grain with a creamy exterior. It is available in supermarkets, Italian groceries, gourmet food stores, and natural food stores.

Rice Cooking Tips

There's no trick to making good rice time after time; it's a matter of measuring carefully and paying attention to timing.

▶ Rice cooked with tomatoes or other high-acid ingredients often requires extra water.

▶ Instead of boiling rice, you can bake it. Combine rice and boiling liquid in an ovenproof baking dish, cover, and bake at 375°F until the liquid is absorbed, 25 to 30 minutes.

▶ For added flavor, replace some or all of the water with chicken broth, beef broth, or vegetable broth. Wine, sherry, or beer can also replace some of the water.

▶ Make sure the pot lid covers the pot tightly.

▶ Unless a recipe says otherwise, don't stir the rice while it cooks.

Cooking Pasta

Cooking dry pasta is as easy as boiling water, but here are a few tips to guarantee that the pasta has a pleasing texture.

▶ Use plenty of water—6 to 8 quarts of water per pound of pasta.

▶ Unsalted water comes to a boil faster than salted water. So bring the water to a boil, then add about 1 tablespoon salt for every 1 gallon of water.

▶ The water should be boiling before you add the pasta. Stir the pasta a few times to keep it moving so it cooks evenly and doesn't stick together.

▶ Cover the pot after adding the pasta to bring the water back to a boil rapidly, then remove the cover.

▶ To tell if the pasta is done, remove a piece and bite into it. Perfectly cooked pasta should be al dente—tender but still firm to the bite. If there is a hard core in the pasta, it is not done.

▶ Drain the pasta thoroughly. Pasta will continue to cook in the strainer unless served immediately or rinsed with cold water.

▶ Because pasta cools rapidly, it is a good idea to serve it in warmed bowls.

▶ If you're cooking with fresh pasta, figure about one-third the cooking time of dry pasta.

CHAPTER ELEVEN

Vegetables

Every year, Thanksgiving tables overflow with a flavorful bounty of scalloped, creamed, and glazed vegetables. After all, this is the way our ancestors cooked every day—not just for special occasions.

In earlier days, fresh-picked vegetables were prepared in ways that brought out their best flavors—baked in a casserole with cream sauce or fried in bacon grease. No one ever had to remind the kids to eat their vegetables!

It all began when the first colonists arrived in the New World looking for fertile land to farm. Without a successful crop, it was nearly impossible for families to thrive and achieve the necessary security and economic independence that were the hallmarks of life in the New World.

And what vegetable wonders the New World could produce! American colonists soon learned to fertilize their staple crops with fish for heartier harvests, and planted beans between the rows of corn. Crops of pumpkins and winter squash could be grown in winter gardens to provide sustenance during seasons of colder weather.

Potatoes, on the other hand, weren't always a popular vegetable. Although they were introduced several times in the United States without success, it wasn't until Scottish-Irish immigrants produced the first abundant potato crops near Boston in 1719 that they finally earned a prominent place on dinner tables across America.

As the United States continued to evolve from a predominantly agrarian society to a more industrialized nation in the nineteenth century, fewer and fewer families had land on which to grow vegetables. But gardens remained an important element of American culture throughout its history, symbolizing such ideas as unity during the grass-roots, "victory garden" movement of both world wars, and today epitomizing "the good life" for suburbanites.

You don't need a farm or garden plot to enjoy fresh vegetables today. Modern processing techniques and worldwide distribution have now made a variety of fresh vegetables available year-round. With fresh, regional produce readily available at farmers' markets, organic grocers, and supermarkets, it's time to bring back the most flavorful ways of cooking!

Basic Cooked Artichokes

It is easy to cook artichokes—just steam them until they are tender. What is tricky is prepping them for steaming. When you are preparing artichokes for yourself and fellow artichoke lovers, just trim the stems to make the artichokes sit level and place them in the pot.

SERVES 4

1 to 2 tablespoons white vinegar
4 large artichokes
½ medium lemon
½ cup (1 stick) butter, melted
2 tablespoons lemon juice

1. Fill a large bowl with water and add 1 tablespoon vinegar per quart of water.

2. Cut each artichoke stem just above the small leaves. If the stem is not too woody, it can also be peeled and cooked. Snap off or cut off the tough dark outer leaves of the artichoke. Stop at the point where the leaves begin to turn yellow, indicating tenderness. Cut off the top of each artichoke with a serrated knife, about ½ inch from the tip. Rub the cut surfaces with lemon. Use scissors to trim the pointed ends of the outer leaves. Place the artichokes in the acidified water until you are ready to cook; this preserves their color.

3. Bring 1 to 2 inches of water to a boil in a large saucepan. Place the artichokes on a rack above the boiling water, cover, and steam for 25 to 45 minutes, depending on size, or until a petal near the center pulls out easily.

4. Combine the melted butter and lemon juice and divide the mixture among 4 small bowls. Serve the artichokes hot with the lemon butter on the side.

TIP: To eat an artichoke, break off one outside leaf with your fingers, dip it in sauce (usually melted butter), and scrape off the fleshy bottom part of the leaf by pulling it through your clenched teeth. Discard the leaf and pull off the next leaf. When you get to the fuzzy choke in the center, use a spoon to scrape away the fuzzy fibers or cut around and under it with a sharp knife. Eat the bottom and stem, again dipping them into the sauce.

Asparagus with Hollandaise Sauce

Asparagus and hollandaise sauce are a perfect flavor combination. When French cooking reigned supreme in American restaurants in the late 1800s, this dish was frequently served.

SERVES 4

24 thick asparagus spears
Hollandaise sauce (page 17), warmed

1. Snap off the woody bottom of each asparagus stalk where it breaks easily. If desired, peel the stems.

2. Bring an inch of water to a boil in a large skillet. Add the asparagus, cover, and boil until the stems are tender, 4 to 8 minutes.

3. Drain off the water. Transfer the asparagus to a serving dish. Spoon the sauce over the top and serve.

Lemon-Butter Asparagus

Although asparagus has become available year-round in supermarkets, locally harvested asparagus has a freshness that you can't beat. Allow 6 to 8 thick spears per person.

SERVES 4

24 thick asparagus spears
2 tablespoons butter
2 tablespoons lemon juice
3 tablespoons toasted flaked almonds

1. Snap off the woody bottom of each asparagus stalk where it breaks easily. If desired, peel the stems.

2. Bring an inch of water to a boil in a large skillet. Add the asparagus, cover, and boil until the stems are tender, 4 to 8 minutes.

3. Drain off the water. Add the butter and let it melt over medium heat. Add the lemon juice and toss gently to coat.

4. Transfer the asparagus to a serving dish. Sprinkle with the almonds and serve.

Parmesan Asparagus

Asparagus can be enjoyed numerous ways. This classic Italian way is simple, and goes well with many meals.

SERVES 4

24 thick asparagus spears
½ cup grated Parmesan cheese

1. Preheat the broiler.

2. Snap off the woody bottom of each asparagus stalk where it breaks easily. If desired, peel the stems.

3. Bring an inch of water to a boil in a large oven-proof skillet. Add the asparagus, cover, and boil until the stems are tender, 4 to 8 minutes.

4. Drain off the water. Sprinkle with the cheese. Broil until the cheese is melted and browned. Serve hot.

Tex-Mex Pinto Beans

Cooked pinto beans make a fine accompaniment to any Tex-Mex meal. Served with grilled steak, this spiced and herbed dish is just what the cowboys ordered.

SERVES 6

2 cups (1 pound) dried pinto beans, debris removed, soaked overnight, and drained
8 cups water
1 medium onion, finely chopped
3 jalapeño chile peppers, finely chopped
2½ teaspoons minced garlic
3 tablespoons chili powder
1 tablespoon ground cumin
1 tablespoon salt, or to taste
2 teaspoons dried oregano
¼ cup chopped fresh cilantro

1. Combine the beans, water, onion, jalapeños, garlic, chili powder, cumin, salt, and oregano in a large saucepan and bring to a boil. Reduce the heat and simmer for 4 hours, until tender, stirring occasionally.

2. Stir in the cilantro. Taste and adjust the seasonings as needed. Serve hot.

TIP: Mash and cook leftover beans in lard (or oil) to make refried beans.

Cuban Black Beans and Rice

This is a typical dish served by immigrants from Cuba or Puerto Rico. It is most often served as a side dish with grilled steak or other entrées, but it also makes a fine vegetarian entrée.

SERVES 4

2 tablespoons oil
½ medium onion, chopped
¼ cup chopped green bell pepper
1 teaspoon minced garlic
1 (15-ounce) can black beans, undrained
¼ cup water
1 tablespoon dry sherry
¼ teaspoon sugar
1 teaspoon ground cumin
1 teaspoon dried oregano
Salt and pepper
Hot cooked white rice, to serve

1. Heat the oil in a medium saucepan over medium-high heat. Add the onion and bell pepper and sauté until the onion is softened, 4 to 5 minutes. Add the garlic and sauté for 1 minute longer.

2. Stir in the beans, water, sherry, sugar, cumin, and oregano. Mash a few of the beans with the back of a spoon to thicken and flavor the sauce. Bring to a boil, then reduce the heat and simmer for 20 minutes, until the flavors have blended.

3. Season to taste with salt and pepper and serve over rice.

Refried Beans

Refried beans can be served as a side dish, a filling for tacos and burritos, or a topping for tortilla chips. You can make a vegetarian version by substituting oil for the lard, but it will not be as flavorful.

SERVES 4 TO 6

1 cup (½ pound) dried pinto beans, debris removed, soaked overnight, and drained
6 cups water, plus boiling water as needed
1 bay leaf
½ cup lard or bacon drippings
1 medium onion, chopped
1 tablespoon minced garlic
1 jalapeño chile pepper, seeded and minced
1 tablespoon chili powder
1 teaspoon ground cumin
½ teaspoon salt, or to taste
Pinch of cayenne pepper
½ teaspoon dried oregano

1. Combine the beans, water, and bay leaf in a large saucepan and bring to a boil. Reduce the heat and simmer, uncovered, stirring occasionally, until the beans are very tender, 1½ to 2 hours, adding boiling water as necessary to keep the beans covered.

2. Remove the bay leaf. Mash the beans in the pot with a potato masher or the back of a spoon.

3. Melt the lard in a large skillet over medium-high heat. Add the onion and sauté until soft, about 3 minutes. Add the garlic, jalapeño, chili powder, cumin, salt, and cayenne pepper and cook, stirring, until fragrant, about 1 minute. Add the beans, any cooking liquid from the pot, and the oregano and stir to combine. Cook, stirring, until the mixture forms a thick purée, 5 to 10 minutes.

4. Taste and adjust the seasoning as needed. Serve hot.

Boston Baked Beans

Boston is called Beantown because beans slow-baked in molasses have been a favorite Boston dish since colonial days, when the city was a major producer of rum. Sugar cane harvested by slaves in the West Indies was turned into molasses and shipped to Boston to be made into rum, which was then sent to West Africa to buy more slaves to send to the West Indies. Even after slavery's end, Boston continued to be a big rum-producing city. The traditional accompaniment is Boston brown bread, which is also flavored with molasses.

SERVES 6

2 cups (1 pound) dried navy beans, debris removed, soaked overnight, and drained
¾ pound salt pork, rinsed and diced
1 medium onion
½ cup molasses
¼ cup brown sugar
1 teaspoon dry mustard
1 teaspoon salt
½ teaspoon black pepper
3½ cups boiling water, plus more as needed

1. Cover the beans with cold water in a large saucepan. Bring to a boil and cook for 10 minutes; drain.

2. Preheat the oven to 325°F.

3. Put half of the salt pork on the bottom of a bean pot or large casserole along with the whole onion. Add the beans and put the remaining salt pork on top.

4. Mix the molasses, brown sugar, mustard, salt, and pepper with 3½ cups boiling water in a small bowl and pour over the beans. The beans should be covered with liquid. If not, add more boiling water. Cover the pot with a lid.

5. Bake for 6 hours, checking periodically and adding boiling water as needed to keep the beans moist; do not flood them. If the beans become too soupy, remove the lid to encourage evaporation. Remove the onion and serve the beans hot.

TIP: To make the beans Vermont style, replace the molasses with pure maple syrup. You can also adjust the seasonings with more salt, pepper, and onion.

Midwestern Baked Beans

These beans have a sweet tomato sauce, a type greatly popularized by Heinz. Serve them mixed with sliced hot dogs for an all-American meal of franks and beans.

SERVES 6

2½ cups (1 pound) dried great Northern beans, debris removed, soaked overnight, and drained
6 cups water, plus boiling water as needed
1 (28-ounce) can tomato sauce
½ cup chili sauce
½ cup firmly packed dark brown sugar
⅓ cup molasses
1 large onion, finely chopped
2 teaspoons salt
1 teaspoon dry mustard
½ pound thick-sliced bacon

1. Cover the beans with cold water in a large saucepan. Bring to a boil and cook for 10 minutes; drain.

2. Preheat the oven to 325°F.

3. Combine the beans and water in a large bean pot or casserole. Mix in the tomato sauce, chili sauce, brown sugar, molasses, onion, salt, and mustard. Arrange the bacon slices on top of the beans.

4. Bake for 6 hours, covered, checking the pot periodically and adding boiling water as needed to keep the beans moist; do not flood them. If the beans become too soupy, remove the lid to encourage evaporation. Serve hot.

Beets in Orange Sauce

Because beets are so easily stored in root cellars, they were once a regular item on the dinner table. Typically, it is the natural sweetness in beets that is enhanced, as in this recipe where the beets are served in a sweet orange sauce. This preparation is sometimes called Yale beets, as opposed to the Harvard beet recipe that follows.

SERVES 4 TO 6

4 medium beets, trimmed
1 cup fresh orange juice (from approximately 3 medium oranges)
2 tablespoons sugar
1½ teaspoons cornstarch dissolved in 1 tablespoon cold water
1 tablespoon grated orange zest
¼ teaspoon salt
2 tablespoons butter

1. Cover the beets with water in a large saucepan. Bring to a boil and cook gently until tender, 30 to 35 minutes. Drain, cool, peel, and slice; set aside.

2. Combine the orange juice, sugar, cornstarch mixture, orange zest, and salt in a medium saucepan. Bring to a boil, remove from the heat, and whisk in the butter, stirring until melted.

3. Add the beets to the sauce, toss gently to combine, simmer for 10 minutes to heat through, and serve.

Harvard Beets

The crimson color of beets evokes the color of the Harvard football team's jerseys, or so the story goes of how this dish of sliced beets in a thickened sweet-and-sour sauce got its name. Harvard beets are served hot as a side dish.

SERVES 4 TO 6

4 medium beets, trimmed
½ cup sugar
1 tablespoon all-purpose flour
½ cup white vinegar
¼ cup water
½ teaspoon salt
2 tablespoons butter

1. Cover the beets with water in a large saucepan. Bring to a boil and cook gently until tender, 30 to 35 minutes. Drain, cool, peel, and slice; set aside.

2. Combine the sugar, flour, vinegar, water, and salt in a medium saucepan. Bring to a boil, reduce the heat, and simmer for 5 minutes, until thickened. Whisk in the butter.

3. Stir in the beets, toss gently to combine, simmer for 10 minutes to heat through, and serve.

Broccoli with Cheese Sauce

Although broccoli was known in England as early as 1699, this vegetable didn't gain popularity in America until Italian farmers started planting it in the 1920s. Broccoli has traditionally been used among Chinese and Italian immigrants, but this recipe is completely American in origin.

SERVES 4 TO 6

3 tablespoons butter
3 tablespoons all-purpose flour
2 cups milk
1 cup shredded Cheddar cheese (about
    4 ounces)
Salt and pepper
2 large broccoli heads, florets and stalks cut
    into bite-size pieces

1. Melt the butter over medium heat in a small saucepan. Stir in the flour to form a smooth paste and cook, stirring, for 2 minutes. Gradually whisk in the milk. Cook, stirring, for 5 to 7 minutes, until thickened. Stir in the cheese until melted. Season to taste with salt and pepper and keep warm.

2. Steam the broccoli over boiling water for 4 to 5 minutes, until tender-crisp.

3. Transfer the broccoli to a serving bowl, pour the cheese sauce over the top, and serve.

TIP: Peel away the tough outer layer of stem and small leaves on the broccoli stalks. Cut off a few inches at the base of the stems if they are dried up.

Broccoli au Gratin

Broccoli and cheese make a perfect combination, so broccoli is often baked in a casserole with a cheese topping, as in this au gratin recipe.

SERVES 6 TO 8

3 large broccoli heads, florets and stalks, cut
    into bite-size pieces
3 tablespoons butter
1 small onion, finely chopped
1 teaspoon minced garlic
2/3 cup sour cream
1 cup grated Parmesan cheese
Salt and pepper

1. Steam the broccoli over boiling water for 4 to 5 minutes, until tender-crisp. Plunge into a bowl of cold water to stop the cooking. Drain well and set aside.

2. Melt the butter in a medium saucepan over medium heat. Add the onion and sauté until softened, about 3 minutes. Add the garlic and sauté for one minute longer. Remove from the heat.

3. Mix in the broccoli, sour cream, and ¾ cup of Parmesan cheese. Season to taste with salt and pepper.

4. Preheat the broiler.

5. Spoon the mixture into a 2-quart gratin or soufflé dish and sprinkle the top with the remaining ¼ cup Parmesan cheese. Place under the broiler for 2 minutes or until the cheese is melted and slightly golden. Serve hot.

Whole Cauliflower with Cheese Sauce

Mark Twain said that cauliflower is nothing more than a cabbage with a college education. That may be so, but cooked cauliflower that is served whole is quite elegant—something people rarely say about cabbage dishes. Add the rich cheese topping of this recipe and the cauliflower is even more delicious.

SERVES 4 TO 6

3 tablespoons butter
3 tablespoons all-purpose flour
2 cups milk
1 cup shredded Gruyère or Swiss cheese (about 4 ounces)
Salt and pepper
1 large cauliflower head

1. Melt the butter over medium heat in a small saucepan. Stir in the flour to form a smooth paste and cook, stirring, for 2 minutes. Gradually whisk in the milk. Cook, stirring, for 5 to 7 minutes, until thickened. Stir in the cheese until melted. Season to taste with salt and pepper and keep warm.

2. Trim the leaves from the cauliflower and cut the stem even with the head. Steam the cauliflower over boiling water for 20 to 25 minutes, until the core is easily pierced.

3. Transfer the cauliflower to a serving bowl, pour the cheese sauce over the top, and serve.

Cauliflower au Gratin

When buying cauliflower, look for evenly colored white "curds," or stem tips. There should be no bruises or brown spots. Store in a plastic bag in the refrigerator for up to 5 days. Novelty cauliflowers come in purple, orange, and green colors, but the flavor is all the same. This dish uses onion, Cheddar cheese, and sour cream in a tasty casserole topped with buttery bread crumbs.

SERVES 4

1 large cauliflower head, broken into florets
4 tablespoons (½ stick) butter
½ medium onion, diced
1½ cups grated Cheddar cheese (about 6 ounces)
1 cup sour cream
Salt and pepper
½ cup dry bread crumbs

1. Cook the cauliflower in a large pot of salted boiling water until tender-crisp, about 10 minutes. Drain well.

2. Preheat the oven to 350°F. Grease a 1½-quart baking dish.

3. Combine the cauliflower with 2 tablespoons of butter, the onion, cheese, and sour cream in a large bowl. Season to taste with salt and pepper.

4. Spoon into the prepared dish. Melt the remaining 2 tablespoons butter and toss with the bread crumbs. Sprinkle over the cauliflower mixture.

5. Bake for 30 minutes, until heated through. Serve hot.

Brussels Sprouts with Bacon and Onions

These little cabbages are delicious when they are not overcooked, and the smoky taste of bacon adds great flavor to this dish. Brussels sprouts are a traditional Thanksgiving dish.

SERVES 4

2 slices bacon, chopped
6 small white boiling onions, peeled and sliced
1 pound (1 pint) Brussels sprouts, trimmed and halved
¼ cup water
1 teaspoon red-wine vinegar
Salt and pepper

1. Fry the bacon in a large skillet over medium heat until crisp, 10 to 15 minutes. Remove the bacon with a slotted spoon and drain on paper towels; set aside. Pour off all but 2 tablespoons of fat.

2. Add the onions to the skillet and sauté just until well coated, about 1 minute. Add the Brussels sprouts and sauté for 2 minutes. Add the water, cover, and steam until the Brussels sprouts are bright green and tender, about 8 minutes.

3. Transfer the Brussels sprouts to a serving bowl. Drizzle the vinegar over the top and season with salt and pepper. Crumble the bacon, sprinkle on top, and serve immediately.

Skillet Cabbage with Bacon

Colonists found that cabbage grew well in the New World, especially in the Mid-Atlantic region, and it stored well in root cellars. German immigrants in the nineteenth century brought many recipes for cabbage, including variations of this one.

SERVES 4

2 slices bacon, chopped
1 medium onion, finely chopped
½ teaspoon minced garlic
1 medium green cabbage head, cored and
    shredded
Salt and pepper

1. Fry the bacon in a large, deep saucepan or Dutch oven over medium heat until crisp, 10 to 15 minutes. Remove the bacon with a slotted spoon and set aside to drain on paper towels. Pour off all but 2 tablespoons of fat.

2. Add the onion and garlic to the skillet and sauté until softened, about 3 minutes. Stir in the cabbage until it is wilted and fits in the pan. Continue to cook, stirring occasionally, until the cabbage is tender, about 10 minutes.

3. Season to taste with salt and pepper, then crumble the bacon and sprinkle over the cabbage. Serve hot.

Braised Cabbage with Apples

You can make this recipe with red cabbage, savoy cabbage, or green cabbage. The slow cooking tenderizes the cabbage, while the apples lend sweetness. This dish goes very well with beef, pork, and veal.

SERVES 4 TO 6

2 tablespoons butter
1 medium cabbage head, shredded
2 large tart apples, such as Granny Smith or
    Rome Beauty, peeled, cored, and sliced
1 bay leaf
¼ cup dry white wine
2 tablespoons cider vinegar
1 teaspoon brown sugar
Salt and pepper

1. Melt the butter in a large, deep saucepan or Dutch oven over medium heat. Stir in the cabbage until it is wilted and fits in the pan. Mix in the apples and bay leaf. Cover and cook over low heat for about 10 minutes, until the cabbage is tender-crisp.

2. Add the wine, vinegar, brown sugar, and salt and pepper to taste; stir to mix well.

3. Cover and cook for 45 to 60 minutes, until the cabbage is tender. Remove the bay leaf. Taste and adjust the seasonings as needed. Serve hot.

Glazed Carrots

Plain cooked carrots aren't very popular, but when they are dressed with a little butter and sugar, everyone is happy. The fresh mint is optional but highly recommended.

SERVES 4

4 medium carrots, sliced
2 tablespoons butter
2 tablespoons brown sugar or pure maple
    syrup
Salt and pepper
1 teaspoon chopped fresh mint (optional)

1. Steam the carrots over boiling water until barely tender, about 3 minutes. Set aside.

2. Melt the butter in a large skillet over medium heat. Stir in the brown sugar and carrots and salt and pepper to taste. Cook until slightly browned and glazed, 3 to 5 minutes.

3. Sprinkle in the mint, if desired. Serve hot.

Bacon-Fried Carrot Curls

*This recipe adheres to two principles of
Southern cooking: Everything tastes better fried,
and everything tastes better with bacon.*

SERVES 6

6 large carrots
8 slices bacon, chopped
½ cup oil
½ cup brown sugar

1. Cut the carrots into curls using a vegetable
peeler. To do so, hold the carrot in one hand and
use solid pressure to make a stroke along its length
and produce a long curl or ribbon of carrot. Continue peeling off curls, rotating the carrot to get
as many curls as possible. When you have finished
with all the carrots, you should have a heaping
bowl of curls. Set aside.

2. Cook the bacon in a large skillet over medium-
high heat until crisp, 10 to 15 minutes. Remove
with a slotted spoon and drain on paper towels.
Break the slices into small bits when cool.

3. Heat the oil in a separate large skillet over
medium-high heat. Carefully add the carrot curls
to the hot oil and toss well. Sprinkle in the brown
sugar and bacon bits. Continue cooking and tossing until the carrots are soft and starting to turn
translucent, about 5 minutes.

4. Remove from the oil with a slotted spoon or
tongs and drain briefly on paper towels. Serve hot.

Chiles Rellenos

*Fried stuffed chile peppers are a classic in Tex–Mex
restaurants throughout the West. The cheese should be
Monterey Jack and the chile peppers should be fresh
Anaheim, New Mexican green, or poblano—large and
green. The batter is made with flat beer. To make beer flat,
pour it into a bowl and stir until the bubbles disappear,
or open a bottle the day before you plan to cook.*

SERVES 6 TO 8

2 cups all-purpose flour
1 teaspoon salt
½ teaspoon black pepper
8 ounces flat beer
1 cup milk
1 tablespoon oil, plus more for frying
12 to 16 chile peppers
2 (8-ounce) packages cream cheese, cut into
    1-ounce strips
4 to 6 cups shredded Monterey Jack cheese
    (1 to 1½ pounds)

1. Combine the flour, salt, pepper, beer, milk,
and oil in a blender and process until smooth.
The mixture should have the consistency of thick
pancake batter. If necessary, adjust the consistency
by adding a little milk or flour. Refrigerate for
30 minutes.

2. Preheat the broiler.

3. Broil the chile peppers, turning often, until
the skins are blistered. Put the chile peppers in
a paper bag or a bowl covered with plastic wrap
and let them steam for 5 to 10 minutes. Wearing
rubber gloves, peel the skin off each chile pepper,
leaving the stem on. Slit the chile peppers from
top to bottom on one side and remove the seeds.

4. Put a strip of cream cheese in each chile pepper, then stuff with the shredded cheese until full.

5. Heat about 2 inches of oil to 365°F in a large,
deep skillet. One by one, use tongs to dip the stuffed
chile peppers into the batter, then lower them carefully into the hot oil. Do not crowd the pan. Fry
until crisp and golden brown, turning as needed,
4 to 8 minutes. Drain on paper towels. Repeat
until all the chile peppers are fried. Serve hot.

Corn on the Cob

Although the new super-sweet varieties of corn hold their sweetness for longer periods of time than the older varieties, freshness is the key to sweetness. Keep corn refrigerated until just before you cook it to maintain its sugar content.

SERVES 4 TO 8

4 to 8 medium corn ears, shucked
Butter, to serve
Salt and pepper, to serve

Bring 2 to 3 inches of salted water to a boil in a large pot. Add the corn, cover, and steam until heated through, about 5 minutes. Serve hot, passing the butter, salt, and pepper at the table.

Sautéed Corn with Bacon and Pepper

This recipe makes a good change of pace from corn on the cob, and it can be made from fresh or frozen corn.

SERVES 4

2 thick slices bacon, chopped
½ medium onion, chopped
1 small red bell pepper, seeded and chopped
1 small green bell pepper, seeded and chopped
1 jalapeño chile pepper, seeded and minced
2 cups fresh or frozen corn
2 tablespoons water
1 tablespoon cider vinegar
Salt and pepper

1. Fry the bacon in a large skillet over medium heat until crisp, 10 to 15 minutes. Remove the bacon with a slotted spoon and drain on paper towels; set aside. Pour off all but 2 tablespoons of fat.

2. Return the skillet to the heat and add the onion, bell peppers, and jalapeño. Sauté until softened, about 4 minutes. Add the corn and water. Cover and steam for 3 to 4 minutes, until the corn is hot.

3. Stir in the bacon, vinegar, and the salt and pepper to taste. Serve immediately.

TIP: One medium ear of corn yields about ½ cup kernels.

Corn Fritters

Corn fritters go by the name of "corn oysters" in some parts of the South. They can be served as breakfast or as a side dish with dinner. Serve with sorghum or pure maple syrup.

SERVES 4

1 (16-ounce) can creamed corn
2 large eggs
1½ cups all-purpose flour
1 teaspoon baking powder
½ teaspoon salt
¼ teaspoon black pepper
Oil, for frying

1. Beat together the corn and eggs in a medium bowl.

2. Sift together the flour, baking powder, salt, and pepper in a separate medium bowl. Fold the flour mixture into the corn mixture.

3. Heat 2 to 3 inches of oil to 365°F in a large, deep skillet.

4. Carefully drop the batter by tablespoon into the hot oil. Fry to a delicate brown, about 2 minutes per side. Drain on paper towels. Serve immediately.

Spoonbread

This custard-like dish is made with cornmeal, like a bread, but it is soft enough to be eaten with a spoon, hence the name.

SERVES 4 TO 6

2 cups milk
½ cup half-and-half
1 tablespoon butter
1 teaspoon salt
½ teaspoon black pepper
1 cup yellow cornmeal
1 cup fresh or frozen corn
1 bunch fresh chives, chopped (about ½ cup)
3 large eggs, separated

1. Preheat the oven to 350°F. Grease an 8-inch square baking dish.

2. Heat the milk, half-and-half, butter, salt, and pepper in a medium saucepan until just boiling. Whisk in the cornmeal in a slow, steady stream, stirring until the mixture is smooth. Remove from the heat and stir in the corn and chives. Let cool slightly.

3. Beat the egg yolks in a small bowl and stir into the corn mixture.

4. Beat the egg whites in a separate small bowl until stiff; fold into the batter. Pour the mixture into the prepared baking dish and lightly smooth the top with a spatula.

5. Bake for 30 minutes, until puffed and golden brown and a knife inserted into the center comes out clean. Serve immediately.

Corn Pudding

Unlike spoonbread, corn pudding doesn't contain any cornmeal, so the texture is smoother. On the other hand, it is not as light because the egg whites are not beaten separately. The two dishes, however, are fairly similar.

SERVES 4 TO 6

2 large eggs
1¼ cups milk
2 tablespoons butter, melted
2 cups fresh or frozen corn (thawed and drained if frozen)
2 tablespoons all-purpose flour
2 tablespoons sugar
¾ teaspoon salt
Pinch of black pepper

1. Preheat the oven to 350°F. Grease an 8-inch square baking dish.

2. Beat the eggs with the milk and butter in a medium bowl. Stir in the corn, flour, sugar, salt, and pepper. Pour into the prepared baking dish.

3. Place the baking dish in a water bath and bake for 50 to 55 minutes, until a knife inserted in the center comes out clean. Serve immediately.

Collard Greens with Ham Hocks

Here is the mess o' greens Southerners love so well. It can be made with collards, kale, turnip greens, or mustard greens. The greens are slowly simmered with a piece of salt pork or ham hock until the texture is no longer tough and any bitterness is gone. Typically, greens are served with freshly baked cornbread to dip into the "pot-likker"—the concentrated, vitamin-filled broth that results from the long cooking of the greens.

SERVES 8

2 smoked ham hocks
4 cups water, or more as needed
2 pounds collard greens
1 medium onion, diced
1 tablespoon salt
1½ teaspoons crushed red pepper
1 tablespoon sugar
¼ cup bacon drippings or oil
Hot pepper vinegar, to serve

1. Cover the ham hocks with water in a large saucepan. Bring to a boil, reduce the heat, cover, and simmer for 45 minutes. Skim the foam from the broth once or twice.

2. Meanwhile, prepare the collard greens. Cut away the very thick part of the stems and discard. Wash thoroughly, drain, and chop into small pieces.

3. Stir the collard greens into the broth and add the onion, salt, crushed red pepper, and sugar. Drizzle with the bacon drippings and cook, covered, at a lively simmer until the collard greens are tender, about 20 minutes.

4. Turn off the heat and adjust the seasonings as needed. Cover the pot and let sit for a few minutes before serving. Serve hot, passing the pepper vinegar at the table.

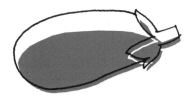

Eggplant Parmesan

Eggplant is not as popular in America as it is in the Middle East and in southern Europe. We have Thomas Jefferson to thank for introducing eggplant to the American garden, but it did not gain much popularity until it started appearing as eggplant Parmesan on the menus of Italian–American restaurants.

SERVES 4 TO 6

4 cups marinara sauce (page 260)
¼ teaspoon salt
3 large eggs
1 cup dry bread crumbs
½ cup oil
2 medium eggplants, peeled and sliced ¼ inch thick
½ cup grated Parmesan cheese
1½ pounds mozzarella cheese, sliced

1. Preheat the oven to 350°F. Lightly grease a 9 x 13-inch baking dish.

2. Mix the sauce with the salt in a medium bowl. Set aside.

3. Beat the eggs in a shallow bowl. Pour the bread crumbs into another shallow bowl. Heat the oil in a large skillet over medium-high heat.

4. Dip each slice of eggplant first into the beaten egg, then into the crumbs. Use tongs to add the slices to the hot oil in a single layer and cook until golden brown on both sides, 2 to 3 minutes per side. Set aside to drain on paper towels.

5. Layer half of the eggplant in the baking dish, sprinkle with half of the Parmesan cheese, cover with half of the mozzarella cheese, then cover with half of the marinara sauce. For the top half, layer the remaining eggplant, followed by the remaining marinara sauce, mozzarella and then Parmesan cheese.

6. Bake for 30 minutes, until the sauce is bubbly and the cheese is melted.

7. Let stand for 10 minutes and serve.

Sautéed Green Beans with Mushrooms

The process of trimming green beans is sometimes called tipping and tailing because you cut off the skinny tips on either end of the bean. At that point, you can leave the beans whole, which looks elegant when the beans are pencil thin, or you can cut the beans into 1½-inch pieces.

SERVES 4 TO 6

1½ pounds green beans, trimmed
¼ cup (½ stick) butter
¼ cup finely chopped onion
2 cups thinly sliced mushrooms
Salt and pepper

1. Steam the green beans over boiling water until tender-crisp, 4 to 8 minutes.

2. Melt the butter in a large skillet over medium heat. Add the onion and mushrooms and sauté until the mushrooms give up their juice, about 8 minutes.

3. Add the green beans and toss to coat. Season to taste with salt and pepper. Serve immediately.

Green Beans Amandine

Green beans with almonds is a classic French preparation. The crisp flaked almonds provide a wonderful texture contrast to the softer beans.

SERVES 4 TO 6

1½ pounds green beans, trimmed
¼ cup (½ stick) butter
1 cup flaked almonds
1 tablespoon lemon juice
Salt and pepper

1. Steam the green beans over boiling water until tender-crisp, 4 to 8 minutes.

2. Melt the butter in a large skillet over medium heat. Add the almonds and sauté until lightly browned, 2 to 3 minutes.

3. Add the green beans and lemon juice and toss to coat. Season to taste with salt and pepper. Serve immediately.

Southern-Style Green Beans

Green beans can be cooked just like greens—very slowly, with flavoring from a ham hock. The best beans for this recipe are older, tougher beans.

SERVES 8

8 cups water
1 ham hock
1 medium onion, finely chopped
1 teaspoon minced garlic
¼ cup white vinegar
1 tablespoon salt
1½ teaspoons black pepper
4 pounds green beans, trimmed and cut into
    1½-inch pieces

1. Combine the water, ham hock, onion, garlic, vinegar, salt, and pepper in a large saucepan. Bring to a boil, reduce the heat, and simmer for 45 minutes.

2. Add the beans, cover, and simmer for 20 minutes.

3. Take out the ham hock, remove the meat from the bone, and slice the meat into small pieces. Discard the bone, return the meat to the beans, and serve.

Green Bean Casserole

In 1955, Campbell Soup Company developed the original recipe for a green bean casserole using cream of mushroom soup. It has become one of the most ubiquitous vegetable recipes around—everyone makes it. This classic version skips the soup and canned onion rings and makes it all from scratch.

SERVES 6

Casserole:
2 pounds green beans, trimmed and cut into
    1½-inch pieces
6 tablespoons (¾ stick) butter
2 cups thinly sliced mushrooms
¼ cup all-purpose flour
3 cups milk
Salt and pepper

Topping:
2 large onions, sliced into thin rings
Milk
1 cup all-purpose flour
1 teaspoon garlic salt
1 teaspoon salt
1 teaspoon black pepper
Oil, for frying

1. To make the casserole, blanch the beans in a large pot of boiling salted water until just tender, about 5 minutes. Drain, plunge into ice water to stop the cooking, drain again, and set aside.

2. Melt the butter in a medium saucepan over medium heat. Add the mushrooms and sauté until they give up their juice, about 8 minutes. Stir in the flour to make a paste and cook for 2 minutes. Whisk in the milk and cook, stirring, until thickened and bubbly. Remove from the heat, season with salt and pepper, and set aside.

3. To make the topping, place the onion rings in a bowl and cover with milk. Refrigerate for at least 10 minutes and up to 1 hour.

4. Mix the flour, garlic salt, salt, and pepper in a medium bowl.

5. Heat 2 to 3 inches of oil to 365°F in a large, deep saucepan.

6. Strain the milk from the onions. Add the flour mixture and toss to coat. Slip a few rings into the hot oil and cook until lightly browned, about 2 to 3 minutes; drain on paper towels. Continue until all the onions are fried.

7. Preheat the oven to 350°F. Lightly oil a 2-quart casserole dish.

8. Combine the green beans, sauce, and 1 cup of onion rings in a large bowl. Adjust the seasoning if necessary. Spoon into the casserole dish and top with the remaining fried onion rings.

9. Bake for about 45 minutes, or until hot, and serve.

Crisp Fried Okra

Okra, a member of the same family as hibiscus and cotton, is a large vegetable plant brought to the United States three centuries ago by African slaves. Many people prefer breaded and fried okra because the slippery texture is less pronounced.

SERVES 4 TO 6

2 large eggs
½ teaspoon hot pepper sauce, such as Tabasco
1 pound okra, trimmed and sliced ½ inch thick
1 cup yellow cornmeal
½ teaspoon salt
½ teaspoon black pepper
Oil, for frying

1. Beat the eggs with the hot pepper sauce in a medium bowl. Add the okra and stir to coat. Set aside.

2. Combine the cornmeal, salt, and pepper in a shallow bowl.

3. Heat 2 to 3 inches of oil to 365°F in a large, deep saucepan.

4. Dip the okra pieces into the cornmeal mixture to coat well, then fry the okra in batches until browned, 4 to 6 minutes for each batch. Drain on paper towels and serve immediately.

TIP: When buying fresh okra, look for young pods that are free of bruises, tender but not soft, and no more than 4 inches long. Okra may be stored in the refrigerator in a paper bag or wrapped in a paper towel in a perforated plastic bag for 2 to 3 days.

Okra with Tomatoes

Cooking okra with acidic ingredients, in this case tomatoes, complements the slippery texture of this vegetable. It is delicious served over rice.

SERVES 6

4 slices bacon, chopped
½ medium onion, chopped
1½ pounds okra, trimmed and sliced about
    ½ inch thick
4 large tomatoes, seeded and diced
Salt and pepper
Cayenne pepper

1. Fry the bacon in a large skillet over medium heat until crisp, 10 to 15 minutes. With a slotted spoon, remove the bacon from the skillet and drain well on paper towels. Drain off all but 2 tablespoons of fat. Crumble the bacon when cool and set aside.

2. Add the onion to the skillet and reduce the heat to low. Cook for 10 to 15 minutes, stirring occasionally, until tender. Add the okra, tomatoes, salt, pepper, and cayenne pepper to taste. Stir well and simmer for about 20 minutes, until the okra and tomatoes are just tender.

3. Spoon the okra into a serving dish, sprinkle with the bacon, and serve.

TIP: To seed tomatoes, cut in half horizontally and squeeze out the seeds.

Creamed Onions

This is a Thanksgiving dinner standard—tiny pearl onions bathed in a creamy sauce. Cover the onions with boiling water and let them cool in the water. The skins will then slip off easily, making this dish very easy to prepare.

SERVES 4 TO 6

1½ pounds white pearl onions, peeled
3 tablespoons butter
3 tablespoons all-purpose flour
2 cups milk
Salt and pepper

1. Cover the onions with cold salted water in a medium saucepan. Bring to a boil, cover, and cook for 20 to 25 minutes, until tender. Drain and set aside.

2. Melt the butter in a medium saucepan over medium heat. Stir in the flour to form a smooth paste and cook for 1 minute. Gradually whisk in the milk. Increase heat to medium-high, cook, stirring occasionally, until the mixture thickens and comes to a boil, about 5 minutes.

3. Add the onions, reduce heat to medium-low, and cook, stirring occasionally, for 10 more minutes. Season to taste with salt and pepper and serve.

Baked Stuffed Onions

Onions are used as a flavoring ingredient so often that it is easy to forget they are a delicious vegetable in their own right. Try these stuffed onions as an accompaniment to steaks or roasts. The dish can be made with regular yellow cooking onions or sweet onions, such as Walla Walla or Vidalia.

SERVES 4

4 large onions
½ cup finely chopped walnuts
½ cup dry bread crumbs
2 tablespoons honey
1 tablespoon red-wine vinegar
2 teaspoons Dijon mustard
½ teaspoon salt
¼ teaspoon black pepper
¼ cup chopped fresh parsley

1. Preheat the oven to 350°F.

2. Slice about ½ inch off the top of each onion. Hollow out a bowl-shaped center to hold about ¼ cup of filling. Slice enough off the bottoms to let the onions stand upright, and set them in a baking dish large enough to hold them all in a single layer. Add 1 inch of water to the dish.

3. Bake for 30 to 45 minutes, until tender, adding more water if the pan dries out.

4. While the onions bake, prepare the stuffing. Combine the walnuts, bread crumbs, honey, vinegar, mustard, salt, and pepper in a small bowl and mix well.

5. Stuff each onion with about ¼ cup of stuffing. Bake for 30 minutes more, until the stuffing is golden.

6. Garnish with parsley and serve warm.

Glazed Onions

The natural sugar in onions will caramelize and add tremendous flavor to this dish. The onions make a wonderful topping for steaks and burgers.

SERVES 4 TO 6

3 tablespoons butter
3 medium onions, sliced and separated into rings
¼ cup dry sherry
1 teaspoon sugar
Salt and pepper

1. Melt the butter in a large skillet over medium heat. Add the onions and sauté for 5 to 8 minutes, until the onions are very soft.

2. Add the sherry, sugar, and salt and pepper to taste. Reduce the heat and simmer, stirring occasionally, until the onions begin to brown, 10 to 20 minutes. Serve hot.

French-Fried Onion Rings

At a county fair, you may encounter these as "broomstick onions," because the onions are threaded onto a broomstick, dipped in batter, then slid off into the deep fryer. When cooking onion rings in vast quantities, you'll find that a broomstick is easier to handle than a simple pair of tongs. Serve these with your favorite dipping sauce, such as ketchup or ranch dressing.

SERVES 4 TO 6

3 to 4 large sweet onions, such as Walla Walla, Maui, or Vidalia, peeled, cut ½ inch thick, and separated into rings
Oil, for frying
2 large eggs
2 cups buttermilk
2 cups all-purpose flour
1 teaspoon baking soda
1 teaspoon salt, plus more to taste

1. Soak the onions in ice water until you are ready to fry them.

2. In a large, deep saucepan, begin heating 2 to 3 inches of oil to 365°F. Preheat the oven to 200°F.

3. Beat together the eggs and buttermilk in a medium bowl. Add the flour, baking soda, and 1 teaspoon salt, and mix well. Set aside.

4. Drain the onions and pat dry with paper towels.

5. Dip a few onion rings into the batter and slip into the hot oil; do not crowd. Fry until golden brown, turning once, 3 to 4 minutes total.

6. Drain the onion rings on paper towels and season with salt. Keep warm in the oven until all the onion rings have been fried. Serve warm.

Glazed Parsnips

Parsnips are often compared to carrots, but they have a unique taste. They are not appealing raw, but when cooked, their flavor is complex, nutty, and sweet.

SERVES 4 TO 6

1½ pounds parsnips, peeled and cut into 2-inch sticks
2 cups water
3 tablespoons butter
1 tablespoon sugar
Salt and pepper

1. Combine the parsnips, water, butter, and sugar in a large skillet over medium-high heat. Bring to a boil, reduce the heat to medium, cover, and simmer 5 minutes, until tender.

2. Uncover, increase the heat to high, and boil off the liquid until the parsnips are coated with a thick glaze, 6 to 8 minutes more.

3. Season to taste with salt and pepper and serve.

Mashed Parsnips and Scallions

Parsnips alone might draw some protests from diners who were expecting mashed potatoes, but mixed with potatoes they create a wonderful flavor combination.

SERVES 4

1 pound parsnips, peeled and cut into 2-inch lengths
½ pound baking potatoes, peeled and sliced 1 inch thick
1 bunch scallions, trimmed and thinly sliced
½ cup milk
¼ cup (½ stick) butter
Salt and pepper

1. Combine the parsnips and potatoes in a medium saucepan and cover with salted water. Bring to a boil and cook until tender, about 15 minutes. Add the scallions and cook for 3 minutes more. Drain well and set aside.

2. Meanwhile, heat the milk and butter in a small saucepan over low heat until the butter melts.

3. Return the vegetables to the saucepan and mash with a potato masher, gradually adding the milk mixture. Continue to mash until the texture is smooth.

4. Season to taste with salt and pepper and serve immediately.

Parsnip Fritters

When made into fritters, even the most unpopular vegetables become appealing. In this case, parsnips are cooked and mashed, made into cakes, coated in bread crumbs, and fried to crispy perfection.

SERVES 4

1 pound parsnips, peeled and sliced
2 tablespoons all-purpose flour
Pinch of ground nutmeg
2 tablespoons butter, melted
Salt and pepper
1 large egg
½ cup dry bread crumbs
¼ cup oil

1. Cover the parsnips with salted water in a medium saucepan and bring to a boil. Boil until tender, about 15 minutes. Drain well.

2. Return the parsnips to the saucepan and mash well with a potato masher. Mix in the flour, nutmeg, and butter. Season to taste with salt and pepper and set aside.

3. Beat the egg in a shallow bowl. Put the bread crumbs in a second shallow bowl. Heat the oil in a large skillet over medium heat.

4. Form the parsnip mixture into small, flat, round cakes. Dip into the beaten egg, then into the bread crumbs. Fry the cakes in the oil until browned on both sides, 3 to 4 minutes per side. Continue until all the fritters are cooked. Serve hot.

Peas and Lettuce

When most Americans had gardens, spring peas were harvested at the same time as early lettuce. The two of them were a cause for celebration. This traditional dish is best made with fresh peas.

SERVES 4

1 cup water
2 tablespoons butter
1 teaspoon sugar
½ teaspoon salt
8 white pearl onions, peeled
2 cups shelled peas (from about 2 pounds in the pod)
6 large romaine leaves or curly leaf lettuce, cut in ½-inch-wide strips
Black pepper

1. Heat the water with the butter, sugar, and salt in a medium saucepan over medium heat until the butter melts. Add the onions, reduce the heat, cover, and simmer for 15 minutes.

2. Add the peas and simmer for 10 minutes.

3. Stir in the lettuce. Cover and cook for 10 minutes more. Season with pepper and serve immediately.

Minted Peas and Shallots

Fresh peas and mint are a classic combination. This dish goes beautifully with roast lamb, another spring dish.

SERVES 4

2 tablespoons butter
⅓ cup finely chopped shallots
3 cups fresh or frozen peas
1 cup chicken broth (page 119)
Pinch of sugar
2 tablespoons shredded fresh mint
Salt and pepper

1. Melt the butter in a large skillet over medium heat. Add the shallots and cook, stirring, until softened and beginning to color, about 3 minutes.

2. Stir in the peas, broth, and sugar. Cover and simmer until the peas are just barely tender, 5 to 15 minutes. Uncover and cook until most of the liquid has evaporated, 5 to 10 minutes more.

3. Stir in the mint, season with salt and pepper, and serve.

Creamed Peas and Onions

Here's a traditional Thanksgiving dish. It is usually made with frozen peas, since fresh peas are generally not available in the fall.

SERVES 4

1 cup white pearl onions, peeled
1 (10-ounce) package frozen peas
1 tablespoon butter
1 tablespoon all-purpose flour
½ teaspoon salt
¼ teaspoon black pepper
1 cup milk

1. Cover the onions with salted water. Bring to a boil, cover, and simmer until tender, 20 to 25 minutes. Add the peas and cook until hot, about 3 minutes. Drain and transfer to a warmed serving bowl.

2. Melt the butter in a small saucepan over low heat. Blend in the flour, salt, and pepper to form a smooth paste. Cook for 1 minute. Gradually whisk in the milk and bring to a boil, stirring constantly. Reduce the heat to medium and cook for 5 minutes, until thick and bubbly.

3. Pour the sauce over the peas and onions and stir gently. Serve hot.

Stuffed Bell Peppers

The thick walls of bell peppers make them ideal for stuffing. You can fill them with any ground beef mixture for a main dish. Here they are stuffed with rice to make a satisfying side dish.

SERVES 4

4 large red or green bell peppers
2 tablespoons butter
¼ cup finely chopped onion
1 teaspoon minced garlic
2½ cups cooked long-grain white rice
1 cup fresh or frozen corn
1 cup diced tomato
2 cups shredded Cheddar cheese (about 8 ounces)
2 tablespoons chopped fresh parsley
Salt and pepper

1. Cut the bell peppers lengthwise into halves and remove the seeds and membranes.

2. Bring a large pot of salted water to a boil. Add the bell peppers and cook for 2 minutes. Drain.

3. Preheat the oven to 375°F. Grease a baking dish large enough to hold the bell peppers in a single layer.

4. Melt the butter in a large skillet over medium-high heat. Add the onion and garlic and sauté until softened, about 3 minutes. Stir in the rice, corn, tomato, and half the cheese; stir until melted and blended. Stir in the parsley and salt and pepper to taste.

5. Fill the bell pepper halves with the rice mixture. Place, stuffed side up, in the baking dish. Top each with the remaining cheese.

6. Bake for 25 minutes, until the bell peppers are tender and the filling is hot. Serve immediately.

Mashed Potatoes

The ultimate comfort food, mashed potatoes are so easy to make yet so easy to abuse. Here are some ground rules: Use russet or baking potatoes for the fluffiest texture; use a potato masher or ricer to break down the potatoes, never a food processor; and heat the milk before you add it to the cooked potatoes. Butter is necessary, so use as much or as little as you please.

SERVES 6

6 medium baking potatoes, peeled and cut into large chunks (about 2 pounds)
3 to 6 tablespoons butter
1 cup milk
Salt
White pepper

1. Place the potatoes in a medium saucepan and cover with cold salted water. Cover, bring to a boil, and cook until tender, 15 to 20 minutes.

2. Drain well and return to the saucepan over low heat to dry.

3. Meanwhile, melt the butter in the milk in a small saucepan over low heat.

4. Mash the potatoes with a potato masher, beat in the butter and milk, and continue to beat for about a minute, until fluffy. Season to taste with salt and pepper and serve hot.

TIP: If the potatoes will be held before serving, make them looser by adding a bit more milk. They will continue to thicken as they sit.

Duchess Potatoes

A very elegant variation on mashed potatoes, this recipe serves as both a side dish and a garnish. For example, surround a broiled steak or platter of carved roast beef with these beautiful piped potatoes.

SERVES 8

6 medium baking potatoes
6 tablespoons (¾ stick) butter, softened
4 large egg yolks
Salt
White pepper
¼ teaspoon ground nutmeg

1. Place the potatoes in a medium saucepan and cover with cold salted water. Cover, bring to a boil, and cook until tender, 15 to 20 minutes. Drain well and set aside.

2. Preheat the oven to 375°F. Grease a rimmed baking sheet.

3. Peel the potatoes and rice with a potato ricer. Mix in the butter, egg yolks, salt, pepper, and nutmeg. The mixture should be thick.

4. Spoon the potato mixture into a pastry bag fitted with a large star tip. Pipe the potato mixture into small mounds onto the baking sheet.

5. Bake for 8 to 10 minutes, until golden brown. Serve hot.

Holiday Potato Cups

For serving mashed potatoes in a slightly different form, these cheese-topped potato cups are a wonderful choice. They hold up better than mashed potatoes on a buffet table, can be made in advance, and look special on a plate.

SERVES 6

4 medium baking potatoes, peeled and cut into large chunks
1 cup heavy cream
1 teaspoon salt
¼ teaspoon black pepper
½ cup grated Parmesan cheese or shredded Cheddar cheese

1. Place the potatoes in a medium saucepan and cover with cold salted water. Cover, bring to a boil, and cook until tender, 15 to 20 minutes. Drain well.

2. Preheat the oven to 375°F. Grease 6 small ramekins or muffin cups.

3. Rice or mash the potatoes with a potato ricer or masher. Mix in ⅔ cup of cream, the salt, and pepper.

4. Spoon the mixture into the prepared ramekins and smooth the tops.

5. Whip the remaining ⅓ cup cream until soft peaks form. Fold in the cheese. Spread evenly over the cups.

6. Bake for 15 minutes, until the tops are browned.

7. Cool the cups on a wire rack for 10 minutes, invert onto a serving platter, turn over, cheese side up, and serve immediately.

Baked Potatoes

There is nothing easier than throwing a few potatoes into the oven to bake while you prepare dinner. Although any potato can be baked, it's best to stick with baking potatoes—the interiors bake up fluffy and moist, ready to soak up all that lovely butter and sour cream. A sprinkling of fresh chopped chives is always a welcome touch.

SERVES 4

4 medium baking potatoes
Salt and pepper, to serve
Butter, to serve
Sour cream, to serve

1. Preheat the oven to 375°F.

2. Poke the potatoes with a fork or knife in several places to prevent them from exploding in the oven. Place directly on the oven rack. Bake for 45 to 60 minutes, until tender. Serve hot with the salt and pepper, butter, and sour cream at the table.

Cheesy Stuffed Baked Potatoes

Consider the baked potato a blank canvas, and paint on it with as many tasty ingredients as you like. Some even turn a simple baked potato into a main dish, mixing in bacon or chopped ham and steamed broccoli.

SERVES 6

6 large baking potatoes
1 tablespoon butter
½ cup finely chopped red bell pepper
¼ cup finely chopped green bell pepper
½ cup finely chopped onion
1½ cups shredded Cheddar cheese (about 6 ounces)
2 tablespoons milk
2 tablespoons sour cream

1. Preheat the oven to 375°F.

2. Poke the potatoes with a fork or knife in several places to prevent them from exploding in the oven. Place directly on the oven rack. Bake for 45 to 60 minutes, until tender.

3. Meanwhile, melt the butter over medium heat in a large skillet. Add the bell peppers and onion and sauté until tender, about 5 minutes. Set aside.

4. Remove the baked potatoes from the oven and reduce the oven temperature to 350°F.

5. Remove a thin slice from the top of each potato; scoop the pulp out into a bowl without disturbing the potato skins. Set the skins aside. Mash the potato pulp with a fork. Stir in 1 cup of cheese, then stir in the milk, sour cream, and sautéed vegetables.

6. Spoon the potato mixture back into the potato skins. Place the filled potato skins, stuffed side up, on a baking sheet. Sprinkle the tops with the remaining ½ cup cheese.

7. Bake for about 20 minutes, until the filling is hot and the cheese is melted. Serve hot.

Potatoes O'Brien

This dish of diced potatoes fried crisp with chopped onions and bell peppers dates back to the turn of the previous century and most likely was made even before that. Who this particular O'Brien was is lost in history. The dish may have received an Irish last name simply because potatoes are so closely associated with the Irish.

SERVES 4 TO 6

6 tablespoons oil
⅔ cup finely chopped onion
⅓ cup finely chopped green bell pepper
⅓ cup finely chopped red bell pepper
4 medium baking potatoes, peeled and diced
Salt and pepper

1. Heat 2 tablespoons of oil in a large skillet over medium heat. Add the onion and bell peppers and sauté, stirring occasionally, until the vegetables are softened, about 5 minutes. Use a slotted spoon to transfer the vegetables to a small bowl. Set aside.

2. Add the remaining 4 tablespoons oil to the skillet and heat over medium-high heat. Add the potatoes and sauté, stirring occasionally, until tender and crisp, 20 to 25 minutes.

3. Stir in the vegetable mixture and add salt and pepper to taste. Heat over medium-low heat until hot. Serve immediately.

Steamed New Potatoes with Parsley and Dill

New potatoes are thin-skinned, so there's no need to peel them—just scrub them well. They have a fresh and lively taste, which is why steaming is a good way to enjoy their natural flavors.

SERVES 4 TO 6

1 pound small new potatoes, quartered or halved
3 tablespoons butter, softened
2 tablespoons chopped fresh parsley
2 teaspoons chopped fresh dill
Salt and pepper

1. Set a steamer basket over boiling water, add the potatoes, cover, and steam for 10 to 12 minutes, just until tender.

2. While the potatoes are steaming, stir together the butter, parsley, and dill in a warmed serving bowl.

3. Add the potatoes to the herb mixture and toss well. Season to taste with salt and pepper. Serve immediately.

Sautéed New Potatoes

Supermarkets will call any small, thin-skinned potato a new potato. But a freshly harvested potato is indeed a treat worth seeking out. This gentle cooking method is perfect for the delicate flavor of new potatoes.

SERVES 4 TO 6

2 tablespoons butter
1 tablespoon oil
1 pound small new potatoes, halved
Salt and pepper

1. Melt the butter with the oil in a large skillet over medium heat.

2. Add the potatoes and coat well with the butter mixture. Cover, reduce the heat to low, and cook until tender and browned, about 25 minutes, shaking the pan frequently. For more browned potatoes, increase the heat in the last 5 to 10 minutes to medium, shaking the pan frequently.

3. Season to taste with salt and pepper and serve hot.

Oven-Roasted Potatoes

A perfectly roasted potato is a wondrous thing to behold—crisp on the outside and tender on the inside. The key is to use potatoes all of the same size, coated with just enough oil, and roasted in a hot oven. A sprinkling of coarse kosher salt after removing from the oven is the perfect finish. Herbs, such as rosemary and thyme, may be added during roasting for extra flavor.

SERVES 4 TO 6

2 tablespoons oil
1 teaspoon salt
¼ teaspoon black pepper
1 pound small new potatoes, halved
1 teaspoon paprika
Coarse or kosher salt

1. Preheat the oven to 500°F. Grease a shallow roasting pan.

2. Combine the oil, salt, and pepper in a large bowl. Add the potatoes and toss well to coat. Transfer to the prepared pan and spread out into a single layer.

3. Roast for 15 to 18 minutes, until the potatoes are tender. Shake once or twice during roasting to cook evenly.

4. Remove from the oven, toss with the paprika, and sprinkle with salt. Serve hot.

Scalloped Potatoes

These potatoes are slowly baked in a white sauce, resulting in an extremely tasty and rich dish. Onions add subtle flavor to the sauce. Choose a potato that will hold its shape when cooked—a boiling or waxy potato. Baking potatoes are not appropriate. Bake and serve in a scalloped dish for a classy presentation.

SERVES 4 TO 6

3 tablespoons butter
¼ cup all-purpose flour
3 cups half-and-half
1 small onion, chopped
1 teaspoon minced garlic
2 teaspoons salt
¼ teaspoon black pepper
6 medium waxy potatoes, such as thin-skinned red or white, peeled and sliced ¼ inch thick

1. Preheat the oven to 350°F. Grease a 2-quart baking dish.

2. Melt the butter in a saucepan over medium heat. Stir in the flour to make a paste and cook for 2 minutes. Slowly add the half-and-half, stirring constantly, until thickened, 5 to 6 minutes. Add the onion, garlic, salt, and pepper.

3. Spread half the potatoes evenly in the prepared baking dish. Cover with half the sauce. Add the remaining potatoes and top with the remaining sauce.

4. Cover and bake for 1 hour. Uncover, increase the oven temperature to 400°F, and bake for 20 to 30 minutes more, until the top is browned.

5. Cool for 10 minutes before serving.

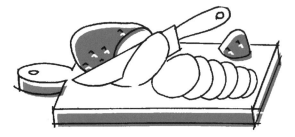

Potatoes au Gratin

Many people confuse potatoes au gratin with scalloped potatoes. Au gratin refers to a baked dish topped with cheese or buttered bread crumbs. Traditionally, scalloped potatoes are made without cheese.

SERVES 4 TO 6

4 tablespoons (½ stick) butter
¼ cup all-purpose flour
3 cups milk
1 small onion, chopped
1 teaspoon minced garlic
2 teaspoons salt
¼ teaspoon black pepper
6 medium waxy potatoes, such as thin-skinned red or white, peeled and sliced ¼ inch thick
1 cup shredded Cheddar cheese (about 4 ounces)
½ cup fresh bread crumbs

1. Preheat the oven to 350°F. Grease a 2-quart baking dish.

2. Melt 3 tablespoons of butter in a saucepan over medium heat. Stir in the flour to make a paste and cook for 2 minutes. Slowly add the milk, stirring constantly, until thickened, 5 to 6 minutes. Stir in the onion, garlic, salt, and pepper.

3. Spread half the potatoes evenly in the prepared baking dish. Cover with half the sauce and sprinkle with ½ cup of Cheddar cheese. Add the remaining potatoes, cover with the remaining sauce, and top with the remaining ½ cup Cheddar cheese.

4. Cover and bake for 1 hour.

5. Melt the remaining 1 tablespoon of butter. Uncover the baking dish, sprinkle with the bread crumbs, and drizzle with the melted butter. Increase the oven temperature to 400°F and bake for 20 to 30 minutes more, until the top is browned.

6. Cool for 10 minutes before serving.

TIP: Add 1 cup diced ham to the white sauce to convert this side dish into a main course.

Cheesy Potato Casserole

Casseroles are perfect for holiday buffet tables because they stay hot and can be stretched to feed a crowd. You can also prepare the casserole early in the day and bake it at the last minute.

SERVES 6 TO 8

5 to 6 medium baking potatoes, peeled and thinly sliced
2 cups (1 pint) cream-style cottage cheese
1 cup sour cream
⅓ cup sliced scallions
½ teaspoon minced garlic
1 teaspoon salt
¼ teaspoon black pepper
½ cup shredded Cheddar cheese
Paprika

1. Boil the potatoes with enough salted water to cover in a large saucepan until just tender, about 10 minutes. Drain well and set aside.

2. Preheat the oven to 350°F. Grease a 9 x 13-inch baking dish.

3. Combine the cottage cheese, sour cream, scallions, garlic, salt, and pepper in a large bowl. Fold in the potatoes. Pour into the prepared baking dish and top with the cheese. Sprinkle paprika over the top.

4. Bake for 40 minutes and serve hot.

Mashed Potato Pancakes

Potato pancakes make a tasty side dish to serve with steaks, roast, baked ham, or your favorite barbecued meat. You can make these with leftover mashed potatoes, but this recipe starts from scratch.

SERVES 6 TO 8

6 medium baking potatoes peeled and cut into chunks
⅓ cup finely chopped onion
3 tablespoons all-purpose flour
1 large egg
1 teaspoon salt
Pinch of black pepper
2 tablespoons butter, plus more as needed

1. Preheat the oven to 250°F.

2. Place the potatoes in a medium saucepan and cover with salted water. Cover the pan and bring to a boil. Cook until tender, 15 to 20 minutes; drain well.

3. Mash or rice the potatoes with a potato masher or ricer. Mix in the onion, flour, egg, salt, and pepper and set aside.

4. Melt the butter in a large skillet over medium heat.

5. Shape half of the potato mixture into 4 to 6 patties and add to the skillet in a single layer. Cook, turning once, until golden brown, 3 to 5 minutes per side.

6. Transfer the pancakes to an ovenproof serving platter and keep warm in the oven. Repeat with the remaining potato mixture, adding more butter to the skillet if needed. Serve hot.

Potato Pancakes

These are the famous latkes served at Hanukkah, the Jewish festival of light. Traditionally they are served with applesauce and sour cream. Use baking potatoes for best results.

SERVES 4

2 medium baking potatoes, grated
1 tablespoon grated onion
2 large eggs
¼ cup all-purpose flour
1 teaspoon salt
⅓ cup oil

1. Combine the grated potatoes, onion, eggs, flour, and salt in a large bowl.

2. Heat the oil in a large skillet over medium-high heat. Carefully drop the potato mixture by the heaping tablespoon into the skillet. Flatten each cake with a spatula and fry until golden brown, 3 to 5 minutes on each side.

3. Drain briefly on paper towels and serve hot.

French Fries

There's no need to fear making french fries at home. What is required is a two-step frying process and careful attention to details. Use baking potatoes soaked in cold water before the first frying. Peeling the potatoes is optional. Serve with ketchup, mayonnaise (the European way), ranch dressing, or a sweet-and-sour sauce.

SERVES 4 TO 6

4 large baking potatoes, cut into 2¼ x ⅜-inch strips
Peanut or other oil with a high smoking point
Salt

1. Soak the potatoes for 30 minutes in enough cold water to cover.

2. Heat 3 inches of oil in a deep, heavy saucepan to 275°F.

3. Drain the potatoes and pat dry with paper towels. Cook in the oil, a few at a time, for about 2 minutes. Remove with a slotted spoon and drain on paper towels; the fries will be pale and limp. Continue until all the potatoes have been fried.

4. Preheat the oven to 250°F.

5. Increase the temperature of the oil to 365°F. Add the fries, a few at a time, and fry a second time to brown to the desired color, 2 to 3 minutes.

6. Drain the fries on fresh paper towels and keep warm in the oven until all the fries have been fried a second time. Sprinkle with salt and serve.

Creamed Spinach

Creamed spinach is a rich, flavorful accompaniment to any steak and is often served as such at traditional steakhouses.

SERVES 4 TO 6

2 (10-ounce) packages fresh spinach, washed and trimmed
3 tablespoons butter
1 small onion, finely chopped
1 teaspoon minced garlic
3 tablespoons plus 1 teaspoon all-purpose flour
2 cups milk
½ cup grated Parmesan cheese
Salt and pepper

1. Bring 1 inch of water to a boil in a large saucepan. Add the spinach, cover, and steam until wilted, 3 to 5 minutes. Drain and press out as much water as possible. If the spinach seems watery, gather it in handfuls and squeeze to remove the excess water. Transfer to a cutting board, chop, and set aside.

2. Melt the butter in a medium saucepan over medium heat. Add the onion and garlic and sauté until softened, about 4 minutes. Stir in the flour to make a paste. Cook for 1 minute. Gradually whisk in the milk and cook until hot and thickened. Stir in the cheese.

3. Stir in the spinach and cook until the spinach is hot, about 2 minutes. Season to taste with salt and pepper and serve.

TIP: If you would like to make this in advance, transfer the creamed spinach to a lightly greased baking dish. Sprinkle the top with buttered bread crumbs. Refrigerate until 40 minutes before serving, then bake at 350°F for about 30 minutes, until hot and bubbly.

Cheesy Spinach Squares

This recipe is lighter than bread and more solid than a soufflé, making it difficult to categorize. Using cheese, bell pepper, and scallions, it is a great way to help kids—and adults—enjoy their spinach.

SERVES 6

2 (10-ounce) packages fresh spinach, washed and trimmed
⅓ cup all-purpose flour
1 teaspoon baking powder
1 teaspoon salt

½ teaspoon black pepper
¼ teaspoon ground nutmeg
2 large eggs
1 cup milk
1 tablespoon butter, melted
2 cups shredded Cheddar cheese (about 8 ounces)
¼ cup finely chopped red bell pepper (optional)
2 scallions, chopped

1. Preheat the oven to 350°F. Grease a 7 x 11-inch baking dish.

2. Bring 1 inch of water to a boil in a large saucepan. Add the spinach, cover, and steam until wilted, 3 to 5 minutes. Drain, rinse with cold water, and press out as much water as possible. If the spinach seems watery, gather it in handfuls and squeeze to remove the excess water. Transfer to a cutting board and chop.

3. Stir together the flour, baking powder, salt, pepper, and nutmeg in a medium bowl.

4. In a separate medium bowl, beat the eggs. Beat in the milk and butter. Stir in the spinach, cheese, bell pepper, if using, and scallions. Pour over the flour mixture and stir until just combined. Transfer to the prepared baking dish.

5. Bake for about 30 minutes, until set.

6. Cool for 10 minutes, slice into squares, and serve.

TIP: To make this recipe with frozen spinach, substitute a 1-pound bag of frozen spinach or two 10-ounce packages. Thaw, squeeze out the excess liquid, chop, and proceed with step 3.

Spanakopita

This Greek spinach pie is made with phyllo dough, which is found in the freezer section of most supermarkets, and spinach flavored with feta cheese, traditionally made with sheep or goat's milk. Spanakopita makes a delicious vegetarian main course.

SERVES 6

5 tablespoons oil
4 (10-ounce) packages fresh spinach, washed and trimmed
1 bunch scallions, chopped
Salt and pepper
½ pound feta cheese, crumbled
2 large eggs, lightly beaten

1. Heat 1 tablespoon of oil in a large skillet over medium-high heat. Add half of the spinach and sauté, tossing with tongs, until wilted, about 2 minutes. Remove from the pan and drain. Repeat with the remaining spinach, using 1 more tablespoon of oil. Squeeze out as much liquid as possible, transfer to a cutting board, and coarsely chop.

2. Pour off any liquid in the skillet and add the remaining 3 tablespoons oil. Add the scallions and sauté until soft, 2 to 3 minutes. Add the chopped spinach and season to taste with salt and pepper. Cook over low heat for 1 to 2 minutes, then set aside to cool.

3. Stir the feta and beaten eggs into the cooled spinach mixture.

4. Preheat the oven to 350°F. Grease a 9 x 13-inch baking dish.

5. Unfold the phyllo dough and lay 6 sheets in the baking dish, brushing each with butter before adding the next. Spoon the spinach filling over the top and cover with 6 more sheets, buttering each sheet. Score the top 3 sheets with a sharp knife to mark the serving pieces.

6. Bake for 40 to 45 minutes, or until the top is golden.

7. Let stand for 15 minutes, cut along the scored lines, and serve warm.

TIP: To make this recipe with frozen spinach, substitute two 1-pound bags frozen spinach or three 10-ounce packages. Thaw, squeeze out the excess liquid, and proceed with step 2.

Pan-Fried Zucchini

People sometimes feel that zucchini and summer squash are too watery. This recipe addresses that problem by coating the zucchini in flour. It gives the zucchini a crisp exterior.

SERVES 4

2 large eggs
½ cup all-purpose flour
2 teaspoons minced fresh parsley
1 teaspoon minced garlic
1 teaspoon salt
½ teaspoon black pepper
1 tablespoon butter, plus more as needed
2 tablespoons oil, plus more as needed
6 small zucchini or yellow summer squash,
    sliced into ¼-inch rounds

1. Beat the eggs in a shallow bowl.

2. Combine the flour, parsley, garlic, salt, and pepper in a second shallow bowl.

3. Melt the butter in the oil in a large skillet and heat over medium-high heat. Dip the zucchini rounds in the egg, then in the flour mixture. Shake off any excess, and place in a single layer in the skillet.

4. Brown on both sides, about 2 minutes per side, taking care not to let the zucchini stick (you may need to add more oil or butter). Continue until all the zucchini is cooked. Serve hot.

Cheese-Stuffed Zucchini

A bacon-cheese filling can make any vegetable a crowd pleaser. Although gardeners might be tempted to use overgrown zucchini here, tender small zucchini taste best.

SERVES 4

4 slices bacon, chopped
2 medium zucchini or yellow summer squash, or
    4 small zucchini or yellow summer squash
2 medium tomatoes, seeded and chopped
1½ cups shredded Cheddar cheese (about
    6 ounces)
½ cup seasoned dry bread crumbs, or more as
    needed

1. Fry the bacon in a medium skillet over medium-high heat until crisp, 10 to 15 minutes. Remove the bacon with a slotted spoon and drain on paper towels; set aside. Reserve 1 tablespoon of the fat in a small bowl and set aside.

2. Bring a large pot of salted water to a boil.

3. Cut the zucchini in half lengthwise and blanch in the boiling water for 3 to 5 minutes, until partially cooked. Drain well.

4. Scoop out the zucchini pulp, leaving a ¼-inch-thick shell. Chop the pulp and combine with the tomatoes and cheese.

5. Preheat the broiler.

6. Place the zucchini, hollowed side up, on a broiler pan. Fill each with the cheese mixture.

7. Mix the bread crumbs with the reserved 1 tablespoon of fat. Crumble the bacon, add to the bread crumb mixture, and mix well.

8. Sprinkle each zucchini with the bread crumb mixture and grill until golden brown, about 3 to 4 minutes.

Batter-Fried Zucchini

These tasty bites can be served plain or with a well-seasoned tomato sauce. They make a tasty appetizer or side dish.

SERVES 4 TO 6

2 cups all-purpose flour
2½ teaspoons salt
¼ teaspoon black pepper
4 large egg yolks, beaten
¾ cup beer
Oil, for frying
2 large egg whites, stiffly beaten
4 medium zucchini or yellow summer squash,
    sliced into ½-inch rounds

1. Combine the flour, 1½ teaspoons of salt, the pepper, egg yolks, and beer in a medium bowl. Stir until no lumps remain. Let rest for 1 hour at room temperature.

2. In a large, deep saucepan, begin heating 2 to 3 inches of oil to 365°F.

3. Fold the egg whites into the batter.

4. Dip the zucchini, one piece at a time, into the batter, then slip into the hot oil. Fry a few pieces at a time until golden, 3 to 4 minutes.

5. Drain on paper towels and serve immediately.

Baked Sweet Potatoes

Sweet potatoes are sometimes called yams in the United States, but the true yam is a product of the tropics and not very sweet. A sweet potato may have yellow-gray to brown or copper to purple skin and the flesh may be white, yellow, or orange. Regardless of its color, a sweet potato has lots of flavor and requires nothing more than a dressing of butter, salt, and pepper.

SERVES 4

4 medium sweet potatoes
Butter, to serve
Salt and pepper, to serve

1. Preheat the oven to 375°F.

2. Poke the sweet potatoes with a fork or knife in several places to prevent them from exploding in the oven. Place on a baking sheet and bake for 45 to 60 minutes, until tender. Serve hot, passing the butter, salt, and pepper at the table.

Mashed Sweet Potatoes

Since sweet potatoes are such powerhouses of nutrition, it makes sense to serve them as frequently as mashed potatoes. They go well with almost any dish that mashed potatoes might accompany, adding a touch of natural sweetness and a welcome change of pace.

SERVES 4 TO 6

6 medium sweet potatoes, peeled
2 tablespoons butter
½ cup heavy cream
Salt
White pepper

1. Cover the sweet potatoes with water in a medium saucepan. Bring to a boil and cook until tender, 15 to 35 minutes. Drain well and set aside.

2. Meanwhile, melt the butter in the cream in a small saucepan over low heat.

3. When the potatoes are cool enough to handle, rice or mash the potatoes with a potato ricer or masher. Whip in the butter and cream and continue to whip for about 1 minute, until fluffy. Season to taste with salt and pepper and serve hot.

Candied Sweet Potatoes

Candied sweet potatoes are a Thanksgiving classic, dating back to the 1880s, though sweet potato cultivation in America goes back much earlier than that. Columbus shipped the first sweet potatoes back to Europe in 1493.

SERVES 6 TO 8

6 medium sweet potatoes
½ cup (1 stick) butter
1 cup firmly packed brown sugar
½ cup water
1 teaspoon salt

1. Steam the sweet potatoes over boiling water for 30 to 40 minutes, until tender. Drain and set aside.

2. Preheat the oven to 350°F. Grease a 9 x 13-inch baking dish.

3. When cool, peel and slice the sweet potatoes into ½-inch slices. Place in the prepared baking dish.

4. Melt the butter in a small saucepan over medium heat. Stir in the brown sugar, water, and salt. Cook until the sugar is dissolved and pour over the potatoes.

5. Bake for 1 hour, basting occasionally with the brown sugar sauce. Serve hot.

Sweet Potato Casserole with Marshmallows

The origin of the sweet potato-marshmallow marriage is lost in time, though marshmallows date back to at least the 1880s. Sweet potatoes are native to South America but they were grown throughout the southern United States at the time of Columbus's arrival. Use either small or large marshmallows.

SERVES 6 TO 8

6 medium sweet potatoes
½ cup milk
¼ cup sugar
½ cup chopped walnuts
¼ cup (½ stick) butter, softened
¼ cup bourbon or other whiskey (optional)
Salt
Marshmallows

1. Steam the sweet potatoes over boiling water for 30 to 40 minutes, until tender. Drain and set aside.

2. Preheat the oven to 350°F. Grease a 2-quart baking dish.

3. When the potatoes are cool enough to handle, scoop out the flesh into a large bowl and discard the skins. Rice or mash the potatoes with a potato ricer or masher.

4. Mix the milk, sugar, walnuts, butter, and bourbon, if using, in a medium bowl and add to the mashed sweet potatoes; blend well. Season to taste with salt and transfer to the baking dish. Top with the marshmallows.

5. Bake for 30 minutes, until the top is light golden brown. Serve hot.

Yankee Sweet Potatoes

Only a Yankee would think to combine sweet potatoes with apples and maple syrup. This is a variation on candied sweet potatoes and a very good one, indeed. Don't use pancake syrup—use pure maple syrup.

SERVES 6 TO 8

3 large sweet potatoes
3 tablespoons butter
3 large tart apples, such as Granny Smith or Rome Beauty, peeled, cored, and sliced
½ cup pure maple syrup

1. Steam the sweet potatoes over boiling water for 30 to 40 minutes, until tender. Drain and set aside.

2. Preheat the oven to 350°F. Grease a 9-inch square baking dish.

3. When the potatoes are cool, peel and cut them into ½-inch slices.

4. Melt 2 tablespoons of butter in a medium skillet over medium heat. Add the apple slices and sauté until tender, about 5 minutes.

5. Alternate layers of sweet potatoes and apple slices in the baking dish, ending with sweet potatoes. Dot with the remaining tablespoon of butter and pour the syrup over all.

6. Bake for 35 minutes, until the potatoes are glazed and browned. Serve hot.

Sweet Potato Pancakes

Pancakes made with sweet potatoes are a terrific, nutritional alternative to regular potato pancakes. These can be served as a side dish with a roast or steak. They also make a fine breakfast, served hot with butter and pure maple syrup or honey.

SERVES 4

2 medium sweet potatoes, peeled and grated
3 tablespoons all-purpose flour
1 tablespoon milk
2 large eggs, lightly beaten
½ teaspoon salt
4 to 6 tablespoons shortening or oil, plus more as needed

1. Preheat the oven to 200°F.

2. Stir together the sweet potatoes, flour, milk, eggs, and salt in a medium bowl.

3. Heat 4 tablespoons of shortening in a large skillet over medium-high heat.

4. Spoon 2 tablespoons of batter into the skillet for each pancake; do not crowd. Press flat with the back of a spatula and cook for about 5 minutes, until the bottom is browned and crisp. Turn carefully and cook the second side, 4 to 5 minutes more. Drain on paper towels. Repeat until all the batter is used, adding shortening as needed.

5. Hold the finished cakes in the oven until all are done. Serve hot.

Winter Squash Purée

A smooth purée of winter squash can be dressed up easily with the addition of a sweetener, butter, and cream. Use whatever winter squash you have on hand.

SERVES 6 TO 8

1 large buttercup or butternut squash
¼ cup (½ stick) butter
¼ cup pure maple syrup or brown sugar
¼ cup half-and-half
Salt and pepper

1. Preheat the oven to 375°F.

2. Cut the squash into quarters. Remove and discard the seeds and fibers. Place, skin side up, in a baking dish and add about 1 inch of water to the dish.

3. Bake until completely tender, 60 to 90 minutes, depending on the size of the pieces.

4. When the squash pieces are cool enough to handle, scoop out the flesh. Use a potato masher to mash the flesh in a large bowl and beat in the butter until smooth. Beat in the maple syrup and half-and-half. Season to taste with salt and pepper. Serve hot.

TIP: You can make this dish in advance and reheat it in the top of a double boiler set over boiling water.

Baked Acorn Squash

The acorn squash is a medium-size squash with a deeply furrowed shape. The skin may be deep green, gold, or white, while the flesh is bright orange to off-white. The flesh is sweet and enhanced here with a sweet-and-spicy sauce.

SERVES 4

1 large acorn squash
1 cup water
½ cup orange juice
¼ cup packed brown sugar
2 tablespoons lemon juice
2 tablespoons butter
1 teaspoon salt
¼ teaspoon ground nutmeg
⅛ teaspoon ground cinnamon
Pinch of ground cloves

1. Preheat the oven to 400°F.

2. Cut the squash into quarters. Remove and discard the seeds and fibers. Place the squash, skin side down, in a 9 x 13-inch baking dish.

3. Combine the water, orange juice, brown sugar, lemon juice, butter, salt, nutmeg, cinnamon, and cloves in a small saucepan and bring to a boil. Pour the mixture evenly over the squash.

4. Cover the dish with aluminum foil and bake for 45 minutes, until the squash is tender when pierced with a fork. Serve hot.

Butternut Squash Casserole

If you like marshmallows on your sweet potato casserole, this combination of sugar, vanilla extract, and vanilla wafers is for you.

SERVES 6 TO 8

1 large butternut squash
¼ cup granulated sugar
1½ cups milk
1 teaspoon vanilla extract
½ teaspoon salt
2 tablespoons all-purpose flour
2 large eggs
¾ cup (1½ sticks) butter, melted
½ (16-ounce) package vanilla wafers, crushed
1 cup firmly packed brown sugar

1. Preheat the oven to 425°F.

2. Cut the squash in half lengthwise and remove and discard the seeds and fibers. Place, skin side up, in a baking dish and add 1 inch of water. Bake for about 1 hour, until tender. Let cool briefly.

3. When the squash is cool enough to handle, scoop out the flesh and discard the skin. Use a potato masher to mash the flesh in a large bowl. Mix in the granulated sugar, milk, vanilla extract, salt, flour, eggs, and ½ cup of melted butter. Transfer to a 2-quart baking dish.

4. Bake for 30 to 40 minutes or until set.

5. In a medium bowl, combine the crushed vanilla wafers, the remaining ¼ cup melted butter, and the brown sugar. Crumble over the top of the casserole and return to the oven to brown, 10 to 15 minutes. Serve hot.

Fried Green Tomatoes

Fried green tomatoes are popular in the South and Midwest, although the first recipe for them comes from New York City in the 1870s. Bacon grease is the traditional frying medium, but butter, or even vegetable oil, can be used.

SERVES 4

4 medium green tomatoes, sliced ½ inch thick
½ cup milk
1 cup all-purpose flour
⅔ cup yellow cornmeal
½ teaspoon salt
¼ teaspoon black pepper
¼ cup bacon grease or butter

1. Pat the tomatoes dry with paper towels and set aside.

2. Pour the milk into one shallow bowl, the flour into another. Mix the cornmeal, salt, and pepper in a third shallow bowl.

3. Heat the bacon grease in a large skillet over medium-high heat.

4. Dip the tomatoes into the flour, tapping off any excess, then dip into the milk, and then into the cornmeal. Place the slices in a single layer in the skillet and fry until golden brown on both sides, 3 to 4 minutes per side. Drain on paper towels. Continue until all the slices are fried. Serve hot.

Broiled Tomatoes

Old-fashioned tomato varieties, full of good flavor, are back in home gardens and farmers' markets. The heirloom varieties are worth seeking out for their superior flavor, particularly for simple recipes such as this one.

SERVES 4

4 medium tomatoes
Dijon mustard
Salt and pepper
3 tablespoons butter, melted
¼ cup seasoned dry bread crumbs
¼ cup grated Parmesan cheese

1. Preheat the broiler.

2. Cut the tomatoes in half horizontally and place, cut side up, on a baking sheet. Spread the cut sides with mustard and sprinkle with a little salt and pepper. Set aside.

3. Combine the melted butter, bread crumbs, and Parmesan cheese in a small bowl. Spoon the crumb mixture over the top of each tomato half, dividing evenly.

4. Broil until the crumbs are browned and the tomatoes are tender, 4 to 5 minutes.

Stewed Tomatoes

In the old days, women often had a "summer kitchen," where they could can vast quantities of tomatoes and other summer vegetables away from the heat of the oven in the main kitchen. Stewed tomatoes was a standard canning recipe, and could be used year-round as a side dish or as the basis for a vegetable soup. It is a good way to use up overripe tomatoes.

SERVES 6

6 to 8 medium tomatoes
2 tablespoons butter
1 medium onion, thinly sliced
1 large celery rib, chopped
½ medium green bell pepper, chopped
3 tablespoons sugar, or to taste
1 bay leaf
Salt and pepper

1. Put the tomatoes in a pot of boiling water for 15 to 20 seconds, then plunge into ice water to cool quickly. Peel, remove and discard the cores, and cut into wedges.

2. Combine the tomatoes, butter, onion, celery, bell pepper, sugar, and bay leaf in a medium saucepan. Add salt and pepper to taste, cover, and simmer on medium heat for 30 minutes.

3. Remove the bay leaf. Taste and adjust the seasoning as needed and serve hot.

Tomatoes au Gratin

Each American eats about 18 pounds of commercially grown fresh tomatoes each year, much of which goes into salads and sandwiches. But old-fashioned dishes like this one combine tomatoes with bread cubes, bacon, a bit of sugar, hot pepper sauce, and a crisp cracker topping.

SERVES 4 TO 6

¼ cup (½ stick) butter
1 cup bread cubes
1 medium onion, chopped
4 slices bacon, cooked crisp and crumbled
2 teaspoons sugar
2½ cups peeled, seeded, and chopped
    tomatoes
1 teaspoon salt
Dash of hot pepper sauce, such as Tabasco
Pinch of dried basil
10 to 12 crushed saltine crackers

1. Preheat the oven to 350°F. Grease a 2-quart baking dish.

2. Melt the butter in a large skillet over medium heat. Add the bread cubes and brown lightly, about 5 minutes.

3. Add the onion and sauté until softened, about 3 minutes.

4. Add the bacon to the bread mixture. Add the sugar, tomatoes, salt, hot pepper sauce, and basil and mix gently. Spoon into the prepared baking dish and top with the crushed crackers.

5. Bake for 45 minutes. Serve hot.

Tomatoes Stuffed with Spinach and Rice

Tomatoes make a handy container for all sorts of fillings. Here the filling is spinach and rice. Choose Parmesan cheese as a topping for an Italian spin on the dish, or add feta cheese for a Greek flair.

SERVES 6

6 large tomatoes, cored
2 (10-ounce) packages fresh spinach, washed and trimmed
2 tablespoons oil
1½ cups sliced mushrooms
1 medium onion, finely chopped
1 teaspoon minced garlic
1 teaspoon dried basil
½ teaspoon salt
¼ teaspoon black pepper
1 cup cooked white or brown rice
6 tablespoons grated Parmesan cheese or crumbled feta cheese

1. Preheat the oven to 400°F.

2. Cut a slice from the top of each tomato. Remove the pulp and seeds, leaving each with a ¼-inch-thick shell. Turn upside down and drain on paper towels. Chop the tomato pulp (makes about 3½ cups) and set aside.

3. Bring 1 inch of water to a boil in a large saucepan. Add the spinach, cover, and steam until wilted, 3 to 5 minutes. Drain, rinse with cold water, and press out as much water as possible. If the spinach seems watery, gather it in handfuls and squeeze to remove the excess water. Transfer to a cutting board and chop.

4. Heat the oil in a large skillet over medium-high heat. Add the mushrooms and onion and cook, stirring, until tender, about 10 minutes. Add the spinach, tomato pulp, garlic, basil, salt, and pepper. Cook over low heat, stirring occasionally, until the flavors blend, about 10 minutes. Stir in the rice and ¼ cup of Parmesan cheese. Remove from the heat, cover, and let stand for 5 minutes.

5. Place the tomato shells in a 9 x 13-inch baking dish. Spoon the hot mixture into each, dividing evenly, then sprinkle each with 1 teaspoon of remaining Parmesan cheese.

6. Bake for about 15 minutes, until the tomatoes are hot and the filling is golden. Serve hot.

TIP: To make this recipe with frozen spinach, substitute one 1-pound bag of frozen spinach or two 10-ounce packages. Thaw, squeeze out any excess liquid, chop, and proceed with step 4.

Creamed Turnips

The closely related turnip and rutabaga are both root vegetables. Turnips are mild flavored and white fleshed. Rutabagas are sweeter and stronger in flavor. They can be used interchangeably in most recipes, and this dish is one such example, combining the vegetable with a simple yet flavorful cream sauce.

SERVES 4 TO 6

6 cups peeled and cubed turnips or rutabagas
2 tablespoons butter
¼ cup half-and-half
Salt and pepper

1. Bring a large pot of salted water to a boil. Add the turnips and boil until tender, 6 to 9 minutes (20 to 30 minutes for rutabagas). Drain well.

2. Return the turnips to the saucepan. Add the butter, half-and-half, and salt and pepper to taste. Simmer over medium heat for 3 to 4 minutes. Serve hot.

Rutabaga Pudding

In the 1880s, savory puddings were commonly served as side dishes alongside roasts. This particular pudding is Irish in origin.

SERVES 4 TO 6

6 tablespoons (¾ stick) butter
4 cups peeled and grated rutabagas or turnips
1 tablespoon grated onion
3 large eggs
1 (3-ounce) package cream cheese, softened
2 cups milk
1 teaspoon salt
1 teaspoon sugar

¼ teaspoon black pepper
Pinch of ground nutmeg
¾ cup dry bread crumbs

1. Preheat the oven to 350°F. Grease an 8-inch square baking dish.

2. Melt 4 tablespoons of butter in a large skillet over medium heat. Add the rutabaga and onion and sauté until softened, about 10 minutes.

3. In a large bowl, beat the eggs and cream cheese until well blended. Gradually beat in the milk. Stir in the rutabaga mixture, salt, sugar, pepper, and nutmeg.

4. Transfer the mixture to the prepared baking dish and top with the crumbs. Dot with the remaining 2 tablespoons butter.

5. Bake for 30 to 45 minutes, until set, and serve.

Succotash with Fresh Lima Beans

The first succotash the Pilgrims enjoyed was made of corn and kidney beans, and perhaps dog meat, all cooked in bear grease. The dish was called "misickquatash" by the Narragansett Indians. This succotash is made with fresh lima beans.

SERVES 4 TO 6

2 pounds lima beans, shelled
2 slices bacon, chopped
6 medium corn ears
¾ cup half-and-half
2 tablespoons butter
Salt and pepper

1. Bring a large pot of salted water to a boil. Add the lima beans and cook until almost tender, about 10 minutes. Drain and set aside.

2. Cook the bacon in the same pot over medium-high heat until lightly browned, about 5 minutes.

3. Cut the corn kernels off the ears into the pot with the bacon and scrape the liquid from the cobs with the dull edge of a knife. Add the lima beans and half-and-half, cover, and simmer over medium heat for about 10 minutes. Add the butter, and salt and pepper to taste. Serve hot.

Mixed Vegetables au Gratin

All vegetables can be prepared au gratin, or baked in a creamy cheese sauce and topped with crispy bread crumbs. Feel free to substitute other vegetables if you wish.

SERVES 4 TO 6

¼ cup (½ stick) butter
¼ cup all-purpose flour
2 cups milk
2 cups shredded Cheddar or Swiss cheese (about 8 ounces)
Salt and pepper
2 tablespoons oil
1 medium onion, thinly sliced
2 cups green beans, trimmed and cut into 2-inch lengths
2 cups sliced zucchini or yellow summer squash
2 cups fresh or frozen corn
Salt and pepper
⅓ cup dry bread crumbs

1. Preheat the oven to 425°F. Grease a 2-quart baking dish.

2. Melt the butter in a medium saucepan over medium heat. Stir in the flour to make a smooth paste and cook for 2 minutes. Gradually whisk in the milk and cook until thickened, 4 to 5 minutes. Stir in the cheese and cook until melted. Season to taste with salt and pepper. Keep warm.

3. Heat the oil in a large skillet over medium-high heat. Add the onion and sauté until softened, about 3 minutes. Add the green beans and sauté until softened, about 4 minutes. Stir in the zucchini and corn and continue to sauté until all the vegetables are tender, about 5 minutes.

4. Spread a little of the cheese sauce in the prepared baking dish and spoon the vegetable mixture on top. Season generously with salt and pepper. Cover with the remaining sauce and top with the bread crumbs.

5. Bake for 20 to 30 minutes, until heated through and browned on top. Serve hot.

Tex-Mex Vegetable Casserole

These spicy, cheesy vegetables make an excellent side dish for grilled or broiled meats and chicken. You can also serve this casserole with broiled or pan-fried sausages, accompanied by warm flour tortillas and guacamole.

SERVES 4 TO 6

2 tablespoons oil
2 small yellow summer squash, sliced
2 small zucchini, sliced
1 medium onion, sliced
1 medium red or green bell pepper, seeded and sliced
1 teaspoon minced garlic
1 teaspoon ground cumin
¼ teaspoon salt
2 cups fresh or frozen corn
1 (4-ounce) can chopped green chile peppers, drained
½ cup shredded Monterey Jack cheese
¾ cup shredded Cheddar cheese

1. Preheat the oven to 400°F. Grease a 2-quart baking dish.

2. Heat the oil in a large skillet over medium-high heat. Add the squash, zucchini, onion, bell pepper, garlic, cumin, and salt and sauté until just soft, about 5 minutes. Mix in the corn and chile peppers.

3. Transfer the vegetables to the prepared baking dish. Toss with the Monterey Jack cheese and ½ cup of Cheddar cheese.

4. Bake for 15 minutes. Sprinkle the remaining ¼ cup Cheddar cheese over the top and bake for 5 more minutes. Serve hot.

Ratatouille

This popular French vegetable stew usually combines eggplant, tomatoes, onions, bell peppers, and zucchini. It can be served hot, at room temperature, or cold. Though it fits the bill as a side dish, it can also be served as an appetizer to spread on toasted baguette or French bread.

SERVES 6

½ cup oil
1 large eggplant, peeled and cut into 1-inch cubes
1 large onion, diced
1 medium green bell pepper, seeded and cut into 1-inch squares
1 medium red bell pepper, seeded and cut into 1-inch squares
3 small zucchini, diced ½ inch
1 teaspoon minced garlic
1 teaspoon dried thyme
2 bay leaves
4 medium tomatoes, cut into 1-inch chunks
¼ cup dry white wine
Salt and pepper
¼ cup chopped fresh basil

1. Heat ¼ cup of oil in a large saucepan over medium-high heat. Add the eggplant and sauté until browned, about 15 minutes. Transfer from the saucepan to an ovenproof dish with a slotted spoon and keep warm.

2. Add 2 tablespoons of oil to the saucepan and heat. Add the onion and bell peppers and sauté until the vegetables are softened, about 5 minutes. Use a slotted spoon to remove them from the saucepan and combine with the eggplant.

3. Add the remaining 2 tablespoons oil to the saucepan and heat. Add the zucchini and sauté until softened, about 5 minutes.

4. Return the sautéed vegetables to the saucepan. Add the garlic, thyme, and bay leaves and cook for about 2 minutes. Add the tomatoes and wine and season to taste with salt and pepper. Cover and simmer for 30 minutes, stirring occasionally.

5. Uncover and simmer until the juices reduce a little, about 15 minutes. Remove the bay leaves and stir in the basil. Serve hot, at room temperature, or slightly chilled.

To cook dried beans, rinse 1 pound beans (about 2 cups) and pick over to remove any debris. Soak the beans overnight in water. Drain. Combine with 8 cups fresh water in a large saucepan and bring to a boil. Skim off any foam that rises to the top. Cover and simmer for the times listed below. If you need to add water at any point, be sure it is boiling hot. Adding cold water will toughen the beans. Cooking beans in acidic ingredients, such as tomato sauce, will also toughen the beans, but adding salt to the cooking water will not. The yields vary depending on the bean, but generally 1 pound of dried beans will yield 6 to 7 cups of cooked beans.

Variety	Cooking Time
Black beans	1 to 1½ hours
Black-eyed peas (Presoaking is not needed)	45 to 60 minutes
Cannellini (white kidney beans)	45 minutes
Cranberry beans	1¼ to 1½ hours
Garbanzos (chickpeas) (Time depends on the age of the bean)	1 to 3 hours
Great Northern beans	1½ hours
Kidney beans	1 hour
Lentils (Presoaking is not needed)	30 to 45 minutes
Lima beans, large	50 to 60 minutes
Lima beans, small	45 to 60 minutes
Lima beans, Christmas	1 hour
Navy or pea beans	1 to 1½ hours
Pink beans	50 to 60 minutes
Pinto beans	1 to 1½ hours
Soybeans	2 to 2½ hours

Guide to Cooking Fresh Vegetables

All vegetables should be washed thoroughly before being cooked. Cooking times will vary depending on the age and size of the vegetables. To boil most vegetables, bring the water to a boil. Add salt, then add the vegetable and boil until tender. Root vegetables, however, should be placed in cold salted water first, then brought to a boil. To steam vegetables, bring a few inches of water to a boil in a saucepan. Add the vegetables in a steamer basket, cover, and steam until tender.

VEGETABLE	PREPARATION	BOIL TIME	STEAM TIME	SAUTÉ TIME
Artichokes	Trim the stems. Cut 1 inch off the tops. Cut off the sharp leaf tips. Rub the cut surfaces with ½ lemon.	20 to 35 minutes	20 to 45 minutes	N/A
Asparagus	Snap off the woody ends. Leave whole or cut into 1-inch pieces.	4 to 8 minutes	4 to 8 minutes	3 to 5 minutes
Beans, green or wax	Trim the ends. Leave beans whole or cut into 1-inch pieces.	2 to 8 minutes	3 to 12 minutes	5 to 10 minutes
Beans in the shell	Shell.	10 to 40 minutes	15 to 35 minutes	N/A
Beets	Cut off all but 1 inch of the stems and roots.	20 to 60 minutes	20 to 60 minutes	N/A
Bell peppers	Remove the stems and seeds. Cut into rings or strips.	N/A	N/A	3 to 5 minutes
Broccoli	Peel the stems. Remove the woody base. Cut lengthwise into spears, or chop, or slice the stems and cut them into florets.	2 to 12 minutes	3 to 12 minutes	N/A
Brussels sprouts	Trim the base and remove the yellowed leaves. Cut in half if they are large.	6 to 12 minutes	6 to 15 minutes	3 to 6 minutes
Cabbage	Remove the wilted outer leaves and the core. Cut into wedges or smaller pieces.	6 to 8 minutes	10 to 12 minutes	6 to 10 minutes
Carrots	Peel, then slice.	4 to 9 minutes	7 to 10 minutes	5 to 8 minutes

Vegetable	Preparation	Boil Time	Steam Time	Sauté Time
Cauliflower	Remove the leaves and the woody stem. Leave whole or break into florets.	3 to 5 minutes	3 to 6 minutes	N/A
Corn on the cob	Remove the husks and silks.	3 to 7 minutes	3 to 10 minutes	N/A
Corn off the cob	Remove the husks and silks. Stand the ear on its stem end and cut off the kernels.	4 to 8 minutes	4 to 8 minutes	3 to 5 minutes
Eggplant	Peel, if desired, then slice or cube.	N/A	N/A	5 to 10 minutes
Greens	Remove the tough stems.	3 to 20 minutes	N/A	2 to 15 minutes
Okra	Cut off the stems. Leave whole or cut ½ inch thick.	3 to 5 minutes	3 to 8 minutes	5 to 10 minutes
Onions	Peel, then slice or dice.	5 to 10 minutes (for boiling onions)	N/A	3 to 5 minutes
Parsnips	Peel and slice.	4 to 9 minutes	5 to 10 minutes	5 to 8 minutes
Pea pods	Remove the tips and strings.	2 to 4 minutes	2 to 4 minutes	2 to 3 minutes
Peas in the pod	Shell.	4 to 12 minutes	5 to 15 minutes	N/A
Potatoes	Peel, if desired, and remove the eyes. Cut into quarters or cubes.	10 to 25 minutes	10 to 25 minutes	10 minutes (for slices)
Rutabagas	Peel and cut into cubes.	18 to 20 minutes	18 to 20 minutes	N/A
Spinach	Wash and trim.	3 to 5 minutes	3 to 5 minutes	3 to 5 minutes
Squash, winter	Halve, then remove the seeds and fibers.	12 to 20 minutes	12 to 20 minutes	3 to 5 minutes
Squash, yellow summer	Slice.	3 to 5 minutes	4 to 6 minutes	N/A
Sweet potatoes	Peel and cut into quarters or cubes.	15 to 35 minutes	15 to 35 minutes	5 to 8 minutes
Turnips	Peel, then slice or cube.	6 to 9 minutes	6 to 9 minutes	3 to 5 minutes
Zucchini	Slice.	3 to 5 minutes	4 to 6 minutes	3 to 5 minutes

CHAPTER TWELVE

Breads and Toppings

Nothing says "home" like the aroma of fresh-baked bread wafting from the kitchen. It draws the whole family to the table, eager to slather fresh, creamy butter onto the warm creations emerging from the oven.

Bread baking used to be a chore every cook had to master. In the 1850s, 90 percent of bread consumed in the United States was baked at home, despite the proliferation of bakeries. In California, gold prospectors made sourdough bread a San Francisco legend. The prospectors' love of the quick starter dough soon earned them the nickname "sourdoughs."

Until 1868, most bread in America was leavened without yeast. In the North, salt-rising bread was common, while baking soda was the leavening of choice in the South. Hungarian still-master Charles Fleischmann changed all that after visiting his sister in Cincinnati. He found American breads inferior to European breads and decided the fault lay with the yeast. Soon he was packaging yeast in foil packets to be shipped everywhere, and people could watch bread and rolls rise with compressed yeast right before their eyes.

The development of the bread-slicing machine in 1928 and the appearance of Wonder Bread in 1930 led to a decrease in bread baking at home. But recent modern conveniences have made bread baking easy. Today, we have reliable yeast for rising, efficient gas and electric ovens to regulate heat, and stand mixers with dough hooks to replace the elbow grease needed to beat yeast dough into submission. For those without the time or inclination to make yeasted breads, there are plenty of biscuits, muffins, and quick breads that can be made in minutes. In recent years, countertop bread makers have brought freshly baked bread to our fingertips at the push of a button.

All the baking in this chapter assumes that the oven rack sits in the middle position of the oven, unless otherwise stated. Always properly preheat your oven, and remember that glass bakeware conducts and retains heat better than metal, so oven temperatures should be reduced by 25°F whenever you use glass. For more even baking, rotate your baking sheets and pans front to back halfway through the baking time. If you have to use more than one rack, make sure the racks are at least 6 inches apart for proper air circulation, and rotate the pans top to bottom halfway through the baking process. If you follow these tips, whatever bread you set out to make should come out delicious!

Baking Powder Biscuits

The classic American biscuit is a light, soft roll that has many uses. It may be split open, buttered, and served with supper instead of bread or dinner rolls. For breakfast it might be halved and served with ham and red-eye gravy or sausage gravy. The dough also makes a fine topping for pot pie, and yet it tastes just as good when baked as shortcake and served with strawberries and whipped cream for dessert.

MAKES ABOUT 8

2 cups all-purpose flour
4 teaspoons baking powder
¾ teaspoon salt
6 tablespoons butter or shortening
¾ cup milk

1. Preheat the oven to 425°F.

2. Sift the flour, baking powder, and salt into a medium bowl. Cut in the butter with a pastry blender or 2 knives until the mixture is crumbly. Add the milk and stir lightly with a fork until the dough clings together.

3. Turn the dough out onto a floured surface. Knead gently a few times, until smooth. Roll out to a thickness of ½ inch. Cut into 2-inch rounds with a biscuit cutter and place on an ungreased baking sheet.

4. Bake for 12 to 15 minutes, until golden brown. Serve hot.

Beaten Biscuits

Featured on breakfast and tea tables of Virginia, beaten biscuits were an essential touch. Unfortunately, with the invention of baking soda, these biscuits have lost their popularity. This version uses a food processor but still results in the crisp exterior, which characterizes this Southern specialty.

MAKES 18 TO 20

3½ cups cake flour
½ teaspoon baking powder
½ teaspoon salt
2 tablespoons sugar
½ cup shortening
¾ cup half-and-half

1. Sift the flour, baking powder, salt, and sugar into a medium bowl. Cut in the shortening with a pastry blender or 2 knives until the mixture is crumbly. Add the half-and-half and stir lightly with a fork until the dough clings together.

2. Use your hands to gather the dough into a ball, place in a resealable plastic bag, and leave in a cool place for several hours or overnight. (If the kitchen is warm, place in the refrigerator, but let the dough stand at room temperature for about 30 minutes before continuing.)

3. Preheat the oven to 325°F.

4. Divide the dough in half. Using a food processor fitted with a plastic dough blade, process each half for 2 minutes.

5. Turn the dough out onto a floured surface and gather into a ball. Roll out to a thickness of ¼ inch. Fold over and roll out again. Continue folding and rolling until the dough is very smooth and pliable, 4 to 6 times. After folding the last time, do not roll out.

6. Cut the dough into 1½-inch circles with a biscuit cutter. Place on an ungreased baking sheet. Prick each biscuit several times with a fork.

7. Bake for 5 minutes on the lowest rack in the oven.

8. Move to the center rack and bake for 20 to 25 minutes, until very pale brown. The inside of the biscuits will be dry and flaky. Serve the same day or place in an airtight container and store for up to 1 week.

Angel Biscuits

The lightest of all biscuits, angel biscuits are made with both yeast and baking powder. Buttermilk adds a moist tang to the batter.

MAKES 24 TO 36

4½ teaspoons (two ¼-ounce packages) active
    dry yeast
¼ cup warm water
2 cups warm buttermilk
5 cups all-purpose flour
¼ cup sugar
1 tablespoon baking powder
1 teaspoon baking soda
1 tablespoon salt
1 cup shortening
Melted butter

1. Grease a baking sheet.

2. Sprinkle the yeast over the warm water, then stir in the buttermilk. Set aside for about 5 minutes, until bubbly.

3. Meanwhile, combine the flour, sugar, baking powder, baking soda, and salt in a large bowl. Cut in the shortening with a pastry blender or 2 knives until the mixture is crumbly. Stir in the yeast mixture, blending well.

4. Turn the dough out onto a floured surface and gather into a ball with your hands. Knead gently for a few turns, then roll out to a thickness of ½ inch. Cut into 2½-inch rounds with a biscuit cutter. Place the biscuits on the prepared baking sheet. Cover with plastic wrap or a clean towel and let rise in a warm place for about 1½ hours.

5. Preheat the oven to 450°F.

6. Bake the biscuits for 8 to 10 minutes, until golden.

7. Brush the tops with the melted butter while still hot. Serve warm.

Cheese Biscuits

Cheese replaces some of the butter in these biscuits. Cheese biscuits are often served as a snack with drinks or coffee, but they also make a fine accompaniment to soup or salad. They can be given a Tex-Mex twist by substituting 2 tablespoons of chopped, roasted green chile peppers for the parsley.

MAKES 12

2 cups all-purpose flour
2½ teaspoons baking powder
½ teaspoon salt
½ teaspoon dry mustard
3 tablespoons butter
⅔ cup shredded sharp Cheddar cheese
2 tablespoons chopped fresh parsley
¾ cup milk, plus more for brushing the biscuit
    tops

1. Preheat the oven to 450°F. Grease a baking sheet.

2. Sift the flour, baking powder, salt, and dry mustard into a medium bowl. Cut in the butter with a pastry blender or 2 knives until the mixture is crumbly. Stir in the cheese and parsley. Add the ¾ cup milk and stir lightly with a fork until the dough clings together.

3. Turn the dough out onto a floured surface and knead gently a few times, until smooth. Roll out to a thickness of ¾ inch. Cut into 2-inch rounds with a biscuit cutter and place on the prepared baking sheet. Brush the tops with milk.

4. Bake for 20 to 25 minutes, until golden brown. Serve warm.

...eberry Scones

*...nd scone dough are virtually the same,
...astry meant to be eaten hot, slathered
...es may be served at breakfast or as a
...ack, particularly with afternoon tea.*

MAKES ABOUT 18

2⅓ cups cake flour
2½ teaspoons baking powder
2 tablespoons plus 2 teaspoons sugar
½ teaspoon salt
6 tablespoons shortening
6 tablespoons milk or half-and-half
2 large eggs (1 separated)
1 cup blueberries (preferably fresh)

1. Preheat the oven to 450°F. Grease a baking sheet.

2. Sift the flour, baking powder, 2 teaspoons sugar, and the salt into a medium bowl. Cut in the shortening with a pastry blender or 2 knives until the mixture is crumbly. Set aside.

3. Mix the milk, 1 egg, and 1 egg yolk in a small bowl. Add to the flour mixture along with the blueberries. Stir lightly with a fork until the dough clings together.

4. Turn the dough out onto a floured surface and knead gently a few times, until smooth. Roll out to a thickness of ½ inch and cut into 3-inch squares. Cut each square in half to make 2 rectangles or 2 triangles. Arrange the scones on the prepared baking sheet.

5. Lightly beat the egg white in a small bowl and brush onto the tops of the scones. Sprinkle with the remaining 2 tablespoons sugar.

6. Bake for 10 to 15 minutes, until golden brown. Serve warm.

Currant-Orange Scones

Dried currants, which often are dried Zante grapes, are smaller than raisins. They are the traditional dried fruit of English scones. You can substitute dried cranberries or finely chopped dried apricots.

MAKES ABOUT 18

3 cups all-purpose flour
⅓ cup sugar
2½ teaspoons baking powder
½ teaspoon baking soda
½ teaspoon salt
¾ cup (1½ sticks) butter, cut into cubes
½ cup dried currants or raisins
1 cup buttermilk (or 1 cup milk with
    1 teaspoon vinegar added)
1 tablespoon grated orange zest

1. Preheat the oven to 450°F.

2. Sift the flour, sugar, baking powder, baking soda, and salt into a medium bowl. Cut in the butter with a pastry blender or 2 knives until the mixture is crumbly. Mix in the currants, then add the buttermilk and orange zest. Stir lightly with a fork until the dough clings together.

3. Turn the dough out onto a floured surface and knead gently a few times, until smooth. Roll out to a thickness of ½ inch and cut into 3-inch squares. Cut each square in half to make 2 rectangles or 2 triangles. Arrange the scones on the prepared baking sheet.

4. Bake for 10 to 15 minutes, until golden brown. Serve warm.

Cinnamon-Apple Streusel Muffins

These muffins are studded with apples and topped with a crumble of cinnamon and sugar. They make a delicious breakfast treat and the perfect after-school snack.

MAKES 12

Topping:
⅓ cup firmly packed brown sugar
3 tablespoons all-purpose flour
2 teaspoons ground cinnamon
2 tablespoons butter, softened

Muffins:
1¾ cups all-purpose flour
⅓ cup granulated sugar
2 teaspoons baking powder
¼ teaspoon salt
1 large egg, beaten
¾ cup apple cider or apple juice
1 large tart apple, such as Granny Smith or
    Rome Beauty, peeled, cored, and diced
1 teaspoon vanilla extract
¼ cup oil

1. Preheat the oven to 400°F. Grease and flour a 12-cup muffin pan or line the pan with paper baking cups.

2. To prepare the topping, stir together the brown sugar, flour, and cinnamon in a small bowl. Mix in the butter with a fork or pastry blender until the mixture is crumbly. Set aside.

3. To make the muffins, stir together the flour, sugar, baking powder, and salt in a medium bowl. Set aside.

4. Stir together the egg, apple cider, diced apple, vanilla extract, and oil in a small bowl until well blended. Add to the flour mixture and stir until just moistened. (The batter should be lumpy.)

5. Spoon about 1 tablespoon of batter into each muffin cup. Sprinkle with 1 teaspoon of the topping. Fill evenly with the remaining batter, then sprinkle the tops with the remaining topping.

6. Bake for about 20 minutes, until golden brown.

7. Cool for 10 minutes, remove from the pan, and cool briefly on wire racks. Serve warm or cooled.

TIP: Muffins are best when served on the day they are made.

Spiced Peach Muffins

These are glorious muffins, bursting with flavor and practically overflowing the muffin cups. The recipe is generous, making larger-than-average muffins.

MAKES 16

4½ cups all-purpose flour
2 cups firmly packed brown sugar
4½ teaspoons baking powder
1 teaspoon salt
1 teaspoon ground cinnamon
½ teaspoon ground allspice
½ teaspoon ground nutmeg
2 large eggs
¾ cup oil
1¼ cups milk
4 large peaches, diced (peeling not necessary)
Granulated sugar

1. Preheat the oven to 400°F. Grease and flour 16 muffin cups or line the cups with paper baking cups.

2. Stir together the flour, brown sugar, baking powder, salt, cinnamon, allspice, and nutmeg in a large bowl. Make a well in the center and add the eggs, oil, and milk. Stir until just moistened. Fold in the peaches.

3. Divide the batter among the muffin cups; they will be very full. Sprinkle the tops with the granulated sugar.

4. Bake for 25 to 30 minutes, until golden brown.

5. Cool for 10 minutes, remove from the pan, and cool briefly on wire racks. Serve warm or cooled.

Almond-Peach Muffins

Canned peaches make a surprisingly tasty addition to muffins. Almonds in this recipe add crunch and even more flavor.

MAKES 12

1½ cups all-purpose flour
1 cup sugar
¾ teaspoon salt
½ teaspoon baking soda
2 large eggs, lightly beaten
½ cup oil
½ teaspoon vanilla extract
⅛ teaspoon almond extract
1¼ cups chopped fresh or canned peaches
   (peeled if fresh)
½ cup chopped almonds

1. Preheat the oven to 375°F. Grease and flour a 12-cup muffin pan or line the pan with paper baking cups.

2. Sift the flour, sugar, salt, and baking soda into a medium bowl. Set aside.

3. Beat together the eggs, oil, vanilla extract, and almond extract in a small bowl. Pour into the flour mixture and stir just until moistened. (The batter will be lumpy.) Fold in the peaches and almonds.

4. Fill the muffin cups three-quarters full with the batter.

5. Bake for 20 to 25 minutes, until golden brown.

6. Cool for 10 minutes, remove from the pan, and cool briefly on wire racks. Serve warm or cooled.

TIP: This same amount of batter will make 24 miniature muffins or 4 jumbo muffins. Generally, miniature muffins are baked for 10 to 17 minutes and jumbo muffins for 30 to 35 minutes, until golden brown.

Best Berry Muffins

You can substitute any berry you have on hand in these delicious muffins. This recipe adds a cinnamon-sugar topping to match the lightly spiced berry batter. You don't have to defrost berries before adding them to muffin batter.

MAKES 12

Topping:
¼ cup all-purpose flour
2 tablespoons packed brown sugar
¼ teaspoon ground cinnamon
2 tablespoons butter, softened

Muffins:
2 cups all-purpose flour
2 teaspoons baking powder
½ teaspoon salt
¼ teaspoon ground cinnamon
½ cup (1 stick) butter, softened
½ cup granulated sugar
1 large egg
¾ cup milk
½ teaspoon vanilla extract
½ cup fresh or frozen blueberries
½ cup fresh or frozen raspberries

1. Preheat the oven to 400°F. Grease and flour a 12-cup muffin pan or line the pan with paper baking cups.

2. To make the topping, combine the flour, brown sugar, and cinnamon in a small bowl. Mix in the butter with a fork or pastry blender until the mixture is crumbly. Set aside.

3. To make the muffins, stir together the flour, baking powder, salt, and cinnamon in a medium bowl. Set aside.

4. Beat the butter and granulated sugar in a medium bowl until light and fluffy. Beat in the egg, milk, and vanilla extract. Add the flour mixture and stir just until moistened. Fold in the berries.

5. Divide the batter evenly among the muffin cups. Sprinkle each with the topping.

6. Bake for 25 to 30 minutes, until golden brown.

7. Cool for 10 minutes, remove from the pan, and cool briefly on wire racks. Serve warm or cooled.

Blueberry Muffins

Blueberry is probably the most popular muffin flavor. A large percentage of America's wild blueberry harvest goes into muffins because commercial bakers prefer their small size. Wild or cultivated, fresh or frozen, blueberries help make an outstanding muffin.

MAKES 12

2 cups all-purpose flour
2 teaspoons baking powder
1 teaspoon salt
¼ cup (½ stick) butter, softened
1 cup sugar
2 large eggs
½ cup milk
1 teaspoon vanilla extract
2 cups (1 pint) fresh or frozen blueberries

1. Preheat the oven to 350°F. Grease and flour a 12-cup muffin pan or line the pan with paper baking cups.

2. Stir together the flour, baking powder, and salt in a medium bowl. Set aside.

3. Beat the butter and sugar in a medium bowl until creamy and light. Beat in the eggs, one at a time, then beat in the milk and vanilla extract until well combined. Add the flour mixture and stir just until moistened. Fold in the berries.

4. Divide the batter evenly among the muffin cups.

5. Bake for 25 to 30 minutes, until golden brown.

6. Cool for 10 minutes, remove from the pan, and cool briefly on wire racks. Serve warm or cooled.

Raspberry Muffins

This recipe makes a simple, classic muffin. Substitute other berries if you don't have raspberries on hand. Remember, muffins are best enjoyed on the day they are made.

MAKES ABOUT 12

2 cups all-purpose flour
1 cup sugar
1 teaspoon baking powder
1 teaspoon baking soda
½ teaspoon salt
2 large eggs, lightly beaten
1 cup buttermilk
¼ cup (½ stick) butter, melted
2 cups (1 pint) fresh or frozen raspberries

1. Preheat the oven to 400°F. Grease and flour a 12-cup muffin pan or line the pan with paper baking cups.

2. Stir together the flour, sugar, baking powder, baking soda, and salt in a medium bowl. Set aside.

3. Beat together the eggs, buttermilk, and butter in a small bowl. Stir into the flour mixture and mix just until moistened. Fold in the berries.

4. Divide the batter evenly among the muffin cups.

5. Bake for 18 to 20 minutes, until golden brown.

6. Cool for 10 minutes. Remove from the pan and cool briefly on wire racks. Serve warm or cooled.

Raisin-Bran Muffins

Start your morning the healthy way with bran muffins. These muffins are sweet and delicious, with the tang of buttermilk.

MAKES 9

1 cup sifted all-purpose flour
½ cup sugar
1 teaspoon baking powder
½ teaspoon baking soda
½ teaspoon salt
1 cup bran flake cereal, crushed
3 tablespoons butter, softened
¼ cup molasses
1 large egg
¾ cup buttermilk
½ cup raisins

1. Preheat the oven to 400°F. Grease and flour 9 muffin cups or line the cups with paper baking cups.

2. Stir together the flour, sugar, baking powder, baking soda, and salt in a medium bowl. Stir in the bran cereal. Set aside.

3. Beat the butter and molasses in a medium bowl until well blended. Beat in the egg and buttermilk until well combined. Add the flour mixture and stir just until moistened. Fold in the raisins.

4. Divide the batter evenly among the muffin cups.

5. Bake for about 25 minutes, until golden brown.

6. Cool for 10 minutes, remove from the pan, and cool briefly on wire racks. Serve warm or cooled.

Sunny Corn Muffins

Corn muffins can accompany any meal, and they make great snacks as well. Using canned corn instead of milk in the batter enhances the corn flavor.

MAKES 12

1 cup yellow cornmeal
1 cup all-purpose flour
4 teaspoons baking powder
½ teaspoon salt
¼ cup oil
½ cup sugar
1 large egg
½ teaspoon vanilla extract
1 cup milk or 1 (10-ounce) can creamed corn

1. Preheat the oven to 350°F. Grease and flour a 12-cup muffin pan or line the pan with paper baking cups.

2. Stir together the cornmeal, flour, baking powder, and salt in a medium bowl. Set aside.

3. Beat the oil, sugar, egg, vanilla extract, and milk in a medium bowl until well blended. Add to the flour mixture and stir just until moistened.

4. Divide the batter evenly among the muffin cups.

5. Bake for about 25 minutes, until golden brown.

6. Cool for 10 minutes, remove from the pan, and cool briefly on wire racks. Serve warm or cooled.

Baked Doughnut Muffins

The sugar-cinnamon coating of these muffins tastes very much like a doughnut coating—without the fuss of frying. These muffins represent the best of both worlds and are perfect with a cup of coffee—morning, noon, or night.

MAKES 10

Muffins:
1½ cups all-purpose flour
2 teaspoons baking powder
¼ teaspoon salt
¼ teaspoon ground nutmeg
¼ cup (½ stick) butter, softened
½ cup sugar
1 large egg
½ cup milk
½ teaspoon vanilla extract

Topping:
⅓ cup sugar
½ teaspoon ground cinnamon
3 tablespoons butter, melted

1. Preheat the oven to 350°F. Grease and flour 10 muffin cups or line the cups with paper baking cups.

2. To make the muffins, stir together the flour, baking powder, salt, and nutmeg in a medium bowl. Set aside.

3. Beat together the butter and sugar in a medium bowl until light and fluffy. Beat in the egg, then beat in the milk and vanilla extract until well blended. Add the flour mixture and stir just until moistened.

4. Divide the batter evenly among the muffin cups.

5. Bake for 20 to 25 minutes, until golden brown.

6. While the muffins bake, make the topping by stirring together the sugar and cinnamon in a small bowl.

7. Remove the muffins from the oven and cool for 10 minutes. Remove from the pan and brush the tops with the melted butter. Roll in the cinnamon-sugar mixture and serve warm.

TIP: An ice-cream scoop works well to portion the muffin batter into the pan.

Popovers

A popover is a hollow quick bread, shaped like a muffin and made from an egg batter that is similar to Yorkshire pudding. The name describes the batter, which rises and pops over the edge of the muffin pan while baking. Be sure to grease the pans thoroughly.

MAKES 8 TO 12

1 cup all-purpose flour
¼ teaspoon salt
2 large eggs
1 cup milk
¼ cup (½ stick) butter, melted

1. Stir together the flour and salt in a large bowl. Add the eggs and milk and whisk to combine. Set aside for 30 minutes at room temperature.

2. Preheat the oven to 450°F. With a pastry brush, generously spread the melted butter on the bottom and sides of each cup in a popover pan so that it puddles in the bottom of each cup.

3. Pour the batter into the prepared pan.

4. Bake for 15 minutes. Reduce the oven temperature to 350°F and bake for 15 to 20 minutes more, until the popovers are browned and crisp.

5. Unmold the popovers onto a wire rack and puncture the sides with a sharp knife to allow the steam to escape. Serve immediately.

Southern-Style Cornbread

In the South, the ideal cornbread is substantial—not at all sweet and light like Northern-style cornbread. It should be made with very little white flour and be very well browned. A cast-iron skillet produces a properly browned crust.

SERVES 6 TO 8

1 tablespoon bacon drippings or butter
1½ cups yellow cornmeal
½ cup all-purpose flour
1 tablespoon sugar
2 teaspoons baking powder
1 teaspoon salt
½ teaspoon baking soda
½ cup boiling water
1½ cups buttermilk
1 large egg, beaten
3 tablespoons butter, melted

1. Preheat the oven to 400°F. Put the bacon grease in an 8- or 9-inch cast-iron skillet and place in the oven to preheat.

2. Stir together 1 cup of cornmeal, the flour, sugar, baking powder, salt, and baking soda in a medium bowl. Set aside.

3. Stir together the remaining ½ cup cornmeal and the boiling water in a medium bowl to make a thick paste. Stir in the buttermilk, egg, and melted butter. Pour into the flour mixture and stir just enough to combine.

4. Remove the preheated skillet from the oven and swirl to coat with the grease. Immediately pour the batter into the skillet.

5. Bake for 20 to 35 minutes, until lightly browned and firm to the touch. Serve warm.

Northern-Style Cornbread

This cornbread is sweet and almost cake-like, in contrast to the denser, heavier, Southern-style cornbread. The light texture and sweeter taste are achieved with the addition of sugar, more eggs, and a greater proportion of white flour.

SERVES 8

1 cup all-purpose flour
1 cup yellow cornmeal
¼ cup sugar
1 tablespoon baking powder
½ teaspoon baking soda
1 teaspoon salt
2 large eggs
⅔ cup buttermilk
⅔ cup milk
¼ cup (½ stick) butter, melted

1. Preheat the oven to 400°F. Grease an 8-inch square baking dish.

2. Stir together the flour, cornmeal, sugar, baking powder, baking soda, and salt in a medium bowl.

3. Whisk together the eggs, buttermilk, and milk in a separate medium bowl. Stir into the flour mixture just enough to thoroughly moisten. Fold in the butter; the batter will be lumpy. Pour into the prepared dish.

4. Bake for 25 to 30 minutes, until a knife inserted into the center comes out clean. Serve warm.

Beantown Brown Bread

The classic accompaniment to Boston baked beans, this dark molasses bread is steamed rather than baked. It also freezes well. To slice without crumbling, use a strong thread, such as unwaxed dental floss, and cut through using a sawing motion.

MAKES 1

½ cup rye flour
½ cup yellow cornmeal
½ cup all-purpose flour
1 teaspoon baking soda
½ teaspoon salt
⅓ cup dark molasses
1 cup buttermilk
½ cup raisins (optional)

1. Grease and flour a 1-pound coffee can or 5-cup pudding mold.

2. Stir together the rye flour, cornmeal, flour, baking soda, and salt in a large bowl. Make a well in the center and add the molasses and buttermilk. Stir just until moistened, then stir in the raisins, if using.

3. Pour the batter into the prepared mold and cover tightly with aluminum foil. Place the mold on a trivet or rack inside a tall pot and weight it down with a saucepan lid. Pour boiling water into the pot until it reaches halfway up the sides of the mold.

4. Steam, with the pot covered, for 3 to 3½ hours, until a knife inserted into the center comes out clean.

5. Cool in the coffee can on a wire rack, uncovered, for 20 minutes.

6. Unmold and serve warm or cooled.

Irish Soda Bread

This traditional Irish quick bread uses baking soda as its leavener and buttermilk as its liquid. Before baking, a cross is sliced into the top of the loaf. According to legend, the cross is supposed to scare away the devil. If you like, add 2 teaspoons of caraway seeds or ¼ cup of dried currants to the batter—two traditional ingredients.

MAKES 1

Bread:
4 cups all-purpose flour
¼ cup sugar
1 tablespoon baking powder
1 teaspoon baking soda
½ teaspoon salt
½ cup (1 stick) butter, softened
1 cup buttermilk
1 large egg, lightly beaten

Glaze:
¼ cup (½ stick) butter, melted
¼ cup buttermilk

1. Preheat the oven to 375°F. Grease a baking sheet.

2. To make the bread, stir together the flour, sugar, baking powder, baking soda, and salt. Mix in the butter, then stir in the buttermilk and egg. Turn the dough out onto a floured board and knead briefly. Form into a ball, flatten slightly, and place on the prepared baking sheet.

3. To make the glaze, combine the melted butter with the buttermilk and brush over the loaf. Use a knife to cut a cross into the top of the loaf.

4. Bake for 35 to 40 minutes, until the bread sounds hollow when tapped on the bottom.

5. Cool on a wire rack. Serve warm or at room temperature, thinly sliced or cut into wedges.

Herbed Square Bread

This savory bread contains all the flavors of a classic turkey stuffing. It makes a fine accompaniment to soup.

SERVES 6 TO 9

1½ cups all-purpose flour
1½ cups yellow cornmeal
2 tablespoons sugar
4 teaspoons baking powder
2½ teaspoons salt
1 teaspoon dried sage
1 teaspoon dried thyme
1½ cups finely chopped onion
1½ cups finely chopped celery
3 large eggs, beaten
1½ cups milk
⅓ cup shortening, melted

1. Preheat the oven to 400°F. Grease a 9-inch square baking dish.

2. Stir together the flour, cornmeal, sugar, baking powder, salt, sage, and thyme. Fold in the onion and celery; set aside.

3. Whisk together the eggs, milk, and shortening in a small bowl. Pour into the dry ingredients and stir only until blended. Pour into the prepared baking dish.

4. Bake for 25 to 30 minutes, until golden and firm to the touch. Serve warm.

Apple-Nut Bread

Is it cake or bread? This is the question asked about many quick breads. The answer, of course, is to serve it however you like. This bread can be served as a dessert, a snack, or breakfast, and it is also delicious toasted.

MAKES 1

2½ cups all-purpose flour
2 teaspoons baking powder
½ teaspoon baking soda
½ teaspoon salt
1 cup sugar
½ cup (1 stick) butter, softened
1 tablespoon light corn syrup or pure maple syrup
2 large eggs
½ cup milk
2 teaspoons grated orange zest
1 cup peeled and grated tart apple, such as Granny Smith or Rome Beauty (about 1 large)
½ cup chopped nuts

1. Preheat the oven to 350°F. Grease a 9 x 5-inch loaf pan.

2. Stir together the flour, baking powder, baking soda, and salt in a medium bowl. Set aside.

3. Combine the sugar, butter, and corn syrup in a large bowl and beat until well blended. Add the eggs, beating after each addition. Beat in the milk and orange zest. Add the flour mixture and stir just until blended. Fold in the apple and nuts, then scrape the batter into the prepared loaf pan.

4. Bake for 45 to 50 minutes, until a toothpick inserted into the center comes out clean.

5. Cool in the pan on a wire rack for 10 minutes before unmolding to cool completely before serving.

Banana-Nut Bread

America's most popular fruit has been present in American markets since the 1800s, and completely ubiquitous since the early 1900s. Some 70 to 80 million bunches of bananas are consumed each year. When they are fully ripe, they turn black, sweet, and mushy. Thrifty cooks learned to use these bananas in bread.

MAKES 1

⅔ cup milk
1 tablespoon lemon juice
2½ cups all-purpose flour
1 teaspoon baking powder
¾ teaspoon salt
½ teaspoon baking soda
½ cup (1 stick) butter, softened
⅔ cup sugar
2 large eggs
2 very ripe medium bananas, peeled
1 cup chopped walnuts or pecans

1. Preheat the oven to 350°F. Grease a 9 x 5-inch loaf pan, line the bottom with wax paper or parchment paper, then grease the paper.

2. Mix the milk and lemon juice in a small bowl and let stand until the milk curdles, about 1 minute. Set aside.

3. Stir together the flour, baking powder, salt, and baking soda in a medium bowl. Set aside.

4. Beat together the butter and sugar in a large bowl until pale and fluffy. Add the eggs, one at a time, beating until just combined. Beat in the bananas until combined. (The mixture will look curdled.)

5. Add the flour mixture to the banana mixture alternately with the soured milk, mixing just until smooth. Fold in the nuts and pour into the prepared loaf pan.

6. Bake for 50 to 55 minutes, until a toothpick inserted into the center comes out clean.

7. Cool in the pan on a wire rack for 10 minutes before unmolding to cool completely before serving. Remove the wax paper before slicing.

Date-Nut Bread

Dates have been grown since the early 1900s in California, where they are made into any number of treats, including milk shakes. Date-nut bread is popular all over, particularly when served with cream cheese for breakfast.

MAKES 1

1 cup packed pitted dates (about
    6 ounces), chopped
¾ cup boiling water
1½ cups all-purpose flour
1 teaspoon baking soda
½ teaspoon salt
½ teaspoon ground cinnamon
½ cup (1 stick) unsalted butter, softened
1 cup packed brown sugar
1 large egg
3 tablespoons lemon juice
1 teaspoon grated lemon zest
1 cup toasted chopped pecans

1. Preheat the oven to 350°F. Grease a 9 x 5-inch loaf pan, line the bottom with wax paper or parchment paper, then grease the paper.

2. Combine the dates and boiling water in a medium bowl. Let stand until the water cools, about 15 minutes.

3. Meanwhile, stir together the flour, baking soda, salt, and cinnamon in a medium bowl. Set aside.

4. Beat the butter with the brown sugar in a large bowl until creamy. Add the egg and beat until well blended. Beat in the lemon juice and lemon zest. Beat in the flour mixture in 3 additions, alternating with the date mixture. Stir in the pecans and pour the batter into the prepared pan.

5. Bake for about 55 minutes, until a toothpick inserted into the center comes out clean.

6. Cool in the pan on a wire rack for 10 minutes before unmolding to cool completely before serving. Remove the wax paper before slicing.

Lemon–Poppy Seed Tea Bread

Lemon tea breads are usually closer to cakes than to breads, and this recipe is no exception. The bread contains lemon zest, but it is the glaze applied after baking that really boosts the lemony flavor. Serve this loaf with coffee or afternoon tea—or as a dessert. The recipe makes two loaves, one for enjoying immediately and one that can be wrapped and stored in the freezer for unexpected guests.

MAKES 2

2 large lemons
3 cups all-purpose flour
2 teaspoons baking powder
½ teaspoon salt
¾ cup (1½ sticks) butter, softened
2½ cups sugar
4 large eggs
1 cup milk
2 teaspoons poppy seeds

1. Preheat the oven to 325°F. Grease two 9 x 5-inch loaf pans, line the bottoms with wax paper or parchment paper, then grease the paper.

2. Finely grate enough zest from the lemons to measure 2 teaspoons. Squeeze enough juice to measure about ½ cup. Set both aside.

3. Stir together the flour, baking powder, and salt in a medium bowl and set aside.

4. Beat together the butter, 2 cups of sugar, and the zest until light and fluffy. Beat in the eggs, one at a time, beating well after each addition. Beat in the flour mixture in three additions, alternating with the milk, just until combined well. Stir in the poppy seeds and 1 tablespoon of reserved lemon juice. Pour the batter into the loaf pans and smooth the tops.

5. Bake for 1 hour, until a toothpick inserted into the centers comes out clean.

6. While the breads are baking, make a glaze by stirring together the remaining lemon juice and ½ cup sugar in a small saucepan over low heat until the sugar is dissolved.

7. Cool in the pans on a wire rack for 15 minutes. Invert the loaves onto the rack and peel off the wax paper. Turn the loaves right side up and pierce the tops all over with a toothpick. Brush the lemon glaze over the tops until all of the glaze is absorbed. Cool completely before serving.

Spiced Pumpkin Bread

An early settler to a New England colony complained about "pumpkins at morning, pumpkins at noon." Doubtless the writer of that complaint wasn't served pumpkin in this delicious form. Pumpkin bread is served at Thanksgiving in some households, though it makes a fine snack any time.

MAKES 2

3 cups all-purpose flour
1 teaspoon baking powder
1 teaspoon baking soda
1 teaspoon ground cinnamon
½ teaspoon ground cloves
½ teaspoon ground nutmeg
½ teaspoon salt
3 cups sugar
1 cup oil
3 large eggs
1 (16-ounce) can solid-pack pumpkin
1 cup coarsely chopped walnuts (optional)

1. Preheat the oven to 350°F. Grease two 9 x 5-inch loaf pans, line the bottoms with wax paper or parchment paper, then grease the paper.

2. Stir together the flour, baking powder, baking soda, cinnamon, cloves, nutmeg, and salt in a medium bowl. Set aside.

3. Beat the sugar and oil in a large bowl until blended. Beat in the eggs, one at a time, until well blended, then beat in the pumpkin. Add the flour mixture and stir until just blended. Fold in the nuts, if using. Pour the batter into the prepared pans.

4. Bake for about 70 minutes, until a toothpick inserted into the centers comes out clean.

5. Cool in the pans on a wire rack for 10 minutes before unmolding to cool completely before serving. Remove the wax paper before slicing.

Zucchini Bread

When home gardeners in America began growing zucchini, they quickly discovered that its bounty could easily overwhelm the cook. Zucchini bread was created as a way of dealing with zucchini that had grown too big to serve as a vegetable.

MAKES 2

3 cups all-purpose flour
1¼ teaspoons baking powder
1 teaspoon baking soda
1 teaspoon salt
2 teaspoons ground cinnamon
½ teaspoon ground nutmeg
1 cup oil
2½ cups sugar
3 large eggs, beaten
2 cups grated zucchini
2 teaspoons vanilla extract

1. Preheat the oven to 350°F. Grease and flour two 8 x 4-inch loaf pans.

2. Stir together the flour, baking powder, baking soda, salt, cinnamon, and nutmeg in a medium bowl. Set aside.

3. Combine the oil and sugar in a large bowl and beat until light. Add the eggs, one at a time, beating well after each addition. Stir in the zucchini and vanilla extract. Add the flour mixture and stir just enough to combine. Pour the batter into the prepared loaf pans.

4. Bake for about 1 hour, until a toothpick inserted into the centers comes out clean.

5. Cool in the pans on a wire rack for 10 minutes, then invert and cool completely before serving.

White Sandwich Bread

Years ago, most women rolled up their sleeves once or twice a week and kneaded loaves of bread to feed their families. They had no bread machines—just powerful arms. It was a relief when white breads started flooding supermarket shelves in the 1930s, but there's no comparison between this soft, fresh loaf and the mass-produced variety.

MAKES 1

2¼ teaspoons (one ¼-ounce package) active dry yeast
¼ cup warm water
1¼ cups buttermilk, at room temperature
3 tablespoons sugar
½ tablespoon salt
6 tablespoons (¾ stick) butter, softened
3½ cups all-purpose flour, or more as needed

1. Sprinkle the yeast over the water and set aside for about 5 minutes, until bubbly.

2. Meanwhile, combine the buttermilk, sugar, salt, and 3 tablespoons of butter in a large bowl. Stir in the yeast mixture. Beat in 3¼ cups of flour, ¼ cup at a time, until the dough begins to pull away from the bowl.

3. Turn the dough out onto a work surface and knead in the remaining ¼ cup flour. Continue to knead for 5 to 7 minutes, until smooth and elastic, adding more flour if necessary until the dough is no longer sticky. Transfer to a greased large bowl, turn to coat, cover with plastic wrap or clean cloth, and set aside in a draft-free place to rise until doubled in size, 1 to 1½ hours.

4. Punch the dough down. Let rest for a few minutes.

5. Return the dough to a floured surface. Form the dough into a rectangle, roll it up, and pinch the ends and seam to seal. Place the roll, seam side down, in a greased 9 x 5-inch loaf pan. Flatten the dough in the pan to fill it evenly. Cover again and set aside at room temperature to rise until the dough reaches the top of the pan, 45 to 60 minutes.

6. Preheat the oven to 375°F.

7. Melt the remaining 3 tablespoons butter. Uncover and cut a ½-inch-deep slash down the center of the risen loaf with the tip of a knife. Brush the melted butter into the crevice and over the top.

8. Bake for 35 to 40 minutes, until deep golden brown or until the loaf sounds hollow when you tap it.

9. Remove the loaf from the pan and cool on a wire rack before slicing. Serve warm or cooled completely.

Whole-Wheat Bread

This loaf is made with a combination of whole-wheat flour and white flour, which makes the texture lighter than a loaf made with 100 percent whole-wheat flour. It is terrific for sandwiches and toast.

MAKES 2

2¼ teaspoons (one ¼-ounce package) active dry yeast
2 cups warm water
¼ cup (½ stick) butter, softened
¼ cup honey
2 tablespoons molasses
2 teaspoons salt
2 cups all-purpose flour, or more as needed
3 cups whole-wheat flour

1. Sprinkle the yeast over the water and set aside for about 5 minutes, until bubbly.

2. Meanwhile, stir together the butter, honey, molasses, and salt in a large bowl. Add the yeast mixture. Beat in the white flour, ½ cup at a time. Beat in 2¾ cups of wheat flour, ½ cup at a time, until the dough begins to pull away from the bowl.

3. Sprinkle the remaining ¼ cup wheat flour onto a work surface. Turn the dough out onto the flour. Knead for 5 to 7 minutes, until smooth and elastic, adding more white flour if necessary until the dough is no longer sticky. Transfer to a greased large bowl, cover with plastic wrap or a clean cloth, and set aside at room temperature to rise until doubled in size, 1 to 1½ hours.

4. Punch the dough down. Let rest for a few minutes.

5. Return the dough to a work surface and divide in half. Form each half into a rectangle, roll it up, and pinch the ends and seam to seal. Place each roll, seam side down, in 2 greased 9 x 5-inch loaf pans. Flatten in the pans to fill evenly. Cover loosely and set aside at room temperature to rise until the dough reaches the tops of the pans, 45 to 60 minutes.

6. Preheat the oven to 375°F.

7. Uncover and bake for 35 to 40 minutes, until deep brown or until the loaves sound hollow when you tap them.

8. Remove the loaves from the pans and cool on a wire rack before slicing. Serve warm or cooled completely.

Egg Bread

The addition of eggs to a yeast bread gives it a yellow color, a richer flavor, and a texture that begs to be torn apart rather than sliced. If you like, divide the dough into thirds, then roll and braid the dough to a make a traditional Jewish challah.

MAKES 1

½ cup (1 stick) butter
1 cup milk
5½ cups all-purpose flour, or more as needed
⅔ cup sugar
1 teaspoon salt
4½ teaspoons (two ¼-ounce packages) active dry yeast
4 large eggs
1 large egg white, beaten

1. Melt the butter in the milk in a small saucepan over low heat. Cool to room temperature.

2. Meanwhile, combine 2 cups of flour, the sugar, salt, and yeast in a large bowl. Add the milk mixture and beat until smooth. Beat in the 4 whole eggs, one at a time, then beat in enough of the remaining flour, ½ cup at a time, to make a soft dough.

3. Place the dough on a floured surface and knead lightly, adding more flour if necessary, until the dough is no longer sticky. Transfer to a greased large bowl, turn to coat, cover, and let rise in a warm, draft-free place until doubled in size, about 1 hour.

4. Punch the dough down. Return the dough to the floured surface and knead gently. Shape into a round loaf and put on a greased baking sheet. Cover again and let rise until doubled, 30 to 45 minutes.

5. Preheat the oven to 325°F.

6. Uncover and brush the dough with the egg white. Bake for 50 to 55 minutes, until golden brown and hollow-sounding when tapped.

7. Cool on a wire rack before slicing. Serve warm or cooled completely.

Gold Rush Sourdough Bread

Baking with sourdough starters is an ancient technique, but it became associated in the 1850s with northern California gold prospectors, who didn't have access to commercial yeasts. Sourdough bread became very popular in San Francisco and remains so today.

MAKES 2

1 cup sourdough starter (recipe follows)
2 cups warm water
1 teaspoon salt
1 teaspoon baking soda
4½ cups all-purpose flour, or more as needed
Yellow cornmeal

1. The night before baking, combine the starter with the warm water. Mix in the salt, baking soda, and 2½ cups of flour. Beat well. Cover and leave in a warm place for 12 hours.

2. Before continuing, take 1 cup of batter and return it to the original starter jug. This will feed the starter and keep it alive for another week.

3. Mix in the remaining 2 cups flour. The dough should be stiff, but not sticky; add more flour if necessary, until the dough is smooth.

4. Turn the dough out onto a floured board and knead for about 10 minutes, until smooth and elastic. Transfer to a greased bowl, turn to coat, cover with plastic wrap or a clean cloth, and let rise in a warm draft-free place until doubled in size, 2 to 4 hours.

5. Punch down the dough and let it rest for a few minutes. Sprinkle 2 baking sheets with cornmeal.

6. Divide the dough evenly and shape into 2 long loaves. Place on the baking sheets, cover again, and let rise for about 2 hours more.

7. Toward the end of the rising period, preheat the oven to 450°F and begin heating a medium kettle or pot of water.

8. Slash the tops of the loaves diagonally with a knife ¼ inch deep every 2 inches and brush with cold water. Place a baking dish on the bottom oven rack and pour in 3 or 4 cups of boiling water. Put the loaves on the rack over the steaming water and close the oven.

9. Bake for about 25 minutes, until golden brown and hollow-sounding when tapped or the internal temperature reads about 200°F.

10. Cool on a wire rack before slicing.

Sourdough Starter

A starter is made from flour or meal and then mixed with other dry and liquid ingredients that are combined with a leavening agent. It is then kneaded, shaped into loaves, and baked. Each time you use the starter, be sure to feed it with 1 cup of fresh batter (see step 2 in the previous recipe).

MAKES ABOUT 2 CUPS

2¼ teaspoons (one ¼-ounce package) active dry yeast
1¾ cups warm water
2 tablespoons honey
2 cups all-purpose flour

1. Dissolve the yeast in the water in a large bowl. Mix in the honey and gradually stir in the flour.

2. Place in an earthenware jug or a half-gallon canning jar. Store at room temperature for 2 days; it should be bubbly. Use immediately or refrigerate for up to 48 hours before using.

Honey Oatmeal Bread

The United States leads the world in oat production, with the oats grown primarily in the Midwest. The Quaker Oats Company made the first trademarked American cereal, Quaker Oats, in 1877. Using rolled oats in bread has long been a favorite way to extend white flour and add a slightly chewy texture and nutty flavor to white bread.

MAKES 2

4½ teaspoons (two ¼-ounce packages) active dry yeast
½ cup warm water
1½ cups hot milk
2 cups rolled oats
⅓ cup shortening
2 teaspoons salt
½ cup honey
4½ to 5 cups all-purpose flour
Melted butter

1. Sprinkle the yeast over the water in a small bowl. Set aside for about 5 minutes, until bubbly.

2. Meanwhile, pour the hot milk over the oats in a large bowl. Stir in the shortening, salt, and honey in a large bowl and continue stirring until the shortening melts. Cool to warm.

3. Stir in 1 cup of flour and the yeast mixture. Then add enough flour (3½ to 4 cups) to make a soft dough.

4. Turn the dough out onto a floured surface and knead until smooth and elastic, about 10 minutes. Form into a ball and place in a greased large bowl; turn to coat, cover, and let rise in a warm, draft-free place until nearly doubled in size, about 1 hour.

5. Punch down the dough, cover again, and let rest for 10 minutes. Grease two 9 x 5-inch loaf pans.

6. Divide the dough evenly and shape into 2 loaves. Place the loaves in the prepared loaf pans and brush the tops with melted butter. Cover a third time and let rise for about 1 hour, until nearly doubled in size.

7. Preheat the oven to 375°F.

8. Uncover and bake for 35 to 40 minutes, until golden brown and hollow-sounding when tapped.

9. Remove the loaves from the pans immediately and cool on wire racks. Brush with more melted butter while hot for a softer crust. Serve warm or cooled completely.

Raisin Bread

This bread makes wonderful French toast. It is also delicious toasted and spread with maple spread.

MAKES 2

2¼ teaspoons (one ¼-ounce package) active
 dry yeast
¼ cup warm water
1 cup raisins
¼ cup (½ stick) butter, softened
¼ cup sugar

1½ teaspoons salt
½ cup hot milk
3¾ cups all-purpose flour, or more as needed
2 large eggs

1. Sprinkle the yeast over the water in a small bowl. Set aside for about 5 minutes, until bubbly.

2. Meanwhile, combine the raisins, butter, sugar, salt, and hot milk in a large bowl. Stir to dissolve the sugar and melt the butter. Let the mixture cool to warm.

3. Stir in the yeast mixture and 1½ cups of flour; beat well. Add the eggs, beating well after each addition. Beat in the remaining 2¼ cups flour, ½ cup at a time, to make a stiff, but not sticky, dough; add more flour if necessary.

4. Turn the dough out onto a floured surface and knead for about 10 minutes, until smooth and elastic. Place in a lightly greased large bowl, turning to coat; cover with plastic wrap or a clean cloth and let stand in a warm draft-free place until doubled in size, about 1½ hours.

5. Punch the dough down and divide in half. Cover again and let rest for 10 minutes. Grease two 8 x 4-inch loaf pans.

6. Shape the dough into 2 equal loaves and place in the prepared pans. Cover a third time and let rise for about 45 to 60 minutes, until almost doubled in size.

7. Preheat the oven to 375°F.

8. Uncover and bake for about 25 minutes, until golden brown and hollow-sounding when tapped. Place aluminum foil over the loaves for the last 10 minutes if they are getting too browned.

9. Remove the loaves from the pans and cool on wire racks before slicing. Serve warm or cooled completely.

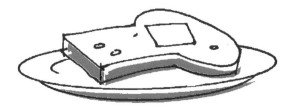

Rye Bread

German-style rye bread like this was brought here by immigrants who settled in the Midwest. It is similar to loaves made by immigrants from Scandinavia, which are hearty and slightly sweet. This is different than the deli sourdough rye to which you may be accustomed.

MAKES 2

4½ teaspoons (two ¼-ounce packages) active dry yeast
2 cups warm water
½ cup molasses
2 tablespoons butter
2 tablespoons sugar
1½ teaspoons salt
3¼ cups rye flour
2 to 2½ cups bread flour, or more as needed

1. Sprinkle the yeast over the water in a small bowl. Set aside for about 5 minutes, until bubbly.

2. Meanwhile, combine the molasses, butter, sugar, and salt in a large bowl. Beat in the yeast mixture and ¾ cup of rye flour. Beat in the remaining 2½ cups rye flour, ½ cup at a time, then beat in enough bread flour to make a stiff, but not sticky, dough.

3. Turn the dough out onto a floured surface. Knead for about 10 minutes, adding bread flour as needed, until smooth and elastic. Transfer the dough to a greased large bowl, turn to coat, cover with plastic wrap or a clean cloth, and let rise in a warm draft-free place until doubled in size, 1 to 1½ hours.

4. Punch down the dough, divide in half, and let rest for 10 minutes. Grease two baking sheets.

5. Form the dough into 2 round loaves and place on the baking sheets. Cover again and let rise until doubled, about 1½ hours.

6. Preheat the oven to 375°F.

7. Uncover and bake for 30 to 35 minutes, until golden brown or hollow-sounding when tapped.

8. Remove the loaves from the baking sheet and cool on wire racks before slicing. Serve warm or cooled completely.

Anadama Bread

Legend has it that the name Anadama was given to this bread by an old New England fisherman, who grew so tired of the cornmeal mush and molasses that his wife served him every night that he mixed it with flour and yeast and baked it for bread, saying, "Anna, damn her!"

MAKES 2

2¼ teaspoons (one ¼-ounce package) active dry yeast
2¼ cups warm water
½ cup (1 stick) butter
¾ cup molasses
1¼ cups yellow cornmeal
2 teaspoons salt
7½ to 8½ cups all-purpose flour, or more as needed

1. Sprinkle the yeast over the water in a small bowl. Set aside for about 5 minutes, until bubbly.

2. Meanwhile, melt the butter in the molasses in a small saucepan over very low heat. Set aside and cool to room temperature.

3. Combine the cornmeal and salt in a large bowl. Beat in the yeast mixture and molasses mixture. Beat in 4 cups of flour, ½ cup at a time, and continue to beat in enough flour to make a stiff, but not sticky, dough.

4. Turn the dough out onto a floured surface. Knead for about 10 minutes, adding flour as needed, until smooth and elastic. Transfer to a greased large bowl, turn to coat, cover with plastic wrap or a clean cloth, and let rise in a warm draft-free place until doubled in size, 1 to 1½ hours.

5. Punch down the dough, divide in half, and let rest for 10 minutes. Grease two 9 x 5-inch loaf pans.

6. Shape the dough into 2 loaves and place in the prepared pans. Cover again and let rise until doubled in size, about 1½ hours.

7. Preheat the oven to 375°F.

8. Uncover and bake for 30 to 35 minutes, until golden brown or hollow-sounding when tapped.

9. Remove the loaves from the pans and cool on wire racks before slicing. Serve warm or cooled completely.

Sally Lunn Bread

This egg bread has its origins in either France or England. One legend says that Sally Lunn, a Huguenot (French Protestant), left her native land to settle in England's West Country, where she sold her rich, buttery cakes in the streets of Bath. Another tale says that Sally Lunn is a corruption of the "soleil et lune" (sun and moon), and refers to the bread's golden color and round shape.

MAKES 1

Bread:
½ cup milk or half-and-half
2 teaspoons vanilla extract
6 tablespoons (¾ stick) butter
¼ cup sugar
2¼ teaspoons (one ¼-ounce package) active
    dry yeast
½ cup warm water
3½ cups all-purpose flour, or more as needed
1½ teaspoons salt
2 large eggs, lightly beaten

Glaze:
3 tablespoons milk
2 tablespoons sugar

1. To make the bread, heat the milk in a small saucepan until tiny bubbles appear around the edge and the first wisps of steam begin to appear. Transfer it to a medium bowl and stir in the vanilla extract, butter, and sugar. Set aside and let the mixture cool to warm.

2. Sprinkle the yeast over the water and set aside for about 5 minutes, until bubbly.

3. When the milk mixture has cooled, beat in the yeast mixture, 2 cups of flour, the salt, and eggs until well combined. Beat in the remaining 1½ cups flour and continue to beat until it becomes a soft, sticky dough; add more flour if necessary.

4. Cover with plastic wrap or a clean cloth and allow to rise in a warm draft-free place for 1 to 1½ hours, or until almost doubled.

5. Grease and flour a 9-inch springform pan. Give the dough a couple of stirs, then place in the pan. Wet your hands and smooth the top.

6. Cover the pan with a damp, clean cloth or greased plastic wrap and set aside to rise until the top crowns over the rim of the pan, 1½ to 2 hours.

7. Place the oven rack in the lowest position and preheat the oven to 350°F.

8. Uncover the bread and bake for 30 to 35 minutes, until golden brown and firm. Loosely cover with aluminum foil after 20 minutes if it seems to be browning too quickly on the top.

9. Meanwhile, make the glaze by combining the milk and sugar in a small saucepan. Bring to a boil and stir until the sugar dissolves. Immediately brush the mixture over the top of the bread. Let the bread cool for 20 minutes before slicing. Serve warm or cooled.

Cheese Bread

Bread comes in many forms—in this case, a yeast-raised cheese bread that makes an excellent accompaniment to drinks and soups. Serve it at your next cocktail party.

MAKES 1

4½ teaspoons (two ¼-ounce packages) active
    dry yeast
2 cups warm milk
2 tablespoons sugar
2 tablespoons butter, melted
¼ teaspoon salt
4½ cups all-purpose flour, or more as needed
6 ounces sharp Cheddar cheese, cut into
    ¼-inch cubes

1. Sprinkle the yeast over the milk in a large bowl. Set aside for about 5 minutes, until bubbly.

2. Add the sugar, butter, and salt and stir to dissolve. Beat in the flour, ½ cup at a time, until smooth; add more flour if necessary until dough is no longer sticky. Add the cheese and mix to thoroughly combine.

3. Pour the batter into a well-greased 1½-quart baking dish and cover loosely with plastic wrap or a clean cloth. Allow to sit in a draft-free place at room temperature until doubled in size, about 1 hour.

4. Preheat the oven to 350°F.

5. Uncover and bake for 50 to 60 minutes, until a toothpick inserted into the center comes out clean.

6. Cool for at least 30 minutes before serving.

Monkey Bread

This sweet yeast bread is made by taking small balls of dough, dipping them in melted butter, and fitting them into a pan. After the dough is allowed to rise, the balls of dough cling together to form a solid loaf, which after baking is easily pulled apart. The bread, also known as bubble loaf, began showing up in women's magazines and community cookbooks in the 1950s. Popularized by Nancy Reagan in the 1980s when she served it at the White House, it remains well liked today.

MAKES 1

2¼ teaspoons (one ¼-ounce package) active dry yeast
4 cups all-purpose flour, or more as needed
½ teaspoon salt
1 tablespoon granulated sugar
½ cup warm milk
½ cup warm water
1 large egg, at room temperature, lightly beaten
1 cup toasted pecans, finely chopped
⅔ cup firmly packed brown sugar
2 teaspoons ground cinnamon
5 tablespoons butter, melted

1. Grease a 9-inch springform or tube pan.

2. Stir together the yeast, flour, salt, and granulated sugar in a large bowl and make a well in the center. Pour in the milk, water, and egg and stir to form a soft dough.

3. Turn the dough out onto a floured surface and knead for about 10 minutes, until smooth and elastic; add more flour if necessary until the dough is no longer sticky. Place in a lightly oiled large bowl, turn to coat, cover with plastic wrap or a clean cloth, and let rise in a warm, draft-free place for 45 to 60 minutes, until doubled in size.

4. While the bread is rising, mix the pecans, brown sugar, and cinnamon in a small bowl. Set aside.

5. Punch down the dough. Turn out onto the floured board and knead gently for 2 minutes. Divide into 30 equal pieces and shape each into a ball.

6. Dip each ball into the melted butter, then roll in the pecan mixture. Place in the prepared pan, leaving some space between each piece. Sprinkle any remaining pecan mixture and melted butter over the dough pieces.

7. Cover again and let rise in a warm place for about 45 minutes, until the dough rises to the top of the pan.

8. Preheat the oven to 375°F.

9. Uncover and bake for 35 to 40 minutes, until golden. The bread should rise a little more in the oven as it bakes.

10. Cool on a wire rack and serve warm or at room temperature.

Butter Dinner Rolls

There's something special about homemade dinner rolls, arranged in a cloth-lined basket at the table, waiting for eager hands. These rolls aren't designed to do double duty in the lunch box or at the breakfast table. They are strictly for your dining pleasure—hot and buttery.

MAKES 12

4½ teaspoons (two ¼-ounce packages) active dry yeast
1¼ cups warm water
3 cups all-purpose flour, or more as needed
1 teaspoon salt
2 tablespoons sugar
¼ cup nonfat dry milk
1 large egg, lightly beaten
½ cup (1 stick) butter, melted

1. Sprinkle the yeast over the water in a large bowl. Set aside for 5 minutes, until bubbly.

2. Stir in 2 cups of flour, the salt, sugar, and dry milk, then beat in the egg. Continue to beat about 150 strokes, frequently scraping the bottom and sides of the bowl. Add half of the melted butter and beat to incorporate. Add the remaining 1 cup flour, about ⅓ cup at a time, beating to incorporate each addition; add more flour if necessary, until the dough is no longer sticky. The dough will be soft. Cover the bowl with plastic wrap or a clean cloth and allow the dough to rise in a warm, draft-free place until doubled in size, about 1 hour.

3. Generously grease the bottoms and sides of a 12-cup muffin pan or line the pan with paper baking cups.

4. Punch down the dough. Drop by hand or spoonfuls into the prepared pan. Brush the tops with half of the remaining melted butter. Let rise, uncovered, in a warm, draft-free place until almost doubled, about 30 minutes.

5. Preheat the oven to 400°F.

6. Bake for 16 to 18 minutes, until golden brown.

7. Brush the tops of the rolls with the remaining melted butter and serve immediately.

Parker House Rolls

These rolls made Boston's Parker House Hotel famous. The rolls were created—some say by accident—by a German baker shortly after the hotel opened in 1855. It is said that in a fit of anger, the baker threw some unfinished rolls in the oven and created the famous purse-like shape.

MAKES 24

4½ teaspoons (two ¼-ounce packages) active dry yeast
1 cup warm milk
1 cup (2 sticks) butter, melted
¼ cup sugar
¼ teaspoon salt
2 large eggs
4½ to 5 cups all-purpose flour

1. Sprinkle the yeast over the milk in a large bowl. Let stand for about 5 minutes, until bubbly.

2. Stir in ½ cup of butter, the sugar, and salt and beat until the sugar is dissolved. Beat in the eggs, then add the flour, ¼ cup at a time, beating on high speed after each addition. If the dough gets too stiff to beat, stir in the rest of the flour by hand until a soft dough forms.

3. Turn the dough out onto a floured surface and knead for 5 minutes, until smooth and elastic. Place in a greased large bowl, turn to coat, cover with plastic wrap or a clean cloth and let rise in a warm, draft-free place until doubled, about 1 hour.

4. Punch down the dough. Grease two 9 x 13-inch baking dishes.

5. Transfer the dough to a lightly floured surface and roll out to a thickness of ½ inch. Cut into 3-inch rounds with a biscuit cutter. Brush each roll with melted butter and fold in half to make half circles. Pinch the edges lightly so the rolls don't unfold as they rise. Place the rolls in a single layer in the prepared pans, cover again, and let rise until doubled in size, 45 to 60 minutes.

6. Preheat the oven to 350°F.

7. Uncover and bake for 20 to 25 minutes, until golden brown. Remove from the pans immediately and brush with more melted butter. Serve warm.

Featherbed Potato Rolls

Potatoes tenderize this dough. Perhaps the recipe was developed to use up leftover mashed potatoes, but don't wait for leftovers to make these tasty morsels.

MAKES 24

1 medium baking potato
2¼ teaspoons (one ¼-ounce package) active dry yeast
¼ cup warm water
⅓ cup sugar
1 teaspoon salt
8 tablespoons (1 stick) butter, melted
1 large egg, beaten
4½ cups all-purpose flour, or more as needed

1. Peel the potato, cover with water in a small saucepan, and cook until tender, about 25 minutes. Remove the potato and mash. Save ¾ cup of potato water and set aside.

2. Sprinkle the yeast over the ¼ cup warm water. Set aside for 5 minutes, until bubbly.

3. Meanwhile, mix the sugar, salt, and 5 tablespoons of butter. Stir in the reserved potato water. Add the yeast mixture, mashed potato, egg, and 2 cups of flour. Beat until smooth. Beat in the remaining 2½ cups flour, ½ cup at a time, to make a soft dough; add more flour if necessary, until the dough is no longer sticky.

4. Turn the dough out onto a floured surface and knead until smooth and elastic. Place in a well-greased large bowl, turn to coat, cover with plastic wrap or a clean cloth, and let rise in a warm, draft-free place until doubled in size, about 1 hour.

5. Punch the dough down. Grease two 9-inch round pans.

6. Divide the dough evenly into 24 pieces and shape into balls. Place 12 dough balls into each pan. Brush the tops with the remaining 3 tablespoons melted butter. Let rise, uncovered, until doubled in size, about 45 minutes.

7. Preheat the oven to 375°F.

8. Bake for 20 minutes, or until lightly browned. Serve warm.

Crescent Rolls

The fun in making rolls lies in all the different shapes you can create. Crescent rolls are made with a flat dough that is cut into wedges, then rolled up.

MAKES 40

2¼ teaspoons (one ¼-ounce package) active dry yeast
¼ cup warm water
1 cup (2 sticks) butter, softened
½ cup sugar
1 cup milk
2 large eggs
4 cups all-purpose flour or bread flour, or more as needed

1. Sprinkle the yeast over the water. Set aside for 5 minutes, until bubbly.

2. Beat in the butter and sugar, then beat in the milk and eggs. Add the flour, ½ cup at a time, beating until smooth; add more flour as necessary, until the dough is no longer sticky.

3. Cover the dough with plastic wrap or a clean cloth and refrigerate overnight.

4. Preheat the oven to 375°F. Grease 2 baking sheets.

5. Divide the dough into 5 equal portions. Roll out each portion on a floured surface into a circle about ¼ inch thick. Divide each circle into 8 wedges, like cutting a pie. Roll up each wedge from the large end to the small, tucking the tip underneath. Place on the prepared baking sheets.

6. Bake until lightly browned, about 12 minutes. Serve warm or cooled.

Herbed Bread Sticks

Bread sticks often accompany drinks. These are particularly tasty, with an assortment of fresh herbs providing flavor.

MAKES 16

2¼ teaspoons (one ¼-ounce package) active
    dry yeast
1 cup warm water
2 tablespoons shortening, melted
1 tablespoon sugar
1½ teaspoons salt, plus more for seasoning
2 tablespoons chopped fresh chives
1 tablespoon chopped fresh parsley
1 teaspoon dill seeds
2½ to 3 cups all-purpose flour
1 large egg, lightly beaten
¼ teaspoon caraway seeds

1. Sprinkle the yeast over the warm water in a large bowl. Set aside for 5 minutes, until bubbly.

2. Beat in the shortening, sugar, salt, chives, parsley, and dill seeds. Add the flour, ½ cup at a time, beating to form a stiff dough. Turn out onto a floured surface and knead until smooth. Place in a greased large bowl, turn to coat, cover with plastic wrap or a clean cloth, and let rise in a warm, draft-free place until doubled in size, about 1 hour.

3. Return the dough to the floured surface and divide into 4 equal portions. Roll out each to form an 8-inch square. Cut the squares into four 2-inch-long strips and twist each strip to form a stick.

4. Place the sticks on a greased baking sheet and brush each with the egg. Sprinkle the tops with salt and caraway seeds. Set aside and let rise, uncovered, in a warm place until doubled in size, 30 to 45 minutes.

5. Preheat the oven to 400°F.

6. Bake for 15 to 20 minutes, until golden brown and firm. Serve warm.

Cheese Rolls

These cheese rolls are the perfect accompaniment to tomato soup. Cheddar cheese can replace American cheese for stronger flavor.

MAKES 12

2¼ teaspoons (one ¼-ounce package) active
    dry yeast
½ cup warm water
⅔ cup shredded American cheese
2 tablespoons sugar
1 teaspoon salt
1 large egg
2 tablespoons butter, melted
2¼ to 2½ cups all-purpose flour

1. Grease a 12-cup muffin pan or line the pan with paper baking cups.

2. Sprinkle the yeast over the water in a large bowl. Set aside for 5 minutes, until bubbly.

3. Mix in the cheese, sugar, salt, egg, butter, and 1 cup of flour. Beat until well blended. Add the remaining flour, ½ cup at a time, beating to form a stiff dough.

4. Divide the dough into 12 equal portions. Roll each into a ball and place in the muffin cups. Cover with plastic wrap or a clean cloth and let rise in a warm, draft-free place until doubled in size, 1 to 1½ hours.

5. Preheat the oven to 375°F.

6. Uncover and bake for 12 to 15 minutes, until golden brown. Serve warm.

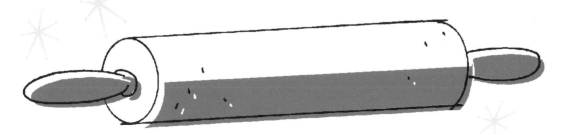

Hot Cross Buns

These buns are traditionally served on Good Friday and during Lent. Traditionally the top of each sweet bun is slashed with a cross, which is later filled with icing.

MAKES 30

Buns:
4½ teaspoons (two ¼-ounce packages) active dry yeast
½ cup warm water
1 cup warm milk
½ cup granulated sugar
¼ cup (½ stick) butter, softened
1 teaspoon vanilla extract
1 teaspoon salt
½ teaspoon ground nutmeg
6½ to 7 cups all-purpose flour
4 large eggs
½ cup dried currants
½ cup raisins

Glaze:
2 tablespoons water
1 large egg yolk

Icing:
1 cup confectioners' sugar
4 teaspoons milk or half-and-half
Pinch of salt
¼ teaspoon vanilla extract

1. To make the buns, sprinkle the yeast over the water in a large bowl. Set aside for 5 minutes, until bubbly.

2. Add the warm milk, sugar, butter, vanilla extract, salt, and nutmeg. Beat in 3 cups of flour, 1 cup at a time, until smooth. Add the eggs, one at a time, beating well after each addition. Stir in the dried currants and raisins and enough of the remaining flour to make a soft dough.

3. Turn the dough out onto a floured surface and knead until smooth and elastic, about 10 minutes. Place in a greased large bowl, turn to coat, cover with plastic wrap or a clean cloth, and let rise in a warm, draft-free place until doubled in size, about 1 hour.

4. Punch the dough down and let rest for 10 minutes. Grease 2 baking sheets.

5. Shape the dough into 30 balls and place on the prepared baking sheets. Cover again and let rise until doubled in size, about 30 minutes.

6. Preheat the oven to 375°F.

7. Using a knife, cut a cross (or X) on the top of each roll. Set aside.

8. To make the glaze, combine the water and egg yolk in a small bowl and beat until smooth. Brush over the buns.

9. Bake the buns for 12 to 15 minutes, until golden brown.

10. Meanwhile, make the icing by combining the confectioners' sugar, milk, salt, and vanilla extract in a small bowl, stirring until smooth.

11. Cool the buns on wire racks and drizzle the icing over the top of each bun, following the lines of the cut cross. Serve warm or cooled.

Cinnamon Buns

There is no aroma more enticing than that of cinnamon buns baking on a frosty morning. This recipe includes an optional glaze to complement the buns' warm, spiced flavor.

MAKES 16

Buns:
4½ teaspoons (two ¼-ounce packages) active dry yeast
2 cups warm milk
½ cup granulated sugar
1½ teaspoons vanilla extract
2 large eggs
½ teaspoon salt
½ cup oil
6 to 7 cups all-purpose flour

Filling:
2 tablespoons ground cinnamon
½ cup (½ stick) sugar
¼ cup butter, softened

Glaze (optional):
1 cup confectioners' sugar
2 tablespoons milk, or more as needed

1. To make the buns, sprinkle the yeast over the warm milk in a large bowl. Set aside for 5 minutes, until bubbly.

2. Add the sugar, vanilla extract, eggs, salt, and oil and mix well. Add the flour, 1 cup at a time, beating until smooth. Use just enough flour to make a soft dough. (The key to making this dough tender and light is to use as little flour as possible so the dough is as soft as possible.)

3. Turn the dough out onto a floured surface and knead until smooth and elastic. Place in a greased bowl, turn to coat, cover with plastic wrap or a clean cloth, and let rise in a warm, draft-free place until doubled in size, about 1 hour.

4. Preheat the oven to 350°F. Grease a baking sheet.

5. To make the filling, mix the cinnamon and sugar in a small bowl. Set aside.

6. Roll out the dough on the floured surface into a rectangular shape 16 inches long. Spread evenly with the butter and sprinkle evenly with the cinnamon-sugar mixture. Roll up, like a jelly roll, starting from the long side. Use a serrated knife to cut into 1-inch sections, then place the rolls, cut side up, on the baking sheet.

7. Bake for 15 to 20 minutes, until golden brown. Serve warm or proceed with making the glaze, if using, while the buns bake.

8. To make the glaze, stir together the sugar and milk in a medium bowl to the desired thinness.

9. Remove the buns from the oven and cool on a wire rack. Drizzle the glaze over the buns while still warm and serve.

Cinnamon-Nut Rolls

Nuts and raisins add to the goodness of these rolls. The sugar topping makes them slightly crunchy on the outside, a marvelous contrast to the pillowy, soft inside.

MAKES 26

2¼ teaspoons (one ¼-ounce package) active
   dry yeast
½ cup warm water
2 large eggs, well beaten
1 cup heavy cream

3 tablespoons granulated sugar, plus more for
   topping
1½ teaspoons salt
1 teaspoon vanilla extract
4½ to 5 cups all-purpose flour
4 tablespoons (½ stick) butter, melted
1 cup firmly packed brown sugar
2 teaspoons ground cinnamon
¾ cup finely chopped nuts (preferably walnuts,
   pecans, or almonds)
⅓ cup raisins, chopped

1. Sprinkle the yeast over the water in a large bowl. Set aside for 5 minutes, until bubbly.

2. Beat in the eggs, cream, granulated sugar, salt, and vanilla extract. Add the flour, 1 cup at a time, beating to form a stiff dough.

3. Turn the dough out onto a floured surface and knead for 2 to 3 minutes, until smooth and elastic. Place in a greased large bowl, turn to coat, cover with plastic wrap or a clean cloth, and set in a warm, draft-free place to rise until doubled in size, about 1½ hours.

4. Place the dough on the floured surface and roll into a 26 x 20-inch rectangle. Brush with 2 tablespoons of butter.

5. Combine the brown sugar and cinnamon in a small bowl and sprinkle half of the mixture over the dough. Fold in half lengthwise, pressing firmly. Fold in half again, lengthwise, and seal the edges.

6. Roll again into a 26 x 12-inch rectangle; brush with the remaining 2 tablespoons butter.

7. Combine the nuts, raisins, and remaining cinnamon mixture in the small bowl and sprinkle over the dough. Roll up, like a jelly roll, starting from the long side. Use a serrated knife to cut into 1-inch slices.

8. Grease 2 baking sheets. Dip one cut side of each roll in granulated sugar and place, sugar side up, on the sheets. Let the rolls rise, uncovered in a warm, draft-free place for at least 15 minutes.

9. Meanwhile, preheat the oven to 375°F.

10. Bake for 15 to 18 minutes, until golden brown. Serve warm.

Glazed Nut Knots

This sweetened, filled dough is cut into strips and tied into knots. Call them love knots and serve them to your sweetheart or loved ones on Valentine's Day.

MAKES 12

Knots:
4½ teaspoons (two ¼-ounce packages) active
    dry yeast
¼ cup warm water
⅓ cup butter
¾ cup hot milk
⅓ cup granulated sugar
2 teaspoons salt
2 teaspoons grated orange zest
2 large eggs
4 to 4½ cups all-purpose flour

Filling:
⅓ cup butter, softened
1 cup confectioners' sugar
1 cup finely chopped nuts

Glaze:
¼ cup orange juice
3 tablespoons confectioners' sugar

1. To make the knots, sprinkle the yeast over the water in a small bowl and set aside for 5 minutes, until bubbly.

2. Combine the butter and hot milk in a large bowl and cool until warm.

3. Beat in the sugar, salt, orange zest, eggs, and yeast mixture. Add the flour, 1 cup at a time, beating well to form a stiff dough. Cover with plastic wrap or a clean cloth and let stand for 30 minutes.

4. To make the filling, combine the butter, confectioners' sugar, and nuts in a small bowl and blend until crumbly. Set aside.

5. Turn the dough out onto a floured surface and roll out to a rectangle approximately 12 x 22 inches. Spread the filling over half of the dough along the long side. Fold the other half of the dough on top of the filling. Cut into 1-inch strips along the short side. Twist each strip a few times and tie one time to resemble a knot.

6. Grease a baking sheet and place each tied piece on the sheet. Cover again and let rise in a warm, draft-free place until doubled in size, 45 to 60 minutes.

7. Preheat the oven to 375°F.

8. Bake for 15 minutes.

9. While the knots bake, make the glaze by stirring together the orange juice and confectioners' sugar until smooth. Brush the glaze on top of the knots and bake for 5 minutes more. Serve warm or cooled.

Maple Spread

There is no substitute for pure maple syrup—pancake syrups with artificial maple flavor just don't work—so be sure to use the real thing. Maple butter is great on toast, pancakes, or French toast. Try it on toasted raisin bread or honey oatmeal bread. A variation follows.

MAKES 1¼ CUPS

¾ cup (1½ sticks) butter, softened
½ cup pure maple syrup

1. Beat the butter and maple syrup until well blended and creamy.

2. Refrigerate until firm.

Honey-Butter Spread

Replace the maple syrup in Maple Spread with ½ cup honey. Complete the recipe as directed.

Apple Butter

Despite the name, there is no butter in apple butter. The name comes from the smooth and buttery texture of this apple purée. A mix of apples creates the best flavor. Baldwin, Braeburn, Cortland, Empire, Golden Delicious, Granny Smith, Gravenstein, Idared, Macoun, McIntosh, Mutsu, Newtown Pippin, Northern Spy, Rhode Island Greening, Winesap, and York are all good choices. Apple butter is delicious on buttered toast or freshly baked rolls. A variation follows.

MAKES 2½ PINTS

4 pounds apples, cored and coarsely chopped
2 cups unsweetened apple juice or apple cider
2 cups sugar
1¼ teaspoons ground cinnamon
¼ teaspoon ground nutmeg

1. Combine the apples and apple juice in a large saucepan. Bring the mixture to a boil, reduce the heat, and simmer until the apples are soft, about 30 minutes.

2. Preheat the oven to 325°F.

3. Strain the mixture through a wire-mesh sieve into a roasting pan. Stir in the sugar.

4. Bake for 3 hours, stirring occasionally.

5. Stir in the cinnamon and nutmeg and bake for about 1 hour more, until the butter mounds up on a spoon and has a glossy sheen. You can also tell that the butter is done when a spoonful placed on a chilled plate does not release any liquid.

6. Ladle the butter into sterilized half-pint or pint jars and wipe the rims with a damp cloth. Place dome lids on the jars and screw on the bands.

7. Process the jars in a boiling water bath, 5 minutes for half-pints or 10 minutes for pints (page 486).

Slow-Cooker Apple Butter

After straining the apple mixture in Apple Butter, place the mixture in a slow-cooker. Stir in the sugar and spices. Cover and cook on low heat for 12 to 14 hours, until thickened. Ladle into canning jars and complete the recipe as directed.

Peach Honey Butter

Peach honey butter is another tasty spread for toast and pancakes. If you have fresh, ripe peaches on hand, use them instead of the canned variety.

MAKES ABOUT 1¾ CUPS

1 (16-ounce) can unsweetened peach halves, drained
2 tablespoons honey
1 teaspoon ground cinnamon
¾ cup (1½ sticks) butter, softened

1. Combine the peaches, honey, and cinnamon in a large bowl. Use a potato masher to mash to the consistency of chunky applesauce.

2. Add the butter and beat until well combined.

3. Refrigerate until firm.

Strawberry Preserves

Before the introduction of powdered and liquid pectin, women cooked their fruit with lots of sugar and for a lengthy amount of time, until the water evaporated and the sugar reached gelling density, particularly when the fruit was naturally low in pectin. This recipe preserves this old-fashioned cooking method.

MAKES 4 PINTS

8 cups crushed strawberries, (fresh or frozen)
6 cups sugar

1. Combine the berries and sugar in a large pot. Bring slowly to a boil over medium-high heat, stirring occasionally, until the sugar dissolves. Cook until thick, about 40 minutes, stirring frequently. Watch carefully; the mixture can scorch easily.

2. Ladle the hot jam into sterilized half-pint or pint jars and wipe the rims with a damp cloth. Place dome lids on the jars and screw on the bands.

3. Process the jars in a boiling water bath, 5 minutes for half-pints, 10 minutes for pints (page 486).

Berry Jam

This recipe is well suited to blackberries, blueberries, boysenberries, dewberries, gooseberries, loganberries, raspberries, and youngberries.

MAKES 3½ TO 4 PINTS

9 cups crushed fresh or frozen berries
6 cups sugar

1. Combine the berries and sugar in a large pot. Bring slowly to a boil over medium-high heat, stirring occasionally, until the sugar dissolves. Cook for 3 to 4 minutes, until the mixture reaches 220°F on a candy thermometer, stirring frequently. Watch carefully; the mixture can scorch easily.

2. Ladle the hot jam into sterilized half-pint or pint jars and wipe the rims with a damp cloth. Place dome lids on the jars and screw on the bands.

3. Process the jars in a boiling water bath, 5 minutes for half-pints, 10 minutes for pints (page 486).

TIPS ON BAKING BREADS

Making your own yeast breads is a rewarding pursuit, one that can offer a lifetime of learning. Here are a few tips to get you started.

▶ Yeast is a living organism that feeds on sugars. When combined with moisture and warmth, it begins to grow, producing carbon dioxide that gets trapped by the gluten in the dough, causing dough to rise.

▶ Store yeast in the refrigerator and use it before the expiration date.

▶ Kneading the dough helps develop the gluten, which traps the carbon dioxide and causes the bread to rise evenly.

▶ When mixing and kneading yeast dough, use as little flour as possible. The dough should be slightly tacky to the touch. The less flour you use, the lighter the loaf.

▶ To knead dough, press down into the dough with the heels of both hands, then push it away from your body. Fold the dough in half, give it a quarter turn, and repeat. Most dough should be kneaded for 5 to 10 minutes.

▶ Dough should usually be left to rise in a warm place; 80°F is the ideal temperature.

▶ The sweeter the dough, the longer the rising time.

▶ To test if the dough has risen enough during the first rise, poke your finger into it. If the indentation remains, the dough is ready. If the dough bounces back, it needs more time.

▶ Don't open the oven door to peek at your bread during the first 20 minutes of baking time. This is when the bread does the most rising, and lowering the temperature could cause it to fall.

Quick breads and muffins are leavened with baking powder, baking soda, and eggs. The batters are similar, if not identical. Here are some baking tips for making both.

▶ Have the oven preheating, the pans greased, and the ingredients assembled before you start. Once the baking powder or baking soda has made contact with the liquid ingredients, it begins to release carbon dioxide, so get the pan into the oven as soon as possible to give the batter a chance to rise properly.

▶ Don't overbeat the batter. The batter should be lumpy. Overbeating will result in a tough, dense product.

▶ a toothpick or knife inserted near the center should come out clean.

▶ A cracked top is perfectly acceptable.

▶ Quick breads can be used to make bread puddings, with excellent results.

CHAPTER THIRTEEN

Pies, Cakes, and Cookies

When the first colonists settled in America, they brought their favorite recipes for pies—both sweet and savory—and served them with almost every meal. Pies later became the focus of contests at county fairs, picnics, and other social events.

Both Pennsylvania Dutch and Southern bakers elevated pie making to an art. From the Pennsylvania Dutch came shoofly pie and various pies enriched with sour cream. The South produced some of the country's finest baked goods, such as pecan pie, chess pie, and key lime pie, in part because white sugar was plentiful there, while the rest of the country relied on molasses and maple syrup.

Cakes were less popular than pies in our country's early history. Cakes were leavened with yeast or eggs; not only did some recipes call for more than a dozen eggs, they also required long hours of beating. This continued until the invention of baking soda in the 1840s, followed by baking powder in the 1860s.

During the early part of the eighteenth century, Americans began to apply the name "cookie" to small, sweet, flat cakes. The word "cookie" appears to come from the Dutch word *koekje* and refers to a small cake that was served as a snack or dessert. The chocolate chip cookie, invented in 1937, is still recognized as the quintessential American cookie.

Fannie M. Farmer's great contribution to American cookery was in standardizing the cups, tablespoons, and teaspoons used to measure ingredients. Once these measurements were standardized, recipes could be written down and shared with some degree of accuracy. But even with written recipes and standardized measurements, it always helps to have an experienced baker in the kitchen.

An experienced baker's instructions are explicit: Always preheat the oven for 10 to 15 minutes before starting to bake; unless a recipe states otherwise, the oven rack should be in the middle position; oven temperatures should be reduced by 25 degrees whenever glass pans are used; unsalted butter is generally fresher tasting and better to use in baked goods; and lard makes the flakiest pie crusts.

There's a wealth of wisdom to be gained by baking with an expert, but such expertise is often not available. Rely on this chapter and its trusted recipes in your kitchen anytime. Using the freshest ingredients is a good place to start.

Apple Pie

Apple pie is the quintessential American pie; no other pie is quite so popular or so esteemed. Because there are so many different apples to use, each pie is different. Particularly good apples for pie include Baldwin, Cortland, Granny Smith, Northern Spy, Rome Beauty, Winesap, and York. Because apples lose volume as they bake, don't hesitate to fill the pie pan extra full.

SERVES 6 TO 8

8 medium tart apples, such as Granny Smith or Rome Beauty, peeled, cored, and thinly sliced
¾ cup plus 1 tablespoon sugar
2 tablespoons all-purpose flour
1 teaspoon ground cinnamon
¼ teaspoon salt
Pinch of ground nutmeg
Dough for 2 (9-inch) pie crusts, refrigerated (page 374)
2 tablespoons butter
1 tablespoon milk

1. Toss the apple slices with ¾ cup sugar, the flour, cinnamon, salt, and nutmeg in a large bowl. Set aside.

2. Preheat the oven to 425°F, with the rack in the lower third of the oven.

3. Roll out half of the dough on a lightly floured surface to a thickness of ⅛ inch. Fit into a 9-inch pie pan, leaving a 1-inch overhang. Fill with the apple mixture. Cut the butter into small pieces and dot it over the filling.

4. Roll out the remaining dough into a circle about 1 inch larger than the pan. Center the crust on top of the pie and trim to ½ inch beyond the edge of the pan. Fold the top crust edge under the bottom crust edge and flute. Cut steam vents in the top crust.

5. Bake for 20 minutes.

6. Reduce the oven temperature to 350°F and continue to bake for 30 minutes.

7. Brush the top crust with the milk and sprinkle with the remaining 1 tablespoon sugar. Bake for 10 to 15 minutes more, until the crust is golden brown. Serve warm or at room temperature.

TIP: Slice apples thin for apple pie. Thick slices promote air space and create a gap between the fruit and the crust.

Sour Cream Apple Crumb Pie

The Pennsylvania Dutch have added immeasurably to the American dessert repertoire. This is one of their famous pies—an apple pie with the added richness of sour cream.

SERVES 6 TO 8

½ cup granulated sugar
5 tablespoons all-purpose flour
¼ teaspoon salt
1 large egg, lightly beaten
¾ cup sour cream
1 teaspoon vanilla extract
6 medium tart apples, such as Granny Smith or Rome Beauty, peeled, cored, and chopped
Dough for 1 (9-inch) pie crust, refrigerated (page 374)
¼ cup firmly packed brown sugar
2 tablespoons butter

1. Preheat the oven to 450°F, with the rack in the lower third of the oven.

2. Blend together the granulated sugar, 1 tablespoon of flour, and the salt in a medium bowl. Stir in the egg, sour cream, vanilla extract, and apples and set aside.

3. Roll out the dough on a lightly floured surface to a thickness of ⅛ inch. Fit into a 9-inch pie pan, leaving a 1-inch overhang. Fold and flute the edge. (Do not prick the bottom.)

4. Pour the apple mixture into the pie crust and bake for 10 minutes.

5. Meanwhile, stir together the remaining 4 tablespoons flour and the brown sugar in a small bowl. Use a fork to mix in the butter until crumbly.

6. Sprinkle the crumb mixture over the pie and reduce the oven temperature to 350°F. Bake for an additional 35 to 40 minutes, until the topping is golden. Serve warm or at room temperature.

Apple Cranberry Pie

If you find apple pie a bit too predictable, this one is full of surprises, with both cranberries and pineapple in the filling. It is just the pie to serve on Thanksgiving in addition to the pumpkin pie.

SERVES 6 TO 8

1 cup fresh or frozen cranberries
5½ cups peeled, cored, and sliced tart apples, such as Granny Smith or Rome Beauty (about 5 to 6 medium)
¼ cup drained crushed pineapple
½ cup firmly packed brown sugar
¼ cup granulated sugar
1 teaspoon grated orange zest
½ teaspoon ground cinnamon
¼ teaspoon ground nutmeg
Dough for 2 (9-inch) pie crusts, refrigerated (page 374)

1. Combine the cranberries, ½ cup of apples, the pineapple, sugars, orange zest, cinnamon, and nutmeg in a food processor. Process until well chopped, but not mushy. Set aside.

2. Preheat the oven to 425°F, with the rack in the lower third of the oven.

3. Roll out half of the dough on a lightly floured surface to a thickness of ⅛ inch. Fit into a 9-inch pie pan, leaving a 1-inch overhang. Spread half of the cranberry mixture in the pie crust. Arrange the remaining apples over this and cover with the remaining cranberry mixture.

4. Roll out the remaining dough into a circle about 1 inch larger than the pie pan. Center the crust on top of the pie and trim to ½ inch beyond the edge of the pan. Fold the top crust edge under the bottom crust edge and flute. Cut steam vents in the top crust.

5. Bake for 15 minutes.

6. Reduce the oven temperature to 350°F and bake for an additional 35 to 40 minutes, until the crust is golden brown. Serve warm or at room temperature.

TIP: If the pie crust edge appears to be browning too rapidly, cover loosely with a ring of aluminum foil.

Whiskey Custard Apple Pie

This custard apple pie is flavored with bourbon, a distinctively American whiskey made from corn. You won't find it at your local diner— sophisticated and elegant, it's perfect for a special occasion.

SERVES 6 TO 8

2 cups peeled, cored, and thinly sliced tart apples, such as Granny Smith or Rome Beauty (about 2 to 3 medium)
¼ cup water
¼ cup bourbon or other whiskey
1 cup firmly packed brown sugar
3 tablespoons butter
Dough for 1 (9-inch) pie crust, refrigerated (page 374)
3 large eggs
1 cup heavy cream
¼ teaspoon ground nutmeg
Whipped cream, to serve

1. Combine the apples, water, and bourbon in a small saucepan over medium heat and cook until soft, about 5 minutes. Stir in the brown sugar and butter until melted. Set aside to cool.

2. Roll out the pie crust on a lightly floured surface to a thickness of ⅛ inch. Fit into a 9-inch pie pan, leaving a 1-inch overhang. Fold and flute the edge. (Do not prick the bottom.) Set aside.

3. Preheat the oven to 450°F, with the rack in the lower third of the oven.

4. In a medium bowl, lightly beat the eggs with an electric mixer. Add the cream and nutmeg and continue to mix until thoroughly combined.

5. Fold in the apple mixture and spoon into the pie crust.

6. Bake for 10 minutes.

7. Reduce the oven temperature to 325°F and bake for an additional 45 minutes, until the filling is set.

8. Cool and serve with whipped cream.

Blackberry Pie

Blackberries are bramble berries; their rambling canes can be found growing throughout America. There are many types of blackberries, including the loganberry, possibly a cross between the blackberry and the raspberry, and the boysenberry, a cross between the loganberry and the blackberry. This pie is lightly sweetened, allowing the berries' natural flavors to come through.

SERVES 6 TO 8

4 cups (2 pints) fresh or frozen blackberries or
    raspberries
3 tablespoons all-purpose flour
1 cup sugar
1 tablespoon lemon juice
¼ teaspoon ground cinnamon
Dough for 2 (9-inch) pie crusts, refrigerated
    (page 374)
1 tablespoon butter, cut into small pieces

1. Combine the blackberries, flour, sugar, lemon juice, and cinnamon in a medium bowl and gently toss to combine. Set aside.

2. Preheat the oven to 425°F, with the rack in the lower third of the oven.

3. Roll out half of the dough on a lightly floured surface to a thickness of ⅛ inch. Fit into a 9-inch pie pan, leaving a 1-inch overhang. Spoon the berry mixture into the pie crust. Dot with the butter.

4. Roll out the remaining dough into a circle about 1 inch larger than the pie pan. Center the crust on top of the pie and trim to ½ inch beyond the edge of the pie pan. Fold the top crust edge under the bottom crust edge and flute. Cut steam vents in the top crust.

5. Bake for 15 minutes.

6. Reduce the oven temperature to 350°F and bake for an additional 35 to 40 minutes, until the crust is golden brown. Serve warm or at room temperature.

Blueberry Pie

Blueberries and huckleberries can both be used in this pie. Huckleberries are very similar to blueberries, but blueberries have a softer texture and many tiny seeds. Both make a delicious, tooth-staining pie. This recipe is lightly spiced with cinnamon and nutmeg.

SERVES 6 TO 8

6 cups (3 pints) fresh or frozen blueberries or
    huckleberries
1 cup sugar
1 tablespoon lemon juice
1 teaspoon ground cinnamon
⅛ teaspoon ground nutmeg
5 tablespoons all-purpose flour
Dough for 2 (9-inch) pie crusts, refrigerated
    (page 374)

1. Combine 3 cups of berries with the sugar, lemon juice, cinnamon, and nutmeg in a medium saucepan. Stir in 4 tablespoons of flour. Cook over low heat just until the mixture bubbles. Remove from the heat and let cool.

2. Preheat the oven to 425°F, with the rack in the lower third of the oven.

3. Roll out half of the dough on a lightly floured surface to a thickness of ⅛ inch. Fit into a 9-inch pie pan, leaving a 1-inch overhang. Sprinkle the remaining 1 tablespoon flour into the pie crust, then spoon in the remaining 3 cups raw berries. Top with the cooked berry mixture.

4. Roll out the remaining dough into a circle about 1 inch larger than the pie pan. Center the crust on top of the pie and trim to ½ inch beyond the edge of the pan. Fold the top crust edge under the bottom crust edge and flute. Cut steam vents in the top crust.

5. Bake for 15 minutes.

6. Reduce the oven temperature to 350°F and bake for an additional 35 to 40 minutes, until the crust is golden brown. Serve warm or at room temperature.

TIP: Place fruit pies on a baking sheet in the oven to avoid
    bubbling fruit juices from spilling onto the oven floor.

Blueberry Cream Pie

Only the crust needs baking in this delicious summer-weather pie. Sweet berries in a cloud of whipped cream make a wonderful Fourth of July dessert. Huckleberries and raspberries are also delicious in this pie.

SERVES 6 TO 8

¾ cup granulated sugar
2½ tablespoons cornstarch
¼ teaspoon salt
⅔ cup water
3 cups (1½ pints) fresh or frozen blueberries
2 tablespoons butter
1½ tablespoons lemon juice
1 cup heavy cream
1 tablespoon confectioners' sugar
½ teaspoon vanilla extract
1 (9-inch) pie crust, baked and cooled
(page 374)

1. Combine the granulated sugar, cornstarch, and salt in a medium saucepan over medium heat. Stir in the water and 1 cup of blueberries. Stirring constantly, bring to a boil and cook until very thick. Add the butter and lemon juice; mix well and let cool. Gently stir in the remaining 2 cups blueberries and refrigerate for at least 1 hour, up to 6 hours.

2. Whip the heavy cream in a large bowl until thick. Beat in the confectioners' sugar and vanilla extract.

3. Cover the bottom of the pie crust with half of the whipped cream, then pour the blueberry filling over the top. Chill for about 2 hours.

4. Top the pie with the remaining whipped cream and serve immediately.

Lattice Cherry Pie

The hint of almonds paired with the taste of cherries is an enticing combination, and traditional lattice topping makes this pie as wonderful to view as it is to eat.

SERVES 6 TO 8

4 cups (2 pints) pie cherries, pitted
3 tablespoons quick-cooking tapioca
1¼ cups sugar
1 tablespoon lemon juice
⅛ teaspoon salt
¼ teaspoon almond extract
Dough for 2 (9-inch) pie crusts, refrigerated
(page 374)

1. Mix the cherries, tapioca, sugar, lemon juice, salt, and almond extract in a large bowl. Let sit for about 10 minutes.

2. Preheat the oven to 425°F, with the rack in the lower third of the oven.

3. Roll out half of the dough on a lightly floured surface to a thickness of ⅛ inch. Fit into a 9-inch pie pan, leaving a 1-inch overhang. Spoon the cherry mixture into the pie crust.

4. Roll out the remaining pie dough into a rectangle about ⅛ inch thick and 11 inches long. Trim the ragged edges. Cut the rectangle lengthwise into 10 equal strips, each about ½ inch wide.

5. To form a lattice, overlap one end of 2 dough strips on a sheet of wax paper, laying them perpendicular to each other in an "L" shape. Working from the overlapped corner, lay another strip parallel to one of the original strips with about ½ inch between them. Overlap the corner opposite (either over or under) the strip next to it. Lay the next strip perpendicular to the last strip and continue to interweave the remaining strips using the over-under pattern.

6. Center the wax paper on top of the pie filling and carefully slide the paper out so that the lattice rests evenly on the filling. Trim the ends of the lattice strips. Moisten the overhanging edge of the bottom crust with water and fold up over the ends of the strips. Flute the edge of the crust.

7. Bake for 15 minutes.

8. Reduce the oven temperature to 350°F and bake for an additional 35 to 40 minutes, until the crust is golden brown. Serve warm or at room temperature.

Cherry Cheese Pie

In the good ol' days, canning cherries was common. Now we can just buy them at the supermarket. This rich, cherry-lovers' dessert is both sweet and tart, with a creamy texture.

SERVES 6 TO 8

2 (1-pound) cans pitted dark sweet cherries
1 cup sugar
3 tablespoons cornstarch
⅛ teaspoon salt
1 tablespoon butter
2 tablespoons lemon juice
1 (3-ounce) package cream cheese, softened
1 (9-inch) pie crust, baked and cooled
   (page 374)

1. Drain the cherries, reserving the juice. Set both aside.

2. Combine ⅔ cup of sugar, the cornstarch, and salt in a medium saucepan. Add 1 cup of reserved cherry juice and cook over medium heat, stirring constantly, until the mixture comes to a boil. Cook for about 2 minutes. Add the cherries and cook for another 2 minutes.

3. Remove the saucepan from the heat and stir in the butter and lemon juice, stirring until the butter melts. Let cool.

4. Whip the cream cheese with the remaining ⅓ cup sugar in a small bowl. Spread over the bottom of the baked pie crust and pour in the cherry mixture.

5. Chill for at least 3 hours and up to 8 hours. Serve cold.

Fresh Peach Pie

Georgia is the Peach State, but fresh peaches are commercially grown all along the East and West Coasts, as well as in Alabama, Michigan, Arkansas, and Colorado. A fresh tree-ripened peach has a gloriously sweet flavor. Nectarines can be substituted in this recipe, which is flavored with ground ginger, lemon zest, and almond extract.

SERVES 6 TO 8

4 medium peaches, peeled, pitted, and sliced
¾ cup firmly packed brown sugar
3 tablespoons quick-cooking tapioca
¾ teaspoon ground ginger
½ teaspoon grated lemon zest
¼ teaspoon almond extract
Dough for 2 (9-inch) pie crusts, refrigerated
   (page 374)

1. Mix the peaches, brown sugar, tapioca, ginger, lemon zest, and almond extract. Let sit for about 10 minutes.

2. Preheat the oven to 425°F, with the rack in the lower third of the oven.

3. Roll out half of the dough on a lightly floured surface to a thickness of ⅛ inch. Fit into a 9-inch pie pan, leaving a 1-inch overhang. Spoon the peach mixture into the pie crust.

4. Roll out the remaining pie dough into a rectangle about ⅛ inch thick and 11 inches long. Trim the ragged edges. Cut the rectangle lengthwise into 10 equal strips, each about ½ inch wide. Set aside.

5. To form a lattice, overlap one end of 2 dough strips on a sheet of wax paper, laying them perpendicular to each other in an "L" shape. Working from the overlapped corner, lay another strip parallel to one of the original strips with about ½ inch between them. Overlap the corner opposite (either over or under) the strip next to it. Lay the next strip perpendicular to the last strip and continue to interweave the remaining strips using the over-under pattern.

6. Center the wax paper on top of the pie filling and carefully slide the paper out so that the lattice rests evenly on the filling. Trim the ends of the lattice strips. Moisten the overhanging edge of the

bottom crust with water and fold up over the ends of the strips. Flute the edge of the crust.

7. Bake for 15 minutes.

8. Reduce the oven temperature to 350°F and bake for an additional 35 to 40 minutes, until the crust is golden brown. Serve warm or at room temperature.

TIP: To peel peaches, dip the peaches in boiling water for 20 to 30 seconds, then plunge into cold water. Use a knife to pull off the skin. Redip any peaches that don't peel easily.

Glazed Peach Pie

This hot-weather pie requires a baked pie crust but very little cooking beyond that. Topped with whipped cream, it is a light and fresh fruit dessert.

SERVES 6 TO 8

6 medium peaches, peeled, pitted, and sliced
1 cup sugar
3 tablespoons cornstarch
¼ teaspoon ground cinnamon
½ cup orange juice
1 (9-inch) pie crust, baked and cooled
    (page 374)
Whipped cream, to serve

1. In a medium bowl, mash enough peaches to measure 1 cup. Set aside.

2. Combine the sugar, cornstarch, and cinnamon in a small saucepan, then stir in the orange juice and mashed peaches. Cook over medium heat until the mixture comes to a boil, stirring occasionally. Continue boiling for 1 minute, until the mixture thickens.

3. Spread half of this glaze over the sides and bottom of the baked crust. Fill with the remaining peach slices and pour the remaining glaze over all.

4. Chill in the refrigerator for at least 3 hours. Serve with whipped cream.

Streusel-Topped Pear Pie

This recipe developed when hardy pioneers found that fruit trees—especially pear—thrived in the southern region of Oregon. Bosc, Anjou, and Bartlett are all good varieties for this pie.

SERVES 6 TO 8

7 medium pears, peeled, cored, and sliced
½ cup granulated sugar
2 tablespoons lemon juice
1½ tablespoons quick-cooking tapioca
½ teaspoon ground cinnamon
⅛ teaspoon ground mace
Dough for 1 (9-inch) pie crust, refrigerated
    (page 374)
½ cup all-purpose flour
½ cup firmly packed brown sugar
¼ cup butter, softened

1. Combine the pears with the granulated sugar, lemon juice, tapioca, cinnamon, and mace in a large bowl. Let sit for 15 minutes.

2. Preheat the oven to 425°F with the rack in the lower third of the oven.

3. Roll out the dough on a lightly floured surface to a thickness of ⅛ inch. Fit into a 9-inch pie pan, leaving a 1-inch overhang. Fold and flute the edge. (Do not prick the bottom.)

4. Spoon the filling into the pie crust and bake for 10 minutes.

5. Meanwhile, stir together the flour and brown sugar in a small bowl. Use a fork to mix in the butter until crumbly.

6. Sprinkle the crumb mixture over the pie and reduce the oven temperature to 350°F. Bake for an additional 35 to 40 minutes, until the topping is golden. Serve warm or at room temperature.

Plum Pie

Across the country, gnarled and scraggly wild plum trees can be found, often with old apple and pear trees. Plums, including the Italian prune plum, have been an important part of country life since the early pioneers traveled from the barely settled eastern United States to what was then called the West: Ohio, Kentucky, Indiana, and Tennessee. This pie is reminiscent of those days—simply seasoned, yet full of flavor.

SERVES 6 TO 8

2½ pounds plums, halved, pitted, and sliced
    (3 to 3½ cups)
1 cup plus 1 tablespoon sugar
¼ cup all-purpose flour
¼ teaspoon ground cinnamon
¼ teaspoon salt
Dough for 2 (9-inch) pie crusts, refrigerated
    (page 374)
2 tablespoons milk

1. Toss the plums with 1 cup sugar, the flour, cinnamon, and salt in a large bowl. Set aside.

2. Preheat the oven to 425°F, with the rack in the lower third of the oven.

3. Roll out half of the dough on a lightly floured surface to a thickness of ⅛ inch. Fit into a 9-inch pie pan, leaving a 1-inch overhang. Fill with the plum mixture.

4. Roll out the remaining dough into a circle about 1 inch larger than the pie pan. Center the crust on top of the pie and trim to ½ inch beyond the edge of the pan. Fold the top crust edge under the bottom crust edge and flute. Cut steam vents in the top crust.

5. Bake for 20 minutes.

6. Reduce the oven temperature to 350°F and continue to bake for 30 minutes.

7. Brush the top crust with the milk and sprinkle with the remaining 1 tablespoon sugar. Continue to bake for 10 to 15 minutes, until the crust is golden brown. Serve warm or at room temperature.

TIP: Fruit pies are wonderful when served
warm with a scoop of ice cream.

Streusel-Topped Rhubarb Pie

It wasn't until rhubarb started showing up in pies that people became interested in this intensely sour plant. Rhubarb pie was so popular in the 1800s that rhubarb became known as the "pie plant." This recipe cuts the tartness with sugar and tapioca in the filling, which is topped by a sweetened, buttery crumble. Use only the stems of the rhubarb; the rest of the plant is poisonous.

SERVES 6 TO 8

Pie:
6 cups sliced rhubarb stems
1¼ cups sugar
¼ cup quick-cooking tapioca
¼ teaspoon salt
1 large egg, beaten
Dough for 1 (9-inch) pie crust, refrigerated
    (page 374)

Topping:
½ cup sugar
½ cup all-purpose flour
⅛ teaspoon salt
¼ cup (½ stick) butter, softened

1. To make the pie, mix the rhubarb, sugar, tapioca, salt, and egg in a medium bowl. Let stand for 15 minutes.

2. Preheat the oven to 425°F.

3. Roll out the dough on a lightly floured surface to a thickness of ⅛ inch. Fit into a 9-inch pie pan, leaving a 1-inch overhang. Fold and flute the edge. (Do not prick the bottom.)

4. Pour the rhubarb mixture into the pie crust and set aside.

5. To make the topping, combine the sugar, flour, and salt in a medium bowl. Mix in the butter with a fork until the mixture is crumbly.

6. Sprinkle the topping over the pie filling and bake for 10 minutes.

7. Reduce the oven temperature to 350°F and continue to bake for 35 to 40 minutes, until the topping is browned and the juices are bubbling. Serve warm or at room temperature.

Strawberry-Rhubarb Pie

Strawberries ripen when rhubarb plants grow vigorously. You might say that the sweet strawberries tame the tart rhubarb, or that the tart rhubarb cuts through the berries' sweetness. It is the best of both worlds.

SERVES 6 TO 8

4 cups diced rhubarb stems
2 cups (1 pint) hulled and sliced strawberries
1¼ cups sugar
⅓ cup all-purpose flour
1 teaspoon ground ginger
Dough for 2 (9-inch) pie crusts, refrigerated
(page 374)

1. Mix the rhubarb, strawberries, sugar, flour, and ginger in a large bowl. Let sit for about 10 minutes.

2. Preheat the oven to 450°F, with the rack in the lower third of the oven.

3. Roll out half of the dough on a lightly floured surface to a thickness of ⅛ inch. Fit into a 9-inch pie pan, leaving a 1-inch overhang. Spoon the fruit mixture into the pie crust.

4. Roll out the remaining pie dough into a rectangle about ⅛ inch thick and 11 inches long.

Trim the ragged edges. Cut the rectangle lengthwise into 10 equal strips, each about ½ inch wide. Set aside.

5. To form a lattice, overlap one end of 2 dough strips on a sheet of wax paper, laying them perpendicular to each other in an "L" shape. Working from the overlapped corner, lay another strip parallel to one of the original strips with about ½ inch between them. Overlap the corner opposite (either over or under) the strip next to it. Lay the next strip perpendicular to the last strip and continue to interweave the remaining strips using the over-under pattern.

6. Center the wax paper on top of the pie filling and carefully slide the paper out so that the lattice rests evenly on the filling. Trim the ends of the lattice strips. Moisten the overhanging edge of the bottom crust with water and fold up over the ends of the strips. Flute the edge of the crust.

7. Bake for 10 minutes.

8. Reduce the oven temperature to 350°F and bake for an additional 35 to 40 minutes, until the crust is golden brown. Serve warm or at room temperature.

Strawberry Custard Pie

If you want an extraordinary pie, look no further than this outstanding strawberry pie. It has a topping made of broiled brown sugar, much like the crème brûlée served at fancy restaurants, and its filling is flavored with kirsch. Kirsch is a brandy distilled from cherries and their pits. It adds an aromatic quality to the filling.

SERVES 6 TO 8

Crust:
¼ cup (½ stick) butter, softened
1 cup all-purpose flour
¼ teaspoon salt
2 tablespoons milk
1 tablespoon granulated sugar

Filling:
2 cups (1 pint) hulled and sliced strawberries
½ cup granulated sugar
3 tablespoons kirsch
1 pint (2 cups) heavy cream
¼ teaspoon salt
6 large egg yolks, lightly beaten
1 teaspoon vanilla extract
1 cup firmly packed brown sugar

1. Preheat the oven to 350°F.

2. To make the crust, use a fork to mix the butter, flour, salt, milk, and sugar in a medium bowl until well blended; the mixture should be crumbly. Press firmly into the bottom and up the sides of a 9-inch pie pan. Bake for 30 minutes, or until firm. Set aside to cool.

3. To make the filling, lightly toss the strawberries with ¼ cup of granulated sugar and the kirsch in a medium bowl. Set aside.

4. Pour the heavy cream into the top of a double boiler set over boiling water. Stir in the salt and remaining ¼ cup granulated sugar. When the sugar has completely melted, gradually stir in the egg yolks and cook over medium heat until the mixture thickens. Remove from the heat and stir in the vanilla extract. Let cool.

5. Drain the berries and spoon into the baked pie crust. Pour the cooled cream mixture over the top and chill well, about 2 hours.

6. Preheat the broiler.

7. Sprinkle the brown sugar over the top of the pie and place under the broiler. Broil for 5 minutes, until the sugar melts and forms a top crust. Serve immediately.

Mincemeat Pie

Mincemeat is traditionally made with beef suet, but beef, lamb, pork, or venison stew meat is also found in many recipes. In colonial times, cooks made mincemeat filling in the fall and stored it for later use in pies.

SERVES 6 TO 8

2 cups beef suet, cut into small pieces
3 cups peeled, cored, and finely chopped tart apples, such as Granny Smith or Rome Beauty (about 3 to 4 medium)
½ cup firmly packed brown sugar
1 teaspoon ground cinnamon
½ teaspoon ground cloves
½ teaspoon salt
¼ cup raisins
¼ cup black cherry wine or sherry
3 tablespoons bourbon or other whiskey
Dough for 2 (9-inch) pie crusts, refrigerated (page 374)

1. Cook the suet in a medium saucepan over medium heat, stirring to break it up into smaller pieces, about 8 minutes. Add the apples, brown sugar, cinnamon, cloves, and salt. Cook over low heat until thoroughly heated, about 10 minutes. Stir in the raisins, wine, and bourbon. Set aside.

2. Preheat the oven to 425°F, with the rack in the lower third of the oven.

3. Roll out half of the dough on a lightly floured surface to a thickness of ⅛ inch. Fit into a 9-inch pie pan, leaving a 1-inch overhang. Fill with the meat mixture.

4. Roll out the remaining dough into a circle about 1 inch larger than the pan. Center the crust on top of the pie and trim to ½ inch beyond the edge of the pan. Fold the top crust edge under the bottom crust edge and flute. Cut steam vents in the top crust.

5. Bake for 15 minutes.

6. Reduce the oven temperature to 350°F and continue to bake for 35 to 45 minutes, until the crust is golden brown. Serve warm.

Shoofly Pie

The Pennsylvania Dutch are credited with the invention of this pie—so sweet with brown sugar and molasses, you have to guard it by shooing away the flies that will be drawn to it.

SERVES 6 TO 8

1¼ cups all-purpose flour
½ cup firmly packed brown sugar
½ teaspoon ground cinnamon
⅛ teaspoon ground ginger
⅛ teaspoon ground nutmeg
⅛ teaspoon salt
¼ cup (½ stick) butter, softened
Dough for 1 (9-inch) pie crust, refrigerated (page 374)
⅔ cup water
½ teaspoon baking soda
⅔ cup molasses

1. Preheat the oven to 450°F, with the rack in the lower third of the oven.

2. Combine the flour, brown sugar, cinnamon, ginger, nutmeg, and salt in a medium bowl. Blend in the butter with a fork until the mixture resembles coarse meal. Set aside.

3. Roll out the dough on a lightly floured surface to a thickness of ⅛ inch. Fit into a 9-inch pie pan, leaving a 1-inch overhang. Fold and flute the edge. (Do not prick the bottom.) Set aside.

4. Heat the water in a small saucepan over medium heat until simmering. Stir in the baking soda and molasses. Stir in ⅔ cup of the flour mixture and pour into the pie crust. Cover with the remaining flour mixture.

5. Bake for 15 minutes.

6. Reduce the oven temperature to 350°F and continue to bake for 35 to 45 minutes, until the filling is set. Serve warm or at room temperature.

Pecan Pie

Pecans are native to America, but it is not clear how long pecan pies have been made. The development of corn syrup in 1906 spread word of pecan pie, so much that in some areas of the country the pie is called "Karo pie," after a major brand of corn syrup. The crunchy-sweet combination is enjoyable, especially when served warm with vanilla ice cream.

SERVES 6 TO 8

3 large eggs, lightly beaten
1 cup light corn syrup
1 cup firmly packed brown sugar
⅓ cup butter, melted
2 tablespoons all-purpose flour
⅛ teaspoon salt
1 teaspoon vanilla extract
Dough for 1 (9-inch) pie crust refrigerated (page 374)
1 cup pecan halves or pieces

1. Preheat the oven to 350°F.

2. Beat together the eggs, corn syrup, brown sugar, butter, flour, salt, and vanilla extract in a medium bowl. Set aside.

3. Roll out the dough on a floured surface to a thickness of ⅛ inch. Fit into a 9-inch pie pan, leaving a 1-inch overhang. Fold and flute the edge. (Do not prick the bottom.)

4. Arrange the pecans in the bottom of the pie crust and pour in the corn syrup mixture.

5. Bake for about 45 minutes, until the crust is golden brown and the filling is firm.

6. Serve slightly warm or at room temperature.

Maple-Nut Pie

The butternut, or white walnut, was the nut of choice for New Englanders, while the pecan was the preferred nut of the South. Today, this sweet pie is most frequently made with walnuts and uses pure maple syrup.

SERVES 6 TO 8

3 large eggs
¾ cup sugar
¾ cup pure maple syrup
3 tablespoons butter, melted
2 tablespoons all-purpose flour
1 tablespoon cider vinegar
⅛ teaspoon salt
Dough for 1 (9-inch) pie crust, refrigerated
    (page 374)
1¼ cups walnut pieces and halves

1. Preheat the oven to 350°F.

2. Beat together the eggs, sugar, maple syrup, butter, flour, vinegar, and salt in a medium bowl. Set aside.

3. Roll out the dough on a lightly floured surface to a thickness of ⅛ inch. Fit into a 9-inch pie pan, leaving a 1-inch overhang. Fold and flute the edge. (Do not prick the bottom.)

4. Arrange the walnuts in the pie crust and pour in the maple syrup mixture.

5. Bake for about 40 minutes, until the crust is golden brown and the filling is firm.

6. Cool to room temperature before slicing.

Peanut Butter Pie

The peanut is actually not a nut, but the underground seed of a legume. Pre-Incan Peruvians called them "ground seeds" and offered them as provisions to help the spirits of the dead on their way to heaven. This recipe may not get you to heaven, but the taste is divine.

SERVES 6 TO 8

1½ cups shelled raw peanuts, blanched
1 cup molasses, sorghum, or corn syrup
½ cup sugar
½ cup (1 stick) butter

4 large eggs
1 teaspoon vanilla extract
⅛ teaspoon salt
¼ teaspoon ground nutmeg
Dough for 1 (9-inch) pie crust, refrigerated
    (page 374)

1. Preheat the oven to 325°F.

2. Spread the peanuts out on a baking sheet and roast for 40 to 45 minutes, until golden and fragrant. Cool. Increase the oven temperature to 375°F.

3. Grind the peanuts in a food processor and pack into a measuring cup to make 1 cup.

4. Beat together the ground peanuts, molasses, sugar, butter, eggs, vanilla extract, salt, and nutmeg in a medium bowl. Set aside.

5. Roll out the dough on a lightly floured surface to a thickness of ⅛ inch. Fit into a 9-inch pie pan, leaving a 1-inch overhang. Fold and flute the edge. (Do not prick the bottom.)

6. Bake for 35 minutes, until the crust is light brown and the filling is set.

7. Cool to room temperature before slicing.

Sugar Pie

Sugar pie is found north to south in the United States—sometimes made with cream, sometimes with eggs. It may have its origins as "tarte au sucre," a recipe that was passed around New England by French Canadians and was brought to the South via the Acadians, who eventually settled in Louisiana. This pie, with its many variations, is also known as chess pie.

SERVES 6 TO 8

Dough for 1 (9-inch) pie crust, refrigerated
    (page 374)
4 large eggs
1 cup granulated sugar
1 cup firmly packed brown sugar
½ cup (1 stick) butter, melted
½ cup milk or half-and-half
¼ cup all-purpose flour
1 tablespoon vanilla extract
½ teaspoon salt

1. Preheat the oven to 350°F.

2. Roll out the dough on a lightly floured surface to a thickness of 1/8 inch. Fit into a 9-inch pie pan, leaving a 1-inch overhang. Fold and flute the edge. (Do not prick the bottom.)

3. Beat the eggs, sugars, butter, milk, flour, vanilla extract, and salt in a medium bowl until thick and well blended. Pour into the pie crust.

4. Bake for about 45 minutes, until the crust is golden brown and the filling is firm.

5. Cool to room temperature before serving.

Pumpkin Pie

It is impossible to think of Thanksgiving without pumpkin pie. Historians suggest that a pumpkin pie–like dessert was served at the first Thanksgiving in 1621.

SERVES 6 TO 8

Dough for 1 (9-inch) pie crust, refrigerated (page 374)
3 large eggs
1½ cups cooked or canned pumpkin
1 cup firmly packed brown sugar
1 teaspoon ground cinnamon
1 teaspoon ground ginger
½ teaspoon ground allspice
½ teaspoon ground nutmeg
½ teaspoon salt
½ cup evaporated milk

1. Preheat the oven to 425°F, with the rack in the lower third of the oven.

2. Roll out the dough on a lightly floured surface to a thickness of 1/8 inch. Fit into a 9-inch pie pan, leaving a 1-inch overhang. Fold and flute the edge. (Do not prick the bottom.) Set aside.

3. Beat the eggs in a medium bowl until light. Beat in the pumpkin, brown sugar, cinnamon, ginger, allspice, nutmeg, and salt. Add the evaporated milk and mix until well blended. Pour into the pie crust.

4. Bake for 15 minutes.

5. Reduce the oven temperature to 350°F. Continue baking for 35 to 45 minutes more, until the

filling is firm and a knife inserted into the center comes out clean.

6. Cool on a wire rack. Serve at room temperature or chilled with whipped cream.

Squash Pie

Pumpkins were one of many winter squashes introduced by the Indians to the colonists. Winter squash could be stored for months and quickly became a staple of the colonists' diet. The number of varieties is now huge and includes many wonderfully sweet, delicately flavored, and fine-textured squash like blue hubbard, sugar baby, butternut, buttercup, and Turk's cap. This pie is similar to pumpkin pie, with a bit more sweetness and spice.

SERVES 6 TO 8

Dough for 1 (9-inch) pie crust, refrigerated (page 374)
3 large eggs
1½ cups cooked and puréed winter squash
1 cup firmly packed brown sugar
2 tablespoons molasses
1 teaspoon butter, melted
1 teaspoon ground ginger
1 teaspoon ground cinnamon
½ teaspoon salt
¼ teaspoon ground nutmeg
1 cup milk

1. Preheat the oven to 425°F, with the rack in the lower third of the oven.

2. Roll out the dough on a lightly floured surface to a thickness of 1/8 inch. Fit into a 9-inch pie pan, leaving a 1-inch overhang. Fold and flute the edge. (Do not prick the bottom.) Set aside.

3. Beat the eggs in a medium bowl until light. Beat in the squash, brown sugar, molasses, butter, ginger, cinnamon, salt, nutmeg, and milk. Pour into the pie crust.

4. Bake for 15 minutes.

5. Reduce the oven temperature to 350°F. Continue baking for another 35 to 45 minutes, until the filling is firm and a knife inserted into the center comes out clean.

6. Cool on a wire rack. Serve at room temperature or chilled.

Sweet Potato Pie

George Washington Carver is responsible for finding hundreds of uses for the peanut. He also turned his inventive mind to the sweet potato, devising more than one hundred uses for it as well. This is one terrific use for the orange tuber, baked in a filling that is minimally sweetened and flavored by brandy, orange zest, and nutmeg.

SERVES 6 TO 8

3 medium sweet potatoes
Dough for 1 (9-inch) pie crust, refrigerated
   (page 374)
¼ cup (½ stick) butter, softened
2 large eggs, separated
½ cup honey
½ cup milk
¼ teaspoon salt
¼ teaspoon ground nutmeg
1 tablespoon brandy
1 teaspoon baking soda
½ teaspoon grated orange zest
3 tablespoons sugar

1. Cover the potatoes with water in a medium saucepan. Bring to a boil, reduce the heat, and simmer until the potatoes are tender, 15 to 35 minutes.

2. Meanwhile, roll out the pie crust on a lightly floured surface to a thickness of ⅛ inch. Fit into a 9-inch pie pan, leaving a 1-inch overhang. Fold and flute the edge. (Do not prick the bottom.) Set aside.

3. Drain the potatoes, remove the flesh from the skin, and press the flesh through a fine-mesh strainer. Cool slightly.

4. Preheat the oven to 425°F, with the rack in the lower third of the oven.

5. In a large bowl, beat together the butter, egg yolks, honey, milk, salt, and nutmeg until the mixture is creamy. Beat in the brandy, baking soda, and orange zest. Fold in the sweet potatoes, then pour into the pie crust.

6. Bake for 15 minutes.

7. Reduce the oven temperature to 300°F. Continue baking for 25 to 35 minutes more, until the filling is set.

8. Meanwhile, beat the egg whites with the sugar in a medium bowl until stiff peaks form. Spread evenly over the baked pie, making sure the meringue meets the crust all around.

9. Bake for 20 minutes, until the meringue is lightly browned.

10. Cool for 2 to 3 hours before serving.

Banana Cream Pie

The creation of a banana cream pie is a remarkable achievement. It should be made with ripe bananas whose skins are heavily flecked with brown. For a wonderful change of pace, replace the pie crust with a chocolate-wafer crumb crust and flavor the custard with white chocolate.

SERVES 6 TO 8

½ cup sugar
¼ cup cornstarch
Pinch of salt
2 cups milk
3 large egg yolks, lightly beaten
1 tablespoon butter
1 teaspoon vanilla extract
1 cup heavy cream
1 (9-inch) pie crust, baked and cooled
   (page 374)
3 medium bananas, peeled and sliced

1. Combine the sugar, cornstarch, salt, and milk in the top of a double boiler set over boiling water. Cook until boiling, stirring constantly. Continue cooking and stirring for another 10 minutes.

2. In a medium bowl, gradually stir about ½ cup of sugar mixture into the egg yolks, then pour back into the sugar mixture. Cook, stirring constantly, for 2 minutes, until thick and smooth. Remove from the heat and stir in the butter and vanilla extract.

3. Pour the custard into a medium bowl, cover the surface with plastic wrap, and refrigerate until completely cooled, 2 to 4 hours.

4. Whip the heavy cream in a small bowl until stiff. Fold half into the custard.

5. Cover the bottom of the pie crust with about ½ inch of custard. Arrange the banana slices over the custard and cover with the remaining custard. Pipe the remaining whipped cream over the top.

6. Chill for 3 to 4 hours before serving.

Coconut Cream Pie

Coconuts were introduced to American bakers in the early 1800s and proved immensely popular in desserts. This classic recipe mixes coconut into a custard filling, which is then topped with freshly whipped cream.

SERVES 6 TO 8

1½ cups sweetened coconut flakes
1 cup sugar
⅓ cup cornstarch
2 tablespoons all-purpose flour
¼ teaspoon salt
3 large eggs, lightly beaten
3 cups milk
1 tablespoon butter
2 teaspoons vanilla extract
1 (9-inch) pie crust, baked and cooled
  (page 374)
1 cup heavy cream

1. Preheat the oven to 325°F.

2. Spread ¼ cup of coconut flakes on a baking sheet and toast for about 10 minutes, until golden. Set aside.

3. Stir together the sugar, cornstarch, flour, and salt in a medium saucepan. Stir in the eggs until the mixture is well blended. Gradually stir in the milk. Cook over medium heat, stirring constantly, until boiling. Boil and stir for 1 more minute.

4. Remove the saucepan from the heat. Stir in the butter and vanilla extract, then stir in the remaining 1¼ cups coconut flakes until blended. Pour into the baked pie crust.

5. Refrigerate for 6 to 8 hours, until set.

6. Whip the cream until stiff and pipe over the top of the pie. Sprinkle with the toasted coconut flakes and serve.

Chocolate Cream Pie

Rich and creamy, this is an American pie fit for any occasion. Use the best chocolate you can find; it will make all the difference.

SERVES 6 TO 8

2 ounces (2 squares) semisweet chocolate, plus more to serve
2 ounces (2 squares) unsweetened chocolate, chopped
1 cup plus 2 tablespoons sugar
¼ cup all-purpose flour
1 tablespoon cornstarch
¾ teaspoon salt
4 large egg yolks
3 cups milk
2 tablespoons butter, cut into small pieces
1½ teaspoons vanilla extract
1 (9-inch) pie crust, baked and cooled
  (page 374)
1 cup heavy cream

1. Chop the semisweet chocolate and put into the top of a double boiler. Add the unsweetened chocolate and cook over barely simmering water, stirring, until smooth. Remove from the heat.

2. Whisk together 1 cup sugar, the flour, cornstarch, salt, and egg yolks in a medium saucepan until well combined. Whisk in the milk. Bring to a boil over medium heat, whisking, and simmer, still whisking, until thick, about 1 minute.

3. Force the custard through a fine-mesh strainer into a medium bowl and whisk in the melted chocolates, the butter, and vanilla extract until smooth. Pour the filling into the crust.

4. Chill the pie, covered, for at least 6 hours or overnight.

5. Beat the cream to soft peaks. Add the remaining 2 tablespoons sugar and beat just until stiff peaks form. Spoon the whipped cream decoratively onto the pie and sprinkle with grated semisweet chocolate. Serve immediately.

Black-Bottom Pie

This classic pie dates from the turn of the twentieth century. Its chocolate custard layer is topped with a layer of rum custard smothered in whipped cream. It is rich and wonderful. (Note: This recipe contains raw eggs. For more information, see page 11.)

SERVES 6 TO 8

1 tablespoon (one ¼-ounce package) unflavored gelatin
¼ cup cold water
1¾ cups milk
1 cup granulated sugar
1 tablespoon cornstarch
⅛ teaspoon salt
4 large eggs, separated
2 ounces (2 squares) semisweet chocolate, plus more to serve
1 teaspoon vanilla extract
1 (9-inch) ginger snap crumb crust, baked and cooled (page 375)
⅛ teaspoon cream of tartar
2 tablespoons rum
1 cup heavy cream
2 tablespoons confectioners' sugar

1. In a small bowl, dissolve the gelatin in the cold water. Set aside.

2. Heat the milk to just boiling in the top of a double boiler set over simmering water. Stir in ½ cup of granulated sugar.

3. Mix the cornstarch with the salt and egg yolks in a small bowl, then slowly add to the milk mixture. Cook, stirring constantly, until the mixture thickens. Stir in the gelatin mixture, then divide evenly between 2 medium bowls.

4. Finely chop the 2 ounces semisweet chocolate and add to one bowl of custard. Add the vanilla extract and stir until the chocolate is completely melted. Pour into the baked pie crust and tip the pan around so the chocolate coats the sides. Set aside.

5. Beat the egg whites with the cream of tartar in a medium bowl until foamy. Gradually add the remaining ½ cup granulated sugar, a little at a time, until stiff. Fold into the remaining bowl of custard, then stir in the rum. Spread over the chocolate layer in the pie pan.

6. Chill well, overnight if possible.

7. Whip the cream with the confectioners' sugar in a small bowl until stiff. Spread over the top of the pie and garnish with grated semisweet chocolate. Serve immediately.

Butterscotch Pie

A cloud of meringue tops a creamy butterscotch pudding in this pie recipe. It is the combination of brown sugar and butter that gives butterscotch its characteristic flavor.

SERVES 6 TO 8

⅓ cup all-purpose flour
1 cup firmly packed brown sugar
Pinch of salt
2 cups milk
3 large eggs, separated
2 tablespoons butter
½ teaspoon vanilla extract
1 (9-inch) pie crust, baked and cooled (page 374)
½ teaspoon cream of tartar
½ cup granulated sugar

1. Preheat the oven to 375°F.

2. Whisk together the flour, brown sugar, and salt in the top of a double boiler over simmering water. Slowly pour in the milk, whisking, and bring to a boil. Boil for 1 minute, whisking constantly.

3. Beat the egg yolks in a small bowl until thick and smooth. Gradually stir a few tablespoons of the hot milk mixture into the beaten egg yolks, mixing constantly until blended. Pour the yolk mixture back into the milk mixture, stirring until combined. Cook, stirring constantly, until thick and smooth, about 2 minutes.

4. Remove the double boiler from the heat, stir in the butter and vanilla extract, and pour into the pie crust.

5. Beat the egg whites with an electric mixer on high speed until foamy. Beat in the cream of tartar. Gradually beat in the sugar, ¼ cup at a time. Continue to beat at high speed until stiff and glossy.

6. Use a rubber spatula to spread the meringue over the pie. Be sure that all edges of the pie crust are sealed with meringue.

7. Bake for 7 to 8 minutes, until the meringue is light golden brown.

8. Cool on a wire rack in a draft-free place. Serve at room temperature.

Lemon Meringue Pie

Once Abe Lincoln was elected to the Illinois Legislature in 1834, he spent many days visiting his constituents around the state during his four two-year terms. Mrs. Nancy Breedlove owned a small hotel where the future president stayed, and she served a delectable lemon meringue pie. Lincoln enjoyed the pie so much that he asked for the recipe and took it with him to the White House. Here is one version of that delicious recipe.

SERVES 6 TO 8

7 large eggs, separated
1¾ cups granulated sugar
1⅔ cups water
¾ cup lemon juice
⅓ cup cornstarch
1½ tablespoons grated lemon zest
3 tablespoons butter
1 (9-inch) pie crust, baked and cooled
    (page 374)
½ teaspoon cream of tartar
1½ cups confectioners' sugar

1. Preheat the oven to 375°F.

2. Whisk together the egg yolks, granulated sugar, water, lemon juice, cornstarch, and lemon zest in a medium saucepan over medium heat. Bring to a boil, whisking constantly, until boiling, about 15 minutes.

3. Remove the saucepan from the heat and whisk in the butter. Continue stirring until the butter is completely melted. Pour into the baked crust.

4. Beat the egg whites with an electric mixer on high speed until foamy. Beat in the cream of tartar, then gradually beat in the confectioners' sugar, ¼ cup at a time. Continue to beat at high speed until the egg whites are stiff and glossy.

5. Use a rubber spatula to spread the egg white over the pie. Be sure that all edges of the pie crust are sealed with meringue.

6. Bake for 7 to 8 minutes, until the meringue is golden brown.

7. Cool on a wire rack. Serve at room temperature.

TIP: Bakers sometimes notice that their meringue "weeps" or "sweats" after baking. Weeping meringue is usually a two-part problem: The egg whites haven't been beaten sufficiently after the sugar is added and/or the pie filling isn't hot enough when the meringue is added.

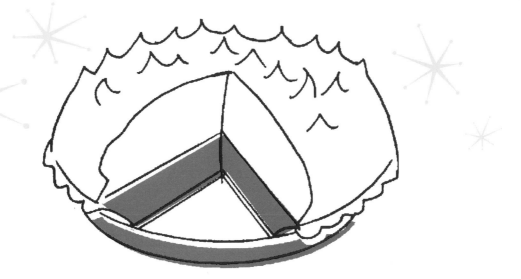

Pineapple Angel Pie

Angel pies date back to at least 1940, when McCall's magazine first featured a lemon angel pie. The angel pie turns meringue–topped pies upside down, using meringue to make the crust, with the filling between layers of whipped cream.

SERVES 6 TO 8

Crust:
4 large eggs, separated
½ teaspoon cream of tartar
1 cup sugar

Filling:
½ cup plus 1 tablespoon sugar
1 tablespoon lemon juice
1 cup well-drained crushed pineapple, (juice reserved)
1 cup heavy cream

1. Preheat the oven to 225°F. Grease and flour a 9-inch pie pan.

2. To make the crust, beat the egg whites with an electric mixer on high speed until foamy. Gradually add the cream of tartar and sugar and continue beating until stiff peaks form. Spread on the bottom and up the sides of the prepared pie pan.

3. Bake for 1½ hours, until the crust is set and very light brown. Cool.

4. To make the filling, combine the egg yolks, ½ cup sugar, the lemon juice, and 2 tablespoons of reserved pineapple juice in the top of a double boiler set over simmering water. Cook until the mixture thickens, about 10 minutes. Remove from the heat and stir in the crushed pineapple. Set aside to cool.

5. Beat the cream with the remaining 1 tablespoon sugar until soft peaks form.

6. Spoon half of the whipped cream into the crust and cover with the pineapple filling. Top with the remaining whipped cream.

7. Refrigerate for several hours or overnight. Serve chilled.

Key Lime Pie

Key lime pies were first made in the 1850s in the Florida Keys, the only place Key limes are grown. It was one of the first and best uses made of the newly created canned sweetened condensed milk. This pie can be made with a crumb crust or a pastry crust. A meringue or whipped cream topping is common. The combination of sweet, tart, and creamy is what makes this pie so popular.

SERVES 6 TO 8

4 large egg yolks
1 (14-ounce) can sweetened condensed milk
½ cup lime juice (preferably from Key limes)
⅓ cup sour cream
1 tablespoon finely grated lime zest
1 (9-inch) pie crust, baked and cooled (page 374)
Whipped cream, to serve (optional)

1. Preheat the oven to 325°F.

2. Beat the egg yolks in a large bowl until thick and pale yellow, 7 to 10 minutes. Add the condensed milk, lime juice, sour cream, and lime zest and beat until blended and smooth. Pour into the crust.

3. Bake for 20 minutes, until the filling is set.

4. Cool on a rack, then refrigerate for 3 to 4 hours.

5. Pipe whipped cream on the top of the pie and serve immediately.

Frozen Lemon Mousse Pie

The light, airy, creamy, lemon–tart filling in this recipe is guaranteed to cool you down in hot weather. It is the perfect ending to an evening of outdoor dining. (Note: This recipe contains raw eggs. For more information, see page 11.)

SERVES 6 TO 8

3 large eggs, separated
⅛ teaspoon salt
½ cup sugar
¼ cup lemon juice
1 teaspoon grated lemon zest
1 cup heavy cream
1 (9-inch) crumb crust, baked and cooled
    (page 374)

1. Beat together the egg yolks, salt, and sugar in the top of a double boiler set over simmering water. Stir in the lemon juice and zest. Cook until the mixture thickens and coats a spoon, about 10 minutes.

2. Remove the double boiler from the heat and refrigerate.

3. In a medium bowl, beat the egg whites until stiff. Set aside.

4. In another medium bowl, whip the cream until soft peaks form. Fold with the egg whites into the chilled lemon mixture. Spoon into the crust.

5. Freeze until firm, 2 to 4 hours.

6. Remove the pie from the freezer about 30 minutes before serving.

Lemon Chiffon Pie

Chiffon pies came into fashion during the 1940s. The light, fluffy filling contains egg whites and gelatin. Here is a classic recipe, but feel free to change the type of juice to create a lime chiffon, orange chiffon, or pineapple chiffon pie. (Note: This recipe contains raw eggs. For more information, see page 11.)

SERVES 6 TO 8

1 cup sugar
1 tablespoon (one ¼-ounce package)
    unflavored gelatin
4 large eggs, separated
⅔ cup water
⅓ cup lemon juice
1 tablespoon grated lemon zest
½ teaspoon cream of tartar
1 (9-inch) pie crust, baked and cooled
    (page 374)

1. Stir together ½ cup of sugar and the gelatin in a small saucepan. Set aside.

2. Blend the egg yolks, water, and lemon juice in a small bowl, then stir into the sugar mixture. Cook over medium heat, stirring constantly, just until boiling. Stir in the lemon zest.

3. Chill the saucepan in the refrigerator, stirring occasionally, until the mixture mounds slightly when dropped from a spoon.

4. Beat the egg whites and cream of tartar in a large bowl until foamy. Beat in the remaining ½ cup sugar, 1 tablespoon at a time, then continue beating until stiff and glossy.

5. Fold the chilled lemon mixture into the egg whites and spoon into the baked pie crust.

6. Chill for at least 3 hours, until set, and serve.

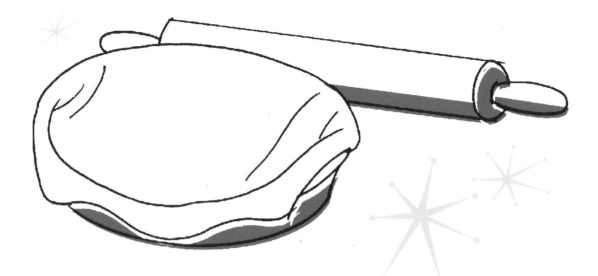

Fried Fruit Pies

Fried pie has been a staple in the South for generations. Its dough takes a lot of overworking and handling; in fact, it needs to be tough enough to hold up to all the rolling, pinching, and crimping necessary to put the pie together, as well as to contain the filling throughout the frying process. The warm, fruity contents and crisp golden crust are well worth the effort.

MAKES 12

Crust:
3 cups all-purpose flour
1 teaspoon salt
¾ cup shortening
1 large egg, lightly beaten
¼ cup cold water
1 teaspoon white vinegar

Filling:
3 cups dried fruit (apricots, peaches, and/or apples)
1½ cups water
6 tablespoons sugar
¼ teaspoon ground allspice
¼ teaspoon ground cinnamon
Oil, for frying

1. To make the crust, stir together the flour and salt in a medium bowl. Cut in the shortening with a pastry blender or 2 knives until the mixture resembles coarse crumbs. Stir the egg with the water and sprinkle over the flour mixture. Sprinkle in the vinegar. Mix lightly until the ingredients are well combined. Form the dough into a ball and wrap in plastic wrap. Refrigerate for at least 1 hour.

2. To make the filling, combine the fruit and water in a small saucepan and simmer over low heat for 30 to 45 minutes, until very tender. Add more water if necessary to prevent scorching. Allow to cool, then mash the fruit slightly. Stir in the sugar, allspice, and cinnamon. Set aside.

3. Remove the dough from the refrigerator and cut it into 12 equal pieces. Form into balls.

4. On a lightly floured surface, roll out each ball into a 5- to 6-inch circle. Spoon 2 generous tablespoons of filling onto half of one circle. Fold over to make a half circle and seal by wetting the inside edge of the dough with water. Press and crimp the dough with the tongs of a fork to ensure a good seal. Repeat until all the dough circles are filled. Set aside.

5. Heat 3 to 4 inches of oil in a large saucepan or deep fryer to 375°F.

6. Using a slotted spoon, lower 3 pies into the oil, one at a time, and cook until golden brown, 3 to 4 minutes. Drain well. Repeat until all the pies are cooked.

7. Cool and drain on wire racks. Serve warm or at room temperature.

Fresh Fruit Tart

Tarts, compared to pies, are generally shallow and have no top crust. The filling in this tart is a classic pastry cream, made with milk and egg yolks. The fruit—suggested here or of your choice—should be arranged decoratively on top of the pastry cream. A light coating of apple jelly and Cognac makes the fruit sparkle.

SERVES 8

Crust:
1¾ cups all-purpose flour
¼ cup sugar
¼ teaspoon salt
10 tablespoons (1¼ sticks) chilled unsalted
    butter, cut into small pieces
1 large egg yolk
3 tablespoons heavy cream

Filling:
1 cup milk
3 large egg yolks
⅓ cup sugar
2 tablespoons cornstarch

Topping:
⅔ cup apple jelly
2 tablespoons cognac or brandy
3 medium kiwifruit, peeled and thinly sliced
1 medium peach or nectarine, peeled, pitted,
    and thinly sliced
1 cup blueberries
1 cup hulled and halved strawberries
Sprigs of fresh mint

1. To make the crust, combine the flour, sugar, and salt in a food processor and pulse to mix. Add the butter and pulse to blend until the mixture resembles coarse crumbs. Whisk the egg yolk and cream in a small bowl and add to the flour mixture; process until moist clumps form. Gather the dough into a ball and flatten into a disk. Cover with plastic wrap and refrigerate for 4 hours.

2. Meanwhile, prepare the filling by bringing the milk to a simmer in a medium, heavy saucepan. Whisk the yolks, sugar, and cornstarch in a medium bowl to blend and gradually whisk the hot milk into the bowl. Return the mixture to the same saucepan. Continue to whisk over medium heat until thickened and boiling. Boil for 1 minute, then pour into a separate medium bowl. Press a sheet of plastic wrap onto the filling surface. Cover and chill until cold, about 4 hours.

3. Preheat the oven to 375°F.

4. Press the dough onto the bottom and up the sides of an 11-inch tart pan with a removable bottom. Line the crust with aluminum foil and fill with dried beans or pie weights. Bake until the sides are set, about 15 minutes. Take the crust out of the oven and remove the foil and beans. Return the crust to the oven and bake, piercing with a fork if bubbles form, until golden, about 15 minutes. Transfer the pan to a cooling rack and cool completely. Remove the sides from the pan.

5. To make the topping, combine the jelly and cognac in a small saucepan. Stir over medium heat until the jelly melts, about 2 minutes. Brush half of the jelly mixture onto the bottom of the crust. Let it stand at room temperature until set, about 5 minutes. Add the filling and spread evenly. Arrange the fruit over the filling and brush the remaining jelly mixture over the top. Garnish with mint sprigs and serve.

Basic Pie Crusts

Pies were first baked in America as soon as settlers arrived from England. They were originally topped with a crust, but over time other toppings (or none at all) became favored. There are many recipes for pie crust. Using butter alone tends to make a more flaky crust than one of shortening alone. This recipe combines both butter and shortening.

MAKES 2 (9-INCH) PIE CRUSTS

2½ cups all-purpose flour
½ teaspoon salt
½ cup (1 stick) butter, cut into small pieces
6 tablespoons shortening
About 6 tablespoons ice water

1. If mixing by hand, stir together the flour and salt in a medium bowl. Cut in the butter with a pastry blender or 2 knives. Add the shortening and blend with a fork until the mixture resembles small peas. Sprinkle the water, 1 tablespoon at a time, over the flour mixture and stir with the fork until the dough holds together and doesn't crumble. Gather into a ball.

If mixing in a food processor, combine the flour and salt in the food processor and process briefly to mix. Add the butter and shortening and pulse intermittently until the mixture has the consistency of coarse meal. Add the water, 1 tablespoon at a time, and pulse intermittently until the mixture begins to hold together. Gather into a ball.

2. Divide the dough equally into 2 balls. Wrap each in plastic wrap and refrigerate for at least 30 minutes.

3. Roll out the dough on a lightly floured surface into two 10-inch circles, about ⅛ inch thick. Fold one circle in half, then gently lift it up and center it in a pie pan. Unfold and ease the dough loosely into place without stretching it. Repeat with the second circle if making single-crust pies.

4. For a single-crust pie, trim the overhanging edge about ½ inch larger than the outside rim of the pan. Fold it under, even with the rim of the pie pan, and crimp or flute the edge. Repeat with the second pie crust. Refrigerate one or both of the crusts for 15 minutes, then fill and bake as directed in the recipe, or see the instructions that follow.

To bake, preheat the oven to 425°F, with the rack in the lower third of the oven. Remove the crust from the refrigerator and prick the bottom and sides with a fork at ½-inch intervals. Fit a large circle of aluminum foil in the bottom and up the sides of the dough. Fill with dried beans or pie weights to prevent the crust from buckling. Bake for 10 to 12 minutes, until golden. Cool on a wire rack, then fill as directed in the recipe.

For a double-crust pie, trim the overhanging edge even with the rim of the pie pan. Add the filling. To make the top crust, roll out the remaining dough into a circle 1 inch larger than the pie pan. Moisten the edge of the bottom crust with water. Fold the dough circle in half, lift it up, place it across the center of the filled pie, and unfold. Trim the edge ½ inch larger than the pie pan. Tuck the overhang under the edge of the bottom crust. Crimp the edges with a fork or make a fluted pattern with your fingers. Cut several decorative slits in the top crust to allow steam to escape. Refrigerate for 15 minutes, then bake as directed.

Lard Pie Crusts

This is still a popular recipe among old-time cooks because lard creates a very flaky texture. You can find lard in the dairy department of the supermarket. Just be sure the lard is ice cold before using.

MAKES 2 (9-INCH) PIE CRUSTS

2⅔ cups all-purpose flour
½ teaspoon salt
1 cup lard
½ cup ice water
8 teaspoons cider vinegar

1. If mixing by hand, stir together the flour and salt in a medium bowl. Cut in the lard with a pastry blender or 2 knives until the mixture resembles small peas. Mix the water and vinegar in a small bowl, then use a fork to blend it into the flour mixture, 1 tablespoon at a time, until the dough holds together and doesn't crumble. Gather into a ball.

If mixing in a food processor, combine the flour and salt in the food processor and process briefly to mix. Add the lard and pulse intermittently until the mixture has the consistency of coarse meal. Mix the water and vinegar in a small bowl, then add to the flour mixture, 1 tablespoon at a time, and pulse intermittently until the mixture begins to hold together. Gather into a ball.

2. Divide the dough equally into 2 balls. Wrap each in plastic wrap and refrigerate for at least 30 minutes.

3. On a lightly floured surface, roll out the dough into two 10-inch circles, about ⅛ inch thick. Fold one circle in half, then gently lift it up and center it in a pie pan. Unfold and ease the dough loosely into place without stretching it. Repeat with the second circle if making single-crust pies.

4. For a single-crust pie, trim the overhanging edge about ½ inch larger than the outside rim of the pie pan. Fold it under, even with the rim of the pan. Crimp or flute the edge. Repeat with the second pie crust. Refrigerate one or both of the crusts for 15 minutes, then fill and bake as directed in the recipe or see the instructions below.

To bake, preheat the oven to 425°F, with the rack in the lower third of the oven. Remove the crust from the refrigerator and prick the bottom and sides with a fork at ½-inch intervals. Fit a large circle of aluminum foil in the bottom and up the sides of the dough. Fill with dried beans or pie weights to prevent the crust from buckling. Bake for 10 to 12 minutes, until golden. Cool on a wire rack, then fill as directed in the recipe.

For a double-crust pie, trim the overhanging edge even with the rim of the pie pan. Add the filling. To make the top crust, roll out the remaining dough into a circle 1 inch larger than the pie pan. Moisten the edge of the bottom crust with water. Fold the dough circle in half, lift up, place it across the center of the filled pie, and unfold. Trim the edge ½ inch larger than the pie pan. Tuck the overhang under the edge of the bottom crust. Crimp the edges with a fork or make a fluted pattern with your fingers. Cut several decorative slits in the top crust to allow steam to escape. Refrigerate for 15 minutes, then bake as directed.

Crumb Crust

Match the crumbs to the pie. Graham crackers are traditional, but any cookie can be used, including vanilla wafers, chocolate wafers, and ginger snaps. A chocolate crust gives great flavor and color contrast.

MAKES 1 (9-INCH) PIE CRUST

1½ cups finely crushed crumbs (made from graham crackers, ginger snaps, vanilla wafers, chocolate wafers, shortbread cookies, or other similar crunchy cookies or wafers)
1 to 3 tablespoons sugar
6 tablespoons butter, melted
1 teaspoon ground cinnamon, ginger, instant coffee, cocoa powder, or nutmeg (optional)

1. Preheat the oven to 375°F.

2. Combine the crumbs, sugar, butter, and spice, if using. Spoon into a 9-inch pie pan and press evenly into the bottom and up the sides.

3. Bake for 7 to 10 minutes. Cool before filling.

Graham Cracker Crust

Graham crackers are made from graham flour, which was named after the health food advocate Reverend Sylvester Graham (1794–1851). Graham believed that white bread and meat were detrimental to good health and stimulated carnal appetites, but this sweet and buttery crust is a tasty temptation.

MAKES 1 (9-INCH) PIE CRUST

1½ cups finely ground graham cracker crumbs
3 tablespoons sugar
6 tablespoons (¾ stick) butter, melted
¼ teaspoon ground cinnamon

1. Preheat the oven to 350°F. Lightly grease a 9-inch pie pan.

2. Combine the graham cracker crumbs, sugar, butter, and cinnamon in a medium bowl and mix until well combined. Press firmly into the bottom and up the sides of the pan.

3. Bake for 8 minutes.

4. Set aside on a wire rack to cool before filling.

White Layer Cake

This is a basic butter cake that differs from a yellow cake because it is made with whole eggs instead of just the yolks. Chocolate frosting is a fine topping for this cake; the filling can be icing, a flavored buttercream, lemon curd, or mousse.

SERVES 10 TO 12

2 cups all-purpose flour
3½ teaspoons baking powder
1 teaspoon salt
½ cup (1 stick) butter, softened
1 cup sugar
2 large eggs, separated
1 teaspoon vanilla extract
1 cup milk
⅛ teaspoon cream of tartar
Frosting of choice (pages 394–395)

1. Preheat the oven to 350°F. Grease and flour two 8-inch round cake pans. Line the bottoms of the pans with parchment paper and grease and flour the paper.

2. Sift the flour, baking powder, and salt into a medium bowl. Set aside.

3. Beat the butter with an electric mixer in a large bowl until creamy. Gradually add the sugar and beat until light and fluffy, then add the egg yolks, one at a time, beating well after each addition. Scrape down the sides of the bowl, then add the vanilla extract and beat until combined.

4. With the mixer on low speed, alternately add the flour mixture and milk to the bowl in 3 additions, beginning and ending with the flour. Set aside.

5. In a small bowl, beat the egg whites until foamy. Add the cream of tartar and continue beating until stiff peaks form.

6. Stir a little of the whites into the batter to lighten it, then fold in the remaining whites until combined.

7. Pour the batter into the prepared pans and smooth the tops.

8. Bake for 25 to 30 minutes, until a toothpick inserted into the cake centers comes out clean.

9. Cool the cakes in their pans on a wire rack for 10 minutes. Invert onto the rack, remove the parchment paper, and cool completely before frosting.

10. Spread the frosting between the layers and over the top and sides. Slice and serve.

Yellow Butter Cake

Cake mixes revolutionized the home kitchen when they first appeared in 1948. Pillsbury and General Mills both came out that year with chocolate, white, and yellow cake mixes. This is the basic cake against which all cake mixes should be judged. It is easy to make and has a light, buttery taste.

SERVES 10 TO 12

3 cups cake flour
4 teaspoons baking powder
¾ teaspoon salt
¾ cup (1½ sticks) butter, softened
1½ cups sugar
6 large egg yolks
2 teaspoons vanilla extract
1 cup milk
Frosting of choice (pages 394–395)

1. Preheat the oven to 350°F. Grease and flour two 9-inch round cake pans. Line the bottoms of the pans with parchment paper and grease and flour the paper.

2. Sift the flour, baking powder, and salt into a medium bowl. Set aside.

3. Beat the butter with an electric mixer in a large bowl until creamy. Gradually add the sugar and beat until light and fluffy. Add the egg yolks, one at a time, beating well after each addition. Scrape down the sides of the bowl, then add the vanilla extract and beat until combined.

4. With the mixer on low speed, alternately add the flour mixture and milk to the bowl in 3 additions, beginning and ending with the flour. Pour into the prepared pans and smooth the tops.

5. Bake for 25 to 35 minutes, until a toothpick inserted into the cake centers comes out clean.

6. Cool the cakes in their pans on a wire rack for 10 minutes. Invert onto the rack, remove the parchment paper, and cool completely before frosting.

7. Spread the frosting between the layers and over the top and sides. Slice and serve.

Chocolate Layer Cake

With the presence of both baking chocolate and cocoa powder, this is an outstanding, tender chocolate cake—perfect for the next birthday. Chocolate cake mixes cannot compare to it.

SERVES 10 TO 12

4 ounces (4 squares) semisweet chocolate, chopped
⅓ cup cocoa powder
1 cup boiling water
2¼ cups all-purpose flour
2 teaspoons baking powder
1 teaspoon baking soda
¼ teaspoon salt
1 cup (2 sticks) butter, softened
2¼ cups sugar
3 large eggs
1½ teaspoons vanilla extract
1 cup milk
Frosting of choice (pages 394–395)

1. Preheat the oven to 350°F. Grease and flour two 9-inch round cake pans. Line the bottoms of the pans with parchment paper and grease and flour the paper.

2. Combine the chopped semisweet chocolate and cocoa powder in a small bowl. Pour in the boiling water and stir until the chocolate is melted. Set aside to cool.

3. Sift the flour, baking powder, baking soda, and salt into a medium bowl. Set aside.

4. Beat the butter with an electric mixer until creamy. Gradually add the sugar and beat until light and fluffy. Add the eggs, one at a time, beating well after each addition. Scrape down the sides of the bowl, then add the vanilla extract and chocolate mixture and beat until combined.

5. With the mixer on low speed, alternately add the flour mixture and milk to the bowl in 3 additions, beginning and ending with the flour. Pour into the prepared pans and smooth the tops.

6. Bake for about 40 minutes, until a toothpick inserted into the cake centers comes out clean.

7. Cool the cakes in their pans on a wire rack for 10 minutes. Invert onto the rack, remove the parchment paper, and cool completely before frosting.

8. Spread the frosting between the layers and over the top and sides. Slice and serve.

Devil's Food Cake

There are two stories associated with how this cake received its name. The first is that the cake is so rich and delicious, it must be sinful. The second is that the tendency of cocoa powder to appear reddish in baked goods gives it a devilish association. Devil's food cake is also known as red velvet cake, red devil's cake, Waldorf Astoria cake, and $100 cake.

SERVES 10 TO 12

2 cups cake flour
¼ cup cocoa powder
1 teaspoon baking soda
1 teaspoon salt
½ cup shortening
1½ cups sugar
1 large egg
2 tablespoons brewed coffee
1 teaspoon vanilla extract
1 teaspoon red food coloring (optional)
1 cup buttermilk
Frosting of choice (pages 394–395)

1. Preheat the oven to 350°F. Grease and flour two 9-inch round cake pans. Line the bottoms with parchment paper and grease and flour the paper.

2. Sift the flour, cocoa powder, baking soda, and salt into a medium bowl. Set aside.

3. Beat the shortening with an electric mixer in a large bowl until creamy. Gradually add the sugar and beat until light and fluffy. Beat in the egg. Scrape down the sides of the bowl, then add the coffee, vanilla extract, and food coloring, if using. Beat until combined.

4. With the mixer on low speed, alternately add the flour mixture and buttermilk to the bowl in three additions, beginning and ending with the flour. Pour into the prepared pans and smooth the tops.

5. Bake for about 40 minutes, until a toothpick inserted into the cake centers comes out clean.

6. Cool the cakes in their pans on a wire rack for 10 minutes. Invert onto the rack, remove the parchment paper, and cool completely before frosting.

7. Spread the frosting between the layers and over the top and sides. Slice and serve.

German Chocolate Cake

This cake isn't German in origin at all, but bears the surname of Sam German, an inventor at the Baker's Chocolate Company. The original recipe appeared in a Dallas newspaper in 1957 using Baker's "German" Sweet Chocolate. As popularity grew for the cake and its main chocolate ingredient, its name was eventually shortened to German chocolate cake. If the cake is baked in a sheet pan, it is called a Texas sheet cake

SERVES 10 TO 12

4 (1-ounce) squares baking chocolate, chopped
½ cup boiling water
2 cups all-purpose flour
1 teaspoon baking soda
½ teaspoon salt
1 cup (2 sticks) butter, softened
2¼ cups sugar
4 large eggs, separated
1 teaspoon vanilla extract
1 cup buttermilk
Coconut pecan frosting (recipe follows)
Pecan halves, to serve (optional)

1. Preheat the oven to 350°F. Grease and flour three 9-inch round baking pans.

2. Stir together the chocolate and boiling water in a small bowl until smooth; set aside.

3. Sift the flour, baking soda, and salt into a medium bowl and set aside.

4. Beat the butter in a large bowl with an electric mixer until creamy. Gradually add the sugar, beating until light and fluffy. Add the egg yolks, one at a time, beating well after each addition. Scrape down the sides of the bowl, then stir in the vanilla extract. Add the flour mixture alternately with the chocolate mixture and buttermilk, beating just enough to blend.

5. In a small bowl, beat the egg whites until stiff peaks form.

6. Stir a little of the whites into the batter to lighten it, then fold in the remaining whites until combined. Pour into the prepared pans.

7. Bake for 25 to 30 minutes, until the cake tops spring back when touched lightly.

8. Cool the cakes in their pans on a wire rack for 10 minutes. Invert onto the rack and cool completely before frosting.

9. Spread the frosting between the layers and over the top and sides. Garnish with the pecan halves, if using, slice, and serve.

Coconut Pecan Frosting

This rich, crunchy frosting is traditional on German chocolate cake; it is also good on spice cake.

MAKES 2⅔ CUPS

1 (14-ounce) can sweetened condensed milk
3 large egg yolks, lightly beaten
½ cup (1 stick) butter
1 teaspoon vanilla extract
1⅓ cups sweetened coconut flakes
1 cup chopped pecans

1. Stir together the condensed milk, egg yolks, and butter in a medium saucepan. Cook over low heat, stirring constantly, until the mixture is thickened and bubbly.

2. Remove the saucepan from the heat. Stir in the vanilla extract, coconut flakes, and pecans and cool to room temperature. Beat until the frosting is of spreading consistency, and use as directed.

Banana Cream Cake

This is a heavenly cake filled with whipped cream and the goodness of bananas. If you like, add almonds as a garnish and flavor the whipped cream with almond extract instead of vanilla extract.

SERVES 10 TO 12

2 cups all-purpose flour
2 teaspoons baking powder
½ teaspoon baking soda
½ teaspoon salt
½ teaspoon ground ginger

½ cup shortening
1 cup granulated sugar
2 large eggs
2 teaspoons vanilla extract
1 cup ripe bananas, peeled and mashed
    (about 1 to 2 medium)
¼ cup buttermilk
1 cup heavy cream
¼ cup confectioners' sugar
2 medium bananas, peeled

1. Preheat the oven to 350°F. Grease and flour two 8-inch round cake pans. Line the bottoms with parchment paper and grease and flour the paper.

2. Sift the flour, baking powder, baking soda, salt, and ginger into a medium bowl. Set aside.

3. Beat the shortening with an electric mixer in a large bowl until creamy. Gradually add the granulated sugar and beat until light and fluffy. Beat in the eggs, one at a time, beating well after each addition. Scrape down the sides of the bowl, then add 1 teaspoon of vanilla extract and beat until combined. Set aside.

4. Combine the mashed bananas and buttermilk in a small bowl and mix until smooth.

5. With the mixer on low speed, alternately add the flour mixture and buttermilk mixture to the shortening mixture in 3 additions, beginning and ending with the flour. Pour into the prepared pans and smooth the tops.

6. Bake for 25 to 30 minutes, until a toothpick inserted into the cake centers comes out clean.

7. Cool the cakes in their pans on a wire rack for 10 minutes. Invert onto the rack, remove the parchment paper, and cool completely.

8. Beat the cream with the confectioners' sugar and remaining 1 teaspoon vanilla extract until stiff.

9. Spread half of the cream mixture on top of one of the cakes. Slice 1 banana and place the slices on the cream layer. Top with the second cake and spread the remaining whipped cream on it. Slice the remaining banana and use the slices as a garnish. Serve immediately.

Boston Cream Pie

Not actually a pie at all, this is a cake filled with custard and frosted with chocolate. At the Parker House Hotel in Boston, where it was created, it was called a Parker House Chocolate Pie. In 1996, it was chosen as the official state dessert of Massachusetts.

SERVES 10 TO 12

Cake:
½ cup all-purpose flour
1 cup cake flour
2 teaspoons baking powder
½ teaspoon salt
½ cup (1 stick) butter, softened
1 cup granulated sugar
2 large eggs
1 teaspoon vanilla extract
¾ cup milk

Filling:
1 cup half-and-half
½ cup milk
⅓ cup granulated sugar
Pinch of salt
2 tablespoons cornstarch
2 large egg yolks, slightly beaten
2 teaspoons vanilla extract

Frosting:
3 ounces (3 squares) semisweet chocolate
2 tablespoons butter
¼ cup half-and-half
½ teaspoon vanilla extract
½ cup confectioners' sugar, sifted

1. To make the cake, preheat the oven to 350°F. Grease and flour two 9-inch round cake pans and line the bottoms with parchment paper. Grease and flour the paper.

2. Sift the flours, baking powder, and salt together into a medium bowl. Set aside.

3. Beat the butter with an electric mixer in a large bowl until creamy. Gradually beat in the sugar until light and fluffy. Beat in the eggs, one at a time, beating well after each addition. Scrape down the sides of the bowl, then add the vanilla extract and beat until combined.

4. With the mixer on low speed, alternately add the flour mixture and milk to the bowl in 3 additions, beginning and ending with the flour. Pour into the prepared pans and smooth the tops.

5. Bake for about 15 to 20 minutes, until the cakes start to shrink away from the sides of the pans and the centers spring back when lightly touched.

6. Cool the cakes in the pans on a wire rack for 10 minutes, then invert onto the rack, remove the parchment paper, and cool completely.

7. To make the filling, combine the half-and-half with ¼ cup of milk in a small saucepan over medium heat and cook until bubbles begin to form along the edge of the mixture. Immediately add the sugar and salt and stir until dissolved. Remove the pan from the heat and set aside.

8. Combine the remaining ¼ cup milk with the cornstarch in a medium bowl and whisk to remove lumps. Whisk in the eggs, then add the hot cream mixture in a thin stream, whisking constantly. Return to the saucepan, place over medium heat, and bring to a boil. Reduce the heat, stirring constantly, until the custard thickens, about 5 minutes. Remove from the heat, stir in the vanilla extract, lay a piece of plastic wrap on top of the custard, and cool to room temperature.

9. To make the frosting, melt the chocolate with the butter in a heavy saucepan over low heat. Remove from the heat and stir in the half-and-half and vanilla extract in a slow, steady stream. When the mixture is smooth, beat in the confectioners' sugar until smooth; cool.

10. Spread the cooled filling over one of the cooled cakes and place the second cake on top. Pour the chocolate frosting evenly over the top, allowing it to spill down the sides.

11. Let the frosting set for about 2 hours before serving.

Coconut Cake

The largest of the nuts, the average coconut weighs 1½ pounds, and one coconut tree will produce thousands of coconuts over its 70-year life span. That is a good thing, since this buttery coconut cake is worth making again and again.

SERVES 10 TO 12

2 cups all-purpose flour
1 teaspoon baking powder
½ teaspoon salt
1 cup (2 sticks) butter, softened
1⅓ cups sugar
3 large eggs
1 teaspoon vanilla extract
1 cup coconut milk or milk, at room
    temperature
1½ cups sweetened coconut flakes
Frosting of choice (pages 394–395)

1. Preheat the oven to 350°F. Grease and flour two 8-inch round cake pans and line the bottoms with parchment paper. Grease and flour the paper.

2. Sift the flour, baking powder, and salt into a medium bowl and set aside.

3. Beat the butter with an electric mixer in a large bowl until creamy. Gradually beat in the sugar on medium speed until light and fluffy. Add the eggs, one at a time, beating well after each addition. Scrape down the sides of the bowl, then beat in the vanilla extract until combined.

4. With the mixer on low speed, alternately add the flour mixture and coconut milk to the butter mixture in 3 additions, beginning and ending with the flour. Fold in the coconut flakes. Pour into the prepared pans and smooth the tops.

5. Bake for 45 to 50 minutes, until a toothpick inserted into the cake centers comes out clean.

6. Cool the cakes in their pans on a wire rack for 10 minutes. Invert onto the rack, remove the parchment paper, and cool completely.

7. Spread the frosting between the layers and over the top and sides. Slice and serve.

TIP: Fresh coconut is superior in flavor to packaged coconut. To prepare a fresh coconut, pierce 2 of the eyes with a metal skewer or ice pick. Shake out the liquid, then bake the coconut at 400°F for 15 minutes. Set the hot coconut on the counter and give it a sharp blow with a hammer in the center of the shell; it should break cleanly in half. Peel away the brown skin with a sharp knife and grate the flesh in a food processor.

Gingerbread Cake

Gingerbread may have been invented by ancient Greeks, but it has evolved over time and place. The earliest settlers to the New World enjoyed gingerbread often; the first recipe appeared in Amelia Simmons' "American Cookery" in 1796. This dark, spiced cake is lovely served plain or accompanied by whipped cream, lemon curd, or applesauce.

SERVES 6

2 cups all-purpose flour
1½ teaspoons ground cinnamon
1 teaspoon baking soda
1 teaspoon ground ginger
¼ teaspoon salt
⅛ teaspoon ground cloves
½ cup (1 stick) butter, softened
½ cup firmly packed brown sugar
2 large eggs
1 tablespoon finely grated lemon zest
½ cup molasses
1 cup milk

1. Preheat the oven to 350°F. Grease and flour an 8-inch square pan.

2. Sift the flour, cinnamon, baking soda, ginger, salt, and cloves into a medium bowl. Set aside.

3. Beat the butter and brown sugar with an electric mixer in a large bowl until light and fluffy, about 3 minutes. Add the eggs, one at a time, beating well after each addition. Add the lemon zest and molasses and beat to combine.

4. With the mixer on low speed, alternately add the flour mixture and milk to the bowl in 3 additions, beginning and ending with the flour. Pour into the prepared pan.

5. Bake for 40 to 45 minutes, until a toothpick inserted into the center comes out clean.

6. Cool the cake on a wire rack. Serve warm or cooled.

Carrot Cake with Cream Cheese Frosting

The Greeks were the first to believe that eating carrots would improve your eyesight. During World War II, the British furthered this belief by saying that British pilots improved their night vision by eating large quantities of carrots. They were, however, only trying to encourage the eating of carrots, as they were one of the few foods that were not in short supply during the war. Regardless, this spiced cake and its rich frosting make a great argument for taste.

SERVES 10 TO 12

2 cups all-purpose flour
1½ teaspoons baking powder
1½ teaspoons ground cinnamon
1 teaspoon baking soda
½ teaspoon salt
4 large eggs
1½ cups sugar
1 cup oil
2 teaspoons vanilla extract
2½ cups finely grated carrots
1 cup pecans or walnuts, toasted and coarsely chopped
Cream cheese frosting (page 394)

1. Preheat the oven to 350°F. Grease and flour two 9-inch round cake pans. Line the bottoms of the pans with parchment paper. Grease and flour the paper.

2. Sift the flour, baking powder, cinnamon, baking soda, and salt into a medium bowl. Set aside.

3. Beat the eggs with an electric mixer in a large bowl until frothy. Gradually add the sugar and beat until the batter is thick and light colored, 3 to 4 minutes. Add the oil in a steady stream, scrape down the sides of the bowl, then beat in the vanilla extract. Add the flour mixture and beat just until blended. Fold in the carrots and nuts. Evenly divide the batter between the 2 prepared pans.

4. Bake for 30 to 35 minutes, until a toothpick inserted into the cake centers comes out clean.

5. Cool the cakes in their pans on a wire rack for 10 minutes. Invert onto the rack, remove the parchment paper, and cool completely.

6. Spread the frosting between the layers and over the top and sides. Slice and serve.

Spice Cake

Spice cakes smell wonderful as they bake, releasing a warm aroma of sugar and spices. As with carrot cake, cream cheese frosting is a perfect choice for this cake.

SERVES 10 TO 12

2 cups all-purpose flour
1½ teaspoons baking powder
1 teaspoon ground cinnamon
½ teaspoon baking soda
¼ teaspoon ground cloves
¼ teaspoon ground ginger
¼ teaspoon ground nutmeg
½ teaspoon salt
½ cup (1 stick) butter, softened
1½ cups sugar
2 large eggs
½ teaspoon vanilla extract
1½ cups buttermilk
Cream cheese frosting (page 394)

1. Preheat the oven to 350°F. Grease and flour two 8-inch round cake pans. Line the bottoms of the pans with parchment paper. Grease and flour the paper.

2. Sift the flour, baking powder, cinnamon, baking soda, cloves, ginger, nutmeg, and salt into a medium bowl. Set aside.

3. Beat the butter with an electric mixer in a large bowl until creamy. Gradually add the sugar and beat until light and fluffy. Add the eggs, one at a time, beating well after each addition. Scrape down the sides of the bowl, then add the vanilla extract and beat until combined.

4. With the mixer on low speed, alternately add the flour mixture and buttermilk to the bowl in 3 additions, beginning and ending with the flour. Pour into the prepared pans and smooth the tops.

5. Bake for 35 to 40 minutes, until a toothpick inserted into the cake centers comes out clean.

6. Cool the cakes in their pans on a wire rack for 10 minutes. Invert onto the rack, remove the parchment paper, and cool completely before frosting.

7. Spread the frosting between the layers and over the top and sides. Slice and serve.

Pumpkin Spice Cake

Pumpkins saved many an early settler from starvation. Today we enjoy many staple desserts using pumpkin—especially cakes. This recipe is delicious and classic, incorporating spices, butter, and brown sugar to enhance the pumpkin's mellow flavor.

SERVES 10 TO 12

Cake:
2 cups sifted cake flour
1 teaspoon baking powder
1 teaspoon baking soda
½ teaspoon salt
½ teaspoon ground cinnamon
¼ teaspoon ground ginger
⅛ teaspoon ground cloves
½ cup (1 stick) unsalted butter, softened
1¼ cups firmly packed brown sugar
2 large eggs
1 cup fresh or canned puréed pumpkin
1 teaspoon vanilla extract
½ cup buttermilk, at room temperature

Frosting:
1 (8-ounce) package cream cheese, softened
¼ cup (½ stick) butter, softened
¼ cup pure maple syrup, at room temperature
1⅓ cups sifted confectioners' sugar

1. Preheat the oven to 350°F. Grease and flour two 8-inch round cake pans. Line the bottoms of the pan with parchment paper. Grease and flour the paper.

2. To make the cake, stir the flour, baking powder, baking soda, salt, cinnamon, ginger, and cloves in a medium bowl. Set aside.

3. Beat the butter and brown sugar until light and fluffy. Add the eggs, one at a time, beating well after each addition. Beat in the pumpkin and vanilla extract until well blended.

4. Add the flour mixture and buttermilk alternately to the pumpkin batter, in 3 additions, beginning and ending with the flour mixture. Pour into the prepared pans.

5. Bake for approximately 30 minutes, until a toothpick inserted into the cake centers comes out clean.

6. Cool the cakes in their pans on a wire rack for 10 minutes. Invert onto the rack, remove the parchment paper, and cool completely.

7. To make the frosting, combine the cream cheese and butter in a food processor and pulse until smooth. Add the maple syrup and confectioners' sugar and process until creamy and well blended.

8. Spread the frosting between the layers and over the top and sides.

9. Refrigerate to set the frosting. Bring to room temperature before slicing and serving.

Black Walnut Cake

*Black walnuts are native to the eastern part of the
United States, growing on trees that can reach 100 feet in
height. They are much stronger in flavor than English walnuts,
but the two can be used interchangeably. This recipe has
a light lemon touch that complements the walnuts,
while its tube shape gives a more elegant presentation.*

SERVES 10 TO 12

1 cup (2 sticks) unsalted butter, softened
2 cups sugar
2 cups sifted all-purpose flour
¼ teaspoon salt
1 cup finely chopped black walnuts or toasted
   English walnuts
1 teaspoon lemon extract
1 teaspoon vanilla extract
5 large eggs

1. Preheat the oven to 350°F. Grease and flour a
10-inch tube pan.

2. In a large bowl, use an electric mixer to beat the
butter with the sugar until light and fluffy. Beat
in the flour, salt, and walnuts on low speed until
well blended. Beat in the lemon extract and vanilla
extract, then add the eggs, one at a time, beating
well after each addition. Increase the speed to
high and beat for 5 minutes. Pour the batter into
the prepared tube pan.

3. Bake for 55 to 65 minutes, until a toothpick
inserted into the cake comes out clean.

4. Cool the cake in the pan on a wire rack for
30 minutes, then invert onto the rack and cool
completely. Slice and serve.

Pound Cake

*Pound cakes were originally made from one pound each
of butter, sugar, eggs, and flour. No leaveners were used
other than the air whipped into the batter. In the days when the
illiteracy rate was high, this simple convention made
it easy to remember the recipe. After the invention of baking
powder, most recipes were altered to make the cake lighter
and less dense, but that hasn't affected the delicious
vanilla-butter taste of this recipe.*

SERVES 10 TO 12

2¼ cups all-purpose flour
2 teaspoons baking powder
½ teaspoon salt
½ cup (1 stick) butter, softened
1½ cups sugar
9 large egg yolks
1 teaspoon vanilla extract
1 cup milk

1. Preheat the oven to 325°F. Grease and flour a
9-inch tube pan.

2. Sift the flour, baking powder, and salt into a
medium bowl. Set aside.

3. Beat together the butter and sugar with an electric mixer in a large bowl until light and fluffy.
Add the egg yolks and continue beating until thick,
about 5 minutes. Beat in the vanilla extract.

4. With the mixer on low speed, alternately add
the flour mixture and milk to the bowl in 3 additions, beginning and ending with the flour. Pour
into the prepared pan.

5. Bake for 50 to 60 minutes, until a toothpick
inserted into the cake comes out clean.

6. Cool the cake in the pan on a wire rack for
30 minutes, then invert onto the rack and cool
completely. Slice and serve.

Angel Food Cake

*Angel food cakes were once known as angel cakes and
foam-style cakes. They are made with a large quantity
of egg whites and no shortening or leavening. There are several
theories as to who invented this cake. Some historians credit
the Pennsylvania Dutch, while other historians credit African-
American slaves in the South. Angel food cakes are also a
traditional African-American favorite for
post-funeral feasting.*

SERVES 10 TO 12

1½ cups confectioners' sugar
1 cup cake flour
¼ teaspoon salt
1½ cups large egg whites (from 11 to 12 large
    eggs), at room temperature
1½ teaspoons cream of tartar
1 cup granulated sugar
1 teaspoon vanilla extract

1. Preheat the oven to 350°F.

2. Sift the confectioners' sugar, flour, and salt into a medium bowl and set aside.

3. Beat the egg whites with an electric mixer in a large bowl until frothy. Add the cream of tartar and beat at medium speed until soft peaks form. Gradually add the granulated sugar, continuing to beat just until soft peaks form. Beat in the vanilla extract.

4. Sprinkle one-fourth of the dry ingredients over the whites and fold in gently but thoroughly. Fold in the remaining dry ingredients, one-third at a time. Pour evenly into an ungreased 10-inch tube pan with a removable bottom.

5. Bake for 40 to 45 minutes, until the top is light gold and the cake shrinks from the sides of the pan and springs back when touched lightly.

6. Thread the pan, upside down, onto the neck of a bottle and cool completely.

7. To remove the cake from the pan, run the tip of a long, narrow knife between the outer edge of the cake and pan. Tilt the pan on its side and gently tap the bottom edge against the counter. Rotate, tapping and turning a few more times, until the cake appears free. Invert onto a wire rack, tap firmly, and lift the pan from the cake.

8. To serve, slice the cake with a serrated knife, using a sawing motion. Pressing down on the knife only flattens the cake because it is so light.

Sponge Cake

Sponge cakes are light, airy cakes leavened with separately beaten egg yolks and beaten egg whites; they are fat free (except for the egg yolks). This sponge cake is flavored with a little orange or lemon zest. You can use sponge cake in trifles with custard and fruit, or it is delicious plain. Serve with fresh strawberries or raspberries in syrup for added flavor and color.

SERVES 10 TO 12

1½ cups large egg whites (from 11 to 12 large
    eggs), at room temperature
1 teaspoon cream of tartar
½ teaspoon salt
1⅓ cups granulated sugar
1⅓ cups sifted all-purpose flour
⅔ cup large egg yolks (from 8 to 9 large eggs),
    at room temperature
1 teaspoon finely grated lemon zest or orange
    zest
Confectioners' sugar

1. Preheat the oven to 325°F. Grease a 10-inch tube pan.

2. Beat the egg whites with an electric mixer in a large bowl until foamy. Add the cream of tartar and salt and beat until the whites begin to hold their shape. Gradually add the granulated sugar, beating until the mixture is stiff and glossy. Carefully fold in the flour and set aside.

3. Beat the egg yolks with the lemon zest in a medium bowl until thick and lemon colored. Gradually fold into the egg white mixture, then pour into the prepared pan.

4. Bake for 50 to 55 minutes, until a toothpick inserted into the cake comes out clean.

5. Thread the pan, upside down, onto the neck of a bottle and cool completely.

6. To remove the cake from the pan, run the tip of a long, narrow knife between the outer edge of the cake and pan. Tilt the pan on its side and gently tap the bottom edge against the counter. Rotate, tapping and turning a few more times, until the cake appears free. Invert onto a wire rack, tap firmly, and lift the pan from the cake.

7. Dust with confectioners' sugar and serve.

Jelly Roll

This tasty sponge cake is rolled up around a filling of jelly. It reveals a lovely pinwheel pattern when cut. The jelly roll has been around since the 1880s.

SERVES 10

¼ cup confectioners' sugar
¾ cup cake flour
¾ teaspoon baking powder
¼ teaspoon salt
2 tablespoons water
4 large eggs, separated
12 tablespoons (¾ cup) granulated sugar
½ teaspoon vanilla extract
½ teaspoon cream of tartar
1 cup tart red jelly, such as currant, raspberry, or strawberry

1. Preheat the oven to 400°F. Line a shallow 15½ x 10½-inch jelly roll pan (or any low-sided baking sheet) with waxed paper so that the paper extends ½ inch over the pan edges. Grease the paper lightly. Prepare a towel by laying it out on a flat, clean surface and sprinkling it evenly with 2 tablespoons of the confectioners' sugar. Set the pan and towel aside.

2. Sift the flour with the baking powder and salt into a small bowl 3 times. Set aside.

3. Combine the water and egg yolks in a large bowl and place over hot water. Beat with a rotary beater until very thick and light colored. Add 6 tablespoons of granulated sugar gradually and continue to beat until thick. Remove the bowl from over the hot water and beat in the vanilla extract.

4. Sift the flour over the yolk mixture in 4 batches, beating until smooth after each addition. Set aside.

5. Beat the egg whites with the cream of tartar in a medium bowl until soft peaks form. Gradually beat in the remaining 6 tablespoons granulated sugar until stiff, shiny peaks form.

6. Fold the yolk mixture into the whites until well blended. Pour into the prepared pan and spread lightly to the edges.

7. Bake for 7 to 8 minutes or until the cake springs back when lightly touched.

8. Remove the cake from the oven and place on a wire rack. Quickly loosen the edges with a thin-bladed knife and turn out onto the prepared towel. Strip off the paper, then roll up evenly, from the narrow side, on the towel. Unroll gently and spread jelly evenly over the top. Reroll and wrap in wax paper. Store in a cool place for 10 to 15 minutes.

9. Dust with the remaining 2 tablespoons confectioners' sugar and serve.

Orange Chiffon Cake

In 1948, the chiffon cake, a cross between a butter and a sponge cake, was hailed by Betty Crocker as the "cake discovery of the century." It was invented in 1927 by an insurance salesman, who sold it to restaurants in the Los Angeles area. Eventually he sold his recipe to General Mills, which printed the recipe and included it in packages of Gold Medal flour. The butter in this recipe is replaced by oil, with the egg whites stiffly beaten and folded into the batter. The result is a very light, moist cake.

SERVES 10 TO 12

7 large eggs, separated
2¼ cups sifted cake flour
1½ cups superfine white sugar
1 tablespoon baking powder
½ teaspoon salt
½ cup oil
¾ cup orange juice
2 tablespoons finely grated orange zest
1 teaspoon vanilla extract
¾ teaspoon cream of tartar

1. Separate the eggs and place the whites in one bowl and 6 egg yolks in another, discarding the last yolk. Cover both with plastic wrap and bring them to room temperature, about 30 minutes.

2. Preheat the oven to 325°F.

3. Stir the flour, 1¼ cups of superfine sugar, the baking powder, and salt into a large bowl.

4. Make a well in the center of the flour mixture and add the egg yolks, oil, orange juice, orange zest, and vanilla extract. Beat for 1 minute with an electric mixer at medium speed until smooth. Set aside.

5. Put the egg whites in a separate medium bowl and beat until foamy. Add the cream of tartar and continue to beat until soft peaks form. Gradually beat in the remaining ¼ cup superfine sugar, beating until stiff peaks form.

6. Gently fold the egg white mixture into the batter just until blended. Pour into an ungreased 10-inch tube pan.

7. Bake for 55 to 60 minutes, until a toothpick inserted into the cake comes out clean and the top of the cake springs back when lightly pressed.

8. Thread the pan, upside down, onto the neck of a bottle and cool completely before removing the cake from the pan, 1½ to 2 hours.

9. To remove the cake from the pan, run a thin-bladed knife around the inside of the tube pan and center core. Invert onto a greased wire rack, cool, and serve.

Pineapple Upside-Down Cake

The classic American pineapple upside-down cake dates to sometime after the introduction of canned pineapple in 1903. The Hawaiian Pineapple Co. (now Dole Pineapple) held a pineapple recipe contest in 1925, and of the more than 60,000 recipes sent in, 2,500 were for pineapple upside-down cake. The glazed, inverted pineapple top is delicious with the tender cake beneath. A variation using apricots follows.

SERVES 8

1 (20-ounce) can pineapple slices
¼ cup (½ stick) butter
1 cup firmly packed brown sugar
16 pecan halves
1 cup all-purpose flour

1 teaspoon baking powder
½ teaspoon salt
3 large eggs, separated
1 cup granulated sugar
Red maraschino cherries, to serve

1. Preheat the oven to 350°F.

2. Drain the pineapple, reserving 5 tablespoons of the juice.

3. Melt the butter in a 9-inch cast-iron skillet over low heat. Stir in the brown sugar and remove from the heat. Arrange 8 pineapple slices in a single layer over the brown sugar mixture. Fill the centers and spaces between the pineapple slices with the pecans placed flat side up. Set aside.

4. Sift the flour, baking powder, and salt into a medium bowl and set aside.

5. In a separate medium bowl, beat the egg yolks with an electric mixer at medium speed until thick and lemon colored. Gradually add the granulated sugar, and continue to beat. Mix in the flour mixture and reserved pineapple juice.

6. Beat the egg whites in a separate medium bowl until stiff peaks form. Fold into the cake batter. Pour the batter evenly over the pineapple slices.

7. Bake for 40 to 45 minutes, until a toothpick inserted into the center comes out clean.

8. Cool the cake in the skillet for 30 minutes, then invert it onto a serving plate. Place a maraschino cherry in the center of each pineapple ring. Serve warm.

Apricot Upside-Down Cake

Replace the pineapple in Pineapple Upside-Down Cake with 8 to 12 peeled apricot halves, placing the apricots, flat side up, in the brown sugar mixture. Replace the pineapple juice with 5 tablespoons apricot nectar. Omit the pecans and the cherries and proceed with the recipe as directed.

...n Spice Cake

...the subtle tart–sweetness of plums
...ile plums can be found in many
...sh plums from local farmers'
...mmer season are best.

5 cups all-purpose flour
2 teaspoons ground cinnamon
½ teaspoon baking soda
½ teaspoon ground allspice
½ teaspoon ground ginger
½ teaspoon ground nutmeg
¼ teaspoon ground cloves
¼ teaspoon salt
1 cup oil
2 cups sugar
3 large eggs
1 teaspoon vanilla extract
1 teaspoon almond extract
Whipped cream, to serve

1. Preheat the oven to 350°F. Line a 9-inch springform pan with aluminum foil and grease the foil.

2. Halve and pit the plums and place them, cut side up, in the bottom of the pan. Set aside.

3. Sift together the flour, cinnamon, baking soda, allspice, ginger, nutmeg, cloves, and salt into a medium bowl and set aside.

4. Beat the oil and sugar with an electric mixer on low speed in a large bowl until well blended. Add the eggs one at a time, beating after each addition, until well blended. Beat in the vanilla extract and almond extract, then add the flour mixture and beat until well blended. Pour slowly over the plums.

5. Bake the cake for 50 to 60 minutes, until a toothpick inserted into the center comes out clean.

6. Set aside to cool for 15 minutes before removing the sides and inverting onto a serving plate. Remove the aluminum foil and serve warm, with whipped cream.

Sour Cream Coffee Cake

Coffee cakes are informal cakes that are often served for breakfast. The sour cream coffee cake, with its topping and filling of nuts and cinnamon streusel, is one of the most popular of the genre. It is similar to a butter cake, but the addition of sour cream gives this cake a richer texture and taste. In recent years, mini chocolate chips have been added to enrich the already tasty streusel topping.

SERVES 12

Cake:
2 cups sifted cake flour
¾ teaspoon baking powder
½ teaspoon baking soda
¼ teaspoon salt
10 tablespoons (1¼ sticks) butter, softened
1 cup granulated sugar
2 large eggs
1½ teaspoons vanilla extract
⅔ cup sour cream

Filling and topping:
¼ cup firmly packed brown sugar
¾ cup toasted and chopped pecans
⅓ cup mini chocolate chips
1 teaspoon ground cinnamon
1 tablespoon all-purpose flour

Crumb Cake

Coffee klatches were informal get-togethers over coffee. Crumb cake is a fitting accompaniment to coffee and conversation because of its buttery, cinnamon-sugar topping. "Coffee klatch" comes from the German word "kaffeeklatsch," meaning "coffee gossip."

SERVES 12

Cake:
3 cups all-purpose flour
1 cup granulated sugar
1 tablespoon baking powder
1 teaspoon salt
2 large eggs
1 cup milk
¼ cup oil
2 teaspoons vanilla extract

Crumb topping:
2½ cups all-purpose flour
1 cup firmly packed brown sugar
2 teaspoons ground cinnamon
1 cup (2 sticks) butter, melted and cooled
Confectioners' sugar

1. Preheat the oven to 350°F. Grease and flour a 9-inch springform pan.

2. To make the cake, stir together the flour, baking powder, baking soda, and salt in a medium bowl. Set aside.

3. Beat the butter with an electric mixer in a large bowl until creamy. Gradually add the sugar and continue to beat until light and fluffy, 3 to 4 minutes. Add the eggs, one at a time, beating well after each addition, then beat in the vanilla extract.

4. With the mixer on low speed, alternately add the flour mixture and sour cream to the bowl in 3 additions, starting and ending with the flour. Mix only until combined and then set aside.

5. To make the filling and topping, stir together the brown sugar, pecans, chocolate chips, cinnamon, and flour in a small bowl. Set aside.

6. Spoon half of the batter into the prepared pan, smoothing the top. Sprinkle half of the nut mixture on top of the batter. Cover with the remaining batter, then top with the remaining nut mixture.

7. Bake for 45 to 50 minutes, until a toothpick inserted into the center comes out clean.

8. Remove from the oven and let rest for about 10 minutes before releasing the sides of the pan. Serve warm or at room temperature.

1. Preheat the oven to 350°F. Grease and flour a 9 x 13-inch baking dish.

2. To make the cake, sift the flour, sugar, baking powder, and salt into a medium bowl.

3. Beat the eggs, milk, oil, and vanilla extract in a large bowl, then fold the flour mixture into the bowl until combined. Do not overmix. Spread the batter evenly in the prepared baking dish.

4. To make the crumb topping, stir together the flour, brown sugar, and cinnamon in a medium bowl. Pour the butter over the mixture and stir until large crumbs form. Sprinkle the crumbs over the cake batter.

5. Bake for 20 to 30 minutes, until a toothpick inserted into the center comes out clean.

6. Cool the cake in the pan on a wire rack for at least 20 minutes. Sprinkle with confectioners' sugar and serve warm or at room temperature.

German Apple Cake

There are probably as many variations of German apple cake as there are bakers of German descent in this country. In this cake, concentric circles of apples top a simple butter cake. It makes a lovely dessert, or it can be served as a coffee cake.

SERVES 10 TO 12

1⅔ cups all-purpose flour
1 teaspoon baking powder
½ teaspoon salt
½ cup (1 stick) butter, softened
1 cup plus 2 tablespoons granulated sugar
3 large eggs
6 to 7 medium tart apples, such as Granny
    Smith or Rome Beauty
½ teaspoon ground cinnamon
Confectioners' sugar

1. Preheat the oven to 375°F. Grease a 9-inch springform pan.

2. Sift the flour, baking powder, and salt into a medium bowl and set aside.

3. Beat the butter and 1 cup granulated sugar in a large bowl until light and fluffy. Add the eggs, one at a time, beating well after each addition. Add the flour mixture and blend well.

4. Spoon the batter into the prepared springform pan. Peel, core, and quarter the apples, then slice evenly. Arrange in concentric circles to cover the batter.

5. Mix the remaining 2 tablespoons granulated sugar and the cinnamon in a small bowl and sprinkle over the apples.

6. Bake for 45 to 60 minutes, until a toothpick inserted into the center comes out clean.

7. Let the cake cool in the pan on a wire rack.

8. Release the sides of the pan, sprinkle the cake with confectioners' sugar, and serve immediately.

Glazed Dutch Apple-Nut Cake

Walnuts, apples, and cinnamon add classic flavor to this simple cake. If you like, substitute pears for the apples.

SERVES 10 TO 12

Cake:
2 cups all-purpose flour
1 teaspoon baking soda
1 teaspoon salt
2 teaspoons ground cinnamon
2 large eggs
1 teaspoon vanilla extract
1 cup oil
1½ cups granulated sugar
4 medium tart apples, such as Granny Smith
    or Rome Beauty, peeled, cored, and finely
    chopped
1 cup walnuts, finely chopped

Glaze:
1 cup sifted confectioners' sugar
¼ teaspoon vanilla extract
Milk

1. Preheat the oven to 350°F. Grease and flour a 9-inch tube pan.

2. To make the cake, sift together the flour, baking soda, salt, and cinnamon into a medium bowl and set aside.

3. Beat the eggs and vanilla extract with an electric mixer on high speed in a large bowl for 2 minutes, until light. Gradually beat in the oil, beating for 2 minutes or until thick, then gradually beat in the sugar. Alternately add the flour mixture, apples, and walnuts, beating well after each addition. Beat at medium speed for 3 minutes and spoon into the prepared pan.

4. Bake for 60 minutes, until a toothpick inserted into the center comes out clean.

5. Cool the cake in the pan on a wire rack for 30 minutes, then invert onto the rack and cool completely.

6. To make the glaze, combine the confectioners' sugar and vanilla extract in a small bowl. Add the milk, 1 tablespoon at a time, until the

glaze is fairly liquid and has a smooth consistency. Drizzle over the cake and let sit for at least 1 hour to set. Slice and serve.

Brandied Fruitcake

Fruitcake has become the topic of jokes, with legends about cakes that are passed from one generation to the next. But spiced, dense, colorful fruitcake has its fans, and for them, no Christmas would be complete without it. Start the fruitcakes about a month before you want to enjoy them or give them away.

MAKES 2

1½ pounds mixed diced candied fruit (about 3 cups)
2½ cups chopped pecans
1 (15-ounce) package golden raisins
2½ cups brandy
2 tablespoons dry bread crumbs
3 cups all-purpose flour
1 teaspoon baking powder
½ teaspoon salt
½ teaspoon ground cinnamon
¼ teaspoon ground allspice
1 cup (2 sticks) butter, softened
2 cups firmly packed brown sugar
4 large eggs
¾ cup cold brewed coffee

1. Combine the fruit, pecans, raisins, and ½ cup of brandy in a large bowl. Toss to mix thoroughly, cover, and let stand for 3 to 5 hours.

2. Preheat the oven to 275°F. Generously butter two 9-inch loaf pans. Sprinkle each with 1 tablespoon of bread crumbs, rotating the pans to coat evenly.

3. Sift the flour, baking powder, salt, cinnamon, and allspice into a medium bowl and set aside.

4. Beat the butter with the brown sugar in a large bowl until smooth. Add the eggs, one at a time, beating well after each addition, and continue to beat until light and fluffy. Add the flour mixture alternately with the coffee, stirring after each addition, until the batter is just blended.

5. Pour the batter over the fruit mixture and mix until well combined. Spoon into the prepared pans.

6. Bake for 1½ hours, until a toothpick inserted into the center comes out clean.

7. Cool in the pans on wire racks for 20 minutes, then invert onto the racks and cool completely.

8. Place each cake on a large sheet of aluminum foil and sprinkle each with ¼ cup of brandy. Wrap the cakes tightly in the foil, sealing well. Store in a cool, dark place for 7 days.

9. Unwrap the cakes and sprinkle each with an additional ¼ cup of brandy. Rewrap. Repeat this procedure each week for the next 2 weeks. Then let the cakes mellow for a final week before serving.

One-Bowl Chocolate Snacking Cake

Even grandmothers resorted to shortcuts once in a while. Combine all the ingredients into one bowl, scrape the batter into the baking pan, and bake. There's no need to frost this cake, as it is rich and moist when served plain. A dusting of confectioners' sugar is a nice but unnecessary touch. Serve with a dollop of ice cream or whipped cream.

SERVES 6

2 cups all-purpose flour
1 cup sugar
1 cup cold brewed coffee
1 cup mayonnaise
¼ cup cocoa powder (preferably Dutch processed)
2 teaspoons baking powder

1. Preheat the oven to 350°F. Grease and flour a 9-inch square baking dish.

2. Combine the flour, sugar, coffee, mayonnaise, cocoa powder, and baking powder in a medium bowl and stir until well blended. Pour into the prepared baking dish.

3. Bake for 30 minutes, until a toothpick inserted into the center comes out clean.

4. Cool before serving.

Applesauce Cake

This tasty cake is made easy by using applesauce. Frosting is not required, but cream cheese frosting is a nice accompaniment to the mild spice, raisins, and chopped walnuts.

SERVES 6

2 cups sifted all-purpose flour
1 cup sugar
1 teaspoon salt
2 teaspoons baking soda
1 teaspoon ground cinnamon
½ teaspoon ground nutmeg
¼ teaspoon ground cloves
2 cups applesauce
½ cup (1 stick) butter, melted
1 cup raisins
1 cup chopped walnuts
Cream cheese frosting (page 394), optional

1. Preheat the oven to 350°F. Grease and flour a 9-inch square baking dish.

2. Sift the flour, sugar, salt, baking soda, cinnamon, nutmeg, and cloves into a medium bowl. Beat in the applesauce and butter until smooth, then fold in the raisins and walnuts. Pour into the prepared pan.

3. Bake for 45 to 50 minutes, until a toothpick inserted into the center comes out clean.

4. Cool in the pan on a wire rack.

5. Spread the frosting over the top and sides, if using. Slice and serve.

New York Cheesecake

New York cheesecakes are rich and creamy, often topped with fruit. This style of cheesecake was made famous by Lindy's restaurant in New York City and is a typical dessert found in American steakhouses.

SERVES 16

1 cup graham cracker crumbs
1 cup plus 3 tablespoons sugar
3 tablespoons butter, melted
5 (8-ounce) packages cream cheese, softened
3 tablespoons all-purpose flour
1 tablespoon vanilla extract
1 cup sour cream
4 large eggs
1 (21-ounce) can cherry pie filling (optional)

1. Preheat the oven to 325°F.

2. Mix the crumbs, 3 tablespoons sugar, and the butter in a small bowl. Press firmly onto the bottom of a 9-inch springform pan. Bake for 10 minutes and set aside.

3. In a large bowl, beat together the cream cheese, remaining 1 cup sugar, the flour, and vanilla extract with an electric mixer on medium speed until well blended. Add the sour cream, then mix in the eggs on low speed just until blended; do not overbeat. Pour over the crust.

4. Bake for 70 minutes, until the center is almost set.

5. Run a knife around the rim of the pan to loosen the cake; cool before removing the pan sides.

6. Refrigerate for 4 hours or overnight. Top with pie filling, if using, before serving.

TIP: Overbeating the batter once the eggs have been added may cause the cake to crack as it cools.

Chocolate Icebox Cake

When a recipe has "icebox" in the title, you know it is an old one. The icebox was invented in 1803 and the Frigidaire refrigerator entered the marketplace in 1919. Sometime between those two milestones, this heavenly chocolate cake was invented.

SERVES 8 TO 10

Cake:
¼ cup water
4 ounces (4 squares) baking chocolate, chopped
½ cup granulated sugar
1 cup (2 sticks) butter, softened
1 cup confectioners' sugar
⅛ teaspoon salt
2 teaspoons vanilla extract
4 large eggs, separated
36 ladyfingers

Topping:
1 cup heavy cream
1 tablespoon confectioners' sugar

1. To make the cake, combine the water, chocolate, and granulated sugar in the top of a double boiler over simmering water. Stir until the chocolate is melted and the mixture is smooth. Set aside to cool.

2. Beat the butter and confectioners' sugar with an electric mixer in a large bowl until smooth. Beat in the salt and vanilla extract and set aside.

3. Lightly beat the egg yolks in a medium bowl, then beat into the cooled chocolate mixture. Pour into the butter mixture and blend well.

4. Beat the egg whites on medium-high speed in a separate medium bowl until stiff peaks form. Fold into the chocolate batter.

5. Line the sides and bottom of a 10-inch springform pan with half of the ladyfingers. Spoon half the chocolate mixture on top and make a second layer of ladyfingers. Top with the remaining chocolate.

6. Refrigerate for 24 hours.

7. To make the topping, whip the cream on medium speed until it thickens. Add the confectioners' sugar, and continue to whip until soft peaks form. Spread on the cake with a spatula and serve immediately.

Babka

Babka is a sweet, spongy, yeast-raised cake that is traditionally baked for Easter Sunday in Russia and Poland; it was also popular in Jewish communities. Babka was introduced to the United States by immigrants and is popular in bakeries around New York City. Babkas can be served plain, dusted with confectioners' sugar, or glazed, as in this recipe.

SERVES 6 TO 8

Babka:
¾ cup milk
2¼ teaspoons (one ¼-ounce package) active
    dry yeast
¼ cup warm water
4 cups all-purpose flour

½ cup granulated sugar
2 teaspoons finely grated lemon zest
½ teaspoon salt
½ cup (1 stick) butter, softened
3 large egg yolks
1 cup raisins

Glaze:
2 tablespoons lemon juice
¼ cup confectioners' sugar
¼ cup water

1. To make the babka, bring the milk to a boil in a small saucepan, then cool to about 130°F.

2. Sprinkle the yeast over the water in a small bowl. Let stand for 5 minutes, until bubbly.

3. Combine 1½ cups of flour with ¼ cup of sugar, the lemon zest, salt, and dissolved yeast in a large bowl. Gradually beat in the warm milk until smooth. Let rest for a few minutes to give the yeast a chance to activate.

4. Beat in the butter, egg yolks, and remaining ¼ cup sugar, then beat in the remaining 2½ cups flour.

5. Cover the bowl loosely with plastic wrap or a clean cloth and let it sit in a warm, draft-free place until the dough has doubled in size, 1 to 1½ hours.

6. Stir the dough down and mix in the raisins.

7. Grease a 9-inch tube pan and turn the dough into the pan. Level the top with a spatula. Cover again and let rise until the dough reaches the top of the pan, 2½ to 3 hours.

8. Preheat the oven to 350°F, with the oven rack in the lower third of the oven.

9. Bake for 30 to 35 minutes, until the top is browned and a toothpick inserted into the cake comes out clean.

10. Cool on a wire rack for 10 minutes.

11. To make the glaze, combine the lemon juice, confectioners' sugar, and water in a small saucepan and bring to a boil. Reduce the heat to a simmer and stir constantly until syrupy, about 5 minutes.

12. Carefully turn the babka out of the pan. Turn right side up and brush the warm cake with the lemon glaze. Cool completely before serving.

Cream Cheese Frosting

This is the classic frosting for carrot cake. It is also wonderful on any spice cake. A variation using lemon follows.

MAKES ENOUGH FOR TWO 9-INCH CAKE LAYERS OR ONE 9 X 13-INCH CAKE

½ cup (1 stick) butter, softened
2 (8-ounce) packages cream cheese, softened
2½ cups sifted confectioners' sugar
1 teaspoon vanilla extract

1. In a medium bowl, beat the butter and cream cheese with an electric mixer on low speed until very smooth and free of lumps.

2. Gradually add the confectioners' sugar and beat on low speed until fully incorporated and smooth. Add the vanilla extract and continue beating until smooth and creamy.

3. Apply the frosting as directed.

Lemon Cream Cheese Frosting

Add the finely grated zest of 1 lemon and 2 table-spoons fresh lemon juice with the vanilla extract in Cream Cheese Frosting. Complete the recipe as directed.

Vanilla Buttercream Frosting

This frosting can be used on any butter cake—white, yellow, chocolate, or spice. Its creamy flavor is complementary but not overpowering. Three variations follow.

MAKES ENOUGH FOR TWO 9-INCH CAKE LAYERS OR ONE 9 X 13-INCH CAKE

1 pound (4 sticks) butter, softened
2 cups sifted confectioners' sugar
1 tablespoon vanilla extract

1. In a medium bowl, beat the butter with an electric mixer on low speed while adding the confectioners' sugar. When all the sugar is mixed in, scrape down the sides of the bowl. Add the vanilla extract and beat on medium speed for 5 to 7 minutes.

2. Fill and frost the cake, then refrigerate for 10 to 20 minutes to set before serving.

Lemon Buttercream

Substitute 2 teaspoons lemon extract for the vanilla extract in Vanilla Buttercream Frosting and complete the recipe as directed.

½ cup (1 stick) butter, softened
2½ cups confectioners' sugar
¼ cup cocoa powder (preferably Dutch processed)
¼ cup heavy cream
1 ounce (1 square) baking chocolate, melted
1 tablespoon light or dark corn syrup

1. Beat the butter with an electric mixer at medium speed in a medium bowl until creamy.

2. Gradually add the confectioners' sugar and cocoa powder alternately with the cream and melted chocolate, scraping the bowl often, until well mixed, 2 to 3 minutes. Beat in the corn syrup and continue beating until smooth and creamy.

3. Apply the frosting as directed.

Seven-Minute Frosting

Simple and fast, this classic, fluffy white frosting is often used on coconut cake.

MAKES ENOUGH FOR TWO 9-INCH CAKE LAYERS OR ONE 9 X 13-INCH CAKE

1½ cups sugar
¼ teaspoon cream of tartar or 1 tablespoon corn syrup
⅛ teaspoon salt
⅓ cup water
2 large egg whites
1½ teaspoons vanilla extract

1. Combine the sugar, cream of tartar, salt, water, and egg whites in the top of a double boiler. Beat with an electric mixer for 1 minute.

2. Place the pan over boiling water, making sure that the boiling water does not touch the bottom of the top pan. (If this happens, it could cause your frosting to become grainy.) Beat constantly on high speed for 7 minutes, then beat in the vanilla extract.

3. Apply the frosting as directed.

Orange Buttercream

Substitute 2 teaspoons orange extract for the vanilla extract in Vanilla Buttercream Frosting and complete the recipe as directed.

Almond Buttercream

Substitute 2 teaspoons almond extract for the vanilla extract in Vanilla Buttercream Frosting and complete the recipe as directed.

Chocolate Buttercream Frosting

This smooth and creamy chocolate frosting is a tasty signature for any cake.

MAKES ENOUGH FOR TWO 9-INCH CAKE LAYERS OR ONE 9 X 13-INCH CAKE

Chocolate Chip Cookies

In 1937, Ruth Wakefield invented the chocolate chip cookie at the Toll House Inn she ran with her husband, Kenneth, near Whitman, Massachusetts. She was trying to make her famous Butter Drop Do cookie, but ran out of baker's chocolate, so she broke up a bar of Nestlé's semisweet chocolate. She didn't melt the chocolate, thinking it would melt during the baking and mix with the batter. Needless to say, it didn't, but the cookies were a huge success. She published the recipe in several newspapers and eventually traded the rights to Nestlé in exchange for a lifetime supply of free chocolate. At first, Nestlé tried to make the recipe easier by including a small chopper in its chocolate packages. Finally, in 1939, the chocolate morsels that we know today were introduced.

MAKES ABOUT 36

2¼ cups all-purpose flour
1 teaspoon baking soda
1 teaspoon salt
1 cup (2 sticks) butter, softened
¾ cup granulated sugar
¾ cup firmly packed brown sugar
1 teaspoon vanilla extract
2 large eggs
2 cups (12-ounce package) semisweet chocolate chips
1 cup chopped nuts of choice

1. Preheat the oven to 375°F.

2. Sift the flour, baking soda, and salt into a medium bowl and set aside.

3. Beat the butter, sugars, and vanilla extract in a large bowl. Add the eggs, one at a time, beating well after each addition. Gradually beat in the flour mixture, then stir in the chocolate chips and nuts.

4. Drop rounded tablespoons of dough onto ungreased baking sheets.

5. Bake for 9 to 11 minutes, until golden brown.

6. Let stand for 2 minutes, then transfer to wire racks to cool completely.

Chocolate Chip Oatmeal Cookies

Crossing an oatmeal cookie with a chocolate chip cookie creates the best of both worlds—oatmeal for chewy, hearty texture and chocolate chips to add sweetness to each bite.

MAKES ABOUT 36

1¼ cups all-purpose flour
½ teaspoon baking soda
1 teaspoon salt
1 cup (2 sticks) butter, softened
1 cup firmly packed brown sugar
½ cup granulated sugar
2 large eggs
2 teaspoons vanilla extract
3 cups quick-cooking oats
1 cup chopped walnuts
1 cup semisweet chocolate chips

1. Preheat the oven to 375°F.

2. Sift the flour, baking soda, and salt into a medium bowl and set aside.

3. Beat together the butter and sugars in a large bowl. Add the eggs, one at a time, beating well after each addition. Beat in the vanilla extract,

then gradually beat in the flour mixture until just blended. Fold in the oats, walnuts, and chocolate chips.

4. Drop rounded tablespoons of dough onto ungreased baking sheets.

5. Bake for 12 to 15 minutes, until golden brown.

6. Let stand for 2 minutes, then transfer to wire racks to cool completely.

Oatmeal Raisin Cookies

The spices in these cookies fill the house with an exquisite aroma as they bake. These are the quintessential school lunchbox cookies.

MAKES ABOUT 36

1½ cups all-purpose flour
1 teaspoon baking soda
1 teaspoon ground cinnamon
½ teaspoon ground cloves
½ teaspoon salt
1 cup (2 sticks) butter, softened
1 cup firmly packed brown sugar
½ cup granulated sugar
2 large eggs
1 teaspoon vanilla extract
3 cups rolled oats
1 cup raisins

1. Preheat the oven to 375°F.

2. Sift the flour, baking soda, cinnamon, cloves, and salt into a medium bowl.

3. In a large bowl, beat together the butter, sugars, eggs, and vanilla extract until smooth. Add the flour mixture to the bowl and blend thoroughly. Stir in the oats and raisins.

4. Drop rounded tablespoons of dough onto ungreased baking sheets.

5. Bake for 12 to 15 minutes, until golden brown.

6. Let stand for 2 minutes, then transfer to wire racks to cool completely.

Peanut Butter Cookies

In 1890, a St. Louis physician encouraged the owner of a food products company, George A. Bayle Jr., to process and package ground peanut paste as a nutritious protein substitute for red meat for people with poor teeth. But it wasn't until it was sold as a concession treat at a stand at the 1904 St. Louis Universal Exposition that peanut butter became popular. The sweet–salty–chewy cookies this recipe produces are perfect with a tall glass of cold milk.

MAKES ABOUT 48

3 cups all-purpose flour
2 teaspoons baking soda
½ teaspoon salt
1 cup shortening
1 cup granulated sugar
1 cup firmly packed brown sugar
1 cup crunchy peanut butter
1 teaspoon vanilla extract
2 large eggs

1. Preheat the oven to 350°F.

2. Sift the flour, baking soda, and salt into a medium bowl and set aside.

3. Beat together the shortening, sugars, peanut butter, and vanilla extract. Add the eggs, one at a time, beating well after each addition. Stir the flour mixture into the bowl and blend thoroughly.

4. Shape the dough into 2-inch balls and place them 2 inches apart on ungreased baking sheets. Press each with the tongs of a fork twice, in opposite directions, to make a crisscross pattern.

5. Bake for 8 to 10 minutes, until golden brown.

6. Let stand for 2 minutes, then transfer to wire racks to cool completely.

Peanut Blossoms

These peanut butter cookies with a giant chocolate chip made of a Hershey's Kiss look beautiful, have a beautiful name, and taste even better.

MAKES ABOUT 48

½ cup shortening
¾ cup creamy peanut butter
½ cup granulated sugar, plus additional for coating
½ cup firmly packed brown sugar
1 large egg
2 tablespoons milk
1 teaspoon vanilla extract
1¾ cups all-purpose flour
1 teaspoon baking soda
½ teaspoon salt
48 solid chocolate-drop candies, such as Hershey's Kisses, unwrapped

1. Preheat the oven to 375°F.

2. Beat together the shortening and peanut butter in a large bowl. Gradually add the sugars, beating until light and fluffy. Beat in the egg, milk, and vanilla extract until well combined. Set aside.

3. In a small bowl, combine the flour, baking soda, and salt. Gradually add to the peanut butter mixture, beating until well combined.

4. Shape the dough into 1-inch balls and roll in granulated sugar. Place 2 inches apart on ungreased baking sheets.

5. Bake for 8 to 10 minutes, until golden brown, and remove from the oven. Immediately top each cookie with a chocolate candy, pressing down firmly until the cookie cracks around the edge.

6. Let stand for 2 minutes, then remove to wire racks to cool completely.

Raisin Cookies

Make sure your raisins are worthy of these delicious cookies. If they are dried out, cover them with boiling water and let stand for 10 minutes, then drain. The raisins should be soft and chewy to complement the golden cookie.

MAKES ABOUT 36

2 cups all-purpose flour
½ teaspoon baking soda
½ teaspoon salt
1½ teaspoons finely grated orange zest
1½ cups raisins
½ cup granulated sugar
¼ cup firmly packed brown sugar
1 cup shortening
1 large egg
⅔ cup sour cream
1 teaspoon vanilla extract

1. Sift the flour, baking soda, and salt into a medium bowl. Stir in the orange zest and raisins and set aside.

2. Beat together the sugars and shortening, then beat in the egg and half the flour mixture until thoroughly blended. Stir in the sour cream, vanilla extract, and remaining flour mixture; blend well.

3. Refrigerate the dough for at least 1 hour, until firm.

4. Preheat the oven to 375°F.

5. Form the dough into 1-inch balls and put on ungreased baking sheets 2 inches apart. Use a fork to flatten each ball to a thickness of ⅛ to ¼ inch.

6. Bake for 10 to 13 minutes, until golden brown.

7. Let stand for 2 minutes, then transfer to wire racks to cool completely.

Pecan Sandies

Rich and buttery, these cookies crumble like sand when bitten into. They are also known as sand tarts. By any name, they are wonderful with tea, coffee, or milk. A variation follows.

MAKES ABOUT 48

2 cups all-purpose flour
1 teaspoon salt
½ teaspoon baking soda
½ cup coarsely chopped pecans
1 cup (2 sticks) butter, softened
¾ cup granulated sugar
½ cup firmly packed brown sugar
1 large egg
1 teaspoon vanilla extract

1. Sift the flour, salt, and baking soda into a medium bowl and stir in the pecans. Set aside.

2. In a large bowl, beat together the butter, ½ cup of granulated sugar, and the brown sugar until light and fluffy. Beat in the egg and vanilla extract until well combined, then add the flour mixture and mix well.

3. Cover and refrigerate the dough for 20 minutes or until it becomes easy to handle.

4. Preheat the oven to 350°F.

5. Shape the dough into 1-inch balls and roll in the remaining ¼ cup granulated sugar. Place 2 inches apart on ungreased baking sheets. Flatten with the bottom of a glass dipped in granulated sugar.

6. Bake for 10 to 12 minutes, until the edges are lightly browned.

7. Let stand for 2 minutes, then transfer to wire racks to cool completely.

Almond Cookies

Replace the pecans in Pecan Sandies with ½ cup chopped slivered almonds and use almond extract instead of vanilla extract. Complete the recipe as directed.

Mexican Wedding Cakes

This recipe is old, but its name is as recent as the 1950s and 1960s, a time when Tex–Mex cuisine was adopted into American cooking. Depending on your ethnic background, you may know these sugar–coated, buttery balls of nuts as Russian tea cakes, Italian butter nuts, Southern pecan butterballs, snowdrops, Viennese sugar balls, or snowballs. They are traditionally served at weddings, Christmas, and other festive occasions.

MAKES 36 TO 48

½ cup toasted nuts (preferably pecans,
    walnuts, and/or hazelnuts)
2 cups confectioners' sugar
1 cup (2 sticks) butter, softened
½ teaspoon vanilla extract
2 cups all-purpose flour
½ teaspoon salt

1. Combine the nuts and ¼ cup of confectioners' sugar in a food processor. Process until the nuts are finely ground; set aside.

2. Beat together the butter and ¾ cup of confectioners' sugar until light and fluffy. Beat in the vanilla extract, then add the flour and salt and beat until combined. Stir in the nut mixture, cover, and refrigerate for about 1 hour, until firm.

3. Preheat the oven to 350°F. Line 2 baking sheets with parchment paper.

4. Form the dough into 1-inch balls and place 2 inches apart on the prepared baking sheets.

5. Bake for 15 to 20 minutes, until lightly browned.

6. While the cookies are baking, place the remaining 1 cup confectioners' sugar in a shallow bowl.

7. Cool the cookies on the baking sheets for a few minutes. While still warm, roll the cookies in the confectioners' sugar and place on wire racks to cool. When the cookies have cooled, roll them again in the confectioners' sugar to give an even coating of sugar.

Ginger Snaps

Ginger snaps came with the colonists from England, but many different countries make similar spiced cookies. The Germans make "pfeffernüsse;" the Scandinavians make "pepparkaka." Ginger snaps are distinctive because the sugar coating ensures that the tops will be covered with little cracks.

MAKES ABOUT 60

2¾ cups all-purpose flour
1½ teaspoons ground ginger
1 teaspoon baking soda
1 teaspoon ground cinnamon
½ teaspoon ground cloves
¾ cup (1½ sticks) unsalted butter, softened
1 cup firmly packed brown sugar
¼ cup molasses
1 large egg
¼ cup granulated sugar

1. Sift the flour, ginger, baking soda, cinnamon, and cloves into a medium bowl and set aside.

2. In a large bowl, beat together the butter and brown sugar until light and fluffy. Add the molasses and beat until well combined. Beat in the egg until well combined. Gather the dough into a ball, cover with plastic wrap, and chill until firm, at least 1 hour.

3. Preheat the oven to 350°F. Line baking sheets with parchment paper and put the sugar in a small, shallow bowl.

4. Pinch off pieces of dough and form into 1-inch balls. Roll each ball in the sugar and arrange 2 inches apart on the baking sheets.

5. Bake for 10 to 12 minutes, until the cookies are flattened and a shade darker.

6. Let stand for 2 minutes, then transfer to wire racks to cool completely.

Snickerdoodles

The meaning of the whimsical name Snickerdoodle is unknown, but it is thought to have originated in England. Known worldwide, these cookies can be made in a variety of ways. This version is perhaps most common, incorporating vanilla with an accent of nutmeg, and a dusting of cinnamon.

MAKES ABOUT 48

2½ cups all-purpose flour
2 teaspoons cream of tartar
1 teaspoon baking soda
½ teaspoon salt
¼ teaspoon freshly grated nutmeg
1 cup (2 sticks) butter, softened
1¾ cups sugar
2 large eggs
1 teaspoon vanilla extract
2 teaspoons ground cinnamon

1. Preheat the oven to 375°F.

2. Sift the flour, cream of tartar, baking soda, salt, and nutmeg into a medium bowl and set aside.

3. Beat the butter and 1½ cups of sugar with an electric mixer in a large bowl until light and fluffy. Beat in the eggs and vanilla extract until creamy, then stir in the flour mixture until completely combined. Set aside.

4. Mix the remaining ¼ cup sugar and the cinnamon in a small, shallow bowl and set aside.

5. Roll the cookie dough into balls the size of small walnuts, then roll the balls in the cinnamon and sugar mixture until well coated. Place 2 inches apart on ungreased baking sheets.

6. Bake for 10 to 12 minutes, until golden brown.

7. Let stand for 2 minutes, then transfer to wire racks to cool completely.

Amish Sugar Cookies

These delicate sugar cookies are drop cookies rather than rolled cookies, so they are a snap to make.

MAKES ABOUT 60

4½ cups all-purpose flour
1 teaspoon salt
1 teaspoon cream of tartar
1 teaspoon baking soda
1 cup (2 sticks) butter, softened
1 cup oil
1 cup granulated sugar
1 cup confectioners' sugar
2 large eggs
1 teaspoon vanilla extract
Colored granulated sugar, for coating

1. Sift the flour, salt, cream of tartar, and baking soda into a medium bowl and set aside.

2. Beat the butter, oil, and sugars in a large bowl until light and fluffy. Add the eggs, one at a time, beating well after each addition. Beat in the vanilla extract, then add the flour mixture and beat until smooth.

3. Gather the dough into a ball, cover with plastic wrap, and refrigerate for at least 1 hour.

4. Preheat the oven to 350°F.

5. With floured hands, shape the dough into 1-inch balls and place 2 inches apart on ungreased baking sheets. Flatten with the bottom of a chilled glass dipped in colored sugar. Sprinkle with the colored sugar.

6. Bake for 10 to 12 minutes, until the edges are golden brown.

7. Let stand for 2 minutes, then transfer to wire racks to cool completely.

Melting Moment Cookies

This recipe, using cornstarch, makes a uniquely tender cookie—one that just about melts in your mouth. Serve with afternoon tea.

MAKES ABOUT 36

1 cup all-purpose flour
½ cup cornstarch
½ cup plus 2 tablespoons confectioners' sugar
¾ cup (1½ sticks) butter, softened
1 teaspoon vanilla extract or almond extract

1. Preheat the oven to 350°F.

2. Sift the flour, cornstarch, and ½ cup confectioners' sugar into a medium bowl. Work in the butter and vanilla extract with a pastry blender to form a soft dough.

3. Shape the dough into 1-inch balls and place 2 inches apart on ungreased baking sheets. Flatten the balls by pressing twice, in opposite directions, with fork tongs dipped in water, leaving a crisscross pattern on top.

4. Bake for 15 to 20 minutes, until the edges are lightly browned. While still hot, sift the remaining 2 tablespoons confectioners' sugar over the cookies.

5. Let stand for 2 minutes, then transfer to wire racks to cool completely.

Chocolate Crinkles

Chocolate lovers delight in this fudgy chocolate cookie dusted with confectioners' sugar. These cookies are best made and served the same day.

MAKES ABOUT 36

¼ cup (½ stick) butter
8 ounces (8 squares) semisweet chocolate, coarsely chopped
1½ cups all-purpose flour
¼ teaspoon salt
½ teaspoon baking powder
½ cup granulated sugar
2 large eggs
2 teaspoons vanilla extract
1 cup confectioners' sugar

1. Melt the butter with the chocolate in the top of a double boiler set over simmering water. Remove from the heat, mix well, and cool.

2. Stir together the flour, salt, and baking powder in a medium bowl and set aside.

3. In a large bowl, beat the granulated sugar and eggs with an electric mixer until pale and fluffy. Beat in the vanilla extract, then stir in the melted chocolate mixture until well blended. Stir in the flour mixture just until incorporated. Cover with plastic wrap and refrigerate until firm, at least 1 hour.

4. Preheat the oven to 325°F. Line 2 baking sheets with parchment paper.

5. Put the confectioners' sugar in a shallow bowl. Shape the dough into 1-inch balls. Roll the balls in confectioners' sugar until completely coated, gently tap off any excess, and place about 2 inches apart on the prepared baking sheets.

6. Bake for 10 to 15 minutes, just until the edges are slightly firm but the centers are still soft.

7. Let stand for 2 minutes, then transfer to wire racks to cool completely.

Thumbprint Cookies

Thumbprint cookies are butter-rich shortbread cookies that have an indentation made with a thumb to hold jam. Some recipes call for filling the centers of the cookies with jam before they are baked. This can be done if you are planning to serve them the same day they are baked. But if you want to store the cookies for several days, it is best to fill them the day of serving to avoid softening the cookies.

MAKES ABOUT 24

1 cup all-purpose flour
⅛ teaspoon salt
½ cup (1 stick) butter, softened
⅓ cup sugar
1 large egg, separated
½ teaspoon vanilla extract
½ cup toasted and finely chopped hazelnuts or almonds
½ cup raspberry jam or jam of choice

1. Preheat the oven to 350°F. Line a baking sheet with parchment paper.

2. Whisk together the flour and salt in a medium bowl and set aside.

3. Beat together the butter and sugar with an electric mixer in a large bowl until light and fluffy. Beat in the egg yolk and vanilla extract until combined. Gradually add the flour mixture and beat just until combined. Set aside.

4. Beat the egg white in a small bowl until frothy and set aside.

5. Place the chopped nuts in a small, shallow bowl.

6. Shape the dough into 1-inch balls. Dip each ball into the egg white and then lightly roll in the chopped nuts. Place on the prepared baking sheet, and repeat, placing the balls about 1 inch apart. Using your thumb or the end of a wooden spoon, make a deep indentation into the center of each cookie.

7. Bake for 9 to 11 minutes, until set and lightly browned on the bottoms.

8. Remove from the oven and place the baking sheet on a wire rack. If the centers of the cookies have risen, use the end of a wooden spoon to gently press in the indentation again.

9. Remove the cookies from the baking sheet and cool completely on a wire rack.

10. When the cookies are cool, spoon a little jam into the center of each one. Serve the same day.

Shortbread Cookies

Simplest of all cookies, shortbread cookies are rich in butter. Traditionally served with tea, especially at Christmas and New Year's, shortbread originated in Scotland and at one time contained oats. It is now usually made with wheat flour, though a small proportion of rice flour may be used to make an especially crisp cookie. A plain shortbread can be dressed up with the addition of spices, chocolate, nuts, dried fruits, and citrus zest. Three variations follow.

MAKES 12 TO 24

2 cups all-purpose flour
¼ teaspoon salt
1 cup (2 sticks) butter, softened
½ cup confectioners' sugar
1 teaspoon vanilla extract

1. Stir together the flour and salt in a medium bowl and set aside.

2. In a large bowl, beat the butter until creamy. Add the confectioners' sugar and beat until smooth. Stir in the vanilla extract, then gently mix in the flour mixture until just incorporated. Flatten the dough into a disk shape, wrap in plastic wrap, and chill for at least 1 hour.

3. Preheat the oven to 300°F. Line 2 baking sheets with parchment paper.

4. Roll out the dough on a lightly floured surface to a thickness of ½ inch. Using lightly floured cookie cutters, cut into rounds or whatever shapes you wish. Place on the prepared baking sheet and refrigerate for about 15 minutes.

5. Bake for 20 minutes, until dry but not brown. (The bottoms will be lightly browned.)

6. Let stand for 2 minutes, then transfer to wire racks to cool completely.

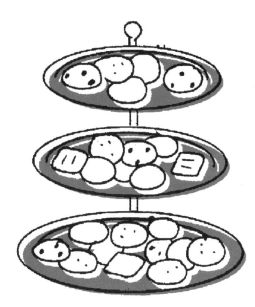

Chocolate-Dipped Shortbread Cookies

Make Shortbread Cookies and allow the cookies to cool. Melt 4 ounces of semisweet or milk chocolate with 1 teaspoon oil in the top of a double boiler set over simmering water. Dip each cookie into the melted chocolate and place on a parchment-lined baking sheet. Chill in the refrigerator until the chocolate is set.

Hazelnut Shortbread Cookies

Replace ¼ cup of confectioners' sugar in Shortbread Cookies with ¼ cup brown sugar. Add ½ cup toasted and finely chopped hazelnuts to the dough and complete the recipe as directed.

Spiced Shortbread Cookies

Add 1 teaspoon ground cinnamon and ¼ teaspoon freshly grated nutmeg to the dough for Shortbread Cookies. Complete the recipe as directed.

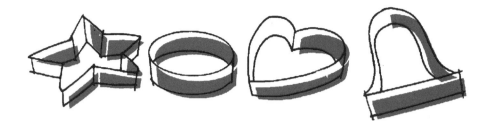

Sugar Cookies

Sugar cookies are blank canvases upon which decorations of all kinds are welcomed. This recipe includes a white glaze, which can be colored with food coloring. While the glaze is still wet, add sprinkles, colored sugar crystals, tiny bits of candy—whatever you wish. And, of course, the choice of cookie cutters is vast.

MAKES 36 TO 48

Cookies:
2 cups all-purpose flour
1 cup granulated sugar
1½ teaspoons baking powder
½ teaspoon salt
¼ cup shortening
¼ cup (½ stick) butter, softened
1 tablespoon milk
2 large eggs
1 teaspoon vanilla extract

Glaze:
1 cup confectioners' sugar, sifted
2 tablespoons half-and-half
½ teaspoon vanilla extract

1. To make the cookies, sift the flour, sugar, baking powder, and salt into a medium bowl and set aside.

2. Beat together the shortening, butter, and milk with an electric mixer in a large bowl. Beat in the eggs and vanilla extract, then gradually stir in the flour mixture to form a dough.

3. Gather the dough into a ball, wrap in plastic wrap, and refrigerate for 1 hour.

4. Preheat the oven to 400°F.

5. Divide the dough in half and form into 2 disks. On a lightly floured surface, roll out one disk to a thickness of ¼ inch. Cut into the desired shapes and use a large spatula to transfer to ungreased baking sheets.

6. Bake for 8 to 12 minutes, until lightly browned.

7. Let stand for 2 minutes, then transfer to wire racks to cool completely.

8. While the cookies cool, make the glaze by beating together the confectioners' sugar, half-and-half, and vanilla extract until smooth. Apply to the cooled cookies and decorate as desired.

Hermit Cookies

It is thought that seamen took these sweet-spiced cookies with them on long voyages because the raisins kept them soft. As to how they got their name, there is no universal agreement among food historians. One theory is that the Moravians, an ethno-religious group well known for thin spice cookies in North Carolina and Pennsylvania, were sometimes called "herrnhutter" in German or Dutch, and that might have sounded like "hermits" to English speakers.

MAKES 36 TO 48

2½ cups all-purpose flour
2 teaspoons baking powder
1 teaspoon ground cinnamon
½ teaspoon ground nutmeg
¼ teaspoon salt
⅛ teaspoon ground mace
⅛ teaspoon ground cloves
½ cup (1 stick) butter, softened
1 cup sugar
2 large eggs
½ cup molasses
2 tablespoons milk
1 teaspoon vanilla extract
1 cup raisins, regular and golden, chopped

1. Sift the flour, baking powder, cinnamon, nutmeg, salt, mace, and cloves into a medium bowl and set aside.

2. Beat the butter and sugar with an electric mixer in a large bowl until creamy and smooth. Beat in the eggs, molasses, milk, and vanilla extract, then add the flour mixture and beat just until combined. Stir in the raisins.

3. Gather the dough into a ball, wrap tightly in plastic wrap, and refrigerate for 2 hours.

4. Preheat the oven to 350°F. Grease 2 baking sheets.

5. Divide the dough evenly and return one portion to the refrigerator. Roll out one half on a lightly floured surface into a sheet about ¼ inch thick. Cut into rounds or squares and place on the prepared baking sheet.

6. Bake for about 10 minutes, until no indentation remains when touched.

7. Let stand for 2 minutes, then transfer to wire racks to cool completely. Repeat with the second ball of dough.

Gingerbread Cookies

What would Christmas be without the chance to decorate gingerbread people? The dough is easy to handle and the frosting is perfect for decorating. If you don't have a pastry bag for applying frosting, fill a small plastic bag with the frosting and snip off a corner for an instant pastry bag.

MAKES ABOUT 48

Cookies:
2 to 2¼ cups all-purpose flour
½ teaspoon baking soda
½ teaspoon ground cinnamon
½ teaspoon ground ginger
½ teaspoon salt
¼ teaspoon ground cloves
½ cup (1 stick) butter, softened
⅓ cup firmly packed brown sugar
3 tablespoons corn syrup
⅓ cup honey
½ teaspoon finely grated lemon zest
½ teaspoon vanilla extract

Frosting:
1½ cups sifted confectioners' sugar
1 large egg white
1 teaspoon lemon juice
Dash of vanilla extract
Food coloring of choice

1. To make the cookies, sift 2 cups of flour, the baking soda, cinnamon, ginger, salt, and cloves into a medium bowl and set aside.

2. Beat the butter and brown sugar with an electric mixer in a large bowl until creamy. Beat in the corn syrup, honey, lemon zest, and vanilla extract, then gradually mix in the flour mixture to make a soft dough. If the dough is too soft, add the remaining ¼ cup flour, 1 tablespoon at a time.

3. Gather the dough into a ball, wrap in plastic wrap, and chill for 1 hour.

4. Preheat the oven to 350°F. Line several baking sheets with parchment paper.

5. Roll out the dough on a lightly floured surface to a thickness of ⅛ inch. Cut into the desired shapes and transfer with a large spatula to the ungreased baking sheets.

6. Bake for about 8 minutes, until puffed and dry.

7. Let stand for 2 minutes, then transfer to wire racks to cool completely.

8. While the cookies cool, make the frosting by beating together the confectioners' sugar, egg white, lemon juice, and vanilla extract until the mixture stands in peaks. If necessary, add a little more sugar or egg white. Divide into separate bowls and color with food coloring as desired. Apply the frosting to the cooled cookies; cover the bowls with a damp cloth when they are not being used.

Rugalach

Rugalach are traditional Hanukkah cookies brought to America by Jewish immigrants from Eastern Europe. They are made with a cream cheese dough and a filling of fruit or chocolate.

MAKES ABOUT 72

2 cups (4 sticks) butter, softened
2 (8-ounce) packages cream cheese, softened
4 cups sifted all-purpose flour
2 cups apricot preserves
1 large egg beaten with 1 tablespoon water
2 cups sugar
1 tablespoon ground cinnamon
2 cups finely chopped walnuts
3 cups raisins
Milk

1. In a large bowl, beat the butter with an electric mixer until smooth. Add the cream cheese and beat until thoroughly blended. Add the flour all at once and beat until the dough comes together.

2. Line a baking sheet with plastic wrap and place the dough in the center. Press into a 9 x 12-inch rectangle, cover with the plastic wrap, and chill for 1 hour or more.

3. Cut the dough into 3 long rectangles, each measuring 3 x 12 inches. Remove one strip and place on a lightly floured work surface. Return the remaining two strips to the refrigerator.

4. Roll out the dough into a 6 x 24-inch rectangle. Spread one-third of the apricot preserves evenly over the dough, leaving a 1-inch border along the long edge closest to you. Brush the egg mixture onto this border.

5. Combine the sugar and cinnamon in a small bowl, and sprinkle almost one-third of it generously over the filling. Top with one-third of the chopped walnuts and raisins.

6. Roll up the dough toward you, making sure it is tight and evenly shaped. Seal the edge that has been brushed with the egg mixture.

7. Brush milk over the roll, sprinkle with a little cinnamon-sugar mixture, and cut into 1-inch cookies. Lay flat on a parchment paper–lined baking sheet and refrigerate for 30 minutes. Repeat with the remaining dough and filling.

8. Preheat the oven to 375°F.

9. Bake the cookies for 30 minutes, until golden brown.

10. Remove the cookies from the baking sheet immediately and cool on wire racks.

Hungarian Nut Crescents

This is another melt-in-your-mouth filled cookie made from a dairy-rich dough. The recipe is often made at Christmastime.

MAKES ABOUT 36

2 cups all-purpose flour
½ teaspoon salt
1 cup (2 sticks) butter
⅔ cup sour cream
1 large egg, separated
½ teaspoon vanilla extract
⅔ cup finely chopped nuts
⅔ cup sugar
1 teaspoon ground cinnamon

1. Mix the flour and salt in a large bowl. Cut in the butter with a pastry blender or 2 knives until the mixture resembles coarse crumbs. Beat in the sour cream, egg yolk, and vanilla extract until well blended. Chill until firm enough to handle, 3 to 4 hours.

2. Preheat the oven to 350°F. Grease 2 baking sheets.

3. Mix the nuts, sugar, and cinnamon in a small bowl and set aside.

4. Divide the dough into thirds and form each portion into a disk. Working with one disk at a time (return the other portions to the refrigerator), roll out the dough on a lightly floured surface into a 9- or 10-inch circle about ⅛ inch thick. Cut into 12 wedges.

5. Sprinkle one-third of the nut mixture all over the tops of the wedges. Starting from the widest end, roll up each wedge. Brush the tips with egg white and seal. Transfer to the prepared baking sheets. Repeat with the remaining dough until all the crescents are rolled.

6. Bake for 18 to 20 minutes, until golden brown.

7. Let stand for 2 minutes, then transfer to wire racks to cool completely.

Spritz Cookies

Producing beautiful-looking cookies is easier with the help of a cookie press. Cookie presses were introduced by Scandinavian immigrants, who called their cookies spritz cookies, from the German word "spritzen," which means to squirt or spray. This recipe makes a lightly sweetened cookie flavored by vanilla and almond extracts. Two variations follow.

MAKES ABOUT 48

4 cups all-purpose flour
1 teaspoon baking powder
½ teaspoon salt
1½ cups (3 sticks) butter, softened
1 cup sugar
1 large egg
1 teaspoon vanilla extract
½ teaspoon almond extract

1. Preheat the oven to 375°F.

2. Sift the flour, baking powder, and salt into a medium bowl and set aside.

3. Beat together the butter and sugar with an electric mixer in a large bowl until creamy. Add the egg, vanilla extract and almond extract and beat until light and fluffy. Stir in the flour mixture, mixing well.

4. Pack the dough into a cookie press fitted with a decorative plate. Press through the cookie press onto ungreased baking sheets, spacing the cookies about 1 inch apart.

5. Bake for 8 to 10 minutes, until the edges are lightly browned.

6. Let stand for 2 minutes, then transfer to wire racks to cool completely.

Spice Spritz Cookies

Sift 1 teaspoon ground cinnamon, ¼ teaspoon ground cloves, and ¼ teaspoon ground nutmeg with the flour mixture in Spritz Cookies. Complete the recipe as directed.

Chocolate Spritz Cookies

Melt 2 squares (2 ounces) baking chocolate, cool slightly, and beat into the batter with the egg in Spritz Cookies. Complete the recipe as directed.

Pecan Icebox Cookies

Whether you call them icebox or refrigerator cookies, the idea is the same. Make a batch of dough, form it into a log, and chill (or freeze) it until it is needed. Then slice, bake, and serve. These cookies are flavored by vanilla and made crunchy by chopped pecans.

MAKES ABOUT 72

3 cups all-purpose flour
1 teaspoon baking soda
1 teaspoon salt
1 cup shortening
2 cups sugar
2 large eggs
1 tablespoon vanilla extract
1 cup chopped pecans

1. Sift the flour, baking soda, and salt into a medium bowl and set aside.

2. Beat the shortening and sugar with an electric mixer in a large bowl until fluffy. Add the eggs, one at a time, beating well after each addition. Beat in the vanilla extract, then stir in the flour mixture, mixing well. Fold in the pecans.

3. Shape the dough into 3 logs (each about 2 inches in diameter), wrap each in wax paper, and refrigerate for at least 2 hours and up to 3 days.

4. When you are ready to bake, preheat the oven to 375°F. Grease several baking sheets.

5. Cut the dough into ¼-inch slices and arrange 2 inches apart on the prepared baking sheets.

6. Bake for about 10 minutes, until lightly golden around the edges.

7. Let stand for 2 minutes, then transfer to wire racks to cool completely.

Brown Sugar Icebox Cookies

Brown sugar gives these slice-and-bake cookies that delicious butterscotch flavor. Keep a roll of this dough in the freezer for unexpected guests, or when your child gives you no advance warning that you need to bring something for a bake sale, class party, or Girl Scout meeting.

MAKES 48 TO 60

1¾ cups all-purpose flour
1 teaspoon baking powder
¼ teaspoon salt
½ cup (1 stick) butter, softened
1 cup firmly packed brown sugar
1 large egg
2 teaspoons finely grated orange zest
1 teaspoon vanilla extract

1. Sift the flour, baking powder, and salt into a medium bowl and set aside.

2. Beat the butter and brown sugar with an electric mixer in a large bowl until fluffy. Add the egg, orange zest, and vanilla extract and beat until well blended. Stir in the flour mixture, mixing well.

3. Shape the dough into 3 logs (each about 2 inches in diameter), wrap each in wax paper, and refrigerate for at least 2 hours and up to 3 days.

4. When you are ready to bake, preheat the oven to 375°F. Grease several baking sheets.

5. Cut the dough into ⅛-inch slices and arrange 2 inches apart on the prepared baking sheets.

6. Bake for 6 to 8 minutes, until lightly golden around the edges.

7. Let stand for 2 minutes, then transfer to wire racks to cool completely.

Almond Biscotti

In Italian-American communities, bakers make biscotti—twice-baked cookies designed for dunking into wine or coffee. Said to have originated during Columbus's time, they are credited to an Italian baker who originally served them with a sweet Tuscan wine. Bakers from around Europe have adopted their own versions of biscotti: The English make rusks; the Germans make zwieback; the Greeks make biskota; and the Jews make mandelbrot. These classic biscotti are mildly sweetened and flavored with almonds.

MAKES ABOUT 30

1 cup whole almonds, blanched
2 cups all-purpose flour
¾ cup sugar
1 teaspoon baking powder
⅛ teaspoon salt
3 large eggs
1 teaspoon vanilla extract
1 teaspoon almond extract

1. Preheat the oven to 350°F.

2. Spread the almonds out on a baking sheet and toast for 8 to 10 minutes, until golden brown. Let cool, then chop coarsely and set aside.

3. Reduce the oven temperature to 300°F. Line a baking sheet with parchment paper.

4. Stir together the flour, sugar, baking powder, and salt in a large bowl. Add the eggs, vanilla extract, and almond extract and beat with an electric mixture until blended. Add the almonds and continue to beat until a stiff dough forms.

5. Transfer the dough to a lightly floured surface and divide in half. Form each half into a log about 10 inches long and 2 inches in diameter. Transfer to the prepared baking sheet.

6. Bake for 35 to 40 minutes, until firm.

7. Cool on a wire rack for about 10 minutes.

8. Transfer the logs to a cutting board and use a serrated knife to cut each diagonally into slices 1½ inches thick. Arrange, cut side up, on the baking sheet.

9. Bake for 10 to 12 minutes, turn the slices over, and bake for 10 minutes more, until firm.

10. Remove from the oven and cool on wire racks.

Whoopie Pies

Whoopie pies are an invention of the Pennsylvania Dutch. They are soft chocolate-sandwich cookies stuffed with sugary white filling.

MAKES ABOUT 24

Cookies:
2¼ cups all-purpose flour
5 tablespoons cocoa powder
1 teaspoon salt
1 teaspoon baking soda
½ teaspoon baking powder
6 tablespoons shortening
1 cup granulated sugar
1 large egg
2 teaspoons vanilla extract
1 cup milk

Filling:
½ cup shortening
1¼ cups confectioners' sugar
1 teaspoon vanilla extract
¾ cup marshmallow cream
1 to 2 tablespoons milk

1. Preheat the oven to 350°F. Grease 2 baking sheets.

2. To make the cookies, sift the flour, cocoa powder, salt, baking soda, and baking powder into a medium bowl and set aside.

3. Beat together the shortening and sugar with an electric mixer in a large bowl. Beat in the egg and vanilla extract, then add the flour mixture alternately with the milk, beating between additions.

4. Drop the dough by tablespoons onto the prepared baking sheets.

5. Bake for 10 to 12 minutes, until firm.

6. Let stand for 2 minutes, then transfer to wire racks to cool completely.

7. To make the filling, beat together the shortening and confectioners' sugar in a medium bowl. Add the vanilla extract, marshmallow cream, and enough milk to make it fluffy. Beat well until smooth.

8. Spread the filling on the flat side of one cookie and top with a second cookie, flat side down. Repeat with the remaining cookies and filling.

Coconut Macaroons

Macaroons are a French cookie made with almond paste or coconut. Because they don't contain any flour, they have been adopted by Jews as a Passover cookie. To get that wonderful, flowery look to your macaroons, use a star tube and twist the pastry tube as you extrude the dough, bringing your hand around in a circle and then upwards to form a peak. When the cookie is baked, the ridges in the swirl design should become golden brown.

MAKES 36 TO 48

2¾ cups sweetened coconut flakes
1¼ cups sugar
3 to 4 large egg whites
1 tablespoon corn syrup
1 teaspoon vanilla extract

1. Preheat the oven to 350°F. Line several baking sheets with parchment paper.

2. Combine the coconut, sugar, 3 egg whites, and corn syrup in the top of a double boiler set over simmering hot water. Stir briskly to form a smooth paste. Remove from the heat and, if necessary, add just enough additional egg white to make a smooth paste. Stir in the vanilla extract.

3. Fill a large pastry bag fitted with a large star tip and pipe macaroons onto the prepared baking sheets.

4. Bake for 8 to 10 minutes, until firm.

5. Immediately transfer to wire racks to cool completely.

TIP: If you don't have a pastry bag, drop the cookies from a teaspoon onto the baking sheets. They won't be as pretty, but they will still taste fine.

Brownies

Legend has it that a Bangor, Maine, housewife was baking chocolate cake one day and it fell. Instead of pitching it out, this frugal cook cut the collapsed cake into bars and served it, apparently to great appreciation. The first published recipe for chocolate brownies appeared in a Sears, Roebuck catalog in 1897. For extra richness, top with a chocolate frosting.

MAKES 16 TO 24

1½ pounds semisweet chocolate, chopped
1 cup (2 sticks) butter, cut into pieces
6 large eggs
2 cups sugar
¼ teaspoon salt
1 tablespoon vanilla extract
1½ cups all-purpose flour
½ cup chopped walnuts

1. Preheat the oven to 350°F. Grease a 9 x 13-inch baking dish.

2. Melt the chocolate and butter in the top of a double boiler set over simmering water. Remove from the heat and set aside.

3. Beat together the eggs, sugar, and salt with an electric mixer in a large bowl. Stir in the melted chocolate mixture and vanilla extract until smooth. Add the flour and mix until well blended. Fold in the walnuts and spoon the batter into the prepared dish.

4. Bake for 45 to 55 minutes, until a toothpick inserted into the center comes out clean.

5. Remove from the oven and let cool on a wire rack. Serve at room temperature or chilled.

TIP: Brownies will cut more evenly
if baked a day before serving.

Lemon Bars

Lemon bars have a shortbread cookie crust and a sweet-tart lemony filling, topped with confectioners' sugar. They are rich and buttery, so cut the bars small. These are best eaten the day they are made.

MAKES ABOUT 25

Crust:
½ cup (1 stick) butter, softened
¼ cup confectioners' sugar
1 cup all-purpose flour
⅛ teaspoon salt

Filling:
1 cup granulated sugar
2 large eggs
⅓ cup fresh lemon juice (from about 2 large lemons)
1 tablespoon grated lemon zest
2 tablespoons all-purpose flour
Confectioners' sugar, to serve

1. Preheat the oven to 350°F. Grease an 8 x 8-inch baking dish.

2. To make the crust, beat together the butter and sugar with an electric mixer in a medium bowl until light and fluffy. Add the flour and salt, beating until the dough just comes together. Press into the bottom of the prepared dish.

3. Bake for 20 to 25 minutes, until lightly browned. Remove from the oven and place on a wire rack to cool while you make the filling.

4. To make the filling, beat the granulated sugar and eggs in a separate medium bowl until smooth. Beat in the lemon juice and zest, then fold in the flour. Pour over the crust.

5. Bake for 20 to 25 minutes, until the filling is just barely set.

6. Sift the confectioners' sugar over the lemon filling while it is still warm, cool for at least 30 minutes, then cut into squares and serve.

TIP: Remove the zest before halving
and squeezing the lemon.

Raspberry Squares

Another classic bar cookie, raspberry squares are a perfect blend of butter, sugar, and fruit. You can also achieve perfection by substituting any berry jam.

MAKES ABOUT 32

1½ sticks (¾ cup) butter, softened
½ cup plus ⅓ cup sugar
2 large eggs, separated
1½ cups sifted all-purpose flour
1 cup finely chopped nuts
1 cup raspberry jam

1. Preheat the oven to 350°F. Grease a 9 x 13-inch baking dish.

2. Beat the butter with ½ cup sugar with an electric mixer in a large bowl until light and fluffy. Beat in the egg yolks, then add the flour and beat until well mixed and a dough forms.

3. Transfer the dough to the prepared dish and pat to make an even layer, building up a ½-inch rim around the sides.

4. Bake for 15 minutes, until the edges just begin to turn golden.

5. Meanwhile, make the meringue by beating the egg whites with an electric mixer in a medium bowl until soft peaks begin to form. Continue beating, gradually adding the remaining ⅓ cup sugar and beating until stiff. Fold in the nuts and set aside.

6. Let the crust cool for 2 to 3 minutes, then spread with the jam. Spread the meringue over the jam, working from the rim of the dish toward the center.

7. Bake for 15 to 20 minutes, until lightly browned.

8. Place the dish on a wire rack and cool before cutting into squares and serving.

Congo Squares

To ensure these soft cookies are cut evenly, line the baking pan with aluminum foil that overhangs the edges. Once cooled, use the overhanging foil as handles and transfer the cookie to a cutting board for slicing.

MAKES ABOUT 32

2⅔ cups all-purpose flour
2½ teaspoons baking powder
½ teaspoon salt
⅔ cup butter, softened

2¼ cups firmly packed brown sugar
3 large eggs
1 cup chopped nuts
1 (6-ounce) package semisweet chocolate chips

1. Preheat the oven to 350°F. Grease a 9 x 13-inch baking dish.

2. Sift the flour, baking powder, and salt into a medium bowl and set aside.

3. Beat the butter and brown sugar with an electric mixer in a large bowl until light and fluffy. Add the eggs, one at a time, beating well after each addition. Beat in the flour mixture, then stir in the nuts and chocolate chips. Spoon into the prepared baking dish.

4. Bake for 20 to 30 minutes, until the contents begin to pull away from the sides of the dish and are still slightly soft in the middle.

5. Place the dish on a wire rack and cool before cutting into squares and serving.

Dream Bars

Also known by the names seven-layer bars and lazy layer bars, these are easy to make.

MAKES ABOUT 32

½ cup (1 stick) butter, melted
1½ cups graham cracker crumbs
1 cup sweetened coconut flakes
1 (6-ounce) package semisweet chocolate chips
1 (6-ounce) package butterscotch chips
1 cup chopped walnuts or pecans
1 (14-ounce) can sweetened condensed milk

1. Preheat the oven to 350°F.

2. Pour the butter into a 9 x 13-inch baking dish and spread evenly. Sprinkle the graham cracker crumbs evenly over the butter and pat to make a firm, level surface. Sprinkle the coconut over the crumbs, then follow with the chocolate chips, butterscotch chips, and nuts. Drizzle the condensed milk over all.

3. Bake for about 20 minutes, until golden.

4. Cool completely on a wire rack before cutting into squares and serving.

TIPS TO BETTER BAKING

The old saying goes "easy as pie," but pies can challenge even the most experienced cook. Here are some tips to help you in your kitchen.

▶ The food processor method for making pie crusts is the easiest. It is faster than mixing by hand, and because the dough is handled less, it keeps the ingredients more chilled.

▶ Replacing 1 tablespoon of water in a pastry recipe with 1 tablespoon cider vinegar or lemon juice relaxes pie dough and makes it easier to roll. It will not diminish the crust's flakiness but will diminish shrinkage as it bakes.

▶ Flour the work surface very lightly. Excess flour will toughen pastry dough. Add additional flour sparingly, as needed. Roll out dough from the center to avoid overworking.

▶ Use the right pie pan. Glass or dull-metal pie pans work the best. Avoid shiny metal or disposable aluminum pans, which reflect heat and prevent crusts from browning. Dark pans may cause crusts to brown too much.

▶ To keep baked edges from getting too brown, cover the edges with aluminum foil after the first 15 minutes of baking. Use a 12-inch square piece of foil. Cut out a 7-inch circle from the center, and gently fold the foil ring around the crust's edge.

▶ If your pie filling tends to be too runny, it may be underbaked. Try baking 5 to 10 minutes longer than normal.

▶ Allow the pie to cool on a wire rack to room temperature, or until barely warm, before slicing to ensure that the filling is set and will not run. This will take between 2 and 4 hours, depending on the thickness of the pie.

Applying frosting is easy. Here are some tips to make the finished cake look professional.

▶ Start with a completely cooled cake. Brush off any crumbs and, if necessary, cut away any crisp edges.

▶ To keep the cake plate clean, place strips of wax paper around the plate edges. These can be removed later.

▶ Place the first cake layer, top side down, on the cake plate. Spread with frosting almost to the edge, using a frosting spatula.

▶ Place the second layer, top side up, on top of the bottom layer.

▶ Spread about three-quarters of the remaining frosting evenly on the sides, holding the frosting spatula so that the tip rests on the wax paper. The straight edge of the blade should be held against the frosting so that the flat side of the blade forms a 30-degree angle with the side of the cake. Don't worry about the ridge of frosting that piles up on the top of the cake; you will use that later.

▶ Spread the remaining frosting on top of the cake, working from the edge to the center, with the spatula held horizontally and level.

▶ Swirl decorative circles and wavy lines in the frosting with the back of a spoon, and pull up for peaks.

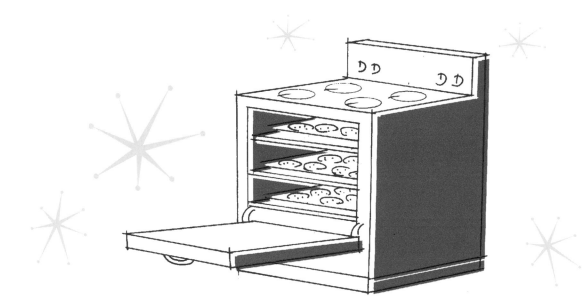

Warm home-baked cookies fresh from the oven are one of life's simple pleasures. Here are some tips to ensure your baking success.

▶ Always start by preheating the oven.

▶ Do not grease the baking sheets unless the recipe tells you to.

▶ Parchment paper prevents cookies from sticking to the pan.

▶ Shiny, light-colored baking sheets do a better job of evenly browning the bottoms of cookies than dark sheets do.

▶ Butter should always be used softened or at room temperature. Cold, hard butter will not cream as easily when you blend it with the sugar, resulting in flat cookies.

▶ If a recipe calls for brown sugar, firmly pack it into the measuring cup for an accurate measurement.

▶ When using nuts, toast them before adding them to the batter for maximum flavor. (Also, taste them before using to make sure they haven't gone rancid.)

▶ Don't use imitation ingredients. Pure vanilla extract and high-quality chocolate do make a difference.

▶ When adding dried fruits like raisins or currants, make sure they are soft, not hard and shriveled. To reconstitute hard, dried fruit, pour boiling water over it, let sit 4 to 5 minutes, then strain. Proceed as the recipe directs.

▶ Keep cookie size consistent. Measure the batter out carefully so all the cookies will be the same size and will bake at the same speed.

▶ A small, 1-ounce ice cream scoop makes portioning out cookie dough easy.

▶ Don't crowd the cookies on a baking sheet. Generally leave 1 to 2 inches of space between them.

▶ Halfway through baking, reverse the top and bottom sheets and rotate each from front to back.

▶ Do not overbake cookies. If a recipe specifies baking for 10 minutes, check after 8 minutes.

▶ Bake no more than one or two baking sheets at a time. If you are making several batches of cookies, make sure you cool the baking sheet completely before using it again or your dough may melt off the pan.

▶ All cookies should be completely cooled before storing. Soft cookies should be stored in an airtight container, while hard cookies should be stored between layers of wax paper or foil in a loosely covered container. For the freshest taste, cookies should be eaten within a few days.

CHAPTER FOURTEEN

Other Desserts and Sweets

Americans love their sweets, and not so very long ago, traditional home-made desserts were a part of daily life. Fancy desserts were reserved for special occasions, but for everyday dining, dessert usually consisted of simple puddings or fruit-laden concoctions. Many of these old-fashioned fruit desserts had curious names like grunts, slumps, and pandowdies, in contrast to the temptingly named crisps, cobblers, and crunches.

But all of these desserts, in their various forms, are really just another form of fruit pie. They recall an earlier time, before the dawn of the supermarket, when one had to make do with the staples on hand—flour, sugar, butter, eggs, and fruit, fresh or preserved.

A sure way to spoil recipes like this is to use immature fruit. These desserts require ripe, juicy fruits that are bursting with flavor; otherwise, the sweeteners and spices tend to overwhelm them. This can be a challenge, given the fact that our supermarkets tend to stock fruit that is grown far away and picked before it is ripe. One way to easily resolve this is to make these desserts with in-season and locally grown produce. Canned or frozen fruit may also be used.

This chapter also includes creamy puddings and ice creams. In the early days of our country—before ready-made mixes—puddings were simple, ordinary desserts. However, once mixes became ubiquitous, people quickly forgot how good puddings made from scratch could be. Ice cream, too, is a special treat when homemade. Modern ice-cream machines remove much of the labor and rock-salt guesswork, and still produce a delicious homemade treat.

Last but not least, sweets and candies wind up this delectable chapter. Creamy fudges and brittle have always held a prominent place in culinary history, tempting America's sweet tooth for generations. Whether the use fruit, nuts, chocolate, or coconut, these all-time favorite treats are the perfect additions to get-togethers and holidays. Whatever treat you decide to make, it's sure to be met with applause.

Applesauce

Applesauce is simply apples cooked down until they form a purée. If you peel the apples first, or use unpeeled green and yellow apples, the applesauce will be yellow. If you cook red apples with their peels on, the applesauce will be pink.

MAKES ABOUT 3 QUARTS

6 cups unsweetened apple cider
5 pounds cooking apples, such as Jonathan or Winesap, quartered
¼ teaspoon salt
½ teaspoon ground cinnamon
Sugar, brown sugar, honey, or pure maple syrup (optional)

1. Bring the cider to a boil in a large saucepan. Continue boiling until reduced by half, 8 to 10 minutes.

2. Add the apples and salt and bring back to a boil. Reduce the heat and simmer, stirring occasionally, for 45 minutes, until the apples break down and the mixture is thick.

3. Run the apples through a food mill to strain out the seeds and skins.

4. Add the cinnamon and sweetener to taste, if using.

5. Store in the refrigerator or freezer; or pour into hot, clean canning jars while hot. Process in a boiling water bath for 20 minutes (page 486).

Baked Apples

This is a good old-fashioned dessert, perfect for a frosty fall evening. Apples particularly good for baking include Cortland, Granny Smith, Northern Spy, Rome Beauty, Winesap, and York Imperial.

SERVES 4

4 large tart apples, such as Granny Smith or Rome Beauty
½ cup firmly packed brown sugar
¼ cup (½ stick) butter, softened
¼ cup raisins
2 teaspoons ground cinnamon
⅔ cup apple cider or water
Half-and-half or ice cream, to serve (optional)

1. Preheat the oven to 350°F.

2. Scoop out the core from the top of each apple, leaving a well. Do not cut all the way through. Cut several shallow slits around the sides of the fruit to allow steam to escape without cracking the skins. Place the apples in a baking dish just large enough to hold them.

3. In a small bowl, mix the brown sugar, butter, raisins, and cinnamon. Stuff one-fourth of the mixture into each apple. Pour the cider around the apples. Cover tightly.

4. Bake for 30 minutes, uncover, baste with the pan liquids, and bake for 10 minutes more, until the apples are tender but not mushy. Serve warm, with half-and-half poured over the tops or with a scoop of ice cream on top, if using.

Apple Snow

Cooked apples in a fluffy cloud of beaten egg whites was a popular dessert in the early 1900s. It was also called apple float. (Note: This recipe contains raw eggs. For more information, see page 11.)

SERVES 6

6 large tart apples, such as Granny Smith or Rome Beauty, peeled, cored, and chopped
3 tablespoons water
1 cup sugar
½ teaspoon ground cinnamon
¼ teaspoon ground cloves
½ teaspoon vanilla extract
2 large egg whites

1. Combine the apples and water in a large saucepan and cook, covered, over low heat until foamy, 15 to 30 minutes. Remove from the heat and stir in the sugar, cinnamon, cloves, and vanilla extract. Let cool.

2. Whip the egg whites until stiff peaks form. Fold into the cooled apple mixture and serve.

Apple Crisp

Although any fruit can be baked under an oat topping, apples seem the most popular for this treatment. Apple crisp is delicious served warm with a scoop of ice cream.

SERVES 6

4 large tart apples, such as Granny Smith or
  Rome Beauty, peeled, cored, and sliced
1 tablespoon lemon juice
1 cup rolled oats
½ cup firmly packed brown sugar
⅓ cup all-purpose flour
1 teaspoon ground cinnamon
½ teaspoon salt
¼ cup (½ stick) butter, melted

1. Preheat the oven to 375°F. Grease an 8-inch square baking dish.

2. In a medium bowl, toss the apples with the lemon juice, then arrange them in the baking dish. Set aside.

3. Combine the oats, brown sugar, flour, cinnamon, and salt in a separate medium bowl. Mix in the butter until the mixture is crumbly. Sprinkle over the apples.

4. Bake for 30 minutes, until the juices are bubbling and the topping is golden. Serve warm or cooled.

Apple Pandowdy

Pandowdy is a deep-dish baked dessert, consisting of fruit, sugar, and spices, with a thick top crust. With a name like pandowdy, this could only be a comforting, old-fashioned dessert. Nathaniel Hawthorne wrote about it in his novel The Blithedale Romance *in 1852.*

SERVES 6

4 medium tart apples, such as Granny Smith
  or Rome Beauty, peeled, cored, and sliced
⅓ cup firmly packed brown sugar
2 teaspoons ground cinnamon
½ teaspoon ground nutmeg
2½ cups all-purpose flour
1 tablespoon baking powder
½ teaspoon salt
1¼ cups (2½ sticks) butter, softened
⅔ cup granulated sugar
1 large egg
1 cup milk
Whipped cream or ice cream, to serve

1. Preheat the oven to 350°F. Grease a 9-inch square baking dish.

2. Place the apples in the dish and sprinkle with the brown sugar, cinnamon, and nutmeg. Set aside.

3. Stir together the flour, baking powder, and salt in a medium bowl and set aside.

4. In a large bowl, cream the butter and granulated sugar until fluffy. Mix in the egg. Add the flour mixture in small quantities, alternating with the milk and ending with the flour mixture.

5. Spread the batter evenly over the apples and bake for about 50 minutes, until golden brown.

6. Cool for at least 10 minutes before serving. You can serve it right out of the pan or inverted onto a serving plate like an upside-down cake. Top with whipped cream or ice cream.

Apple Brown Betty

Apple brown betty—a dish of sliced apples and crumbled topping, but no oats—might be the precursor of apple crisp. The dish was first popular in the 1800s, but its origins are unknown. Top with whipped cream, half-and-half, or ice cream.

SERVES 8

11 medium tart apples, such as Granny Smith or Rome Beauty, peeled, cored, and sliced
2 teaspoons ground cinnamon
1½ cups all-purpose flour
1⅓ cups firmly packed brown sugar
½ cup (1 stick) butter, softened
¼ cup hot water
Juice of ½ medium lemon

1. Preheat the oven to 350°F. Grease a 9 x 13-inch baking dish.

2. Arrange the apples in the baking dish and sprinkle the cinnamon over the top. Set aside.

3. In a medium bowl, mix the flour and ⅔ cup of brown sugar. Mix in the butter until crumbly; set aside.

4. Make a syrup by combining the remaining ⅔ cup brown sugar with the hot water and lemon juice in a small bowl.

5. Pour half the syrup over the apples. Sprinkle the crumble mixture evenly over the apples, then pour the remaining syrup over the topping.

6. Bake for 60 to 75 minutes, until the top is golden brown. Serve warm.

Apple Strudel

Apple strudel came to this country with immigrants from Germany, Austria, and central Europe. Those bakers had to painstakingly roll out their paper-thin strudel dough. Fortunately, we can use phyllo dough, found in the freezer section of most supermarkets.

SERVES 12

⅓ cup granulated sugar
2 tablespoons cornstarch
½ cup brandy or apple juice
5 cups peeled, cored, and sliced tart apples, such as Granny Smith or Rome Beauty (about 5 medium)
⅓ cup firmly packed brown sugar
1 teaspoon ground cinnamon
Pinch of ground nutmeg
½ cup raisins
½ cup chopped walnuts
12 (12 x 16-inch) phyllo pastry sheets
¾ cup (1½ sticks) butter, melted
¾ cup fine dry bread crumbs

1. Preheat the oven to 375°F. Cover a baking sheet with aluminum foil.

2. Combine the granulated sugar, cornstarch, and brandy in a small saucepan over medium heat and bring to a boil. Cook until the mixture becomes thick. Remove from the heat.

3. Toss the apples with the brown sugar, cinnamon, and nutmeg in a large bowl. Pour in the brandy mixture and toss to coat. Fold in the raisins and walnuts and set aside.

4. Unfold the phyllo sheets and brush one sheet with melted butter. Sprinkle with the bread crumbs. Layer the sheets, continuing to brush with the butter and sprinkle with the crumbs.

5. Spoon the apple mixture along the long edge of the stacked layers and roll up. Fold in the ends before the last roll to secure the filling within the pastry. Carefully transfer the strudel to the baking sheet and brush with the remaining butter.

6. Bake for 35 minutes, until the pastry is golden brown.

7. Slice when warm or cooled completely and serve immediately.

Apple Dumplings

Apples encased in pastry dough, a variation on apple pie, is a food tradition that goes back to the Old World. Apple dumplings are best if served warm, with pan juices spooned over the top and vanilla ice cream on the side.

SERVES 6

2¼ cups all-purpose flour
2 teaspoons baking powder
½ teaspoon salt
⅔ cup shortening
½ cup milk
2 cups sugar
1 teaspoon ground cinnamon
½ teaspoon ground nutmeg
2 cups water
¼ cup (½ stick) butter
6 small tart apples, such as Granny Smith or
    Rome Beauty, peeled and cored

1. Stir together the flour, baking powder, and salt in a medium bowl. Cut in the shortening with a pastry blender or 2 knives until the mixture looks like coarse crumbs. Add the milk and mix just until moistened. Form the dough into a ball, wrap in plastic wrap, and refrigerate for 30 minutes.

2. Combine 1½ cups of sugar, ½ teaspoon of cinnamon, ¼ teaspoon of nutmeg, and the water in a medium saucepan. Bring to a boil, reduce the heat, and simmer for 5 minutes. Remove from the heat and stir in the butter. Set aside.

3. Preheat the oven to 375°F.

4. Roll out the dough on a lightly floured surface into a 12 x 18-inch rectangle. Cut into six 6-inch squares.

5. Combine the remaining ½ cup sugar, ½ teaspoon cinnamon, and ¼ teaspoon nutmeg in a shallow bowl. Roll each apple in the sugar and spice mixture until well coated. Place an apple in the center of a pastry square. Moisten the edges of the dough, fold each corner up to the top and center of the apple, and pinch the edges together. Place in a 9 x 13-inch baking dish and repeat with the remaining apples. Pour the cinnamon syrup over the dumplings.

6. Bake for 40 to 45 minutes, until the pastry is golden brown and the apples are tender when tested with a knife. Serve warm.

Apricot Whip

Whips are fruit purées blended into whipped cream or beaten egg whites to make a very light, airy dessert. Apricots or prunes are often used. (Note: This recipe contains raw eggs. For more information, see page 11.)

SERVES 4

½ cup dried apricots
½ cup water
1 tablespoon orange juice
¼ cup firmly packed brown sugar
½ cup heavy cream
2 large egg whites
2 tablespoons granulated sugar

1. Combine the apricots and water in a small saucepan. Cover and simmer over low heat for 15 minutes, until the apricots are soft. Drain.

2. Purée the apricots in a blender or food processor. Mix in the orange juice, brown sugar, and cream. Chill for at least 4 hours.

3. Beat the egg whites in a medium bowl until soft peaks form. Slowly add the granulated sugar and continue beating until stiff peaks form. Fold the egg whites into the apricot mixture.

4. Spoon into individual dishes and serve.

Berry Cobbler

As pioneers traveled west in the second half of the nineteenth century, cooks had to adapt traditional oven–baked pie recipes to use quick biscuit doughs that could be cooked in Dutch ovens. The cobbler is thought to be one of those products of American culinary ingenuity. It is a deep–dish pie made from whatever fruit is available and covered with a quick–cooking crust. Serve with half–and–half, whipped cream, or ice cream.

SERVES 6

Filling:
½ cup sugar
2 tablespoons all-purpose flour
4 cups (2 pints) mixed fresh or frozen berries, such as blueberries, raspberries, blackberries, and boysenberries
1 tablespoon butter

Cobbler dough:
¼ cup (½ stick) butter, softened
½ cup sugar
1 large egg, well beaten
1½ cups all-purpose flour
2 teaspoons baking powder
½ teaspoon salt
½ cup milk

1. Preheat the oven to 400°F.

2. To make the filling, add the sugar and flour to the berries in a large bowl and mix gently. Pour the mixture in the bottom of a greased, wide, and deep 2-quart baking dish. Dot the top with the butter and set aside.

3. To make the cobbler dough, cream the butter in a medium bowl, add the sugar and egg, and mix well. In a small bowl, sift together the flour, baking powder, and salt. Alternately add the flour mixture and milk to the butter mixture to form a batter.

4. Cover the berries with the batter and bake for 50 to 60 minutes, until the top is lightly browned. Serve warm.

TIP: If using frozen berries, remember to thaw and drain before using.

Mixed Berry Crisp

Although apples are traditionally used in crisps, berries are equally delicious. Use whatever berries you have on hand, and serve with cream or ice cream.

SERVES 8

1½ cups fresh or frozen blackberries
1½ cups fresh or frozen raspberries
1½ cups fresh or frozen blueberries
¼ cup granulated sugar
2 cups all-purpose flour
2 cups rolled oats
1½ cups firmly packed brown sugar
1 teaspoon ground cinnamon
½ teaspoon ground nutmeg
1½ cups (3 sticks) butter

1. Preheat the oven to 350°F. Grease a 9 x 13-inch baking dish.

2. In a large bowl, gently toss together the berries and granulated sugar and set aside.

3. Combine the flour, oats, brown sugar, cinnamon, and nutmeg in a separate large bowl. Cut in the butter with a pastry blender or 2 knives until crumbly. Press half of the mixture in the bottom of the prepared baking dish. Cover with the berries. Sprinkle the remaining crumble mixture over the top.

4. Bake for 30 to 40 minutes, until the fruit is bubbly and the topping is golden brown. Serve warm or cooled.

Blueberry Buckle

Buckles are fruit-filled cakes that have the unfortunate tendency to collapse, or buckle, under the weight of their crumb topping. You can substitute an equal quantity of strawberries, sliced plums, raspberries, or blackberries for the blueberries.

SERVES 6

Cake:
2 cups all-purpose flour
2 teaspoons baking powder
½ teaspoon salt
¼ teaspoon ground nutmeg
¼ cup (½ stick) butter, softened
1 cup sugar

1 large egg
1 teaspoon almond extract
½ cup milk
3 cups (1½ pints) fresh or frozen blueberries

Topping:
½ cup sugar
⅓ cup all-purpose flour
1 teaspoon ground cinnamon
¼ cup (½ stick) butter, softened

1. Preheat the oven to 375°F. Grease and flour a 9-inch square baking dish.

2. To make the cake, sift the flour, baking powder, salt, and nutmeg into a medium bowl. Set aside.

3. Beat together the butter and ¾ cup of sugar in a medium bowl until light and fluffy. Beat in the egg and almond extract. Alternately add the flour mixture and the milk, starting with the flour and incorporating well after each addition.

4. Toss the berries with the remaining ¼ cup sugar in the prepared baking dish. Spoon the batter over the berries.

5. To make the topping, mix the sugar, flour, and cinnamon in a small bowl. Mix in the butter until the mixture is crumbly. Sprinkle on top of the cake.

6. Bake for 45 to 50 minutes, until the top is a rich, golden brown. Serve warm or cooled.

Blackberry Slump

The dough can be expected to rise and then slump into the berries in this aptly named, old-fashioned fruit dessert. Substitute other berries, or peaches or plums, if you wish, and serve warm with cream, whipped cream, or ice cream.

SERVES 6

4 cups (2 pints) fresh or frozen blackberries
1¾ cups sugar
1 cup all-purpose flour
1½ teaspoons baking powder
½ teaspoon salt
½ cup milk
¼ cup (½ stick) butter, melted

1. Preheat the oven to 375°F. Grease an 8-inch square baking dish.

2. Pour the berries into the baking dish and sprinkle with 1½ cups of sugar. Set aside.

3. In a medium bowl, stir together the flour, baking powder, salt, and remaining ¼ cup sugar. Mix in the milk and butter, then pour over the berries.

4. Bake for 40 to 45 minutes, until the crust is golden and the filling is bubbly. Serve warm or cooled.

Blueberry Grunt

Grunts are an old New England dessert of steamed fruit and dough. The dough is said to grunt and sigh as it rises with the steam.

SERVES 6

1 cup all-purpose flour
2 teaspoons baking powder
¼ teaspoon salt
½ cup half-and-half
2 cups (1 pint) fresh or frozen blueberries
½ cup sugar
1 cup water
Heavy cream or whipped cream, to serve

1. Sift together the flour, baking powder, and salt into a medium bowl. Add the half-and-half and stir briskly until smooth. Set aside.

2. Combine the blueberries with the sugar and water in a large, nonreactive saucepan. Bring to a boil over high heat and boil for 1 minute.

3. Drop the dough into the saucepan by the tablespoon, spacing the dumplings about 1 inch apart. Reduce the heat to low, cover tightly, and simmer undisturbed for 20 minutes, until the dumplings are puffed and a toothpick inserted into the center of a dumpling comes out clean.

4. Spoon the dumplings into dessert bowls, pour the blueberry sauce over them, and serve. Pass the cream at the table.

Cherry Crunch

*Crunch or crisp? The two recipes are pretty similar,
but most crunch recipes sandwich the fruit
between two layers of crunchy oats.*

SERVES 6

4 cups pie cherries, pitted
3 tablespoons quick-cooking tapioca
1¼ cups granulated sugar
2 cups rolled oats
1 cup firmly packed brown sugar
⅔ cup all-purpose flour
2 teaspoons ground cinnamon
¼ teaspoon ground nutmeg
½ teaspoon salt
½ cup (1 stick) butter, melted

1. Preheat the oven to 375°F. Grease an 8-inch
square baking dish.

2. Toss the cherries with the tapioca and granulated sugar in a medium bowl and set aside.

3. Combine the oats, brown sugar, flour, cinnamon, nutmeg, and salt in a large bowl. Mix in the
butter until crumbly.

4. Press half of the oat mixture into the bottom of
the baking dish and top with the cherry mixture.
Sprinkle the remaining oat mixture on top.

5. Bake for 30 minutes, until the juices are bubbling and the topping is golden. Serve warm or
cooled.

Ambrosia

*Ambrosia is the food of the gods, according to Greek
mythology. But in America it is a dessert of chilled fruit,
usually oranges and bananas, mixed with coconut.*

SERVES 6

1 cup orange juice
3 medium oranges, peeled and sectioned
1 (8-ounce) can pineapple chunks
2 medium bananas, peeled and sliced
½ cup sweetened coconut flakes

1. Combine the juice, orange sections, pineapple,
and bananas in a large bowl, stirring gently to
blend. Refrigerate until serving time.

2. Fold in the coconut just before serving.

Broiled Peaches

*Broiled peaches make a simple but elegant finale to a dinner.
Serve with a dollop of whipped cream, if you like.*

SERVES 4

4 medium peaches
8 whole cloves
2 tablespoons butter, melted
½ cup sugar
1 teaspoon ground cinnamon
¼ cup brandy

1. Dip the peaches in boiling water for 10 seconds. Chill immediately in a bowl of ice water.
Drain and peel right away; the skins should slip
off easily. Halve the peaches, remove the pits, and
stick 1 clove in the cut side of each half. Place the
peaches in a shallow baking dish or sheet tray.
Brush the outside of the peach halves with the
melted butter. Sprinkle sugar in the cavity of each
half and follow with a light sprinkle of cinnamon.
Fill each peach half with a spoonful of brandy and
any remaining butter.

2. Broil the peaches 6 inches from the heat and
watch carefully. The peaches are done when the
tops turn light brown. Remove the cloves and
serve warm.

Peach Cobbler

*It is thought that the name "cobbler" derives from the idea
that the baked crust looks like a cobblestone road when it is
baked. Whether this is true or not, there is no doubt that peach
cobblers are terrific, down-home comfort desserts.
A variation using raspberries follows.*

SERVES 8

Filling:

6 large peaches, peeled, pitted, and cut into
    slices or chunks

½ cup sugar

1 tablespoon cornstarch or quick-cooking
    tapioca

1 tablespoon lemon juice

½ teaspoon ground cinnamon

¼ teaspoon salt

Pinch of ground nutmeg

Crust:

½ cup shortening

¼ cup sugar

1 large egg

½ teaspoon vanilla extract

¾ cup all-purpose flour

½ teaspoon baking powder

¼ teaspoon salt

2 tablespoons milk

Vanilla ice cream or whipped cream, to serve

1. Preheat the oven to 375°F. Grease a 9 x 13-inch baking dish.

2. To make the filling, combine the peaches, sugar, cornstarch, lemon juice, cinnamon, salt, and nutmeg in a medium bowl. Toss gently to mix. Transfer to the prepared baking dish and set aside.

3. To make the crust, beat together the shortening and 3 tablespoons of sugar in a medium bowl until light and fluffy. Beat in the egg and vanilla extract. Add the flour, baking powder, salt, and milk and mix well. Gather the dough into a ball.

4. Roll out the dough on a lightly floured surface until rectangular and slightly bigger than the baking dish. Roll the dough onto the rolling pin, unroll over the peach filling, and seal around the edges. Poke a few holes in the top to allow steam to escape, and sprinkle the remaining 1 tablespoon sugar on top.

5. Bake for about 1 hour, until the crust is light brown and the filling is bubbling. Serve warm with a scoop of vanilla ice cream or whipped cream.

Peach Raspberry Cobbler

Replace the 6 peaches in Peach Cobbler with 3 cups sliced peaches and 2 cups fresh or frozen raspberries. Proceed with the recipe as directed.

Peach Crumble

Corn flakes add the crunch in this rustic fruit dessert. It is best made with fresh, juicy peaches, but the peach season is short, so enjoy it with canned peaches if you must.

SERVES 6

1 cup all-purpose flour

½ teaspoon baking soda

½ teaspoon salt

½ teaspoon ground cinnamon

¼ teaspoon ground nutmeg

½ cup (1 stick) butter, softened

½ cup firmly packed brown sugar

1 teaspoon finely grated lemon zest

1 teaspoon lemon juice

½ cup corn flakes, crushed

9 medium fresh or canned peach halves (peeled
    and pitted if fresh, drained if canned)

Whipped cream, to serve

1. Preheat the oven to 350°F. Grease an 8-inch square baking dish.

2. Sift the flour, baking soda, salt, cinnamon, and nutmeg into a medium bowl and set aside.

3. In a large bowl, beat the butter, brown sugar, lemon zest, and lemon juice until light. Add the flour mixture and corn flakes and stir until the mixture becomes crumbly.

4. Press half of the mixture into the bottom of the prepared pan. Arrange the peach halves on top, cut side down. Sprinkle the remaining mixture over the top.

5. Bake for 45 to 50 minutes, until the topping is golden. Serve warm with whipped cream.

Baked Prune Whip with Custard Sauce

Prunes may not be your first thought when planning dessert, but this light whipped dish is uncommonly good.

SERVES 6

Prune whip:
1 cup pitted prunes
½ cup firmly packed brown sugar
3 large egg whites (yolks reserved)
¼ teaspoon salt
1 tablespoon lemon juice

Custard sauce:
2 tablespoons granulated sugar
1 teaspoon cornstarch
⅛ teaspoon salt
1¼ cups milk
3 large egg yolks, beaten
½ teaspoon vanilla extract

1. Preheat the oven to 325°F.

2. To make the prune whip, cover the prunes with boiling water in a small bowl and let stand for 5 minutes. Drain and chop.

3. Combine the prunes, brown sugar, egg whites, and salt in a large bowl. Beat until stiff enough to hold peaks. Fold in the lemon juice, then spoon into a shallow, 1-quart baking dish. Set the baking dish in a large pan filled with 1 inch of hot water.

4. Bake for 40 minutes, until the mixture puffs and forms a thin crust. Remove from the water bath and cool.

5. To prepare the custard sauce, combine the sugar, cornstarch, and salt in a small saucepan. Stir in the milk. Heat to boiling over medium heat, stirring constantly. Stir 1 cup of hot milk mixture, a little at a time, into the egg yolks. Return the egg yolk mixture to the saucepan and cook for 1 minute over low heat, stirring constantly. Do not boil.

6. Remove from the heat and stir in the vanilla extract. Serve the prune whip at room temperature with the warm sauce, or chill both the whip and the sauce and serve cold.

Rhubarb Compote

Rhubarb was commonly found in the kitchen gardens of early settlers because it could be harvested throughout the growing season. Think of this dish as rhubarb sauce, similar to applesauce. It is delicious when served warm over ice cream or cold with shortbread cookies, or simply top with whipped cream and enjoy.

SERVES 4

4 cups finely chopped fresh or frozen rhubarb stems
1 cup sugar
½ cup orange juice or water
1 teaspoon ground cinnamon
½ teaspoon ground ginger

Combine all the ingredients in a large saucepan over high heat until boiling. Reduce to medium heat. Cook for 15 minutes, stirring frequently, until the rhubarb is soft and the sauce is thickened. Serve warm or cold.

Strawberry Shortcake

There are some who remember strawberry shortcake as strawberries over a white or yellow cake, while there are others who remember it as strawberries served over biscuits. This recipe follows the biscuit tradition.

SERVES 9

2 quarts strawberries
¼ cup plus 3 tablespoons sugar
3 cups all-purpose flour
4½ teaspoons baking powder
¾ teaspoon salt
¾ cup (1½ sticks) butter, cut into small pieces
1½ cups heavy cream
1½ teaspoons vanilla extract
Whipped cream, to serve

1. Remove the hulls from the strawberries and thinly slice. Combine the strawberries with ¼ cup sugar in a large bowl. Set aside at room temperature to macerate (which will allow the strawberries to release their juices).

2. After about 20 minutes, crush half the berries with a potato masher to release more juice. Do not mash all of them. Set aside.

3. Sift the flour, remaining 3 tablespoons sugar, the baking powder, and salt into a large bowl and toss to combine. Cut in the butter with a pastry blender or 2 knives until the mixture has the consistency of small peas.

4. Make a well in the center of the flour mixture and pour in the cream and vanilla extract. Mix until the dough is evenly moistened and just combined; it will look shaggy and still feel a little dry. Gently knead by hand 5 or 6 times to create a loose ball.

5. Transfer the dough to a lightly floured surface and pat it into an 8-inch square, ¾ to 1 inch thick. Transfer the dough to a baking sheet lined with parchment paper, cover with plastic wrap, and chill for 20 minutes in the refrigerator.

6. Preheat the oven to 425°F.

7. Cut the dough into 9 even squares and spread them 2 inches apart from each other on the baking sheet.

8. Bake until the biscuits are medium golden brown, 18 to 20 minutes.

9. Split open the biscuits and arrange the bottom halves in serving bowls. Ladle some of the strawberries onto each half along with some of their juices. Top with the remaining halves and spoon a little more juice over the biscuits. Add a dollop of whipped cream and serve at once.

Strawberry Fool

This dish is a traditional English dessert, and its name probably comes from the French word "fouler," which means "to mash." It consists of sweetened puréed fruit that is folded into stiffly beaten whipped cream. It is lovely when showcased in long-stemmed parfait or wine glasses, garnished with fresh fruit. A variation using raspberries follows.

SERVES 4

1 (1-pound) bag frozen unsweetened
  strawberries
½ cup sugar, or more to taste
1 cup heavy cream
4 fresh strawberries (optional)

1. Process the thawed strawberries in a food processor until the berries are puréed. Transfer to a large bowl and stir in 6 tablespoons of sugar. Taste and add more sugar if necessary. Refrigerate for several hours or overnight.

2. Whip the cream in a large bowl until soft peaks form. Add the remaining 2 tablespoons sugar and continue to whip until stiff peaks form. With a rubber spatula, gently fold in the strawberry purée.

3. Spoon the mixture into 4 long-stemmed parfait or wine glasses. Cover and refrigerate until serving time, up to 4 hours before serving. Garnish with the fresh strawberries, if using.

Raspberry Fool

Substitute 1 (1-pound) bag frozen raspberries for the strawberries in Strawberry Fool. Complete the recipe as directed, using fresh raspberries to garnish if you wish.

Strawberries Romanoff

Strawberries and cream make a wonderful combination. Add orange and vanilla, and strawberries Romanoff comes to life. Many stories of its origin abound, but one thing is for certain—this dessert is fit for royalty.

SERVES 6

4 cups (2 pints) strawberries, hulled
Juice of 1 medium orange (about ½ cup)
¼ cup Grand Marnier
1 cup heavy cream, well chilled
¼ cup superfine or confectioners' sugar
½ teaspoon vanilla extract

1. Combine the strawberries, orange juice, and Grand Marnier in a large bowl, cover, and refrigerate for an hour or more.

2. Whip the cream in a medium bowl until stiff, gradually adding the sugar and vanilla extract.

3. Spoon the berries with their juice into dessert dishes (preferably chilled silver) and serve with the sweetened whipped cream on top.

Fruit Fritters

These tasty morsels are proof that everything tastes better fried. Fruit fritters make a wonderful accompaniment to ice cream instead of cookies.

SERVES 4 TO 6

Oil, for frying
1 cup all-purpose flour
1 tablespoon granulated sugar
1 teaspoon baking powder
½ teaspoon salt
2 large eggs, separated
½ cup milk
4 cups apple chunks, banana chunks, fresh
    berries, nectarine slices, peach slices, and/
    or plum slices
Confectioners' sugar, to serve

1. Begin heating 3 to 4 inches of oil in a large, deep saucepan to 425°F. Preheat the oven to 250°F.

2. Sift together the flour, granulated sugar, baking powder, and salt into a medium bowl. Set aside.

3. In a large bowl, beat together the egg yolks, milk, and 1 tablespoon of oil. Stir in the flour mixture until well blended. Set aside.

4. Beat the egg whites in a small bowl until stiff peaks form. Fold into the batter.

5. When the oil is hot, dip a few pieces of fruit in the batter and let any excess drip off. Use tongs to carefully slide into the hot oil and fry, turning once, until golden brown and puffed, 3 to 4 minutes. Drain on paper towels and keep warm in the oven until all are fried.

6. Sprinkle with confectioners' sugar and serve warm.

Chocolate Pudding

Before there were mixes, there was cornstarch pudding: rich, smooth pudding that was irresistible in any flavor and easy to make. Just be sure to use a heavy-bottomed saucepan and cook over medium-low heat to avoid scorching or causing lumps.

SERVES 6 TO 8

¾ cup sugar
3 tablespoons cornstarch
⅓ cup cocoa powder (preferably Dutch
    processed)
⅛ teaspoon salt
2½ cups milk
4 large egg yolks
½ cup heavy cream
4 ounces (4 squares) semisweet chocolate,
    chopped
1½ teaspoons vanilla extract
1 tablespoon butter, cut into small pieces
Whipped cream, to serve

1. Whisk together the sugar, cornstarch, cocoa powder, and salt in a medium, heavy-bottomed saucepan. Beat in ½ cup of milk to make a smooth paste. Beat in the egg yolks, one at a time, until well blended. Set aside.

2. Combine the remaining 2 cups milk with the cream in a separate medium saucepan. Bring just to a boil, then remove from the heat. (The milk will foam up to the top of the pan when done, so watch carefully.) Gradually pour the milk into the egg mixture, whisking constantly, until the mixture is smooth.

3. Place the saucepan over medium-low heat. Cook, stirring constantly, until the mixture thickens, about 5 minutes. Remove from the heat and pour through a strainer to remove any lumps that may have formed during cooking.

4. Stir in the chocolate, vanilla extract, and butter, stirring gently with a rubber spatula until the mixture is smooth.

5. Pour into dessert bowls or long-stemmed wine glasses. Serve warm or chilled, topped with a dollop of whipped cream.

TIP: Make sure you reach the bottom, sides, and corners of the saucepan when stirring to prevent the pudding from sticking and scorching.

Vanilla Pudding

This sweet, creamy, simply flavored pudding is elegant and sure to please most palates. If you like your pudding warm, then by all means eat it right away. But if you like it cold, press plastic wrap onto the surface and refrigerate until firm, which will take a couple of hours. If you leave the pudding unwrapped, it will develop a skin on top—which some people love and others don't.

SERVES 6

¼ cup cornstarch
½ cup sugar
¼ teaspoon salt
3 cups half-and-half or milk
2 teaspoons vanilla extract
Whipped cream, to serve

1. Whisk together the cornstarch, sugar, and salt in a small bowl. Beat in ½ cup of half-and-half to make a smooth paste and set aside.

2. Put the remaining 2½ cups half-and-half into a medium, heavy-bottomed saucepan and bring just to a boil, then remove from the heat. Stir the cornstarch paste into the half-and-half and cook over medium-low heat, whisking constantly, until the mixture is smooth and thick. Continue cooking for about 5 minutes to thoroughly cook the cornstarch, stirring constantly.

3. Remove from the heat and stir in the vanilla extract.

4. Pour into 6 dessert bowls or long-stemmed wine glasses. Serve warm or chilled, topped with a dollop of whipped cream.

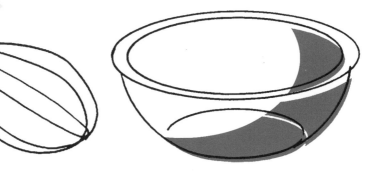

Banana Pudding

Banana pudding is an old Southern favorite consisting of layers of vanilla pudding, sliced bananas, and vanilla wafers under a meringue topping. A simplified version using instant pudding has appeared on the back of pudding and cookie boxes, but the homemade version is best.

Pudding:
About 44 vanilla wafers (half a 12-ounce box)
1 cup sugar
½ cup all-purpose flour
½ teaspoon salt
4 large egg yolks (whites reserved)
2 cups milk
1 tablespoon butter
1 teaspoon vanilla extract
4 to 5 medium bananas, peeled and sliced
    about ⅜ inch thick

Topping:
4 large egg whites, at room temperature
¼ teaspoon cream of tartar
5 tablespoons sugar
½ teaspoon vanilla extract

1. Preheat the oven to 375°F.

2. To make the pudding, line the bottom of a 9-inch square baking dish with a layer of vanilla wafers; set aside.

3. Stir together the sugar, flour, and salt in a small bowl.

4. Combine the egg yolks and milk in a heavy-bottomed saucepan and whisk to combine. Whisk in the flour mixture and bring to a boil over medium heat, stirring constantly. When the mixture begins to thicken, stir in the butter. Continue to cook, stirring constantly, until the mixture is smooth and thick. Remove from the heat and stir in the vanilla extract. Set aside.

5. Place a layer of banana slices in the baking dish on top of the vanilla wafers, lining the banana slices up edge to edge. Pour half of the pudding over the banana layer, spreading with a rubber spatula to make an even layer. Arrange another layer of vanilla wafers, another layer of banana slices, and cover with the remaining pudding.

6. To make the topping, beat the egg whites in a medium bowl at medium speed with an electric mixer until they form soft peaks. Add the cream of tartar. Beating at high speed, gradually add the sugar, a tablespoon at a time, and continue beating until stiff peaks form. Fold in the vanilla extract and spread the topping over the pudding, sealing it at the sides of the dish.

7. Bake for 12 to 15 minutes, until the top is browned. Serve warm or cooled.

Butterscotch Pudding

Brown sugar and butter give this pudding its unique flavor; packaged mixes taste artificial by contrast. If you'd like to make a parfait, layer the pudding with toffee bits and whipped cream in a parfait glass.

⅔ cup firmly packed brown sugar
2 tablespoons cornstarch
1 (12-ounce) can evaporated milk
⅓ cup water
1 large egg
3 tablespoons butter, cut into small pieces
½ teaspoon vanilla extract
Whipped cream, to serve

1. Combine the brown sugar and cornstarch in a medium, heavy-bottomed saucepan. Stir in the evaporated milk and water. Cook over medium heat, stirring constantly, until the mixture comes to a boil. Remove from the heat and set aside.

2. Beat the egg in a small bowl. Stir in ½ cup of the milk mixture until smooth. Pour back into the milk mixture and cook over medium heat, stirring constantly, until just boiling.

3. Remove the pan from the heat and stir in the butter and vanilla extract. Pour into dessert dishes and refrigerate for at least 1 hour, until firm. Serve chilled, topped with whipped cream.

Rice Pudding

Rice pudding is nursery food that was brought over from Europe by early settlers. It is also a comforting dessert—starchy, sweet, and smooth. In Greek diners throughout the Northeast, it competes with pies as a favorite dessert.

SERVES 6

4 cups milk
2 cups uncooked long-grain rice
Pinch of salt
½ cup raisins (optional)
1 cup evaporated milk or heavy cream
2 large eggs
½ cup sugar
½ teaspoon vanilla extract
Pinch of ground cinnamon
Pinch of ground nutmeg
Whipped cream, to serve

1. Mix the milk, rice, salt, and raisins, if using, in the top of a double boiler set over simmering water. Cover and simmer over medium-high heat, stirring occasionally for 30 minutes.

2. Beat together the evaporated milk, eggs, sugar, and vanilla extract in a medium bowl. Stir into the rice mixture and cook, stirring constantly, until the rice is tender and the mixture is thickened, about 10 minutes.

3. Remove from the heat and stir in the cinnamon and nutmeg. Refrigerate until thick, at least 1 hour.

4. Spoon into individual dessert dishes, garnish with whipped cream, and serve.

Tapioca Pudding

Once instant tapioca found its way onto the grocery shelves, knowledge of how to cook large-pearl tapioca almost disappeared. This recipe is the real thing. If you have trouble finding pearl tapioca at your local supermarket, look for it wherever Asian foods are sold.

SERVES 4 TO 6

⅓ cup large-pearl tapioca (not quick-cooking)
2¼ cups milk
¼ teaspoon salt
½ cup sugar
2 large eggs
½ teaspoon vanilla extract

1. Soak the tapioca in enough water to cover for 8 hours, until translucent. Drain.

2. Combine the tapioca, milk, and salt in a large, heavy-bottomed saucepan. Bring to a boil, reduce the heat, and simmer, uncovered, for 50 minutes, stirring frequently. Stir in the sugar and remove from the heat.

3. Beat the eggs in a small bowl. Stir in about ½ cup of the hot tapioca mixture. Return the mixture slowly to the saucepan. Bring to a boil, stirring constantly, and boil for 3 minutes, until thick.

4. Reduce the heat to low and cook, stirring constantly, for 15 minutes. Remove the pan from the heat and stir in the vanilla extract.

5. Chill until firm, at least 2 hours, and serve.

Bread Pudding

Bread pudding will only be as good as the bread that goes into it. Brioche, challah, and egg breads make rich bread puddings. Quick breads, such as banana nut bread, add interesting and unexpected flavors. If you prefer, remove the crusts before cubing the bread.

SERVES 6

3 large eggs
3½ cups milk
¾ cup sugar
1 teaspoon vanilla extract
¼ teaspoon salt
4 cups cubed stale bread (about 1-inch cubes)
¾ cup raisins
Cinnamon
Ice cream or whipped cream, to serve

1. Preheat the oven to 325°F. Grease a 2-quart baking dish.

2. In a medium bowl, beat the eggs, milk, sugar, vanilla extract, and salt until well blended. Mix in the bread cubes and raisins. Pour into the prepared baking dish and sprinkle the top with cinnamon.

3. Bake for 45 to 50 minutes, until the pudding is puffed up and brown and a knife inserted into the center comes out clean.

4. Top with ice cream or whipped cream and serve warm.

Baked Custard

The earliest and most simple of all puddings, baked custard goes back to at least the Middle Ages, when custard was typically baked after breads were taken out of the oven and the oven cooled. The trick with baking custard is to keep the heat slow and steady, which is why the custard cups are placed in a hot water bath.

SERVES 6

4 large eggs
½ cup sugar
½ teaspoon salt
2½ cups half-and-half
1 teaspoon vanilla extract
Ground nutmeg

1. Preheat the oven to 350°F.

2. Beat the eggs, sugar, and salt in a large bowl, then beat in the half-and-half and vanilla extract until mixed.

3. Pour into six 6-ounce custard cups and sprinkle with the nutmeg. Place the cups in a 9 x 13-inch baking dish. Fill the baking dish with 1 inch of hot water.

4. Bake for 30 to 45 minutes, until a knife inserted near the center of one of the cups comes out clean.

5. Transfer the cups to a wire rack to cool completely, then refrigerate. Serve cold.

Indian Pudding

Some Native Americans might know this pudding as sagamite; a colonist might know it as hasty pudding. But in time, anything that was made with "Indian corn," as corn was called, acquired the word "Indian" in its title. This is a hearty cornmeal pudding sweetened with molasses.

SERVES 6

4 cups milk
2 tablespoons butter
½ cup yellow cornmeal
3 large eggs
½ cup sugar
1 tablespoon ground cinnamon
1½ teaspoons ground ginger
1 teaspoon salt
1 cup molasses
Vanilla ice cream, to serve

1. Preheat the oven to 400°F. Grease a 2-quart baking dish.

2. Bring the milk and butter to a boil in a large, heavy-bottomed saucepan over medium heat. Stir in the cornmeal in a slow, steady stream, stirring constantly, until smooth, well blended, and slightly thickened, about 5 minutes.

3. Remove the pan from the heat. Beat in the eggs, sugar, cinnamon, ginger, and salt, then beat in the molasses. Pour into the prepared baking dish. Cover with a piece of wax paper cut to fit the top of the pudding. Place the baking dish in a large pan and add 1 inch of hot water to the larger pan.

4. Bake for about 1 hour, until the wax paper can be lifted without the pudding sticking to it. Serve hot with vanilla ice cream on top.

Mexican Flan

"Flan de leche" is the national dessert of Mexico, but it is frequently cooked north of the border as well. Here is a recipe for this baked custard, with its delicious caramelized sugar sauce.

SERVES 8

1 cup sugar
3 cups milk
1 teaspoon vanilla extract
5 large eggs

1. Preheat the oven to 350°F.

2. Sprinkle ½ cup of sugar in a medium, heavy skillet. Cook over medium heat, stirring constantly, until the sugar melts and turns a light golden brown. Immediately pour into a 6-cup tube pan. Let the mixture cool.

3. Meanwhile, combine the remaining ½ cup sugar, the milk, vanilla extract, and eggs in a blender and process until the sugar dissolves.

4. Pour the mixture into the tube pan and place the pan in a larger baking dish. Pour hot water into the larger baking dish to a depth of 2 inches.

5. Bake for 45 to 50 minutes, until a knife inserted into the center comes out clean.

6. Carefully remove the tube pan from the water bath and cool on a wire rack. Cover and chill for 8 hours.

7. Invert the flan onto a serving dish, letting the browned sugar mixture drizzle over the top, and serve.

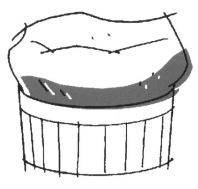

Chocolate Soufflé

Soufflés are impressive-looking desserts, yet they are easy to make. Slightly undercooking the soufflé will give a desirable, custard-like center. For best results, eat the soufflé soon after pulling it out of the oven.

SERVES 4

½ cup granulated sugar, plus more for dusting
3 ounces (3 squares) semisweet chocolate, chopped
5 large eggs, separated (discard 2 yolks)
Confectioners' sugar (optional)
Whipped cream, to serve (optional)

1. Preheat the oven to 350°F. Grease a deep 2-quart baking dish or four 1½-cup ramekins and dust with granulated sugar, tapping out any excess. Set aside.

2. Place the chocolate in the top of a double boiler over barely simmering water. Stir until melted, then remove from the heat. Add ¼ cup of granulated sugar, stirring to combine, then whisk in the 3 egg yolks.

3. In a medium bowl, beat the egg whites with the remaining ¼ cup granulated sugar until they hold stiff, glossy peaks. With a rubber spatula, fold about 1 cup of the egg whites into the chocolate mixture. Gently fold in the remaining egg whites until the white streaks are gone. Spoon the mixture into the baking dish or ramekins.

4. Bake in the middle of the oven until the top has a crust and the center jiggles, 25 to 30 minutes.

5. Remove from the oven, dust with confectioners' sugar, if using, or dollop with a large spoonful of whipped cream, if using. Serve immediately.

Lemon Sponge Pudding

Sometimes this dish is called lemon pudding cake. The batter separates during baking into a soufflé-like topping, with a lemon sauce underneath.

SERVES 4 TO 6

1 cup sugar
¼ cup all-purpose flour
¼ teaspoon salt
¼ cup lemon juice
1 tablespoon finely grated lemon zest
1 tablespoon butter, melted
1 cup milk
2 large eggs, separated

1. Preheat the oven to 350°F. Grease a 1½-quart baking dish.

2. Stir together the sugar, flour, and salt in a medium bowl. Stir in the lemon juice, zest, butter, and milk; set aside.

3. Beat the egg yolks in a small bowl until thick and pale. Stir into the lemon mixture and set aside.

4. Beat the egg whites until stiff but not dry in a separate small bowl. Fold into the lemon mixture.

5. Pour the mixture into the prepared baking dish. Place the baking dish in a larger pan and pour 2 inches of hot water into the larger pan.

6. Bake for about 40 minutes, until the topping is set and golden. Serve warm.

Upside-Down Chocolate Pudding

Like lemon sponge pudding, this recipe makes a two-layered confection of gooey pudding and sauce. It is rich and chocolatey.

SERVES 6

1 ounce (1 square) baking chocolate
2 tablespoons butter
1 cup all-purpose flour
1½ cups granulated sugar
2½ teaspoons baking powder
¼ teaspoon salt
½ cup milk
1 teaspoon vanilla extract
½ to ⅔ cup coarsely chopped nuts
¼ cup firmly packed brown sugar
2 tablespoons cocoa powder (preferably Dutch processed)
1 cup cold water

1. Preheat the oven to 350°F. Grease an 8-inch square baking dish.

2. Melt the chocolate and butter in a small saucepan over low heat.

3. Meanwhile, stir together the flour, ¾ cup of granulated sugar, the baking powder, and salt in a medium bowl. Stir in the milk and vanilla extract, then add the chocolate mixture and beat until smooth. Stir in the nuts and pour the batter into the prepared baking dish.

4. In a small bowl, stir together the remaining ¾ cup granulated sugar, the brown sugar, and cocoa powder until smooth. Sprinkle evenly over the pudding batter. Pour the water evenly over all.

5. Bake for 40 to 50 minutes, until the top layer appears set. Serve warm.

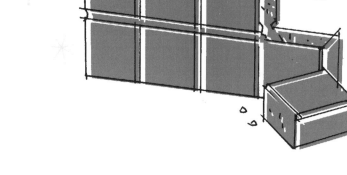

Chocolate Mousse

The word "mousse" derives from a French word meaning "foam." It is applied to all sorts of light and airy dishes, particularly desserts. Chocolate mousse is a great dessert, with a custard-like quality, that is light and ever so chocolatey. It can be made in advance to ease meal preparation.

SERVES 8

2 cups heavy cream
4 large egg yolks
¼ cup sugar
6 ounces (6 squares) semisweet chocolate, chopped

1. Heat 1 cup of cream in a medium saucepan over medium heat until hot. Do not boil.

2. Meanwhile, beat the egg yolks in a small bowl until thick and yellow colored. Add the sugar and mix well. Slowly add the hot cream, whisking continuously. Pour back into the saucepan and cook over medium-low heat for about 5 minutes, stirring constantly, until thickened.

3. Stir in the chocolate pieces until completely melted and smooth. Set aside to cool.

4. Whip the remaining 1 cup cream in a small bowl until stiff. Fold into the custard in 2 equal parts.

5. Spoon into individual dessert bowls or stemmed glasses. Refrigerate for up to 4 hours and serve.

Simple Chocolate Mousse

This mousse is an easier version of the classic mousse. It is really just chocolatey whipped cream.

SERVES 4 TO 6

3 ounces (3 squares) baking chocolate, broken into small pieces
2 cups heavy cream
½ cup sugar

1. Melt the chocolate in a double boiler over simmering water and stir until smooth. Pour in a large bowl and set aside.

2. Beat the cream with the sugar in a large bowl until soft peaks form.

3. Whisk one-third of the whipped cream into the melted chocolate until smooth and completely incorporated. Fold the lightened chocolate into the remaining whipped cream until smooth.

4. Spoon into individual dessert bowls, or stemmed glasses. Refrigerate for up to 4 hours and serve cold.

Coffee Mousse

Coffee is a delicious and sophisticated flavor to serve at the end of a fine dinner party. This is a particularly rich mousse. (Note: This recipe contains raw eggs. For more information, see page 11.)

SERVES 4

½ cup (1 stick) butter, softened
2 tablespoons instant espresso powder
2 tablespoons warm water
¾ cup sugar
5 large egg whites
¼ cup finely grated dark or semisweet chocolate

1. Beat the butter in a medium bowl until light and fluffy; set aside.

2. Dissolve the espresso powder in the water in a small bowl. Add to the butter along with ¼ cup of sugar and beat to blend. Set aside.

3. In a separate medium bowl, beat the egg whites until soft peaks form. Gradually add the remaining ½ cup sugar, beating constantly, until stiff peaks form.

4. Add half of the egg whites to the espresso mixture and mix until well blended. Fold in the remaining egg whites, then fold in the grated chocolate.

5. Spoon into individual dessert bowls or stemmed glasses. Refrigerate for up to 4 hours and serve cold.

Charlotte Russe

A charlotte is a dessert that can be filled with a variety of fruits, custards, puddings, or creams, and then chilled. A charlotte Russe is a simple, lemon-flavored version, the origins of which remain uncertain.

SERVES 6

1 tablespoon (one ¼-ounce package) unflavored gelatin
2 tablespoons cold water
1 cup milk
4 large egg yolks
½ cup sugar
¼ teaspoon salt
Grated zest of 1 medium lemon
¼ cup lemon juice
6 ladyfingers, split in half lengthwise
1 cup heavy cream

1. Sprinkle the gelatin over the cold water in a small bowl to soften. Set aside.

2. Heat the milk in a small saucepan over medium heat until bubbles appear along the edges of the milk.

3. Stir together the egg yolks, sugar, and salt in a medium, heavy-bottomed saucepan. Beat in the hot milk, a little at a time. Cook over low heat, stirring constantly, until the mixture is smooth and slightly thickened.

4. Remove the pan from the heat, stir in the gelatin mixture, and continue to stir until the gelatin dissolves. Stir in the lemon zest and juice.

5. Refrigerate until cold but not set, about 30 minutes.

6. Line a 1-quart mold or bowl with the ladyfingers, placing some on the bottom and the remainder upright around the sides. Some of the ladyfingers may have to be cut to make them fit.

7. In a medium bowl, beat the cream until it forms soft peaks. Gently fold the whipped cream into the gelatin mixture and pour into the mold.

8. Chill for 2 to 3 hours, until firm. To serve, unmold onto a platter or cake stand.

French Vanilla Ice Cream

French-style ice creams descended from medieval custards and creams; freezing was just the next step. Thomas Jefferson is credited with bringing French-style ice cream, made with egg yolks, to America, but ice cream was enjoyed as early as 1744 in Maryland. It was also made by a confectioner in New York City "almost every day," according to an ad placed in the New York Gazette. *First Lady Dolley Madison was a big fan of ice cream and served it frequently at the White House between 1809 and 1817. You will need an ice-cream maker to prepare this recipe. Three variations follow.*

MAKES 1 ½ QUARTS

2 cups milk
8 large egg yolks
¾ cup sugar
Pinch of salt
2 cups heavy cream
2 teaspoons vanilla extract

1. Heat the milk in a medium, heavy-bottomed saucepan over medium heat until bubbles form along the edges of the milk. Remove from the heat.

2. In a large bowl, beat together the egg yolks, sugar, and salt until thick. Gradually whisk in ½ cup of milk mixture. Pour this back into the hot milk mixture, stirring constantly.

3. Cook over low heat, stirring until the custard thickens. Do not allow it to boil. Remove the saucepan from the heat when you can see a thick film form over the back of a spoon. Let cool.

4. Stir the cream and vanilla extract into the custard and refrigerate until cold.

5. Transfer the mixture to an ice-cream maker and process according to the manufacturer's directions.

Chocolate Ice Cream

Make French Vanilla Ice Cream through step 4. Melt 2 ounces (2 squares) unsweetened chocolate and 3 ounces (3 squares) semisweet chocolate in the top of a double boiler over simmering water. Add to the warm vanilla mixture and stir until combined. Refrigerate until cold, then transfer to an ice-cream maker and process according to the manufacturer's directions.

Strawberry Ice Cream

Make French Vanilla Ice Cream through step 4. While the vanilla mixture chills in the refrigerator, combine 2 cups coarsely chopped strawberries with ¼ cup sugar in a medium bowl and let stand for 30 minutes. Stir into the vanilla mixture, transfer to an ice-cream maker, and process according to the manufacturer's directions.

Peach Ice Cream

Make French Vanilla Ice Cream through step 4. While the vanilla mixture chills in the refrigerator, combine 2 cups peeled and coarsely chopped ripe peaches with ¼ cup sugar in a medium bowl and let stand for 30 minutes. Stir into the vanilla mixture, transfer to an ice-cream maker, and process according to the manufacturer's directions.

Butter Pecan Ice Cream

Butter pecan is an old flavoring that is becoming quite rare in the ice-cream world. Buttery and crunchy, it is a flavor worth reviving.

MAKES 1 ½ QUARTS

2 cups half-and-half
1 cup firmly packed dark brown sugar
2 tablespoons butter
2 cups heavy cream
1½ teaspoons vanilla extract
½ cup chopped pecans

1. Combine the half-and-half, brown sugar, and butter in a medium saucepan over low heat. Stir until the mixture starts to bubble around the edges. Remove the saucepan from the heat and allow to cool.

2. Stir in the heavy cream and vanilla extract.

3. Refrigerate until cold.

4. Transfer the mixture to an ice-cream maker and process according to the manufacturer's directions, adding the pecans as the ice cream starts to harden.

Raspberry Ice Cream

Here's a recipe for ice cream that doesn't require an ice-cream maker. It won't have the same creamy texture of machine-made ice cream, but it will be a homemade treat worth savoring on a hot summer day. Substitute blackberries if you like.

SERVES 6

2 cups fresh or frozen raspberries
1 cup sweetened condensed milk
¼ cup water
2 tablespoons lemon juice
½ cup heavy cream

1. Mash the berries with a potato masher in a medium bowl or purée in a food processor. Pass through a food mill or strainer to remove the seeds, if desired, and set aside in a large bowl.

2. Combine the condensed milk, water, raspberries, and lemon juice in a large bowl. Chill in the refrigerator for 1 to 2 hours.

3. In a separate small bowl, whip the cream until it forms soft peaks. Fold into the raspberry mixture, pour into a freezer tray, and place in the freezer.

4. When the mixture is half frozen, scrape it away from the sides and bottom and beat until smooth but not melted.

5. Return to the freezer and freeze until firm. Serve cold.

Orange Sherbet

Sherbet is generally lighter than ice cream and sits well in the stomach after a large meal. Here it contains egg whites rather than whole eggs. (Note: This recipe contains raw eggs. For more information, see page 11.)

MAKES 1½ QUARTS

1 cup water
1½ cups sugar
1 tablespoon finely grated orange zest
4 large egg whites
2⅔ cups orange juice
2 tablespoons lemon juice
1 cup heavy cream

1. Combine the water and sugar in a medium saucepan over medium heat and cook until the sugar dissolves. Simmer for 10 minutes. Add the orange zest and continue simmering for another 5 minutes. Remove from the heat and cool.

2. In a small bowl, beat the egg whites until foamy. Set aside.

3. Mix the orange juice and lemon juice in a large bowl, then stir in the cooled sugar mixture. Fold in the beaten egg whites along with the cream.

4. Transfer the mixture to an ice-cream maker and process according to the manufacturer's directions.

Raspberry Sherbet

If you want to use this refreshing, creamy raspberry sherbet to make watermelon bombe, you may want to add food coloring to brighten the color. (Note: This recipe contains raw eggs. For more information, see page 11.)

MAKES 1½ QUARTS

1 cup water
1½ cups sugar
2 pints red raspberries
4 large egg whites
2 tablespoons lemon juice
1 cup heavy cream

1. Combine the water and sugar in a medium saucepan over medium heat and cook until the sugar dissolves. Stir in the berries and simmer for 10 minutes. Pass through a food mill or strainer to remove the seeds, transfer to a large bowl, and let cool.

2. In a small bowl, beat the egg whites until foamy. Set aside.

3. Stir the lemon juice into the berry mixture, then fold in the beaten egg whites along with the cream.

4. Transfer the mixture to an ice-cream maker and process according to the manufacturer's directions.

Ice Cream Bombe

Sometimes a dish is more than the sum of its parts, and surely that is the case with an ice cream bombe. Freeze three different flavors of ice cream in layers in a bowl, and you have bombe! This is an exciting, beautiful way to serve good old ice cream. A variation follows.

SERVES 10 TO 12

2 pints chocolate ice cream (page 435), softened
1½ pints French vanilla ice cream (page 434), softened
1 pint strawberry ice cream (page 435), softened

1. Line an 8-inch bowl with plastic wrap, making sure the wrap overhangs the edges. Chill in the freezer.

2. Scoop the chocolate ice cream into the bowl of an electric mixer fitted with the paddle attachment. Beat on low speed until the ice cream is soft enough to spread easily, 20 to 30 seconds. Remove the prepared bowl from the freezer. With a rubber spatula or spoon, coat the inside of the bowl with an even layer of the ice cream. Return the bowl to the freezer to refreeze the ice cream, 30 to 60 minutes.

3. Soften the vanilla ice cream in a clean bowl with the electric mixer on low speed for 20 to 30 seconds. Spread on top of the chocolate ice cream and freeze for 30 to 60 minutes more, until firm.

4. Soften the strawberry ice cream in a clean bowl with the electric mixer on low speed for 20 to 30 seconds. Spoon in enough strawberry ice cream to fill the bowl. Freeze until hard, several hours or overnight.

5. To unmold, place a serving plate upside down on top of the bowl. Holding the plate against the bowl, invert the bowl on top of the plate. Use a hair dryer on low or a hot, wet towel placed over the metal bowl for a few seconds to loosen the bowl from the ice cream. Remove the metal bowl and plastic wrap and place the bombe back in the freezer until serving time.

6. Slice the bombe into wedges and serve.

TIP: It is essential to use premium ice cream. Bargain brands contain too much air and will deflate when softened and packed into the mold. Let the ice cream soften, but do not let it liquefy or it will be become coarse and icy in texture.

Watermelon Bombe

Replace the chocolate ice cream in Ice Cream Bombe with lime sherbet. Fold ½ cup chocolate chips into the softened raspberry sherbet (to resemble watermelon seeds) and use it to replace the strawberry ice cream. Form, freeze, and serve as directed.

Hot Fudge Ice Cream Sundaes

The history of the ice cream sundae has many versions. The most popular story suggests it was invented in the late 1800s after the consumption of "sinfully" rich ice cream sodas on Sundays. Confectioners concocted a substitute of ice cream and syrup and called it a "Sunday soda," later changing it to an "ice cream sundae." The hot fudge sundae is probably the most popular version.

SERVES 4

French vanilla ice cream (page 434)
Hot fudge sauce (recipe follows)
Whipped cream
¼ cup chopped walnuts (optional)
4 red maraschino cherries

1. Layer scoops of ice cream and fudge sauce in parfait glasses, ending with fudge.

2. Top each with whipped cream, a sprinkling of nuts, if using, and a cherry. Serve immediately.

Hot Fudge Sauce

This sweet and simple sauce has a variety of uses, from topping ice cream to your favorite desserts.

MAKES ABOUT 2½ CUPS

¼ cup (½ stick) butter
4 ounces (4 squares) unsweetened chocolate, chopped
⅔ cup boiling water
2 cups sugar
¼ cup light corn syrup
¼ teaspoon salt
2 teaspoons vanilla extract

1. Melt the butter in a large, heavy saucepan over low heat. Add the chocolate and cook, stirring, until melted.

2. Stir the boiling water, sugar, corn syrup, and salt into the saucepan. Bring to a boil over medium heat and cook, without stirring, until the sauce is thickened and glossy, about 8 minutes.

3. Remove from the heat and stir in the vanilla extract. Serve hot. Leftover sauce can be stored in the refrigerator for later use. Just reheat over very low heat, stirring in a little hot water if necessary.

Butterscotch Sundaes

Homemade butterscotch and vanilla ice cream come together in a perfect marriage.

SERVES 4

French vanilla ice cream (page 434)
Butterscotch sauce (recipe follows)
Whipped cream
¼ cup chopped pecans (optional)
4 red maraschino cherries

1. Layer scoops of ice cream and butterscotch sauce in parfait glasses, ending with the sauce.

2. Top each with whipped cream, a sprinkling of nuts, if using, and a cherry. Serve immediately.

Butterscotch Sauce

This old-fashioned soda-fountain recipe is a favorite among butterscotch lovers.

MAKES ABOUT 2 CUPS

1 cup firmly packed brown sugar
⅔ cup light corn syrup
¼ cup (½ stick) butter
⅔ cup evaporated milk
⅛ teaspoon baking soda
1 teaspoon vanilla extract

1. Combine the brown sugar, corn syrup, and butter in a medium saucepan over medium heat. Cook, stirring constantly, until the brown sugar dissolves and the mixture comes to a full rolling boil. Boil, without stirring, for 1 minute.

2. Remove the pan from the heat and let stand for 5 minutes.

3. Meanwhile, combine the evaporated milk, baking soda, and vanilla extract in a small bowl. Stir into the slightly cooled brown sugar mixture.

4. Serve warm. Store any leftover sauce in the refrigerator. Reheat over very low heat, stirring in a little hot water if necessary.

Banana Splits

The creation of the banana split is claimed by several people in different locations. According to one story, the banana split was created in Latrobe, Pennsylvania, in 1904. Pharmacy apprentice David Strickler placed three scoops of ice cream on a split banana. He was soon imitated by other soda jerks; and the banana split has evolved over time to include three different ice cream flavors—vanilla, chocolate, and strawberry—topped with chocolate syrup, strawberries, crushed pineapple, nuts, whipped cream, and a cherry. Serve in glass banana split dishes if you have them.

SERVES 4

4 medium bananas, peeled and split
   lengthwise
4 scoops French vanilla ice cream (page 434)
4 scoops chocolate ice cream (page 435)
4 scoops strawberry ice cream (page 435)
1 cup frozen strawberries in syrup, thawed
1 cup canned crushed pineapple
1 cup chocolate syrup
Whipped cream
1 cup chopped walnuts
12 red maraschino cherries

1. Line 2 banana halves in the bottom of 4 banana split dishes.

2. Add a scoop each of the vanilla, chocolate, and strawberry ice creams on top of the banana halves in each dish.

3. In one dish, spoon ¼ cup of strawberries over one scoop, ¼ cup of pineapple over one scoop, and ¼ cup of chocolate syrup over the last scoop. Repeat with the other dishes.

4. Spoon a generous dollop of whipped cream on each scoop in each dish. Sprinkle chopped nuts over all and top with 3 cherries per sundae. Serve immediately.

Baked Alaska

Baked Alaska—a baked ice cream pie with a meringue top—was a favorite gourmet dish in the 1950s. Its invention is often attributed to American scientist Benjamin Thompson Rumford (1753–1814) when he was experimenting with the insulating properties of egg whites. A purchased pound cake works just fine if you do not wish to trouble with baking one from scratch.

SERVES 8 TO 10

1 (8-ounce) piece pound cake (page 384), edges trimmed and cut into ¼-inch-thick slices
2 pints chocolate ice cream (page 435), slightly softened
1 pint French vanilla ice cream (page 434), slightly softened
6 large egg whites
¼ teaspoon cream of tartar
1⅓ cups sugar

1. Line a 9-inch pie pan with the pound cake slices, overlapping the pieces as little as possible. Cover with plastic wrap and use your hands to flatten the cake into the contours of the plate. Trim the top edges as needed. Freeze until solid, about 3 hours.

2. Spoon the chocolate ice cream into the frozen cake shell. Smooth the top, shaping it into a dome. Freeze until hard, about 2 hours.

3. Spoon the vanilla ice cream over the chocolate ice cream, shaping it into a dome. Freeze until hard, about 2 hours.

4. Preheat the oven to 475°F, with the rack in the lower third of the oven.

5. In a large bowl, beat the egg whites with an electric mixer at medium speed until foamy. Add the cream of tartar. Beating on high speed, gradually add the sugar, beating until the egg whites form stiff peaks.

6. Spread the meringue over the hard ice cream; swirl with a spoon to make a decorative pattern. Alternately, you can spread a ½-inch-thick layer of meringue over the hard ice cream and smooth with a long spatula. Spoon the remaining meringue into a pastry bag with a large star tip; decorate the top with large rosettes. Make sure the ice cream is completely covered.

7. Bake the dessert for 3 to 5 minutes, until the meringue is lightly browned. Serve immediately.

Bananas Foster

In the 1950s, New Orleans was the major port of entry for bananas shipped from Central and South America. Owen Edward Brennan, the owner of Brennan's restaurant in New Orleans, challenged his talented chef, Paul Blangé, to include bananas in a new culinary creation. The resulting dessert of ice cream topped by bananas in a butter-rum sauce was named for Richard Foster, a friend of Brennan's who served on the New Orleans Crime Commission, a civic effort to clean up the French Quarter.

SERVES 4

4 scoops French vanilla ice cream (page 434)
¼ cup (½ stick) butter
1 cup firmly packed brown sugar
½ teaspoon ground cinnamon
¼ cup banana liqueur
4 medium bananas, peeled and cut in half lengthwise, then halved crosswise
¼ cup dark rum

1. Place the ice cream on 4 dessert plates and place in the freezer.

2. Combine the butter, brown sugar, and cinnamon in a medium skillet over low heat and cook, stirring, until the sugar dissolves. Stir in the banana liqueur. Add the bananas and sauté until the bananas soften and begin to brown, 3 to 5 minutes.

3. Pour in the rum and continue to cook until the rum is hot. Remove from the heat.

4. Immediately ignite the rum with a match. When the flames subside, lift the bananas out of the pan and place 4 pieces over each portion of ice cream. Generously spoon the warm sauce over the top of the ice cream and serve immediately.

Cherries Jubilee

Cherries jubilee was created with Queen Victoria's favorite fruit to honor her and celebrate the occasion of her Golden Jubilee in 1887. The original dish did not call for ice cream, just poached sweet cherries in a thickened syrup that was flambéed with brandy. Soon, however, ice cream was added and became the perfect accompaniment. Anything flambéed was the rage of dinner parties in the 1950s. Use caution when preparing this recipe. Be sure there are no flammable materials or children nearby.

SERVES 4

4 scoops French vanilla ice cream (page 434)
1 (16-ounce) can pitted dark sweet cherries
¼ cup sugar
2 tablespoons cornstarch
¼ cup kirsch or cherry brandy

1. Place the ice cream on 4 dessert plates and place in the freezer.

2. Drain the cherries, reserving the syrup. Set aside the cherries and add enough water to the syrup to make 1 cup. Pour the liquid into a small saucepan and set aside.

3. Mix the sugar and cornstarch in a small bowl. Stir into the saucepan and cook over medium heat until the sauce is thick and bubbly. Remove from the heat and stir in the cherries. Transfer the mixture to a large bowl and set aside.

4. Heat the brandy in a small skillet.

5. Remove the brandy from the heat, ignite it with a match, and pour or ladle it over the cherry mixture.

6. Spoon the cherry mixture over the ice cream and serve immediately.

Frozen Orange Cups

Florida orange growers dread a freeze during the growing season, but this way of freezing oranges makes a sophisticated dinner party dessert. Serve with a plate of cookies. This dessert is sometimes called orange surprise.

SERVES 4

4 large oranges
1 cup heavy cream
4 teaspoons sugar
¼ cup finely crushed cookies, candy bar, or
    miniature semisweet chocolate pieces
    (optional)

1. Slice off the upper third of each orange and discard. Carefully remove and drain the pulp from the peels, reserving the juice for another use. Reserve the orange cups. Cut the pulp into bite-size pieces and set aside.

2. Beat the cream with the sugar in a medium bowl until stiff peaks form. Fold in the orange pulp and crushed cookies, if using.

3. Spoon the mixture into the orange cups. Cover with plastic wrap and freeze for about 3 hours, until firm.

4. Let stand at room temperature for 15 to 20 minutes before serving.

Funnel Cakes

Funnel cakes are made by pouring batter through a funnel into a deep pan of hot fat. This was once a Pennsylvania Dutch breakfast treat. Today, you are most likely to encounter funnel cakes at carnivals and fairs.

MAKES 20 TO 30

Oil, for frying
4 cups all-purpose flour
⅓ cup granulated sugar
1 tablespoon baking powder
½ teaspoon salt
3 large eggs
3 cups milk
Sifted confectioners' sugar

1. Begin heating 3 to 4 inches of oil in a large, deep saucepan to 365°F.

2. Sift together the flour, granulated sugar, baking powder, and salt into a medium bowl. Set aside.

3. Beat the eggs with the milk in a large bowl, then beat in the flour mixture until very smooth.

4. When the oil is hot, fill a large funnel with the batter, holding one finger over the bottom of the funnel to keep the opening closed. Remove your finger to open the end of the funnel and allow the batter to run out in a steady stream into the hot fat, moving the funnel from the center, swirling outward in a circular pattern. Fry for 2 to 3 minutes, until golden brown.

5. Transfer the fried funnel cakes to paper towels to drain. Shake confectioners' sugar over the drained cakes. Repeat until all the batter is used. Serve while the cakes are still hot.

Beignets

"Beignet" translates as "fritter" from French, but in New Orleans a beignet is more like a raised doughnut. It is sold in the French Quarter as a breakfast treat or snack with coffee—preferably chicory coffee.

MAKES 48 TO 60

2¼ teaspoons (one ¼-ounce package) active dry yeast
1½ cups warm water
½ cup granulated sugar
1 teaspoon salt
2 large eggs, lightly beaten
1 cup evaporated milk
7 cups all-purpose flour
¼ cup shortening
Oil, for frying
Sifted confectioners' sugar

1. Sprinkle the yeast over the warm water in a large bowl, stir to dissolve, and let stand for 5 minutes, until foamy.

2. Beat in the granulated sugar, salt, eggs, and evaporated milk. Add 4 cups of flour and beat until smooth. Beat in the shortening, then gradually mix in the remaining flour.

3. Cover with plastic wrap and refrigerate for at least 4 hours or overnight.

4. Roll out the dough on a lightly floured surface to a thickness of ¼ inch. Cut into 2½- to 3-inch squares and set aside.

5. Heat 3 to 4 inches of oil in a large, deep saucepan to 375°F. Use tongs to add the beignets, a few at a time, and fry for 2 to 3 minutes, until lightly browned on both sides.

6. Drain on paper towels and sprinkle generously with confectioners' sugar. Serve hot.

Sopaipillas

While the Louisianans were enjoying their beignets, folks in the Southwest were enjoying sopaipillas—deep-fried fritters served with honey. "Sopaipilla" means "pillow" in Spanish.

MAKES ABOUT 24

2 cups all-purpose flour
1½ teaspoons salt
1 teaspoon sugar
½ teaspoon baking powder
2 tablespoons warm water
1 tablespoon heavy cream
2 teaspoons oil, plus more for frying
Honey, to serve

1. Mix the flour, salt, sugar, and baking powder in a large bowl. Stir in the water, cream, and 2 teaspoons oil to make a soft dough.

2. Turn the dough out onto a lightly floured surface and knead lightly. The dough will be sticky. Cover with a dish towel and let rest for 30 minutes.

3. Heat 3 to 4 inches of oil in a large, deep saucepan or deep fryer to 375°F.

4. Roll out the dough into a rectangle about 9 x 12 inches and ¼ inch thick. Let the dough rest for a few minutes, then fold it in half. Roll out again until it is ¼ inch thick. Cut into 3-inch squares.

5. Use tongs to carefully add the squares to the hot oil, 2 or 3 at a time. Use a fork to press them down into the oil so they'll puff. Fry until golden brown, about 3 minutes, turning once.

6. Drain well on paper towels and serve hot, passing the honey at the table.

Buttermilk Doughnuts

Who invented the doughnut? While ancient Romans were known to fry sweet breads, it was probably the Pennsylvania Dutch who first put holes in the centers of their doughnuts. There is a story told in Rockport, Maine, that a sea captain named Hanson Gregory poked out the soggy centers of his wife's fried cakes so that he could slip them over the spokes of his ship's wheel. Regardless of origin, these tender, sugary doughnuts are a wonderful treat.

MAKES 12 TO 14

¾ cup buttermilk
¼ cup (½ stick) butter, melted
3 large eggs (2 whole, 1 separated)
3½ cups all-purpose flour, or more as needed
1 cup granulated sugar
2 teaspoons baking powder
1½ teaspoons ground nutmeg
1 teaspoon salt
½ teaspoon baking soda
Shortening or oil, for frying
Confectioners' sugar

1. Whisk together the buttermilk, melted butter, 2 whole eggs, and 1 yolk in a small bowl. Set aside.

2. Combine 1 cup of flour, the granulated sugar, baking powder, nutmeg, salt, and baking soda in a large bowl. Add the buttermilk mixture and beat with a mixer on medium speed for 10 seconds, until well blended. Add 2 cups of flour and mix on low speed just until combined, about 30 seconds. The dough should be moist and sticky, somewhere between thick cake batter and cookie dough.

3. Begin heating 3 to 4 inches of shortening in a large, deep saucepan to 375°F.

4. Generously dust a work surface and a rolling pin with flour, using some of the remaining ½ cup flour. Roll out the dough to a thickness of ½ inch, adding flour only as needed to keep the dough from sticking. Dip a 2½-inch doughnut cutter in flour and cut out the doughnuts. Gather the scraps, roll them out, and cut more doughnuts. Let sit for 5 minutes before frying.

5. Use tongs to add the doughnuts to the hot oil, 3 or 4 at a time. As the doughnuts rise to the top, flip them with a slotted spoon. Cook for 50 seconds, until well browned, and flip again. Fry for the same amount of time on the other side, remove, and drain on paper towels. Let the fat return to 365°F before frying subsequent batches.

6. Dust the doughnuts with confectioners' sugar, if using, and eat warm or cool.

Cider Doughnuts

Cider doughnuts are a New England tradition and a variation on the buttermilk doughnut. The key to success with doughnuts is to maintain a steady 375°F oil temperature. If the oil cools down, the doughnuts will absorb oil and become greasy "sinkers."

MAKES ABOUT 20

Doughnuts:
1 cup apple cider
¼ cup shortening or oil, plus more for frying
3½ cups all-purpose flour
2 teaspoons baking powder
1 teaspoon baking soda
½ teaspoon ground cinnamon
½ teaspoon salt
¼ teaspoon ground nutmeg
1 cup granulated sugar
2 large eggs
½ cup buttermilk

Glaze:
2 cups confectioners' sugar
¼ cup apple cider

1. To make the doughnuts, boil the cider in a small saucepan until it is reduced to ¼ cup, 8 to 10 minutes. Let cool.

2. Begin heating 3 to 4 inches of shortening in a large, deep saucepan to 375°F.

3. Stir together the flour, baking powder, baking soda, cinnamon, salt, and nutmeg in a medium bowl. Set aside.

4. Beat the sugar with the ¼ cup shortening in a large bowl until smooth. Beat in the eggs, buttermilk, and reduced cider. Add the flour mixture and mix just enough to combine.

5. Transfer the dough to a lightly floured board and pat to ½-inch thickness. Cut with a 2½- to 3-inch doughnut cutter. Gather the scraps, roll them out, and cut more doughnuts. Let sit for 5 minutes before frying.

6. Use tongs to add the doughnuts to the hot oil, 3 or 4 at a time. As the doughnuts rise to the top, flip them with a slotted spoon. Cook for about 1 minute, until well browned, and flip again. Fry for the same amount of time on the other side. Drain on paper towels. Let the fat return to 375°F before frying subsequent batches. Repeat until all the doughnuts are fried.

7. To make the glaze, combine the confectioners' sugar and cider in a shallow bowl and stir until smooth. Dip the doughnuts in the glaze while warm, and serve.

Baklava

Baklava—a rich dessert of thin, layered pastry drenched in butter and layered with spices, nuts, and honey—is popular in both Greece and Turkey. In the United States, it can be found wherever there is a Greek community. You should be able to find frozen phyllo dough in most supermarkets.

MAKES ABOUT 36

1 teaspoon ground cinnamon
1 pound chopped walnuts
1 (16-ounce) package phyllo dough, thawed
1 cup (2 sticks) butter, melted
1 cup sugar
1 cup water
½ cup honey
1 teaspoon grated lemon zest

1. Preheat the oven to 350°F. Grease a 9 x 13-inch baking dish.

2. Toss together the cinnamon and nuts in a small bowl.

3. Unroll the phyllo dough and cut the whole stack in half to fit the dish. Cover the dough with a damp cloth while assembling the baklava, to keep it from drying out.

4. Place 2 sheets of phyllo in the bottom of the prepared dish. Brush generously with butter. Sprinkle 2 to 3 tablespoons of the nut mixture on top. Repeat the 3 layers until all ingredients are used, ending with about 6 sheets of phyllo. Using a sharp knife, cut the baklava (all the way through to the bottom of the dish) into 4 long rows, then (9 times) diagonally to make about 36 diamond shapes.

5. Bake for 50 minutes, until golden and crisp.

6. While the baklava is baking, combine the sugar and water in a small saucepan over medium heat and bring to a boil. Stir in the honey and lemon zest. Reduce the heat and simmer for 20 minutes.

7. Remove the baklava from the oven and immediately spoon the syrup over it. Cool completely before serving.

Rum Balls

A cross between a cookie and a candy, these no-bake treats are a Christmas tradition. Buy fancy confectioners' paper cups for serving them.

MAKES ABOUT 30

1½ cups vanilla wafer crumbs (about 50 wafers)
¼ cup dark or amber rum
¼ cup honey
2 cups ground walnuts (about 8 ounces)
Confectioners' sugar

1. Combine the wafer crumbs, rum, honey, and walnuts in a large bowl and blend thoroughly. Shape into 1-inch balls and roll in the confectioners' sugar until well coated.

2. Store in an airtight container. They improve in flavor after a few days of resting.

TIP: A food processor does the best job of pulverizing the cookies to make crumbs.

Bourbon Balls

Bourbon balls, made with chopped pecans and cocoa powder, are a variation on rum balls. Bourbon, of course, is the spirit of choice in the South.

MAKES ABOUT 36

1 cup finely crushed vanilla wafers
1 cup finely chopped pecans
1½ cups confectioners' sugar
2 tablespoons cocoa powder (preferably Dutch processed)
2 tablespoons bourbon or other whiskey
1½ tablespoons light corn syrup

1. Combine the wafer crumbs, pecans, 1 cup of confectioners' sugar, and the cocoa powder in a large bowl. Set aside.

2. Stir together the bourbon and corn syrup in a small bowl. Stir into the dry mixture, cover, and refrigerate for at least 1 hour.

3. Form the mixture into 1-inch balls and roll in the remaining ½ cup confectioners' sugar until well coated.

4. Store in an airtight container. They improve in flavor after a few days of resting.

Butterscotch Haystacks

Chow mein noodles give this easy no-bake treat the look of haystacks. These are so simple to make you can enlist your children's help.

MAKES ABOUT 50

⅔ cup peanut butter
1 (12-ounce) package butterscotch chips
1 (3-ounce) can chow mein noodles
1 cup chopped walnuts or peanuts

1. Melt the peanut butter and butterscotch chips in a medium, heavy saucepan over low heat and stir until smooth. Stir in the noodles and nuts until well coated.

2. Drop by the teaspoon onto a baking sheet lined with wax paper.

3. Chill in the refrigerator until set and serve.

Chocolate Haystacks

For chocolate lovers, butterscotch haystacks can be made with chocolate. The chow mein noodles add an appealing salty crunch.

MAKES ABOUT 60

1 (12-ounce) package semisweet chocolate chips
1 (12-ounce) package butterscotch chips (or peanut butter chips)
½ teaspoon vanilla extract
3 cups chow mein noodles

1. Melt the chocolate and butterscotch chips in a medium, heavy saucepan over low heat and stir until smooth. Stir in the vanilla extract, then stir in the noodles until well coated.

2. Drop by the teaspoon onto a baking sheet lined with wax paper.

3. Chill in the refrigerator until set.

Crispy Rice Squares

Neither a candy nor a cookie, these crunchy treats were invented by the Kellogg Company to make use of their famous rice cereal. These squares are sticky, sweet, and a favorite for kids of all ages.

MAKES ABOUT 24

¼ cup (½ stick) butter
1 (10-ounce) package marshmallows
6 cups crisp rice cereal

1. Grease a 9 x 13-inch baking dish.

2. Melt the butter in a large saucepan over low heat. Stir in the marshmallows and blend well.

3. Remove from the heat, add the cereal, and stir until the cereal is coated.

4. Transfer to the prepared baking dish and press evenly into the dish.

5. Cool, cut into squares, and serve.

Popcorn Balls

Popcorn balls were first made with molasses in the 1870s; later the recipe was refined with granulated sugar. Popcorn balls were a popular trick-or-treat giveaway in the good old days.

MAKES ABOUT 20

5 quarts freshly popped corn
4 cups sugar
2 teaspoons salt
1 cup water
2 tablespoons butter
¼ teaspoon cream of tartar

1. Pour the popcorn into a large bowl and set aside.

2. Combine the sugar, salt, water, butter, and cream of tartar in a large saucepan over medium heat. Stir constantly until the mixture reaches the firm-ball stage, 244°F on a candy thermometer.

3. Pour the syrup over the popcorn and stir gently with a large spoon to coat well.

4. Lightly butter your hands and shape the popcorn into 3-inch balls. Place on a greased baking sheet or wax paper. Let cool and serve.

Caramel Corn

Caramel corn is a delicious treat that is absolutely addictive. Add peanuts and bury a few prizes in the bowl and you'll have Cracker Jack, a ballpark tradition.

MAKES 5 CUPS

5 cups freshly popped corn
1 cup (2 sticks) butter
½ cup light corn syrup
2 cups firmly packed dark brown sugar
1 teaspoon salt
½ teaspoon baking soda

1. Preheat the oven to 250°F.

2. Spread the popcorn in a large, shallow baking pan and put it in the oven to keep warm and crispy.

3. Combine the butter, corn syrup, brown sugar, and salt in a large saucepan. Cook over medium heat, stirring until the sugar is dissolved. Bring to a boil and continue to cook until the syrup reaches the firm-ball stage, 245°F on a candy thermometer. Continue cooking for 5 minutes more.

4. Remove the syrup from the heat and stir in the baking soda. The syrup will foam.

5. Remove the popcorn from the oven and drizzle the syrup over it. Mix well.

6. Return the popcorn to the oven for 45 to 50 minutes more, stirring every 15 minutes. Cool and serve or store in an airtight container.

Crunchy Candied Pecans

Candied nuts make an irresistible holiday snack, perfect for gift giving. They are terrific plain and also make a wonderful topping for ice cream.

MAKES 6 CUPS

2 large egg whites
2 cups firmly packed brown sugar
2 tablespoons all-purpose flour
¼ teaspoon salt
2 teaspoons vanilla extract
5½ to 6 cups pecans

1. Preheat the oven to 250°F. Grease 2 baking sheets.

2. Whip the egg whites until foamy. Gradually beat in the brown sugar and flour, then beat in the salt and vanilla extract. Fold in the pecans with a rubber spatula until the pecans are thoroughly coated.

3. Transfer the mixture to the prepared baking sheets and arrange in a single layer.

4. Bake for 45 minutes, stirring every 15 minutes, until browned and crisp. Let cool before serving or storing in an airtight container.

Candied Apples

Candied apples are a specialty of carnivals and street fairs, but kids appreciate them any time. They are also popular around Halloween.

.MAKES 6

6 medium apples
6 craft sticks
2 cups sugar
2 cups corn syrup
⅓ cup cinnamon candies
1 cup water
¾ teaspoon red food coloring
¾ teaspoon ground cinnamon
½ teaspoon vanilla extract
¼ teaspoon ground cloves

1. Remove the stems from the apples, wash, and pat dry with paper towels. Insert a craft stick into the bottom of each apple, running through to the stem end without protruding all the way through the top. Line a baking sheet with wax paper, stand the apples on it, stick side up, and set aside.

2. Combine the sugar, corn syrup, cinnamon candies, and water in a medium saucepan over medium heat. Cook until the candies dissolve, stirring constantly. Be careful not to boil. Stir in the food coloring, cinnamon, vanilla extract, and cloves.

3. Bring to a boil and continue to boil, without stirring, until the syrup reaches the hard-crack stage, 300°F on a candy thermometer.

4. Remove the mixture from the heat and quickly dip each apple, one at a time, into the mixture, swirling until thoroughly coated. Set the coated apples, standing on their tops with the sticks pointing up, back on the baking sheet until the coating hardens.

5. Let the apples cool to room temperature before eating.

Caramel Apples

The caramel apple is a variation on the candied apple. Choose a tart apple to create a crisp contrast with the soft, sweet coating.

MAKES 10 TO 12

10 to 12 medium tart apples, such as Granny
   Smith or Rome Beauty
10 to 12 craft sticks
1 cup firmly packed brown sugar
1 cup (2 sticks) butter
1 cup corn syrup
1 (14-ounce) can sweetened condensed milk
1 teaspoon vanilla extract

1. Remove the stems from the apples, wash, and pat dry with paper towels. Insert a craft stick into the bottom of each apple, running through to the stem end without protruding all the way through the top. Line a baking sheet with wax paper, stand the apples on it, stick side up, and set aside.

2. Combine the brown sugar, butter, corn syrup, and condensed milk in a medium saucepan over medium heat. Cook until the sugar dissolves, stirring constantly.

3. Bring to a boil and continue to boil, without stirring, until the mixture reaches the soft-ball stage, 234°F on a candy thermometer. Add the vanilla extract and continue to cook to 238°F.

4. Remove the mixture from the heat and quickly dip each apple, one at a time, into the mixture, swirling until thoroughly coated. Set the coated apples, standing on their tops with the sticks pointing up, on the baking sheet.

5. Refrigerate until the coating hardens, and serve.

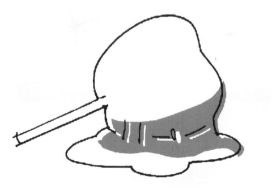

Chocolate-Dipped Apricots

Apricots are prized for their delicate, velvety skin and intensely sweet fragrance and flavor, but their season is all too brief. Most of the time, apricots are enjoyed dried—as in this holiday treat.

MAKES ABOUT 40

½ cup semisweet chocolate chips
1½ tablespoons brandy
1 (6-ounce) package dried apricots (about 40)

1. Line a baking sheet with wax paper.

2. Combine the chocolate chips and brandy in the top of a double boiler and heat until melted and smooth.

3. Dip half of each apricot into the chocolate mixture and place on the wax paper.

4. Refrigerate for 1 to 2 hours, until the chocolate is firm, and serve. Store any leftovers in a cool place.

Chocolate Peanut Butter Balls

Chocolate and peanut butter make a great combination. Soft and crunchy on the inside and topped with chopped peanuts, these snacks will disappear as fast as you make them.

MAKES ABOUT 40

1 cup chunky peanut butter
½ cup corn syrup
1 cup crisp rice cereal
½ pound milk chocolate, chopped
¼ cup finely chopped peanuts

1. Beat the peanut butter and corn syrup in a medium bowl until smooth. Stir in the cereal until well mixed. Set aside.

2. Line a baking sheet with wax paper. Shape the peanut butter mixture into 1-inch balls and place on the wax paper.

3. Refrigerate until firm, 2 to 3 hours.

4. Melt the chocolate in the top of a double boiler over simmering water and stir until smooth.

5. Use a skewer to dip each ball into the chocolate, swirling to coat. Allow any excess to drip back into the pan. Place the dipped ball on the wax paper and continue until all the balls have been dipped.

6. Let stand for 2 hours, until the chocolate is almost firm. Sprinkle the peanuts over each and let stand for 1 more hour, until the chocolate is set. Arrange on a serving plate and serve.

Chocolate Crunchies

Milk chocolate and raisins with rice cereal crunch—these candies are surprisingly easy to make and deliver a nice contrast of textures and flavors.

MAKES ABOUT 30

14 ounces milk chocolate, chopped
1½ cups crisp rice cereal
1 cup raisins

1. Generously grease an 8-inch square baking dish.

2. Melt the chocolate in the top of a double boiler over simmering water. Stir until smooth. Stir in the cereal and raisins until well mixed. Spoon into the prepared dish.

3. Refrigerate until firm, about 2 hours.

4. Cut into squares and serve.

Chocolate Fudge

Candy making was very popular among coed college students in the late nineteenth century. One of the earliest records of fudge making is found in a letter written by a student at Vassar College in Poughkeepsie, New York. Emelyn Battersby Hartridge wrote that her schoolmate's cousin made fudge in Baltimore in 1886 and sold it for 40 cents a pound. Miss Hartridge secured the recipe, and in 1888, she made 30 pounds of this delicious fudge for the Vassar Senior Auction. Word spread of the confection to other women's colleges, and the candy gained great popularity.

MAKES ABOUT 50

2 cups sugar
1 cup heavy cream
2 ounces (2 squares) baking chocolate, chopped
1 tablespoon butter

1. Grease an 8-inch square baking dish.

2. Combine the sugar and cream in a medium saucepan over medium heat. Cook until hot, then stir in the chocolate until melted. Wash down the sides of the pan with a wet pastry brush to dissolve any sugar crystals.

3. Stirring constantly, continue to cook until the mixture reaches the soft-ball stage, 234°F on a candy thermometer.

4. Remove the pan from the heat and stop the cooking by plunging the pan into a basin of cold water for 1 minute. Add the butter but do not stir.

5. When the temperature of the fudge reaches 110°F, stir without stopping until the fudge thickens and loses its sheen.

6. Pour into the prepared baking dish.

7. Cut into squares before the fudge hardens completely and serve.

TIP: To test for the soft-ball stage, drop a small amount of the mixture into a glass of chilled water. The mixture should form a ball that is soft enough to flatten when picked up with the fingers (234° to about 240°F).

Vanilla Fudge

Although we think of fudge as chocolate, this candy can be any flavor. Vanilla is especially popular. American confectioners helped to spread the popularity of fudge by introducing it to resort-area vacationers in the 1880s. Mackinac Island in Michigan is particularly known for this confection.

MAKES ABOUT 50

1 cup heavy cream
2 cups sugar
½ cup (1 stick) butter
1 tablespoon corn syrup
1 teaspoon vanilla extract

1. Grease an 8-inch square baking dish.

2. Combine the cream, sugar, butter, and corn syrup in a heavy saucepan over low heat. Stir constantly until the sugar dissolves and the butter melts. Wash down the sides of the pan with a wet pastry brush to dissolve any sugar crystals.

3. Bring to a boil and cook until the mixture reaches the soft-ball stage, 234°F on a candy thermometer.

4. Remove the pan from the heat and stop the cooking by plunging the pan into a basin of cold water for 1 minute.

5. When the temperature of the fudge reaches 110°F, stir in the vanilla extract and continue to stir without stopping until the fudge thickens and loses its sheen.

6. Pour into the prepared baking dish.

7. Cut into squares before the fudge hardens completely and serve.

Easy Peanut Butter Fudge

Making fudge can be tricky without professional equipment. In candy stores, professionals use huge marble tables to work their confections into the right consistency. Home cooks simply pour their mixed ingredients directly into baking pans and hope for the best. Recipes that contain marshmallow cream, like this one, seem easiest to make.

MAKES ABOUT 100

4 cups granulated sugar
1 cup firmly packed brown sugar
½ cup (1 stick) butter
1½ cups heavy cream
1 (7-ounce) jar marshmallow cream
1 (18-ounce) jar peanut butter

1. Grease a 9 x 13-inch baking dish.

2. Combine the sugars, butter, and heavy cream in a large, heavy saucepan over medium heat. Bring to a boil, stirring constantly, for 7 minutes.

3. Remove the pan from the heat and stir in the marshmallow cream and peanut butter until smooth.

4. Spoon into the prepared baking dish and let cool.

5. Cut into small squares and serve.

Creamy Chocolate-Nut Fudge

This delicious, creamy fudge is especially welcome during the holidays or as a special treat. Once the chocolate is melted, kids will enjoy getting involved in mixing, refrigerating, and serving it.

MAKES ABOUT 50

1 (7-ounce) jar marshmallow cream
1½ cups sugar
⅔ cup evaporated milk
¼ cup (½ stick) butter
¼ teaspoon salt
1 cup semisweet chocolate chips
2 cups milk chocolate chips
½ cup chopped nuts
1 teaspoon vanilla extract

1. Grease an 8-inch square baking dish.

2. Combine the marshmallow cream, sugar, evaporated milk, butter, and salt in a large saucepan. Bring to a full boil and cook for 5 minutes, stirring constantly.

3. Remove the pan from the heat and stir in the semisweet chocolate chips and milk chocolate chips until the chocolate is melted and the mixture is smooth. Stir in the nuts and vanilla extract.

4. Pour the mixture into the prepared pan and chill in the refrigerator for at least 2 hours, until firm.

5. Cut into squares and serve.

Divinity Fudge

Divinity fudge (also known as divinity and divinity candy) is an early-twentieth-century American creation. One of the primary ingredients is corn syrup, a product actively marketed to (and embraced by) American consumers as an affordable sugar substitute. Karo brand corn syrup, introduced by the Corn Products Refining Company in 1902, promoted its use in recipe booklets, with divinity fudge as one of their recipes. It's not hard to imagine how this richly flavored candy got its name!

MAKES ABOUT 24

2 cups sugar
½ cup corn syrup
½ cup water
2 large egg whites
Pinch of salt
½ cup chopped pecans
¼ cup halved candied cherries
2 teaspoons vanilla extract

1. Grease an 8-inch square baking dish.

2. Combine the sugar, corn syrup, and water in a large saucepan over medium heat. Cook, stirring, until the sugar dissolves. Wash down the sides of the pan with a wet pastry brush to dissolve any sugar crystals.

3. Bring to a boil and cook, without stirring, to the firm-ball stage, or 244°F on a candy thermometer.

4. While the syrup is cooking, beat the egg whites with the salt in a small bowl until stiff but not dry.

5. While beating constantly, drizzle in the hot syrup, pouring slowly at first, and then a little faster. When the mixture is stiff, beat until creamy. Stir in the nuts, cherries, and vanilla extract.

6. Pour the mixture into the prepared dish and let cool.

7. Cut into 1-inch squares when firm and serve.

Penuche

Penuche is basically fudge made with brown sugar. This version also contains the light crunch of pecans. The texture will be firmer than most fudge.

4½ cups (2 pounds) firmly packed brown
   sugar
1 cup evaporated milk
½ cup (1 stick) butter
¼ teaspoon salt
1 teaspoon vanilla extract
1½ cups chopped pecans

1. Grease a 9-inch square baking dish.

2. Combine the brown sugar, milk, butter, and salt in a large saucepan over medium heat. Cook, stirring, until the sugar is dissolved. Wash down the sides of the pan with a wet pastry brush to dissolve any sugar crystals.

3. Cook, without stirring, until the mixture reaches the soft-ball stage, 234°F on a candy thermometer.

4. Remove the pan from the heat and plunge into a basin of cold water for 1 minute to stop the cooking. Cool to 110°F.

5. Mix in the vanilla extract and pecans and beat until thick.

6. Pour into the prepared baking dish.

7. Cut into squares when firm and serve.

Maple Fudge

If a candy can be made with syrup instead of sugar, it will be made with pure maple syrup—at least in Vermont, where maple syrup is a prized commodity. Traditionally this fudge is made with butternuts, which are hard-shelled walnuts found in New England.

2 cups pure maple syrup
1 tablespoon corn syrup
¾ cup half-and-half
1 teaspoon vanilla extract
¾ cup coarsely chopped butternuts or walnuts

1. Grease a 9-inch square baking dish.

2. Combine the maple syrup, corn syrup, and half-and-half in a large saucepan over medium heat. Cook, stirring, until the sugar dissolves. Wash down the sides of the pan with a wet pastry brush to dissolve any sugar crystals.

3. Cook, without stirring, until the mixture reaches the soft-ball stage, 234°F on a candy thermometer.

4. Remove the pan from the heat and plunge into a basin of cold water for 1 minute to stop the cooking. Cool to 110°F.

5. Mix in the vanilla extract and butternuts and beat until thick.

6. Pour into the prepared baking dish and cool.

7. Cut into squares when firm and serve.

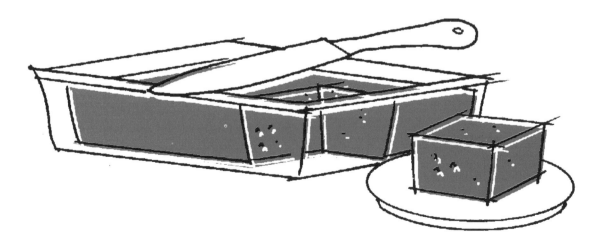

Peanut Brittle

This is a traditional holiday classic that was invented sometime around 1900; its brittle texture prompted its name. Brittles should be broken into pieces because they will shatter if you attempt to cut them with a knife.

MAKES 1½ POUNDS

2 cups sugar
1 cup corn syrup
1 cup water
½ teaspoon salt
2 cups raw peanuts
2 tablespoons butter
2 teaspoons baking soda

1. Grease two 15-inch jelly-roll pans.

2. Combine the sugar, corn syrup, water, and salt in a large saucepan over medium heat and cook, stirring, until the sugar dissolves. Wash down the sides of the pan with a wet pastry brush to dissolve any sugar crystals.

3. Cook, without stirring, until the mixture reaches the soft-ball stage, 234°F on a candy thermometer. Continue cooking, then add the peanuts when the mixture reaches 250°F.

4. Continue to cook to the hard-crack stage, 300°F, stirring often. Remove from the heat.

5. Quickly stir in the butter and soda and beat to a froth for a few seconds. Pour at once onto the prepared pans, spreading the mixture with a rubber spatula. If desired, cool slightly and pull with forks to stretch thin.

6. Break into pieces when cooled and serve.

Pralines

These French candies are a particular favorite in the South, especially in New Orleans, where they are most often made with pecans. Crushed pralines are often used as a mix-in or topping for vanilla ice cream.

MAKES ABOUT 36

2½ cups sugar
1 cup half-and-half
1 tablespoon butter
2 cups pecan halves or almonds

1. Combine 2 cups of sugar with the half-and-half and butter in a large saucepan over medium heat. Bring to a boil.

2. Meanwhile, melt the remaining ½ cup sugar in a large, heavy skillet over medium heat and cook until caramel colored. Add the cream mixture to the caramelized sugar. Stir in the pecans and cook to the soft-ball stage, 234°F on a candy thermometer.

3. Remove the pan from the heat and beat the mixture until it thickens.

4. Drop spoonfuls of the mixture onto wax paper to form hard candy disks 2 to 3 inches in diameter.

5. Let the pralines harden and serve.

TIPS FOR SWEET PERFECTION

The easiest and best no-cook summer desserts are simple combinations of whipped cream and fruit. Here are some tips for making good whipped cream.

▶ Choose a bowl large enough to hold the cream when doubled in volume.

▶ A small amount of cream (less than 1 cup) will whip better in a deep, narrow bowl than in a wide, shallow one.

▶ For the best volume, chill the bowl and beaters in the freezer for 15 minutes before whipping the cream.

▶ Whip the cream to soft peaks before adding sugar or flavorings.

▶ Confectioners' sugar leaves no unpleasant grit in whipped cream, and the cornstarch in it helps to stabilize the whipped cream.

▶ A little pure maple syrup, honey, or vanilla extract gives whipped cream added flavor.

▶ Pasteurized cream whips up higher and tastes fresher than the easier-to-find ultrapasteurized cream.

Candy making is one of the more difficult cooking skills to acquire. It requires precision, good equipment, good weather, and a little luck. Here are some tips.

▶ You will need a medium, heavy-bottomed saucepan large enough to hold 3 to 4 times the volume of the ingredients to prevent them from boiling over.

▶ A candy thermometer is key. If possible, buy one equipped with a metal clamp that attaches to the side of the pan.

▶ Test your candy thermometer to make sure it is accurate every time you use it. Immerse it in a pan of water, and bring the water to a boil. If the temperature doesn't read 212°F when the water boils, adjust your candy-making temperatures accordingly.

▶ A long-handled wooden spoon will keep you from burning yourself while stirring.

▶ Never use margarine in a recipe that calls for butter. Margarine has a higher water content than butter, and this will significantly affect the cooking time.

▶ Make candy on clear, crisp days. On rainy or humid days, the cooking time can increase substantially, or the candy may never set up at all, because sugar attracts water.

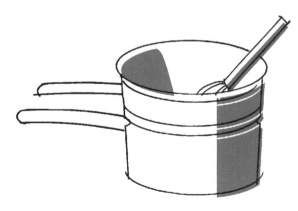

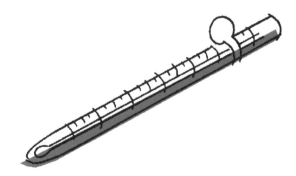

Egg whites are beaten until stiff and then used to make mousses or meringues. Here are a few helpful tips to ensure the proper consistency every time.

▸ For the best results, beat egg whites in a deep bowl with a rounded bottom.

▸ Copper bowls react chemically with egg whites to form fluffy, well-beaten whites. You get the same results by adding cream of tartar (⅛ teaspoon per 2 egg whites).

▸ The bowl must be clean, with no trace of fat.

▸ Egg whites beaten without sugar will not peak as firmly as those beaten with sugar.

▸ When folding egg whites into a thick or heavy mixture, first stir in a quarter of the whites to lighten the mixture. Then fold in the remainder.

▸ To fold in egg whites, use a large rubber spatula and quickly but gently cut into the middle of the mixture. Bring the bottom of the batter up and over the remaining mixture. Rotate the bowl a quarter turn and repeat. Fold gently to retain as much air as possible. Stop folding when no white streaks remain.

In the old days, people made candy without the help of a candy thermometer. They just dropped a small amount of the mixture into a glass of cold water and then examined the reaction. Remove the pan from the heat while testing to avoid overcooking the candy and use a fresh glass of water for each test.

STAGE	TEMPERATURE	INDICATOR
THREAD	Begins at 230°F (110°C)	Forms a short, coarse thread
SOFT-BALL	Begins at 234°F (112°C)	Forms a ball that flattens when removed from the water
FIRM-BALL	Begins at 244°F (117°C)	Forms a ball that will not flatten unless pressed
HARD-BALL	Begins at 250°F (121°C)	Forms a rigid but still pliable ball
SOFT-CRACK	Begins at 270°F (132°C)	Separates into hard threads that bend
HARD-CRACK	Begins at 300°F (149°C)	Separates into hard, brittle threads

CHAPTER FIFTEEN

Drinks

The sun hovers over the trees. Grandfather, father, and the boys amble in from the barn. The hay is safe under cover and everyone looks forward to a tall glass of freshly made lemonade. The sound of rattling ice in a cool glass pitcher hurries their footsteps to the kitchen. Haying is hot work and creates a mighty thirst that only a tart-sweet glass of lemonade can quench.

Move ahead to the suburbs of the 1950s. The porch is replaced by a patio in the backyard and mother has a steak marinating in the refrigerator. The kids are at the malt shop, sipping brown cows and root beer floats. Now there is just enough time to set up a mini bar by the grill so father can make the martinis—shaken, not stirred.

Leap ahead to today. Many things have changed in our lives, but we still get hungry and thirsty. New cocktails are created and popularized all the time, but the classics—martinis, Manhattans, margaritas, bloody Marys—never go out of fashion. The Kentucky Derby wouldn't be the Kentucky Derby without mint juleps, and Christmas wouldn't be Christmas without eggnog. Homemade lemonade still tastes better than anything out of a can or jar, and iced tea is still the preferred drink throughout the South.

These days, in our go-go world, coffee seems to be the drink of choice. It fuels our mornings and keeps us up working late at night. When King George found it convenient to tax tea in the colonies, and protest took place in the form of the Boston Tea Party, patriots found it more expedient to drink coffee or something called "patriot's tea," brewed from sage leaves. Despite the ubiquitous presence of coffee shops on every street corner in modern urban America, most people still take pride in serving a good "cuppa joe" and enjoy after-dinner drinks, such as Irish coffee.

On the weekends, we may attend parties and celebrations where punch is served. These punch recipes are still based on the rule of five: something sweet, something sour, something strong, something weak, and the addition of spices.

Let's lift our glasses to tradition, and the ties that bind us to our past as well as to our future. Where there is food and fellowship, there will always be satisfying drinks nearby!

Alexander

This recipe is for the original Alexander, which has spawned many variations (one variation follows). It is generally served as an after-dinner drink.

SERVES 1

¾ ounce gin
¾ ounce white crème de cacao
2 ounces half-and-half

Shake the gin, crème de cacao, and half-and-half in a cocktail shaker filled with ice. Strain into a chilled cocktail glass and serve.

Brandy Alexander

In the original Alexander, replace the gin with brandy and the white crème de cacao with dark crème de cacao. Complete the recipe as directed.

Black Russian

Russia and Mexico come together in this simple cocktail. It is a dessert lover's delight. A variation follows.

SERVES 1

2 ounces vodka
1 ounce Kahlúa

Pour the vodka, then the Kahlúa into a glass filled with ice. Serve immediately (do not stir).

White Russian

Make a Black Russian, then top off the glass with half-and-half. Serve at once without stirring.

Bloody Mary

The classic brunch drink, the bloody Mary was invented in Harry's New York Bar in Paris in the 1920s. The tomato juice drink was later brought to the King Cole Bar in New York City at the St. Regis Hotel, where it was known as the red snapper. Several variations follow.

SERVES 1

2 ounces vodka
2 dashes Worcestershire sauce
2 dashes hot pepper sauce, such as Tabasco
Dash of lemon juice
Pinch of salt
Pinch of black pepper
Tomato juice
1 medium celery stalk, to serve

Stir the vodka, Worcestershire sauce, hot pepper sauce, lemon juice, salt, and black pepper in a highball glass with ice. Fill the glass with tomato juice, then garnish with the celery and serve.

Bloody Maria

Replace the vodka in a Bloody Mary with tequila and replace the lemon juice with lime juice. Complete the recipe as directed.

Bloody Mary Quite Contrary

Replace the vodka with sake in a Bloody Mary and complete the recipe as directed.

Virgin Mary

Eliminate the vodka in a Bloody Mary and complete the recipe as directed.

Brooklyn

This sister cocktail to the Manhattan uses Campari, a mild bitters–type aperitif. The result is a smooth whiskey drink with a hint of orange peel.

SERVES 1

½ ounce bourbon or other whiskey
½ ounce vermouth
½ ounce Campari

Shake the bourbon, vermouth, and Campari in a cocktail shaker filled with ice. Strain into a chilled rocks glass or cocktail glass and serve.

TIP: One ounce equals one normal shot glass.

Cape Codder

Many things made with cranberry juice get the inevitable name of Cape Cod. This drink is as refreshing as a Cape sea breeze.

SERVES 1

1 ounce vodka
5 ounces cranberry juice
1 lime wedge, to serve

Pour the vodka and cranberry juice into a highball glass with ice and stir. Garnish with the lime wedge.

Cosmopolitan

There is some debate as to whether a cosmopolitan should be flavored with lemon or lime and whether to stir or shake. The stirrers claim that stirring produces a clearer drink, while the shakers claim that all fruit juice martinis should be shaken.

SERVES 1

2 ounces vodka
1 ounce Cointreau
2 to 3 ounces cranberry juice
2 lime or lemon wedges

Stir or shake the vodka, Cointreau, and cranberry juice in a cocktail shaker filled with ice. Squeeze in 1 wedge of lime and strain into a chilled martini glass. Garnish with the remaining lime wedge and serve.

Cuba Libre

This cocktail probably dates from the Spanish–American War, when Cuba was liberated from Spanish rule. The rum-and-cola drink was very popular with American soldiers, who brought the drink home.

SERVES 1

Juice of ½ medium lime
2 ounces light rum
Cola
1 lime twist, to serve

Pour the lime juice into a highball glass over ice cubes. Add the rum, fill with the cola, stir, and serve with the lime twist.

TIP: Make ice cubes festive for a party by freezing sprigs of mint, maraschino cherries, or strips of lemon or orange zest in them.

Daiquiri

This cocktail is named after the town of Daiquiri in Cuba. Daiquiris were served in F. Scott Fitzgerald's novel This Side of Paradise, *further popularizing the drink. Two variations follow.*

2 ounces light rum
2 teaspoons lime juice
½ teaspoon superfine sugar

Shake the rum, lime juice, and sugar in a cocktail shaker filled with ice. Strain into a chilled cocktail glass and serve.

Frozen Daiquiri

Combine the rum, lime juice, and sugar in a Daiquiri with ¼ cup of ice cubes in a blender. Pulverize the ice and pour into a chilled cocktail glass; serve immediately.

Frozen Strawberry Daiquiri

This is a classic summer cool-off drink. Without the rum, it makes a popular kids' drink, too. Just double the recipe, pour the child's drink first, then add the rum, blend, and serve yourself.

SERVES 1

1½ ounces light rum
¾ ounce strawberry liqueur
3 large strawberries, hulled
1½ ounces lemon juice
¼ cup ice cubes

Combine all the ingredients in a blender and pulverize the ice. Pour into a chilled cocktail glass and serve.

Gimlet

This is a classic gin-based cocktail, of which there are many variations in the proportions. Some bartenders add carbonated water, while others do not. A vodka variation follows.

SERVES 1

2 ounces gin
1 ounce lime juice
1 red maraschino cherry, to serve
1 lime wedge, to serve

Shake the gin and lime juice in a cocktail shaker filled with ice. Strain into a chilled cocktail glass. Garnish with the cherry and lime wedge and serve.

Vodka Gimlet

Replace the gin in a Gimlet with vodka and complete the recipe as directed.

Gin Fizz

This refreshing citrus drink was invented in the late 1880s by Henry C. Ramos, a New Orleans tavern keeper. The key is to make it creamy, and that's all in the generous shaking. A variation follows. (Note: This recipe contains raw eggs. For more information, see page 11.)

SERVES 1

2 ounces gin
2 ounces half-and-half
1 tablespoon superfine sugar
1 tablespoon lemon juice
1 tablespoon lime juice
1 large egg white
Club soda
1 slice orange, to serve
1 red maraschino cherry, to serve

Combine the gin, half-and-half, sugar, lemon juice, lime juice, and egg white in a cocktail shaker filled with ice and shake well. Strain into a chilled highball glass and top with a splash of club soda. Garnish with the slice of orange and the cherry and serve.

Sloe Gin Fizz

Replace the gin in a Gin Fizz with 1 ounce gin and 1 ounce sloe gin. Omit the half-and-half and egg white and complete the recipe as directed.

Gin and Tonic

Gin originated in the seventeenth century in the Netherlands. From there it spread to England, where it was inexpensively produced and thus extremely popularized. Later, when the British were in the Far East and became susceptible to malaria, they discovered that quinine (an ingredient in tonic water) was useful in treating the disease. Because of quinine's bitter taste, the addition of gin made it much more palatable, and a new cocktail was invented.

SERVES 1

1 ounce gin
3 ounces tonic water
1 slice lime, to serve

Pour the gin and tonic over ice in a highball glass and stir. Garnish with the slice of lime and serve.

Golden Cadillac

This is a creamy gold-colored cocktail often served after a meal. The citrus and cream flavors complement each other well.

SERVES 1

2 dashes Galliano
½ ounce orange juice
1 ounce Cointreau or Triple Sec
1 ounce half-and-half
1 ounce white crème de cacao

Shake the Galliano, orange juice, Cointreau, half-and-half, and crème de cacao in a cocktail shaker filled with ice. Strain into a chilled cocktail glass or Champagne flute and serve.

Grasshopper

Like the pie, a grasshopper cocktail is minty and sweet, going down as easily as a dessert.

SERVES 1

1 ounce crème de menthe
1 ounce white crème de cacao
1 ounce half-and-half
Grated chocolate, to serve

Shake the crème de menthe, crème de cacao, and the half-and-half in a cocktail shaker filled with ice. Strain into a chilled cocktail glass, garnish with a little grated chocolate, and serve.

Hurricane

The hurricane was invented during World War II at Pat O'Brien's French Quarter Bar in New Orleans. It was named after the shape of a hurricane lamp and gave rise to the hurricane glass in which it is served. Pat O'Brien's bar is still open today in New Orleans' famous French Quarter, selling its original hurricane cocktail mix at the bar.

SERVES 1

2 ounces light rum
2 ounces dark rum
2 ounces passion fruit juice
1 ounce orange juice
½ ounce lime juice
1 tablespoon simple syrup (page 476)
1 tablespoon grenadine
1 red maraschino cherry, to serve
1 slice orange, to serve

Shake the rums, passion fruit juice, orange juice, lime juice, simple syrup, and grenadine in a cocktail shaker filled with ice. Strain into a chilled hurricane glass, garnish with the cherry and the slice of orange, and serve.

Kir Royale

This recipe mixes crème de cassis, a liqueur made from black currants, with Champagne for a refreshing, bubbly drink. Two variations follow.

SERVES 1

1 ounce crème de cassis
5 ounces Champagne

Pour the crème de cassis into a chilled Champagne flute. Gently pour Champagne on top (do not stir) and serve.

Kir

Replace the Champagne in Kir Royale with white wine and complete the recipe as directed.

Kir Imperial

Replace the crème de cassis in Kir Royale with framboise liquor and complete the recipe as directed.

Long Island Iced Tea

The splash of cola in this cocktail gives it the appearance of iced tea, though it doesn't contain any tea.

SERVES 1

1 ounce vodka
1 ounce gin
1 ounce rum
1 ounce tequila
1 ounce Cointreau
Juice of ¼ medium lemon
Cola

Fill a highball glass halfway with ice. Add the vodka, gin, rum, tequila, Cointreau, and lemon juice (in that order). Top with a splash of cola (do not stir) and serve.

Mai Tai

This drink was created near the end of World War II by Victor Bergeron, the founder of the restaurant Trader Vic's. It can be found on virtually every known tropical drink menu.

SERVES 1

1 ounce dark rum
1 ounce amber rum
1 ounce orange juice
½ ounce Cointreau or Triple Sec
½ ounce lime juice
1 teaspoon orgeat syrup or 1 drop almond
    extract
1 teaspoon superfine sugar
Dash of grenadine
1 slice orange, to serve

Shake the rums, orange juice, Cointreau, lime juice, orgeat syrup, sugar, and grenadine in a cocktail shaker filled with ice. Strain into a highball glass filled with more ice. Garnish with the slice of orange and serve.

Manhattan

The Manhattan began to appear sometime around the 1880s, but its exact origins are convoluted. One account places its invention in New York at a banquet given by Winston Churchill's American mother at the Manhattan Club.

SERVES 1

2 ounces bourbon or other whiskey
1 ounce sweet vermouth
Angostura bitters
Red and green maraschino cherries, to serve

Stir the bourbon, vermouth, and a few drops of bitters with ice and strain into a chilled cocktail glass. Garnish with the cherries and serve.

Margarita

There are many claims regarding the origins of this classic tequila cocktail, most of which trace it back to Mexico in the 1930s. It is the cocktail of choice with Tex-Mex foods.

SERVES 1

Salt
1½ ounces tequila
1 ounce lime juice
½ ounce Cointreau or Triple Sec
1 lime twist, to serve

Chill a large, stemmed cocktail glass and dip the rim in salt. Shake the tequila, lime juice, and Cointreau in a cocktail shaker filled with ice. Strain into the glass and serve with the lime twist.

TIP: The best salt rim is made by rubbing the outside of the glass with a lime wedge, turning the glass upside down, and sprinkling salt onto the outside of the rim.

Martini

This is the classic recipe, complete with olives. James Bond's martini was shaken, not stirred. Three variations follow.

SERVES 1

2 ounces gin
½ ounce vermouth
Pitted green olives, to serve

Shake the gin and vermouth in a cocktail shaker filled with ice. Strain into a chilled martini glass. Garnish with a spear of olives and serve.

Dry Martini

Omit the vermouth in a Martini and complete the recipe as directed. Garnish with a lemon twist and serve.

Vodka Martini

Substitute vodka for the gin in a Martini and complete the recipe as directed.

Gibson

Mix a Martini, then substitute a pickled onion for the olive garnish.

Smoking Martini

Variations of the martini abound. This combination creates a dry, smoky-flavored drink.

SERVES 1

4 ounces gin
1 ounce bourbon or other whiskey
1 red maraschino cherry or slice lemon, to serve

Shake the gin and bourbon in a cocktail shaker filled with ice and strain into a chilled martini glass. Garnish with the cherry or lemon slice and serve.

Mojito

This citrus concoction traces back to Cuba around the turn of the twentieth century. Its bubbly, minty-sweet character makes the drink go down easily.

SERVES 1

3 sprigs fresh mint
2 teaspoons superfine sugar
1½ ounces lemon juice
1½ ounces light rum
Club soda or seltzer water
1 slice lemon, to serve

In a tall, thin glass, crush some of the mint leaves with a fork to coat the inside of the glass. Add the sugar and lemon juice and stir thoroughly. Fill with ice. Add the rum and stir. Top off with club soda. Add the slice of lemon and the remaining mint and serve.

Old Fashioned

When a drink has its own glass, you know it's timeless. This bittersweet cocktail originated at the Pendennis Club in Louisville, Kentucky, sometime in the 1890s.

SERVES 1

1 teaspoon superfine sugar
2 dashes angostura bitters
Dash of water
1 red maraschino cherry
1 orange wedge
2 ounces bourbon or other whiskey

Mix the sugar, bitters, and water in an old fashioned glass. Drop in the cherry and orange wedge. Muddle the mixture into a paste using a muddler or the back of a spoon. Pour in the bourbon, fill with ice cubes, stir, and serve.

Piña Colada

This blender drink tastes like a vacation in the Caribbean, where coconut and pineapple are used fresh from the trees.

SERVES 1

3 ounces light rum
3 tablespoons coconut milk
3 tablespoons crushed pineapple
1 slice pineapple, to serve

Combine the rum, coconut milk, and pineapple in a blender with 2 cups of crushed ice and briefly blend at a high speed. Pour into a chilled hurricane glass, garnish with the slice of pineapple, and serve.

Pink Lady

Many of our most famous and beloved cocktails date back to the Prohibition era, when cocktails were devised to disguise the taste of unskillfully and illicitly made liquors. This fruity cream drink is from that era. (Note: This recipe contains raw eggs. For more information, see page 11.)

SERVES 1

1 ounce gin
1 teaspoon grenadine
1 teaspoon half-and-half
1 large egg white

Shake the gin, grenadine, half-and-half, and egg white in a cocktail shaker filled with ice. Strain into a chilled cocktail glass and serve.

Planters Punch

Despite the name, this lemon drink is really a cocktail, not a punch.

SERVES 1

1 ounce brandy
½ ounce light rum
½ ounce bourbon or other whiskey
Juice of ½ medium lemon
1 tablespoon superfine sugar
Seltzer water

Shake the brandy, rum, bourbon, lemon juice, and sugar in a cocktail shaker filled with ice. Strain into a Collins glass over more ice cubes. Fill with the seltzer water, stir, and serve.

Rob Roy

A Rob Roy, named after the legendary hero of Sir Walter Scott's novel, is basically a Manhattan made with Scotch.

SERVES 1

2 ounces Scotch
1 ounce sweet vermouth
2 dashes angostura bitters
1 red maraschino cherry or lime wedge, to serve

Shake the scotch, vermouth, and bitters in a cocktail shaker filled with ice. Strain into a chilled cocktail or rocks glass, garnish with the cherry, and serve.

Rum and Coke

The all-American cocktail: Rum is the drink of our forefathers, cola is the drink of today. Add lime juice and you get a Cuba libre.

SERVES 1

1 ounce rum
5 ounces cola

Fill a highball glass two-thirds full with ice. Add the rum, then the cola. Stir briskly and serve.

Scarlett O'Hara

This cocktail is named for the famous heroine of Gone with the Wind. *It's a clean, refreshing drink on a hot summer day.*

SERVES 1

1½ ounces Southern Comfort
1½ ounces cranberry juice
1 ounce lime juice

Shake the Southern Comfort, cranberry juice, and lime juice in a cocktail shaker filled with ice. Strain into a rocks glass with ice or into a chilled cocktail glass without ice. Serve.

Screwdriver

Enhance this classic orange juice and vodka drink by adding a dash of Cointreau for more citrus taste.

SERVES 1

2 ounces vodka
Orange juice
1 slice orange, to serve
1 red maraschino cherry, to serve

Pour the vodka into a highball glass with a few ice cubes and top with the orange juice. Garnish with the slice of orange and the cherry and serve.

Shirley Temple

*This sparkling cherry beverage was invented
for the famous underaged star.*

SERVES 1

Dash of grenadine
Ginger ale
1 slice orange, to serve

Pour the grenadine into a highball glass packed
with ice cubes and top with the ginger ale. Garnish
with the slice of orange and serve with a straw.

Sidecar

*Sometime between World War I and 1934, this citrus drink
was invented. The stories of its origins generally involve a
customer who arrived at a bar in a sidecar attached
to a motorcycle. Three variations follow.*

SERVES 1

1½ ounces brandy
½ ounce Triple Sec
½ ounce lemon or lime juice

Shake the brandy, triple sec, and lemon juice in a
cocktail shaker filled with ice. Strain into a chilled
cocktail glass and serve.

Havana Sidecar

Replace the brandy in a Sidecar with light rum
and complete the recipe as directed.

Boston Sidecar

Add 1 ounce of rum to the Sidecar and reduce
the brandy to ½ ounce. Complete the recipe as
directed.

Louisville Slugger

Replace the brandy in the Sidecar with bourbon
and complete the recipe as directed.

Singapore Sling

*This is a cocktail of gin, cherry brandy, Cointreau,
Benedictine brandy, and citrus juices. It was created
at the Long Bar in Singapore's Raffles Hotel around 1915.*

SERVES 1

1 ounce gin
½ ounce cherry brandy
¼ ounce Cointreau
¼ ounce Benedictine
Dash of angostura bitters
4 ounces pineapple juice
½ ounce lime juice
⅓ ounce grenadine
1 slice pineapple, to serve
1 red maraschino cherry, to serve

Shake the gin, cherry brandy, Cointreau, Benedictine, bitters, pineapple juice, lime juice, and
grenadine in a cocktail shaker filled with ice.
Strain into a highball glass packed with ice, garnish
with the slice of pineapple and the cherry, and
serve with a straw.

Stinger

*This potent after-dinner drink is meant to be sipped.
It's perfect for a cold winter night.*

SERVES 1

2 ounces brandy
¾ ounce white crème de menthe
Sprigs fresh mint, to serve

Shake the brandy and crème de menthe in a
cocktail shaker filled with ice. Strain into a chilled
cocktail glass, garnish with the sprigs of mint,
and serve.

Tequila Sunrise

This colorful cocktail is perfect on a hot, sultry afternoon. If you pour carefully, you will get the layered effect of a sunrise.

SERVES 1

1½ ounces tequila
3 ounces orange juice
1 ounce grenadine
1 slice lime, to serve

Place ice in a highball glass, then add the tequila, orange juice, and grenadine. Garnish with the slice of lime and serve.

Tom Collins

This drink goes back to the post–Civil War era and was made with Old Tom gin to distinguish it from a John Collins, which was made with Holland gin. Today the drink is made with any gin and a carbonated citrus soda sold as Collins mix.

SERVES 1

2 ounces gin
1 ounce lemon juice
1 teaspoon superfine sugar
3 ounces club soda
1 red maraschino cherry, to serve
1 slice orange, to serve

Fill a cocktail shaker halfway with ice cubes. Add the gin, lemon juice, and sugar and shake well. Strain into a Collins glass or a highball glass almost filled with ice cubes. Add the club soda. Stir, garnish with the cherry and the slice of orange, and serve.

Whiskey Sour

This simple concoction is a great go-to for the occasion when all that's on hand is whiskey, a lemon, and some sugar.

SERVES 1

2 ounces bourbon or other whiskey
Juice of ½ medium lemon
½ teaspoon superfine sugar
1 lemon wedge, to serve
1 red maraschino cherry, to serve

Shake the bourbon, lemon juice, and sugar in a cocktail shaker filled with ice. Strain into a chilled whiskey sour glass. Garnish with the lemon wedge and cherry and serve.

Zombie

This drink was created in the late 1930s by Don the Beachcomber at his restaurant in Los Angeles. Supposedly, he developed the drink for a friend. His friend later reported that the drink made him feel like a zombie. Many variations of this drink exist.

SERVES 1

1 ounce light rum
1 ounce añejo rum
½ ounce 151-proof rum
1 ounce apricot brandy
2 ounces orange juice
1 ounce pineapple juice
1 ounce lime juice
1 teaspoon superfine sugar
1 red maraschino cherry, to serve
1 slice orange, to serve
1 sprig fresh mint, to serve

Blend the rums, apricot brandy, orange juice, pineapple juice, lime juice, and sugar with crushed ice at low speed in a blender. Strain into a chilled Collins glass. Garnish with the cherry, the slice of orange, and the sprigs of mint and serve with a straw.

Iced Coffee

Since iced coffee is generally diluted with milk or cream, you need to start with very strong coffee. When you brew your coffee, increase the proportion of ground coffee to water.

SERVES 1

1 cup cold, strong brewed coffee
Half-and-half or milk
Heavy cream (optional)
Grated chocolate, to serve (optional)

Put a little crushed ice into a tall glass mug. Fill it two-thirds full with the coffee, then add the half-and-half. Top the glass with ¼ inch of cream, if using, and a little grated chocolate, if using. Serve with a long spoon.

TIP: Freeze leftover coffee and tea in ice cube trays. Use these cubes to cool down iced beverages without diluting them.

Iced Tea

The 1904 St. Louis World Fair helped popularize iced tea. It continues to be especially popular in the South, but iced tea can be found on menus just about everywhere.

SERVES 8

4 tea bags, such as orange pekoe
2 cups cold water
Simple syrup (page 476; optional)
Lemon wedges, to serve (optional)

1. Remove any paper wrapped around or attached to the tea bags; tie the strings together. Place the bags in a heatproof, 2-quart pitcher.

2. Bring the 2 cups cold water to a boil in a medium saucepan. Remove from the heat and immediately pour over the tea bags.

3. Allow the tea to steep for 20 minutes or more.

4. Remove the tea bags, squeeze out the excess liquid into the tea, and discard the bags. Fill the pitcher with enough water to equal 2 quarts. Add simple syrup to sweeten the tea to taste, if using.

5. Cover and refrigerate until well chilled.

6. Pour the chilled tea over ice cubes in tall glasses and serve with lemon wedges, if desired.

Minted Iced Tea

Orange pekoe tea in its ingredients is not orange flavored at all. The "orange" refers to the grade of tea. You must use fresh mint leaves for this recipe; dried won't do.

SERVES 4

2 tablespoons fine orange pekoe tea
4 cups boiling water
2 cups fresh mint leaves
Simple syrup (page 476; optional)
4 slices lemon, to serve
4 sprigs fresh mint, to serve

1. Combine the tea in a heatproof 2-quart pitcher with the boiling water. Steep for 10 minutes; cool slightly.

2. Fill a glass pitcher with ice and the mint leaves. Strain the tea over the ice and mint and sweeten to taste with the simple syrup, if desired.

3. Garnish each glass with a lemon slice and mint sprig and serve.

Lemonade

Real lemonade is nothing more than fresh lemon juice, water, and sugar, but it is the freshness of the lemon juice that makes all the difference. You can adjust the sweetness of the recipe by adding simple syrup or more lemon juice. A dash of grenadine transforms it into pink lemonade.

SERVES 8 TO 10

1¾ cups sugar
8 cups water
1½ cups lemon juice (preferably fresh)
Thin slices lemon, to serve

1. Combine the sugar and 1 cup of water in a small saucepan. Bring to a boil and stir to dissolve the sugar. Cool to room temperature, cover, and refrigerate until chilled.

2. Remove the seeds from the lemon juice but leave any pulp.

3. Stir together the chilled syrup, lemon juice, and remaining 7 cups water in a large pitcher. Garnish with the slices of lemon and serve.

TIP: Before juicing lemons or limes, roll them on the counter while pressing down with your palm to help break down the interior membranes and make juicing easier. Then cut them in half around the middle, and press and twist against a reamer to release the juice.

Limeade

Limeade is a wonderfully refreshing change of pace from lemonade. If you like, make it with seltzer water for a sparkling version, using 1 cup water and 7 cups seltzer water to replace the 8 cups water. Figure that you will need approximately 10 medium limes to make 1½ cups of juice.

SERVES 8 TO 10

1¾ cups sugar
8 cups water
1½ cups lime juice (preferably fresh)
Thin slices lime, to serve

1. Combine the sugar and 1 cup of water in a small saucepan. Bring to a boil and stir to dissolve the sugar. Cool to room temperature, cover, and refrigerate until chilled.

2. Stir together the chilled syrup, lime juice, and remaining 7 cups water in a large pitcher. Garnish with the slices of lime and serve.

Orange Julius

In 1926 Julius Freed opened a modest orange juice stand in downtown Los Angeles. Freed's friend Bill Hamlin helped Freed jazz up the juice by making it frothy and consistent, and, inevitably, more popular. Customers would belly up to the counter saying "Give me an orange Julius."

SERVES 4

⅔ cup (6 ounces) frozen orange juice concentrate
1 cup milk
1 cup water
½ cup sugar
1 teaspoon vanilla extract

Combine the orange juice, milk, water, sugar, and vanilla extract in a blender. Add 10 to 12 ice cubes, cover, and blend on medium speed until smooth, about 30 seconds. Serve immediately.

Raspberry Shrub

In colonial times, "shrubs" were made from a mixture of rum, sugar, and orange or lemon juice that was aged in crocks, then strained and served over ice. We drink less rum these days, so shrubs have become drinks made from fruit, sugar, and water.

SERVES 4

1 (10-ounce) package frozen raspberries
¾ cup orange juice
½ cup milk
¼ cup sugar
2 cups club soda
6 to 8 fresh mint leaves, to serve (optional)

1. Purée the raspberries, orange juice, milk, and sugar in a blender for about 30 seconds, until smooth.

2. Strain the mixture through a wire mesh strainer into a medium bowl to remove the seeds.

3. Place the bowl in the freezer until the mixture becomes thick and slushy.

4. Dilute the mixture to taste with about 1 part club soda to 2 parts shrub.

5. Garnish each glass with a mint leaf, if desired, and serve.

Switchel

Before there was Gatorade, there was switchel, also known as haymaker's punch. This drink was kept cool in the cellar and hauled out to relieve the thirst of the men and women who worked the fields. This version is sweetened with sugar; in the old days, molasses was more commonly used.

SERVES 12

1 gallon cold water
1 cup cider vinegar
½ cup superfine sugar
Pinch of ground ginger

1. Combine the water, vinegar, sugar, and ginger in a large bowl and stir until the sugar dissolves.

2. Chill well before serving.

Vanilla Milk Shake

The old soda fountain specialized in ice-cream drinks. One of these was the white cow, otherwise known as a vanilla milk shake.

SERVES 1

4 scoops French vanilla ice cream (page 434)
1½ cups milk
1 tablespoon vanilla extract

Combine the ice cream, milk, and vanilla extract in a blender and blend until smooth. Serve immediately with a straw.

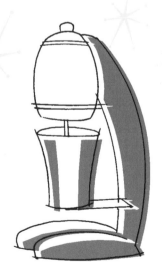

Chocolate Milk Shake

Whether you call it a chocolate frappé, a chocolate frosted, or a chocolate milk shake, it is all the same—ice cream, chocolate syrup, and milk blended into a frothy, creamy drink.

SERVES 1

4 scoops French vanilla ice cream (page 434)
1½ cups milk
¼ cup chocolate syrup

Combine the ice cream, milk, and chocolate syrup in a blender and blend until smooth. Serve immediately with a straw.

Black-and-White

As with many traditional recipes, there is some controversy regarding the contents of a black-and-white. Some say it is a milk shake made with vanilla ice cream and chocolate syrup, though that is also the recipe for a chocolate shake. Others say the shake is made with vanilla ice cream plus vanilla extract or syrup and chocolate syrup. Here's another delicious version.

SERVES 1

4 scoops chocolate ice cream (page 435)
1½ cups milk
1 tablespoon vanilla extract

Combine the ice cream, milk, and vanilla extract in a blender and blend until smooth. Serve immediately with a straw.

Vanilla Malted

When scoop shops separated from pharmacies to serve ice cream to customers away from the medicinal atmosphere, they called themselves malt shops, after the malted milk shake, a wildly popular preparation. Malt is a powdered extract of wheat or malted barley combined with milk, originally created as an easily digested food for infants.

SERVES 1

4 scoops French vanilla ice cream (page 434)
1½ cups milk
2 tablespoons malted milk powder
1 tablespoon vanilla extract

Combine the ice cream, milk, malted milk powder, and vanilla extract in a blender and blend until smooth. Serve immediately with a straw.

Chocolate Malted

There are chocolate malted milk powders available, but they don't taste chocolatey enough to use in an ice-cream malted. Stick with the plain malt powder and chocolate syrup, as in this recipe.

SERVES 1

4 scoops French vanilla ice cream (page 434)
1½ cups milk
3 tablespoons chocolate syrup
2 tablespoons malted milk powder
1 teaspoon vanilla extract

Combine the ice cream, milk, chocolate syrup, malted milk powder, and vanilla extract in a blender and blend until smooth. Serve immediately with a straw.

Double Chocolate Malted

In the language of soda fountains, this chocolatey delight is known as a "burn one all the way."

SERVES 1

4 scoops chocolate ice cream (page 435)
1½ cups milk
2 tablespoons chocolate syrup
2 tablespoons malted milk powder
1 teaspoon vanilla extract

Combine the ice cream, milk, chocolate syrup, malted milk powder, and vanilla extract in a blender and blend until smooth. Serve immediately with a straw.

Egg Cream

In New York City, egg creams (or phosphates, as they were also known) are made with chocolate syrup, milk, and seltzer water, but no eggs. The trick is in the preparation—if made just right, there should be a foamy head at the top of the glass, supposedly resembling beaten egg whites. The best way to add the seltzer water is to squirt it in. But if you don't have charged seltzer water, use highly carbonated seltzer water.

SERVES 1

2 tablespoons chocolate syrup (preferably Fox's U-bet)
⅓ cup milk
⅔ cup ice-cold, charged seltzer water

Pour the chocolate syrup into a large soda fountain glass. Add the milk and stir to blend (don't worry if a few streaks of unblended chocolate remain in the bottom of the glass). Add the seltzer water and stir vigorously. A foamy head will rise to the top. Serve immediately.

Chocolate Ice-Cream Soda

When ice cream meets soda, a reaction occurs that creates a foamy head. Add chocolate syrup and you have a frothy treat.

SERVES 1

2 tablespoons chocolate syrup
Seltzer water
1 scoop French vanilla ice cream (page 434), frozen solid
Whipped cream, to serve

1. Pour the chocolate syrup into a large glass.

2. Add the seltzer water, stirring as you pour, to within 2 inches of the rim of the glass.

3. Carefully add the ice cream, trying to straddle the rim of the glass and still submerge enough to begin reacting with the carbonation. If the ice cream is too deep in the flavored seltzer water, the soda will overflow. If it doesn't touch the seltzer water at all, a foamy head will not be produced.

4. Top with whipped cream and serve.

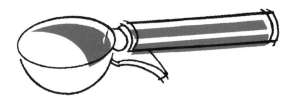

Brown Cow

This combination of chocolate syrup, cola, and ice cream is unusual but very delicious.

SERVES 1

1 tablespoon chocolate syrup
Cola
1 scoop French vanilla ice cream (page 434), frozen hard
Whipped cream, to serve

1. Pour the chocolate syrup into a large glass.

2. Add the cola, stirring as you pour, to within 2 inches of the rim of the glass.

3. Carefully add the ice cream, trying to straddle the rim of the glass and still submerge enough to begin reacting with the carbonation. If the ice cream is too deep in the flavored cola, the soda will overflow. If it doesn't touch the cola at all, a foamy head will not be produced.

4. Top with whipped cream and serve.

Root Beer Float

The root beer must be very cold when you make this float, or the ice cream will melt too quickly. A chilled glass beer stein is the appropriate glass.

SERVES 1

Root beer
1 scoop French vanilla ice cream (page 434), frozen hard

1. Pour about ½ cup of root beer into the bottom of a glass.

2. Carefully add the ice cream, then fill the glass with more root beer. Serve immediately with a spoon.

Irish Coffee

Chef Joe Sheridan invented this drink in 1942 at Foynes Dock, a flying boat dock during World War II. In 1947, it became the official welcoming beverage of Shannon Airport just outside Limerick, Ireland.

SERVES 1

1½ ounces Irish whiskey
6 ounces hot brewed coffee
1 teaspoon sugar
1 tablespoon heavy cream

Pour the whiskey into a warmed Irish coffee glass or mug. Stir in the coffee and sugar, then pour the cream over the back of a spoon to give a thick coating on the top (do not stir). Serve hot.

Café Brûlot

Café (meaning "coffee") and brûlot (meaning "burnt brandy") has been a New Orleans tradition since the 1890s. Flameproof brûlot bowls were made especially for the recipe sometime before 1900. Use caution when preparing this recipe. Be sure there are no flammable materials or children nearby.

SERVES 4

1 cinnamon stick, roughly broken
4 whole cloves
Zest of ½ medium orange
Zest of ½ medium lemon
4 sugar cubes
¼ cup cognac
2 tablespoons Grand Marnier or other orange liqueur
2 cups hot brewed coffee

1. Combine the cinnamon, cloves, orange zest, lemon zest, and sugar in a small saucepan over low heat. Stir in the cognac and Grand Marnier.

2. Using a long match, carefully ignite the mixture. Immediately, but slowly, pour in the coffee, stirring until the flames subside.

3. Remove cinnamon sticks. Pour into small coffee cups and serve.

Herbal Tea

Herbal teas are made by infusion—that is, steeping the herbs in hot water.

SERVES 4

4 cups boiling water
½ cup dried herbs (mint, lemon verbena, chamomile, etc.)

Combine the water and herbs in a teapot. Steep for about 5 minutes. Remove the tea leaves or strain them out. Serve at once.

Hot Cocoa

American hot cocoa, or hot chocolate, is distinguished by its use of cocoa powder, whereas Mexican hot chocolate and European hot chocolates use solid chocolate.

SERVES 4

6 tablespoons cocoa powder
6 tablespoons sugar
Pinch of salt
2½ cups milk
1 teaspoon vanilla extract
2½ cups half-and-half
Whipped cream, to serve

1. Mix the cocoa powder, sugar, and salt in a medium, heavy-bottomed saucepan. Slowly stir in 1 cup of milk and whisk until the cocoa dissolves. Add the vanilla extract.

2. Stir in the remaining 1½ cups milk and the half-and-half. Heat to just before boiling, stirring constantly.

3. Pour the hot cocoa into 4 mugs, top each with whipped cream, and serve.

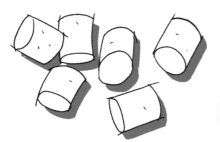

Mexican Hot Chocolate

Mexican hot chocolate is much richer than its north-of-the-border counterpart, using chopped chocolate, cinnamon, and eggs to enhance the flavor.

SERVES 6

6 cups milk
½ cup sugar
3 squares (3 ounces) baking chocolate, chopped
1 teaspoon ground cinnamon
2 large eggs
2 teaspoons vanilla extract
Whipped cream, to serve

1. Combine 1 cup of milk, the sugar, chocolate, and cinnamon in a large, heavy-bottomed saucepan. Cook over medium-low heat, stirring constantly, until the chocolate is melted. Gradually stir in the remaining 5 cups milk. Cook, stirring, until the milk is very hot. Do not allow the mixture to boil. Remove from the heat and set aside.

2. Beat the eggs in a small bowl. Gradually stir 1 cup of hot milk mixture into the eggs, then transfer the entire mixture to the saucepan. Cook and stir for 2 minutes over low heat.

3. Remove the pan from the heat and stir in the vanilla extract. Beat with a hand beater until very frothy.

4. Pour the hot chocolate into mugs, dollop each with whipped cream, and serve.

Hot Mulled Cider

Cold cider—the juice of pressed apples—is a refreshing fall drink. Hot mulled cider is cider heated with spices. It may be spiked with rum or made nonalcoholic. Either way it is the perfect seasonal drink for Halloween.

SERVES 8

2 quarts apple cider
¼ cup firmly packed light brown sugar
2 cinnamon sticks
½ teaspoon whole cloves
½ teaspoon ground cardamom
½ teaspoon ground nutmeg
Zest of 1 medium orange
8 ounces rum, brandy, or Calvados (optional)

1. Combine the cider, brown sugar, cinnamon sticks, cloves, cardamom, nutmeg, and orange zest in a large pan. Bring to a boil, reduce the heat, and simmer for 30 minutes.

2. Strain out the spices and zest and discard. Return the cider to the pan and keep warm.

3. Serve as is or make alcoholic by pouring 1 ounce of the preferred liquor into each serving mug and topping off with the hot cider.

Mulled Wine

Early settlers had a tool called a "muller" that looked like a fireplace poker. Its purpose was to be heated at the fireplace, then plunged into a tankard of cider, wine, or ale to warm it. Mulled wine is warmed wine with spices.

SERVES 4

1 (750-millileter) bottle medium or full-bodied red wine
2 cups water
2 cups orange juice
½ cup sugar
2 medium lemons, thinly sliced
12 whole cloves
6 whole allspice berries
1 cinnamon stick
1 slice fresh ginger root

1. Combine the wine, water, orange juice, sugar, lemons, cloves, allspice, cinnamon, and ginger in a large saucepan. Heat until almost boiling; do not allow it to boil.

2. Strain and discard the spices. Serve warm.

Grog

Grog, a seaman's drink, is a mixture of rum and hot water, which was often used to try to prevent scurvy. Americans began sweetening the grog with molasses, but you can choose sugar, if you like.

SERVES 1

1½ ounces rum
1 teaspoon molasses or superfine sugar
½ ounce lemon juice
Hot water

Pour the rum, molasses, and lemon juice into a coffee mug, then top off with the hot water. Stir and serve.

Hot Toddy

There are no rules when it comes to a hot toddy. It is a cocktail made of any spirit—whiskey, brandy, rum, gin, or vodka—plus hot water or tea, sugar, and spices. It's a drink to soothe the spirit and send one on to a peaceful rest.

SERVES 1

1½ ounces bourbon or other whiskey
¼ ounce lemon juice
¾ ounce simple syrup (page 476)
4 ounces hot water
1 slice lemon, to serve
1 whole clove, to serve

Combine the bourbon, lemon juice, and simple syrup in a heatproof glass or mug. Fill the mug with hot water, add the slice of lemon speared with the clove, and serve.

Hot Buttered Rum

This Christmas Eve classic hits the spot on any cold winter night. Some make it with apple cider to add the sweetness. This old-world recipe instead uses a simple syrup.

SERVES 1

½ tablespoon butter
½ ounce simple syrup (page 476)
Pinch of ground nutmeg
2 ounces dark rum
Boiling water

Put the butter, simple syrup, and nutmeg in a coffee mug. Pour in the rum and stir well. Fill the mug with boiling water, stir again, and serve.

Iced Tea Punch

Some speculate that the word "punch" derives from the Hindi word "panch," meaning five, which refers to the five initial ingredients—arrack (fermented palm sap), tea or spices, sugar, water, and lemon. The recipe has been generalized to become a "rule of five," which is something sweet, something sour, something strong, something weak, and spices. This punch fits the classic formula.

SERVES 16 TO 20

8 tea bags, such as orange pekoe, or 8 teaspoons loose black tea
2 cups boiling water
2 cups sugar
2 cups cold water
2 cups lemon juice
1 large banana, peeled and sliced
1 cup strawberries, hulled and sliced
2½ cups fresh or canned pineapple chunks
2 large oranges, peeled and thinly sliced
2 cups melon balls or cubes (preferably honeydew or cantaloupe)
1 (28-ounce) bottle ginger ale

1. Steep the tea bags in the boiling water for about 5 minutes.

2. Strain the tea into a large pitcher or crock and mix in the sugar. Stir until the sugar is dissolved. Add the cold water and lemon juice and chill.

3. Pour the tea into a punch bowl, add the fruit and ginger ale, and serve immediately.

Tropical Fruit Punch

The foundation for this punch is frozen, which guarantees that the punch will be icy cold when served.

SERVES 16

6 cups water
4 cups sugar
3 cups orange juice
½ cup lemon juice
2 (46-ounce) cans pineapple juice
3 (2-liter) bottles ginger ale

1. Combine the water and sugar in a large pot and bring to a boil. Simmer until the water is reduced to a syrup (about 30 minutes). Remove from the heat and cool.

2. Mix in the orange juice, lemon juice, and pineapple juice. Freeze.

3. When you are ready to serve, thaw until slushy. Place in a large punch bowl, add the ginger ale, and serve immediately.

Orange Sherbet Punch

Make a particularly fine presentation for this punch by packing the sherbet into a ring mold, freezing it, then unmolding the ring into the punch bowl before adding the liquid ingredients.

SERVES 12 TO 16

4 cups cold orange juice
1 cup milk
3 tablespoons superfine sugar
½ teaspoon ground nutmeg
1 cup cold seltzer water
1 quart orange sherbet

1. Combine the orange juice, milk, sugar, and nutmeg in a large pitcher. Mix until the sugar dissolves.

2. Pour in the seltzer water and stir to blend.

3. Scoop the sherbet into a large glass punch bowl, pour the punch over the top, and serve.

Citrus Punch

One theory suggests that the word "punch" is simply the short version of the word "puncheon," which refers to a wooden cask that holds 70 to 80 gallons. This refreshing recipe makes considerably less than that.

SERVES 16 TO 20

3 (28-ounce) bottles lemon-lime soda
18 ounces frozen orange juice concentrate
18 ounces frozen lemonade concentrate
18 ounces frozen limeade concentrate
3 quarts cold water
2 pints lemon sherbet or lime sherbet

1. Make an ice ring with as much soda as will fit in your mold. Freeze.

2. Combine all the juice concentrates with the water in a large punch bowl, and stir to dissolve. Add the remaining soda.

3. Add the ice ring, scoop the sherbet into the punch bowl, and serve.

Sangria

There are probably as many ways to mix this classic Spanish punch as there are Spanish bartenders, but it always contains red wine and fruit. "Sangria" is Spanish for "bleeding" and refers to the color of the punch.

SERVES 8

3 cups dry red wine
1½ cups lemon-lime soda
1½ cups orange juice
1 medium lime, thinly sliced
1 medium lemon, thinly sliced
1 medium orange, thinly sliced
½ cup brandy
¼ cup sugar
2 tablespoons Cointreau or other orange liqueur
2 tablespoons grenadine
2 tablespoons lemon juice
2 tablespoons lime juice

Combine all the ingredients in a large pitcher and let stand for 30 minutes. Serve in wine glasses over ice.

Fish-House Punch

The original recipe for the famous fish-house punch dates back to prerevolutionary times and is credited to a fishing and social club in Schuylkill, Pennsylvania. The North American colonies were well stocked with rum and lemons as a result of trading with the Caribbean colonies. This particular punch became popular because it met a need. There were no restaurants in those days, just inns and fish houses. Lunch was a busy time, and the fish houses kept bowls of fish-house punch in their entryways to occupy their clientele until they were seated.

SERVES 40

1⅔ cups superfine sugar
6 cups water
3 cups lemon juice
1 (750-millileter) bottle Jamaican rum
1 (750-millileter) bottle light rum
½ cup peach brandy
1 medium lemon, sliced

1. Dissolve the sugar in the water and lemon juice in a large punch bowl. Add the rums and brandy, cover the punch bowl with plastic wrap, and let it sit for 3 to 4 hours.

2. Add a block of ice and float the lemon slices as a garnish, then serve.

Martha Washington's Rum Punch

Rum was a spirit of choice for our founding fathers, and both Martha and George Washington had a way with spirits. George Washington made whiskey at his estate in Mt. Vernon, and Martha concocted a recipe much like this one later found written down in her journals.

SERVES 6 TO 10

3 medium lemons, quartered
1 medium orange, quartered
3 cinnamon sticks, broken
6 whole cloves
½ teaspoon ground nutmeg
4 ounces simple syrup (page 476)
4 ounces lemon juice
4 ounces orange juice
12 ounces boiling water
3 ounces light rum
3 ounces dark rum
3 ounces Curaçao
1 medium orange or lemon, thinly sliced, to serve

1. Mash the lemons, orange, cinnamon sticks, cloves, and nutmeg in a heatproof pitcher. Add the simple syrup, lemon juice, and orange juice. Pour the boiling water over the mixture and cool for a few minutes. Chill for 2 to 3 hours.

2. Strain the mixture into a punch bowl, then add the rums and the Curaçao.

3. Garnish with the slices of orange, add ice, and serve.

Mimosa Punch

Flavored with orange juice and sparkling with club soda and Champagne, this is the perfect punch to serve at a brunch.

SERVES 40

2 (12-ounce) cans frozen orange juice concentrate, thawed
2 quarts club soda
3 (750-millileter) bottles Champagne or sparkling white wine

1. Scoop the orange juice concentrate into a punch bowl and stir to soften. Stir in the club soda and continue to stir until blended. Add the Champagne, stirring gently.

2. Float an ice mold in the punch and serve immediately.

Strawberry Champagne

Champagne punches are often served at weddings. This particular recipe uses strawberries and is perfect for a June celebration.

SERVES 40

2 (10-ounce) packages frozen sweetened strawberries, thawed
2 (750-millileter) bottles rosé wine
1½ cups lemon juice
Confectioners' sugar or simple syrup (page 476)
3 (750-millileter) bottles Champagne or sparkling white wine

1. Purée the strawberries in a blender or food processor, adding a little of the rosé wine if too thick. Chill for 2 to 3 hours.

2. Sweeten the lemon juice to taste with confectioners' sugar and pour it into a punch bowl. Stir in the puréed strawberries and the wine.

3. Pour in the Champagne, float an ice mold in the punch, and serve immediately.

Bombay Punch

Bombay punch is a recipe that dates back to the sixteenth century. Today, you are more likely to find it served at a party than at a tavern frequented by British seamen.

SERVES 40

2 cups lemon juice
Confectioners' sugar or simple syrup (recipe follows)
3 cups brandy
3 cups dry sherry
⅓ cup maraschino liqueur
⅓ cup orange liqueur
3 (750-millileter) bottles Champagne or sparkling white wine
40 ounces club soda
1 medium orange thinly sliced, to serve

1. Pour the lemon juice into a large punch bowl and sweeten to taste with sugar or simple syrup.

2. Stir in the brandy, sherry, maraschino liqueur, and orange liqueur.

3. Pour in the Champagne and club soda and stir gently. Float an ice mold, garnish with the slices of orange, and serve.

Simple Syrup

This all-purpose sweetener is especially useful for cold drinks, and it will store for several weeks in the refrigerator.

MAKES 2 CUPS

2 cups water
2 cups sugar

1. Mix the sugar and water in a medium saucepan over medium heat. Cook, stirring, until the sugar is completely dissolved.

2. Remove the pan from the heat and cool to room temperature. Pour into a covered container and refrigerate.

Eggnog

No winter holiday gathering is complete without this rich brew. Eggnog is related to various milk and wine punches that came to the New World with early English settlers, who replaced the wine with rum and other spirits later on. A nonalcoholic variation follows. (Note: this recipe contains raw eggs. For more information, see page 11.)

SERVES 8

6 large eggs, separated
¾ cup granulated sugar
1½ cups brandy
½ cup rum
4 cups milk
4 cups heavy cream
½ cups confectioners' sugar
Grated nutmeg

1. Beat the egg yolks in a large bowl while adding the granulated sugar until the mixture is pale and light. Slowly beat in the brandy and rum, then beat in the milk and 2 cups of cream. Chill.

2. Just before serving, beat the egg whites until stiff but not dry. Fold them into the eggnog mixture and set aside.

3. In a medium bowl, whip the remaining 2 cups cream and the confectioners' sugar until soft peaks form. Fold into the eggnog mixture.

4. Pour the eggnog into a punch bowl, sprinkle with nutmeg, and serve.

Teetotalers' Eggnog

Omit the brandy and rum in Eggnog and beat 1 teaspoon vanilla extract with the egg yolks. Complete the recipe as directed.

MAKING THE PERFECT DRINK

Bartending is both an art and a science. Here are a few tips for the artist and the chemist.

▶ Even professionals measure ingredients. Here are some standard bar measures.

> Shot = 1 ounce (2 tablespoons)
> Jigger = 1½ to 2 ounces
> Pony = 1 ounce
> Dash = ⅙ ounce
> Teaspoon = ⅛ ounce

▶ Always put ice in the glass or shaker before pouring in the liquor and mixer. This chills the liquids as they are poured in.

▶ Serve cocktails icy cold. Chill the glasses in the refrigerator, or let them sit in shaved ice before using them.

▶ When the recipe calls for a twist, rub a narrow strip of zest around the rim of the glass. Twist the zest and drop in the twist as a garnish.

▶ Stir drinks that are made of clear liquids. If the drink has a carbonated drink (soda, seltzer water), stir gently to preserve the bubbles.

▶ Shake drinks that contain fruit juices, sugar, eggs, or cream.

▶ For a sugar-frosted glass, moisten the rim of a prechilled glass with a lemon or lime wedge and then dip the rim into confectioners' sugar (before the alcohol is poured).

Preparing a good cup of coffee should be easy; all you have to do is combine ground coffee beans with hot water. Different coffee makers will require different techniques, however, so here are a few helpful tips for all makes and models.

▶ Coffee beans are perishable. For the best coffee, grind the beans just before brewing.

▶ Coffee beans should be kept in an airtight container.

▶ Choose the correct grind for your machine. A mill or burr grinder (as opposed to a blade grinder) grinds the beans more precisely. For drip machines, use a medium-fine grind (grinding too fine can actually cause overextraction and your coffee will taste bitter).

▶ Measure the coffee and water accurately. Use 2 level tablespoons of coffee to 6 ounces of water.

▶ Start with fresh water from the cold tap. Hot water can pick up impurities in the pipes, and water that has been sitting loses its oxygenation. Make sure you heat the water to 195° to 205°F, but not boiling.

▶ Store freshly brewed coffee in a vacuum container or insulated beverage container. Preheat the vacuum container with hot water, then pour in your coffee immediately after it is finished brewing. Brewed coffee maintains its best flavor for about 20 minutes on the hot plate of a coffee maker.

Tea bags are an American invention of convenience. They are generally filled with tea dust rather than whole leaves and are lower in quality than tea leaves. Also they tend to go stale more quickly than loose tea. So use loose tea leaves for the best results.

▶ Brew with filtered or bottled water for the best flavor, and heat the water to a rolling boil.

▶ Use 1 teaspoon of loose tea for each 6 ounces of hot water, plus 1 teaspoon for the pot. If you are using a metal infuser or tea ball, make sure it is large enough to allow the tea leaves to fully expand by not overpacking the tea.

▶ Preheat the teapot by rinsing with hot water.

▶ Use time, not color, as your guide to correctly brew tea. Steep green tea for 3 minutes and black tea for 5 minutes.

▶ Remove tea leaves by removing the tea ball or straining the brewed tea into a clean teapot. Tea should not brew for longer than 5 minutes or it will become bitter.

▶ Freshly brewed tea tastes best, so make only as much as you can drink in 20 minutes. After that, brew a new pot.

▶ Serve tea with milk or half-and-half, a sweetener (honey or sugar), and lemon wedges, if desired.

Whether it's a new recipe or old, punch is the perfect party drink. It is an easy, festive, inexpensive crowd-pleaser.

▶ When estimating quantities, figure 1 gallon (16 cups) punch for every ten people. That's assuming your guests will drink about three 4-ounce servings during the party.

▶ Mix all the ingredients in the order given in the punch recipe. Champagne, sparkling wine, seltzer water, soda—anything carbonated—goes in just before serving, after the other ingredients are mixed. Stir it sparingly to preserve the fizz.

▶ Use simple syrup (page 476) instead of sugar, which doesn't dissolve well in cold liquids.

▶ Chill all the ingredients before mixing (unless you're making a hot punch recipe). If possible, chill the punch bowl also.

▶ Use large blocks of ice or ice molds instead of ice cubes, which melt quickly and dilute the punch. Tea, juice, or any nonalcoholic ingredient can be frozen in an ice mold.

▶ Add whole strawberries, raspberries, cranberries, mint leaves, citrus slices, or maraschino cherries to your ice mold for added color and a touch of extra flavor.

▶ To freeze fruit into an ice mold, pour ½ to 1 inch of liquid into the bottom of the mold, top with fruit, and freeze. (If you are freezing water, use only distilled water, for the sake of clarity.) Remove the mold from the freezer, add more liquid to cover well, and freeze again. Allow several hours for the process. When ready, run warm water over the bottom of the mold to loosen it. Invert and float the mold in the punch bowl.

Champagne Flute

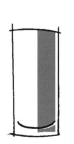

Collins Glass

Highball Glass

Hurricane Glass

Irish Coffee Glass

Martini Glass

Old Fashioned Glass

Rocks Glass

Whiskey Glass

Utensils and Equipment

Having all the right equipment in your kitchen makes cooking a pleasure rather than a chore. While you may not need everything mentioned here, this list serves as a helpful reference as you begin equipping your kitchen with the basics. Always buy the best that you can afford; quality equipment will last a lifetime.

POTS AND PANS

Prices range considerably for pots and pans. High-quality pans distribute heat evenly and are less likely to burn your food. Sometimes you can get a nice deal by buying a set, but it can also make sense to buy one pot to see how well you like it before committing to an expensive set. Here's the minimum you will need.

BAKING DISHES: A 9 x 13-inch nonstick or glass baking dish is essential for a one-layer sheet cake and brownies. This size pan is also great for macaroni and cheese and dishes like scalloped potatoes. You should have two or three baking dishes or casseroles in various sizes. A lidded casserole dish is especially handy.

BAKING SHEETS: Baking sheets have rims, cookies sheets do not. Generally they can be used interchangeably. A nonstick cookie sheet that is light in color and does not darken with use is ideal for cookies. How many to have depends on whether or not you plan to bake a lot. You will need an absolute minimum of two.

CAKE PANS: For layer cakes, you will need two or three 9-inch round, nonstick pans.

DUTCH OVEN: This is a covered metal (preferably cast-iron) casserole that can cook on top of the stove and in the oven. It should have a 6-quart to 8-quart capacity and a lid.

LARGE POTS: An 8-quart pot is big enough to cook pasta, but if you're going to make stock, buy a 16-quart pot.

LOAF PANS: Most recipes require two 9 x 5-inch loaf pans. Nonstick metal is best.

MUFFIN PANS<Heavy-duty, nonstick muffin pans work fine, but aluminum pans work just as well (and they're cheaper).

PIE PAN: Every cook should have at least one 9-inch pie pan.

ROASTING PANS: At a minimum, you will need a 9 x 13-inch metal roasting pan that can double as a baking dish. You can use it to make most casseroles, roast a chicken, etc. For turkeys and larger roasts, you will need a larger roasting pan.

SAUCEPANS: Heavy saucepans are less likely to result in burnt foods. Basic sizes are small (2-cup and 4-cup capacity), medium (2- to 3-quart), and large (8-quart). Saucepans should all have lids. You will need at least one in each size.

SKILLETS: Skillets and frying pans are the same thing. You can definitely use a large one (12-inch diameter). It is good to also have a medium one (10-inch) and a small one (6- or 8-inch). Cast-iron is the best, though some people prefer heavy-duty aluminum nonstick skillets. Cast-iron does require seasoning and special handling, so follow the manufacturer's directions when cleaning. The same is true with nonstick skillets.

SPRINGFORM PANS: These are cake pans with removable sides. They are useful if you plan to do a lot of baking. Springform pans that are 9 inches in diameter are most useful.

TUBE PAN: If you plan to bake sponge cakes or angel food cakes, you will need one 10-inch, ring-shaped pan with the hole in the center. Buy one with a removable bottom for easy removal of the cake.

BASIC TOOLS AND UTENSILS

If you've chosen pots and pans with a nonstick finish, be sure to use plastic utensils. These are less likely to scratch, which helps to protect the finish and is safe for your health.

BRUSHES: These are great for spreading oil, melted butter, marinades, etc. It is a good idea to reserve one strictly for pastries so it doesn't pick up odors.

CUTTING BOARDS: Wood or plastic is fine. Plastic is dishwasher safe.

MIXING BOWLS: You will need several in small, medium, and large sizes. Stainless steel is inexpensive and useful. Stoneware is nice but does get chipped; plastic bowls stain. Opt for nesting bowls no matter what, as they are easy to store.

HEATPROOF RUBBER SPATULAS: Use for scraping— at least two, a small one and a larger one.

LONG-HANDLED FORK

LONG-HANDLED, HEAVY-DUTY SOUP LADLE

LONG-HANDLED, HEAVY-DUTY SPOONS: At least one should be a slotted spoon. Wooden spoons are also useful because they will not damage a nonstick coated pan.

WHISK: For heavy beating and/or blending when a fork is not sufficient.

WIDE SPATULA: Also called a pancake turner.

MEASURING TOOLS

MEASURING CUPS: You will need a 2-cup glass measuring cup for liquids. A 4-cup measuring cup for liquids is useful as well. Plastic, even clear plastic, tends to scratch and become discolored and hard to read. You will also need a set of 1/8- to 1-cup dry measuring cups for dry ingredients— either metal or plastic is fine here.

MEASURING SPOONS: Buy two sets so you can use one for liquid ingredients and one for dry.

THERMOMETERS: An instant-read (digital or dial) thermometer is necessary for judging when meats and roasts are done. A candy thermometer is very useful for making candy.

KNIVES

A good set of knives is essential for chopping, dicing, and slicing. High-carbon steel knives are preferred by many chefs and experienced cooks alike. Buy the very best you can afford. Start with an 8-inch chef's knife, which will take care of your basic chopping and slicing needs. Don't bother with a carving or slicing knife right away—you won't use it very often, and your chef's knife can handle most of those duties for a while. A paring knife, 3 or 4 inches long, is needed for peeling,

trimming, and other precise cutting. A serrated knife is a must for slicing bread. A swivel-bladed vegetable peeler is not absolutely necessary but is very handy. Buy a blade sharpener and learn how to use it to keep your knives working at peak efficiency—sharpening stone works best. Also invest in a wooden storage block; knives should not be stored loose in a drawer.

MISCELLANEOUS TOOLS AND UTENSILS

Some may seem obvious, but all should have a home in your kitchen.

Bottle opener
Box or other hand grater
Can opener
Colander
Corkscrew
Lemon reamer
Pastry blender
Pepper grinder
Potato masher
Ricer
Rolling pin
Strainer, wire-mesh
Timer
Vegetable steamer insert
Whisk
Wire racks
Zester

SMALL APPLIANCES

FOOD PROCESSOR: There are very few tools as valuable as this. It can grate large amounts of anything in short order, and it can make pie and bread dough in minutes. It can purée as well as a blender, and it can chop vegetables and grate hard cheeses.

ELECTRIC MIXER: A standing mixer is very handy, especially if you plan to bake a lot. It does the best job on egg whites and whipping cream. You can get by with a handheld mixer, however.

BLENDERS: A blender does the best job of puréeing soups. It is also needed for making milk shakes, smoothies, and other drinks.

TOASTER: What would breakfast be without toast?

Cooking Terms

If you are new to cooking, you may find some of the recipe language confusing. Here are some of the cooking terms you'll encounter.

AL DENTE: Doneness for pasta is defined by the Italian term *al dente*, meaning "to the tooth." The pasta is cooked just enough to maintain this firm, chewy texture.

BASTE: To brush or spoon liquid fat or juices over meat during cooking, to add flavor and to prevent it from drying out.

BATTER: A semi-liquid mixture of flour, fat, and liquid that is thin enough in consistency to require a pan or bowl to encase it. A batter is different from dough, which maintains its shape.

BEAT: To mix ingredients by briskly whipping or stirring them with a spoon, fork, whisk, rotary beater, or electric mixer.

BLANCH: To pour boiling water over food to loosen skin, partially cook, and remove or set color. When blanching fruits or vegetables you generally plunge the food into ice water to stop the cooking action.

BLEND: To mix or fold two or more ingredients together to obtain equal distribution throughout the mixture.

BRAISE: A cooking technique that requires browning meat or vegetables. They are then covered and cooked slowly in a small amount of liquid. The effect of braising is to tenderize and imbue with flavor.

BREAD: To coat the food with crumbs (usually with fresh or dry bread crumbs).

BROIL: To cook food directly under the oven's heat source. This technique only cooks/browns the top surface of the food while the inside remains cool.

BROTH: A flavorful liquid (stock) made by gently cooking meat, seafood, or vegetables (and/or their by-products, such as bones and trimming), often with herbs, in liquid, usually water. The pieces are then strained from the liquid.

BROWN: To cook food quickly to produce a browned exterior while the interior remains moist.

BRUSH: To use a pastry brush to coat a food such as meat or bread with melted butter, glaze, or other liquid.

BUTTERFLY: To cut open foods, such as shrimp, down the center without cutting all the way through, and then spread apart.

CHOP: To cut into irregular pieces. Finely chopped pieces are ¼ to ½ inch in size. Large pieces are coarsely chopped. Very fine chopping is called mincing.

COAT: To evenly cover food with flour, crumbs, or a batter before cooking.

CODDLE: To cook an egg by placing the egg in its shell in water just below the boiling point.

COMBINE: To blend two or more ingredients into a single mixture.

CORE: To remove the inedible center of fruits and vegetables, such as apples and cabbage.

CREAM: To beat shortening or butter, with or without sugar, until light and fluffy. This process traps in air bubbles, which will later create height in cookies and cakes.

CRIMP: To create a decorative edge on a pie crust. On a double pie crust, this will seal the edges together.

CURE: To preserve or add flavor with an ingredient, usually salt or sugar.

CUSTARD: A thick, creamy mixture of beaten egg, milk, and other ingredients, cooked with gentle heat, often in a water bath or double boiler. As pie filling, custard is frequently cooked and chilled before being layered into a prebaked crust.

CUT IN: To work shortening or butter into dry ingredients using two knives, a fork, or a pastry blender.

DASH: A measure approximately equal to ¹⁄₁₆ teaspoon. Used for liquid ingredients.

DEEP FRY: To cook by completely submerging food in hot oil.

DEGLAZE: To add liquid to a pan in which foods have been fried or roasted, in order to dissolve the caramelized juices stuck to the bottom of the pan. The flavorful liquid is then used to make a sauce or gravy.

DICE: To cut into small cubes ⅛ to ¼ inch in size.

DOT: To sprinkle food with small bits of an ingredient, such as butter, to allow for even melting.

DOUGH: A combination of ingredients including flour, liquid, and sometimes a leavener, producing a firm mixture which holds it shape for making baked goods, especially bread.

DREDGE: To lightly coat food, usually with flour or cornmeal, often in preparation for frying.

DRIPPINGS: Used for gravies and sauces, drippings are the liquids left in the bottom of a roasting or frying pan after meat is cooked.

DRIZZLE: To pour a liquid such as a sweet glaze or melted butter in a slow, light trickle over food.

DUST: To sprinkle food with spices, sugar, or flour for a light coating.

EGG WASH: A mixture of beaten eggs (yolks, whites, or both together) with either milk or water. Used to coat baked goods, to seal and/or give them a shine when baked.

FILET: A boneless cut of meat or poultry.

FILLET: To remove the bones from meat or fish for cooking. It also refers to a boneless piece of fish.

FLAMBÉ: To ignite a sauce or other alcoholic liquid so that it flames.

FLUTE: To create a decorative scalloped or undulating edge on a pie crust or other pastry.

FOLD: To mix lightly with a spoon or rubber spatula to keep as much air in the mixture as possible.

FRY: To cook food in hot butter or oil, usually until a crisp brown crust forms. Food may be deep fried (immersed in oil) or pan fried (cooked in a shallow amount of oil).

GEL: To cause a food to set or solidify, usually by adding gelatin.

GLAZE: A liquid that gives an item a hardened, shiny surface, such as chocolate thinned with melted shortening. Also, to cover a food with such a liquid.

GRATE: To shred or cut into fine pieces by rubbing against a rough surface with holes.

GRILL: To cook over a heat source (traditionally over wood coals) in the open air.

GRIND: To cut a food into small pieces with a food processor, chopper, grinder, or mortar and pestle.

HULL: To remove the leafy parts of soft fruits, such as strawberries.

ICE: To cool down cooked food by placing in ice; also, to spread frosting on a cake or other foods.

INFUSE: To extract flavors by soaking them in liquid heated in a covered pan. Herbal teas are infused.

JULIENNE: To cut into long, thin strips, like matchsticks.

KNEAD: To work dough with the heels of your hands, using a pressing and folding motion, until the dough becomes smooth and elastic.

LEAVEN: To produce air bubbles in and cause the rising of baked goods, such as cookies and cakes.

LINE: To place layers of edible (cake or bread slices) or inedible (aluminum foil or wax paper) ingredients in a pan to provide structure for a dish or to prevent sticking.

LUKEWARM: Neither hot nor cold, a temperature of about 95°F.

MARINATE: To soak meat, poultry, fish, or vegetables in seasoned liquid to add flavor.

MASH: To beat or press a food to remove lumps and make a smooth mixture.

MINCE: To chop food into tiny, irregular pieces.

MIX: To beat or stir two or more foods together until they are thoroughly combined.

MOISTEN: To add enough liquid to dry ingredients to dampen but not soak them.

MULL: To slowly heat wine or cider with spices and sugar.

NONREACTIVE: Made of stainless steel, ceramic, or glass.

PAN FRY: To cook in a hot pan with a small amount of hot oil, butter, or other fat, turning the food over once or twice until done.

PARBOIL: To partially cook food (usually vegetables) in boiling liquid.

PARCHMENT PAPER: A heavy, heat-resistant paper used in cooking, particularly for lining baking sheets.

PEAKS: The mounds made in a mixture, for example, egg white that has been whipped to stiffness. Peaks are "stiff" if they stay upright or "soft" if they curl over.

PINCH: A very small amount, a bit less than ⅛ teaspoon, that can be held between a thumb tip and forefinger. Used for dry ingredients, such as spices.

PIPE: To force a semisoft food through a bag (either a pastry bag, or a plastic bag with one corner cut off).

PIT: To remove the center stone or seed of a fruit, such as a peach or an avocado, usually with a knife.

POACH: To simmer in liquid.

PURÉE: To finely blend and/or mash food into a thick, smooth consistency.

REDUCE: To cook a liquid over high heat so that some of the water evaporates, resulting in decreased volume and intensified flavor.

ROAST: To cook uncovered in the oven.

ROUX: A cooked paste, usually made from flour and butter, used to thicken sauces and soups.

SAUTÉ: To cook foods quickly in a small amount of oil in a skillet over direct heat.

SCALD: To heat a liquid, such as milk, to just below the point of boiling.

SCORE: To cut shallow lines in meat, fish, or dough.

SEAR: To cook quickly over very high heat so that a crust forms.

SHRED: To cut or tear into long narrow strips, either by hand or by using a grater or food processor.

SHUCK: To peel off or remove the shell or husk from oysters, clams, or an ear of corn.

SIFT: To remove large lumps from a dry ingredient, such as flour or confectioners' sugar, by passing it through a fine mesh. This process also incorporates air into the ingredients, making them lighter.

SIMMER: To cook in gently bubbling liquid.

SIMPLE SYRUP: A solution of equal parts sugar dissolved in water.

STEAM: To cook food in either a steamer or strainer insert over boiling water in a covered pan.

STEEP: To soak dry ingredients, such as tea leaves, in liquid until the flavor is infused into the liquid.

STEW: To slowly cook food in liquid in a covered pot or pan.

STRAIN: To remove particles from a liquid by pouring it through a wire-mesh strainer or piece of cheesecloth.

THIN: To reduce a mixture's thickness with the addition of more liquid.

TOSS: To thoroughly combine several ingredients by mixing lightly.

WATER BATH: A gentle cooking technique in which a container is in a pan of water, which simmers throughout the cooking process.

WHIP: To incorporate air into ingredients, such as cream or egg whites, by beating until light and fluffy; also refers to the utensil used for this action.

WHISK: To mix or fluff by beating; also refers to the utensil used for this action.

ZEST: The thin, brightly colored outer part of the rind of citrus fruits (the white meat of the rind is bitter). It contains volatile oils, used as a flavoring.

Herbs and Spices

For the best flavor, buy dried herbs and spices in small quantities, and throw out anything that is older than six months. You should always store herbs and spices in a cool, dark place. A shelf over the stove is not a good place because the heat rising from the stove will cause deterioration in flavor and color.

SPICING IT UP

Until very recently, many Americans preferred mildly flavored foods. Mexican and Tex-Mex foods were found only in the Southwest, and spicy Cajun food was only found in Louisiana. The cooking of New England, the South, and the Midwest in particular was gently seasoned. This cookbook is devoted to re-creating dishes from that older tradition of cooking, but there are ways you can spice it up to suit your individual tastes.

If you can find fresh herbs, always use them instead of dried herbs. For every teaspoon of dried herbs, use one tablespoon of chopped fresh herbs. Basil and mint, in particular, are two herbs that have much more punch when used fresh.

Make sure your spices are fresh. It is even better to grind your own in a spice mill. Freshly grated nutmeg, for example, is far superior to ground nutmeg.

Make sure you have added enough salt and pepper. The first and best way to punch up the flavor of a dish is to add enough salt to suit your palate.

Other flavor enhancers include vinegar and lemon juice (especially with dishes that contain tomatoes and other acidic ingredients), wine or sherry (particularly with rich, meaty dishes), and hot sauce (if you like hot sauce, you like it with everything!).

HERBS AND SPICES

The list below contains the herbs and spices used in this book. Herbs are dried and crumbled, unless otherwise noted. Spices are ground unless otherwise noted.

Allspice
Basil
Bay leaves (whole)
Black pepper
Capers
Caraway seeds
Cardamom
Cayenne pepper
Celery salt
Celery seeds
Chervil
Chili powder
Chives
Cilantro
Cinnamon (sticks and ground)
Cloves
Coriander
Crushed red pepper
Cumin
Curry powder
Dill
Dill seed
Fennel
Filé powder
Garlic
Ginger
Juniper berries
Mace
Marjoram
Mint
Mustard (dry)
Mustard seed
Nutmeg
Oregano
Paprika
Parsley
Poppy seeds
Rosemary
Saffron (threads and crushed)
Sage
Savory
Tarragon
Thyme
Turmeric

Canning and Pickling

Home cooks have been preserving foods by canning and pickling for years. In the days before supermarkets and year-round distribution of local and imported produce, canning was the only way to guarantee a variety of foods, particularly fruits and vegetables, in the diet. Because canning is no longer necessary, some fear it is becoming a lost art. The instructions here are very basic and it is probably a good idea, if you plan to do any canning, to get a book on food preservation or consult your county extension agricultural agent for more information.

Canning involves putting foods into jars and heating them to a temperature that destroys the microorganisms that could be a health hazard or cause the foods to spoil. Air is driven from the jar during heating and a vacuum seal is formed as it cools. The vacuum seal prevents air from getting back into the jar and contaminating the food.

SAFE CANNING METHODS

Many people today still use some of the out-dated methods of canning and others have experimented with microwaves and slow cookers, but boiling water-bath canning and pressure canning are the most effective.

Because pressure canning requires special equipment and is potentially dangerous, we will only deal with boiling water-bath canning here.

Boiling water-bath canning is safe for fruits, tomatoes, and pickles, as well as jams, jellies, and other preserves. In this method, jars of food are heated by being completely submerged in boiling water (212°F at sea level).

CANNING EQUIPMENT

Apart from ladles, funnels, and sieves, which you may already own, you need the following canning equipment. Most supermarkets and hardware stores stock canning equipment, especially in late summer.

BOILING WATER-BATH CANNER: Get one with a wire rack to hold the jars.

CANNING JARS: Use quart, pint, and half-pint sizes. Canning jars are made from glass tempered to withstand high heat during processing. They can be reused year after year if undamaged. Do not use jars in which you bought commercially prepared sauce or jam because the glass may not be strong enough.

TWO-PIECE LID: Consisting of a flat disk called a dome lid that sits on top of the jar and a screw ring to hold it in place. The flat disk lid cannot be reused; undamaged screw rings can be used again.

JAR LIFTER: Allows you to handle hot jars.

THE RULE FOR TOMATOES

Because the acidity of tomatoes varies, safe canning requires that tomatoes be acidified to maintain a safe pH and prevent the growth of bacteria. In the case of many preserves, the acid is part of the recipe—as in the case of ketchup, which contains vinegar. Otherwise, acidify tomatoes by adding 2 tablespoons bottled lemon juice or ½ teaspoon citric acid to each quart jar.

HOW TO CAN USING A BOILING WATER-BATH

For safe canning, follow these directions, based on USDA recommendations:

1. Prepare the pickles, tomatoes, or sauce according to the recipe.

2. Prepare the lids and rings by putting them in a pan of boiling water. Keep them in the boiling water for 10 minutes. Do not remove them until you are ready to put them on the jars.

3. Prepare the jars. You do not have to sterilize jars used for food processed in a boiling water-bath for more than 10 minutes. Simply wash them in soapy water or in a dishwasher, then rinse thoroughly to remove all traces of soap. For boiling water-bath processing times of less than 10 minutes, sterilize the prewashed jars by submerging them in a canner filled with hot (not boiling) water, making sure the water rises 1 inch above the jar top. At sea level, boil the jars for 10 minutes; at higher elevations, boil for an

additional minute for every 1,000 feet, as indicated in the information on this page. Some dishwashers also have a sterilizing cycle you can use.

4. Fill the jars, leaving a ½-inch headspace or the headspace indicated in your recipe. Wipe away any drips on the rim. If bubbles appear as you fill the jars, run a clean spatula or chopstick inside the jar edge to release them. Do not stir, which could create more bubbles.

5. Place the lids on top and secure with a metal ring, tightening it so it grips. (You do not need to exert extra pressure to make it extremely tight.) Load the jars into the canner rack.

6. Fill the canner half full with water and preheat to 180 degrees. Lift the rack by its handles and set it in the canner.

7. Add more boiling water, if necessary, to bring the water level to 1 inch above the jars.

8. Turn the heat as high as possible and wait until the water is boiling vigorously. Cover the canner with the lid. Reduce the heat to maintain a moderate boil. As soon as you have covered the canner, set a timer for the recommended processing time. If you live at a high elevation, increase the processing time as necessary, using the information on this page.

9. Have more boiling water on hand to counteract any evaporation that makes the water fall below the recommended level. Arrange folded towels on a counter where you can place the finished jars for cooling.

10. When the jars have boiled for the recommended time, remove them from the canner using a jar lifter. Set them on the towels, right side up, placing them at least 1 inch apart.

11. Let the jars cool for 12 hours, and then test to establish that you have a good seal. Look at the middle of the lid; it should be slightly concave. Press the center hard with your thumb; if it does not move downward or "give," it is sealed. You can also tap the lid with the rounded bowl of a teaspoon. If it is correctly sealed, it will ring clearly; if not, it will sound dull. If the seal is faulty, the tomatoes or pickles inside the jar are not spoiled, but they cannot be kept for long periods. Store them in the refrigerator and use within a week.

PROCESSING TIMES

Each food has its own processing time. The length of time required varies with the denseness of the food, its packing liquid, and its pH. There are many good books devoted to preserving foods, which you can consult for specific times. Your county extension service will also have information on preserving food by canning.

ADJUSTING CANNING TIMES FOR ALTITUDE

At sea level, water boils at 212°F; at higher elevations, it boils at lower temperatures. In these higher regions, foods must be processed for longer to ensure that harmful organisms are destroyed. The USDA recommends that you add 1 minute for every 1,000 feet above sea level when processing foods that require less than 20 minutes in the boiling water-bath. Add 2 minutes for every 1,000 feet for foods that must be processed for more than 20 minutes.

TROUBLESHOOTING

In general, it is not difficult to detect when a canning job has gone bad. The first sign that a jar of food is no good is that the lid will pop up (or bulge); there might also be seeping around the seal. Mold growing on the surface of the food is a sure sign of a problem. Abnormal colors in the brine of pickles, cloudiness in the brine, and a white colored film on the surface of the food are additional indications of contamination.

Do not eat contaminated food. It invariably will cause harm. Reheating the food—even boiling it for long periods—is not a solution, as botulism is not the living part of the *Clostridium botulinum* but a byproduct of its lifecycle in the form of spores. Botulism is in fact a deadly form of food poisoning in low-acid foods, such as vegetables, that produces toxins that are dangerous to people as well as animals.

It is best to store canned foods at relatively low temperatures, as this helps to prevent any activity by microorganisms that might have survived the heating process. Keeping jars in dark, cool places also helps to preserve vitamins and taste.

Freezing and Thawing

Whether you have an excess of leftovers, a bumper crop of berries from your own berry patch, or a great supermarket deal on chicken breasts, freezing can be a safe, easy, and convenient way to preserve foods.

Most foods, including fruits, vegetables, meat, and prepared soups and stews, can be safely frozen. Some foods require special preparation, such as blanching (most vegetables) or packing in a sugar syrup (most fruit). Foods that do not tolerate freezing well include salad vegetables, mushrooms, and raw potatoes. In general, foods made with eggs and dairy products do not freeze well.

Most foods can be safely kept in the home freezer for 3 to 12 months without loss of quality. Best keeping times vary depending on the food; with time, all frozen foods will deteriorate in quality until they are unacceptable for use.

GENERAL TIPS

▶ Freezers should be kept at or below 0°F.

▶ In contrast to refrigerators, deep freezers should be packed tightly, as this allows the freezer to function better.

▶ Using appropriate packaging, such as freezer bags and plastic containers, will help protect foods and prevent "freezer burn."

▶ When the surface of frozen foods comes in contact with the air, freezer burn (grayish-brown leathery spots) occurs. Freezer burn does not make food unsafe, but heavily freezer-burned foods may have to be discarded due to a loss of quality. Cut freezer-burned portions away either before or after cooking the food.

▶ Avoid placing hot foods straight into the freezer because this will raise the freezer temperature and may adversely affect other foods. Cool foods before freezing.

▶ Make sure that frozen food is completely thawed before cooking.

▶ Don't forget to label and date your packages, using waterproof pens or permanent markers.

FREEZING FRUITS

Fruits are generally pretty easy to freeze. Many go straight from the berry bush and into the freezer bag. However, every fruit is different, and some require special handling for best results. When using freezer containers instead of plastic bags, remember to leave ½ to 1 inch of headroom to provide for expansion.

Fruit generally has a better texture when tossed with sugar or packed in a sugar syrup before freezing. Ascorbic acid is added to some fruits to prevent browning. Here are preparation instructions for most fruits.

APRICOTS: Rinse and pit. Cut in half or leave whole. Blanch by dipping in boiling water for 30 seconds, then peel. For best results, toss with ½ cup sugar per quart.

BERRIES: Rinse berries, drain well, and hull when appropriate. Spread on a tray and freeze until solid, then pour into a plastic freezer bag or a freezing container. For best results, toss with ¼ to ½ cup sugar per quart.

CHERRIES: Rinse, remove stems, and pit. Tray-freeze, then put into bags (as with berries). For best results, toss with ⅔ cup sugar per quart.

MANGOES: Rinse, peel, and cut into pieces. Avoid the flesh near the pit. Mix slices with ¼ teaspoon ascorbic acid and ½ cup sugar. Make sure the sugar dissolves. Pack in freezer bags or containers.

MELONS: Cut the melons in half and remove the seeds. Cut again into quarters and eighths, then peel and cut into cubes. Pack in freezer bags or containers.

PEACHES AND NECTARINES: Peel peaches by dipping in boiling water for 1 minute, then placing under cold water. The skins should slip off easily. You may leave on the skins of nectarines. Toss with ¼ teaspoon ascorbic acid and ½ cup sugar per quart.

PEARS: Peel, halve, and core. Prepare a syrup of 1¾ cups sugar to 4 cups water and bring to a boil. Add ¾ teaspoon ascorbic acid per quart syrup. Add pears to the boiling syrup and heat for about 1½ minutes. Pack in freezer containers with syrup.

PINEAPPLE: Peel and remove eyes and cores. Cut into wedges, slices, etc. Dry-pack in freezer bags or containers.

PLUMS: Rinse and dry, then slice or pit, if desired. Dry-pack or sugar-pack with ½ cup sugar per quart.

RHUBARB: Rinse and remove the leaves (leaves are poisonous). Cut stems into ½ to 1 inch pieces, then dry-pack or toss with 1 cup sugar per quart.

FREEZING VEGETABLES

Most vegetables require blanching before freezing. When using freezer containers instead of plastic bags, remember to leave ½ to 1 inch of headroom to provide for expansion.

To blanch, add the vegetables to boiling water and blanch for the time suggested below. Remove from the boiling water or drain and immediately plunge in ice water to stop the cooking. Drain the vegetables well. If possible, pat dry with clean paper towels before packing into bags and freezing.

VEGETABLE PREPARATION

ASPARAGUS: Cut off tough ends, if any. Blanch for 2 to 4 minutes.

GREEN BEANS: Snap off ends and cut into 2-inch lengths. Blanch for 3 minutes.

BEETS: Cut into slices or wedges and cook for 30 to 45 minutes.

BROCCOLI: Trim ends and rinse. Cut into small pieces (about 2 inches or heads no more than 1½ inches across). Blanch for 3 minutes.

CARROTS: Peel and cut to desired size (generally no bigger than 3 or 4 inches in length). Blanch for 2 to 5 minutes depending on size.

CORN: For corn on the cob, cook for 7 to 11 minutes. For kernels, place the whole cob in boiling water for 4 minutes, then cut off the kernels with a knife.

ONIONS: Peel and chop. No cooking or blanching is necessary.

PEAS: Shell and freeze on a tray. When frozen, pour into freezer bags.

SUMMER SQUASH AND ZUCCHINI: Cut into ½-inch slices and blanch for 3 minutes.

TOMATOES: Scald in boiling water to loosen the skin. Peel and cut off the stems. Cut to desired size and heat through. Cool and then pack.

FREEZING MEAT

Meat should be wrapped in freezer paper, aluminum foil, or plastic wrap. Do not remove the wrapping from meats purchased at the supermarket.

Maintain the freezer at or below 0°F.

Frozen ground meat should be used within 3 months.

Pork can be frozen for 6 to 8 months.

Beef, lamb, veal, and venison can be frozen for 8 to 12 months.

Poultry and other birds can be frozen for about 12 months.

PACKAGING AND LABELING

To speed up freezing and to retain the natural color, flavor, and texture of food, cool all foods and syrup before packaging. Pack food tightly in the container to leave as little air as possible. Most foods do require headspace between the packed food and the lid of the container to allow for expansion of the food as it freezes. A ½- to 1½-inch headspace is generally acceptable.

It is safe to freeze meat or poultry directly in its supermarket wrapping. Since this type of wrap is permeable to air, use the food within 2 months or overwrap these packages as you would any food for long-term storage, using airtight heavy-duty aluminum foil, plastic wrap, or freezer paper, or place the package inside a plastic bag.

Use low-temperature tape to seal plastic and aluminum-foil containers tightly and to label the contents of the container. Use a wax or soft-lead pencil, a crayon, or a special waterproof marking ink on a low-temperature label or tape. Include on the label the name of the product, date frozen, and weight or number of servings.

THAWING FOODS SAFELY

There are only three ways to safely thaw food: in the refrigerator; in cold, frequently changed water; or in the microwave. Do not thaw foods at room temperature or outside. These methods may result in food that can cause food-borne illness. The only exceptions are pastries, bread, and fruit, which can be thawed at room temperature.

REFRIGERATOR THAWING

This is the preferred method of thawing, and it is the slowest method. Small food items may defrost overnight in the refrigerator, but most foods require a day or two.

All meats, fish, shellfish, poultry, and vegetables should be thawed in the refrigerator. Bacteria capable of causing illness are common on these foods, and many bacteria on fresh food will still be present when food is thawed. The refrigerator's temperature should not exceed 40°F when thawing these types of food.

For turkey, place the wrapped bird in the refrigerator on a tray or in a pan to catch moisture that accumulates as it thaws, allowing 24 hours for every 5 pounds of bird. A 20-pound bird will take 4 full days and nights to defrost.

COLD-WATER THAWING

This method is faster than refrigerator thawing, but it requires more attention. Food should be placed in a leakproof plastic bag and immersed in cold water. Make sure the bag doesn't leak, as bacteria from the air or surrounding environment could be introduced into the food. Also, food tissues absorb water and can result in watery, lower-quality food. Change the water frequently, at least every 30 minutes. After thawing, refrigerate the food until ready for use.

MICROWAVE THAWING

Use this method to defrost food only when you plan to cook it immediately. Some areas of the food may become warm and begin to cook during microwaving. Microwave thawing does not destroy bacteria, so the food still needs to be thoroughly cooked.

POWER OR EQUIPMENT FAILURE

If power for your freezer is interrupted, do not open the freezer door. Food in a loaded freezer will usually stay frozen for 2 days, even in the summertime. If service is not restored within 1 to 2 days, use dry ice to keep the food frozen. Discard any foods that have been warmer than 40°F for more than two hours. Discard any foods that have been contaminated by meat juices.

If it is freezing outside or there is snow on the ground, you may be tempted to keep food frozen outside until the power is restored. However, foods stored outside are exposed to the sun, environmental contamination, and roaming animals and birds. Keep food indoors.

REFREEZING THAWED FOODS

You may safely refreeze frozen foods that have thawed if they still contain ice crystals or if they are still cold (about 40°F) and have not been in the refrigerator for more than one day. In general, if a food is safe to eat, it is safe to refreeze. Partial thawing and refreezing will lower the quality of fruits and vegetables. Meats may be cooked and then frozen again with little loss of quality. Use refrozen foods as soon as possible to maintain an acceptable quality.

COOKING FROZEN FOODS

Raw or cooked meat, poultry, and casseroles can be cooked or reheated from the frozen state. It will take approximately one and a half times the usual cooking time. Discard any wrapping or absorbent paper from meat or poultry. When cooking whole poultry, remove the giblet pack from the cavity as soon as it becomes loose. Cook the giblets separately.

Almost all vegetables cooked before serving may be taken directly from the freezer, unpacked, and then steamed, boiled, or microwaved. Spinach and corn on the cob are better if first thawed for 4 hours in the refrigerator. Package directions should be followed for exact times.

Presentation and Garnishing

Making food look attractive is as much a part of the cook's job as making it taste delicious. A pleasing food presentation announces that something enjoyable is about to happen, and it is so simple to do.

Good food presentation starts with menu planning. A plate of pork chops, mashed potatoes, and corn does not offer enough color contrast. But change the mashed potatoes to sweet potatoes and the corn to peas and you have an attractive plate of food. So think about colors as you plan your menu.

If you want to stick to those mashed potatoes anyway, think about adding color to them with chopped fresh chives. Consider adding color to the corn with diced pimentos or red bell pepper. Likewise, instead of plain white rice, make rice pilaf. Cook the rice in broth and add finely chopped herbs. The next time you make a salad, toast and then chop a small handful of pecans, almonds, or walnuts. All you have to do is sprinkle them on top of your salad for a special touch, and the added crunch makes it much more pleasing. Any or all of these little touches add up to a beautiful plate of food.

In addition to color, think about the shapes of the food you are serving. A boneless chicken breast is just a mound on the plate. But if you slice the breast and fan out the pieces, the chicken looks much more appealing. When plating foods, alternate the heights of the food. For example, lean a lamb chop or slices of steak against a mound of potatoes instead of just laying the two side by side.

Garnishing plates or platters does not necessarily require special skills. A garnish can be as simple as a sprig of a fresh herb. Top a platter or individual plates of pasta with a few whole herb leaves. Sprinkle chopped herbs on fish or meat or float them in soups. The simplest garnishes are often the most elegant, and gardeners have a world of choices outside their door.

When you choose a garnish, consider four things: color, texture, shape, and taste.

Oranges and lemons are available year-round and are wonderful to use as garnishes. In Grandmother's day, rings of cinnamon-flavored candied apples often served as garnishes. Today you can use a slice of kiwifruit or starfruit for interesting shapes and colors. Strawberries are available almost year-round and are a natural garnish for anything chocolate. They're also perfect with breakfast entrées, such as omelets or quiches.

Vegetable garnishes don't have to be carved by a master crafter. Carrots, celery, squash, zucchini, bell peppers, tomatoes, radishes, broccoli, cauliflower, and beets—these can be sliced, julienned, grated, curled, or left whole to provide color and accent to the plate.

To make carrot curls float in a soup or to top a casserole, slice a carrot lengthwise into thin slices with a vegetable peeler. Steam the carrots with a tablespoon of water in the microwave for 30 seconds. They'll go limp and be easy to curl and drape on a plate or dish.

For dessert at home, don't overlook the impact of a few berries or nuts adorning the plate of something as simple as ice cream. Or use shaved chocolate curls on a chocolate cake (just use a vegetable peeler on a block of room-temperature chocolate).

The more complex the dish is, the simpler the garnish should be. Chopped parsley in a beef stew makes sense, just as a combination of finely chopped tomatoes, carrots, and zucchini could top a plain chicken breast.

Just remember that you can have too much of a good thing. It is not necessary to surround a plate with a border of green; a sprig can have equal if not greater effect. Don't lose the beauty of the dish in an overabundance of garnishment. Above all, let the food speak for itself.

Holiday Menus

Are you at a loss for what to serve at your next gathering? Here are a few suggestions to inspire you. Obviously, there are many more recipes to choose from. These ideas are provided as a means to get you started.

JANUARY

NEW YEAR'S EVE PARTY: Festivities abound in celebration of a new year! Here is a selection of fun appetizers and easy treats to serve to a crowd of well-wishers.

> Strawberry Champagne
> Tropical Fruit Punch
> Spiced Nuts
> Cheese Straws
> Marinated Olives
> Texas Caviar
> Hot Artichoke Dip
> Stuffed Mushrooms
> Sweet-and-Sour Meatballs
> Brownies

FEBRUARY

VALENTINE'S DAY DINNER: Here's a romantic dinner for you and your partner. Just add candlelight and mood music.

> Kir Royale
> French Onion Soup
> Mushroom-Stuffed Roast Chicken
> Mashed Potatoes
> Green Beans Amandine
> Parker House Rolls
> Devil's Food Cake

MARCH/APRIL

ST. PATRICK'S DAY DINNER: The proper drink to serve with this delicious meal is Guinness.

> Limeade
> Corned Beef and Cabbage
> Steamed New Potatoes with Parsley and Dill
> Rutabaga Pudding
> Irish Soda Bread
> Key Lime Pie

PASSOVER DINNER: Jews celebrate their freedom from slavery in Egypt with a table ceremony called a "seder" and a meal that is without bread.

> Wine
> Chicken Soup with Matzo Balls
> Beef Brisket with Dried Fruit
> Oven-Roasted Potatoes
> Mixed Green Salad
> Sautéed Green Beans with Mushrooms
> Baked Apples

EASTER DINNER: Easter is an occasion to celebrate spring and the renewal of the earth.

> Wine
> Deviled Eggs
> Stuffed Cucumbers
> Baked Glazed Ham
> Wild Rice
> Ginger Ale and Fruit Salad Mold
> Minted Peas and Shallots
> Sweet Potato Casserole with Marshmallows
> Lemon Meringue Pie

MAY/JUNE

CINCO DE MAYO PARTY: Mexicans and Americans everywhere celebrate Cinco de Mayo, which translates as the fifth of May and marks a battle that took place in 1862.

> Margaritas
> Mojitos
> Guacamole
> Pico de Gallo
> Mexican Tortilla Soup
> Posole
> Sopaipillas

MEMORIAL DAY COOKOUT: Roll out the grill for the first outdoor meal of the season. This holiday marks the unofficial start of summer.

> Iced Tea Punch
> Juicy Grilled Burgers
> Patio Hot Dogs
> Creamy Pea Salad
> Macaroni Salad
> Strawberry Custard Pie

JULY

FOURTH OF JULY DINNER: Observe this all-American holiday with an all-American menu.

> Lemonade
> Sangria
> Pimento Cheese
> Pico de Gallo
> Beer-Basted Grilled Chicken
> Barbecued Beef Short Ribs
> Potato Salad
> Sliced Tomato Salad
> Corn on the Cob
> Watermelon Bombe

AUGUST/SEPTEMBER

LABOR DAY DINNER: Bid farewell to summer with a dinner celebrating the bounty of the season.

> Minted Iced Tea
> Piña Colada
> Gazpacho
> Grilled Halibut with Garlic-Basil Butter
> Grilled Corn
> Grilled Garlic Bread
> Three Bean Salad
> Mixed Berry Crisp
> French Vanilla Ice Cream

OCTOBER

HALLOWEEN PARTY: Scatter bowls of candy around the room, and decorate with cobwebs and monsters. This is no time for serious formal dining!

> Zombie
> Party Cheese Ball
> Nutty Popcorn
> Autumn Fruit Salad
> Tex-Mex Chili
> Frozen Orange Cups

NOVEMBER

THANKSGIVING DINNER: This combination of classic dishes will give your family lots to be thankful for.

> Wine
> Cape Codder
> Roast Turkey with Giblet Gravy
> Basic Bread Stuffing
> Cranberry-Nut Gelatin Salad
> Brussels Sprouts with Bacon and Onion
> Candied Sweet Potatoes
> Glazed Carrots
> Featherbed Potato Rolls
> Pumpkin Pie

DECEMBER

HANUKKAH DINNER: Here is a delicious Jewish-American feast to celebrate the lighting of the menorah.

> Wine
> Hot Mulled Cider
> Roast Chicken with Pan Gravy
> Cheddar Cheese Soup
> Potato Pancakes
> Creamy Pea Salad
> Applesauce
> Beets in Orange Sauce
> Jelly Roll

CHRISTMAS DINNER: After a busy morning of opening gifts, everyone will be joyous when feasting on this scrumptious spread. The drinks are definite warmers on a cold winter night.

> Eggnog
> Grog
> Grapefruit and Avocado Salad
> Standing Rib Roast with Horseradish
> Sauce
> Holiday Potato Cups
> Creamed Spinach
> Baked Acorn Squash
> Herbed Bread Sticks
> Brandied Fruitcake

THE RECIPE TESTERS

⬛⬛⬛⬛⬛⬛⬛⬛⬛⬛

Sarah Absher MI, Kay Adams WA, Jeanne Ahearn CA, Dorinne Albright RI, Ron Alexander MI, Crystal Alford TN, Carole Allen WI, Debra Allen CA, John & Patricia Alles WI, Barbara Amidon UT, Barbara Anderson CA, Jennifer Anderson UT, Valeri Anderson LA, Eric Aragon UT, Barbara Archer IL, Melissa & Carolyn Aughe IN, Nancy Babineau VT, Francine Bagwell LA, Natalie Bailey PA, Rosemary Baldwin IL, Shelley Baltz TN, Chris Banas NJ, Kathryn Barbasiewicz WI, David Barch VT, Kari Barrett MD, Pamela Barton WA, Richard Baumann WI, Sharon L. Baver NY, Judy Bay WI, Clare Becker Egypt, Peggy Becker WI, Patti Bell CA, Ann-Marie Bergman WI, Linda Bernskoetter KS, Barbara Berry DE, Ann Besaw MI, Cynthia Best PA, Joann Betschart CA, Susan Beuel NY, Susan Bingaman IA, Bryan Blazek WI, Heather Bley MN, Kathy Block-Brown OR, Lisa Bodamer WI, Sirena Boden CA, Maryellen Boderck NJ, Carole Cotter Bodner MI, Daniel Boese WI, Isabelle Bolton FL, Ashley Boncimino TX, Boschulte Family WI, Christine-Sara Bosinger CA, Cyndi Bowan PA, Andy Boynton WA, Britt Brady IL, Beth Brann CA, Judith Bratek CO, Lisa Braunreiter WI, Mike Brenwald GA, Emily Bridges VT, Anita Brinton WI, Janel Brock CA, Lynette Brooks WI, Michelle Brost IL, Deanna Brown IL, Jonquil Brown ID, Sharon Brown WI, Linda Brunner WI, Ruth Buchholz ND, Christy Buchta WI, Christi Buell OR, Donna & Gary Buell AZ, Gerald Buller KS, Stephanie Bunn TN, Kristin Burns CA, Barbara Buscher NV, Melissa Bustle NC, Daryl Byers GA, Patricia Cahalan CA, Laurie Cain TN, Jan Caldwell CA, Cheryl Cambron TN, Kay Campbell IL, Arlene Canitz WI, Laurel Casale IL, Kathy Casey IL, Walt Caudle VA, Claudia M. Cepeda NY, Estelle Chalfin CA, Patti Chambers IN, Carol Chan CA, Winter Chan UT, Randi Chen CA, Nancy Chin UK, Bethany Christiansen UT, Brenda Christiansen UT, Elizabeth Clarke WA, Emmy Clausing CA, Joyce A. Clauson WI, Kristy Clayman WI, Arlene Coco Buscombe MN, Bettina Cohen CA, Jesse Colby UT, Patton Conner MD, Wendy Lee Connors WA, Mary Connolly NY, Genna Cookson RI, Rosie Cooley WY, Joan Cooper WI, Judi Copping VT, Lisa Cramm VT, Laurie Crass WI, Dr. Don & Janis Crego WI, Denis Crevier WI, Julie Crocfer CO, Heather Cross NY, Chris Crytzer PA, Lynn Cunliffe UT, Peggy Curtis WA, Susan Dahlem LA, Lisa Dambach WI, Erin Darling WA, Tracy Davis MI, Mandy Davis-Hanson IL, Gregory Dayton WI, Stephanie Dean CA, Dawn DeFraties IL, Claudia M. DeLatorre NJ, Noli Delo WI, Brittney Deming OR, Joann Denby MI, Shannon Lee Denney WI, Lynda DeRushia UT, Suzanne DeVoe UT, Judy DeWar WI, Peter & Karen Diamond PA, Eileen Diaz RI, Stephanie Dickison OH, Lynn Dieckmann CA, Cheryl Diener IL, Peggy Dillon CA, Amy Dimitoulis NJ, Toni Disano MO, Debra Dishaw White CA, Nancy Dotson WI, Judy Draper CA, Donna Drawbridge IL, Fanchon DuGarm ND, Donna Dull CA, Sylvia Dunne MO, Jon Dunning TN, Tom Dusing SD, Kerry Dwyer WI, Cindy Dziedzic WI, Susan Easterbrooks WA, Todd Eberhard UT, Jean Ecos WI, Linda Eide WI, Dan Eisenhut WI, Gloria Elizabeth CA, Tammy Engstler WI, Jessica Erdman WA, Freya Erickson UK, Paula Erickson WI, Gwen Essegian CA, Dianne Essex TN, Pamela Essmann WI, Ember Ete UT, Caroline Etzkorn IL, Gloria Evans VA, Donna Everett MN, Sandra Fair MI, Janna Fakier CA, Rita Farkas CA, Connie Farmer VA, Shelley Feingold NJ, Michael Ferrin UT, Peter Fessenbecker WI, Adam Fields NY, Merry Filo WI, Kim Fisch IL, Daniel Fisher WV, Stacey FitzSimmons MD, Van Fitzsimmons FL, Phyllis Flanigan TN, Nellmary Fledderman LA, Scott Fleischmann WI, Christine Fleissner WI, Molly Fleming CA, James Fletcher WI, Susan Flint CA, Steven Fluder WI, Carol Flynn CO, Karen Fohey WI, Linda Follett AK, Linda Follis AR, Laura Fosgate TN, Pam Foutch IL, Jay Freck WI, Barbara French VA, Marta Freud IL, Anne Fricker TN, C.C. Fridlin AL, Bruce Gaber MD, Lawrence Galbraith MI, Paula Gasvoda MT, Michelle Gawe VT, Melanie Gering WA, Tracy Gigliello CA, Amanda Gilleard OR, Rod Gillette WI, Virginia Gleason LA, Jennifer Goddard WV, Susan Godwin IL, Priscilla Gold-Darby AL, Leslie Goldenberg MA, Risa Golding NJ, Terri Golner WI, Margie Gonzales CA, Sherry Gonzales LA, Patricia Gonzalez WI, Sherri Goodwin WI, Danelle Graham OR, Kim Graham CA, Colleen Grant NV, Betty Gregg WI, Patricia Griffith NE, Pamela Grow PA, Donna Marie Guerrero WI, Rosa Lee Guillette VT, Susie Guyton GA, Holly Hahl WA, Natalie Hala CA, Ginny Hall RI, Janet Hall SD, Joan Hallford TX, Jennifer Alys-Jane Hamilton Canada, Aurore Hamzaoui NY, Thomas Hanewall WI, Lisa Hardebeck MO, Steve Hares CA, Jennifer Harris CO, Jo-Ann Harrison MI, Peg Harvey WI, Julie Hawkes CA, Barbara Hayler IL, Brenda Haynes MN, Mary Healy MI, Maria Hecker CA, Roger Heilman UT, Cindi Heimlich WI, Turi Henderson WA, Garner Hendrick CA, Kathy Henry PA, Pat Hepp WI, Holly Herpich LA, Anthony Herrera WI, Chrissy Hiebert WI, Anita Hirsch PA, Joan Hong CA, Linda Hopkins UT, Jennifer Hopper TN, Theresa Horton GA, Veronica Hoyle-Kent CA, Christy Hudson AR, Betty Hurlburt VT, Lois Inouye HI, Brenda Jackson RI, Nan Jacob CA, Paula Jacobson MD, Sharron Jahnke WI, Susan Johnsen OR, Angela Johnson CA, Kerry Johnson CO, Thomas Johnson CT, Doug Jones OK, Kay Jones IL, Jean Jordan WI, Joanna Jost CA, Janyse Judy NY, Stacy Judy HI, Kathy Kahler WI, Chantill Kahler-Royer MN, Kelly Kaiser FL, Brian Kane MA, Laura Kastens NE, Allison Katen IL, Annie Katzer WA, Elsie Keith GA, Carol Killingsworth CO, Kathleen Kinnear CA, Penny Kipp AK, Linda Kirchner WI, Marti Kirsch CO, Susan Kirtley CA, Arlene Kissack WI, Nupur Kittur NY, LisaBeth Klein OR, Kathy Klimpel TX, Darlene Knese IL, Bonnie Knight CA, Betty Joe Kobierski IL, Richard Koehn UT, Katherine J. Koetting WI, Jill Koloske WI, Mary Ellen Komac NV, Trish Kosmach PA, Mary Kotek WI, Kimberly Krasley PA, Alice Krelo UT, Cindy Krenke WI, Thomas Kriese CA,

Tom Kroc MO, Nicki Kroll WI, Rich Kroll CA, Heather Krueger MN, Geralyn Krzywda WI, Charlotte Kubsh MO, Mary Agnes Kuehmichel WI, Bob Kurzmann MI, Linda Lamm WI, Sue LaMunyon AK, Gisele Landry LA, Mary Anne Larimore CA, Geraldine Larson SD, Molli Larson IL, Joan Laube MS, Phoebe Lawless NC, Joy Layne TN, Adrienne Lee CO, Felicia Lee CA, Jim Lee WV, Maurice Lee CA, Samantha Lee NJ, Carleen Lehouiller VT, Robin Lepolds CA, David Levine NJ, Gail Levitt WA, Roxanne Lewandowski WI, Cathe Lieb CA, Evelyn Liggett MO, Jo Anne Lightfoot IL, Laurel Lindner CA, Cynthia Lloyd UT, Dolores Loberg ND, Elizabeth Lombardo MO, Frank Loose FL, Jim Lorenzen WI, Andrea Love NY, Betty J. Love CO, Paul Lovoi CA, Matthew Lyon UT, Susan Mackowiak WI, Cheryl Maguire CT, Thomas Malmevik WA, Barbara A. Mapp NC, Jennifer Marcum CA, Mr. Leslie Marks FL, Mary Ann Marschhauser NY, Louise Marston CA, Linda Martin NY, Michelle Martin WI, Roanne Martin Switzerland, Diane Master CA, JoAnn Matsko PA, Lesley Maul CA, Lisa Maxon WI, Kathleen Maxwell TN, Jerry Mayberry TN, Miriam Mazliach CA, Kathy McCann VT, Heather McClatchey UT, Jane McCurdy CA, Kelly McDonald MO, Terese McGrath MO, Cathy McGregor VT, Tammy McGuire IL, Angela McHugh FL, Jeff McKee MO, Rick McKee CA, Mike and Mary McLarty UT, Terry McLaughin WI, Judy McMahon CA, Susann McMichael PA, Joyce McMillan CO, Kelly McNamara CA, Margaret McNeil TN, Carroll McNeill CA, Audrey Mercer GA, Kristen Merrell AK, Sharon Merrell AK, Donna Meyer IL, Kathleen Meyer WI, Rebecca Meyer MS, Rebecca Michaels PA, Amy Miller Canada, Deborah Miller CA, Cheryl Milner WI, Diane Mincher VT, Sharon Minnich PA, Brenda Minster WI, Heather Mitzel ND, Kathleen Momoi WI, Linda Moody FL, Stephanie Morey WI, Evelyn Morgan WI, Frances Morgan CA, Margaret Morrison CA, Debra Moskyok CA, Carol Moss VA, Danya Moss MI, Mandie Moss UT, Pat Motheral CA, Elena Mou CA, Robert & Rena Mullins TX, Laura Murdoch UT, Marianne Murphy IL, Edwina Nakano HI, Alexia Nalewaik CA, Anne Napolitano NY, Shannon Nascimento CA, Catherine Nash CA, Barry Nass NY, Elaine Nelson WA, Mary Nelson WI, Diane Niemchick TN, Marcia Nosko WI, Nina Notaro Canada, Linda Noyes VA, Kim Obernberger WI, Eric O'Brien OR, Shannon Bow O'Brien TX, Linda Odum NH, Anna Ohly WI, Karl Ohly WI, Laureen Ojalvo NY, L. Peat O'Neil MD, Dee O'Reilly IL, Paige Orloff CA, Sharon Osborne ND, Michael Otto WI, Laura Owens TN, Lisa Owens WA, Jackie Padesky OH, Jeff Page CT, Elizabeth Pankow WI, Melissa Parish UT, Marilyn Parks MI, Barbara Parysek CA, Stephanie Patag PA, Harriet Patrick WI, Cathleen Patterson WI, Jennifer Patterson WI, Sara Zoe Patterson NH, Kate Patton NY, Trudy Schafer Paul CA, Laura Pellizzi NY, Rebecca Penovich MD, Michael Perket WI, Marcella Perodo Italy, Philip Perschetz VA, Raquel Pestana MA, Rochelle Peterson CA, Melanie Peterson MI, Valerie Pigg Rozzi AK, Nancy Piontkowski WI, Carolyn Piotrowski WI, Susan Plattner IL, Roselle Ponsaran OH, Franklin Poole, Jr. LA, Mary Poulsen IL, Amy Powell NY, Jeanie Prince WV, Janet Quarles LA, Connie Quenemoen CA, Kelly Quick WI, Linda Raether WI, Shyamala Ramanathan-Edwards UK, Gary Rara CA, Pat Rataczak WI, Heather Ratcliff WA, Vickie Rayburn IL, Gwynneth Rayer CA, Tammy Raymond WI, Sandra Rebiger WI, Candyce Rector TN, Andrea Reiff IL, Ann Marie Rembert IL, Christopher Reyes CA, Rhonda Rhodes NY, Robyn Rice-Foster IN, Susan Rieder WI, Sindy Riedman ND, Leta Riemenschneider TN, Sherry Riesterer WI, John Ritzman WI, Jean Robertson UT, Cindi Robinson-Sim WI, Erica Rogers MO, Waunita Roggenbuck AK, Peggy Rohde WI, Karen Rohlin CA, Cheryl Rojic CO, Leanne M. Roman MI, Jerry Ronaghan NY, Brandon Root MI, Holly Rosby OH, Dede Rose CO, Sallie Rosenow WI, Susan Ross WI, April Rowland MO, Mary & Nancy Roycraft MI, Rucks Family WI, Helene Rude NY, Jennie Rudolph KY, Sara Russ MI, Susan Ryan CA, Bonnie Salopek WI, Andrew Sampson WA, Jody Sanden OR, Patricia Sanford UT, Jason Santistevan UT, Dale Sapp MO, Janine Sarach VA, Jason Sarnowski WI, Cynthia Sasaki CA, Leslie Saviage CA, Sherry Schare CA, Cathy Schauer OH, Pam Schoechert WI, Matt Schreiner TX, Marianne Schultz HI, Jan Schwartz WI, Shelley Schweitzer IL, Kimberly Scully AK, Darlene Seelos MN, Ruth Selmo MI, Christy Serafini FL, Susan Shaw IL, Janet Shelly IL, Dolores Shemes CA, Diane Sheya UT, Stephanie Shiffert PA, Erma Shipley TN, Marcelyn Shuler MI, Lisa Sidhu UT, Cathie Sikora AK, David Silva UT, Karissa Silva NY, Harvey Simmons TX, Bob & Carol Sippel CA, Mike Sixta NM, Jeremy Smith FL, Laura J. Smith CA, Mary Lou Smith CO, Sarah Smith Canada, Sheila Smith WI, Sue & Jeff Smith WI, Whitney Smith MO, Jane Sogge IL, Jason Sopel Canada, Theresa Soto NY, Alicia Spivak CA, Inge Spotnitz CA, Ailas Stafford TN, Cheryl Stalans GA, Adrianna Standiford MT, Diane Stardy WI, Mary Stassi MO, Leith Steel CA, Jolene Steele WA, Pat Steele WA, Anna Stewart CA, Ann Marie Stone NY, Linda Stonestreet WV, Sara Stong CO, Pat Stratton MT, Jeanne Strepacki IL, Laraine Stummer AK, Lana Stutzman CA, Charlene Sutherby MI, Cindy Sutherland MS, Marlys & Bob Swanson WI, Fern Swenson WI, Ellen Swirsky IL, Lynn Sylver IL, Mark Szocik WI, Joyce Takaki CA, Troy Takao CA, Marjorie Talley OK, Renee Tarshis CA, Andrea Taylor WI, Pattie Taylor MI, Edward Templin SC, Rene Tennant CA, Margaret Terakawa HI, Susan Theusch WI, Candy Thomas VT, Kristen Thomas NC, Raymond Thomas NC, Connie Thomason WI, Sharon Thompson IL, Sally Tiemann CA, Donna Tingley CA, Deb Tischendorf WI, Deirdre Todd HI, Annette Tomei CA, Ana Topolovec NY, Tourdots Family WI, Bob Townsend WI, Patti Triska NV, Mary Troll MO, Jennifer Tsay CA, Rebecca Tyson Smith AK, Walter & Jill Unglaub WI, Nancy Valuet MI, Carrie Vandal ND, Alexia Vanides Gentry CA, Clara Varner WY, Lisa Vasquez WI, Mukta Verma CA, Kathy Vetro NJ, Kay Vickery TN, Diane Villanueva WI, Pam Volkert WI, Sandra Voss MO, Vossekuils Family WI, Paul Wagner MT, Jeanine Walentoski WI, Jill Walker UT, Joan Wallis MA, Wendy Wallis WI, Amy Wallow WI, Margo Warren IL, Robert Watts NJ, Nancy Weber NY, Jane Wegner WI, Ilene Weiser PA, Diane Weissman IA, Shirley Wells FL, Carole Wenthe IL, Nicole Weston CA, Andrea White VA, Anna White LA, Carol White WI, J.B. White WI, Joyce White MD, Maxine White NY, T. White WI, Pam Whiteside-Morrison CO, Heather Whitney TX, Kristy Wilce CA, Becky Willett WI, Jeff Williams TN, Jennifer Williams CA, Kimberly Williams FL, Linda & Rick Williams CA, Marilyn Williams UT, Rosalie Williams TN, Claire Willmore UT, Meg Wilson SC, Megan Wilson TN, Ron Wilson CA, Brenda Winkelman PA, Barbara Winschel IL, Connie Winters TN, Fred Wishnie WI, Robin Wolf WI, Ted Wolf IL, Anna Wolfe ME, Diane Wolfert CO, Sheila Wyum ND, Faye Yang CA, Cindy Yap Australia, Barbara & John Yingling WI, Jeremy Youde CA, Debbie Zambetti CA, Rick Zeek CA, Mary Zick ND

A

acorn squash, baked, 313
aebleskivers, 28
Alexander, 456
all-American cheeseburgers, 51
all-American hamburgers, 50
almond(s)
    biscotti, 408–409
    buttercream frosting, 395
    cookies, 399
    green beans amandine, 296
    and peach muffins, 328
altitude and canning times,
    487
ambrosia, 422
American Cookery (Simmons), 8
American goulash, 269
American home cooking, 9
American pizzas, 44–45
Amish sugar cookies, 401
anadama bread, 340
angel biscuits, 325
angel food cake, 384–385
angel pie, about, 370
antipasto tray, 71
appetizers
    antipasto tray, 71
    beef jerky, homemade, 70–71
    caramel corn, 61
    caraway sticks, 63
    cheese ball, 58–59
    cheese quesadillas, 67
    cheese spreads, 57–58
    cheese straws, 62–63
    chopped chicken livers, 60
    choux pastry, 65
    clam puffs, crunchy, 67
    clams casino, 68
    cocktail sauce, 65
    cold cuts and cheese tray, 71
    crudités, 71
    deviled eggs, 64
    dips, 57–59
    fruit and cheese tray, 71
    Greek meatballs, 69
    guacamole, 56
    kal-bi short ribs, 70
    lobster puffs, 64–65
    marinated mushrooms, 64
    marinated olives, 64
    nutty party mix, 62
    oysters Rockefeller, 68
    pico de gallo, 56
    pigs in a blanket, 70
    popcorn, 61
    prosciutto with melon, 71
    roasted chestnuts, 62
    salsa cruda, 56
    shrimp cocktail, 65
    smoked salmon spread, 59
    spiced nuts, 60
    stuffed cucumbers, 63
    stuffed grape leaves, 66–67
    sweet-and-sour meatballs, 69
    Texas caviar, 57
    toasted pumpkin seeds, 60
apple(s)
    baked, 416
    and braised cabbage, 292
    brown Betty, 418
    butter, slow-cooker, 349
    candied, 446
    caramel, 446
    cinnamon streusel muffins,
      327
    cornmeal pancakes, 26
    cranberry pie, 355
    crisp, 417
    crumb pie with sour cream,
      354
    dumplings, 419
    Dutch apple nut cake, glazed,
      390–391
    fried, New Hampshire, 36
    German apple cake, 390
    grilled, 257
    nut bread, 333
    pandowdy, 417
    pie, 354
    potato, sausage, and apple
      stuffing, 179
    and sausage stuffing, 176–177
    snow, 416
    strudel, 418
    stuffed pork crown roast,
      204–205
    whiskey custard pie, 355
applesauce, 416
applesauce cake, 392
appliances, small, 481
apricot(s)
    chocolate-dipped, 447
    grilled, 257
    upside-down cake, 387
    whip, 419
arroz con pollo, 274
artichoke dip, hot, 59
artichokes, 286
asparagus
    with hollandaise sauce, 286
    lemon-butter, 286
    Parmesan, 287
    quiche, 25
    salad with lemon-mustard
      dressing, 76–77
autumn fruit salad, 83
avgolemono, 114
avocado and grapefruit salad, 83
avocados, about, 56

B

babka, 393
baby back ribs, grilled, 235
bacon
    about, 37
    carrot curls, fried, 293
    and cheese breakfast strata, 23
    cheeseburgers, 51
    chicken livers and, 170–171
    Hangtown fry, 22
    horseradish dip, 58
    hot brown sandwiches, 46–47
    lettuce, and tomato sandwiches
      (BLT), 41
    oysters wrapped in, 248
    and peanut butter sandwich,
      spicy, 43
    pork tenderloin, wrapped,
      206
    shrimp wrapped in, 248
    trout, wrapped, 132
baked Alaska, 439
baked apples, 416
baked beans, 288–289
baked potatoes, grilled, 250–251
baked potatoes, stuffed, cheesy,
    304
baking powder biscuits, 324
baklava, 443
banana(s)
    cream cake, 379
    cream pie, 366–367
    Foster, 439
    grilled, 257
    nut bread, 334
    pudding, 428
    splits, 438
barbecue
    brisket, 232–233
    brisket, oven-barbecued, 192
    chicken, 242
    chicken, baked, 154
    mops, 253
    pulled pork, 236–237

Conversion Chart

Unless you have finely calibrated measuring equipment, conversions between U.S. and metric measurements will be inexact. It's important to convert the measurements for all of the ingredients in a recipe to maintain the same proportions as the original.

Measurement	Conversion
Ounces to grams	Multiply ounces by 28.35
Grams to ounces	Multiply grams by 0.035
Pounds to grams	Multiply pounds by 453.6
Pounds to kilograms	Multiply pounds by 0.45
Fahrenheit to Celsius	Subtract 32 from Fahrenheit temperature, multiply by 5, then divide by 9
Celsius to Fahrenheit	Multiply Celsius temperature by 9, divide by 5, then add 32

By Volume

U.S.	Metric
⅕ teaspoon	1 ml
¼ teaspoon	1.25 ml
½ teaspoon	2.5 ml
1 teaspoon	5 ml
1 tablespoon	15 ml
1 fluid ounce	30 ml
¼ cup	60 ml
⅓ cup	80 ml
½ cup	120 ml
⅔ cup	160 ml
¾ cup	180 ml
1 cup	240 ml
2 cups	475 ml
1 quart (4 cups)	1.1 liters
.91 quart	1 liter
4 quarts (1 gallon)	3.78 liters
½ inch	1.27 cm
1 inch	2.54 cm

By Weight

U.S.	Metric
¼ ounce	7 grams
½ ounce	14 grams
1 ounce	28 grams
1¼ ounces	35 grams
1½ ounces	42 grams
2½ ounces	70 grams
4 ounces	112 grams
5 ounces	140 grams
8 ounces	227 grams
10 ounces	280 grams
15 ounces	420 grams
16 ounces (1 pound)	453 grams
1.1 pounds	500 grams
2.2 pounds	1 kilogram

Equivalents

3 teaspoons	1 tablespoon
4 tablespoons	¼ cup
8 tablespoons	½ cup
12 tablespoons	¾ cup
16 tablespoons	1 cup
1 cup	½ pint
2 cups	1 pint
2 pints	1 quart
4 quarts (liquid)	1 gallon
1 pound	16 ounces